ELEMENTS OF LAW

ELEMENTS OF LAW

Second Edition

Eva H. Hanks
Dr. Samuel Belkin Professor of Law and Society
Benjamin N. Cardozo School of Law
Yeshiva University

Michael E. Herz
Professor of Law
Benjamin N. Cardozo School of Law
Yeshiva University

Steven S. Nemerson, Ph.D., J.D.

ISBN: 978–1–4224–7676–5

Library of Congress Cataloging-in-Publication Data
Hanks, Eva H.
Elements of law / Eva H. Hanks, Michael E. Herz, Steven S. Nemerson. -- 2nd ed.
p. cm.
Includes index.
ISBN 978-1-4224-7676-5 (casebound)
1. Law--United States--Cases. I. Herz, Michael E. II. Nemerson, Steven S. III. Title.
KF385.A4H36 2010
349.73--dc22
2010004277

NOTE TO USERS
To ensure that you are using the latest materials available in this area, please be sure to periodically check the LexisNexis Law School web site for downloadable updates and supplements at www.lexisnexis.com/lawschool.

Editorial Offices
121 Chanlon Rd., New Providence, NJ 07974 (908) 464-6800
201 Mission St., San Francisco, CA 94105-1831 (415) 908-3200
www.lexisnexis.com

MATTHEW◆BENDER

(2010–Pub.3534)

DEDICATIONS

To John
— EHH

To Jean, Daniel, Zachary, and Rachel
— MEH

To Sara, Leah, and David
— SNN

ACKNOWLEDGMENTS
(Second Edition)

This second edition of *Elements of Law* reflects a few large changes and countless minor revisions and updates. Many of these are the result of input from other readers. Our colleague Jonathan Silver was particularly generous with his time and attention, providing uniquely precise, and enormously valuable, suggestions and corrections. We also benefitted from the thoughtful comments of Myriam Gilles, Alex Reinert, and Edward Stein, all of whom taught from the first edition and initial versions of the second. Cardozo students Jennifer Congregane and Arthur Oder were a great help in performing additional research, obtaining copyright clearances, proofreading, and citechecking. We extend sincere thanks to all of them.

We reprint below the acknowledgements from the first edition. The debts we incurred in producing that edition remain, even though not all the material referenced does, and we renew our thanks to the many friends and colleagues who provided their support and assistance.

EHH
MEH

* * *

The authors gratefully acknowledge the permission of the copyright holders to reprint excerpts from the following works:

Benjamin N. Cardozo, The Nature of the Judicial Process 112–115, 141, 166–168 (1921). Copyright © 1921 by the Yale University Press. Reprinted with permission.

Paul D. Carrington, Book Review, 72 California L. Rev. 477, 490–491 (1984). Reprinted by permission of University of California Berkeley School of Law and Paul Carrington.

Ronald Dworkin, Law as Interpretation, 60 Tex. L. Rev. 527, 541–543 (1982). Reprinted with permission of the Texas Law Review and Ronald Dworkin.

Lon Fuller, The Morality of Law 33–34, 38–39 (rev. ed. 1969). Copyright © 1969 by The Yale University Press. Reprinted with permission.

Joseph C. Hutcheson, Jr., The Judgment Intuitive: The Function of the "Hunch" in Judicial Decision, 14 Cornell Law Quarterly 274, 275–279 (1928). Reprinted by permission of the Cornell Law Review.

"The Reception of the Common Law in the United States, in Political Separation and Legal Continuity," by Harry W. Jones, pp. 93–94, 96–99, 105, published by the American Bar Association. Copyright © 1976 by the American Bar Association. Reprinted with permission. This information or any portion thereof may not be copied or disseminated in any form or by any means or stored in an electronic database or retrieval system without the express written consent of the American Bar Association.

Harry W. Jones, Some Causes of Uncertainty in Statutes, 36 A.B.A. J. 321, 321 (1950). Reprinted by permission of the American Bar Association.

ACKNOWLEDGMENTS *(Second Edition)*

Anthony Kronman, Precedent and Tradition, 99 Yale L.J. 1029, 1031–32, 1034, 1038–39, 1067–68 (1990). Reprinted by permission of The Yale Law Journal Company, Inc., from The Yale Law Journal, Vol. 99, pp. 1029.

Karl N. Llewellyn, The Bramble Bush: On Our Law and Its Study 17–18, 38–40, 42–45, 48–49, 55, 66–67 (1960). Reprinted by permission of the copyright holder, Oxford University Press.

Daniel John Meador, American Courts 1–8 (West Publishing Co. 2d ed. 2000). Reprinted with permission.

Margaret Radin, The Liberal Conception of Property: Cross Currents in the Jurisprudence of Takings, 88 Columbia Law Review 1667, 1680–1684 (1988). Reprinted by permission of the Columbia Law Review Association, Inc. and Margaret Radin.

Hart Pomerantz & Steve Breslin, Regina v. Ojibway, 8 Criminal Law Quarterly 137 (1965). Reproduced from 8 Criminal Law Quarterly 137 with the permission of Canada Law Book, A Division of The Cartwright Group Ltd. (1-800-263-3269, www.canadalawbook.ca) and the authors of the article, H. Pomerantz and S. Breslin.

Frederick Schauer, Precedent, 39 Stanford Law Review 571, 572–580, 582, 587, 591, 595–598, 600 (1987). Copyright © by the Stanford Law Review. Reprinted by permission of the Stanford Law Review.

Kathleen M. Sullivan, The Supreme Court, 1991 Term — Foreword: The Justices of Rules and Standards, 106 Harvard Law Review 22, 57–59 (1992). Copyright © 1992 by the Harvard Law Review Association. Reprinted by permission of the Harvard Law Review and the author.

James B. White, Talk to Entering Students, University of Chicago, The Law School, Occasional Paper No. 13 (1977), pp. 1-6, 13-14. Reprinted by permission of James B. White and the University of Chicago Law School.

ACKNOWLEDGMENTS
(First Edition)

We leaned heavily on many wonderful colleagues for advice, insight, and correction in this project. Richard Weisberg and Charles Yablon shared their extraordinary knowledge and insights, and their contributions left a deep mark on all that is best about Part I. Thank you! Marci Hamilton, John McGinnis, and Stewart Sterk were kind enough to slog through all of Part II and provided extremely valuable comments. Rebecca Brown, of the Vanderbilt School of Law, and Abner Greene steered us away from several errors in Part II. Laura Cunningham provided the tax code problem in chapter [10] and Mark Squillace of the Wyoming School of Law was good enough to review the Clean Air Act problem in that chapter. John Hanks provided an extraordinary, almost unseemly, amount of help with the chapter on law and economics. Thanks also to Drucilla Cornell, who shared her encyclopedic knowledge of feminist scholarship, and Elbert Gates, on whose judgment we drew in the Critical Race Theory chapter. We greatly benefitted from many discussions with Paul Shupack, who has thought long and hard about this course. Arthur Jacobson helped make the "Anderson Connection," which he (rightly) thought would be good for both sides, and was a fruitful source of ideas in conversation.

We also wish to express our gratitude to the Benjamin N. Cardozo School of Law of Yeshiva University, Dean Monroe Price, and Dean Frank J. Macchiarola for their generous help in the form of a sabbatical, reduced teaching loads, summer research stipends, funds for research assistants, and other support. We especially thank Dean Macchiarola for teaching a section of the *Elements* course and sharing his insights with us.

Thank you to Judge Jack Weinstein for valuable comments and suggestions.

Kaaron Saphir typed more versions of this manuscript than she cares to remember and never lost her good humor and patience.

We acknowledge our enormous debt to the writers of the first *Elements* materials — Karl Llewellyn and Soia Mentschikoff — and to the justly famous "Columbia legal method materials" prepared by Noel Dowling, Edwin Patterson, and Richard Powell and redone by Harry W. Jones, John M. Kernochan, and Arthur W. Murphy.

Finally, we thank our students. We are particularly indebted to the Fall 1991 Legal Process Workshop,[1] an intrepid band that convened as an editorial board, coped with raw text and unedited articles, shared thoughts and opinions, contributed ideas and materials, and more. We like to think they would approve of the final product. A thank you, too, to the many *Elements* students who have kept the course fresh and challenging through the years, particularly those unsuspecting (and generally uncomplaining) souls who used

---

[1] They were, in alphabetical order: Simon Anolick, A.C. Biddle, Melinda Cody, Peter Fante, Lisa Foy, Jennifer Geller, Sara Goldstein, Suzanne Kazenoff, Susan Kent, Victoria Kummer, Barry Marenberg, June Raegner, Judy Ross, James Schwalbe, Allen Sragow, and Mary Watson. Ms. Kummer, of course, wrote the Civil Procedure section in Chapter 1. Alan Wolf, our physicist-student-contributor (see the note on law and science in Chapter 1 and the footnote on the quark in Chapter 6) participated as an auditor.

ACKNOWLEDGMENTS (First Edition)

these materials in draft form.

EHH
MEH
SSN

I wish to offer a personal note of thanks to several people.

Research assistants. Amy Trakinski in the early days of this venture; Barry Marenberg who for two years was always there when needed and for whose loyalty and help I am grateful; and the resplendent troika of (in alphabetical order) Tim Hamilton, Betty Hyman, and Agnes McCarthy, ably assisted by Juan Otero, who took over proofreading, cite-checking, copyright clearances, and my office where my presence, so they made clear, was a hindrance to their work. I thank each and every one of them.

Others. Barbara Bryce Herrington and Dora Young Spofford, my extraordinary Maine friends, who so often kept body and soul together in the long summers of "the book." Phineas Finn and Tom Jones.

I dedicate my work to my friend John Hanks. You supported me from the first moment we spoke of this book until the day the manuscript finally was mailed. I am deeply grateful.

Eva Hanks
New York City
Gouldsboro, Maine

Michael Jaffe (Cardozo '94) took on an eclectic array of research assignments with diligence, good humor, and intelligence. Adina Lewis (Cardozo '95) and Jason Levine (Cardozo '94) showed the same qualities in additional research and in the chores of proofreading, cite-checking, and securing copyright clearances. (As legions of copyright holders can attest, Ms. Lewis displayed particular tenacity in the last of those tasks.) Thanks to all of you.

Michael Herz
New York City

I am most grateful to my exceptional research assistants, Henry Katz (Cardozo '94) and Tammy Bieber (Cardozo '95).

Steven Nemerson
Northport, NY

EDITORIAL NOTE

We have deleted footnotes and citations in excerpted material without any indication. Additions are indicated by brackets, deletions by three asterisks (though deleted paragraphs are not separately indicated). Where the excerpt is itself quoting another source from which *it* has made a deletion, such a deletion is indicated by three dots.

We have numbered all footnotes, including those that are part of an excerpt, consecutively through each chapter. Thus, footnotes that are part of an excerpt do not bear their original numbers. A footnote within an excerpt is part of the original unless specifically indicated as "Ed. Fn."

FOREWORD

What do fear, frustration, anger, and a sense of isolation have to do with the study of law?

They are feelings experienced by almost all law students (including most likely your teachers, and most assuredly your authors, when they were students). They are feelings endemic to the first year and especially the first semester of law school.

We hope this book ameliorates those feelings. In our view the most important remedy for your law student's alienation and confusion is to understand what it is you are doing. *That is what this whole course is about.*

What follows are excerpts from a *Talk to Entering Students*, given some time ago at a renowned law school (the University of Chicago Law School) by a renowned member of its faculty (Professor James B. White). We use these extracts not primarily because they say what needs saying uncommonly well, although they do. The point is to show you that what is unsettling about this new experience is not caused by *your* being at *your* law school, but is near universal to all future lawyers at all law schools. We use Professor White's eloquence to show you that the suggested remedy is not merely the idiosyncratic prescription of your quixotic authors.

> I don't want to attribute to any of you the sort of ignorance I once had, but it is possible that some of you think — as many non-lawyers do — that the law is at bottom very simple. I once thought that what the word "law" referred to was, obviously enough, the laws themselves. And I naturally expected that the laws were all written down somewhere to be looked up and applied to life. The rules, once found, were simple enough; the mystery of the law had to do with their location. What mainly distinguished me from the lawyer, I thought, was that he knew where to find the rules and how to be sure he had found all of them. * * *

start here ←

> But this simple view does not account for all the ways in which the law works, and omits entirely what is most interesting, difficult, and important in what we do. Think for a moment what would follow if it were true that the activity of law consisted of nothing more than memorizing certain clear rules and learning where to find the others. First, both law school and the practice of law would be intolerably boring. On the face of it, few things could be more dull than simply memorizing large numbers of rules or learning one's way about a bibliographical system. But the fact is that for many people the study and practice of law are both difficult and fascinating. Second, since the rules that must be memorized are not invented at the law schools but exist outside of them, generally available to the world at large, there would be no substantial or interesting difference between a good legal education and a poor one. (Indeed, it would not be plain under these circumstances why we should have law schools or formal legal training at all. We could publish lists of rules and examine students on their "knowledge" of them at a bar examination.) And if this view of the law were accurate, there would be little to distinguish a good lawyer from a poor one. But there is general agreement, among those who claim to know, that a good legal education is something important and special, something very difficult to attain; that a good lawyer has capacities and powers the poor one

FOREWORD

lacks; and that in this field as in others excellence is rare and valuable.

The third consequence of this simple view of the law would be that the case method — "learning the law by reading cases" — would seem bizarre and perhaps sadistic. Why should one read these complicated and difficult cases simply to discover the general propositions for which they stand? But a great many lawyers regard their experience of learning how to read a case as a step of huge importance in their education as minds and as people, involving much more than learning to discover and repeat rules. Some, at least, would say that this training has helped them to find in the material of their daily professional existence a set of puzzles and difficulties that can interest them for life. * * *

Let me suggest that you regard the law not as a set of rules to be memorized but as an activity, as something that people do * * *. The law is a set of social and intellectual practices that defines a universe or culture in which you will learn to function; like other important activities, it offers its practitioner the opportunity to make a life, to work out a character, for herself or for himself. What you will learn in law school, on this view, is not information in the usual sense, not a set of repeatable propositions, but how to do something. Our primary aim is not to transmit information to you, but to help you learn how to do what it is that lawyers do with the problems that come to them. * * *

It might help if you were to compare the process of learning law * * * [to] learning a language. One must of course know the rules of grammar and the meanings of terms, but to know those things is not to know how to speak the language; that knowledge comes only with use. The real difficulties and pleasures lie not in knowing the rules of French or of law, but in knowing how to speak the language, how to make sense of it, how to use it to serve your purposes in life. * * *

In both language and law, learning has a double focus: if one is to live and act competently in a particular culture, one simply must learn how the language — or the law — is in fact spoken by others, by those whom one wishes to address, to persuade, to learn from, and to live with. But one also wishes to learn how to turn the language, or the law, to one's own purposes: to invent new sentences, to have new ideas, to do new things, perhaps to change the nature of the language itself. Your concern in law school is thus a double one: to learn as completely as you can how the legal culture functions; and to establish a place for yourself in relation to it from which you can attempt to use it in your own ways — in ways that increase your capacities and powers, ways that enable you to speak truthfully to the conditions of the world and to take positions (and offer them to others) which seem to you to be right.[2]

Like learning a language, we would add, learning law requires your participation. It is not passive. So speak up in class. A law school class is a joint undertaking between you and your classmates. *You will educate one another.* Each and every contribution is valuable — "right" or "wrong," especially since, as you will come to understand, in an important sense there are no "right" or "wrong" answers. For that matter, as you will also come to understand, it is the questions more than the answers that concern us.

[2] James B. White, *Talk to Entering Students*, Occasional Papers, The Law School, The University of Chicago (1977), pp. 2–4, 12–14.

FOREWORD

If you and your classmates will educate one another, what does your teacher do? She ~~The teacher~~ will guide you, with your active assistance. She knows, in a general way, what troubles you, what is difficult for you. But in a general way only, not at any given moment your particular trouble: is it that you do not understand a question or an answer or where the conversation is headed? That you think the court is wrong (legally? factually? ethically?), or your classmate is wrong or your teacher? Raise your hand and speak up: unless you do, your teacher cannot know what you think.

Professor White again:

> Of course, your first efforts will be halting, you will misunderstand things, you will make errors. That is not your fault; it resides in the nature of things.
>
> Your teachers know all this, and while you may sometimes understandably feel that the persistent and impossible demands of the classroom are intended to operate as a sort of bootcamp discipline or hazing exercise, that is not our purpose at all. The cases are hard for us as well as for you, sometimes I think harder for us than for you; our task is to lead a conversation, by question and observation, which will expose the difficulties of our common circumstance, the perplexities that do not at first appear. It is important for you to know that these are perplexities for all of us, and that your teachers have no handy solutions to purvey. * * * The difference between your teacher and you, after all, is only that he has read the case more often, thought about it longer, and has a somewhat larger set of legal materials to bring to bear on it. He has no patent from above that will guarantee his being right. And you can have no assurance, whatever he says, that he will not change his mind. The legal mind is marked, one might say, by an odd combination of three things: a capacity to organize the materials of argument, with great force, on either side of a question; a willingness to reach and state a conclusion; and an openness to persuasion that one is wrong. Law school is among other things an experience of making up and changing your mind. Behind all the rhetorical force is a deep sense of the tentative.
>
> The truth is that there are no experts in the law, in the sense that there are no persons upon whose judgment you may rely without understanding it; each of us is responsible for what he thinks and says, and it is no discharge of your duty to repeat to your professor what he has told you he thinks. You must make your own way.
>
> It may or may not be comforting to hear this, but the sense of inadequacy and isolation which you should have as you now contemplate this process will always, in one form or another, be with you. One never knows all the law; one never feels wholly confident about any step taken in the law. The lawyer lives in an uncertain and indeterminate world, and his profession is to survive and flourish in it.

Reread these paragraphs whenever you are in danger of forgetting that it is a *process* in which you are engaged. *Forgive yourself for not being able to immediately do perfectly what you could not possibly do perfectly, or perhaps even well, as you begin your journey.* As Justice Brandeis reportedly said to his daughter, "My dear, if you would only recognize that life is hard, things would be so much easier for you."[3]

---

[3] Anthony A. Lewis, *In Memoriam: Paul A. Freund*, 106 HARV. L. REV. 16, 18 (1992).

FOREWORD

Finally, the world of law is a world of words. "Law is the intersection of language and power."[4]

Power clearly entails ethical responsibilities for those who exercise it. But so does language. Listen to Václav Havel, once dissident convict, then President of his country, and one of the few authentic moral heroes of the latter part of the 20th century:

> At the beginning of everything is the word.
>
> It is a miracle to which we owe the fact that we are human.
>
> But at the same time it is a pitfall and a test, a snare and a trial.
>
> More so, perhaps, than it appears to you who have enormous freedom of speech, and might therefore assume that words are not so important.
>
> They are.
>
> They are important everywhere.
>
> The same word can be humble at one moment and arrogant the next. And a humble word can be transformed easily and imperceptibly into an arrogant one, whereas it is a difficult and protracted process to transform an arrogant word into one that is humble. I tried to demonstrate this by referring to the tribulations of the word "peace" in my country.
>
> As we approach the end of the second millennium, the world, and particularly Europe, finds itself at a peculiar crossroads. It has been a long time since there were so many grounds for hoping that everything will turn out well. At the same time, there have never been so many reasons to fear that if everything went wrong the catastrophe would be final.
>
> It is not hard to demonstrate that all the main threats confronting the world today, from atomic war and ecological disaster to a catastrophic collapse of society and civilization — by which I mean the widening gulf between rich and poor individuals and nations — have hidden deep within them a single root cause: the imperceptible transformation of what was originally a humble message into an arrogant one.

Arrogantly, man began to believe that, as the pinnacle and lord of creation, he understood nature completely and could do what he liked with it.

> Arrogantly, he began to think that as the possessor of reason, he could completely understand his own history and could therefore plan a life of happiness for all, and that this even gave him the right, in the name of an ostensibly better future for all — to which he had found the one and only key — to sweep from his path all those who did not fall for his plan.
>
> Arrogantly, he began to think that since he was capable of splitting the atom, he was now so perfect that there was no longer any danger of nuclear arms rivalry, let alone nuclear war.
>
> In all those cases he was fatally mistaken. That is bad. But in each case he is already beginning to realize his mistake. And that is good.

---

[4] Fred R. Shapiro, *Preface, in* THE OXFORD DICTIONARY OF AMERICAN LEGAL QUOTATIONS ix (Fred R. Shapiro ed. 1993).

FOREWORD

Having learned from all this, we should all fight together against arrogant words and keep a weather eye out for any insidious germs of arrogance in words that are seemingly humble.

Obviously this is not just a linguistic task. Responsibility for and toward words is a task which is intrinsically ethical.

As such, however, it is situated beyond the horizon of the visible world, in that realm wherein dwells the Word that was in the beginning and is not the word of man.[5]

We wish you luck (one always needs a bit of that), fortitude, and courage. Mostly we wish you joy and excitement during the journey you are about to begin.

The Authors

---

[5] From Havel's acceptance speech upon being presented (*in absentia* — the "Velvet Revolution" was yet to take place) the Peace Prize of the German Bookseller Association on October 15, 1989. Václav Havel, *A Word About Words*, *in* OPEN LETTERS 377, 388–389 (Paul Wilson ed. & A.G. Brain trans. 1991).

TABLE OF CONTENTS

Appendix A, B, C + D

Part I	**THE COMMON LAW**	**1**

Chapter 1	**CASES**	**3**
A.	THE COMMON LAW	3
B.	"CASES"	7
C.	COURTS	15
D.	JUDGES	17
E.	LITIGATION: HOW A DISPUTE BECOMES A "CASE"	20
F.	JUDGMENTS AND THEIR EFFECTS — HEREIN OF RES JUDICATA, AND SOME OTHER IMPORTANT WORDS	28
1.	*Reversing and Overruling*	28
2.	*Res Judicata and Stare Decisis*	30

read
VIP
a few words

Chapter 2	**READING AND BRIEFING CASES**	**31**
A.	THE CASE	32
	Marie E. Kelly, Plaintiff-Appellant v. Donald C. Gwinnell and Paragon Corp., Defendants-Appellants, and Joseph J. Zak and Catherine Zak, Defendants-Respondents	32
B.	THE BRIEF	47
1.	*Heading*	49
2.	*Statement of the Case*	50
3.	*The Facts*	54
4.	*Procedural History and Outcome Here*	57
5.	*Issue or Issues (and Holding)*	61
6.	*Holding (and Issue or Issues)*	63
7.	*Reasoning*	66
8.	*Separate Opinions and Dissents*	67
9.	*Other Items of Note*	67
C.	A SAMPLE BRIEF	68

ALL OF iT

Chapter 3	**JUDGING**	**73**
A.	THE BASES OF JUDICIAL DECISIONS	74
B.	EMPATHY, PASSION, REASON: TWO EXAMPLES	91
	Hynes v. New York Central Railroad	91
	Palsgraf v. Long Island Railroad	93
C.	A FINAL NOTE	102

read

TABLE OF CONTENTS

Chapter 4   **A CASE SEQUENCE** 103

Barrett v. Southern Pacific Co. 106
Sample Brief 109
Notes and Questions 111
Peters v. Bowman 112
Notes and Questions 115
Peters v. Bowman 116
Questions 118
Sanchez v. East Contra Costa Irrigation Co. 118
Notes and Questions 119
Copfer v. Golden 121
Wilford v. Little 124
Notes and Questions 126
Knight v. Kaiser 132
Notes and Questions 138
Reynolds v. Willson 142
Notes and Questions 150
Garcia v. Soogian 152
Questions 156
King v. Lennen 156
Notes and Questions 158

Chapter 5   **A THEORY OF PRECEDENT** 163

A.   INTRODUCTION 164
B.   WHAT IS PRECEDENT? 165
   1.   Precedent as a Rule 165
   2.   What in a Precedent Binds? 166
      Questions 168
C.   CAN PRECEDENT CONSTRAIN? 170
   1.   Introduction 170
   2.   Categories and Characterizations 171
      Notes and Questions 174
   3.   Decisions Without Characterizations 174
      Robins Dry Dock & Repair Co. v. Flint 175
      Notes and Questions 176
   4.   Categories of Assimilation 177
   5.   Do Some Precedents Constrain More Than Others? 179
      Questions 179
D.   WHY A DOCTRINE OF PRECEDENT? 180
   1.   Criticisms 180

TABLE OF CONTENTS

2.   *Utilitarian Defenses* 183

   (a)   Fairness 183

   (b)   Predictability 184

   (c)   Efficiency 186

   (d)   Legitimacy 188

          Planned Parenthood v. Casey 189

          Notes and Questions 191

3.   *Burkean "Conservatism"* 193

4.   *Are Courts Constitutionally Required to Adhere to Precedent?* 196

          Anastasoff v. United States 196

          Notes and Questions 199

E.   "LIVING LAW" AND THE "DEAD HAND" 200

          Butler v. McKellar 202

          NOTES 205

          Planned Parenthood v. Casey 206

Chapter 6   **WHAT JUDGES DO — A CODA** **207**

A.   INTRODUCTION 207

B.   PENNSYLVANIA COAL V. MAHON 207

          Pennsylvania Coal Co. v. Mahon 208

C.   NOTE ON THE JURISPRUDENCE OF "TAKINGS" 212

D.   IN SEARCH OF LODESTARS: ECONOMICS 214

E.   IN SEARCH OF LODESTARS: POLITICS 216

F.   IN SEARCH OF LODESTARS: "PROPERTY" 218

G.   IN SEARCH OF LODESTARS: "A LAW OF RULES" 223

H.   IN SEARCH OF LODESTARS: "DEMOCRACY" 227

I.   A (SOMEWHAT LENGTHY) EPILOGUE 229

          Keystone Bituminous Coal Association v. Debenedictis 229

          Notes and Questions 233

Part II   **IN THE DOMAIN OF STATUTES** **235**

Chapter 7   **STATUTES V. THE COMMON LAW** **239**

A.   A COMMON LAW RULE 239

          Filmore v. Metropolitan Life Insurance Co. 239

          Notes and Questions 240

B.   THE STATUTORY COMPLICATION 241

          Deem v. Millikin 241

          Notes and Questions 242

          Riggs v. Palmer 242

          Notes and Questions 245

TABLE OF CONTENTS

C.   THE LEGISLATIVE RESPONSE 246
     Wadsworth v. Siek 246
     Questions 247
     NOTE ON STATUTES AND PRECEDENTS 248
     Shrader v. Equitable Life Assurance Society 250
     Notes and Questions 251

Chapter 8   THEORIES OF STATUTORY INTERPRETATION 253

A.   COURTS AS AGENTS OF THE LEGISLATURE 255
    1.   *Traditional Intentionalism* 255
    2.   *Doubts About the Focus on Legislative Intent* 257
      (a)   *Fictional Intent* 258
      (b)   *Public Choice* 259
    3.   *Agents of a Principal without Intent* 261
      (a)   *Broadening Intentionalism* 261
        (i)   *"Imaginative Reconstruction"* 261
        (ii)   *Purposivism* 264
      (b)   *Narrowing Intentionalism — Herein of "The New Textualism"* 266
B.   COURTS AND LEGISLATURES AS LAWMAKING PARTNERS . . . 269
    1.   *Independent Judicial Judgment* 269
    2.   *Dynamic Statutory Interpretation* 271
    3.   *Legislative Supremacy* 272

Chapter 9   SOURCES OF STATUTORY INTERPRETATION 275

     Church of the Holy Trinity v. United States 275
     BACKGROUND NOTE 280
     THE SOURCES OF INTERPRETATION 282
    1.   *Text* 282
    2.   *Beyond Text* 283
    3.   *Title* 283
    4.   *Purpose* 284
    5.   *Historical and Legislative Context* 286
    6.   *Legislative History* 288
    7.   *Later Amendments* 291
    8.   *Public Policy and the Nature of Things* 291

Chapter 10   READING STATUTORY TEXTS 297

A.   THE PRIMACY OF THE TEXT 297
    1.   *The Internal Revenue Code* 298

TABLE OF CONTENTS

2.		*Building an Incinerator*	299
3.		*A Violent Felony*	301
4.		*The Case of the Suspended Teacher*	302
5.		*"Using a Gun"*	303
6.		*Using a House*	304
B.		STATUTORY UNCERTAINTY	305
1.		*Why Aren't Statutes Clearer?*	305
2.		*Vagueness*	310
		Regina v. Ojibway	310
		Questions	311
		Notes and Questions	313
		NOTE ON VAGUENESS AND DELEGATION	316
3.		*Ambiguity*	316
		Nix v. Hedden	317
		Notes and Questions	318
		University of Utah Hospital v. Bethke	320
		Notes and Questions	321
4.		*Punctuation and Grammatical Uncertainty*	321
5.		*Context*	323
		United States v. Ressam	323
		Notes and Questions	326
6.		*Canons of Construction*	329
	(a)	Invoking Canons	329
		United States v. Scrimgeour	329
	(b)	*Types of Canons*	332
	(c)	A Linguistic Canon — *Expressio Unius*	333
		NOTE ON THE LIMITS OF *EXPRESSIO UNIUS*	334
	(d)	A Substantive Canon — The Presumption Against Interference with State Governmental Operations	336
		Gregory v. Ashcroft	337
		Notes and Questions	339
C.		IGNORING UNAMBIGUOUS MEANING	340
		United States v. Locke	340
		Notes and Questions	342
		United States v. Wells Fargo Bank	346
		Notes and Questions	347

Chapter 11	**STATUTORY PURPOSE**	**349**

Heydon's Case	349
Christiansburg Garment Co. v. EEOC	351

TABLE OF CONTENTS

Notes and Questions 353

Friedrich v. City of Chicago 354

Questions 356

West Virginia University Hospitals, Inc. v. Casey 356

Notes and Questions 359

NOTE ON DETERMINING, OR ATTRIBUTING, PURPOSE 361

NOTE ON PURPOSE AND THE PROPER JUDICIAL ROLE 363

In Re House Bill No. 1,291 364

Notes and Questions 364

Chapter 12   LEGISLATIVE HISTORY **367**

A.   INTRODUCTION 367

B.   USING LEGISLATIVE HISTORY 368

  1.   *The Plain Meaning Rule* 368

  2.   *A Hierarchy of Legislative Sources* 370

        Question 372

  3.   *Legislative History in Practice* 372

    (a)   Air Quality Standards 372

          Questions 373

    (b)   Liability for Hazardous Waste Cleanup 373

          Notes and Questions 374

    (c)   *Gregory v. Ashcroft* 375

          Gregory v. Ashcroft 376

          Notes and Questions 380

C.   THE ASSAULT ON JUDICIAL RELIANCE ON LEGISLATIVE
        HISTORY 381

  1.   *Constitutional Illegitimacy* 381

  2.   *Inaccurate Evidence of Members' Actual Views* 382

  3.   *Indeterminacy* 384

  4.   *Unavailability and Cost* 386

        Notes and Questions 386

        NOTE ON LEGISLATIVE HISTORY AND "DEMOCRATIC
        EXEGESIS" 387

Chapter 13   STATUTES IN THE ADMINISTRATIVE STATE **391**

A.   INTRODUCING ADMINISTRATIVE AGENCIES 391

B.   AGENCY INTERPRETATIONS 393

C.   DEFERENCE TO AGENCY INTERPRETATIONS 395

        Skidmore v. Swift & Co. 395

        Chevron U.S.A. Inc. v. NRDC 397

        Notes and Questions 399

TABLE OF CONTENTS

D.   AN AGENCY (IN)ACTION 402
     Massachusetts v. EPA 402
     Notes and Questions 409

Chapter 14   STABILITY AND CHANGE IN STATUTORY LAW . . . 413

A.   *STARE DECISIS* IN STATUTORY CASES 413
     Patterson v. McLean Credit Union 413
     Notes and Questions 417
B.   CHANGING STATUTORY MEANING 421
     Li v. Yellow Cab Co. 422
     Notes and Questions 425
     Saint Francis College v. Al-Khazraji 426
     Notes and Questions 427
     Bob Jones University v. United States 428
     Notes and Questions 432
C.   "DESUETUDE" — HEREIN OF STATUTORY OBSOLESCENCE . . . 434
     Franklin v. Hill 434
     Notes and Questions 436

**Chapter 15   SUMMARY AND CONCLUSION: THE ROLE OF JUDGES
                  IN A DEMOCRATIC SOCIETY 439**

     Gregory v. Ashcroft 439
     Notes and Questions 441
     Chisom v. Roemer 443
     Notes and Questions 449

TABLE OF CONTENTS

EPILOGUE **455**

Appendix A   **THE FEDERAL COURTS** **457**

Appendix B   **NEW YORK STATE COURTS** **459**

Appendix C   **CALIFORNIA STATE COURTS** **461**

Appendix D   **GEOGRAPHIC BOUNDARIES OF THE FEDERAL COURTS** **463**

Appendix E   **THE LEGISLATIVE PROCESS** **465**

Appendix F   **TWO STATUTORY PROBLEMS** **479**

          Problem 1 479
          Problem 2 480

Table of Cases **TC-1**

Index **I-1**

Part I

THE COMMON LAW

Chapter 1

CASES

A. THE COMMON LAW

Should we ask, what is "law"? (Did you ask yourself that when you decided to "study law"?) Richard Posner, noted teacher and scholar, and since 1981 also a judge on the United States Court of Appeals for the 7th Circuit, has said that "what is law?" is a "question that has little practical significance if, indeed, it is a meaningful question at all." He said this in an article entitled *The Decline of Law as an Autonomous Discipline.*[1] What do you suppose it means to speak of law as "autonomous"? Surely one cannot think about "law's" autonomy without thinking about what "law" is. Hence, how can it possibly not be meaningful to ask precisely that question? And how can it not be of the greatest practical significance: how can you learn to "do law" if you do not know what it is you are learning to do? Or will you learn what it is by doing it?

Assuming that at least for the time being we cannot or should not ask what law is, let's start with a narrower question: what are the components of American law? The usual, formal answer is that they are three. *Constitutional law,* which is outside the scope of this book, consists of the federal and state constitutions and the judicial decisions interpreting and applying them. In general, constitutional law concerns the structure and powers of government, particularly vis-à-vis the individual. *Statutory law* consists of laws enacted by a legislature. Statutes have become an increasingly central part of our legal system, both at the federal and the state level. Statutory interpretation is a complex and controversial matter, which we address in Part II. (Tied to statutes are *regulations*; these are rules promulgated by administrative agencies pursuant to statutory authority that flesh out, clarify, or implement statutes.) The third distinct body of law is the *common law*. It is that part of the legal system of the United States that consists in its entirety of a body of past judicial decisions, as those decisions were rendered in particular "cases." Part I of this book is devoted to the methods of the common law.

Unlike statutory and constitutional law, the common law rests on no authoritative text external to the judiciary. The law is knowable only by reading past "cases"; it is not to be found anywhere other than in those very cases (and in *non* authoritative summaries of them). What marks common law as distinct, then, is its self-generating aspect. That is, "appropriate references for justifying legal decisions are prior legal decisions of the same order, and . . . every decision serves as

---

[1] Richard A. Posner, *The Decline of Law As an Autonomous Discipline: 1962-1987*, 100 Harv. L. Rev. 761, 765 (1987).

by persuading the judges!

a reference for future decisions."[2] (You will learn more about this when we discuss precedent in Chapter 5.) The motor of this "common law self-generativity . . . [is] the role of individuals — ordinary legal persons — in generating legal norms, and the need of individuals to keep transforming them,"[3] in other words, the role of ordinary legal persons in bringing about the "cases" you will study. Or, in still other words, *you as lawyers will make "the law"*: in the cases you will bring, the advice you will give, the arguments you will make, you will generate the precedents that will guide the next generation of lawyers. Thus, one possible answer to our initial question ("what is law?") is that, at least in "common law," *law is application —* application of legal norms by individuals in ordinary interactions.[4]

You should note that "common law" is unique to Anglo-American law. Other countries, even those that have similar democratic aspirations, do not produce a "common law." They (Western Europe, all of Central and South America, many parts of Asia and Africa, and even a few enclaves in the common law world, namely, Louisiana, Quebec, and Puerto Rico) have instead a "civil law" system.[5] Such a system relies primarily on comprehensive, though highly generalized, written codes, rather than on the accumulated body of judicial decisions. It has its origins in Roman Law (which has influenced Anglo-American law as well).[6] The broad acceptance of the civil law is worth remembering, because, as the great Karl Llewellyn[7] admonishes us:

---

[2] Arthur J. Jacobson, *Autopoietic Law: The New Science of Niklas Luhmann*, 87 MICH. L. REV. 1647, 1677 (1989).

[3] *Id.* at 1681.

[4] *Id.* at 1681.

[5] *See* JOHN HENRY MERRYMAN, THE CIVIL LAW TRADITION 3 (1969). The recent emergence of market economies in Eastern Europe has involved the restoration of certain civil law traditions. Note that "civil" has several different legal meanings, each most easily understand in opposition to something else. First, as indicated, there are "civil law" systems as opposed to common law ones. Second, civil can mean "non-criminal." For example, the course in "civil procedure" covers the rules for litigating civil cases as opposed to criminal cases, the latter being prosecutions brought by the government against those charged with violating the criminal law in which the state seeks a criminal punishment such as imprisonment. Litigation between private parties is always "civil," in this sense (though often not "civil" in the etiquette sense). Third, "civil" (more often, "civilian") can mean non-military. "Civil officers" are government employees outside the military; the civil courts (the ones you study in law school) handle litigation involving civilians, as opposed to the military courts, or courts martial, which apply military law and hear cases involving members of the armed forces.

[6] The influence of Roman law derives almost entirely from a single collection, the *Corpus Juris Civilis*, in which the sixth-century Emperor Justinian assembled the works of earlier jurists and emperors. Medieval legal scholars rediscovered and were preoccupied by a particular text from the *Corpus* known as *The Digest*. From the eleventh to the eighteenth century, the central aspect of legal development in Western Europe was the reception of Roman law. This culminated with the idea, borrowed from the *Corpus*, that law should be systematically codified and that Roman law offered the analytic tools for successful codification. The influence of Roman law on the common law is more uncertain; historians agree, however, that Roman and civil law did supply particular doctrines, terms, and perspectives to the common law, especially in such areas as mercantile and family law.

[7] Karl Nickerson Llewellyn (1893-1962), whom you will meet repeatedly in these materials, is generally considered one of the foremost legal scholars of the 20th century. A professor at the Columbia and University of Chicago Law Schools, he was among the most prominent and influential of the "legal realists." He is best-known today as the principal drafter and driving force behind the Uniform Commercial Code and as the author of *The Bramble Bush* (1930), a useful introductory guide for

Llewellyn

Nowhere more than in law do you need armor against that type of ethnocentric and chronocentric snobbery — the smugness of your own tribe and your own time: We are the Greeks; all others are barbarians.[8]

Although American jurists have always been ambivalent toward the English inheritance, American common law has been importantly shaped by its "reception" of the English common law. You have perhaps already noticed that all of your casebooks contain English cases, many of them decided after independence but nevertheless treated as groundbreakers for their particular patch of the law.[9] Indeed, the term "common law" is itself borrowed from England, where it referred to that body of customary law that was shared, or common to, the entire Kingdom (as opposed to idiosyncratic local customs or rules). About reception, you should know at least this:[10]

> How did the common law of England get over here, and to stay? In an opinion written a little more than fifty years after the Declaration of Independence, Justice Story said of the common law that "our ancestors brought with them its general principles and claimed it as their birthright." This is at best a figure of speech, and I greatly doubt that Story meant it as more than that. If there had been lawyers among those who sailed to Virginia in 1607 and to Plymouth in 1620, they would undoubtedly have brought the principles of the common law along with them as their most precious baggage, but the time for lawyers in America had not yet come. The historian-jurist Daniel J. Boorstin gives us a better picture of colonial law as it was in the beginning:

> > Legal proceedings of the early years give us the impression of a people without much legal training and with few lawbooks who were trying to reproduce substantially what they knew 'back home.' Far from being a crude and novel system of popular law, or an attempt to create institutions from pure Scripture, what they produced was instead a layman's version of English legal institutions. * * *

> Colonial law and judicial administration became increasingly profession-alized in the first half of the eighteenth century. The evolution towards regularity and formal rationality in the operation of legal institutions was not as rapid in some colonies as in others, but it is discernible to a substantial degree everywhere. This is always true in developing countries,

---

first-year law students. His two other most important works are *The Common Law Tradition* (1960), which examines appellate decisionmaking, and *The Cheyenne Way*, an interdisciplinary study, well ahead of its time, of dispute resolution among the Cheyenne. The standard biography is WILLIAM TWINING, KARL LLEWELLYN AND THE REALIST MOVEMENT (1973).

[8] KARL N. LLEWELLYN, THE BRAMBLE BUSH: ON OUR LAW AND ITS STUDY 44 (Oceana Pubs. 1960; 1st published 1930). The snobbery seems evenly and equally distributed. Merryman notes that "many people believe the civil law to be culturally superior to the common law, which seems to them to be relatively crude and unorganized." MERRYMAN, *supra* note 5, at 3.

[9] *See,* for just one example, a case most likely at least noted in your Torts casebook: *Rylands v. Fletcher,* In the House of Lords, 3 L.R.-E. & I. App. 330 (1868). It shaped the law dealing with abnormally dangerous activities conducted by an owner on his land.

[10] Harry W. Jones, *The Reception of the Common Law in the United States, in* POLITICAL SEPARATION AND LEGAL CONTINUITY 93–94, 96–99, 105 (Harry W. Jones ed., 1976).

as America then was. Every colony had its substantial property holders who looked to law for the security of their expectations. Commerce was on the rise, not only local business but also intercolonial bargains and overseas trade with England, and commercial undertakings, then as now, required reasonably certain law — and competent lawyers to structure transactions in sensible and effective form. The stage is now set in the colonies for the historically demonstrable cycle: (1) the security of interests and transactions requires some regularization of the law; (2) but the regularization of law creates an urgent need for lawyers; and (3) lawyers, when they come, bring about law's further regularization. * * *

The common law thus came to the colonies of British North America not in the ideological baggage of the first settlers but a century or so later, with the emergence of an accredited and active legal profession, the development of reasonable competence in the judiciary and the regularization of adversary procedures and precedent-based methods of legal reasoning. The principles of the English common law are now to be drawn on as sources of guidance for colonial decision-making. * * *

[I]ndependence made it necessary to formulate a theory of reception. English case-law was presumably applicable, within limits, so long as what were now American states had been colonies of the British Crown. But why and by what mandate should English law be any more authoritative in the now independent states than the law of any other foreign country? In state after state, efforts were made to state the theory and the limits of the reception in explicit terms. This proved to be a difficult drafting assignment, largely because the enacting state conventions and legislatures were by no means sure how much of the English law they wanted to receive and how much to reject. * * *

As a matter of pure theory, American reception may have been limited to the English law as it existed on some set date — 1775, 1776 or whatever — but as a matter of demonstrable fact, English judicial decisions handed down long after 1776 exerted a profound influence on nineteenth century American adjudication. The reception of the common law in the United States remained unfinished business long after American independence was established. Whatever cut-off date may have been recited in this or that state reception statute, American courts did not regard the spring of English common law doctrine as one that went dry for them on the day American independence was proclaimed. Throughout the formative period of American law and well into the later years of the nineteenth century, what was received here was not the closed book of English law as of 1776 but the open book of developing English common law doctrine.

The most important "reception" from England was perhaps not any particular body of doctrine but a way of thinking about law which made it easier for our great jurists (such as Story) to create an indigenous American jurisprudence.[11]

---

[11] A quite wonderful (and very readable) book that tells you more about our legal traditions is GRANT GILMORE, THE AGES OF AMERICAN LAW (1977) (see especially Chapter Two, "The Age of Discovery"). *See*

(handwritten margin notes, top:) e.g. are a **fool** a **pond** "similar"?   why the date? (stare decisis)

B. "CASES"

When a lawyer talks of a "case," she most often means a past judicial decision that once and for all settled a dispute (a lawsuit) between two contending parties — a plaintiff and a defendant, as they most often are called. So one refers to the "case of" *Brown v. Board of Education of Topeka*, 347 U.S. 483 (1954), in which the Supreme Court held that segregated public schools were unconstitutional. The reference tells us that the case was a lawsuit between Brown on the one hand and the Board of Education on the other, that the written opinion announcing and explaining the ruling can be found in volume 347 of the United States Reports (the set of books in which the United States Supreme Court reports its decisions) at page 483, and that the decision occurred in 1954.

(handwritten:) when are facts similar?   all cts? no

But in talking of a "case," a lawyer might also be referring to a particular legal claim, the strength of which, in the common law system, can be evaluated only in light of prior "cases" — that is prior decisions made by courts when faced with situations with similar facts. Thus, suppose you consulted your lawyer about a dispute between you and X, whom you wish to sue. If she were to say, "I don't think you have much of a case," she would mean something like this: I have listened to your story, your tale of the events that transpired as you perceived them. I have done so with a measure of skepticism — because I know only too well that what you have told me is affected by whatever limits your perception and is undoubtedly shaped, consciously or not, by your aims, goals and desires. I have, nevertheless, converted your story into a chapter of the emerging law-story that we lawyers call "facts" and I have then put these facts into legally relevant categories drawing on my understanding of past cases that involved similar factual categories. Next I ascertained that the appropriate court or courts in those cases refused relief to the plaintiff and that they did so recently, firmly, unequivocally, and perhaps even unanimously. Or she means: there are prior, factually similar cases in which the plaintiff prevailed, but they all contained an important factual element that, in my judgment, was crucial to why they were decided the way they were and that element is missing in your case. Or your story contains a factual element never present in those factually similar cases in which the plaintiff prevailed, and its presence here throws off all bets, because, frankly, I judge it to be quite detrimental to your cause, and I think the court will also think it to be detrimental to your cause.

(handwritten margin notes, left:) invited   Use: Π drowning in neighbor pool   e. Π was a child   child trespassed

(handwritten margin numbers, right:) ① ② ③

In short, concludes your lawyer, I am predicting that you would lose this suit against X at this time with your specific facts. If you ask her, why should prior decisions determine the fate of my current dispute with X, she will answer: our legal system says that prior, *factually* similar cases constitute "precedent" for subsequent cases, and a doctrine called stare decisis dictates that courts must follow precedent. Of that, more later; for now, simply accept it (and note only the careful hedging in your lawyer's statement) because we must learn many other things about cases before dealing with stare decisis.

(handwritten right margin:) ❶

---

also MORTON J. HORWITZ, THE TRANSFORMATION OF AMERICAN LAW, 1780-1860 (1977) (especially Chapter One, "The Emergence of an Instrumental Conception of Law").

Cases as a Method of Instruction

Perhaps you now think that the reason you are carrying several pounds of cases into each of your courses is that they contain "The Law of" Contracts or Property or Torts or Civil Procedure or Whatever — and you attend those classes to learn The Law.

Wrong — as you know from the Foreword which warned you that there is no such thing as "The Law of" in the sense in which you probably still think of it: something stored in little black boxes to which your instructors refuse to give you the keys, probably because they want to keep their jobs! And even if such a body of law did exist, your casebooks would be an exceedingly poor tool for teaching it. As Karl Llewellyn observed long ago, "it is obvious that man could hardly devise a more wasteful method of imparting *information about subject matter* than the case-class. Certainly man never has."[12] Worse, the case method is misleading, because the cases you study are virtually all cases which the parties have carried, at great expense in time and money, to the highest tribunal that could or would hear them. By focusing almost exclusively on appellate opinions, you are studying only the very small tip of the very large iceberg of "law" or "the legal system."

Why study only the tip? Perhaps it is because

> many law professors experience vertigo when they open the doors and look outside appellate courtrooms. There is too much to look at, and it becomes difficult to produce elegant theories of law. * * * Those whose personalities need order slam the door quickly and turn back to rules and great cases decided by elite appellate courts.
>
> If we mustered our courage and lifted our eyes from the pages of appellate reports and books written by famous dead Europeans, what might we see? Jerome Frank, with little success, long ago tried to provoke the academy to pay attention to trial judges.[13]

Nevertheless, "the academy" largely persists in making appellate opinions the virtually exclusive vehicle of law studies, at least in the first year. Is the reason really no more than vertigo?

The "case class" approach to legal education was largely the creation of Christopher Columbus Langdell (yes, that really was his name), the first dean of the Harvard Law School. You owe your present enrollment in law school to Dean Langdell:

> Langdell was hired by Charles Eliot, Harvard's new president, because twenty years earlier, when he was a student at Harvard, Eliot had been extraordinarily impressed by Langdell's approach to legal study. When Eliot later recruited Langdell, Harvard's Law School was in serious trouble with declining enrollments and widespread dissatisfaction with its quality.

---

[12] Karl N. Llewellyn, *The Current Crisis in Legal Education*, 1 J. Legal Ed. 211, 215 (1948).

[13] Stewart Macaulay, *Popular Legal Culture: An Introduction*, 98 Yale L. J. 1545, 1546–1547 (1989). The reference is to Jerome Frank, a noted, some would say "extreme," Legal Realist, and his book, *Courts on Trial* (1949).

If Eliot had not met Langdell two decades earlier, he might have succumbed to the view that education of lawyers did not belong in the university. Eliot might have closed Harvard's Law School, just as it had been shut down in 1829 when enrollment fell to one student. In closing Harvard Law School, Eliot might logically then have instructed the departments of philosophy and political economy to deal with whatever they considered important and legitimate about law. If this hypothetical set of events had occurred, there could have been a decoupling of the universities and the legal education of people eager to become practicing lawyers. If so, both legal education and university scholarship about law would have evolved in very different patterns.[14]

One way of legitimizing law as an academic field worthy of university instruction as an autonomous discipline was to align or associate it with the natural sciences. Langdell's central innovation growing out of this conception was the case method. In the preface to his original contracts casebook, Langdell explained:

> Law, considered as a science, consists of certain principles or doctrines. To have such a mastery of these as to be able to apply them with constant facility and certainty to the ever-tangled skein of human affairs, is what constitutes a true lawyer; and hence to acquire that mastery should be the business of every earnest student of law. Each of these doctrines has arrived at its present state by slow degrees; in other words, it is a growth, extending in many cases through centuries. This growth is to be traced in the main through a series of cases; and much the shortest and best, if not the only way of mastering the doctrine effectually is by studying the cases in which it is embodied. But the cases which are useful and necessary for this purpose at the present day bear an exceedingly small proportion to all that have been reported. The vast majority are useless and worse than useless for any purpose of systematic study. Moreover, the number of fundamental legal doctrines is much less than is commonly supposed * * *. It seemed to me, therefore, to be possible to take such a branch of the law as Contracts, for example, and, without exceeding comparatively moderate limits, to select, classify, and arrange all the cases which had contributed in any important degree to the growth, development, or establishment of any of its essential doctrines; and that such a work could not fail to be of material service to all who desire to study that branch of law systematically and in its original sources.[15]

Langdell's novel approach to legal education initially drove virtually every student at the school out of his classroom. But Langdell had the last laugh, and the case method has certainly carried the day. The question is whether it makes sense.

Edwin W. Patterson, the late Cardozo Professor of Jurisprudence at Columbia University Law School, enumerated four benefits claimed by advocates of the case method: (1) *historical*, because it best enables students to grasp the development of the law; (2) *pedagogical*, because it forces students to participate actively in their

---

[14] David Barnhizer, *The Revolution in American Law Schools*, 37 Clev. St. L. Rev. 227, 261 (1989).

[15] Christopher Columbus Langdell, Selection of Cases on the Law of Contracts vi–vii (1870).

education; (3) *pragmatic*, because it gives early training in what lawyers do; and (4) most importantly, *scientific*, in that it focuses on the raw materials of "the science of law."[16]

The first of these justifications is a makeweight; historical understanding is neither a necessary part of, nor unique to, the case method. The second is in our view correct, although slightly overstated. Unfortunately, the case method does not in fact "force" you to participate intellectually; it only creates an incentive to do so. In some cases the incentive backfires; the case method can actively discourage students. In any event, this is a question of pedagogy more than one about the nature of law.

The most interesting defenses of the case method are the third and fourth. In our view, the third is the central justification for the continuing use of the method; the fourth in large measure an anachronistic and wrongheaded misconception. We will consider them in reverse order.

The Law as Science

Consider the following debunking:

Christopher Columbus Langdell, who in 1870 became the first dean of the Harvard Law School, has long been taken as a symbol of the new age [— an age of faith and blind self-confidence among lawyers and legal academics]. A better symbol could hardly be found; if Langdell had not existed we would have had to invent him. Langdell seems to have been an essentially stupid man who, early in his life, hit on one great idea to which, thereafter, he clung with all the tenacity of genius. Langdell's idea evidently corresponded to the felt necessities of the time. However absurd, however mischievous, however deeply rooted in error it may have been, Langdell's idea shaped our legal thinking for fifty years.

Langdell's idea was that law is a science. He once explained how literally he took that doubtful proposition:

[A]ll the available materials of that science [that is, law] are contained in printed books. . . . [T]he library is . . . to us all that the laboratories of the university are to the chemists and physicists, all that the museum of natural history is to the zoologists, all that the botanical garden is to the botanists.[17]

Regarding the idea of a "science of law" Judge Posner has said:

The idea that law is an autonomous discipline, by which I mean a subject properly entrusted to persons trained in law and in nothing else, was originally a political idea. The judges of England used it to fend off royal interference with their decisions, and lawyers from time immemorial have

---

[16] Edwin W. Patterson, *The Case Method in American Legal Education: Its Origins and Objectives*, 4 J. Leg. Educ. 1, 2–10 (1951).

[17] Grant Gilmore, The Ages of American Law 42 (1977) (quoting A. Sutherland, The Law at Harvard 175 (1967)).

used it to protect their monopoly of representing people in legal matters.[18]

As an example, Judge Posner offers a well-known statement by Sir Edward Coke, at the time Chief Justice of the English Court of Common Pleas:

[T]hen the King said, that he thought the law was founded upon reason, and that he and others had reason, as well as the Judges: to which it was answered by me, that true it was, that God had endowed his Majesty with excellent science, and great endowments of nature; but His Majesty was not learned in the laws of his realm of England, and causes which concern the life, or inheritance, or goods, or fortunes of his subjects, are not to be decided by natural reason but by the artificial reason and judgment of law, which law is an act which requires long study and experience, before that a man can attain to the cognizance of it: and that the law was the golden met-wand and measure to try the causes of the subjects; and which protected his Majesty in safety and peace.[19]

Judge Posner continues:

Langdell in the 1870s made [the conception of law as an autonomous discipline] an academic idea. He said that the principles of law could be inferred from judicial opinions, so that the relevant training for students of the law was in reading and comparing opinions and the relevant knowledge was the knowledge of what those opinions contained. He thought that this procedure was scientific, but it was not, not in the modern sense at any rate. It was a form of Platonism; just as Plato had regarded particular chairs as manifestations of or approximations to the concept of a chair, Langdell regarded particular decisions on contract law as manifestations of or approximations to the legal concept of contract.[20]

Judge Posner goes on to call this a "perverse or at best incomplete way of thinking about law."[21] In what lies the perversity? Or, less damning, the incompleteness?

At this point we ought to ask the logical corollary: is it equally perverse or incomplete to view *science* as science?[22]

---

[18] Posner, *supra* note 1, at 762.

[19] *Id.* at 762, n.1 (quoting Prohibitions Del Roy, 6 Coke Rep. 280, 282 (1608)). Lord Coke (1552-1634) was an early collector of precedents; through his own reports, he was largely responsible for the now standard practice of reporting opinions fully. He is best-known for his assertions of the primacy of the common law, both over the King (in the quoted excerpt) and over Parliament (in the celebrated, but long since abandoned, 1610 decision in *Dr. Bonhman's Case*).

Coke's independent stance was successful only up to a point; in 1616 King James I removed him from office, essentially for insufficient malleability. Should judges be removable from office? By the President or Governor? The legislature? The public? Other judges?

[20] *Id.* at 762.

[21] *Id.*

[22] Alan Wolf, Professor of Physics at Cooper Union and, at the time, our student, presented the authors with what follows.

You may have come to law school with the idea that law is "scientific" in the following sense. The applier of law (judge, scientist) looks up the existing rules (precedents, equations) and applies them to particular situations (appellate cases, laboratory experiments). Often a "blind" application of the rules succeeds (justice is done, correct predictions are made), but sometimes a more creative effort is required. When old rules fail to meet our needs (society changes, new experimental realms are explored), we create new rules or modify old ones. We hope that the rules generally improve with changes, but we suspect that our work will never be finished (society is always evolving, there are ever more subtle physical phenomena to understand).

Langdell's method of case law study is said to be a scientific one, so you might expect legal study to resemble your study of, say chemistry. In chemistry you were told that $PV = NRT$ was the relationship between gas pressure, volume, and temperature. Class discussion focused primarily on how to apply the rule, and interesting consequences of the rule. Legal case analysis couldn't be more different. You are given no lists of rules, instead you are asked to deduce the rules from an analysis and comparison of cases. Such a "discovery" method of teaching is rare, but not unheard of in science. In a discovery course, students perform classic scientific experiments, unaware of the results they should obtain.

The far more common method of teaching science is to *present* the fundamental rules (these cannot be derived from more elementary principles, we must appeal to experimental confirmation), and to *derive* the applied rules (these are essentially combinations of the fundamental rules). So the law/science analogy seems to break down. The rules of law are confusing and uncertain, and you are asked to play games to find them. The rules of science are simple (in the sense that they can be expressed concisely and unambiguously) and they are universally True. The most important equation of physics is Newton's Second Law of motion, $F=ma$. It says that the harder I kick an object, the faster it will fly away. Simple and True.

A month or two into the frustrating process of case analysis, you will suspect that cases are decided, not according to rules, but according to judicial whim, lawyer ineptitude, political pressures, and likely the phase of the moon. At this point science and law stand in sharp contrast. Science is Truth (logic, rigor, consistency), and law is a mess (human foibles, politics, economics). If it made any sense quantitatively to compare the truth of science to the truth of law, most everyone would agree that science has a dramatic lead, but it may interest (and dismay? comfort?) you to know that science is not as perfect as you may have thought.

The fundamental physical laws are based on neither logic nor mathematics, they are simply "thought up" and found to be consistent with a set of experiments. Newton's Second Law was "the law" for centuries, but the more precise experiments of modern physics (circa 1900) disproved the law, so Truth was replaced by "approximately true under certain circum

Now the doctor sentence. "Take 2 aspirins + call me in the morning."

Sign: "Right lane MUST turn right"

stances." More accurate versions of Newton's Second Law are far more complex mathematically, but no more logically provable than F=ma.

The applied rules of science rest on the shaky foundation of the fundamental laws, but the applied rules are more than a simple combination of these laws. Approximations of many types are required, each of which limits the accuracy and applicability of the results. Often it is necessary to make assumptions that are not testable or even plausible, simply to be able to proceed with a computation.[23] Bertrand Russell said "All exact science is dominated by the idea of approximation." Students of science, but also scientists and science teachers have a largely unconscious tendency to forget about the approximations and limitations, and to think of and present their results as more True than they really are.

Understanding the imperfections of science should make you feel more forgiving toward law, which, after all, has to solve problems far more complex than science.

Professor Patterson raised a different objection to the idea of "law as science":

End of Wolf

[I]n none of these discussions [of law as science] was it recognized that a rule or principle of law is primarily normative or prescriptive in meaning, whereas scientific propositions are either true or false upon the basis of empirical observations.[24]

The normative quality of law is an essential concept to understand — both because such an understanding will help you to decipher cases, and because it will lead you to think more clearly about what "law" is.

Suppose you enter a classroom and see a sign on the wall that reads "No Smoking." Is it appropriate for you to say about the words, "No Smoking," "That is not true" (or, "That is true")? If it is not appropriate, what does that imply about the nature of the words, "No Smoking"? If you cannot say the *legend* is true or false, what observations can you make about it? Can you say about the *sign,* "That is not true," and what would you mean by that? Do you understand the difference between commenting on the *legend* and on the *sign?*

Presumably, no one will be smoking in the room. What observations can you make about that? If someone is smoking, does that act now make the words "No Smoking" "not true," "false" or what?

If you sue the cement factory next door because it emits dust that settles on your house, and the court says: "We find that the cement factory has (does not have) a right to do that," is that like saying "No Smoking" or is it like saying, "In the United

---

[23] Here are *some* of the approximations used in PV = NRT, the "ideal gas *law*":

1) that the gas molecules occupy no space (wrong);

2) that the huge number of molecules bouncing off the container walls define a constant value for the pressure (wrong); and

3) that there are an infinite number of gas molecules — hence a statistical approach is correct (wrong).

[24] Patterson, *supra* note 16, at 4.

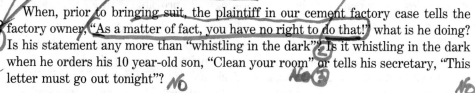

States the 4th of July is a national holiday"?

When, prior to bringing suit, the plaintiff in our cement factory case tells the factory owner, "As a matter of fact, you have no right to do that!" what is he doing? Is his statement any more than "whistling in the dark"? Is it whistling in the dark when he orders his 10 year-old son, "Clean your room" or tells his secretary, "This letter must go out tonight"? NO

Is to say "as a matter of fact, I have the right to do that" a nonsensical sentence? Always? Sometimes? Never? In the factory example, is "as a matter of fact you have no right to do that" a meaningful utterance before the court has spoken? After the court has spoken? yes   NO

What does all this have to do with Professor Patterson's observation? With your understanding of cases? Your understanding of what "law" is about?

Suppose you understand that an opinion in a given case is a mixture of descriptive language, verifiable as true or not, and normative language, verifiable, if that is the right word ("legitimated"?) by standards other than empirical ones.[25] What do you gain from that understanding?

Practical Benefits of the Case Method of Instruction

Although decided cases are obviously essential (if incomplete) data for understanding what judges do and what the law requires, it is rare that anyone now defends the case method on the basis that it is the most scientific approach to a scientific discipline. Rather, the central modern justification relies on a vision of law school as professional training.

> [The case method] has survived because it has been widely esteemed as an efficient and effective means of inculcating intellectual skills, or habits of thinking, which are deemed valuable in the practice of law. People who have studied cases are changed by the experience; the change is often substantial, and may be more profound than that usually wrought by any other experience provided in higher education.

> Case method instruction develops several types of important legal intellectual skills. Such instruction gives a practical bent to the student's thinking; cases are problems, and students reading cases are also trying to solve problems. The activity hones the student's sense of relevance as he acquires the habit of distinguishing between ideas that are useful and those that are not. . . . Additionally, such study helps develop greater balance in thinking. Discussion and analysis of cases require the student to consider both sides of issues. A student who has considered both sides of several thousand cases is less likely to engage in self-deception about the strength and righteousness of his position. * * * Tolerance for ambiguity also improves; professional instinct is heightened.

---

[25] R.M. HARE, THE LANGUAGE OF MORALS (1952), deals with the distinction between descriptive and prescriptive language. It is a wonderful and accessible book that you might want to look at.

Case study is also important as a means of elevating such basic skills as reading, speaking, and listening. This results from the extensive dialogue between teacher and students, and among students, which is greatly facilitated by the framework for discussion provided by the cases being read together by the group. * * *

Students who acquire these intellective traits and habits in adequate supply have also acquired the capacity to become their own professional teachers. To the extent that a person has achieved competence in case method instruction, he is capable of mastering large amounts of new legal material with little or no help. * * * While bare doctrine can be simplified and confined in study outlines and thus assimilated more efficiently than by the case method, understanding of doctrine and underlying policy is enhanced and deepened if the understanding is acquired as a result of the student's own synthesis in the course of problem solving. A student who has read and discussed a hundred antitrust cases, for example, will generally have a much firmer grip on that field, and its difficulties and ambiguities, than one who has invested equal time in passive submission to lecture, outline, and text.[26]

Because at least one of the schools' missions is to train students for the "business of law," that is, for *practice*, it is safe to predict that cases will indeed remain a foundational part of your legal education and, for that matter, will accompany you through your professional life as a lawyer.

C. COURTS

Cases are decided, and decisions issued, of course, by courts. The United States contains a vast number and variety of courts, many operating in distinct but overlapping systems. There is no such thing as "the American judicial system" as such. As Daniel Meador has explained:

The great divide in the American legal landscape is the state-federal line. It derives from the United States constitution, pursuant to which the federal government was created in 1789 to "form a more perfect Union" of the existing states. The federal government and the state governments coexist, with a broad range of powers delegated to the former and all others reserved to the latter, although there are certain powers that can be exercised concurrently. Each of these governments has its own court system, autonomous and self-contained. * * *

The federal judiciary and the fifty state judicial systems are each constructed like a pyramid. In broad outline these systems are similar, but they vary in the details of their organization and business. Across the base are the trial courts, and the courts of first instance. At the apex is the court of last resort, usually called the Supreme Court [though in New York State, oddly, the Supreme Court is the trial-level court and the highest court is

---

[26] Paul D. Carrington, *Book Review*, 72 CAL. L. REV. 477, 490–491 (1984) (reviewing Robert Stevens, Law School: Legal Education in America from the 1850s to the 1980s (1983)).

called the Court of Appeals]. In most states and in the federal system there
is a middle tier, the intermediate appellate courts. * * *

When opinions of American courts are published, they are collected in
various sets of bound volumes known as reports. Most states have their
own official reports, and decisions from all states are included in regional
reports provided by private publishers for the convenience of users. There
are other reports for federal decisions. * * * In addition to being published
in bound volumes, court decisions, statutes, and regulations are now
available nationwide through electronic data retrieval systems * * *.

American courts adhere to the adversary process, as distinguished from
the inquisitorial process that prevails on the continent of Europe and in
numerous countries elsewhere. In both civil and criminal cases, the parties
through their lawyers are solely responsible for presenting the facts to the
court * * * [though most cases are settled and] only some 5 to 10% of cases
actually go to trial. At trial, the lawyers call and question the witnesses.
The testimony elicited in court, along with all other items admitted into
evidence by the judge (e.g. documents), forms the trial record. Based on
this adversarial "party presentation," the trial court makes determinations
of fact, applies the pertinent law, and enters judgment accordingly. . . .

In civil cases, any party dissatisfied with the outcome of the case may
appeal, but in practice only a small percentage of judgments are taken
beyond the trial court. In criminal cases, a high percentage of all
convictions is appealed by defendants (normally the prosecution cannot
appeal an acquittal). Appeals are based solely on the record made in the
trial court. No witnesses appear and no new evidence can be offered at the
appellate level; normally no questions can be raised there for the first time.
Unlike trial courts, over which a single judge presides, appellate courts are
multi-judge forums acting collegially. Appellate courts generally confine
themselves to reviewing questions of law raised in the trial court proceedings; factual determinations made by the trial court are not normally
disturbed. The appellate court's sole function is to determine whether, as a
matter of law, the trial court's judgment should be affirmed, reversed, or
modified in some way. If the appellate court concludes that the lower court
erred in its application of the law, the appellate court may reverse the lower
court's decision. It will do so unless the reviewing judges conclude that the
error was relatively minor and probably did not affect the outcome in the
trial court [i.e., was "harmless error"]. . . .

The state courts are the front-line adjudicators in the United States.
They overshadow the federal courts both in the number of cases they
handle and in the number of persons involved as litigants, lawyers, and
judges. In the trial courts of the fifty states, more than 30,000,000 cases,
civil and criminal, are filed annually, compared with fewer than 314,000 in
the principal federal trial courts (the district courts) and 1,300,000 in the
federal bankruptcy courts. In numbers of judges the state courts likewise
eclipse the federal. There are over 29,800 judges in the state trial courts,

while there are fewer than 1,500 federal trial judges (district, bankruptcy, and magistrate judges).[27]

Within a single jurisdiction (e.g. the State of New York, or the federal system) courts are organized hierarchically, as the foregoing excerpt indicates. This arrangement is illustrated in Appendices A (federal courts), B (New York state courts), and C (California courts). In addition, judicial jurisdiction is subdivided geographically. So a trial court will have jurisdiction of cases arising within the geographic area in which it sits. Appellate courts cover a larger area than trial courts; the Supreme Court covers the entire jurisdiction. This arrangement for the federal courts is illustrated in Appendix D.

D. JUDGES

Courts have fairly large staffs, but, of course, their key members are the judges themselves. Unlike many countries, the United States has no professional track for judges; future judges receive no special education or training and follow no special career path. Judges are lawyers who at some point were appointed or elected to the bench. We offer only three quick observations about the American judiciary here.

First, with regard to *independence*. As part of the general concept of "separation of powers," government authority in the states and at the federal level is divided into three separate branches: legislative, executive, and judicial. Professor Meador again:

> Each part must be in the hands of different officials of official bodies. Put in its simplest form, the doctrine requires that the legislative branch make the law through the passage of statutes, the executive branch enforce the law, and the judicial branch interpret and enunciate the meaning of the law through the adjudication of disputes. By this dividing power, the doctrine aims to protect citizens from abuse of official authority stemming from its concentration in the hands of too few persons or in a single body. In the mystique of American politics, this arrangement is viewed as fundamental to liberty and to government under law. It is embodied in all American government structures; hence, the federal and state courts function as separate branches of government, independent of the legislative and executive branches.[28]

Essential to this arrangement is protection of the courts from oversight or retribution from the other branches — that is, the existence of an independent judiciary. The legislative and executive branches cannot alter a judicial ruling; there is no appeal from the courts to the other branches; and judges cannot be penalized for ruling in a way disfavored by the other branches. (The legislature can, of course, modify the legal rule applied or articulated by the court in its ruling; that is its function as the lawmaking institution of government. But it cannot adjudicate or review judicial adjudications.) At the *federal* level, this independence is constitutionally protected by "life tenure" (judges hold their positions for life; they can be

---

[27] DANIEL JOHN MEADOR, AMERICAN COURTS 1–8 (2d ed. 2000). Reprinted with permission.

[28] *Id.* at 2.

removed from office only through impeachment) and a guarantee that their salaries will not be diminished.[29] *State* judges generally hold office for a specific term of years, after which they must be reappointed or re-elected.

Second, with regard to *selection*. How should judges be selected? The basic methods are three. First, all federal judges, and the judges of some states, are appointed by the head of the executive branch (the President or the Governor). Federal judges are, to be precise, *nominated* by the President and *confirmed* by the Senate. See U.S. Const., art. II, sec. 2. Second, many states use what is commonly referred to as "merit selection," which is a variation on gubernatorial appointment in which a bipartisan commission draws up a short list of names from which the Governor must select. Third, most states hold elections for at least some of their judges. In most instances, these are partisan (i.e., the candidates identify what political party they belong to and run as the nominees of their parties); some states require that judicial elections be nonpartisan.

The choice between appointing and electing judges has been a matter of longstanding, and continuing, debate. In part, this disagreement reflects a contest over what it is judges actually do (or should do). The standard justification for *electing* judges is that "judges make policy [and] * * * like other policymakers, they should be accountable to the people in a representative political system."[30] The standard justifications for *appointing* judges are that judges ought to be independent from politics and the popular will, pursuing the law where it leads rather than yielding to popular pressure, and that the general public is not well-equipped to evaluate judicial ability. During debate over ratification of the Federal Constitution James Madison noted that, while in general high-ranking governmental officers ought to be selected by the people,

> [s]ome deviations . . . from the principle must be admitted. In the constitution of the judiciary department in particular, it might be inexpedient to insist rigorously on the principle: first, because peculiar qualifications being essential in the members, the primary consideration ought to be to select that mode of choice which best secures these qualifications; second, because the permanent tenure by which the appointments are held in that department must soon destroy all sense of dependence on the authority conferring them.[31]

Both the election and the appointment of judges are, at this point in American history, quite politicized and polarizing.

Third, with regard to *composition*. Historically, both the federal and state judiciaries were composed of successful, white, male lawyers. In the last generation or two, there has been a significant increase in the diversity of the bench, with an increasing number of women and minority judges drawn from a variety of practice

---

[29] "The Judges, both of the supreme and inferior Courts, shall hold their Offices during good Behaviour, and shall, at stated Times, receive for their Services, a Compensation, which shall not be diminished during their Continuance in Office." U.S. Const., art. III, § 1.

[30] David Adamany & Philip Dubois, *Electing State Judges*, 1976 Wis. L. Rev. 731, 772.

[31] The Federalist No. 51, at 321 (James Madison) (Clinton Rossiter ed., 1961).

backgrounds. To most, this seems a salutary change. But why, exactly? Consider the following:

> [It is a common] complaint that the judiciary is not adequately "representative" of society as a whole. Advocates of a more representative bench often fail to identify precisely the value of such diversity. Three overlapping justifications are implicit. First, the bench, like any profession, should be open to all regardless of race or gender. * * * Second, a "representative" judiciary (or Congress or school board) has symbolic value. Those subject to the commands of a governing body will have more confidence in and respect for that body if it includes a member or members who are "like" them. Third, representativeness will affect substantive outcomes; that is the basic realist critique and the assumption, or hope, underlying much reluctant support for the [Clarence] Thomas nomination. These latter two justifications are linked. It is because decisions are affected by the decisionmaker's background and group membership that "representativeness" has symbolic value. Public confidence in governing bodies hinges much more on their representativeness than does public confidence in, say, the space program. Thus, the reason "representativeness" matters with regard to judges is that they *do* act on behalf of the public and they do so through the elaboration of norms that are not wholly objective.[32]

As was keenly illustrated during the 2009 confirmation hearings for Justice Sotomayor, most people are more comfortable with the first two justifications than with the third. The nominee spent a large portion of her testimony backtracking from, spinning, and contradicting this statement from a 2002 speech:

> [O]ur experiences as women and people of color affect our decisions. The aspiration to impartiality is just that — it's an aspiration because it denies the fact that we are by our experiences making different choices than others.

> Whether born from experience or inherent physiological or cultural differences * * * our gender and national origins may and will make a difference in our judging. Justice O'Connor has often been cited as saying that a wise old man and wise old woman will reach the same conclusion in deciding cases. * * * I am * * * not so sure that I agree with the statement. First, * * * there can never be a universal definition of wise. Second, I would hope that a wise Latina woman with the richness of her experiences would more often than not reach a better conclusion than a white male who hasn't lived that life.[33]

---

[32] Michael Herz, *Choosing Between Normative and Descriptive Versions of the Judicial Role*, 75 MARQUETTE L. REV. 726, 746–747 (1992).

[33] Sonia Sotomayor, *A Latina Judge's Voice*, 13 BERKELEY LA RAZA L.J. 87, 91–92 (2002).

E.   LITIGATION: HOW A DISPUTE BECOMES A "CASE"[34]

As said earlier, the cases you will read in law school (and as a practicing lawyer) are, for the most part, appellate decisions. That is, the case has been brought to trial, a verdict rendered by the factfinder (either a judge or jury), one party (or both) has appealed the decision to the next higher court in that jurisdiction. What question is before the court on appeal? Who has brought the appeal, and what happened in the court below? The answer to these questions will tell you the *procedural posture* of the case you are reading and, ultimately, shed light on exactly what issue(s) the case does — *and does not* — address.[35]

Your ability to read and understand a case thoroughly will depend in no small measure on your understanding of how cases are brought, tried, and appealed — in short, Civil Procedure. The following discussion is provided to assist you in your general understanding of how a lawsuit is brought in court.[36] We will trace the steps involved in bringing a civil action in the context of a simple hypothetical.[37]

Victim v. Driver

You are a lawyer in the State of Euphoria. Victim comes to you with a problem. She was getting onto her motorcycle in front of the local DVD store, having just rented an instructional DVD on tree house renovation, when Driver rounded the corner in his '57 Edsel, lost control of the wheel, and slammed into Victim and her bike. Victim lists for you all of the troubles she has suffered as a result of the accident: her back and neck were sprained, her motorcycle was totaled, she missed three weeks of work as an aerobics instructor, and she never got to see the DVD she had rented. You take notes during the interview and tell Victim you will get back to her. Now, alone in your office, what do you do?

Is there a cause of action?

Your first job as a lawyer is to determine if Victim has a legally cognizable claim, or *cause of action* — that is, has she suffered something at the hands of Driver for which the courts will grant her relief? As a practical matter, you must also assess her chances of winning even if her claim is legally sufficient. Remember, in our system of justice, a plaintiff must prove that the defendant has done what is

---

[34] (c) 1992 Victoria A. Kummer. Ms. Kummer was a student in our Legal Process Workshop. She undertook the task of preparing the following pages. Her goal was to render a complex process understandable to raw novices without distorting it. We obviously believe that she succeeded splendidly. We would only add this caveat: the goal here is to give you a "palm-of-the-hand" view of matters procedural. Inescapably, some finer points and distinctions have been ignored. You will learn about all of them in due course in Civil Procedure.

[35] Remember, a court can only make a binding ruling on a question that is squarely before it. Musings by a court on an issue outside the specific question it faces are called *dicta* and, while persuasive, do not carry the authority of an actual holding.

[36] As you undoubtedly know by now, Civil Procedure is a fascinating and complex area of study to which law schools typically devote an entire semester, or even a year. This rudimentary outline is merely an introduction to the basic concepts of Civil Procedure.

[37] Our concern at this juncture is only civil cases. The somewhat different procedures of a criminal action, in which the State brings a case against a defendant for criminal wrongdoing, will not be treated here.

claimed, while the defendant is not required to prove anything. Before Victim can recover a judgment against Driver, for example, she must prove her case against him by a "preponderance" of the evidence — the factfinder (either judge or jury) must find it "more likely than not" that Driver "caused" Victim's injuries and did so in a manner giving rise to legal liability.

You have looked through the law books and your old Torts class notes, and you have finally determined that Victim's injuries may be redressed — that is, the law does provide relief for the injuries Victim claims to have suffered at Driver's hands. You have also learned that a nearby motorcycle gang saw the whole thing, so you have a flock of witnesses to help you prove your case. You describe your ordinary fee scale to Victim, who says it sounds reasonable. In your infinite wisdom, you take Victim's case.

What forum?

Now that you have a case to bring, the next logical question is, *where* do you bring it? The court you choose is called the *forum*, and there are many different *fora* from which to choose — municipal, county, district, federal, etc. Where do you go? A court can only hear a case if it is empowered to do so — i.e., if it has "jurisdiction" over the subject matter of the case and over the parties involved. When we say "jurisdiction," we are really talking about two distinct kinds of power: *subject matter jurisdiction* and *personal jurisdiction*. Whether or not a court is empowered to hear a case — whether it has "jurisdiction" — turns on issues such as the nature of the claim, how much money is at stake, where the claim arose, and the state citizenship of the parties.

The competence of a court to hear certain kinds of cases depending on the nature of the claims asserted and the amount in controversy is called the *subject matter jurisdiction* of a court. *Common law* claims are almost always based on *state* common law (federal common law exists, but it is quite rare), and therefore come within the subject matter jurisdiction of the state court. The typical Tort or Contract lawsuit will usually be a *state* claim, arising under state law, and is properly brought in a state court of general jurisdiction.[38]

The subject matter jurisdiction of federal courts is generally limited to cases that arise under federal law. For example, if Victim were claiming that Driver was involved in monopolistic trade practices, then *Victim v. Driver* would be a case arising under federal law (the Sherman Antitrust Act), and would properly belong in federal court. There is one major exception to this limitation of federal jurisdiction: federal courts also have subject matter jurisdiction in cases involving state law claims if the parties are from different states, or if one of the parties is from a foreign country, *and* the amount in dispute exceeds $75,000. In such "diversity cases" (i.e. cases involving parties of "diverse" citizenship), which account for roughly a quarter of the federal docket, the court will apply the law of the state in which it sits.

---

[38] "General jurisdiction" as opposed to "limited jurisdiction." "Courts of limited jurisdiction" — Surrogate's Court, Family Court, Criminal Court, etc. — are usually courts which are empowered to hear only certain kinds of claims such as administration of estates, child custody, and murder, to name a few.

In our case, suppose Victim and Driver are from different states. We know that Victim is a citizen of the State of Euphoria. If Driver was a citizen of the State of Grace, and Victim's claim was for $1,000,000, Victim would have her choice of fora: she may bring suit against Driver in either state or federal court. Choosing the forum for your client's case is a strategic decision which you will make based on a variety of factors, such as which forum's procedural rules could be best used to your client's benefit,[39] which forum can get Victim a trial most quickly, or which forum would provide Victim with the most generous jury. Whichever forum Victim chooses, Driver may be entitled to contest Victim's choice and may try to move the case to the other forum.

Still supposing that Victim and Driver are from different states, what happens if you decide that it is best for Victim to sue in state court? Would it do Victim any good to simply go into the Euphoria state court and bring a claim against Driver? The historical answer would have been no. Since Driver is not from the State of Euphoria, the State of Euphoria may not subject Driver to its judicial process — it lacks *personal jurisdiction* over Driver. Driver may only be hauled into court in his own state, the State of Grace. For this reason, Victim must go to the State of Grace, and sue in Grace's state court if Victim wants to bring her case against Driver in state court. However, at present state statutes almost always provide for jurisdiction over out-of-state drivers who have accidents within the state. Under "long arm statutes," this has been expanded to include all tortious conduct within the state. The out of state driver statutes rely on a concept of "implied consent" that makes all drivers subject to personal jurisdiction.[40]

Bringing the Suit

As it turns out, both Victim and Driver live in Euphoria, so your options for a forum are limited to the Euphoria state court. How do you commence the suit? There are formal procedures, the details of which will vary from state to state, but which will in most respects follow one of two general patterns.

In many jurisdictions (including the federal trial courts), the lawsuit is commenced by *filing a complaint* with the court. If Euphoria were such a "file and serve" state, you would commence your case by first filing the complaint with the Euphoria state court. Afterwards, you would *serve* upon Driver a *summons* which directs Driver to come to court to defend himself. Included with the summons would be a copy of the complaint.

If, on the other hand, Euphoria were a "serve and file" state, you would commence your case by first serving Driver (by mail or by a professional process-server) with the summons and a copy of the complaint. You would not file copies with the court until later, at such time as either you or Driver needed a judge

---

[39] The body of substantive law that applies to any given case is not necessarily the law of the forum. Determining which jurisdiction's substantive law will apply is the subject of a fascinating course entitled Conflict of Laws. However, a case in a particular forum will be subject to the *procedural* law of that forum regardless of what substantive law applies.

[40] You will learn about other exceptions to the "rule" regarding personal jurisdiction in Civil Procedure.

to take action of some kind (for example, to decide something or to order the other party to do something).

The Complaint

The complaint informs the court and Driver of Victim's claims — e.g., "Driver negligently failed to keep control of his automobile and drove it into me, causing the following injuries." The complaint will also outline the relief Victim is seeking from Driver — in this case, an amount of money. If Driver ignores the summons and complaint, the court will render a *default judgment* against him, and the case is over — Victim wins.

The Answer

If Driver is wise, he will avoid a default by responding to the complaint with an *answer*. The answer is a formal document responding to, and often denying outright, each of the specific allegations made in the complaint. It may include one or more *affirmative defenses*, stating in essence "yes, but" (that is, the events occurred as Victim says, but other facts negate Driver's liability), or it may even raise a *counterclaim*, seeking to impose a liability on Victim. Demurrer

Before or after answering, Driver could also move to dismiss *for failure to state a claim upon which relief can be granted* (also called a *demurrer*, stating in essence "so what?" — even if the events occurred exactly as Victim says, the actions by Driver or injuries to Victim are not anything for which the law grants relief) or *for lack of jurisdiction* (stating in essence, "you can't touch me" or "you can't hear this kind of case").

In general, if the facts are undisputed, and the case hinges solely on a question of law, the judge can decide the case alone and prior to trial on a *motion to dismiss*, or on a *motion for summary judgment*. These pre-trial motions, as well as the *motion for judgment as a matter of law* (formerly called a directed verdict motion) *during* the trial, and the *renewal of motion for judgment after trial* (formerly called a judgment notwithstanding the verdict or a J.N.O.V.[41]) share the same basic argument: they ask the court to enter judgment for the moving party *as a matter of law* — because the facts alleged by plaintiff do not amount to a cognizable claim, or because the law does not recognize the defense advanced by the defendant, or because no facts are in dispute and the judge can determine the winner as a matter of law.

Where a question of fact exists, however, the parties must be given the opportunity to prove the facts they have asserted in their complaint and answer. The proving ground is, of course, the trial itself, and the outcome of the case is placed in the hands of the factfinder — either the judge sitting as a trier of fact (the parties having waived their rights to a jury trial) or the jury.

In our case, Driver raises several defenses in his answer. He claims that Victim was wrong in her recital of the facts, asserting that he was driving carefully at the

---

[41]   J.N.O.V. stands for "judgment *non obstante veredicto*." The Federal Rules of Civil Procedure were amended in 1991 to eliminate some of the more archaic terminology found within our federal system. Some state courts still use these older terms, however, and you will still find them mentioned in the cases pre-dating the 1991 amendment.

time of the accident, and denying all fault. In addition, he alleges that Victim herself caused the accident by slamming into Driver's Edsel, and that Driver is therefore not liable for Victim's injuries.[42] Driver also moves to dismiss Victim's claim for injuries stemming from the fact that she never got to view her instructional DVD, arguing that "deprivation of DVD watching" is not a legal claim recognized by the State of Euphoria.

The judge agrees with Driver and dismisses ("throws out" is how laypersons and newspaper reporters tend to put it) Victim's "deprivation of DVD watching" claim. The other claims, however, are legally cognizable and involve disputed facts, thus requiring a trial before a factfinder.

Discovery

Despite what you may think as a result of seeing the "surprise witness" or the metaphorical "smoking gun" evidence on television, the opposing sides in a lawsuit not only share information with each other, they are actually under an obligation to do so. The pre-trial exchange of information is called *discovery*, and in both the federal and state courts a significant portion of the procedural rules is devoted to governing this process. The rules provide a variety of methods to assist the lawyers in their search. *Interrogatories* are written questions served on the opposing party, to which a written response is required to be produced by the party with the aid of her lawyer. *Depositions* are oral examinations of witnesses and parties conducted by the opposing party before a court reporter — a stenographer who (for a fee) produces a transcript of the deposition for each side. Parties may also request the *production of documents* relating to the opposing party, witnesses, the event itself, insurance coverage, and related information.

In this case, you call in Driver for an oral deposition, in which he again insists on his version of the story. You request the production of documents from his car mechanic relating to the service history of the Edsel as well as a copy of Driver's insurance policy.[43] Driver, for his part, deposes Victim as well as every member of the motorcycle gang that will be testifying on her behalf. He also requests the production of documents from her employer (the aerobics fitness center), relating to her health evaluations and her job performance. You refuse this request as totally irrelevant to the dispute, and Driver files a motion asking the court to compel you to comply with the request for document production. The judge agrees with you that Victim's job performance history is irrelevant to the proceedings and denies that portion of the motion, but orders you to comply with the request for documents relating to her health evaluation, since Victim has put her health "in issue" by claiming personal injury and damages from loss of work.

Summary Judgment

---

[42] Driver's claim that Victim is responsible could form the basis for a *counterclaim* by Driver against Victim — a new lawsuit, tried at the same time, in which Driver is the plaintiff suing Victim for damage to his Edsel and any personal injuries he sustained. Let's keep things simple, however, and assume that Driver suffered no personal or property injury in the accident, and therefore has no interest in counterclaiming against Victim.

[43] Why do you think these documents would be helpful to your case?

All during Discovery, at any point until the trial starts, either party may move for *summary judgment*. The question before the court on summary judgment is: for each and every claim in the complaint, is there any genuine issue of material fact for which a trial is required and, if not, is the moving party entitled to judgment as a matter of law? Each claim resolution of which turns on a disputed material fact must be resolved by a factfinder after a trial. In essence then, the question raised by a motion for summary judgment is whether there is anything for a jury (or a judge as fact-finder) to do.

The Jury

Your case against Driver is going to be tried before a jury of six people.[44] When Discovery is completed and the parties are ready for trial, the court will empanel a jury. Many lawyers insist that they have won (or lost) certain cases at this stage of the proceedings. Choosing a jury provides you as the lawyer with strategic opportunities to begin trying your case. You are presented with the opportunity to hear the potential jurors answer questions addressed to them by the judge or by the lawyers. This allows you, first, to select only those jurors who you are confident will see the evidence in the light most favorable to Victim. Second, it allows you, in a setting somewhat less formal than the trial, to begin subtly to lay out your vision of the case for them. The question and answer session between the judge, attorneys, and potential jurors is known as *voir dire*.[45]

The Trial

Your jury is empanelled, and you are ready for trial. You make your opening statement, and Driver's attorney makes his. As the attorney for the plaintiff, you present your case first. You call your first witness, Victim, and ask her questions on *direct examination*. The attorney for Driver questions Victim on *cross examination*. When Driver's attorney asks a question or introduces evidence in a manner which you believe violates the rules of evidence, you *object* in very specific terms so that the record reflects your objection and the reasons for it. In this way, you have ensured that the trial record preserves your objection so that, if necessary, you may raise this point on appeal.

After you have presented all of your witnesses, and Driver's attorney has cross examined each of your witnesses, plaintiff will *rest*. This marks the close of the plaintiff's case. Driver may now move for a *judgment as a matter of law* (formerly: move for a directed verdict), arguing essentially the same thing that he argued at the (pre-trial) summary judgment stage of the proceedings: that, even if the court accepts all of the evidence which the Plaintiff has just presented, the court must still direct a verdict for the defendant Driver as a matter of law because, in light of the proof presented up to this point, no reasonable jury could render a verdict for the plaintiff Victim. If you have not presented any evidence which tends to prove the

---

[44] The size of a civil jury will vary from jurisdiction to jurisdiction.

[45] "Voir dire" translates literally, from modern French, as "to see speak," which is indeed what happens during voir dire. That is not actually what it means, however. The "voir" is a corruption of "vrai," which means "true." So what is really happening in voir dire, at least from an etymological perspective, is not that the lawyers are seeing prospective jurors speak, but rather that the prospective jurors are speaking the truth — or so it is hoped.

facts as alleged in Victim's complaint, then you have not established a *prima facie* case — a case which, on the face of it, is legally sufficient to form the basis of Driver's liability. If you have not "made out" your prima facie case, Driver may very well win his motion, and the case will be over before Driver even presents his defense. The case is "taken away from the jury," a permissible outcome because the jury could only have either (a) reached the same outcome or (b) acted unreasonably.

In this case, the court finds that you have made out your prima facie case on the claim regarding Victim's totaled motorcycle, but the court is not certain you have made out your case regarding the personal injury suffered by Victim. Driver's motion for judgment as a matter of law is therefore denied as to the motorcycle claim, but the court *reserves* judgment regarding the personal injury claim. This claim will still go to the jury along with the rest of the case at the close of Driver's case, but by "reserving" judgment, the court has essentially reserved the right to change its mind after the jury deliberates.

After the plaintiff rests, it is Driver's turn to present his case. He calls and examines his witnesses who are in turn subjected to your searing cross examination. At the close of Driver's case, *both* parties are permitted to move for a directed verdict. Driver renews his motion for directed verdict, arguing that on the proof presented no reasonable trier of fact could find for the Victim. You argue simply that even if the court were to accept Driver's version of the facts as true, that is no defense so Victim must win. Let's assume the judge denies the motions (except for the claim on which the court previously reserved judgment, which is really just a conditional denial), and both sides present their closing arguments to the jury.

Your final opportunity to influence the jury takes place in the form of the judge's instructions, or "charge" to the jury. The jury's determination is limited to questions of fact. The judge's charge states the law, which the jury will apply in reaching its ultimate conclusion as to liability. Before your closing arguments, both you and Driver's attorney will have submitted to the court proposed jury instructions which present the law in a manner most favorable to your respective clients and which, you hope, the judge will adopt in charging the jury. After the jury is charged, they deliberate, and you bite your nails.

The jury comes back, and they have found in favor of Victim on all of her claims — including the claim for personal injury. Driver, however, is permitted to renew his motion for judgment after trial. He does so, and the court grants the motion. Therefore, even though the jury found in favor of Victim on her claim for personal injury, the judge "takes the claim away from the jury" and directs the entry of judgment for Driver on that claim, concluding that Driver is not legally liable for Victim's sprained back and neck.

Appeal

You are not satisfied with the outcome of this case, because you believe that the claim for personal injury and the claim for loss of "DVD watching" should have been left for the jury to decide. You and Victim therefore decide to file an *appeal*. Driver is happy with the dismissal of those two claims, and does not believe that he will get anywhere if he tries to appeal the other claims (on which he lost), so Driver does not file a cross-appeal. He merely "responds" to the appeal as the *Appellee*, or

Respondent, while Victim is in the position of the *Appellant*, or *Petitioner*.

The appeal is a direct attack on the final judgment of the trial court. You claim that the trial court committed an error of law in the proceedings below. For our appeal, you file your papers with the Euphoria Supreme Court arguing that the trial court's dismissal of the "DVD watching" claim, and the grant of Driver's renewed motion for judgment after trial on Victim's personal injury claim, constituted "reversible error,"[46] and therefore the jury's original verdict on the personal injury claim should be reinstated and the plaintiff should be granted a new trial on the "DVD watching" claim.[47]

In Euphoria, there are three levels of courts, as is standard. Thus, appeals go initially to the "intermediate" appellate court; after a decision is rendered there the parties may seek review by the state's highest court (or "court of last resort"). In general, the loser on appeal does not have a right to this further appeal; the highest court chooses which cases to hear (it has a "discretionary docket") and will agree to hear only those of sufficient importance to merit its attention. Similarly, in the federal system, for example, the losing party in the District (trial) Court can appeal as of right to the Court of Appeals, or Circuit Courts. If the losing party wishes to pursue its claims further, in almost all cases it must petition the U.S. Supreme Court for a *writ of certiorari*, the mechanism by which the Court brings the case to it from a lower court. Issuing the writ is completely discretionary, and the Court grants only a tiny portion of "cert" petitions.

You now write a *brief* for the appellate court, a long document (despite its name) outlining the errors of the court below. Driver's attorney files a brief arguing that the court made no errors or that any it made did not affect the outcome. You both submit your briefs, and on the day for oral argument you come to court, stand before the panel of judges (appellate courts typically consist of a panel of three judges), and argue your position.

In this case, you argue that a claim based on "deprivation of DVD watching" is or should be a cognizable claim in the State of Euphoria, and you detail for the court your reasons, pointing to cases that allow such a claim or analogous claims and to policy reasons why doing so would be a good idea. Relying on the trial record, you also argue that Victim's claim for personal injury to her neck and back was fully substantiated by the evidence at trial so that the jury verdict in that claim should not have been set aside by the trial court. Driver's attorney then argues the opposing side, pointing out all of the reasons that "deprivation of DVD watching" should not be considered a legally compensable injury in this state and all the reasons that your evidence in the personal injury claim was legally insufficient.

---

[46] Error that is merely "harmless" is insufficient to cause the appellate court to reverse a lower court's ruling. The moving party must have suffered some *prejudice* as a result of the error for the court to impose a remedy so drastic as reversal.

[47] Courts are always interested in time-saving measures. The appeal of a *judgment after trial* presents a wonderful opportunity to appeal a judgment without asking the appellate court to order a time-consuming new trial. If a judgment after trial is reversed, the original jury verdict can simply be reinstated. On the other hand, the DVD-watching claim has never been litigated, so there is no *judgment* to reinstate if Victim wins her appeal on that claim. If Victim wants to collect on this issue, she must go to trial and win again.

The disposition in an appeal is delivered in the form of a written opinion — the very appellate opinions to which most of your law school reading will be devoted. The court will explain its decision to affirm or reverse, often placing its decision in the context of a wealth of common law authority for its conclusion.

Assume that in the case of *Victim v. Driver*, the court finds that the trial court committed errors of law in setting aside the jury's verdict on the personal injury claim. It will then *reverse* the lower court's ruling. It will not itself enter a new judgment. Instead, it will "remand" the case to the trial court, with instructions to enter judgment for the plaintiff. On the other hand, assume also that the appellate court agrees with the trial court with regard to the "DVD watching" claim, concluding that under Euphoria state law "deprivation of DVD watching" does not present the kind of loss that is legally redressable. Accordingly, it will *affirm* the lower court in this respect, and there the matter ends (unless, of course, Victim seeks review by the state supreme court).

Res Judicata

The case of *Victim v. Driver* is complete, and the judgments are final. Victim's claims against Driver arising out of this accident have been exhausted by this lawsuit, and Victim is *barred* from bringing a new lawsuit in the future based on any claim (either a new one, or one of the claims on which she previously sued) arising from the same accident. We say that the decision of the court in *Victim v. Driver* has "*res judicata*" effect, meaning that the judgment is final and cannot be challenged in a later proceeding. Victim cannot later sue Driver, and Driver cannot later sue Victim, on any *claim or defense* that was raised in this case. The parties are also barred from later raising claims or defenses that were not raised here but could have been. We say that such claims and defenses are *merged* in the judgment. Nor may the parties relitigate any issue in any later disputes between them, if that issue was actually litigated, and was essential to the judgment, in *Victim v. Driver*.

F. JUDGMENTS AND THEIR EFFECTS — HEREIN OF RES JUDICATA, AND SOME OTHER IMPORTANT WORDS[48]

We need to talk about four words, or rather about two sets of two words each, about which we must be clear. They are:

reversing and overruling

res judicata and stare decisis

1. *Reversing and Overruling*

Let us follow the fate of a *single* lawsuit between plaintiff X and defendant Y. As we saw in *Victim v. Driver*, it will begin in a "lower court," typically a trial court of the appropriate jurisdiction. If one or the other or both of the parties are

---

[48] We are indebted to Jones, Kernochan, and Murphy's *Legal Method* for the thought of attempting to clear up this particular bit of endemic beginning law student confusion. *See* HARRY W. JONES ET AL., LEGAL METHOD 7–8 (1980).

dissatisfied with the decision of the lower court, they will take their dispute to a "higher court"; that is, they will appeal, claiming that the lower court was wrong on certain matters, it "erred." Often, the "higher court" is not the highest court of the jurisdiction, in which case the plaintiff or the defendant, or both, if they are still not satisfied after the ruling of the intermediate court, may seek to have the highest court in the jurisdiction — e.g., the "Supreme Court of California," "The New York Court of Appeals" (do you know what it is called in your state?) — hear the case.[49]

The language alone — higher, lower — tells you that the structure is hierarchical. The highest court issues orders to the "lower court" (e.g., hold a new trial, enter judgment for the plaintiff, conduct further proceedings consistent with this opinion, etc.) and the lower court must obey. If the higher court concludes that the lower court reached the correct result, it will *affirm*. On the other hand, we use the magic word "reverse" (as in "We hereby reverse" or "Judgment reversed") when a higher court decides that the court one step below on the hierarchical ladder in the suit between X and Y erred in a non-harmless way.

What, then, is "overruling"?

Suppose that the controversy between our friends X and Y takes place in the State of New Jersey, and that the New Jersey Supreme Court has agreed to review the case, one or both of the parties being unhappy with the decision below. Suppose further that at a time past the New Jersey Supreme Court heard a different case, a dispute between A and B, and "ruled" in favor of B. If the X-Y dispute is factually similar to the A-B dispute, then the decision in the case of *A v. B* is a "precedent" for the case of *X v. Y*. Under the doctrine of stare decisis, the Supreme Court of New Jersey "is bound" to follow the rule of *A v. B* and it must render judgment for defendant Y — *unless*. Unless, that is, it decides to "overrule" *its own prior* decision, in the case of *A v. B*. Should it not overrule, we say it "followed," "stood by," or "adhered to" *A v. B*. Note that the lower court in *X v. Y* was also "bound" by the case of *A v. B*; indeed, more meaningfully than was the state Supreme Court. Because *A v. B* was decided by a higher court, overruling was simply not an option for the lower court.[50]

To put it as succinctly as possible: a court *reverses* the decision of a (lower) court *in the same controversy*; it *overrules* itself, that is, it disavows in a *later, different* case, what *it itself* had ruled in a *prior, different, but factually similar case*.

---

[49] The United States Supreme Court building contains a rather primitive gymnasium, including a basketball court. The gym is on the building's top floor, and is accordingly often referred to as "the highest court in the land."

[50] Or so "the law." But note:

> Some time ago, a handful of judges on the local superior court bench began deciding summary judgment motions without according the parties the benefit of oral argument. * * * In *Mediterranean Construction Co. v. State Farm Fire & Casualty Co.*, this court took a long, hard look at the language of Code of Civil Procedure section 437c, and came to the inescapable conclusion that, as now drafted, it requires oral argument on summary judgment motions * * *.

> We thought — incorrectly, as it turned out — that the trial courts would simply follow our opinion even if they disagreed with it. Stare decisis and all that stuff. But sometimes it seems as though we have to remind the lower court there is a judicial pecking order.

Gwartz v. Superior Court, 71 Cal. App.4th 480, 83 Cal Rptr.2d 865 (1999) (Sills, J.).

The case of *X v. Y*, we said, takes place in New Jersey. Suppose *A v. B* was a New York decision and it was the New York Court of Appeals that gave judgment for B. Must New Jersey now, in *X v. Y*, follow New York? The answer is *no* — stare decisis has territorial limitations. The New York Court of Appeals can only *bind* itself and New York's lower courts. It cannot *bind* the New Jersey Supreme Court or any other tribunal in any other state. Decisions of courts in other jurisdictions are considered "persuasive authority," but *not* binding precedent.

(2.)   Res Judicata *and* Stare Decisis

Let us assume that our hypothetical dispute resulted in a final judgment in the New Jersey Supreme Court for defendant Y. The case is now "res judicata." What that means is that X may not ever again sue Y *over this particular dispute*. This is true even if the rule which is the reason for the outcome of the *X v. Y* dispute is later abandoned; indeed, it is true even if *X v. Y* is itself overruled.

Suppose X is a tenant and Y his landlord. X is suing Y to recover for personal injuries suffered when an intruder entered the apartment building where X lives and injured X in the hallway of the building in the course of a robbery. The Supreme Court of New Jersey ultimately decides in the case that landlords owe no duty to protect tenants against the criminal actions of third parties. Therefore, judgment is for defendant Y.

Some time after the *X v. Y* litigation has concluded, X is again injured in the same apartment building, perhaps even by the same robber. X again sues Landlord Y. The lower courts rule in favor of the landlord — stare decisis requires that they follow "the law," the rule laid down by the Supreme Court of New Jersey in *X v. Y I*. Plaintiff X again asks the New Jersey Supreme Court to review the case. (Why would the plaintiff persist? For that matter, what made him bring the suit in the first place?) The Supreme Court agrees to hear it: it believes its decision in *X v. Y I* may have been wrong and intends to use *X v. Y II* to re-examine the problem. As we have seen, the principle of stare decisis is not absolute with regard to the Court's own prior decisions. Indeed, in this case it declares that landlords *do* have a duty to protect tenants against criminal intruders.

May X now, on the basis of *X v. Y II*, sue Y again to recover for the *first* assault? The answer is a categorical no. Why? *Res judicata*. Think about it. To permit X to sue again after the law has changed would mean that no lawsuit is *ever* truly over. The law is constantly changing, constantly favoring one point of view and then another. It would be manifestly unfair to the litigants on *either* side of a lawsuit to keep them in suspense, forever anticipating the next change in the law which would permit an old adversary to crop up and reinstate a lawsuit that everyone thought had been put to rest.

In sum, in *X v. Y II* the Court *reverses* the lower courts' decisions and *overrules* its own decision in *X v. Y I*. It can do so because *stare decisis* is not absolute; but X cannot sue again to recover for the first assault, notwithstanding the change in the law, because that claim is *res judicata*.

Chapter 2

READING AND BRIEFING CASES

INTRODUCTION

In this chapter we show you, step by step, how to *read* a case, how to *brief* it, how to *analyze* it, how to *think* about it. That is what you will be doing for the next three years — and for the rest of your professional life. The case on which we will focus is edited very lightly in contrast to most of the cases in your casebooks. The reason: in the so-called real world, you have to do your own editing. More immediately, you'll have to cope with unedited cases in Legal Writing and Moot Court.

Our first step is to *read* the case. Of the *reading* of cases, Llewellyn had this to say:

> Now the first thing you are to do with an opinion is to read it. Does this sound commonplace? Does this amuse you? There is no reason why it should amuse you. You have already read past seventeen expressions of whose meaning you have no conception. So hopeless is your ignorance of their meaning that you have no hard-edged memory of having seen unmeaning symbols on the page. You have applied to the court's opinion the reading technique that you use upon the Satevepost. Is a word unfamiliar? Read on that much more quickly! Onward and upward — we must not hold up the story.
>
> That will not do. It is a pity, but you must learn to read. To read each word. To understand each word. You are outlanders in this country of the law. You do not know the speech. It must be learned. Like any other foreign tongue, it must be learned: by seeing words, by using them until they are familiar; meantime, by constant reference to the dictionary. What, dictionary? Tort, trespass, trover, plea, assumpsit, nisi prius, venire de novo, demurrer, joinder, traverse, abatement, general issue, tender, mandamus, certiorari, adverse possession, dependent relative revocation, and the rest. Law Latin, law French, aye, or law English — what do these strange terms mean to you? Can you rely upon the crumbs of language that remain from school? Does *cattle levant and couchant* mean *cows getting up and lying down*? Does *nisi prius* mean *unless before*? Or *traverse* mean an upper gallery in a church? I fear a dictionary is your only hope — a law dictionary — the one-volume kind you can keep ready on your desk. Can you trust the dictionary, is it accurate, does it give you what you want? Of course not. No dictionary does. The life of words is in the using of them, in the wide network of their long associations, in the intangible something we denominate their feel. But the bare bones to work with, the dictionary offers; and

without those bare bones you may be sure the feel will never come.[1]

A. THE CASE

MARIE E. KELLY, PLAINTIFF-APPELLANT v. DONALD C. GWINNELL AND PARAGON CORP., DEFENDANTS-APPELLANTS, AND JOSEPH J. ZAK AND CATHERINE ZAK, DEFENDANTS-RESPONDENTS
96 N.J. 538, 476 A.2d 1219 (1984)

WILENTZ, C.J.

This case raises the issue of whether a social host who enables an adult guest at his home to become drunk is liable to the victim of an automobile accident caused by the drunken driving of the guest. Here the host served liquor to the guest beyond the point at which the guest was visibly intoxicated. We hold the host may be liable under the circumstances of this case.

At the trial level, the case was disposed of, insofar as the issue before us is concerned, by summary judgment in favor of the social host. The record on which the summary judgment was based (pleadings, depositions, and certifications) discloses that defendant Donald Gwinnell, after driving defendant Joseph Zak home, spent an hour or two at Zak's home before leaving to return to his own home. During that time, according to Gwinnell, Zak, and Zak's wife, Gwinnell consumed two or three drinks of scotch on the rocks. Zak accompanied Gwinnell outside to his car, chatted with him, and watched as Gwinnell then drove off to go home. About twenty-five minutes later Zak telephoned Gwinnell's home to make sure Gwinnell had arrived there safely. The phone was answered by Mrs. Gwinnell, who advised Zak that Gwinnell had been involved in a head-on collision. The collision was with an automobile operated by plaintiff, Marie Kelly, who was seriously injured as a result.

After the accident Gwinnell was subjected to a blood test, which indicated a blood alcohol concentration of 0.286 percent.[2] Kelly's expert concluded from that reading that Gwinnell had consumed not two or three scotches but the equivalent of thirteen drinks; that while at Zak's home Gwinnell must have been showing unmistakable signs of intoxication; and that in fact he was severely intoxicated while at Zak's residence and at the time of the accident.

Kelly sued Gwinnell and his employer; those defendants sued the Zaks in a third party action; and thereafter plaintiff amended her complaint to include Mr. and Mrs. Zak as direct defendants. The Zaks moved for summary judgment,

---

[1] KARL N. LLEWELLYN, THE BRAMBLE BUSH: ON OUR LAW AND ITS STUDY 39–40 (Oceana Pubs. 1960; 1st published 1930). What is "Satevepost"? We add this, just in case: reading cases the Llewellyn way includes each and every footnote!

[2] Under present law, a person who drives with a blood alcohol concentration of 0.10 percent or more violates N.J.S.A. 39:4-50 as amended by L. 1983, c. 129, the statute concerning driving while under the influence of intoxicating liquor.

contending that as a matter of law a host is not liable for the negligence of an adult social guest who has become intoxicated while at the host's home. The trial court granted the motion on that basis. While this disposition was interlocutory (plaintiff's claim against Gwinnell and his employer still remaining to be disposed of), the trial court entered final judgment in favor of Zak pursuant to Rule 4:42-2 apparently in order to allow an immediate appeal. Pressler, *Current N.J. Court Rules*, Comment R.4:42-2. The Appellate Division affirmed, *Kelly v. Gwinnell*, 190 N.J. Super. 320 (1983). It noted, correctly, that New Jersey has no Dram Shop Act imposing liability on the provider of alcoholic beverages, and that while our decisional law had imposed such liability on licensees, common-law liability had been extended to a social host only where the guest was a minor. *Id.* at 322–23. (But *see Figuly v. Knoll*, 185 N.J. Super. 477 (Law Div.1982).) It explicitly declined to expand that liability where, as here, the social guest was an adult. *Id.* at 325–26.

The Appellate Division's determination was based on the apparent absence of decisions in this country imposing such liability (except for those that were promptly overruled by the Legislature).[3] *Id.* at 324–25. The absence of such determinations is said to reflect a broad consensus that the imposition of liability arising from these social relations is unwise. Certainly this immunization of hosts is not the inevitable result of the law of negligence, for conventional negligence analysis points strongly in exactly the opposite direction. "Negligence is tested by whether the reasonably prudent person at the time and place should recognize and foresee an unreasonable risk or likelihood of harm or danger to others." *Rappaport v. Nichols*, 31 N.J. 188, 201 (1959); *see also Butler v. Acme Mkts., Inc.*, 89 N.J. 270 (1982) (supermarket operator liable for failure to provide shoppers with parking lot security). When negligent conduct creates such a risk, setting off foreseeable consequences that lead to plaintiff's injury, the conduct is deemed the proximate cause of the injury. "[A] tortfeasor is generally held answerable for the injuries which result in the ordinary course of events from his negligence and it is generally sufficient if his negligent conduct was a substantial factor in bringing about the injuries." *Rappaport, supra*, 31 N.J. at 203; *see Ettin v. Ava Truck Leasing Inc.*, 53 N.J. 463, 483 (1969) (parking tractor-trailer across street is substantial factor in cause of accident when truck with failed brakes collides into trailer).

Under the facts here defendant provided his guest with liquor, knowing that thereafter the guest would have to drive in order to get home. Viewing the facts

---

[3] The Appellate Division noted that several state court decisions imposing liability against social hosts under circumstances similar to those in this case were abrogated by later legislative action. We note that legislation enacted in Oregon did not abrogate the state court's holding in Wiener v. Gamma Phi Chapter of Alpha Tau Omega Fraternity, 258 Or. 632, 485 P.2d 18 (1971). The court found that a host directly serving liquor to a guest has a duty to refuse to serve the guest when it would be unreasonable under the circumstances to permit the guest to drink. Eight years later the legislature enacted Or. Rev. Stat. § 30.955, limiting a cause of action against a private host for damages incurred or caused by an intoxicated social guest to when the host "has served or provided alcoholic beverages to a social guest when such guest was visibly intoxicated." The legislature did not, therefore, preclude liability of private hosts under a negligence theory but instead decided that the social guest must be visibly intoxicated before the host will be held accountable for injuries caused by the guest's intoxicated conduct.

Nevertheless, we acknowledge that many jurisdictions have declined to extend liability to social hosts in circumstances similar to those present in this case. *See, e.g.*, Klein v. Raysinger, 504 Pa. 141, 470 A.2d 507, 510 (1983), and collected cases cited therein.

most favorably to plaintiff (as we must, since the complaint was dismissed on a motion for summary judgment), one could reasonably conclude that the Zaks must have known that their provision of liquor was causing Gwinnell to become drunk, yet they continued to serve him even after he was visibly intoxicated. By the time he left, Gwinnell was in fact severely intoxicated. A reasonable person in Zak's position could foresee quite clearly that this continued provision of alcohol to Gwinnell was making it more and more likely that Gwinnell would not be able to operate his car carefully. Zak could foresee that unless he stopped providing drinks to Gwinnell, Gwinnell was likely to injure someone as a result of the negligent operation of his car. The usual elements of a cause of action for negligence are clearly present: an action by defendant creating an unreasonable risk of harm to plaintiff, a risk that was clearly foreseeable, and a risk that resulted in an injury equally foreseeable. Under those circumstances the only question remaining is whether a duty exists to prevent such risk or, realistically, whether this Court should impose such a duty.

In most cases the justice of imposing such a duty is so clear that the cause of action in negligence is assumed to exist simply on the basis of the actor's creation of an unreasonable risk of foreseeable harm resulting in injury. In fact, however, more is needed, "more" being the value judgment, based on an analysis of public policy, that the actor owed the injured party a duty of reasonable care. *Palsgraf v. Long Island R.R. Co.*, 248 N.Y. 339, 162 N.E. 99 (1928). In *Goldberg v. Housing Auth. of Newark*, 38 N.J. 578, 583 (1962), this Court explained that "whether a *duty* exists is ultimately a question of fairness. The inquiry involves a weighing of the relationship of the parties, the nature of the risk, and the public interest in the proposed solution."

When the court determines that a duty exists and liability will be extended, it draws judicial lines based on fairness and policy. In a society where thousands of deaths are caused each year by drunken drivers,[4] where the damage caused by such deaths is regarded increasingly as intolerable, where liquor licensees are prohibited from serving intoxicated adults, and where long-standing criminal sanctions against drunken driving have recently been significantly strengthened to the point where the Governor notes that they are regarded as the toughest in the nation, see Governor's Annual Message to the N.J. State Legislature, Jan. 10, 1984, the imposition of such a duty by the judiciary seems both fair and fully in accord with the State's policy. Unlike those cases in which the definition of desirable policy is the subject of intense controversy, here the imposition of a duty is both consistent with and supportive of a social goal — the reduction of drunken driving — that is practically unanimously accepted by society.

---

[4] From 1978 to 1982 there were 5,755 highway fatalities in New Jersey. Alcohol was involved in 2,746 or 47.5% of these deaths. Of the 629,118 automobile accident injuries for the same period, 131,160, or 20.5% were alcohol related. The societal cost for New Jersey alcohol-related highway deaths for this period has been estimated as $1,149,516,000.00, based on statistics and documents obtained from the New Jersey Division of Motor Vehicles. The total societal cost figure for all alcohol-related accidents in New Jersey in 1981 alone, including deaths, personal injuries and property damage was $ 1,594,497,898.00. New Jersey Division of Motor Vehicles, *Safety, Service, Integrity, A Report on the Accomplishments of the New Jersey Division of Motor Vehicles* 45 (April 1, 1982 through March 31, 1983). These New Jersey statistics are consistent with nationwide figures, Presidential Commission on Drunk Driving, *Final Report* 1 (1983).

[handwritten annotation: All this now is an analysis, a probing of whether a duty SHOULD exist !]

While the imposition of a duty here would go beyond our prior decisions, those decisions not only point clearly in that direction but do so despite the presence of social considerations similar to those involved in this case — considerations that are claimed to invest the host with immunity. In our first case on the subject, *Rappaport, supra,* 31 N.J. 188, we held a licensee liable for the consequences of a customer's negligent operation of his automobile. The customer was a minor who had become intoxicated as a result of the consumption of liquor at various premises including the licensee's. While observing that a standard of conduct was contained in the statute prohibiting licensees from serving liquor to minors and in the regulation further prohibiting service to any person actually or apparently intoxicated, our decision that the licensee owed a duty to members of the general public was based on principles of common-law negligence.[5]

[handwritten margin notes: licensee "clearly"? / Rappaport "clearly"? / See your Torts course!]

We later made it clear that the licensee's duty is owed to the customer as well, by holding in *Soronen v. Olde Milford Inn, Inc.,* 46 N.J. 582 (1966), that the licensee who served liquor to an intoxicated customer was liable to that customer for the death that resulted when the customer fell in the licensed premises while leaving the bar. While the situation of a licensee differs in some respects from that of a social host, some of the same underlying considerations relied on here in disputing liability are present in both: the notion that the real fault is that of the drunk, not the licensee, especially where the drinker is an adult (as he was in *Soronen*); and the belief — not as strong when applied to licensed premises as when applied to one's home — that when people get together for a friendly drink or more, the social relationships should not be intruded upon by possibilities of litigation.

[handwritten margin notes: licensee "clearly"? / Soronen / Same 2?]

The Appellate Division moved our decisional law one step further, a significant step, when it ruled in *Linn v. Rand,* 140 N.J. Super. 212 (1976), that a social host who serves liquor to a visibly intoxicated minor, knowing the minor will thereafter drive, may be held liable for the injuries inflicted on a third party as a result of the subsequent drunken driving of the minor. There, practically all of the considerations urged here against liability were present: it was a social setting at someone's home, not at a tavern; the one who provided the liquor to the intoxicated minor was a host, not a licensee; and all of the notions of fault and causation pinning sole responsibility on the drinker were present. The only difference was that the guest was a minor — but whether obviously so or whether known to the host is not disclosed in the opinion.[6]

[handwritten margin notes: social host / is that proper role of App. Div.? / Linn App Div]

In *Rappaport,* we explicitly noted that the matter did not involve any claim against "persons not engaged in the liquor business." 31 N.J. at 205. We now approve *Linn* with its extension of this liability to social hosts. In expanding liability, *Linn* followed the rationale of *Rappaport* that the duty involved is a common law duty, not one arising from the statute and regulation prohibiting sales

[handwritten margin notes: Again: common law duty]

[handwritten margin note: etc]

---

[5] We noted that the statutory and regulatory violations could properly be considered by a jury as evidence of the licensee's negligence. *Rappaport,* 31 N.J. at 202–203.

[6] The case was decided on a motion for summary judgment. The court noted that the record did not indicate the minor's age. The opinion does not rely at all on the host's ability easily to determine the fact that the guest was a minor, a factor relied on to some extent in the arguments seeking to distinguish the present case from *Linn.*

of liquor to a minor, neither of which applies to a social host.[7] *Cf. Congini v. Portersville Valve Co.*, 504 Pa. 157, 470 A.2d 515, 517–18 (1983) (in which the Pennsylvania Supreme Court relied exclusively on statutes criminalizing the provision of alcohol to minors as the basis for extending liability to a social host). The fair implication of *Rappaport* and *Soronen*, that the duty exists independent of the statutory prohibition, was thus made explicit in *Linn*. As the court there noted: "It makes little sense to say that the licensee in *Rappaport* is under a duty to exercise care, but give immunity to a social host who may be guilty of the same wrongful conduct merely because he is unlicensed." 140 N.J. Super. at 217.[8]

The argument is made that the rule imposing liability on licensees is justified because licensees, unlike social hosts, derive a profit from serving liquor. We reject this analysis of the liability's foundation and emphasize that the liability proceeds from the duty of care that accompanies control of the liquor supply. Whatever the motive behind making alcohol available to those who will subsequently drive, the provider has a duty to the public not to create foreseeable, unreasonable risks by this activity.

We therefore hold that a host who serves liquor to an adult social guest, knowing both that the guest is intoxicated and will thereafter be operating a motor vehicle, is liable for injuries inflicted on a third party as a result of the negligent operation of a motor vehicle by the adult guest when such negligence is caused by the intoxication. We impose this duty on the host to the third party because we believe that the policy considerations served by its imposition far outweigh those asserted in opposition. While we recognize the concern that our ruling will interfere with accepted standards of social behavior; will intrude on and somewhat diminish the enjoyment, relaxation, and camaraderie that accompany social gatherings at which alcohol is served; and that such gatherings and social relationships are not simply tangential benefits of a civilized society but are regarded by many as important, we believe that the added assurance of just compensation to the victims of drunken driving as well as the added deterrent effect of the rule on such driving outweigh the importance of those other values. Indeed, we believe that given society's extreme concern about drunken driving, any change in social behavior resulting from the rule will be regarded ultimately as neutral at the very least and not as a change for the worse; but that in any event if there be a loss, it is well worth the gain.[9]

---

[7] We note that the Senate and Assembly have recently passed a bill that, if signed into law, would make it a disorderly persons offense knowingly to offer or serve an alcoholic beverage to a person under the legal drinking age. Senate Bill No. S. 1054.

[8] While *Linn*'s statement of the legal rule does not explicitly go beyond the situation in which the social guest was a minor (140 N.J. Super. at 217, 219, 220), its reasoning would apply equally to an adult guest.

[9] We note that our holding and the reasoning on which it is based may be regarded as inconsistent with Anslinger v. Martinsville Inn, Inc., 121 N.J. Super. 525 (App. Div. 1972), certif. den., 62 N.J. 334 (1973). There, the court refused to impose liability on business associates for the injuries a drunken guest suffered after leaving their social affair. The guest died when the car he was driving rammed into a truck on a highway. That court also ruled that decedent's drunkenness constituted contributory negligence, available to the business (or social) host as a defense (as distinguished from its unavailability where defendant is a licensee; *see Soronen, supra*, 46 N.J. 582). We express no opinion on that question, which

The liability we impose here is analogous to that traditionally imposed on owners of vehicles who lend their cars to persons they know to be intoxicated. [Citations omitted.] If, by lending a car to a drunk, a host becomes liable to third parties injured by the drunken driver's negligence, the same liability should extend to a host who furnishes liquor to a visibly drunken guest who he knows will thereafter drive away.

Some fear has been expressed that the extent of the potential liability may be disproportionate to the fault of the host. A social judgment is therein implied to the effect that society does not regard as particularly serious the host's actions in causing his guests to become drunk, even though he knows they will thereafter be driving their cars. We seriously question that value judgment; indeed, we do not believe that the liability is disproportionate when the host's actions, so relatively easily corrected, may result in serious injury or death. The other aspect of this argument is that the host's insurance protection will be insufficient. While acknowledging that homeowners' insurance will cover such liability[10] this argument notes the risk that both the host and spouse will be jointly liable. The point made is not that the level of insurance will be lower in relation to the injuries than in the case of other torts, but rather that the joint liability of the spouses may result in the loss of their home and other property to the extent that the policy limits are inadequate.[11] * * * It may be that some special form of insurance could be designed to protect the spouses' equity in their homes in cases such as this one. In any event, it is not clear that the loss of a home by spouses who, by definition, have negligently caused the injury, is disproportionate to the loss of life of one who is totally innocent of any wrongdoing.

---

is not before us since Gwinnell's only claim against Zak is for contribution or indemnification and not for personal injuries. While, as noted *infra*, Zak and Gwinnell may be liable as joint tortfeasors as to Kelly, any right of contribution or indemnification between the two will have to be determined by the trial court on remand. That determination presumably will require consideration of the effect, if any, of *Soronen, Anslinger*, and the Comparative Negligence Act, N.J.S.A. 2A:15-5.1-5.3 (which was not in effect at the time of those decisions).

The *Anslinger* court also discussed, in dictum, the policy against imposing liability on hosts in social or quasi-business settings. Today, the facts of the case before us persuade us that policy considerations warrant imposing such a duty on a social host. We note also the case of Figuly v. Knoll, 185 N.J. Super. 477 (Law. Div. 1982), which, on facts substantially similar to those before us, held the social host liable.

[10] The dissent challenges our assumption that present homeowners' policies cover the liability imposed by this decision. At oral argument, counsel for both sides indicated that they believe typical homeowners' policies would cover such liability. Even if that is so, however, says the dissent, the homeowner/social host is unable "to spread the cost of liability." *Post* at 568. The contrast is then made with the commercial licensee who "spreads the cost of insurance against liability among its or her customers." *Id.* But the critical issue here is not whether the homeowner can pass the cost on or must bear it himself, but whether tort law should be used to spread the risk over a large segment of society through the device of insurance rather than imposing the entire risk on the innocent victim of drunken driving. Obviously there will be some additional insurance premium at some point that homeowners and renters will have to bear. Their inability to pass that cost on to others, however, is no more persuasive than that same argument would be as to the "average citizen's" automobile liability insurance or, for that matter, for homeowners' insurance as it now exists.

[11] We need not, and do not, reach the question of which spouse is liable, or whether both are liable, and under what circumstances.

Given the lack of precedent anywhere else in the country, however, we believe it would be unfair to impose this liability retroactively. *Merenoff v. Merenoff*, 76 N.J. 535 (1978); *Darrow v. Hanover Twp.*, 58 N.J. 410 (1971); *Willis v. Department of Conservation & Economic Dev.*, 55 N.J. 534 (1970). Homeowners who are social hosts may desire to increase their policy limits; apartment dwellers may want to obtain liability insurance of this kind where perhaps they now have none. The imposition of retroactive liability could be considered unexpected and its imposition unfair. We therefore have determined that the liability imposed by this case on social hosts shall be prospective, applicable only to events that occur after the date of this decision. We will, however, apply the doctrine to the parties before us on the usual theory that to do otherwise would not only deprive the plaintiff of any benefit resulting from her own efforts but would also make it less likely that, in the future, individuals will be willing to claim rights, not yet established, that they believe are just.

The goal we seek to achieve here is the fair compensation of victims who are injured as a result of drunken driving. The imposition of the duty certainly will make such fair compensation more likely. While the rule in this case will tend also to deter drunken driving, there is no assurance that it will have any significant effect. The lack of such assurance has not prevented us in the past from imposing liability on licensees. Indeed, it has been only recently that the sanction of the *criminal* law was credited with having some significant impact on drunken driving.[12] We need not, however, condition the imposition of a duty on scientific proof that it will result in the behavior that is one of its goals. No one has suggested that the common-law duty to drive carefully should be abolished because it has apparently not diminished the mayhem that occurs regularly on our highways. We believe the rule will make it more likely that hosts will take greater care in serving alcoholic beverages at social gatherings so as to avoid not only the moral responsibility but the economic liability that would occur if the guest were to injure someone as a result of his drunken driving.

We do not agree that the issue addressed in this case is appropriate only for legislative resolution. Determinations of the scope of duty in negligence cases has traditionally been a function of the judiciary. The history of the cases cited above evidences a continuing judicial involvement in these matters. Without the benefit of any Dram Shop Act imposing liability on licensees, legislation that is quite common

---

[12] Within the last year those laws have been strengthened and officials have stepped up enforcement efforts. Since 1980, the number of drunk driving arrests in New Jersey has increased by approximately 40%. The number of drunk driving deaths has decreased in this State from a high of 376 deaths in 1981 to a reported preliminary total of 270 deaths in 1983. Since the State minimum drinking age was returned to 21 years in 1983, the number of fatal accidents involving people under the age of 21 has dropped significantly. In 1982, drunken drivers between the ages of 18 and 20 were responsible for 67 highway fatalities. Preliminary figures for 1983 show that this age group was responsible for 38 drunk driving deaths that year. There has been a corresponding drop in the number of injuries sustained in accidents involving drunk drivers. New Jersey Division of Motor Vehicles, *Safety, Service, Integrity, A Report on the Accomplishments of the New Jersey Division of Motor Vehicles, supra,* at 44. Law enforcement officials believe that the decrease in accidents and injuries is attributable to the recent changes in these laws. See Comments of Attorney General, *quoted in* "Highway Carnage," *Herald News,* Mar. 13, 1984, p. A-10; Comments of Director, Division of Motor Vehicles, *quoted in* "Teen Road Carnage Drops Sharply in First Year of Higher Drinking Age," *The Star-Ledger,* Mar. 8, 1984, p. 1.

in other states, this Court determined that such liability nevertheless existed.[13] We did so in 1959 and have continued to expand that concept since then. We know of no legislative activity during that entire period from 1959 to date suggesting that our involvement in these matters was deemed inappropriate; even after the judiciary expanded this liability to include social hosts in its decision in *Linn*, there was no adverse reaction on the part of the Legislature. In fact, the Legislature's passage of S. 1054, imposing criminal liability on anyone who purposely or knowingly serves alcoholic beverages to underage persons, indicates that body's approval of the position taken eight years earlier in *Linn*. The subject matter is not abstruse, and it can safely be assumed that the Legislature is in fact aware of our decisions in this area. Absent such adverse reaction, we assume that our decisions are found to be consonant with the strong legislative policy against drunken driving.

The dissent relies on two related grounds in concluding this matter should be resolved by legislation: the superior knowledge of the legislature obtained through hearings and other means enabling it better to balance the interests involved and to devise an appropriate remedy, and the ruling's potential "extraordinary effects on the average citizen." Many of the cases cited in support of this view, however, are from jurisdictions in which a Dram Shop Act was in effect and are therefore clearly distinguishable. [Citations omitted.]

Whether mentioned or not in these opinions, the very existence of a Dram Shop Act constitutes a substantial argument against expansion of the legislatively-mandated liability. Very simply, when the Legislature has spoken so specifically on the subject and has chosen to make only licensees liable, arguably the Legislature did not intend to impose the same liability on hosts * * *.[14]

In only four of the jurisdictions cited in the dissent did the courts rule, despite the absence of a Dram Shop Act, that a host should not be liable. [Citations omitted.]

Whether our ruling will have such an "extraordinary" impact on "the average citizen" in his or her social and business relations (presumably the premise for the conclusion that judicial action is inappropriate) depends to some extent on an initial evaluation of the matter. We suspect some of the extraordinary change is already taking place, that it is not unusual today for hosts to monitor their guests' drinking to some extent. Furthermore, the characterization of the change as one demanding prior legislative study and warranting action only after such, implies that its effects on balance may be seriously adverse. Given our firm belief that insurance is available, that compensation of innocent victims is desirable, and that the added deterrence against drunken driving is salutary, we do not perceive the potential

---

[13] Justice Jacobs adverted to this fact in his opinion in *Soronen, supra:* "Many states have dram shop acts in which the legislature has specifically fixed the scope and extent of the tavern keeper's civil responsibility for injuries which result from his service of alcoholic beverages to an intoxicated person. We have no such act and must therefore deal with the common law principles of negligence and proximate causation." 46 N.J. at 592.

[14] The dissent's reference to Oregon statutes as abrogating or restricting a prior judicial determination in favor of the cause of action is incorrect. The Oregon statute accepted the judicial determination similar to that made in this case; its effect, as noted *supra* at n. [3], was only to prevent further expansions of liability beyond that allowed by this Court today.

revision of cocktail-party customs as constituting a sufficient threat to social well-being to warrant staying our hand. Obviously the Legislature may disagree.

This Court has decided many significant issues without any prior legislative study. In any event, if the Legislature differs with us on issues of this kind, it has a clear remedy. See, *e.g.*, *Van Horn v. Blanchard Co.*, 88 N.J. 91 (1981) (holding that under Comparative Negligence Act, a plaintiff could recover only from those defendants that were more negligent than was the plaintiff); N.J.S.A. 2A:15-5.1 as amended by L. 1982, c. 191 § 1 eff. Dec. 6, 1982 (under which a plaintiff may recover from all defendants if plaintiff's negligence is less than or equal to the *combined* negligence of all defendants); *Willis v. Department of Conservation and Economic Dev.*, 55 N.J. 534 (1970) (abolishing the State's sovereign immunity from tort claims), N.J.S.A. 59:1-1 *et seq.*, L. 1972, c. 45 (reestablishing and defining immunity for all New Jersey governmental bodies); *Dalton v. St. Luke's Catholic Church*, 27 N.J. 22 (1958), *Collopy v. Newark Eye & Ear Infirmary*, 27 N.J. 29 (1958), *Benton v. Y.M.C.A.*, 27 N.J. 67 (1958) (abolishing charitable immunity), N.J.S.A. 2A:53A-7, L. 1959, c. 90 (reestablishing charitable immunity); *cf. Immer v. Risko*, 56 N.J. 482 (1970) (abolishing interspousal immunity in automobile negligence cases); *France v. A.P.A. Transport Corp.*, 56 N.J. 500 (1970) (abolishing parent-child immunity in automobile negligence cases) (no subsequent legislative action on issue of familial immunity).

We are satisfied that our decision today is well within the competence of the judiciary. Defining the scope of tort liability has traditionally been accepted as the responsibility of the courts. Indeed, given the courts' prior involvement in these matters, our decision today is hardly the radical change implied by the dissent but, while significant, is rather a fairly predictable expansion of liability in this area.[15]

It should be noted that the difficulties posited by the dissent as to the likely consequence of this decision are purely hypothetical. Given the facts before us, we decide only that where the social host directly serves the guest and continues to do so even after the guest is visibly intoxicated, knowing that the guest will soon be driving home, the social host may be liable for the consequences of the resulting drunken driving. We are not faced with a party where many guests congregate, nor with guests serving each other, nor with a host busily occupied with other responsibilities and therefore unable to attend to the matter of serving liquor, nor with a drunken host. We will face those situations when and if they come before us,

---

[15] In view of the arguments set forth, the dissent's approval of the decision in *Linn* is difficult to understand. The difference between that case and the instant case is simply one of degree. There a social host was held liable for the consequences of drunken driving by a minor who had been served by the host in a social setting. The legislative indicator of liability was not significantly stronger (in *Linn* a statutory and regulatory prohibition was involved, applicable, however, only to licensees; here only a regulatory prohibition); in both cases social habits may be affected, substantial economic consequences may result, and in both the court acts without the advantage of a legislative inquiry. The dissent's notion that *Linn* can be distinguished because "minors occupy a special place in our society and traditionally have been protected by state regulation from the consequences of their own immaturity" fails to acknowledge that the thrust of the case was to provide compensation for an innocent victim of a drunken driver where the driver happened to be a minor and not even a party to the action. The entire rationale of the opinion is that there is no sound reason to impose liability on a licensee and not on a social host. There is not a word nor the slightest implication in the opinion suggesting that the underlying purpose of the decision was to protect minors.

** the classic response to the slippery slope

we hope with sufficient reason and perception so as to balance, if necessary and if legitimate, the societal interests alleged to be inconsistent with the public policy considerations that are at the heart of today's decision. The fears expressed by the dissent concerning the vast impact of the decision on the "average citizen's" life are reminiscent of those asserted in opposition to our decisions abolishing husband-wife, parent-child, and generally family immunity in *France v. A.P.A. Transport Corp.*, 56 N.J. at 500, and *Immer v. Risko*, 56 N.J. at 482. In *Immer*, proponents of interspousal immunity claimed that abandoning it would disrupt domestic harmony and encourage possible fraud and collusion against insurance companies. 56 N.J. at 488. In *France*, it was predicted that refusal to apply the parent-child immunity would lead to depletion of the family exchequer and interfere with parental care, discipline and control. 56 N.J. at 504. As we noted there, "[w]e cannot decide today any more than what is before us, and the question of what other claims should be entertained by our courts must be left to future decisions." *Immer*, 56 N.J. at 495. Some fifteen years have gone by and, as far as we can tell, nothing but good has come as a result of those decisions.

We recognize, however, that the point of view expressed by the dissent conforms, at least insofar as the result is concerned, with the view, whether legislatively or judicially expressed, of practically every other jurisdiction that has been faced with this question. It seems to us that by now it ought to be clear to all that the concerns on which that point of view is based are minor compared to the devastating consequences of drunken driving. This is a problem that society is just beginning to face squarely, and perhaps we in New Jersey are doing so sooner than others.

For instance, the dissent's emphasis on the financial impact of an insurance premium increase on the homeowner or the tenant should be measured against the monumental financial losses suffered by society as a result of drunken driving. By our decision we not only spread some of that loss so that it need not be borne completely by the victims of this widespread affliction, but, to some extent, reduce the likelihood that the loss will occur in the first place. Even if the dissent's view of the scope of our decision were correct, the adjustments in social behavior at parties, the burden put on the host to reasonably oversee the serving of liquor, the burden on the guests to make sure if one is drinking that another is driving, and the burden on all to take those reasonable steps even if, on some occasion, some guest may become belligerent: those social dislocations, their importance, must be measured against the misery, death, and destruction caused by the drunken driver. Does our society morally approve of the decision to continue to allow the charm of unrestrained social drinking when the cost is the lives of others, sometimes of the guests themselves?

morally

If we but step back and observe ourselves objectively, we will see a phenomenon not of merriment but of cruelty, causing misery to innocent people, tolerated for years despite our knowledge that without fail, out of our extraordinarily high number of deaths caused by automobiles, nearly half have regularly been attributable to drunken driving. *See supra*, at n.3. Should we be so concerned about disturbing the customs of those who knowingly supply that which causes the offense, so worried about their costs, so worried about their inconvenience, as if they were the victims rather than the cause of the carnage? And while the dissent

is certainly correct that we could learn more through an investigation, to characterize our knowledge as "scant" or insufficient is to ignore what is obvious, and that is that drunken drivers are causing substantial personal and financial destruction in this state and that a goodly number of them have been drinking in homes as well as taverns. Does a court really need to know more? Is our rule vulnerable because we do not know — nor will the Legislature — how much injury will be avoided or how many lives saved by this rule? Or because we do not know how many times the victim will require compensation from the host in order to be made whole?

This Court senses that there may be a substantial change occurring in social attitudes and customs concerning drinking, whether at home or in taverns. We believe that this change may be taking place right now in New Jersey and perhaps elsewhere. It is the upheaval of prior norms by a society that has finally recognized that it must change its habits and do whatever is required, whether it means but a small change or a significant one, in order to stop the senseless loss inflicted by drunken drivers. We did not cause that movement, but we believe this decision is in step with it.

We are well aware of the many possible implications and contentions that may arise from our decision. We express no opinion whatsoever on any of these matters but confine ourselves strictly to the facts before us. We hold only that where a host provides liquor directly to a social guest and continues to do so even beyond the point at which the host knows the guest is intoxicated, and does this knowing that the guest will shortly thereafter be operating a motor vehicle, that host is liable for the foreseeable consequences to third parties that result from the guest's drunken driving. We hold further that the host and guest are liable to the third party as joint tortfeasors, *Malone v. Jersey Central Power & Light Co.*, 18 N.J. 163, 171 (1955); *Ristan v. Frantzen*, 14 N.J. 455, 460 (1954); *Matthews v. Delaware, L. & W. R.R.*, 56 N.J.L. 34 (Sup. Ct. 1893), without implying anything about the rights of the one to contribution or indemnification from the other. *See supra* at n. 8.

Our ruling today will not cause a deluge of lawsuits or spawn an abundance of fraudulent and frivolous claims. Not only do we limit our holding to the situation in which a host directly serves a guest, but we impose liability solely for injuries resulting from the guest's drunken driving. Automobile accidents are thoroughly investigated by law enforcement officers; careful inquiries are routinely made as to whether the drivers and occupants are intoxicated. The availability of clear objective evidence establishing intoxication will act to weed out baseless claims and to prevent this cause of action from being used as a tool for harassment.

We therefore reverse the judgment in favor of the defendants Zak and remand the case to the Law Division for proceedings consistent with this opinion.

GARIBALDI, J., dissenting.

Today, this Court holds that a social host who knowingly enables an adult guest to become intoxicated knowing that the guest will operate a motor vehicle is liable for damages to a third party caused by the intoxicated guest. The imposition of this liability on a social host places upon every citizen of New Jersey who pours a drink for a friend a heavy burden to monitor and regulate guests. It subjects the host to

substantial potential financial liability that may be far beyond the host's resources.

My position as a strong advocate of legal measures to combat drunk driving is established. *See In re Kallen*, 92 N.J. 14 (1983). The majority need not parade the horrors that have been caused by drunk drivers to convince me that there is always room for stricter measurers [*sic*] against intoxicated drivers. I too am concerned for the injured victim of a drunken driver. However, the almost limitless implications of the majority's decision lead me to conclude that the Legislature is better equipped to effectuate the goals of reducing injuries from drunken driving and protecting the interests of the injured party, without placing such a grave burden on the average citizen of this state.

I

Prior to today's decision, this Court had imposed liability only on those providers of alcoholic beverages who were licensed by the State. *See Rappaport v. Nichols*, 31 N.J. 188 (1959). The Appellate Division also had expanded the liability to a social host who served liquor to a minor. *Linn v. Rand*, 140 N.J. Super. 212 (App.Div.1976).[16] Although both of these cases were based on common-law negligence, the courts deemed the regulations restricting the service of alcohol to minors significant enough evidence of legislative policy to impart knowledge of foreseeable risk on the provider of the alcohol and to fashion a civil remedy for negligently creating that risk.

Many other states have considered the problem before us today but no judicial decision establishing a cause of action against a social host for serving liquor to an adult social guest is currently in force. Any prior judicial attempts to establish such a cause of action have been abrogated or restricted by subsequent legislative action. *See, e.g.*, Cal. Civ. Code § 1714 (as amended Stats.1978, ch. 929, § 2, p. 2904); Or. Rev. Stat. § 30.955 (1979).

State courts have found that imposition of this new form of liability on social hosts is such a radical departure from prior law, with such extraordinary effects on the average citizen, that the issue is best left to a legislative determination. [Citations omitted.]

I agree with the holdings of our sister states and with their misgivings about the judicial imposition of the duty that the majority today places on social hosts. * * *

---

[16] If this case involved service of alcohol by a social host to a minor guest, I would vote with the majority in approving *Linn v. Rand, supra*, 140 N.J. Super. 212, to the extent it has been interpreted as applying only to social hosts who serve liquor to minors. The distinction I draw is based on the clearly and frequently expressed legislative policy that minors should not drink alcoholic beverages, *see, e.g.*, N.J.S.A. 33:1-77, and on the fact that minors occupy a special place in our society and traditionally have been protected by state regulation from the consequences of their own immaturity. Although the majority sees no basis for this distinction, I am not alone in making it. *Compare* Klein v. Raysinger, 504 Pa. 141, 470 A.2d 507 (1983) (in which the Supreme Court of Pennsylvania refused to extend liability to a social host who serves an adult guest) *with* Congini v. Porterville Valve Co., 504 Pa. 157, 470 A.2d 515 (1983) (decided on the same day as *Klein* by the same court but extending liability to a social host who served liquor to a minor guest); *see also* Senate Bill S-1054 (recently passed by the Senate and Assembly imposing criminal liability on social hosts who serve liquor to minors but not mentioning hosts who serve liquor to adults).

II

My reluctance to join the majority is not based on any exaggerated notion of judicial deference to the Legislature. Rather, it is based on my belief that before this Court plunges into this broad area of liability and imposes high duties of care on social hosts, it should carefully consider the ramifications of its actions. The Court acts today with seemingly scant knowledge and little care for the possible negative consequences of its decision.

The magnitude of the problem with which we are dealing is entirely unknown. As the Illinois Appellate Court noted in *Miller v. Moran, supra,* 96 Ill. App.3d at 600, 421 N.E.2d at 1049, the injured party normally has a remedy against the direct perpetrator of the injury, the intoxicated driver. The majority's portrayal of the specter of many innocent victims with no chance of recovery against drunk drivers is specious. * * *

As stated earlier in this dissent, this Court has, in the past, imposed civil liability on commercial licensees who serve alcoholic beverages to intoxicated patrons. Commercial licensees are subject to regulation by both the Alcoholic Beverage Commission (ABC) and the Legislature. It is reasonable to impose tort liability on licensees based on their violation of explicit statutes and regulations.

I have no quarrel with the imposition of such liability because of the peculiar position occupied by the licensee. A social host, however, is in a different position. A brief discussion of the dissimilarities between the licensee and the private social host will illustrate the many problems this Court is creating by refusing to distinguish between the two in imposing liability upon them.

A significant difference between an average citizen and a commercial licensee is the average citizen's lack of knowledge and expertise in determining levels and degrees of intoxication. Licensed commercial providers, unlike the average citizen, ·deal with the alcohol-consuming public every day. This experience gives them some expertise with respect to intoxication that social hosts lack. A social host will find it more difficult to determine levels and degrees of intoxication.

The majority holds that a host will be liable only if he serves alcohol to a guest knowing both that the guest is intoxicated and that the guest will drive. Although this standard calls for a subjective determination of the extent of the host's knowledge, a close reading of the opinion makes clear that the majority actually is relying on objective evidence. The majority takes the results of Gwinnell's blood alcohol concentration test and concludes from that test that "the Zaks must have known that their provision of liquor was causing Gwinnell to become drunk * * *."

Whether a guest is or is not intoxicated is not a simple issue. Alcohol affects everyone differently. "[T]he precise effects of a particular concentration of alcohol in the blood varies from person to person depending upon a host of other factors. See generally Perr, 'Blood Alcohol Levels and "Diminished Capacity",' 3 (No. 4) J. Legal Med. 28–30 (April 1975)." *State v. Stasio,* 78 N.J. 467, 478 n. 5 (1979). One individual can consume many drinks without exhibiting any signs of intoxication. Alcohol also takes some time to get into the bloodstream and show its outward effects. Experts estimate that it takes alcohol twenty to thirty minutes to reach its highest level in the bloodstream. See American Medical Association, *Alcohol and*

the Impaired Driver (1968). Thus, a blood alcohol concentration test demonstrating an elevated blood alcohol level after an accident may not mean that the subject was obviously intoxicated when he left the party some time earlier. "Moreover, a state of obvious intoxication is a condition that is very susceptible to after the fact interpretations, *i.e.*, objective review of a subjective decision. These factors combine to make the determination that an individual is obviously intoxicated not so obvious after all." Comment, "Social Host Liability for Furnishing Alcohol: A Legal Hangover?" 1978 Pac. L.J. 95, 103. Accordingly, to impose on average citizens a duty to comprehend a person's level of intoxication and the effect another drink would ultimately have on such person is to place a very heavy burden on them.

The nature of home entertaining compounds the social host's difficulty in determining whether a guest is obviously intoxicated before serving the next drink. In a commercial establishment, there is greater control over the liquor; a bartender or waitress must serve the patron a drink. Not so in a home when entertaining a guest. At a social gathering, for example, guests frequently serve themselves or guests may serve other guests. Normally, the host is so busy entertaining he does not have time to analyze the state of intoxication of the guests. Without constant face-to-face contact it is difficult for a social host to avoid serving alcohol to a person on the brink of intoxication. Furthermore, the commercial bartender usually does not drink on the job. The social host often drinks with the guest, as the Zaks did here. The more the host drinks, the less able he will be to determine when a guest is intoxicated. It would be anomalous to create a rule of liability that social hosts can deliberately avoid by becoming drunk themselves.

The majority suggests that my fears about imposition of liability on social hosts who are not in a position to monitor the alcohol consumption of their guests are "purely hypothetical" in that the present case involves a host and guest in a one-to-one situation. It is unrealistic to assume that the standards set down by the Court today will not be applied to hosts in other social situations. Today's holding leaves the door open for all of the speculative and subjective impositions of liability that I fear.

A more pressing distinction between the social host and commercial licensees is the host's inability to fulfill the duty the majority has imposed even if the host knows that a particular guest is intoxicated. It is easy to say that a social host can just refuse to serve the intoxicated person. However, due to a desire to avoid confrontation in a social environment, this may become a very difficult task. It is much easier in a detached business relationship for a bartender to flag a patron and either refuse to serve him or ask him to leave. We should not ignore the social pressures of requiring a social host to tell a boss, client, friend, neighbor, or family member that he is not going to serve him another drink. Moreover, a social host does not have a bouncer or other enforcer to prevent difficulties that may arise when requesting a drunk to stop drinking or not to drive home. We have all heard of belligerent drunks.

Further, it is not clear from the Court's opinion to what lengths a social host must go to avoid liability. Is the host obligated to use physical force to restrain an intoxicated guest from drinking and then from driving? Or is the host limited to

delay and subterfuge tactics short of physical force? What is the result when the host tries to restrain the guest but fails? Is the host still liable? The majority opinion is silent on the extent to which we must police our guests.

III

The most significant difference between a social host and a commercial licensee, however, is the social host's inability to spread the cost of liability. The commercial establishment spreads the cost of insurance against liability among its customers. The social host must bear the entire cost alone. While the majority briefly discusses this issue, noting that it may result in a catastrophic loss of a home to a husband and wife, it apparently does not consider this much of a problem to the average New Jersey citizen. It assumes that such liability is now covered or will be covered under the homeowner's insurance policy.

The majority cites no authority for its belief that actions against social hosts will be covered under homeowner's insurance. This new cause of action will be common and may result in large awards to third parties. Even if it is assumed that homeowner's insurance will cover this cause of action, it is unrealistic to believe that insurance companies will not raise their premiums in response to it.

Furthermore, many homeowners and apartment renters may not even have homeowner's insurance and probably cannot afford it. Other homeowners may not have sufficient insurance to cover the limitless liability that the Court seeks to impose. These people may lose everything they own if they are found liable as negligent social hosts under the Court's scheme. The individual economic cost to every New Jersey citizen should be weighed before today's result is reached. * * *

Recently, our Legislature has enacted laws making New Jersey the unchallenged leader in the national crackdown on drunken driving. Evidence that the Legislature is still vitally interested in the area of drunken driving is Senate Bill S–1054, recently passed by the Senate and Assembly. It provides a criminal penalty for a social host who serves alcohol to a minor. The absence of any similar imposition of criminal liability on social hosts who serve adult guests should be instructive as to the Legislature's intent on the matter before the Court.

IV

In conclusion, in trivializing these objections as "cocktail party customs" and "inconvenience" the majority misses the point. I believe that an in depth review of this problem by the Legislature will result in a solution that will further the goals of reducing injuries related to drunk driving and adequately compensating the injured party, while imposing a more limited liability on the social host. Imaginative legislative drafting could include: funding a remedy for the injured party by contributions from the parties most responsible for the harm caused, the intoxicated motorists; making the social host secondarily liable by requiring a judgment against the drunken driver as a prerequisite to suit against the host; limiting the amount that could be recovered from a social host; and requiring a finding of wanton and reckless conduct before holding the social host liable.

I do not propose to fashion a legislative solution. That is for the Legislature. I merely wish to point out that the Legislature has a variety of alternatives to this Court's imposition of unlimited liability on every New Jersey adult. Perhaps, after investigating all the options, the Legislature will determine that the most effective course is to impose the same civil liability on social hosts that the majority has imposed today. I would have no qualms about that legislative decision so long as it was reached after a thorough investigation of its impact on average citizens of New Jersey.

B. THE BRIEF

What, then, is a brief?[17]

Suppose you were to tell us that you saw a movie last night and we asked, what was it about? Only in the most unusual circumstances would you retell it frame by frame. Instead, you would begin by assigning the movie to a *genre*, a "category * * * characterized by a particular style, form or content,"[18] for instance, adventure story, love story, or murder mystery. The purpose this categorizing serves is to locate us in the world of possible stories. It presupposes, of course, that we have common cultural referents. A Martian might find your answer, "it was a murder mystery," incomprehensible.

Beyond locating the story in its proper genre, you may offer a *précis* of your movie, a "concise summary of essential points, statements, or facts."[19]

But now note: how concise, or, in other words, how "précis" your *précis* is, will depend upon many variables. Who we are, who you are, why we asked, why you answered, whether you or we have an agenda in the asking or the answering, and so forth; and you will exercise your judgment accordingly. But however abbreviated your *précis*, *it must be a linear narrative with a beginning, a middle, and an end or it will be incomprehensible!*

A brief is nothing more mysterious than a précis of a case, more or less extensive and detailed as the context requires, and following certain conventions as to form.

Why do law students and lawyers "brief" cases? Most obviously, first-year law students do it so as not to be embarrassed in class. Your teachers will question you about the "relevant" and "material" facts; the procedural history of the case; the "holding"; the reasoning; etc. They will expect you to have the answers ready — *from your brief*. More than that, the *process* of briefing forces you to come to grips with, to master, the case you are briefing. *Having* a brief (your classmate's, one from a book) is helpful, but much less so than *preparing* a brief.

Finally, briefing enables you to talk about past cases. In a system of stare decisis, "prior cases," that is, cases that have been finally decided, do not go away but

---

[17] This kind of "brief" — one made when reading a case for the purpose of recalling and understanding what you have read — is different from another kind of "brief," which is a lawyer's written argument presented to a court.

[18] WEBSTER'S NINTH NEW COLLEGIATE DICTIONARY (9th ed. 1989).

[19] *Id.*

remain, or at least are capable of remaining, a part of the living organism of the law. Not only do old cases, like old soldiers, never die — they exert a *normative* force because the system says they are binding on the later court in a factually similar case.

Hence we always need to talk about past cases — but surely not frame by frame, although, just as a frame in a movie can be very powerful, so a single fact in a case can go a long way to explaining the result.

So let's brief *Kelly v. Gwinnell.*

We will assume that you have read the entire case (majority, dissent, footnotes) the Llewellyn way, much or all of it more than once. Take notes and organize the tale chronologically if the court has not done so. (In some cases it may be helpful to draw a picture or a diagram).

The person who brings the appeal is the appellant; she may have been either the plaintiff or the defendant below, but by definition she lost (at least in part). The one responding to the appeal is the appellee or, rarely, the respondent, and again she may have been either the plaintiff or the defendant below. Courts may call a party either by the proper designation at the trial level (plaintiff, defendant) or by the designation on appeal (appellant, appellee or respondent), and they sometimes switch back and forth between the two designations in the same narrative, making it easy to grow confused.

A court may also, having initially identified the cast of characters, use the names of the parties, as the *Kelly* court does. At an absolute minimum, you will be expected to know who is who and who is suing whom. Frequently that will be easy to do: there is one plaintiff suing one defendant. Then again it may get more complicated. Let's take *Kelly*.

In *Kelly*, the plaintiff is Marie Kelly, seriously injured by a drunken driver named Gwinnell. Marie sued Gwinnell and his employer (under certain circumstances employers *may* be "vicariously" liable for torts committed by their employees). Incidentally, why would she sue the employer? If you suspect it is because employers tend to have more money, including insurance, than do their employees, you are on target.

Gwinnell and his employer (aside from answering Marie's complaint) turned around and filed what is called a "third party action," bringing the Zaks into this suit or, to use the technical term, "impleading" them. (You will learn about this in Civil Procedure. For now just accept that such a procedure exists). And who are the Zaks? They are the folks said to have provided Gwinnell all that alcohol. The court calls them "social hosts," to distinguish them from "commercial hosts," that is those, like bar and tavern owners, who are in the business of selling alcohol by the drink to their paying customers.

Why are Gwinnell and his employer doing this?

Well, if, in addition to Gwinnell and maybe his employer, the Zaks, too, are found liable, then perhaps Gwinnell and employer can demand that the Zaks and, possibly,

their insurance company, contribute to paying any damages that Marie recovers.[20]

Apparently Marie — or rather, Marie's lawyer — had not initially thought to make the Zaks co-defendants with Gwinnell and his employer. Why not? Perhaps she had a dumb lawyer; the thought never occurred. Or the thought did occur but was dismissed because the lawyer thought (correctly) that no New Jersey case — or any other case for that matter — had allowed a suit against a social host, at least not where the guest was an adult. To put it differently, there was no precedent, no authority, for holding the Zaks liable.

But then why did the lawyers for Gwinnell and his employer "implead" the Zaks? Short answer: they were better lawyers; they were better at reading the cases and better at "reading" their own Supreme Court; they had more imagination; they were more creative.

In any event, Marie now amends her complaint and adds the Zaks as defendants. *This opinion is only about Marie and the Zaks.*

We are now ready to prepare our "official" brief. Its format looks like this:

1)   **Heading**

2)   **Statement of the Case**

3)   **Facts**

4)   **Procedural History and Outcome Here**

5)   **Issue or Issues [or: Question or Questions Presented]**

6)   **Holding**

7)   **Reasoning**

8)   **Separate Opinions and Dissents**

9)   **Other Items of Note**

There is no "law" prescribing the precise format of a brief. There are individual variations on the basic theme of: facts, procedure, issue, ruling, reasons. For present purposes, follow our format, until you develop your own style. But remember that you should be able to answer specific questions asked in class about the case directly from your brief; if you must alter the format to serve that purpose, by all means do so.

1. *Heading*

The Heading is simply the name of the case, "cited" in a rigorously prescribed format (which you will learn about in your legal writing course). Use the last name of the first-listed party on each side of the "v." to indicate the name of the case.

---

[20] You will learn about the relations among "joint tortfeasors" (defendants "jointly and severally liable") in your Torts course. You need not know anything more about it for our purposes than what we say in the text.

There is no artistic license for you to rearrange the heading, except you may wish to indicate the author of the court's opinion (as well as any separate opinions) and/ or the vote.

Thus, here the heading is: Kelly v. Gwinnell, 96 N.J. 538, 478 A.2d 1219 (1984) (6-1) (opinion for the Court by Wilentz, C.J.; dissent by Garibaldi, J.)

comment

2. *Statement of the Case*

The Statement of the Case is typically a one-sentence capsule version of what the case is "about."

Experience teaches that to formulate that capsule version gives you trouble — as much trouble as articulating the "issue" and the "holding" of the case. The reason? All three demand that you truly grasp the core, the essence of just what it was the court decided and what it did not decide, the latter being *at least* as important as the former! And grasping the core of a decision is very hard to do. Yet you must master this skill among other reasons for a very simple and practical one: when lawyers discuss cases they do not read their briefs to one another, or to the court for that matter. Rather, they put the case, that is, what it was "about," into the proverbial nutshell. And that nutshell looks very much like the Statement of the Case.

Suppose you were to say: *Kelly* is about the potential tort liability of social hosts for their drunken guests.

Is that accurate? Is it acceptable? Yes and No.

Why yes? Well, *Kelly is* about social hosts (the Zaks) and about their drunken guest (Gwinnell) and your description does locate the case on that large map we call "law" and gives it an address: it is a torts case; it is a torts case about social hosts, alcohol, and drunken guests of social hosts. We have now eliminated all the cases in our legal universe that are not torts cases and we have eliminated all cases in our torts universe that are not about social hosts and alcohol and drunken guests. But what we said ("*Kelly* is about the potential tort liability of social hosts for their drunken guests") will not do. Why not?

Our statement has three serious shortcomings:

(1) First, it says nothing about what connection if any, there must exist between the social host and the drunken state of the guest. Yet isn't it crucial to the case that the Zaks "provided liquor directly" (the court's words) to Mr. Gwinnell, serving him "beyond the point at which the guest was visibly intoxicated" (again the court's words)?

the typo exam!

Suppose you were to imagine that the day after *Kelly* is decided by the New Jersey Supreme Court, a visibly drunken Mr. Gwinnell shows up at the Zaks' home, perhaps to commiserate with them. This time the Zaks give him a mug of black coffee to drink; however, it fails to sober him up. A short while later, still drunk, Gwinnell gets into his car. The Zaks make no attempt to stop him and then Gwinnell drives into — lo and behold — Marie Kelly, out in her new S.U.V. The car is totaled and Marie is again seriously injured.

As Marie's lawyer, perhaps you take the position that Marie can sue the Zaks again. You might argue that the Supreme Court of New Jersey "clearly" (a word courts and lawyers tend to use when the matter at hand is anything but clear!) is "bound" to permit her to do so on the basis of *Kelly v. Gwinnell I*.

You would be right IF *Kelly v. Gwinell I* said: a social host of a drunken guest is responsible for injuries that drunken guest inflicts on third parties (when driving an automobile) — *regardless of whether the social host enabled the guest to become drunk* — which is what we implied with our first, too sweeping Statement of the Case. — A p. 50

But is there not a difference between actively doing something and passively standing by and letting something happen? Might we have an easier time — morally, ethically, legally — saying to someone: You may not do that and if you do it anyway we will subject you to legal processes, than saying to someone: You must act and if you fail to act your omission will subject you to legal processes?

If this distinction rings true (*you* kicked the football through the neighbor's window; you didn't stop the class bully from doing so) then you know that the result in *Kelly v. Gwinnell II* is not dictated by *Kelly v. Gwinnell I*; that *Kelly II* is not *Kelly I* and that we must amend our Statement of the Case to read: "*Kelly* is about the potential tort liability of a social host who serves his guest alcohol beyond the point of visible intoxication."

One added note of caution: might the Supreme Court of New Jersey in *Kelly II* hold the Zaks liable "on the authority of our decision in *Kelly I*"? Of course it might! And, of course, it might not! Either is within the court's power. But the court, not we, decrees the future fate of *Kelly I*, decrees how broadly or how narrowly it will sweep. Our job when we read *Kelly I* is to give it as accurate, as objective, as honest a reading as we are capable of — even while we know its uncertainty and ponder at the same time its implications and the arguments we as lawyers could make about it in future cases. Or to put the same thing differently, how we could argue to make future cases "like" *Kelly I*.   *key word*

Let us turn to the second shortcoming of our original Statement, namely: we never say what it was that Gwinnell did, namely, that while drunk *he drove an automobile*.   (2)

Suppose we again imagine ourselves the day after *Kelly* has been decided. Again the Zaks serve alcohol to Gwinnell beyond the point of visible intoxication (some folks are incorrigible). But this time Gwinnell decides to walk home. On the way he passes a house that happens to belong to Marie Kelly and, "for the fun of it" he heaves rocks through her lighted windows. He causes about $10,000 worth of property damages and in addition, one of the rocks hits Marie in the head, causing a severe concussion.[21]

As Marie's lawyer, would you make the Zaks co-defendants with Gwinnell?

You, again, study *Kelly I*. You, again, ponder all the footnotes. Do you think the majority saw the core of the case as being *drinking* and was on some sort of

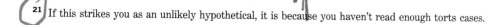

---

[21] If this strikes you as an unlikely hypothetical, it is because you haven't read enough torts cases.

temperance campaign? Or did it see the social problem as one of *drunken driving*? For that matter, note that the court explicitly says, "We impose liability solely for injuries resulting from the guest's *drunken driving*." And note further that Justice Garibaldi agreed with the court about the nature of the problem; she disagrees only as to who the appropriate agency is to address it.

Perhaps you think it should not matter whether Gwinnell drove or walked, in either case he was intoxicated and caused harm. Yet consider: holding social hosts liable for tortious acts of their drunken guests imposes a substantial burden on them and the *Kelly* court was well aware of that. We think we can justify the imposition of that burden because the benefit we hope to get — fewer drunken drivers killing or maiming people with their now deadly weapons — outweighs the burden, at least in the majority's judgment and, if you agree with the outcome of *Kelly*, in yours. But if the benefit (avoided harms) was less or the burden greater, that calculus might come out differently.

Would you give the same overriding weight to the benefit side if the mischief came about as we just hypothesized? Should it matter that, as the footnotes testify, we have a great deal of solid evidence on the consequences of drunken driving, but probably very little on the consequences to third parties of drunken walking? Would you be increasing the burden on the social host by too much? (What is "too much"?) Can the host prevent drunken walking as effectively, with the same amount of effort, as drunken driving?

The two cases (driving and walking) are alike and not alike; they have similarities and dissimilarities. They are similar, but not congruent. Which should prevail and how do we decide the question?

The third shortcoming of our Statement of the Case is that it is silent about the nature of the injury — that is, was the injury one to the plaintiff's person or to her property (or, of course, to both)? In our "walking" hypothetical Gwinnell caused both sorts of damages. Or suppose everything again happened as it did in *Kelly I* except that Marie miraculously walked away from the collision without a scratch — only her car is totaled.

What would you argue for and against the proposition that we should make a distinction between the two kinds of injury? How would your respective positions affect our cost-benefit analysis?

Whatever you conclude, unless you believe that drawing a distinction between personal injuries and property damage is totally irrational and without merit (in which case you must say why), must you not amend your Statement of the Case one more time to read:

> *Kelly* is about the potential tort liability of a social host who serves his (adult?) guest alcohol beyond the point of visible intoxication, knowing that his guest will shortly thereafter drive and who in so doing inflicts personal injuries on third parties.

Did you notice that we just "snuck" something past you? We said, injuries inflicted "on third parties." How about liability of the social host for personal

i.e., Gwinnell — and he be able to sue Zak?

injuries suffered by his drunken guest as a consequence of having served him alcohol beyond the point of intoxication knowing that his guest would shortly be driving his automobile?

You are thinking this is a great deal of energy to spend on getting one sentence right. But of course you are not getting one sentence right — you are getting a case right! Besides, the time and effort we just expended will be amply returned to us when we come to the Issue and the Holding. And meticulous care, bordering on nit-picking, throughout your First Year will make all the rest of your professional life easier.

A final observation regarding our Statement of the Case: do not start your sentence with: "This is an action by Marie Kelly. . . ." It is pointless to do this: (a) we haven't a clue who Marie Kelly is and (b) it tells us nothing of what is normatively significant — legally relevant, if you prefer — about Marie Kelly. She did not bring suit because of an injury to her name. Rather, she wishes to be put into a category of persons which the legal system is willing to protect — here "persons injured because a social host has plied a guest with alcohol beyond intoxication knowing the guest will then drive." It is that categorical trait that you must, in a system of stare decisis, isolate and present when you introduce the story of this case.

Only in the event that the dispute centers around the very words, "Marie Kelly" would you have to say, "Marie Kelly" or, better, "a Marie Kelly" or "one Marie Kelly." Better because most likely you don't mean to imply this is about "*the* Marie Kelly."

Remember: courts fashion general rules while resolving particular controversies.

We can think of two exceptions or modifications:

a) It is Oprah Winfrey — *the* Oprah Winfrey — who is suing for the alleged unauthorized use of her name, for example. You may then say "This is an action by Oprah Winfrey. . . ." But note that the rule of the case would still be a general rule, namely, a rule for people who have become "legends" on the order of Oprah Winfrey.

b) If the plaintiff is a large corporation "everyone" has heard of, it is a great deal more efficient to say "Microsoft," for instance, than it would be to give an identifying description of Microsoft.

What we have said about a plaintiff applies equally to a defendant.

It should be clear to you that it is not the least bit helpful to say: "The plaintiff is bringing suit . . ." as you are, unfortunately, wont to do. There is no known case in which a defendant initiated a lawsuit. The same, needless to say, applies the other way around ("This is a suit against a [the] defendant . . .").

On occasion, plaintiffs and defendants are known by different names — e.g., as libellant and libellee in admiralty proceedings. Apply the proper designation. All else follows as above.

From Manuel: go there!

3. The Facts

What, we might ask first, is the relationship between "the brute raw events" that happened perhaps years ago and "the facts" as they appear in your casebook?

Here is Llewellyn:

> What is left in men's minds as to those raw events has been canvassed, more or less thoroughly, more or less skillfully, by two lawyers. But canvassed through the screen of what they considered *legally* relevant, and of what each considered legally relevant to win his case. It has then been screened again in the trial court through the rules about what evidence can be admitted. The jury has then reached its conclusion, which — for purposes of the dispute — determines contested matters for one side. The two lawyers [who may or may not be the same lawyers that tried the case] have again sifted — this time solely from the record of the trial — what seemed to bear on points upon appeal. Finally, with the decision already made, the judge [really, of course, the judges of the final tribunal in the case] has sifted through these "facts" again, and picked a few which he puts forward as essential — and whose legal bearing he then proceeds to expound. It should be obvious that we may now be miles away from life. Again, we may not. By some miracle it may be there is no distortion. Or by some other each successive distortion may have neatly canceled out the last. But it is current doctrine that the age of miracles is past.[22]

Those then are what we call "the facts of the case" — the final version of the "real" events.

Yet *you* must now "sift" once more: you must put only those facts into your brief that were "material" and "relevant" to the court's decision, the facts on which the decision "turned," without which the court could not, would not, have decided as it did. And again you must do so because you live in a system of stare decisis.

Llewellyn again:

> The plaintiff's name is Atkinson and the defendant's Walpole. The defendant, despite his name, is an Italian by extraction, but the plaintiff's ancestors came over with the Pilgrims. The defendant has a schnauzer-dog named Walter, red hair, and $30,000 worth of life insurance. All these are facts. The case, however, does not deal with life insurance. It is about an auto accident. The defendant's auto was a Buick painted pale magenta. He is married. His wife was in the back seat, an irritable, somewhat faded blonde.[23] She was attempting back-seat driving when the accident occurred. He had turned around to make objection. In the process the car

---

[22] LLEWELLYN, *supra* note 1, at 38.

[23] [Ed. Fn.] In later years, Professor Llewellyn was married, by all accounts happily, to the near legendary Soia Mentschikoff, one of the first women law professors in the country (at the University of Chicago Law School), Dean of Miami University Law School, an important scholar, and a truly formidable woman. She was (she died in 1984) often referred to as "The Russian Bear," with a mixture of affection, admiration, and, last but not least, awe. The point of this footnote obviously is to prevent the delegitimization of Karl Llewellyn.

↑ what allows you to do that ??
b/c you are NOT a Martian!

swerved and hit the plaintiff. The sun was shining; there was a rather lovely dappled sky low to the West. The time was late October on a Tuesday. The road was smooth, concrete. It had been put in by the McCarthy Road Work Company. How many of these facts are important to the decision? * * *

Is it not obvious that as soon as you pick up this statement of the facts to find its legal bearings you must discard some as of no interest whatsoever, discard others as dramatic but as legal nothings?[24]

Which of Llewellyn's hypothetical facts would you discard "as of no interest whatsoever" to this controversy, or as "dramatic but as legal nothings"? Articulate the reasons for your choices. Have you, in the midst of that articulation, also begun to articulate the "rule," the "norm" you are about to fashion?

As for the remaining facts, which you must regard as relevant because we only have two classes, relevant and irrelevant, "you suddenly cease to deal with them in the concrete and deal with them instead in categories which you, for one reason or another, deem significant."[25]

Take
4y - VIP

And again, will your "one reason or another" reflect the rule, the norm, you are in the process of fashioning or believe the court has fashioned?

and again

A normative proposition is general or law-like — is a standard — insofar as it *abstracts* from the wealth of detail found in live social contexts, picking out a few features of a case or situation *normatively significant.*[26]

The more orderly among you will object to this discussion because we were supposed to speak of "The Facts." Yet to what extent can we identify the "relevant facts" of a case without an inkling of what the applicable norm *is* or *should be*? By the same token, can we put down the norm, "the holding," of our case before we grasp the facts?

Your goal, in any event, is clear: to try and determine which facts (or "facts," if you prefer) in the court's narrative you believe to have been "normatively significant."

But take heed:

(bathroom mirror!)

I warn you, I warn you strongly, against cutting the facts down too far. If you cherish any hope of insight into *what difference the rules make* to people, you will have to keep an eye out to some of the more striking details of the facts, as the court gives them. * * * *You will be impatient with the facts to the precise extent to which you need them.*[27]

You should understand this warning, so strongly delivered, from our Statement of the Case. *When in doubt, put it in!* It is better to err by overly narrowing the

why "narrowing"?
MUST DO!

---

[24] LLEWELLYN, *supra* note 1, at 48.

[25] *Id.*

[26] Frank I. Michelman, *The Supreme Court, 1985 Term — Foreword: Traces of Self-Government*, 100 HARV. L. REV. 4, 29 (1986) (emphasis added).

[27] LLEWELLYN, *supra* note 1, at 55.

Go Here the as Briefed about Kelly

sweep of a case (by putting in too many facts) than to err by overly broadening the sweep of a case (by omitting facts that prove to have been important).

Now how about *Kelly*? If you think about our discussion of the Statement of the Case then you know we must say something like this: The plaintiff in this suit is one Marie Kelly who was seriously injured in a head-on collision with one Gwinnell. Immediately prior to the accident Gwinnell had spent an hour or two at the home of Mr. and Mrs. Zak. During that time and according to Gwinnell and the Zaks, Gwinnell had consumed 2 or 3 drinks of scotch on the rocks (query: do we have to be that specific? Would it be OK to say 2 or 3 drinks? 2 or 3 alcoholic drinks?) A blood test administered after the accident showed a blood alcohol concentration of 0.286 percent. A blood alcohol concentration of 0.10 or more violates New Jersey's DWUI statute. Plaintiff's expert concluded that Gwinnell had consumed the equivalent of 13 drinks and that he must have shown unmistakable signs of intoxication while at the Zaks' home. The suit seeks to charge the Zaks with liability for Marie Kelly's injuries as joint tortfeasors with Gwinnell and his employer.

the 1ˢᵗ omission

Do you think we said all we needed to say? (More than we needed to say?) Here is one thing we omitted: Mr. Zak accompanied Gwinnell outside to his car, chatted with him and watched Gwinnell drive off. Is that "relevant" and "material"? How do you think about that question? You ask yourself whether you believe — on the basis of the court's opinion and your common sense and your membership in this society at this time — that had Mr. Zak *not* accompanied Gwinnell outside and *not* chatted with him and *not* watched him drive off, the court would *not* have found the Zaks liable. Preposterous? Irrational? Without rhyme or reason? Then why does the court tell us this fact? This is again a question of identifying the core, or essence, of a decision.

the 2ᵈ

We also omitted that Mr. Zak telephoned Gwinnell's home 25 minutes after Gwinnell drove off to make sure he had arrived safely. Relevant and material? In or out? Why does the court tell us? Does it want us to draw this sort of inference: Zak called because he knew that Gwinnell was drunk and he worried about him getting into an accident?

Assuming the answer is yes — on what aspect of the case could it have a bearing? To show that Zak knew that Gwinnell was drunk? According to the court, we have better evidence than that. That Zak "foresaw" or "should have foreseen" that there might be an accident? True, foreseeability is an element of a negligence cause of action — but it is measured by whether the reasonable prudent person in Mr. Zak's circumstances (and not Mr. Zak himself) should have foreseen that what happened might happen. It is an objective standard, not a subjective one, as you will learn in Torts.

So whether the court meant to signal something or not, we don't need it for our "Facts," right? But harking back to Llewellyn's warning, we repeat: when in doubt put it in. No great harm is done by doing so — but great harm would be done if you omitted to mention, for example, that it was the Zaks who furnished all that liquor to Gwinnell.

walk them through 4.

As to (4) Proced[u]
need to be walked [t]
"precedent" out of *rocedural History and Outcome Here*

You cannot ever properly comprehend a common law case unless you understand its procedural history and its precise procedural posture before the appellate tribunal.

To begin, no one ever "appeals a case." The plaintiff, or the defendant, or both, appeal one or more "reversible errors of law" that they claim the lower court made.

if there are reversible error, then there must be non-reversible - i.e. harmless, - error!

Assume that eventually the "court of last resort," in *Kelly* the Supreme Court of New Jersey, agrees to hear the case. What it can and cannot do by way of "appellate review" is governed by what kind of reversible error is being claimed.

To illustrate: every law suit involves "the facts" and "the law" applicable to these facts. Sometimes the parties "stipulate" to the facts (that is, they agree on what happened) but more often than not, the facts are contested. (You say I had 13 drinks, I say I had two or three). In that event, the "trier of fact" must "find" the facts on the basis of the evidence brought forth by the parties (and there are rules which determine who, plaintiff or defendant, must prove what). The United States, unlike any other country of which we are aware, assigns this task to the jury even in civil cases. Sometimes the parties agree to have the trial judge fulfill this function and she will then wear two hats: as the trier of facts she will make "findings of fact"; as the dispenser of law, she will state "conclusions of law."[28]

there had been J/T

note: Suppose on appeal the defendant claims that the judge wrongfully denied his motion for judgment after trial (formerly called a judgment n.o.v.) because there was insufficient evidence to support a jury verdict for the plaintiff. How much room should we allow the appellate court in reviewing this alleged error? Would it be all right if the appellate court reviewed the case as though the jury had never spoken, never, in effect, been a player? Start "de novo," in legal jargon?

key

discuss! (A) p. 23

If we were to say yes, then what is the point of having a jury in the first place? Yet clearly we consider it important that the larger community, as represented by the jury, participates meaningfully not just in criminal but also in civil proceedings.

a)

There is in addition this: we need someone to judge the credibility of the witnesses. The jury sees them and hears them and observes them. (The same, of course, holds for the trial judge sitting as trier of fact.) The appellate tribunal only has the record. Who is better capable of evaluating credibility? And is it necessary that one have a law degree and be a judge to determine whether someone is telling the truth or is lying or is, perhaps, mistaken?

b)

Finally, we cannot relitigate every case completely — the burden would overwhelm our appellate tribunals. So the division of labor makes sense from an efficiency point of view as well.

c)

---

[28] Note that in general when a jury finds facts it does not tell us its findings; it simply states its ultimate conclusion as to liability. In unusual circumstances, the judge may ask the jury to render a "special verdict," which includes determinations as to specific facts. In addition, when a case is tried to a judge rather than a jury, the judge does generally set out factual findings; indeed, she is often required to do so. *See* Fed. R. Civ. Pro. 52(a)(1).

It won't surprise you then to learn that *in this context* we confine the role of the appellate tribunal; we demand that it show "deference" to the trier of fact. How? By telling it: you must limit your review to the question, was there sufficient evidence for the *jury* (or the judge sitting as trier of fact) to find as it did. *You may not ask, would I (we) have found the way the jury did?* That is not your job. We do not care what you, appellate tribunal, would have done — we care about the integrity of the process and that the vital division of power between the judge (law) and the jury (fact) be respected.

like in K v G

By contrast: suppose the defendant appeals because there is no cause of action against a social host for injuries inflicted by their drunken guests on third persons. However many drinks the defendant served and whether he knew or should have known his guest was intoxicated and about to drive, he owned no duty to Marie Kelly. Therefore the trial court erred when it denied his motion to dismiss for failure to state a claim upon which relief can be granted.[29]   GO TO P. 34

why should "Z"?

The question, is there or is there not (really, *should* there or should there *not* be) a cognizable claim, is there (should there be) a "cause of action" is a *question of law* and thus falls uniquely within the province of lawgiving courts. The appellate tribunal has the final, authoritative word. The jury has no say in it and what the trial court or, for that matter, the intermediate appellate court thought has no binding or limiting effect on the Supreme Court of New Jersey. It alone decides whether there should be such a cause of action.

In the case proper, of course, the trial court had granted the motion for summary judgment in favor of the social host-defendant and it was the plaintiff who appealed.

Now note: the *Kelly* court says: "Viewing the facts most favorably to plaintiff (as we must, since the complaint was dismissed on a motion for summary judgment [by the defendant]), one could reasonably conclude . . ." (emphasis added). It then goes on to enumerate that "one could reasonably conclude" *not "must"*

1) "that the Zaks must have known that their provision of liquor was causing Gwinnell to become drunk, yet they continued to serve him after he was visibly intoxicated";

2) that "[b]y the time he left, Gwinnell was in fact severely intoxicated";

3) that "[a] reasonable person in Zak's position could foresee quite clearly that this continued provision of alcohol to Gwinnell was making it more and more likely that Gwinnell would not be able to operate his car carefully"; and

4) that "Zak could foresee that unless he stopped providing drinks to Gwinnell, Gwinnell was likely to injure someone as a result of the negligent operation of his car."

---

[29] You might here reread the discussion of "The Answer" at *supra* page 29. These things are difficult to keep straight.

[handwritten margin note at top: "harder for Πs or Δs to get sum. jt.? Burden of proof! Answer: Π bk ↑"]

These "facts"[30] suffice, says the court, to sustain a cause of action for negligence: "The usual elements of a cause of action for negligence are clearly present: an action by defendant creating an unreasonable risk of harm to plaintiff, a risk that was clearly foreseeable, and a risk that resulted in an injury equally foreseeable."

You understand clearly, do you not, that these facts have never been "found" to be so by a jury — there never was a jury; *Kelly* was decided on a pre-trial motion.

Did then the judges of the Supreme Court of New Jersey "find the facts"? No, no, and no. Appellate tribunals are not in that business. So what did they do? In their chambers, they sat down and looked at all they knew about the case from the record (which, the court tells us, included "pleadings, depositions, and certifications") and constructed the best case that could be made for the (non-moving) plaintiff (see the italicized part of the quote from the opinion above) and having done so decided whether a plaintiff so situated has, or *should* have, a cause of action against defendants situated like the Zaks: "Under those circumstances the only question remaining is whether a duty exists to prevent such risk or, *realistically, whether this court should impose such a duty*." (Emphasis added).

[handwritten margin note: "non-moving below"]

Suppose that instead of the Zaks it is Marie Kelly who moves for summary judgment, asserting that the facts necessary for her to win are undisputed and that *as a matter of law* the defendants are liable. Now the facts on the basis of which the court will rule change kaleidoscopically. Why? Because (1) Summary judgment may not take from the non-moving party (now the Zaks) something to which they are entitled; (2) the Zaks are entitled to a trial in open court and a jury verdict; (3) therefore the judge must give Zaks everything they could conceivably have gotten from a jury trial. She must construct, on the basis of the available record, the best version of the facts for the Zaks that a jury *reasonably* could find. That story will often differ significantly from the best version of the facts for the plaintiff.

*[handwritten margin note: "raise issue *↑"]*

Returning to the case as it was, on the Zaks' motion for summary judgment, is the lawsuit over once the court says, Marie Kelly, you have a cause of action against the Zaks? In theory, no. To "have [or state] a cause of action" does not mean the plaintiff wins the case; it only means that she can go to trial to present evidence in support of the allegations of the complaint. In short, the appellate court has not "found" any facts, it has only concluded that *if* Marie Kelly establishes the facts she alleges a reasonable jury could find the Zaks liable.

What happens now? The court says: "We . . . remand the case to the Law Division [i.e., the trial court] for proceedings consistent with this opinion." Thus, Marie Kelly can proceed with a trial against the Zaks (and the other defendants); the trial that was precluded when the trial court (incorrectly) granted the Zaks' motion to dismiss. Such a trial will probably not take place, however. In practice,

---

[30] Note that we put the word "facts" in quotation marks. Why? Well, item (2) looks like a "fact" to us — but does item (3)? Does not (3) look more like a standard than a fact? Or at least a "mixed" question of standard and fact? If so and if we let the jury determine it, then we apparently invite the community, by way of the jury and by way of calling (3) a fact, to function as the arbiter of standards of appropriate behavior, at least in this case! You will pursue these matters in your Torts and Civil Procedure courses. We merely want to alert you to the complexities lurking behind the simple "factfinders do facts, judges do law" formula.

especially once the court has ruled on pre-trial motions, the parties have a lot of incentive to settle so as to avoid the time, expense, and risk of going to trial.[31]

The moral of the story: under the heading of, Procedural History and Outcome Here, you must specify what rulings the court or courts below made, the precise error or errors alleged to have been committed, what the reviewing court did regarding those rulings, and what disposition ("affirmed," or "reversed" or "reversed and remanded") it made of the case.

In *Kelly* we would say:

> The trial court granted defendant social hosts' motion for summary judgment. The Appellate Division affirmed. The Supreme Court of New Jersey reverses the judgment in favor of defendants and remands for proceedings consistent with its opinion.

A final word: the procedural history of *Kelly v. Gwinnell* tells us that we have a new precedent, a new rule of law. Future plaintiffs situated as Marie Kelly was can rely on the case as having established that social hosts under "like" circumstances owe a duty to injured third parties.[32]

Suppose, on the other hand, the Supreme Court of New Jersey rules on the disposition of a motion challenging the sufficiency of the evidence in a given case. In other words, whether this jury on the basis of this evidence could have reached the verdict it did. What is the precedential value of such a decision?

So heed Llewellyn's warning:

> I say procedural regulations are the door, and the only door, to make real what is laid down by substantive law. Procedural regulations enter into and condition all substantive law's becoming actual when there is a dispute. . . . Everything that you know of procedure you must carry into every substantive course. You must read each substantive course, so to speak, through the spectacles of that procedure. For what substantive law says should be means nothing except in terms of what procedure says that you can make real.

---

[31] Indeed, less than a year after the New Jersey Supreme Court's ruling in *Kelly*, the parties settled. Marie Kelly received $100,000 from Gwinnell's insurance company and $72,500 from the Zaks' insurance company. "If the whole thing can save one life, it's worth it," *Time* magazine quoted her as saying. *See Expensive Pour: Beware of Drunken Guests*, TIME 73 (Mar. 4, 1985).

[32] Unless, of course, the legislature gets into the act. In New Jersey, the legislature modified *Kelly* in several ways: liability does not extend to the drunken guest; anyone who tests at less than 0.10% is irrebuttably presumed not to be visibly intoxicated; anyone who tests between 0.10% and 0.15% is rebuttably presumed not to be visibly intoxicated; the social host is not jointly and severally liable. A brief explanation of the last point: suppose Marie Kelly gets a judgment for 3 million dollars. If defendants are "jointly and severally liable," then each one is responsible for the entire 3 million dollars (even though Marie cannot, of course, collect more than 3 million dollars altogether). If the Zaks are only severally liable, then they are responsible only for their share in the damages, so to speak. Assume that is 1.3 million. If Marie cannot collect 1.7 million from Gwinnell (who is broke) or perhaps his employer (who has filed for bankruptcy) then that is bad luck for her — the most she is entitled to collect from the Zaks is 1.3 million dollars.

Is the legislative response to *Kelly* a refutation of the court? Or is it an endorsement?

To Issue or Issues (and Holding), page 61, a[...] important points must be made. One is the i[...] elements of a case. The other is embedded in t[...] 61-63 demand class discussion. They are too d[...] use Kelly and as a second example the first of th[...] 63-66.

The rest of the "brief" discussion is easily [...] student asked one of us why we say "*can a* [...]s the descriptive language? Shouldn't it be "*should* [...]ase is should be given a gold star. Then you might [...]ainly) while asking for a normative answer and thu[...] at once — making both circumlocutions acceptable.

[...]nt social host who, knowing his adult guest would shortly be driving his automobile, provided liquor to said guest beyond the point of visible intoxication, in a suit by a third party for injuries sustained as the consequence of the guest's drunken driving, or should the conduct of the social host instead have been subjected to the jury's judgment guided in its deliberations by the trial court's instruction as to the law?

This formulation heeds our warning not to lose sight of the procedural posture of the case by stating explicitly the error charged (and reminds you that the ultimate question is *whether this case should have gone to the jury!*). But it would be permissible to say it differently:

Can a plaintiff who suffers personal injuries inflicted by a drunken driver maintain suit against the driver's social host who, knowing his guest would shortly be driving, provided liquor to his guest beyond the point of visible intoxication?

Or we could say:

Is a social host who serves his adult guest liquor beyond the point of visible intoxication, knowing that the guest will shortly be driving his automobile, under a duty to third parties suffering injuries due to the drunken driving of said guest?

In addition, we must now also grasp two different ways of thinking and speaking about issues and holdings. The words we use to express what we mean are "broad" (or "maximum") and "narrow" (or "minimum"); that is, we speak of a "broad" (or maximum) statement of the issue, the holding; and of a "narrow" (or minimum) statement of the issue, the holding.

It would help if you visualized an inverted pyramid. Or:

Imagine standing in the middle of the field in a stadium and looking at the seats. If you focus on one seat on the lower level, the angle between you and the seat is rather slight; if you look at a seat in the upper level, it's a larger angle.[34]

---

[33] LLEWELLYN, *supra* note 1, at 17–18.

[34] Ruggero J. Aldisert, *Precedent: What It Is and What It Isn't; When Do We Kiss It and When Do We Kill It?*, 17 PEPPERDINE L. REV. 605, 616 (1990). Judge Aldisert was Senior United States Circuit Judge of the U.S. Court of Appeals for the Third Circuit. The stadium metaphor is from a classic piece on stare decisis: Herman Oliphant, *A Return to Stare Decisis*, 14 A.B.A.J. 71 (1928).

The bottom

It is the point at the bottom of the inverted pyramid, the focus on the one seat on the lower level, the minimum, the narrowest point that we want to talk about first.

The court, at the absolute *minimum* must decide *"the dispute that is before it. It cannot refuse because the job is hard, or dubious, or dangerous."*[35]

The narrowest possible question to ask the court, the narrowest formulation of the issue in *Kelly* is:

> Can Marie Kelly, who was seriously injured in a head-on collision with one Gwinnell, maintain an action against Mr. and Mrs. Joseph Zak where a jury could find that Gwinnell after driving Joseph Zak home, stayed at the Zaks and where his hosts served him enough liquor for his blood alcohol to register at 0.286% etc. etc. etc.

You get the point: the "etceteras" stand in for all the further details, including, for instance, the phone-call Zak made to Gwinnell's home. If we included all of these in our (very long) statement of the issue we would then have the narrowest possible articulation of that issue. We would be at the very bottom of our inverted pyramid. (The same is true if we were talking about the Holding).

But we know already — from our Statement of the Case — that some of these details are irrelevant, are immaterial, are of no precedential significance. That we could not think of a single good moral, ethical, policy or justice reason for limiting recovery in future cases to those in which, to take the most extreme example to make the point, the social host's first is name Joseph or the plaintiff's Marie.

To see the true core of the case, and so to be useful for future cases we need to move up from the very bottom of our inverted pyramid, we must "broaden" our Statement of the Issue.

toward the top

It is crucial for you to see that we accomplish this by omitting facts from the case — for example, that Mr. Zak's first name is Joseph; the plaintiff's Marie, etc. Doing so expands the reach, or scope, of the case as a precedent. The question becomes whether there are limits to this shedding process. Is there a "maximum" question that can, *on these facts*, legitimately be said to have been before the court? A "maximum" rule legitimately issued, on these facts, by a court adhering to the rules of the game of our system?

In *Kelly* the court says or, better perhaps, warns:

> We are well aware of the many possible implications and contentions that may arise from our decision[36] We express no opinion whatsoever on any of these matters but confine ourselves strictly to the facts before us. We hold only that where a host provides liquor directly to a social guest and continues to do so even beyond the point at which the host knows the guest is intoxicated, and does this knowing that the guest will shortly thereafter

---

[35] LLEWELLYN, *supra* note 1, at 42.

[36] [Ed. Fn.] We played with some of these — for example, Gwinnell walks home and heaves rocks through Marie Kelly's windows; Gwinnell arrives drunk, is served black coffee, fails to sober up, and the Zaks let him drive home.

the lawyer as advisor as advocate in the suit

be operating a motor vehicle, that host is liable for the foreseeable consequences to third parties that result from the guest's drunken driving.

Try your hand on this simple example: an eight-year old boy asks permission of his parents to stay up until 10:00 p.m. on a school night; his usual bedtime is 8:00 p.m. The reason he gives is that he wants to watch an educational program on television that his teacher mentioned favorably in class. They allow him to watch the show. *the bed=time typo*

1. What is this "case" about?

2. Are any of even these few facts not relevant?

3. What, precisely, is the issue put to the parents? (And by implication, therefore, the breadth of the ruling?)

If there is a continuum that flows from narrow to broad, from minimum to maximum, and back, then where on that continuum do you locate yourself in your brief?

The answer must be that you will locate yourself at the point most appropriate for your purposes, and those purposes will depend on who you are: the plaintiff's lawyer in this case, a plaintiff's lawyer in the next case, the defendant's lawyer in this case, a defendant's lawyer in the next case, the court now or in the next case, a scholar examining the case — a law student preparing for class. Within the boundaries of legitimacy and reasonableness, all are right, none are wrong. *VIP*

6. *Holding (and Issue or Issues)*

If you correctly identified what the case "was about," if, in other words, you got your Statement of the Case right, and if you correctly identified the error charged on appeal, then you have your issue — and your holding. Everything we said just above about "broad" and "narrow" applies with equal force here. Who are you: tinker, tailor, soldier, spy — a plaintiff's lawyer in a subsequent non-driving case ("*Kelly* established a duty of care for all social hosts for the drunken behavior of their guests"); defendant's lawyer in that case ("*Kelly* is limited to cases in which the guest's alcohol level exceeds 0.286% and is further limited to drunken driving"); a court; a scholar; a lawyer being consulted by a client champagne and fine wines wholesaler whose business requires frequent and lavish entertaining of potential customers; a legislator besieged by both MADD and the liquor lobby who wants to know the precise "state of the law"; or last but not least a law student preparing for class — in which latter case it is obvious, is it not, that you should prepare appropriate statements for everyone in this cast of characters! Do it before class and do it in writing to get the maximum benefit out of this exercise, which is to see, by doing it yourself, the multiple legitimate holdings for which a case may stand.  *take up!*

Beyond that, some special, important things need to be said about the holding.

First, we need two more words. The fancy Latin phrase for "holding" is *ratio decidendi*, which translates roughly to "the ground, or reason, of decision." It is a common misunderstanding to think of "decidendi" as being the same word as "descend" (one sometimes hears reference to a case's "ratio descendi" — a term

that just does not exist). This is incorrect; "decidendi" is etymologically related to "decision," not "descend." But you can see how in a system based on stare decisis that misconception would arise. The holding, the ratio decidendi, of a prior case is its central feature from the point of view of those who come later and are trying to determine "the law"; it is what descends from one case to the next. But to say that the holding descends does not tell us what a holding *is*. The true meaning of "decidendi" provides a better clue: it suggests that the holding is the basis for the decision, the thing(s) on which the result turned.

The ratio decidendi is to be distinguished from *obiter dicta* — generally referred to simply as "dicta" ("dictum" in the singular). These are the words in the opinion on which the result *did not* turn; passing observations, generalizations, analogies, illustrations, or asides not necessary to the resolution of the case. Judicial opinions are often larded with dicta; however fascinating or learned they may be, strictly speaking they are not binding in any subsequent case.

We also need two of Llewellyn's "canons":

> *The court can decide only the particular dispute which is before it.*

Everything, everything, everything, big or small, a judge may say in an opinion, is to be read with primary reference to the particular dispute, the particular question before him.[37]

Llewellyn goes on:

[A]s a practiced campaigner in the art of exposition, [the judge] has learned that one must prepare the way for argument. You set the mood, the tone, you lay the intellectual foundation — all with the case in mind, with the conclusion — all, because those who hear you also have the case in mind, without the niggling criticism which may later follow. You wind up, as a pitcher will wind up — and as in the pitcher's case, the wind-up often is superfluous. As in the pitcher's case, it has been known to be intentionally misleading.

With this it should be clear, then, why our canons thunder. Why we create a class of dicta, of unnecessary words, which later readers, their minds now on quite other cases, can mark off as not quite essential to the argument. Why we create a class of *obiter dicta*, the wilder flailings of the pitcher's arms, the wilder motions of his gum-ruminant jaws.[38] Why we set about, as our job, to crack the kernel from the nut, to find the true rule the case in fact decides: the *rule of the case*.[39]

But ponder this anecdote, told by Judge Weinstein:

---

[37] LLEWELLYN, *supra* note 1, at 42–43.

[38] [Ed. Fn.] For example, suppose in Llewellyn's "Magenta Buick" case, the court found Mr. Walpole liable for negligently causing the plaintiff's injury and added: "Of course, if the defendant's steering wheel had been defective, he would not be liable." Or suppose in *Kelly* the court had said, "The defendant would not be liable if the guest had helped himself to the liquor at an open bar the defendant had set up."

[39] LLEWELLYN, *supra* note 1, at 45.

Judge Fuld also taught me that some first year knowledge needs to be handled carefully. "Why did you strike out this citation in the draft of this opinion?" he sternly asked one day.

"It's only a dictum, judge, not a holding. You can't cite it as you have."

"Who wrote it?"

"You did."

"If I said it, it's the law. Put it back in."

Before you rejoice, however, take note that Judge Weinstein went on to tell his listeners (an entering class of Columbia Law School students): "Since you are not judges yet, I suggest that it might be wise to know the difference between holding and dictum."[40]

Let us return to Llewellyn:

> Now for a while I am going to risk confusion for the sake of talking simply. I am going to treat as the rule of the case, the *ratio decidendi*, the rule *the court tells you* is the rule of the case, the ground, as the phrase goes, upon which the court itself has rested its decision. For there is where you must begin, and such refinements as are needed may come after.[41]

Llewellyn implies that what the court *says* is the rule, may not *be* the rule. From where, then, is the "authoritative," the canonical statement of the rule to come? Surely not from you? From the next decision in a factually similar dispute in which the court tells us what it "really" decided in the first case — and which might or might not involve some creative "moving around" of some "dictum" and "holding" (or at least you thought it was "dictum" and "holding," respectively) in the first case.[42] If, as Llewellyn suggests, we can't trust it in the first case, how can we trust it in the second? The answer is, of course, that you cannot; but the better you learn to read cases as judges read them, the closer you will come to trusty readings.

You should now understand why we said at the very beginning of Chapter 1, "unlike statutes and constitutions the common law rests on no authoritative text external to the judiciary." The point is not just that the common law is "judge-made"; in addition, it is perpetually evolving (*see, e.g., Kelly*) and therefore never knowable. One can no more "know" the common law than one can know every single eating establishment in Manhattan.

As for the holding in *Kelly*, the rule of *Kelly*, might we be able to use the court's own statement:

---

[40] Taken from *The Mansion of the Law*, Address to First Year Law Students, Columbia Law School (Sept. 9, 1992). Judge Fuld was a distinguished member (and Chief Judge) of the New York Court of Appeals, for whom Judge Weinstein had clerked. We thank Judge Weinstein for making his speech available to us.

[41] LLEWELLYN, *supra* note 1, at 45.

[42] You could profitably look at KARL N. LLEWELLYN, THE COMMON LAW TRADITION: DECIDING APPEALS (1960).

We hold . . . that where a host provides liquor directly to a social guest and continues to do so even beyond the point at which the host knows [query: should we add, "or should know"?] the guest is intoxicated, and does this knowing that the guest will shortly thereafter be operating a motor vehicle, that host is liable for the foreseeable consequences to third parties that result from the guest's drunken driving.

Yet even this statement requires "refinements," in Llewellyn's phrase. The court here speaks of "foreseeable consequences"; earlier it had said, "Zak could foresee that unless he stopped providing drinks . . . Gwinnell was likely to *injure* someone. . . ." And in its recital of the facts the court says: "The collision was with an automobile operated by plaintiff, Marie Kelly, who was *seriously injured* as a result."

What is the difference between saying, "foreseeable consequences" and saying, "injured"? The word "injured" primarily connotes personal injuries, not damages to property. On the other hand, the "foreseeable consequences" of drunken driving surely encompass both injuring or even killing another driver (or a pedestrian, for that matter) and damaging or totally destroying that driver's car with all that is in it.[43] We don't know whether the court meant that a social host is liable for (serious?) personal injuries only, or that the social host is liable also for property damage accompanying personal injuries, or that a social host is liable even if there is only property damage.[44]

So what do we do? The case, it seems, was about a plaintiff "seriously injured." Hence we, in our statement of the rule of *Kelly*, will move down a notch on our inverted pyramid and will say that social hosts are liable to third parties "suffering serious personal injuries" due to the guest's drunken driving, and will let the question of liability for example for property damage *only* await another day or, rather, another case.

7. *Reasoning*

The most important point about this part of your brief is that you *must* forbid yourself simply to *quote* the court's opinion, as you almost inevitably do at this juncture. Discipline yourself to state *in your own words* what you believe to be the gist of the court's argument, its premises, its reasons for why it decided the case the way it did. And practice doing so as *concisely* as possible. To quote Justice Ginsburg (during her confirmation hearings): "Get it right and keep it tight."

---

[43] Even extremely unlikely events are arguably "foreseeable" in some sense. For example, you hit a world-famous violinist and he had his two Stradivarius's in the limousine.

[44] We are not told what relief the plaintiff sought; i.e., whether in her complaint she asked for compensation for her personal injuries only or for personal injuries and property damage. If the latter, the question would seem to be answered.

8. Separate Opinions and Dissents

Judges who disagree with the majority's reasoning or result may write their own opinions. A judge might simply "concur," meaning that she essentially agrees with, and may well join, the majority opinion, but feels moved to explain or emphasize or qualify a particular aspect of the case or point in the majority opinion. Or a judge might "concur in the result," meaning that she agrees with, and votes for, the *outcome* the majority reaches (e.g., "affirmed") but not with its *reasoning*. Or a judge might dissent, meaning that she disagrees with the outcome and, by definition, at least some aspect of the reasoning, of the majority. It is tempting to ignore these opinions; after all, "the law" is what the majority says it is. Don't! Separate opinions generally do not merit as much attention in your brief as the opinion for the court. But you should read them carefully and describe them in your brief, paying particular attention to how and why they diverge from the majority opinion.

This is for two reasons. First, separate opinions will help to illuminate what it is the court did. It is much easier to understand an opinion when another judge is objecting to it and pointing out its flaws. And the concurring or dissenting judges' explanations or objections may say something about the scope and precedential value of the case.

Second, dissenting opinions, as you will see in at least one instance in the case sequence in Chapter 4, can be every bit as important, or even more important, than the court's opinion to the development of the law. They may foreshadow a new approach, a new or at least different perception of justice, an imminent shift in a legal rule. In law, then, history is sometimes written by the losers.

Over time you will learn to assess dissents critically and to distinguish the impending revolution, which merits close attention, from the more or less graceful rear guard action, which justifies no more than a note in your brief that the court's opinion was accompanied by a dissent or dissents. For now, you must pay close attention and *in your own words* articulate the nub of the disagreement between the dissenter or dissenters and the court.

In *Kelly*, you learn from the dissent all the counter-arguments one can make against the majority's taking the initiative on what both majority and dissent agree is an evil that must be addressed: drunken driving. The quarrel is over who is best qualified to do that. The disagreement thus serves as a fine vehicle to get you started on thinking about the respective roles of courts and legislatures as lawgivers in a system that both boasts of being a representative democracy and has an entrenched common-law tradition.

9. Other Items of Note

Here you can account for anything else in the case that strikes you as interesting or important and that does not properly belong in any of the other parts of your brief. More often than not you will omit item 9. *Kelly* raises at least one issue that might appropriately be included here: the court's decision to apply its ruling prospectively only.

P.I. manual

Common law decisions have a retroactive effect: when Zak poured those scotches for Gwinnell, indeed, until the day *Kelly* was decided, no social host had reason to think he would be held liable for injuries inflicted on third parties by his drunken adult guests with their automobiles. Now Zak learns that he *is* liable for something that happened years ago. His insurance policy may or may not cover him and the insured amount may or may not be adequate.

Is that entirely fair?[45] If not, what could the court do about it? Well, it could say: we hereby announce a new rule but it will apply only to injuries occurring after today's date. Thank you, Ms. Kelly, for having called our attention to a rule (social hosts owe no duty) we no longer think is appropriate. As a civic-minded person you surely do not begrudge future plaintiffs the thousands of dollars you have spent pursuing this case all the way to us, the Supreme Court of New Jersey.

How many people would there be, do you suppose, willing to play the Good Samaritan? If you think virtually none — isn't that rather a problem? We want a "living law" that reflects our present reality; we don't want to be tethered by rules reflecting values we have come to reject. Yet we said early on that common law is *application*; that it is self-generating.[46] In short, we depend on plaintiffs to bring cases that will challenge old rules (e.g., separate but equal is constitutional) and will claim new rights. And given the scarcity of Saints among us, at least *this* plaintiff should (must?) get her just desserts — i.e., the new rule should apply to her.

But *must* we extend it to all the other victims of negligent social hosts who did not come forth and bring suit? Must we let them free-ride, as it were, on the efforts of the one who did?

Note the answer the court gives in *Kelly*:

> The imposition of retroactive liability could be considered unexpected and its imposition unfair. We therefore have determined that the liability imposed by this case on social hosts shall be prospective, applicable only to events that occur after the date of this decision. We will, however, apply the doctrine to the parties before us on the usual theory that to do otherwise would not only deprive the plaintiff of any benefit resulting from her own efforts but would also make it less likely that, in the future, individuals will be willing to claim rights, not yet established, that they believe are just.

This aspect of *Kelly* is a very important one — so important that one might consider including it in the Holding. But if not there then it should be noted here.

C. A SAMPLE BRIEF[47]

Heading: Kelly v. Gwinnell, 96 N.J. 538, 476 A.2d 1219 (1984) (6-1) (opinion for the court: Wilentz, C.J.; dissenting opinion: Garibaldi)

---

[45] For a memorable argument that it is not, see the excerpt from Jeremy Bentham at *infra* page 180.

[46] *See supra* pages 3–4.

[47] *Sample*, not model. "Model" would imply this is the only way to do it; "sample" makes clear that this is *one* way to do it.

Statement of the Case: This is a case about the potential tort liability of a social host who serves his adult guest alcohol beyond the point of visible intoxication, knowing that his guest will shortly thereafter drive, where the guest inflicts serious personal injuries on third parties.

Facts: The plaintiff is one Marie Kelly, who was seriously injured in a head-on collision with one Gwinnell. Immediately prior to the accident Gwinnell had been at the home of Mr. and Mrs. Zak for an hour or two. The Zaks knew that Gwinnell planned to drive home from their house.

According to Gwinnell and the Zaks, the Zaks had served and Gwinnell had consumed 2 or 3 alcoholic drinks. However, a blood test administered after the accident showed a blood alcohol concentration of 0.286 percent. (A blood alcohol concentration of 0.10 or more violates New Jersey's driving while under the influence statute). Plaintiff's expert concluded that Gwinnell had consumed the equivalent of 13 drinks and that he must have shown unmistakable signs of drunkenness while at the Zaks' house.

The suit seeks to charge the Zaks with liability for the plaintiff's injuries, as joint tortfeasors with Gwinnell and his employer.

Procedural History and Outcome Here: The trial court granted defendants Zaks' motion for summary judgment. The Appellate Division affirmed. The Supreme Court of New Jersey reverses and remands.

Issue or Issues (3 versions):

(a) Did the courts below err in granting defendants' motion for summary judgment where a plaintiff who suffers personal injuries inflicted by a drunken driver, seeks to maintain an action against the driver's social host who, knowing his guest would shortly thereafter drive, serves liquor to his guest beyond the point of visible intoxication?

(b) Can a plaintiff who suffers personal injuries inflicted by a drunken driver maintain a negligence suit against the driver's social host who, knowing his guest would shortly thereafter drive, serves liquor to his guest beyond the point of visible intoxication?

(c) Is a social host who serves his guest liquor beyond the point of visible intoxication, knowing that the guest will shortly drive home, under a duty of care to third parties suffering personal injuries due to the drunken driving of said guest?

non-reautison — See p. 108!

Holding (3 versions):

(a) Where a social host provides liquor directly to a guest and continues to do so beyond the point at which the host knows the guest is intoxicated, and does so knowing that the guest will shortly thereafter be operating a motor vehicle, the lower courts erred in granting summary judgment for defendant-host in a suit by a third party who suffered serious personal injuries as a consequence of the guest's drunken driving.

(b) Where a social host provides liquor directly to a guest and continues to do so beyond the point at which the host knows the guest is intoxicated, and does this knowing that the guest will shortly thereafter be operating a motor vehicle, that

Ditto

host is liable for foreseeable consequences to third parties in suffering injuries due to the guest's drunken driving.

(c) A social host who serves his guest liquor beyond the point of visible intoxication, knowing that the guest is planning shortly thereafter to drive, is under a duty to third parties suffering personal injuries due to the guest's drunken driving.

Reasoning: Many jurisdictions have refused to extend liability to social hosts in similar circumstances and state court decisions which did impose such liability were subsequently abrogated or at least modified legislatively. However, conventional negligence law, far from immunizing social hosts, points to the very opposite. We test negligence by asking whether a reasonable and prudent person under like circumstances should recognize and foresee an unreasonable risk or likelihood of harm. Under the circumstances here there can be no doubt that the risk of harm was foreseeable. That being so, the crucial question to decide is whether the court *should* say that a social host *should* owe the injured party a duty of reasonable care. The imposition of such a duty seems both fair and "fully in accord with the State's policy" — as witnessed by recently strengthened criminal sanctions which make New Jersey the "toughest" state in regard to drunk driving. Furthermore the social goal at stake, the reduction of drunk driving, is one that is "practically unanimously" accepted by society.

Prior decisions, as well as an important Appellate Division case which, despite the absence of a Dram Shop Act in New Jersey (a) held licensees liable for the consequences of a minor customer's negligent operation of his automobile; (b) extended that duty to the licensee's customer and (c) held a social host liable for injuries inflicted on a third party as a result of subsequent drunk driving by his — minor — guest support the decision.

The issue is not appropriate only for legislative resolution — after all, there had been *no* legislative activity during the entire period from 1959 (when the first case on the subject of the liability of a licensee was decided) to date. "Obviously the Legislature may disagree" — that is, it can abrogate the ruling.

Going beyond legal principles: "Does our society morally approve of the decision to continue to allow the charm of unrestrained social drinking when the cost is the lives of others, sometimes the guests themselves?" Further: "This court *senses* that there may be a substantial change occurring in social attitudes and customs concerning drinking, whether at home or in taverns." (Emphasis added).

Separate Opinions: There are no concurrences. Justice Garibaldi dissented.

Justice Garibaldi's essential argument is that the legislature and not the court should address the "horrors" of drunken driving, for a number of reasons: the "limitless implications" of the majority's decision; the heavy burden imposed on social hosts to monitor and regulate their guests; the fact that the injured party has a remedy against the drunken driver; the significant dissimilarities between a commercial licensee and a social host, most importantly the social host's inability to spread the cost of insurance; and the possible loss of the family home. Finally, unlike the court, the legislature can hold hearings, debate the policy considerations

and then draft legislation which would "adequately meet the needs of the public in general."

Other Items of Note: The Supreme Court applies the new rule prospectively only but allows Marie Kelly the benefit of her suit.

Chapter 3

JUDGING

We here offer you a highly unsystematic — if you like, arbitrary — selection of statements about what judges do, or ought to do. You have so far read only a handful of cases and you may feel ill equipped to answer the questions we raise. But we do not expect you to "answer" them; they are not in any event "answerable." We only expect that you give them serious thought. We have a fairly modest aim: to introduce you to some of the questions asked and some of the observations made, to acquaint you with the issues that face a judge and surround the judicial process, and perhaps to stimulate a desire for more concentrated study at a later time.

We also wish to inspire you to empathy with the task of judging. Too often, students impatiently dismiss judges' efforts because they do not "like" the opinions — sometimes out of disappointed idealism, sometimes out of a "gut reaction," a direct pipeline from stomach to mouth bypassing both the heart (which has its reasons, after all) and the head, and sometimes out of the opposite, a purely intellectual conviction that may indicate narrow-mindedness more than learning.

Several of the quotations that follow appear in Cardozo's *The Nature of the Judicial Process*,[1] a set of lectures setting out his philosophy of adjudication. They were, in other words, of concern to Cardozo. Try to think of why that was so.

---

[1] BENJAMIN N. CARDOZO, THE NATURE OF THE JUDICIAL PROCESS (Yale University Press 1921) [hereafter cited as *NJP*]. Benjamin N. Cardozo (1870-1938) was and is one of the most revered American jurists. The literature on Cardozo is extensive. The definitive biography is ANDREW L. KAUFMAN, CARDOZO (1998). You might enjoy an essay including personal reminiscences of the Justice by Milton Handler & Michael Ruby, *Justice Cardozo, One-Ninth of the Supreme Court*, 10 CARDOZO L. REV. 235 (1988). RICHARD POSNER, CARDOZO: A STUDY IN REPUTATION (1990) is just what its subtitle says it is; Posner offers many cites to the literature, including some to the inevitable "debunkers." Cardozo had his greatest impact as Chief Judge of the New York Court of Appeals (the state's highest court), which, under his leadership, became the preeminent common law court in the country. His tenure on the United States Supreme Court was too brief for him to leave as large a mark there, although no less an authority than Justice Frankfurter wrote: "What is unparalleled in the history of the Supreme Court, is the impress he made on his judicial brethren during the less than six full terms that he served on the Court and the influence that he has left behind him." Felix Frankfurter, *Benjamin Nathan Cardozo*, *in* FELIX FRANKFURTER, OF LIFE AND LAW AND OTHER THINGS THAT MATTER 185, 187 (Philip P. Kurland, ed., 1965). Even allowing for the exaggeration that attends assessments of Cardozo, *see* POSNER, *supra*, it might fairly be said that Cardozo's Supreme Court stint was unusually significant given its brevity. For such an argument, *see* Richard D. Friedman, *On Cardozo and Reputation: Legendary Judge, Underrated Justice?*, 12 CARDOZO L. REV. 1923 (1991).

Cardozo was "the first modern judge to tell us how he decided cases, how he made law, and, by implication, how others should do so." KAUFMAN, *supra*, at 199. Many students who, at our urging, read *The Nature of the Judicial Process* (it is a slim volume) have told us how helpful they found it and how much it illuminated their law school experience in all their courses but especially in the first year.

A. THE BASES OF JUDICIAL DECISIONS

Holmes[2]

The first requirement of a sound body of law is, that it should correspond with the actual feelings and demands of the community, whether right or wrong.[3]

Gray[4]

We all agree * * * that many cases should be decided by the courts on notions of right and wrong, and, of course, everyone will agree that a judge is likely to share the notions of right and wrong prevalent in the community in which he lives; but suppose in a case where there is nothing to guide him but notions of right and wrong, that his notions of right and wrong differ from those of the community — which ought he to follow — his own notions, or the notions of the community? * * * I believe that he should follow his own notions.[5]

Are Holmes and Gray saying the same thing? If not, how do they differ?

What was the basis of the court's decision in *Kelly v. Gwinnell*? The "feelings and demands of the community" or the Justices' "notions of right and wrong"? Could it be both? Is there a problem when the two conflict?

Suppose that your community is empathetic and deeply compassionate toward people dying of AIDS. A landlord has evicted such a person. The law is "open" as to whether he may or may not do so. You are the judge. Will you follow *your* notions, *your community's* notions, or those of the *larger community* in which, let us stipulate, it is universally felt that the landlord should have the right to do what he did. What should you do if that were also "the law"?

---

[2] Justice Oliver Wendell Holmes, Jr. (1841-1935) is an American legal figure of mythic but controversial proportions. Holmes was a thrice-wounded Civil War veteran, and his experiences in the war were to color his view of the world ever after. (When asked, years later, for the facts of his life he is said to have commented: "Since 1865 there hasn't been any biographical detail.") Holmes was a Judge on the Supreme Judicial Court of Massachusetts prior to his appointment to the U.S. Supreme Court, on which he sat from 1902-1932. The best-known American jurist of his day, if not in the nation's history, he has been both deified and reviled. The fluctuations in Holmes's reputation are described in G. Edward White, *The Rise and Fall of Justice Holmes*, 39 U. CHI. L. REV. 51 (1971). For an interesting discussion and rich cites to the literature, *see* G. Edward White, *Holmes' "Life Plan": Confronting Ambition, Passion, and Powerlessness*, 65 N.Y.U. L. REV. 1409 (1990). The many biographies of Holmes (not to mention a movie and a Broadway play) include SHELDON M. NOVICK, HONORABLE JUSTICE (1989), and LIVA BAKER, THE JUSTICE FROM BEACON HILL (1991). A useful collection of Holmes's writings is THE ESSENTIAL HOLMES: SELECTIONS FROM THE LETTERS, SPEECHES, JUDICIAL OPINIONS, AND OTHER WRITINGS OF OLIVER WENDELL HOLMES, JR. (Richard Posner ed. 1997).

[3] OLIVER WENDELL HOLMES, JR., THE COMMON LAW 41 (1881).

[4] John Chipman Gray (1839-1915) served with Holmes in the Union Army and they were fellow students at Harvard Law School. After practicing in Boston, Gray became a law professor at Harvard, where he was a leading advocate of the "case method." He wrote two treatises in the field of property law, *Restraints on Alienation* (1883) and *The Rule Against Perpetuities* (1886), but is today best remembered for his jurisprudential work, *The Nature and Sources of the Law.*

[5] JOHN CHIPMAN GRAY, THE NATURE AND SOURCES OF THE LAW § 610 (1909), *quoted in* NJP at 107–108.

Is Holmes saying that the law should simply adopt and legitimize majoritarian prejudices, however unreasoned or immoral? Does this sentence "reduce[] all of jurisprudence to a single, frightening statement" that legitimizes any and all persecution of minorities?[6] Does congruence between the law and "the actual feelings and demands of the community" frighten you? Writing in 1945, one observer suggested: "If totalitarianism comes to America it will not come with saluting, 'heiling,' marching uniformed men * * * [but] through dominance in the judiciary of men who have accepted a philosophy of law that has its roots in Hobbes[7] and its fruition in implications from the philosophy of Holmes."[8]

If the linkage of Hitler and Holmes (or for that matter Hitler and Hobbes) shocks you (it does us) what follows sheds some light. In her biography of Holmes, Liva Baker writes:

> His patrician genealogy, his influence on American legal thought and jurisprudence, his sharply worded opinions read from the United States Supreme Court bench, particularly the dissents, even his more or less regular trips to a Washington burlesque house, had acquired a larger-than-life quality. It was said at the time that if you asked your neighbor to name the justices of the Supreme Court, he might name the chief justice, he might think of Louis Brandeis, but surely he would name Oliver Wendell Holmes. Holmes's birthdays were celebrated on the front pages of the *New York Times*. There was an Oliver Wendell Holmes Parent-Teacher Association in Cleveland, Ohio. And in 1946, Emmet Lavery wrote the popular Broadway play *The Magnificent Yankee*; Holmes was the first Supreme Court justice to be so portrayed.

> It is unusual for a judge to capture the imagination and affection of the American people, to translate into a genuine folk hero. * * *

> Then in the 1940s, as Hitler's hordes threatened to destroy what men who had been constructing it for at least five thousand years called civilization, a cult of detractors, led by a group of Jesuit professors scandalized by Holmes's lack of religious faith, formed to demythologize him. When they were through, his democratic sensitivities, his scholarship, and his standards were all found wanting, his work the mechanistic mischief of a materialist. In their zeal to create a modern Antichrist, these critics, like Holmes's admirers, also had distorted the picture.

---

[6] GRANT GILMORE, THE AGES OF AMERICAN LAW 49 (1977).

[7] [Ed. Fn.] Thomas Hobbes (1588-1679). Hobbes's best-known work, *Leviathan*, is an effort to articulate and justify a vision of strong sovereignty. Hobbes begins with two premises: (1) the state of nature, in which life was "solitary, poor, nasty, brutish, and short" (I *Leviathan* ch. 13), was intolerably anarchic, and (2) motivated by appetite and self-interest, mankind has as its primary goal self-preservation and the avoidance of violent death. To obtain peace and order, people give up certain natural rights, make a social contract, and create a sovereign. Readers of Hobbes vary in their assessment of just how all-powerful his sovereign is; detractors view Hobbes's vision as absolutist and totalitarian, supporters stress that Hobbes believed that the sovereign was limited by its own self-interest and deemed resistance permissible if the subject's life were in danger (for then the sovereign would not be performing the function for which it existed).

[8] Ben W. Palmer, *Hobbes, Holmes, and Hitler*, 31 A.B.A. J. 569, 573 (1945).

In an easy effort of transference, Holmes's capacity for deferring to legislative enactment as an expression of majority will became an expression of authoritarianism, might makes right. Supported by an occasional secular scholar, this group created out of Holmes's writings a judicial monster whose jurisprudence came closer to the philosophy of the German dictator than to that of America's Founding Fathers.[9]

Consider the following story, told by Judge Learned Hand, for half a century a federal district and court of appeals judge and sometimes referred to as the single individual most nominated for the Supreme Court by others than the President of the United States:

> I remember once I was with [Justice Holmes]: it was a Saturday when the Court was to confer. It was before we had a motor car, and we jogged along in an old coupe. When we got down to the Capitol, I wanted to provoke a response, so as he walked off, I said to him: "Well, sir, goodbye. Do justice!" He turned quite sharply and he said: "Come here. Come here." I answered: "Oh, I know, I know." He replied: "That is not my job. My job is to play the game according to the rules."[10]

Does this anecdote confirm or refute the picture of Holmes, totalitarian? In its light, could the quote from Montesquieu immediately following be just as readily attributed to Holmes? The quote from Blackstone?

Montesquieu

> In certain cases the law, which is both clairvoyant and blind, may be too harsh. But the judges of the nation * * * are only the mouths that pronounce the words of the law; inanimate beings who can moderate neither its force nor its rigor.[11]

Blackstone[12]

---

[9] BAKER, *supra* note 2, at 8, 10. For a more recent treatment that shares some of the doubts about Holmes voiced by his 1940s detractors, *see* ALBERT ALSCHULER, LAW WITHOUT VALUES: THE LIFE, WORK, AND LEGACY OF JUSTICE HOLMES (2000) (a portrait stressing Holmes's tendencies toward social Darwinism, eugenics, and the belief that might makes right).

[10] LEARNED HAND, THE SPIRIT OF LIBERTY 306–307 (Irving Dilliard ed., 3d ed. 1960). This story has been told, and modified, by many people for many purposes. For an overview and analysis of the different versions, *see* Michael Herz, *Do Justice! Variations on a Thrice-Told Tale*, 82 VIRGINIA L. REV. 11 (1996).

[11] CHARLES DE SECONDAT DE MONTESQUIEU, DE L'ESPRIT DES LOIS, bk. 11, ch. 6 (1748) (translated from the French), *quoted in part in* NJP at 169.

[12] You will come across Sir William Blackstone (1723-1780), an English lawyer, professor, and judge, with surprising frequency.

> Blackstone's *Commentaries on the Laws of England* (1765-1769) is the most important legal treatise ever written in the English language. It was the dominant lawbook in England and America in the century after its publication and played a unique role in the development of the fledgling American legal system. The book went through eight editions during Blackstone's lifetime; innumerable editions, revisions, abridgments, and translations appeared thereafter. Astonishingly, it can still be read with pleasure in the late twentieth century.

Stanley N. Katz, *Introduction* to 1 WILLIAM BLACKSTONE, COMMENTARIES ON THE LAWS OF ENGLAND at iii (1979).

[A] very natural, and very material, question arises: how are these customs or maxims [that form the common law] to be known, and by whom is their validity to be determined? The answer is, by the judges in the several courts of justice. They are the depositary of the laws; the living oracles, who must decide in all cases of doubt, and who are bound by an oath to decide according to the law of the land. * * * [J]udicial decisions are the principal and most authoritative evidence, that can be given, of the existence of such a custom as shall form a part of the common law. * * * [I]t is not in the breast of any subsequent judge to alter or vary from [these prior decisions], according to his private sentiments: he being sworn to determine, not according to his own private judgment, but according to the known laws and customs of the land; not delegated to pronounce a new law, but to maintain and expound the old one. Yet this rule admits of exception, where the former determination is most evidently contrary to reason; much more if it be contrary to the divine law. But even in such cases the subsequent judges do not pretend to make a new law, but to vindicate the old one from misrepresentation. For if it be found that the former decision is manifestly absurd or unjust, it is declared, not that such a sentence was *bad law*, but that it was *not law*; that is, that it is not the established custom of the realm, as has been erroneously determined.[13]

Were the majority of the judges on the New Jersey Supreme Court "only the mouths" that pronounced "the words of the law" in *Kelly v. Gwinnell*? If so, where did that law come from? Is there preexisting law, perhaps a just, "natural" law separate from, and external to, the law of the State of New Jersey and its judges? How would we go about discovering such a body of law?

Suppose there is an eternal body of law; must such a body necessarily contain a specific *rule* for the *Kelly* case — a rule, for example, which says: Where a social host provides liquor directly to a guest and continues to do so beyond the point at which the host knows the guest is drunk and does this knowing that the guest will shortly thereafter be operating a motor vehicle, the trial court should not grant summary judgment for defendant-host in a suit by a third party who suffered serious personal injuries as a consequence of the guest's drunken driving?

If that seems asking a bit much, then how about a background *principle* or *standard* — for instance, society has an interest in deterring behavior that is of little social utility but that endangers life and limb of innocent third parties? Or, principles of justice and fairness require that innocent third parties be compensated for injuries they sustain at the hands of actors whose behavior is of little social utility?

Perhaps some external and eternal body of law does contain such standards or principles. But stated at this level of generality, how do they help us to decide the case of Marie Kelly v. Mr. and Mrs. Joseph Zak?

And what explains the inability of dissenters to discover these rules (if they exist) or principles, and their insistence on disagreeing even when these rules and principles are pointed out?

---

[13] 1 William Blackstone, Commentaries on the Laws of England *69–*70.

A Detour into Rules and Standards

We suggest above that "rules" are something different from "standards" and "principles," from which it would follow that one cannot use these terms interchangeably. However, courts sometimes do so — see the first case in the Chapter 4 case sequence, *Barrett v. Southern Pacific Co.*, and especially Question (2) following the case.[14] It seems appropriate to try and get it straight now. The following may be helpful:[15]

   I. Definitions. — Here is the rules and standards debate in a nutshell. Law translates background social policies or political principles such as truth, fairness, efficiency, autonomy, and democracy into a grid of legal directives that decisionmakers in turn apply to particular cases and facts. In a non-legal society, one might apply these background policies or principles directly to a fact situation. But, in a society with laws, using the intermediary of legal directives is thought to make decisionmakers' lives easier, improve the quality of their decisions, or constrain their naked exercises of choice.

   These mediating legal directives take different forms that vary in the relative discretion they afford the decisionmaker. These forms can be classified as either "rules" or "standards" to signify where they fall on the continuum of discretion. Rules, once formulated, afford decisionmakers less discretion than do standards. Although the terms "rules" and "standards" are not everyone's favorites,[16] I hope we can stipulate to their definition as follows:

   (a) Rules. — A legal directive is "rule"-like when it binds a decisionmaker to respond in a determinate way to the presence of delimited triggering facts. Rules aim to confine the decisionmaker to facts, leaving irreducibly arbitrary and subjective value choices to be worked out elsewhere. A rule captures the background principle or policy in a form that from then on operates independently. A rule necessarily captures the background principle or policy incompletely and so produces errors of over- or under-inclusiveness. But the rule's force as a rule is that decisionmakers follow it, even when direct application of the background principle or policy to the facts would produce a different result.

   (b) Standards. — A legal directive is "standard"-like when it tends to collapse decisionmaking back into the direct application of the background

---

[14] *Infra* page 106.

[15] Kathleen M. Sullivan, *The Supreme Court, 1991 Term — Foreword: The Justices of Rules and Standards*, 106 Harv. L. Rev. 22, 57–59 (1992). Professor Sullivan is a distinguished constitutional law scholar and appellate litigator and the former dean of the Stanford Law School.

[16] First, the ambiguity of the terms breeds confusion. Some people call both rules and standards "principles"; some (notably Ronald Dworkin) call rules "rules" and standards "principles"; some (again, notably Dworkin) use the term "standard" as a broad genus subsuming the species of rules, standards, principles, and policies; and some use rules and standards as synonyms rather than antonyms.

   Second, the rule/standard distinction deceptively appears to be a dichotomy. In fact, there is only a continuum of greater or lesser "ruleness."

principle or policy to a fact situation. Standards allow for the decrease of errors of under- and over-inclusiveness by giving the decisionmaker more discretion than do rules. Standards allow the decisionmaker to take into account all relevant factors or the totality of the circumstances. Thus, the application of a standard in one case ties the decisionmaker's hand in the next case less than does a rule — the more facts one may take into account, the more likely that some of them will be different the next time.

Let us give you an easy example: the point of imposing a speed limit presumably is to make highway travel safer and to reduce accidents and their attendant social costs. The usual way of trying to achieve these social ends is to fix on a number, let's say 65 miles per hour, and to post signs along the route to which that number applies. If you get caught traveling faster than 65 miles per hour, you will get a ticket. The law enforcement officers may have some enforcement discretion in deciding whether to ticket you or not. But there is no judgment call, no discretion, involved in determining whether you broke the law: you either observed the numerical speed limit or you didn't.

Let us look again at how Dean Sullivan describes a rule-like legal directive, of which this is a classic example: "it binds a decisionmaker [here the police officers] to respond in a determinate way to the presence of delimited triggering facts" — you went 70 mph, you get a ticket. "Rules aim to confine the decisionmaker to facts" — did you or did you not travel 70 mph? "A rule captures the background principle or policy . . ." — we (i.e., the legislature in this instance) believe that a speed limit of 65 mph strikes the appropriate balance of safety and convenience. "A rule necessarily . . . produces errors of over- or under-inclusiveness." Suppose you are in the middle of Montana on an empty stretch of a well-maintained Interstate; there isn't another car around as far as the eye can see; you are driving a late model Lincoln Town car; you have been a professional chauffeur for 20 years and you have never even gotten a parking ticket; it is a clear, dry, crisp day, early in the morning and you are traveling west. Under these circumstances the rule (65 mph) is surely overinclusive; that is, it prohibits conduct that should be permitted in light of "the background principle or policy" in that our societal goal would not be endangered by letting you drive 70 mph or maybe even 75 (80? 100? 120?)

Suppose instead you are in New Jersey on a crowded two-lane highway, none too well maintained; you are driving a 1987 Rattletrap; you just got your first driver's license; it is evening and it is raining heavily. Under these circumstances the rule is surely underinclusive, permitting conduct that should be prohibited, because our societal goal is endangered by your driving more than 40 mph (35? 30?).

If all rules share the characteristics of producing "errors of over- or under-inclusiveness," and if we know that and yet still choose a rule as our "mediating legal directive," then it must be because we want to "afford decisionmakers less discretion"; because we want to "constrain their naked exercises of choice."

Suppose we post a sign saying not "Speed Limit 65 MPH," but this:

"Reasonable and prudent" is a standard, not a rule. It is a legal directive that "collapse[s] decisionmaking back into the direct application of the background principle or policy" — that is, we want people to drive safely and prudently because we want to prevent accidents (within limits) but instead of translating that policy into a number, we state it directly.[17]

Assume now that the police stop you. They say you were speeding. You, of course, protest that you were driving in a "reasonable and prudent" manner. You point to the condition of the road, the time of day, the weather, the condition of your car, your prior driving record, and other traffic. All of these factors are presumably relevant and have a bearing on whether you drove reasonably and prudently.

"Standards allow the decisionmaker [here in the first instance the Highway Patrol and eventually, if you contest your ticket, perhaps the Montana Supreme Court] to take into account all relevant factors or the totality of the circumstances," to quote Dean Sullivan again. We now also decrease "errors of under- and over-inclusiveness by giving the decisionmaker more discretion than do rules." But do we want to do that? Granting such discretion has costs. Our answer might well depend on the context, and on our feelings about the particular decisionmaker. Note that this particular level of discretion is that given to juries in civil cases.

---

[17] In 1995, Montana adopted precisely this approach, becoming the first and only state to eliminate a numerical speed limit. In Montana v. Stanko, 974 P.2d 1132, 55 Mont. St. Rep. 1302 (1998), the Supreme Court of Montana held the speed law to be unconstitutionally vague under the Montana constitution; the Montana legislature then re-established numerical speed limits. *See* Robert E. King & Cass R. Sunstein, *Doing Without Speed Limits*, 79 B.U. L. Rev. 155 (1999). Montana and its highway culture made it repeatedly into *The New York Times* and, under the title *Postcard from Montana*, into the June 7, 1999 issue of *The New Yorker*.

Note one other consequence of using a standard rather than a rule: "the more facts one may take into account, the more likely that some of them will be different the next time" and the consequence of *that* is that "the application of a standard in one case ties the decisionmaker's hand in the next case less than does a rule." To put it differently: cases that are decided on the basis of standards yield less precedential value than cases decided by the application of rules.

Let us return to our main subject.

e . g., Torts

Saleilles

One wills at the beginning the result; one finds the principle afterwards; such is the genesis of all juridical construction. Once accepted, the construction presents itself, doubtless, in the ensemble of legal doctrine, under the opposite aspect. The factors are inverted. The principle appears as an initial cause, from which one has drawn the result which is found deduced from it.[18]

Was the result in *Kelly* deduced from principle or did the majority "will at the beginning the result"?

Is not Saleilles' account a perversion of the very ideal of judging, a corruption? How would you defend such a process? Do you believe many judges go about their task in precisely the manner described by Saleilles? Consider:

Any lawyer or judge who is honest with himself knows that he often intuits a conclusion and then goes to work to see if legal reasoning supports it. But the original intuition arises out of long familiarity with the structure and processes of law. A judge will have such intuitions in cases where he has not the remotest personal preference about the outcome. A process like that must occur in all intellectual disciplines. But the honest practitioner, including the lawyer or the judge, also changes his mind when the materials with which he works press him away from his first tentative conclusion. I have had, as many other judges have, the experience of reaching one result after reading the briefs and reversing my position at oral argument, or of voting one way at the judges' conference after argument and then changing my mind in the process of reading, discussion, and writing. I have had the even less pleasurable experience of publishing my opinion and then concluding I was wrong upon reading the petition for rehearing and having to change the result of the case. Many judges can testify to similar experiences. If that is true, and it is, then it is not true that all judges choose their results and reason backward.

But it is true for some judges.[19]

And, Judge Bork charges, *that* view of the judicial process is "profoundly cynical."[20] Do you agree?

---

[18] RAYMOND SALEILLES, DE LA PERSONNALITÉ JURIDIQUE 45–46 (1922) (translated from the French), *quoted in* NJP at 170.

[19] ROBERT M. BORK, THE TEMPTING OF AMERICA: THE POLITICAL SEDUCTION OF THE LAW 71 (1990).

[20] *Id.*

Hutcheson[21]

Perceiving the law as a thing fullgrown, I believed that all of its processes were embraced in established categories, and I rejected most vigorously the suggestion that it still had life and growth, and if anyone had suggested that the judge had a right to feel, or hunch out a new category into which to place relations under his investigation, I should have repudiated the suggestion as unscientific and unsound, while as to the judge who dared to do it, I should have cried "Away with him! Away with him!"

I was too much influenced by the codifiers, by John Austin and Bentham, and by their passion for exactitude. I knew that in times past the law had grown through judicial action; that rights and processes had been invented by the judges, and that under their creative hand new remedies and new rights had flowered.

* * * [B]ut I believed that creation and evolution were at an end, that in modern law only deduction had place, and that the judges must decide "through being long personally accustomed to and acquainted with the judicial decisions of their predecessors." * * *

I knew, of course, that some judges did follow "hunches" – "guesses" I indignantly called them. I knew my Rabelais,[22] and had laughed over without catching the true philosophy of old Judge Bridlegoose's trial, and roughly, in my youthful, scornful way, I recognized four kinds of judgments; first the cogitative, of and by reflection and logomachy; second, aleatory, of and by the dice; third, intuitive, of and by feeling or "hunching;" and fourth, asinine, of and by an ass; and in that same youthful, scornful way I regarded the last three as only variants of each other, the results of processes all alien to good judges. * * *

I came to see that instinct in the very nature of law itself is change, adaptation, conformity, and that the instrument for all of this change, this adaptation, this conformity, for the making and the nurturing of the law as a thing of life, *is the power of the brooding mind*, which in its very brooding makes, creates and changes jural relations, establishes philosophy, and drawing away from the outworn past, here a little, there a little, line upon line, precept upon precept, safely and firmly, bridges for the judicial mind to pass the abysses between that past and the new future. * * *

And so, after eleven years on the Bench following eighteen at the Bar, I, being well advised by observation and experience of what I am about to set down, have thought it both wise and decorous to now boldly affirm that

---

[21] Joseph C. Hutcheson (1879-1973) was Mayor of Houston when, in 1918, he was appointed to the United States District Court for the Southern District of Texas. He was elevated to the U.S. Court of Appeals for the Fifth Circuit in 1930. He was Chief Judge from 1948 until 1959, when he took senior status.

[22] [Ed. Fn.] Rabelais was probably the most famous French writer of his generation (around 1494-1553) and the creator of a number of fantastic fictional characters — in addition to Judge Bridlegoose — such as Gargantua and Pantaguel.

"having well and exactly seen, surveyed, overlooked, reviewed, recognized, read and read over again, turned and tossed about, seriously perused and examined the preparitories, productions, evidences, proofs, allegations, depositions, cross speeches, contradictions * * * and other such like confects and spiceries, both at the one and the other side, as a good judge ought to do, I posit on the end of the table in my closet all the pokes and bags of the defendants — that being done I thereafter lay down upon the other end of the same table the bags and satchels of the plaintiff."

Thereafter I proceeded "to understand and resolve the obscurities of these various and seeming contrary passages in the law, which are laid claim to by the suitors and pleading parties," even just as Judge Bridle-goose did, with one difference only. "That when the matter is more plain, clear and liquid, that is to say, when there are fewer bags," and he would have used his "other large, great dice, fair and goodly ones," I decide the case more or less offhand and by rule of thumb. While when the case is difficult or involved, and turns upon a hairsbreadth of law or of fact, that is to say, "when there are many bags on the one side and on the other" and Judge Bridlegoose would have used his "little small dice," I, after canvassing all the available material at my command, and duly cogitating upon it, give my imagination play, and brooding over the cause, wait for the feeling, the hunch — that intuitive flash of understanding which makes the jump-spark connection between question and decision, and at the point where the path is darkest for the judicial feet, sheds its light along the way.

And more, "lest I be stoned in the street" for this admission, let me hasten to say to my brothers of the Bench and of the Bar, "my practice is therein the same with that of your other worships." * * *

Further, at the outset, I must premise that I speak now of the judgment or decision, the solution itself, as opposed to the apologia for that decision; the decree as opposed to the logomachy, the effusion of the judge by which that decree is explained or excused. I speak of the judgment pronounced, as opposed to the rationalization by the judge on that pronouncement.[23]

Was the result in *Kelly* arrived at by cogitation; by dice; by hunch? Why should it matter that you understand how the decision was arrived at so long as you know the result?

Judge Bridlegoose has two sets of dice — "large, great dice, fair and goodly ones" and "little small" ones. The large he uses for matters "plain, clear and liquid," the "little small dice" when "there are many bags on the one side and on the other," or, in Judge Hutcheson's words, "when the case is difficult or involved, and turns upon a hairsbreadth of law or of fact." As for Judge Hutcheson, instead of using dice, large or little, he decides the one case "more or less offhand and by rule of thumb," and the other by imagination, brooding, hunch — "that intuitive flash of understanding."

---

[23] Joseph C. Hutcheson, Jr., *The Judgment Intuitive: The Function of the "Hunch" in Judicial Decision*, 14 CORNELL L.Q. 274, 275–279 (1928) (emphasis added).

There are, apparently, "easy cases" and "hard cases."

Suppose a plaintiff brings suit for injury to a fetus in a jurisdiction in which case law has held in the past that unborn children are not persons and have, therefore, no cause of action. Is this an easy case or a hard case? How would we know this? Who would decide it?[24]

Are the abortion cases "easy" or "hard?" The surrogate mother cases? The "right to die" cases?

Do we mean by "hard" that the case falls into lacunae in the legal system? If so, then must we draw on extra-legal sources, e.g., our system of ethics, morals, ideology, what have you? (Or, of course, toss dice — but that, too, reflects a value system, does it not?)

Why should judicial behavior differ, as Judge Hutcheson tells us it does, depending on whether the case is easy or hard, assuming "we" can decide the threshold question?

Was *Kelly* an "easy" or a "hard" case? If you have difficulty deciding whether it was one or the other — does the difficulty lie with you or with the task of sorting cases into "easy" and "hard" ones?

Is reliance on intuition, on that "flash of understanding," as Hutcheson calls it, merely avoidance (out of arrogance, laziness, concern for convenience, or possibly wisdom) of the task of finding not the "rule" governing the case, since there does not seem to be one, but the "principle" or "standard"?

What did the *Kelly* court mean by the following: "This Court *senses* that there may be a substantial change in social attitudes and customs concerning drinking, whether at home or in taverns. We *believe* that this change may be taking place right now in New Jersey and perhaps elsewhere."[25]

If Hutcheson is correct and the law is not deductive, does that leave any basis for decision other than the hunch? Consider what is perhaps Justice Holmes's most famous nonjudicial statement:

The life of the law has not been logic: it has been experience.[26]

Could Holmes mean that logic has *no* place in the law? As a lawyer, wouldn't you hope that logical argument might carry some weight?

Holmes's writings were in large measure a reaction to a view of the law we have already considered: that of Dean Langdell, in which law is self-contained and governed by strictly logical considerations. You will recall Langdell's conception of law as a science. On this account, the judge's task is to reason from prior decisions, the dominant mode of legal reasoning being the syllogism. Holmes insisted that judicial decisionmaking was not so rarified or abstract; he saw the common law as

[24] The example is taken from Richard Taylor, *Law and Morality*, 43 N.Y.U. L. Rev. 611, 624–625 (1968), and is discussed in Anthony D'Amato, *The Limits of Legal Realism*, 87 Yale L.J. 468, 478–491 (1978).

[25] *See supra* page 42 (emphasis added).

[26] Holmes, *supra* note 3, at 1.

the pursuit (sometimes unconscious) of sound public policy.

Holmes develops his theme elsewhere in *The Common Law*:

> The felt necessities of the time, the prevalent moral and political theories, intuitions of public policy, avowed or unconscious, even the prejudices which judges share with their fellow-men, have had a good deal more to do than syllogism in determining the rules by which men should be governed. * * *

> [There exists a] paradox of form and substance in the development of law. In form its growth is logical. The official theory is that each new decision follows syllogistically from existing precedents. But just as the clavicle in the cat only tells of the existence of some earlier creature to which a collar-bone was useful, precedents survive in the law long after the use they once served is at an end and the reason for them has been forgotten. The result of following them must often be failure and confusion from the merely logical point of view.

> On the other hand, in substance the growth of the law is legislative. And this in a deeper sense than that what the courts declare to have always been the law is in fact new. It is legislative in its grounds. The very considerations which judges most rarely mention, and always with an apology, are the secret root from which the law draws all the juices of life. I mean, of course, considerations of what is expedient for the community concerned. Every important principle which is developed by litigation is in fact and at bottom the result of more or less definitely understood views of public policy; most generally, to be sure, under our practice and traditions, the unconscious result of instinctive preferences and inarticulate convictions, but none the less traceable to views of public policy in the last analysis.[27]

If Holmes is correct, why do we have judges making law? In trying to "legislate" effectively, they are surely handicapped by inadequate training, resources, expertise, and opportunities. Moreover, doesn't Holmes's view fly in the face of basic democratic principles, under which the electorate controls policymakers?

Re-examine *Kelly* (both the majority and the dissent) in light of Holmes and in light of our questions. What would you now add to your thoughts about the case?

Cardozo

We shall next listen at some length to Cardozo. First of all, we should treasure all judges' explications of what they do; they are, after all, the ones doing it! More often, academics are the ones who debate what judges do and should do. But more importantly, Cardozo, in the words of Justice Brennan, "was able, in a slim volume of near lyric prose [*The Nature of the Judicial Process*] to alter the course of American legal thought":

> [T]o an extent almost unimaginable today, the legal and popular culture of Cardozo's day denied the relevance of the human dimension of the judicial process. * * * [T]he judge was thought to be no more than a legal

---

[27] HOLMES, *supra* note 3, at 1, 35–36.

pharmacist, dispensing the correct rule prescribed for the legal problem presented. It was supposed that judges decided cases in mechanical, "scientific" fashion. * * *

Into this formalistic conception of law Cardozo breathed the wisdom of human experience.[28]

Here then is Cardozo:

Repeatedly, when one is hard beset, there are principles and precedents and analogies which may be pressed into the service of justice if one has the perceiving eye to use them. It is not unlike the divinations of the scientist. His experiments must be made significant by the flash of a luminous hypothesis. For the creative process in law, and indeed in science generally, has a kinship to the creative process in art. Imagination, whether you call it scientific or artistic, is for each the faculty that creates. * * * Learning is indeed necessary, but learning * * * is the springboard by which imagination leaps to truth. The law has its piercing intuitions, its tense, apocalyptic moments. We gather together our principles and precedents and analogies, even at times our fictions, and summon them to yield the energy that will best attain the jural end. * * * "When, again, I asked an American judge, who is widely admired both for his skill and for his impartiality, how he and his fellows formed their conclusions, he also laughed, and said that he would be stoned in the street if it were known that, after listening with full consciousness to all the evidence, and following as carefully as he could all the arguments, he waited until he 'felt' one way or the other." * * * "When the conclusion is there," says William James, "we have already forgotten most of the steps preceding its attainment."[29]

One of the most fundamental social interests is that law shall be uniform and impartial. * * * Uniformity ceases to be a good when it becomes uniformity of oppression. The social interest served by symmetry or certainty must then be balanced against the social interest served by equity and fairness or other elements of social welfare.[30]

If you ask how [the judge] is to know when one interest outweighs another, I can only answer that he must get his knowledge just as the legislator gets it, from experience and study and reflection; in brief, from life itself. Here, indeed, is the point of contact between the legislator's work and his. * * * Each indeed is legislating within the limits of his competence. No doubt the limits for the judge are narrower. He legislates only between gaps. He fills the open spaces in the law. How far he may go without traveling beyond the walls of the interstices cannot be staked out for him

---

[28] William J. Brennan, Jr., *Reason, Passion and "The Progress of Law"*, 10 CARDOZO L. REV. 3, 4 (1988). Professor Gilmore put the point this way: "Cardozo's hesitant confession that judges were, on rare occasions, more than simple automata, that they made law instead of merely declaring it, was widely regarded as a legal version of hardcore pornography." GILMORE, *supra* note 6, at 77.

[29] BENJAMIN N. CARDOZO, THE PARADOXES OF LEGAL SCIENCE 59–61 (1928).

[30] BENJAMIN N. CARDOZO, THE NATURE OF THE JUDICIAL PROCESS 112–113 (Yale University Press 1921). This and later excerpts reprinted with permission.

upon a chart. He must learn it for himself as he gains the sense of fitness and proportion that comes with years of habitude in the practice of an art. * * * None the less, within the confines of these open spaces and those of precedent and tradition, choice moves with a freedom which stamps its action as creative. The law which is the resulting product is not found, but made. The process, being legislative, demands the legislator's wisdom.[31]

Or, as Holmes said:

[J]udges do and must legislate, but they can do so only interstitially; they are confined from Molar to molecular motions. * * * The common law is not a brooding omnipresence in the sky but the articulate voice of some sovereign or quasi-sovereign that can be identified.[32]

We return to Cardozo:

I was much troubled in spirit, in my first years upon the bench, to find how trackless was the ocean on which I had embarked. I sought for certainty. I was oppressed and disheartened when I found that the quest for it was futile. * * * As the years have gone by, and as I have reflected more and more upon the nature of the judicial process, I have become reconciled to the uncertainty, because I have grown to see it as inevitable. I have grown to see that the process in its highest reaches is not discovery, but creation.[33]

Again, compare Holmes:

The training of lawyers is a training in logic. The processes of analogy, discrimination, and deduction are those in which they are most at home. The language of judicial decision is mainly the language of logic. And the logical method and form flatter that longing for certainty and for repose which is in every human mind. But certainty is generally an illusion, and repose not the destiny of man. Behind the logical form lies a judgment as to the relative worth and importance of competing legislative grounds, often inarticulate and unconscious judgment, it is true, and yet the very root and nerve of the whole proceeding.[34]

Adrift on the trackless ocean the judge may be, but, wrote Cardozo,

[h]e is not a knight-errant, roaming at will in pursuit of his own ideal of beauty or of goodness.[35]

Perhaps not usual for the time and place, Cardozo spoke of the unconscious:

Deep below consciousness are other forces, the likes and the dislikes, the predilections and the prejudices, the complex of instincts and emotions and habits and convictions, which make the man, whether he be litigant or

---

[31] NJP at 113–115.

[32] Southern Pac. Co. v. Jensen, 244 U.S. 205, 221–222 (1917) (Holmes, J., dissenting).

[33] NJP at 166.

[34] Oliver Wendell Holmes, Jr., *The Path of the Law, in* COLLECTED LEGAL PAPERS 167, 177 (1920).

[35] NJP at 141.

judge. * * * There has been a certain lack of candor in much of the discussion of the theme, or rather perhaps in the refusal to discuss it, as if judges must lose respect and confidence by the reminder that they are subject to human limitations. I do not doubt the grandeur of the conception which lifts them into the realm of pure reason, above and beyond the sweep of perturbing and deflecting forces. None the less, if there is anything of reality in my analysis of the judicial process, they do not stand aloof on these chill and distant heights; and we shall not help the cause of truth by acting and speaking as if they do. The great tides and currents which engulf the rest of men, do not run aside in their course and pass the judges by.[36]

Cardozo speaks of the need for candor in contemplating the judicial role. What role should candor play in the writing of opinions? Is it good or bad to erect a rationalizing screen, to quote Judge Hutcheson, between "the decree" and the "logomachy, the effusion * * * by which that decree is explained or excused"?

To put the question more sharply:

If the [Legal] Realists were right, if the legal rules applicable to most cases are indeed indeterminate, and such decisions therefore almost always the result of factors other than the mere application of doctrinal categories, then aren't judges lying when they seek to present their decisions as the determinate result of the application of preexisting rules?[37]

* * * [W]hat are judges doing when they write about law in their opinions? They are not describing the state of the law, nor are they describing their own internal thought processes. Rather, they are making arguments * * * [to the judges' of the appellate court] to persuade them that the * * * decision should be affirmed [and to t]he lawyers, litigants and public at large * * * to *explain* and *justify* the judge's decision.

* * * [T]he whole question of "truth" and "belief" in connection with legal argument is rather complex and vexing. When I think about myself as a lawyer making arguments to a court, I find that I can easily make statements like "The law requires a judgment in favor of my client" or "The precedent on which my opponent relies is clearly distinguishable from the case at bar." In short, I find myself phrasing my arguments in the same language of determinacy and clear meaning that seems so problematic when expressed in judicial opinions.

Do I believe it? Do I really believe that the law requires a judgment in favor of my client? Well, yes, but not in quite the same way I believe that

---

[36] NJP at 167–168.

[37] [Ed. Fn.] "Legal realism" was a large and complicated "school" of jurisprudential thought which had its heyday in the 1930s. Rejecting the view of legal reasoning as purely deductive, the legal realists "denied that the actions of legal decisionmakers were the determinate results of applying general legal rules. * * * [They] asserted that in virtually every case the legal decisionmaker * * * was free to decide the case in directly contradictory ways * * * and then find adequate grounds for justifying either result." Charles M. Yablon, *Justifying the Judge's Hunch: An Essay on Discretion*, 41 HASTINGS L.J. 231, 236 (1990). *See also* Charles M. Yablon, *The Indeterminacy of the Law: Critical Legal Studies and the Problem of Legal Explanation*, 6 CARDOZO L. REV. 917 (1985).

the train will arrive at 3:30. I believe that I have made a good argument, that a ruling for my client would be sensible and just and supportable on the basis of prior precedent, but I am perfectly aware that nothing actually *requires* the judge to rule my way, that other arguments have been made by my opponent, and that it is possible that the judge will rule against my client.

Then why do I speak in the language of requirement, compulsion and determinacy? In part, because those are simply the conventions of my language game. No one expects me to say, indeed they would be somewhat surprised if I said, "Truthfully, the precedents could support a ruling either way in this case, but I believe it would be desirable and appropriate to rule for my client." The judge knows very well that when I say the law "requires" or "compels" a given result, I am not denying that she has a choice in the matter. The judge, and everyone else in the process, knows that those words are part of the conventions of making a forceful argument. This in turn makes it impossible for me to express my argument in more ordinary language, closer to my actual belief, that a ruling for my client would be "desirable" or "appropriate," because the conventions of legal argument make those terms seem exceedingly weak. * * *

It is possible to view judicial language as expressing something quite different from the reasons which floated to the top of the judge's mind as she rendered her decision. Rather, the conventions of legal argument may well lead judges to express their decisions in terms of determinate results of legal rules, although the participants in the process understand these statements as explanations and justifications of the judge's choice in ruling for one side or the other, not as a description of the way in which the judge discovered the "right answer" to the legal problem presented by the case before her.[38]

Cardozo spoke of the "grandeur of the conception" that lifts judges into "the realm of pure reason" but dismissed it as unattainable, accepting the presence of the "human" as inevitable. In our own time, Justice William Brennan, invoking Cardozo, has called for the judge to combine passion and reason not because doing so is unavoidable, but rather because "this interplay of forces, this internal dialogue of reason and passion, does not taint the judicial process, but is in fact central to its vitality."[39] By the beginning of this century, he writes, the greatest threat to judicial legitimacy

lay in the legal community's failure to recognize the important role that qualities other than reason must play in the judicial process. In ignoring these qualities, the judiciary had deprived itself of the nourishment essential to a healthy and vital rationality. I shall refer to these qualities

[38] Charles M. Yablon, *Are Judges Liars? A Wittgensteinian Critique of* Law's Empire, 3 Can. J. Jur. 123, 124–125, 135–138 (1990).

[39] Brennan, *supra* note 28, at 3. For a glowing tribute to Justice Brennan, *see* Frank I. Michelman, *Mr. Justice Brennan: A Property Teacher's Appreciation*, 15 Harv. C.R.-C.L. L. Rev. 296 (1980). For a typical less sanguine view of "activist" judges as undermining self-government, *see* Louis Lusky, Our Nine Tribunes: The Supreme Court in Modern America (1993).

under the rubric of "passion," a word I choose because it is general and conveys much of what seems at first blush to be the very enemy of reason. By "passion" I mean the range of emotional and intuitive responses to a given set of facts or arguments, responses which often speed into our consciousness far ahead of the lumbering syllogisms of reason. Two hundred years ago, these responses would have been called the responses of the heart rather than the head. Indeed, to individuals such as Thomas Jefferson, the faculty of reason was suited to address only questions of fact or science, while questions of moral judgment were best resolved by a special moral sense, different from reason, and often referred to as the "heart." In his well-known *Dialogue Between My Head & My Heart*, Jefferson stated that "[m]orals were too essential to the happiness of man to be risked on the incertain combinations of the head. [Nature] laid their foundation therefore in sentiment, not in science."

An appreciation for the dialogue between head and heart is precisely what was missing from the formalist conception of judging. Indeed, Cardozo's own appreciation for it was slow in developing. In *The Nature of the Judicial Process* he appeared to accept with resignation the inevitability of such a dialogue, and did not value or encourage it. He adhered to pure reason as the goal toward which judges, flawed humans though they were, should continue to aspire. Some years later, however, he would come to champion the role of intuition. "The law has its piercing intuitions," he wrote, "its tense, apocalyptic moments." "Imagination, whether you call it scientific or artistic, is for [both law and science] the faculty that creates." The well-springs of imagination, of course, lie less in logic than in the realm of human experience — the realm in which law ultimately operates and has meaning. Sensitivity to one's intuitive and passionate responses, and awareness of the range of human experience, is therefore not only an inevitable but a desirable part of the judicial process, an aspect more to be nurtured than feared.[40]

Passion, however, is not to be confused with "impassioned judgment." Brennan continues:

> It is of course one thing for a judge to recognize the value that awareness of passion may bring to reason, and quite another to give way altogether to impassioned judgment. Cardozo, as usual, said it best:
>
> > [The judge] is not a knight-errant roaming at will in pursuit of his own ideal of beauty or of goodness. He is to draw his inspiration from consecrated principles. He is not to yield to spasmodic sentiment, to vague and unregulated benevolence.
>
> It is often the highest calling of a judge to resist the tug of such sentiments. There is no better example than the criminal law, where the awareness of the brutality of the underlying crime often threatens to overwhelm the mind and discretion of even the most seasoned judge. Yet the judge's job is not to yield to the visceral temptation to help prosecute the criminal, but

---

[40] Brennan, *supra* note 28, at 9–10.

to preserve the values and guarantees of our system of criminal justice, whatever the implications in an individual case. Indeed, the judge who is aware of the inevitable interaction of reason and passion, and who is accustomed to conscious deliberation and evaluation of the two, is the judge least likely in such situations to sacrifice principle to spasmodic sentiment.[41]

Holmes, Cardozo, and Brennan each reject the view that the judge's task is purely logical or syllogistic. How do their views of the inadequacies of reason differ? How do their prescriptions of what judges ought to bring to their task besides pure reason differ?

B. EMPATHY, PASSION, REASON: TWO EXAMPLES

Here are two Cardozo opinions through which to digest and evaluate the foregoing.

HYNES v. NEW YORK CENTRAL RAILROAD
231 N.Y. 229, 131 N.E. 898 (1921)

On July 8, 1916, Harvey Hynes, a lad of sixteen, swam with two companions from the Manhattan to the Bronx side of the Harlem River, or United States Ship Canal, a navigable stream. Along the Bronx side of the river was the right of way of the defendant, the New York Central Railroad, which operated its trains at that point by high tension wires, strung on poles and crossarms. Projecting from the defendant's bulkhead above the waters of the river was a plank or springboard, from which boys of the neighborhood used to dive. One end of the board had been placed under a rock on the defendant's land, and nails had been driven at its point of contact with the bulkhead. Measured from this point of contact the length behind was 5 feet; the length in front 11. The bulkhead itself was about 3½ feet back of the pier line as located by the government. From this it follows that for 7½ feet the springboard was beyond the line of the defendant's property and above the public waterway. Its height measured from the stream was 3 feet at the bulkhead, and 5 feet at its outermost extremity. For more than five years swimmers had used it as a diving board without protest or obstruction.

On this day Hynes and his companions climbed on top of the bulkhead intending to leap into the water. One of them made the plunge in safety. Hynes followed to the front of the springboard, and stood poised for his dive. At that moment a crossarm with electric wires fell from the defendant's pole. The wires struck the diver, flung him from the shattered board, and plunged him to his death below. His mother, suing as administratrix, brings this action for her damages. Thus far the courts have held that Hynes at the end of the springboard above the public waters was a trespasser on the defendant's land. They have thought it immaterial that the board itself was a trespass, an encroachment on the public ways. They have

---

[41] *Id.* at 11–12. If questions of reason and passion and their relationship to judging and judges interest you, you may want to peruse other contributions to Symposium, *Reason, Passion, and Justice Brennan*, 10 Cardozo L. Rev. 1 (1988).

thought it of no significance that Hynes would have met the same fate if he had been below the board and not above it. The board, they have said, was annexed to the defendant's bulkhead. By force of such annexation, it was to be reckoned as a fixture, and thus constructively, if not actually, an extension of the land. The defendant was under a duty to use reasonable care that bathers swimming or standing in the water should not be electrocuted by wires falling from its right of way. But to bathers diving from the springboard, there was no duty, we are told, unless the injury was the product of mere willfulness or wantonness — no duty of active vigilance to safeguard the impending structure. Without wrong to them, cross-arms might be left to rot; wires highly charged with electricity might sweep them from their stand and bury them in the subjacent waters. In climbing on the board, they became trespassers and outlaws. The conclusion is defended with much subtlety of reasoning, with much insistence upon its inevitableness as a merely logical deduction. A majority of the court are unable to accept it as the conclusion of the law. * * *

Rights and duties in systems of living law are not built upon such quicksands.

Bathers in the Harlem River on the day of this disaster were in the enjoyment of a public highway, entitled to reasonable protection against destruction by the defendant's wires. They did not cease to be bathers entitled to the same protection while they were diving from encroaching objects or engaging in the sports that are common among swimmers. Such acts were not equivalent to an abandonment of the highway, a departure from its proper uses, a withdrawal from the waters, and an entry upon land. A plane of private right had been interposed between the river and the air, but public ownership was unchanged in the space below it and above. The defendant does not deny that it would have owed a duty to this boy if he had been leaning against the springboard with his feet upon the ground. He is said to have forfeited protection as he put his feet upon the plank. Presumably the same result would follow if the plank had been a few inches above the surface of the water instead of a few feet. Duties are thus supposed to arise and to be extinguished in alternate zones or strata. * * *

The truth is that every act of Hynes from his first plunge into the river until the moment of his death was in the enjoyment of the public waters, and under cover of the protection which his presence in those waters gave him. The use of the springboard was not an abandonment of his rights as bather. It was a mere by-play, an incident, subordinate and ancillary to the execution of his primary purpose, the enjoyment of the highway. * * * We think there was no moment when he was beyond the pale of the defendant's duty — the duty of care and vigilance in the storage of destructive forces.

This case is a striking instance of the dangers of "a jurisprudence of conceptions" (Pound, Mechanical Jurisprudence, 8 Columbia Law Review, 605, 608, 610), the extension of a maxim or a definition with relentless disregard of consequences to "a dryly logical extreme." The approximate and relative become the definite and absolute. * * * In one sense, and that a highly technical and artificial one, the diver at the end of the springboard is an intruder on the adjoining lands. In another sense, and one that realists will accept more readily, he is still on public waters in the exercise of public rights. The law must say whether it will

subject him to the rule of the one field or of the other, of this sphere or of that. We think that considerations of analogy, of convenience, of policy, and of justice, exclude him from the field of the defendant's immunity and exemption, and place him in the field of liability and duty.

PALSGRAF v. LONG ISLAND RAILROAD
248 N.Y. 339 (1928)

Plaintiff was standing on a platform of defendant's railroad after buying a ticket to go to Rockaway Beach. A train stopped at the station, bound for another place. Two men ran forward to catch it. One of the men reached the platform of the car without mishap, though the train was already moving. The other man, carrying a package, jumped aboard the car, but seemed unsteady as if about to fall. A guard on the car, who had held the door open, reached forward to help him in, and another guard on the platform pushed him from behind. In this act, the package was dislodged, and fell upon the rails. It was a package of small size, about fifteen inches long, and was covered by a newspaper. In fact it contained fireworks, but there was nothing in its appearance to give notice of its contents. The fireworks when they fell exploded. The shock of the explosion threw down some scales at the other end of the platform, many feet away. The scales struck the plaintiff, causing injuries for which she sues.

The conduct of the defendant's guard, if a wrong in its relation to the holder of the package, was not a wrong in its relation to the plaintiff, standing far away. Relatively to her it was not negligence at all. Nothing in the situation gave notice that the falling package had in it the potency of peril to persons thus removed. Negligence is not actionable unless it involves the invasion of a legally protected interest, the violation of a right. * * * The plaintiff as she stood upon the platform of the station might claim to be protected against intentional invasion of her bodily security. Such invasion is not charged. She might claim to be protected against unintentional invasion by conduct involving in the thought of reasonable men an unreasonable hazard that such invasion would ensue. These, from the point of view of the law, were the bounds of her immunity * * *.

A different conclusion will involve us, and swiftly too, in a maze of contradictions. A guard stumbles over a package which has been left upon a platform. It seems to be a bundle of newspapers. It turns out to be a can of dynamite. To the eye of ordinary vigilance, the bundle is abandoned waste, which may be kicked or trod on with impunity. Is a passenger at the other end of the platform protected by the law against the unsuspected hazard concealed beneath the waste? If not, is the result to be any different, so far as the distant passenger is concerned, when the guard stumbles over a valise which a truckman or a porter has left upon the walk? The passenger far away, if the victim of a wrong at all, has a cause of action, not derivative, but original and primary. His claim to be protected against invasion of his bodily security is neither greater nor less because the act resulting in the invasion is a wrong to another far removed. * * * [T]he orbit of the danger as disclosed to the eye of reasonable vigilance would be the orbit of the duty. One who jostles one's neighbor in a crowd does not invade the rights of others standing at the outer fringe when the unintended contact casts a bomb upon the ground. The wrongdoer as to them is the man who carries the bomb, not the

one who explodes it without suspicion of the danger. Life will have to be made over, and human nature transformed, before provision so extravagant can be accepted as the norm of conduct, the customary standard to which behavior must conform.

The argument for the plaintiff is built upon the shifting meanings of such words as "wrong" and "wrongful," and shares their instability. What the plaintiff must show is "a wrong" to herself, *i.e.*, a violation of her own right, and not merely a wrong to someone else, nor conduct "wrongful" because unsocial, but not "a wrong" to anyone. We are told that one who drives at reckless speed through a crowded city street is guilty of a negligent act and, therefore, of a wrongful one irrespective of the consequences. Negligent the act is, and wrongful in the sense that it is unsocial, but wrongful and unsocial in relation to other travelers, only because the eye of vigilance perceives the risk of damage. If the same act were to be committed on a speedway or a race course, it would lose its wrongful quality. The risk reasonably to be perceived defines the duty to be obeyed, and risk imports relation; it is risk to another or to others within the range of apprehension. * * * This does not mean, of course, that one who launches a destructive force is always relieved of liability if the force, though known to be destructive, pursues an unexpected path. * * * Here, by concession, there was nothing in the situation to suggest to the most cautious mind that the parcel wrapped in newspaper would spread wreckage through the station. If the guard had thrown it down knowingly and willfully, he would not have threatened the plaintiff's safety, so far as appearances could warn him. His conduct would not have involved, even then, an unreasonable probability of invasion of her bodily security. Liability can be no greater where the act is inadvertent.

Negligence, like risk, is thus a term of relation. Negligence in the abstract, apart from things related, is surely not a tort, if indeed it is understandable at all.

The judgment of the Appellate Division and that of the Trial Term should be reversed, and the complaint dismissed, with costs in all courts.

---

1. *(Com)passionate judging.* What are we to make of these two contrasting opinions, so different at least in tone, and perhaps in substance? *Hynes* is often seen as a case of (com)passionate judging; *Palsgraf* as a case of dispassionate distancing. It has been described as an example of "the judge cleaning and polishing principles with his back turned to the parties."[42] The comment was intended as a criticism, but is this not precisely what we want judges to do? To decide, *impartially*, on the basis of general principles, regardless of the wealth, race, or identity of the parties. Why, after all, does Justitia wear a blindfold?

For that matter, make an argument that if *Hynes* is a passionate case, so too is *Palsgraf.*

2. *Is judicial passion dangerous?* Justice Brennan seems to propose that passion is an essential ingredient of justice. But might not passion produce *in*justice? We have all seen people act unreasonably (unjustly?) when overwhelmed by passion.

---

[42] Catherine Weiss & Louise Melling, *The Legal Education of Twenty Women*, 40 STAN. L. REV. 1299, 1350 (1988).

Would legitimizing judicial passion give a valid passport to judicial tyranny?

Consider the response to Justice Brennan by Judge Richard Cudahy of the U.S. Court of Appeals for the Seventh Circuit:

> During the last fifty or so years, the growing acceptance of passion or intuition in the law seems generally to have favored "liberal" outcomes and been approved by liberal theoreticians. I do not think there are any iron laws of history, however, that dictate the immutability of these relations. * * *
>
> My own instincts tell me, nonetheless, that in the long run the judges who invoke a measure of intuition and passion are somehow more likely to benefit the powerless than the powerful. This may be Justice Brennan's underlying hunch although he does not articulate it. And perhaps this is merely an illustration of flawed induction from my own life experiences. But I expect there will always be groups too small, diffuse, or reviled to obtain redress for their real grievances through majoritarian processes. These groups will continue to prefer judges whose logic is informed by their sensitivity to the plight of the dispossessed and underrepresented, as opposed to judges who confine themselves to passive roles guided by principles thought to be congenial to the status quo. This is all speculation, of course; nevertheless, it is a surmise deserving of consideration. * * *
>
> In summary, I find myself in general agreement with Justice Brennan's thesis. I must note in candor, however, that the passions and intuitions that he perceives as legitimate and constructive are those that correspond to his own point of view. A passion for capital punishment is not something that he would easily see as legitimate or constructive within the reason-passion paradigm.[43]

Reviewing Ingo Müller's *Hitler's Justice, The Courts of the Third Reich*,[44] Professor Berghahn writes:

> On Dec. 22, 1943, the executioner at the county prison of Wolfenbüttel, some 50 miles east of Hanover in Germany, had to work particularly hard. As the prison chaplain recorded in his death register, the guillotine fell in swift succession that evening at 6:35, 6:38, 6:40, 6:42 and 6:44.
>
> Unlike the thousands of other men, women and children who also died on that day in all parts of Nazi-occupied Europe in the concentration camps, as hostages or as innocent bystanders in military operations, the victims at Wolfenbüttel had been sentenced to death by ordinary courts — courts that had never ceased to operate throughout the Nazi period. These courts were manned by judges who had gone through the traditional law schools, often with excellent examination results, and who, according to conservative estimates, handed down 40,000 to 50,000 death sentences in the 12 years of Hitler's rule of terror. Around 80 percent of these sentences were carried

---

[43] Richard D. Cudahy, *Justice Brennan: The Heart Has Its Reasons*, 10 CARDOZO L. REV. 93, 102–103 (1988).

[44] (Deborah Lucan Schneider trans. 1991).

out, often within hours of the verdict being rendered. University-trained lawyers also imposed over 12,000 death sentences as members of military courts-martial, of which a mere 10 percent were ultimately commuted. If one adds also the reprisal executions of so-called "Night and Fog" prisoners, mainly in occupied Western Europe, and the sentences of special courts set up in Nazi-occupied Eastern territories, at least 80,000 people can be assumed to have died at the hands of Hitler's hanging judges.[45]

How many of these death sentences were handed out by judges full of passion for the Neue Reich?[46] If you do not consider this a fair comment, why not? "The best lack all conviction, while the worst/Are full of passionate intensity."[47]

If you are, by now, thoroughly disquieted, perhaps there is some comfort at least in this:

> The ultimate check, however, upon the passions, intuitions and emotions of one judge is the same faculties of another judge. That is why there is appellate review. It also explains why those reviewing courts always contain more than one member.[48]

Then again, if passions can "sweep" whole countries, why can they not sweep whole courts, or at least five lonely figures?

3. *Empathy.* If "passion" is not unproblematic, will "empathy" serve us better?

Barack Obama, both as Senator and as President, has stressed the importance of empathy in judging. Explaining his vote against the confirmation of John Roberts as Chief Justice of the United States, he stated:

> The problem I face * * * is that while adherence to legal precedent and rules of statutory or constitutional construction will dispose of 95 percent of the cases that come before a court, * * * what matters on the Supreme Court is those 5 percent of cases that are truly difficult. In those cases, adherence to precedent and rules of construction and interpretation will only get you through the 25th mile of the marathon. That last mile can only be determined on the basis of one's deepest values, one's core concerns, one's broader perspectives on how the world works, and the depth and breadth of one's empathy.

> In those 5 percent of hard cases, the constitutional text will not be directly on point. The language of the statute will not be perfectly clear. Legal process alone will not lead you to a rule of decision. In those * * * difficult cases, the critical ingredient is supplied by what is in the judge's

---

[45] Berghahn, *The Judges Made Good Nazis*, N.Y. TIMES BOOK REV., Apr. 28, 1991, at 3.

[46] Regarding law and legal rhetoric in Vichy France see *Avoiding Central Realities: Narrative Terror and the Failure of French Culture Under the Occupation* and *Legal Rhetoric Under Stress: The Example of Vichy*, both in RICHARD WEISBERG, POETHICS AND OTHER STRATEGIES OF LAW AND LITERATURE (1992). *See generally* RICHARD H. WEISBERG, VICHY LAW AND THE HOLOCAUST IN FRANCE (1996).

[47] William Butler Yeats, *The Second Coming*, lines 7–8 (1920).

[48] Cudahy, *supra* note 43, at 103–104.

heart.[49]

As a candidate, he returned to this theme: "[W]e need somebody who's got the heart, the empathy, to recognize what it's like to be a young teenage mom. The empathy to understand what it's like to be poor, or African-American, or gay, or disabled, or old. And that's the criteria by which I'm going to be selecting my judges."[50] And when Justice Souter announced his resignation, giving President Obama his first Supreme Court vacancy, the President said this with regard to what sort of person he would nominate:

> I will seek somebody with a sharp and independent mind and a record of excellence and integrity. I will seek someone who understands that justice isn't about some abstract legal theory or footnote in a case book. It is also about how our laws affect the daily realities of people's lives — whether they can make a living and care for their families; whether they feel safe in their homes and welcome in their own nation.

> I view that quality of empathy, of understanding and identifying with people's hopes and struggles as an essential ingredient for arriving at just decisions and outcomes.[51]

The President's emphasis on empathy provoked a powerful reaction, pro and con, in the media, the public, and the Senate. The negative reaction was strong enough that during the Sotomayor confirmation process the White House came to avoid the word "empathy" as too charged and politically problematic.[52] The nominee herself did not use it a single time during her testimony and expressly disavowed the President's account of what a judge is supposed to do.

Why the flight from empathy? The anti-empathy flank derided it as a code-word for activism, bias, feelings, emotions, and favoritism — in short, decisionmaking based on grounds other than law. Consider this summary of the standard account of the disconnect between empathy and even-handed judging.

> The Rule of Law is the reification of rules governing rights and duties to which we pay homage: thus, this is a "government of laws, not men";[53] the Rule of Law transcends humans and is superior to them. The virtue of the Rule of Law is that it is ostensibly "neutral" and prevents abuse of persons. The neutrality and generality of the Rule of Law seek to serve the goals of protecting individuals from arbitrary treatment and of respecting people as autonomous and equal. As such it is not in direct opposition to empathy. Yet

---

[49] 151 Cong. Rec. S10,366 (daily ed. Sept. 22, 2005) (statement of Sen. Obama).

[50] *See* Edward Whelan, *Obama's Constitution: The Rhetoric and the Reality*, WKLY. STANDARD, Mar. 17, 2008, at 12.

[51] The President's Remarks on Justice Souter, available at http://www.whitehouse.gov/blog/09/05/01/The-Presidents-Remarks-on-Justice-Souter/.

[52] *See* Sheryl Gay Stolberg, *Say It With Feeling? Not This Time Around*, N.Y. TIMES, May 29, 2009, at A15 ("Empathy was all the rage in Washington only a few weeks ago, . . . [b]ut now that conservatives have cast empathy as an epithet when it comes to the judiciary . . . Mr. Obama seems to have dropped it from his confirmation lexicon.").

[53] [Ed. Fn.] This much invoked aspiration originated in the Massachusetts Constitution of 1780, in a provision guaranteeing the separation of governmental powers.

to the extent the concern is with perpetuating the Rule of Law for its own sake, the importance of empathic understanding can disappear.

Essential to legality is the premise that fidelity to the law is necessary for predictability and control over outcomes and for social ordering. The Rule of Law provides us with an anchor, a grounding, that otherwise would not exist in modern postindustrial society; it keeps chaos and anarchy away from our door. Rules — whether explicit or open-textured — provide the illusion, if not the reality, of certainty; that certainty is reason enough to obey or acquiesce to the Rule of Law without question. For this reason the narrative of the suffering caused by the law to the Other can be ignored or suppressed.[54]

Is *Hynes* a case of "empathic understanding"? If so, is it (therefore) a case cut loose from the anchorage of the rule of law? Is it, not to put too fine a point on matters, essentially a lawless, albeit just decision? But is to speak of "lawless but just" decisions not an oxymoron?[55] It seems to come more naturally to speak of "lawful but unjust" decisions. Why?

How do the answers you just gave apply to *Palsgraf*? Where does *Kelly* fit in?

4. *Empathy and Impartiality.* In part, the 2009 empathy debate turned on a disagreement over whether empathy is a neutral characteristic, a turn of mind, or whether it is simply a substantive preference for particular individuals or groups. One empathy skeptic wrote:

> President Obama says he wants judges who have the "empathy to understand what it's like to be poor, or African American, or gay, or disabled, or old." But if judges who feel empathy for these groups can legitimately base decisions on it, the same goes for the considerably larger number of jurists who most easily empathize with what it's like to be rich, or white, or straight, or able-bodied. If we weaken the norm of judicial impartiality in favor of greater emphasis on empathy, minorities and the poor are unlikely to benefit.[56]

Do you agree? If not, how would you respond?

Which way does empathy cut in a case about affirmative action? When a judge must decide whether to suppress illegally seized evidence in a murder trial?

"Empathy" can be variously defined.

---

[54] Lynne N. Henderson, *Legality and Empathy*, 85 Mich. L. Rev. 1574, 1587–1588 (1987).

[55] Before you say yes too quickly, think of that great icon of American (and world) popular culture: the gun that brings justice to the lawless town. Think of the American Western! *See generally* André Bazin, *The Western, or the American Film* par excellence, in II What is Cinema? (1971).

[56] Ilya Somin, *How empathy can distort judges' thinking and lead to bad decisions*, L.A. Times (on-line edition), May 28, 2009, at http://www.latimes.com/news/opinion/opinionla/la-oew-chemerinsky-somin28-2009may28,0,4921073.story. Professor Somin was writing as part of a "Point/Counterpoint" exchange with Dean Erwin Chemerinsky; the whole exchange is worth reading. For an endorsement of empathic judging written against the background of the Sotomayor hearings, *see* Susan A. Bandes, *Empathetic Judging and the Rule of Law*, 2009 Cardozo L. Rev. De Novo 133.

While the word ["empathy"] often appears to be used interchangeably with "love," "altruism," and "sympathy," it actually encompasses specific psychological phenomena. Although the literature of empathy manifests disagreement about what is or is not "empathy," rather than projection, sympathy, or what have you, there are three basic phenomena captured by the word: (1) feeling the emotion of another; (2) understanding the experience or situation of another, both affectively and cognitively, often achieved by imagining oneself to be in the position of the other; and (3) action brought about by experiencing the distress of another (hence the confusion of empathy with sympathy and compassion). The first two forms are ways of knowing, the third form a catalyst for action.[57]

Which, if any, of these three phenomena (none of which equates to bias, sympathy, or preference) are relevant to deciding cases? Note the stress on understanding both "affectively" *and* "cognitively." (Is this the difference between passion and empathy?)

Lawsuits by definition involve two sides. Can a judge be empathetic toward both? If empathy is a thumb on the scale, a preference for one set of interests over another, the answer is no. But if empathy is "a way of knowing," a more complete understanding of the relevant, and competing, interests, the answer might be yes.

5. *"Real people."* It is sometimes said, almost always as a compliment, of a particular judge that he or she does not lose sight of "the people behind the cases," or of how the court's decisions "will affect real people." Consider the following information about the real person behind *Palsgraf.* Does it change your view of the decision? If so, should Cardozo have included some or all of it in the opinion?

"Mrs. Palsgraf" bore the Christian name of Helen. She was forty-three and the mother of three children, of whom the younger two, then fifteen and twelve, were with her at the time of the accident. She was married, but neither side judged it desirable to ask who her husband was or where he was. It may be inferred that they had separated. She testified that she paid the rent, that she had always worked, and that she was "all alone."

At the time of the accident Helen Palsgraf lived in a basement flat at 238 Irving Avenue in Ridgewood [Brooklyn], performing janitorial work in the apartment building, for which she was allowed ten dollars a month on her rent. She did day work outside the apartment, earning two dollars a day or about eight dollars a week. She spoke English intelligibly but not with complete grammatical correctness.

The day of the accident was a hot Sunday in August. She was taking Elizabeth and Lilian to the beach. It was ten o'clock. She carried a valise. She bought their tickets and walked onto the station platform, which was crowded. Lilian went for the Sunday paper. As a train started to pull out, there was the noise of an explosion. Then, "Flying glass — a ball of fire came, and we were choked in smoke, and I says 'Elizabeth turn your back,' and with that the scale blew and hit me on the side." * * *

---

[57] Henderson, *supra* note 54, at 1579.

In 1924 the Long Island's total assets were valued at $114 million of which $98 million was the valuation set on track and equipment. Net income from railroad operations was just over $4 million, reflecting a return just over the 4 percent that was usual for railroads of the period to show. Over 60 percent of the operating income was from passenger traffic. The parent Pennsylvania [Railroad] had a net income of $48 million and assets of $1.7 billion, of which almost one half billion represented capital stock and surplus.[58]

Does *Palsgraf* reflect an appropriate, indeed necessary, judicial detachment? After all, aren't such factors as the relative wealth of the parties legally irrelevant? Or, given the above, might one conclude that Cardozo was not merely not empathetic toward Mrs. Palsgraf, but that the decision *does* reflect "passion" as well as reason, though passion directed *against* the plaintiff? Alternatively, perhaps Cardozo was entirely empathetic, but his empathy was for the Long Island Railroad and its employees.

In *Hynes*, Cardozo says that Harvey Hynes was in "the enjoyment of the public waters," painting a nearly bucolic picture of a boy swimming in the river. In *Palsgraf*, he does not mention that Helen Palsgraf and her children were on their way to the beach on a hot August day. The fact that it was hot is

> a detail of consummate irrelevance in terms of any legal principles but suggestive of the circumstances in which urban users of public transportation need to travel, a reminder of the innocence of Helen Palsgraf's seaside excursion. How such a fact should affect the outcome is nondemonstrable, yet it will play a part in the process by which judgment is reached.[59]

Should Cardozo have mentioned the August heat? If you were Palsgraf's attorney, would you have, even though it is legally irrelevant? Perhaps the ability to identify such factors distinguishes effective litigators from ineffective ones even more than skill at "legal reasoning" (which might, after all, lead an advocate to ignore such factors as the temperature). Does this mean that the most effective advocate is the one with the least sophisticated legal understanding? Or does it overstate the importance of such factors "in the process by which judgment is reached"?

Consider one last aspect of *Palsgraf*:

> Severe impartiality led in *Palsgraf* to the aspect of the decision which seemed least humane: the imposition by Cardozo of "costs in all courts" upon Helen Palsgraf. Under the New York rules of practice, [awards of court] costs [which does *not* include attorney's fees,] were, in general, discretionary with the court. An old rule, laid down in 1828, was that when the question was "a doubtful one and fairly raised, no costs will be allowed." In practice, the Court of Appeals tended to award costs mechanically to the party successful on the appeal. Costs here amounted to $142.45 in the trial

---

[58] John T. Noonan, Jr., Persons and Masks of the Law 126–128 (1976).

[59] *Id.* at 141–142.

court and $100.28 in the appellate division. When the bill of the Court of Appeals was added, it is probable that costs in all courts amounted to $350, not quite a year's income for Helen Palsgraf. She had a case which a majority of the judges who heard it [counting those on the lower courts] thought to constitute a cause of action. By a margin of one, her case had been pronounced unreasonable. . . . The effect of the judgment was to leave the plaintiff, four years after her case had begun, the debtor of her doctor, who was still unpaid; her lawyer, who must have advanced her the trial court fees at least; and her adversary, who was now owed reimbursement for expenditures in the courts on appeal. Under the New York statute the Long Island could make execution of the judgment by seizing her personalty. Only a judge who did not see who was before him could have decreed such a result.[60]

6. *Judging.* Finally: if *you* were a judge, how would you go about judging and, particularly, how would you go about judging when the case before you is not "controlled" by a prior, "precedential," case or statute? Do you know your predilections and prejudices, your "complex of instincts," your "subconscious loyalties" to the groups "in which the accident of birth or education or occupation or fellowship" have placed you? Do you know your passions? Do you trust your *reason*? (What do you mean by reason?) Do you trust your *intuition*? (What do you mean by intuition?) Do you simply rely on your *judgment*? (What do you mean by judgment?[61])

Is the injunction, "Judge, Know Thyself" sufficient?

Can you ask only "What should *I* do in this case? What do *I* think is 'best' in this case?" If you answer yes, are you then not assuming a legislative mantle? And if so, then we can no longer evaluate your decision in terms of its correctness or incorrectness vis-à-vis any preexisting "law" but only in terms of its foolishness or wisdom — is that not so?

Or should you ask, "What can and should I, *a judge*, do in this case?" If you deem that the correct question, are you then not asserting that there is always "something else" for which a judge can reach to help her decide the case? That is, that "there is some aspect of judicial decisionmaking which renders it *qualitatively* different from legislative decisions,"[62] even in a case of "first impression," that is, a case not controlled by precedent. Ought you, in other words, seek to experience "the legal rule structure * * * simultaneously as an 'internal' source of obligation and an 'external' institutional constraint"?[63] And if so, then we could evaluate your decision not only as "wise or foolish, but in terms of some notion of 'correctness' or

---

[60] *Id.* at 144.

[61] Judge Posner calls "good judgment" a "cousin of intuition and another major factor in judicial decisions" where legal materials leave significant judicial discretion. He describes it as "an elusive faculty best understood as a compound of empathy, modesty, maturity, a sense of proportion, balance, a recognition of human limitations, sanity, prudence, a sense of reality, and common sense." RICHARD A. POSNER, HOW JUDGES THINK 117 (2008).

[62] *See generally* Charles M. Yablon, *Judicial Process As an Empirical Study: A Comment on Justice Brennan's Essay,* 10 CARDOZO L. REV. 149, 56 (1988) (emphasis added).

[63] *Id.*

'appropriateness' within the prevailing rule system"[64] — is that not so?

C. A FINAL NOTE

"On July 8, 1916, *Harvey Hines*, a *lad* of sixteen, swam with two companions"; they "intend[ed] *to leap* into the water"; the wires "*flung him* from the *shattered* board, and *plunged* him to his death below."

You knew by the time you reached "plunged" that Harvey Hines would win, right? Probably you guessed it at "lad."

In contrast: "Plaintiff was standing on a platform of defendant's railroad after buying a ticket to go to Rockaway Beach."

Things do not look as promising for "plaintiff," do they?

Is this a difference of form (or style) or one of substance? Cardozo himself doubted the distinction: "The strength that is born of form and the feebleness that is born of the lack of form are in truth qualities of the substance."[65]

Assignment 1

Identify the "strength that is born of form" in *Hynes* and contrast it with the "feebleness that is born of the lack of form" in *Palsgraf*.

Assignment 2

Take an imaginative leap: you are no longer a first-semester law student. You have just become an appellate judge. You look for guidance, for a model, to help you be the kind of judge you feel you want to be and should be.

Reread the excerpts in Section A. Identify those that most nearly embody *your* ideal of what a great judge should be like and that you therefore want to take as a lodestar.[66] Explain your choice. Do the same with those excerpts that you consider at the farthest remove from your vision of the great judge you would like to be. Explain your choice.

---

[64] *Id.*

[65] Benjamin N. Cardozo, Law and Literature 6 (1931).

[66] A lodestar is a star that leads or guides, especially the North Star.

Chapter 4

A CASE SEQUENCE

A case sequence is a series of cases that all address the same question. Here that question, broadly speaking, is the division of responsibility for the safety of children between their parents and landowners onto whose property they (the children) "trespass."

What distinguishes this sequence is that the nine cases in the series come from a single jurisdiction, California, and that seven of the nine were decided by the "same" court, the Supreme Court of California. This allows us, without distraction from the fact that different courts may see cases differently, to concentrate on the fundamental question that all first-year courses, at least, are about: *how do courts go about their business?* Or, to put the same question in other words: *what makes judges rule as they do in individual cases?* We gain greater understanding of that process by watching one *court* over time (here from 1891 to 1959) than one *doctrine* over time — frequently the organizing principle in your substantive courses. In addition, there are three other goals that we have in mind.

On the practical level, you will learn how to read cases against one another: how to read the first case, standing by itself; how to read the next case in relation to the preceding case; to read the third in light of the prior two, the fourth against the prior three, etc. — all the time articulating and rearticulating, shaping and reshaping "the rule of law" evolving under the court's jurisprudence. You are, in a word, to *synthesize* all the cases. Synthesis, the dictionary tells us, is "the composition or combination of parts or elements so as to form a whole."[1] In law, the evolving rule is the whole, the parts or elements are the cases, and the composition or combination of the parts is your active, creative contribution.

On a more poetic level, you will learn to tell a story, for cases are stories, and law and narrative are "inseparably related."[2] About the telling of stories, Lon Fuller had this to say:

> If I attempt to tell a funny story which I have heard, the story as I tell it will be the product of two forces: (1) the story as I heard it, the story *as it is* at the time of its first telling; (2) my conception of the point of the story, in other words, my notion of the story *as it ought to be.* As I retell the story I make no attempt to estimate exactly the pressure of these two forces, though it is clear that their respective influences may vary. If the story as I heard it was, in my opinion, badly told, I am guided largely by my conception of the story as it ought to be, though through inertia or

---

[1] WEBSTER'S NINTH NEW COLLEGIATE DICTIONARY 1198 (9th ed. 1989).

[2] Robert M. Cover, *The Supreme Court, 1982 Term — Foreword: Nomos and Narrative,* 97 HARV. L. REV. 4, 5 (1983).

imperfect insight I shall probably repeat turns of phrase which have stuck in my memory from the former telling. On the other hand, if I had the story from a master raconteur, I may exert myself to reproduce his exact words, though my own conception of the way the story ought to be told will have to fill in the gaps left by faulty memory. These two forces, then, supplement one another in shaping the story as I tell it. It is a product of the *is* and the *ought* working together. There is no way of measuring the degree to which each contributes to the final result. The two are inextricably interwoven, to the point where we can say that "the story" as an entity really embraces both of them. Indeed, if we look at the story across time, its reality becomes even more complex. The "point" of the story, which furnishes its essential unity, may in the course of retelling be changed. As it is brought out more clearly through the skill of successive tellers it becomes a new point; at some indefinable juncture the story has been so improved that it has become a new story. In a sense, then, the thing we call "the story" is not something that is, but something that becomes; it is not a hard chunk of reality, but a fluid process, which is as much directed by men's creative impulses, by their conception of the story as it ought to be, as it is by the original event which unlocked those impulses. The *ought* here is just as real, as a part of human experience, as the *is*, and the line between the two melts away in the common stream of telling and retelling into which they both flow.

Exactly the same thing may be said of a statute or a decision. It involves two things, a set of words, and an objective sought. This objective may or may not have been happily expressed in the words chosen by the legislator or judge. This objective, like the point of the anecdote, may be perceived dimly or clearly; it may be perceived more clearly by him who reads the statute than by him who drafted it. The statute or decision is not a segment of being, but, like the anecdote, a process of becoming. By being reinterpreted it becomes, by imperceptible degrees, something that it was not originally. The field of possible objectives is filled with overlapping figures, and the attempt to trace out distinctly one of these figures almost inevitably creates a new pattern. By becoming more clearly what it is, the rule of the case becomes what it was previously only trying to be. In this situation to distinguish sharply between the rule as it is, and the rule as it ought to be, is to resort to an abstraction foreign to the raw data which experience offers us.[3]

Or, in Professor Cover's words:

> We inhabit a *nomos* — a normative universe. We constantly create and maintain a world of right and wrong, of lawful and unlawful, of valid and void. * * *

> In this normative world, law and narrative are inseparably related. Every prescription is insistent in its demand to be located in discourse — to be supplied with history and destiny, beginning and end, explanation and

---

[3] Lon Fuller, The Law in Quest of Itself 8–10 (1940).

purpose. And every narrative is insistent in its demand for its prescriptive point, its moral. History and literature cannot escape their location in a normative universe, nor can prescription, even when embodied in a legal text, escape its origin and its end in experience, in the narratives that are the trajectories plotted upon material reality by our imaginations. * * *

The codes that relate our normative system to our social constructions of reality and to our visions of what the world might be are narrative. The very imposition of a normative force upon a state of affairs, real or imagined, is the act of creating narrative. The various genres of narrative — history, fiction, tragedy, comedy — are alike in their being the account of states of affairs affected by a normative force field. To live in a legal world requires that one know not only the precepts, but also their connections to possible and plausible states of affairs. It requires that one integrate not only the "is" and the "ought," but the "is," the "ought," and the "what might be." Narrative so integrates these domains. Narratives are models through which we study and experience transformations that result when a given simplified state of affairs is made to pass through the force field of a similarly simplified set of norms.

The intelligibility of normative behavior inheres in the communal character of the narratives that provide the context of that behavior. Any person who lived an entirely idiosyncratic normative life would be quite mad. The part that you or I choose to play may be singular, but the fact that we can locate it in a common "script" renders it "sane" — a warrant that we share a *nomos*.[4]

Finally, you are simultaneously involved with a larger project: to understand a "case law system."

This brings us at last to the case system. For the truth of the matter is a truth so obvious and trite that it is somewhat regularly overlooked by students. *That no case can have a meaning by itself!* Standing alone it gives you no guidance. It can give you no guidance as to how far it carries, as to how much of its language will hold water later. What counts, what gives you leads, what gives you sureness, *that is the background of the other cases* in relation to which you must read the one.[5]

Think back to the pages we devoted to the *Kelly* case. Make an argument, based on that discussion, that Llewellyn is right: *"no case can have a meaning by itself!"* Make an argument, based on that discussion, that Llewellyn is wrong: a case *can* have a meaning by itself! Is there support for either or both positions in the case itself?

There is a moral here and it is simple: *In this course*, do not concentrate your focus on the substantive law. It is useless to read a Torts hornbook or treatise or

---

[4] Cover, *supra* note 2, at 4–10. *See also* the excerpt from Dworkin's *Law as Interpretation*, *infra* pages 170–71.

[5] KARL N. LLEWELLYN, THE BRAMBLE BUSH: ON OUR LAW AND ITS STUDY 48–49 (Oceana Pubs. 1960; first published 1930).

one of many law review articles on "attractive nuisance," per chance the substantive doctrine involved in this case sequence. "Per chance" because we chose the sequence as an effective illustration of the processes by which a court struggles to an inevitably fleeting "solution"; any other sequence supplied with the same attributes would have done as well, regardless of the substantive law involved. If you want to read for our purposes, then read *The Nature of the Judicial Process*, read *The Bramble Bush*, read *An Introduction to Legal Reasoning*;[6] read a novel that says something about law either as a matter of jurisprudence or practice (why not *Bleak House* or *The Brothers Karamazov*?). All of these go to the point of this enterprise; reading "Torts" does not.

We will now read and synthesize nine cases. After each and every case, you should ask yourself these questions:

1) Had I been the plaintiff's lawyer, how would I have argued this case *at the time*?

2) Had I been the defendant's lawyer, how would I have argued this case *at the time*?

3) Were I a judge, how would I have voted *at the time*?

4) An anxious landowner with an enclosed private swimming pool asks me the day after the decision in each of these cases: "What is my potential liability? What is the law?" What do I answer?

5) The parent of a child who has drowned in a neighbor's enclosed pool asks me: "based on the 'existing law,' should I sue?" What do I tell her?

6) How is (5) different from (4)?

BARRETT v. SOUTHERN PACIFIC CO.
91 Cal. 296, 27 P. 666 (1891)

DE HAVEN, J.

This is an action to recover damages for personal injuries alleged to have been sustained by plaintiff through the negligence of defendant. The plaintiff recovered a judgment for $8,500, and from this judgment, and an order denying its motion for a new trial, the defendant appeals.

It was shown upon the trial that defendant maintained a railroad turn-table upon its own premises in the town of Santa Ana. This table was about 150 yards from defendant's depot, and near its engine-house, and distant 72 feet from a public street, and it was not protected by any inclosure, nor did the defendant

---

[6] EDWARD H. LEVI, AN INTRODUCTION TO LEGAL REASONING (1949). Levi was a professor of law, Dean of the Law School, and President at the University of Chicago, as well as Attorney General of the United States during the Ford Administration. This book is a brief, classic text that describes the variations in judicial approaches in common law, statutory, and constitutional cases.

employ any person whose special duty it was to guard it. It was provided with a latch and slot, such as is in common use on such tables, to keep it from revolving. There were several families with small children residing within a quarter of a mile from the place of its location, and previous to the time when plaintiff was hurt, children had frequently played around and upon it, but when observed by the servants of defendant were never permitted to do so. At the date of plaintiff's injury he was eight years of age, and on that day he, with his younger brother, saw other boys playing with the turn-table, and, giving them some oranges for the privilege of a ride, got upon it, and while it was being revolved plaintiff's leg was caught between the table and the rail upon the headblocks, and so severely injured that it had to be amputated. The defendant moved for a nonsuit, which motion was denied. This ruling of the court, and certain instructions given to the jury, present the questions which arise upon this appeal.

The appellant contends that it was not guilty of negligence in thus maintaining upon its own premises, for necessary use in conducting its business the turn-table in question, and which was fastened in the usual and customary manner of fastening such tables; that the plaintiff was wrongfully upon its premises, and therefore a trespasser, to whom the defendant did not owe the duty of protection from the injury received, and that the court should have so declared, and nonsuited the plaintiff. This view seems to be fully sustained by the case of Frost v. Railroad Co., decided by the supreme court of New Hampshire, 9 Atl. Rep. 790. But, in our judgment, the rule as broadly announced and applied in that case cannot be maintained without a departure from well-settled principles. It is a maxim of the law that one must so use and enjoy his property as to interfere with the comfort and safety of others as little as possible consistently with its proper use. This rule, which only imposes a just restriction upon the owner of property, seems not to have been given due consideration in the case referred to. But this principle, as a standard of conduct, is of universal application, and the failure to observe it is, in respect to those who have a right to invoke its protection, a breach of duty, and, in a legal sense, constitutes negligence. Whether, in any given case, there has been such negligence upon the part of the owner of property, in the maintenance thereon of dangerous machinery, is a question of fact dependent upon the situation of the property and the attendant circumstances, because upon such facts will depend the degree of care which prudence would suggest as reasonably necessary to guard others against injury therefrom; "for negligence in a legal sense is no more than this: the failure to observe for the protection of the interests of another person that degree of care, precaution, and vigilance which the circumstances justly demand, whereby such other person suffers injury." Cooley on Torts, 630. And the question of defendant's negligence in this case was a matter to be decided by the jury in view of all the evidence, and with reference to this general principle as to the duty of the defendant. If defendant ought reasonably to have anticipated that, leaving this turn-table unguarded and exposed, an injury, such as plaintiff suffered, was likely to occur, then it must be held to have anticipated it, and was guilty of negligence in thus maintaining it in its exposed position. It is no answer to this to say that the child was a trespasser, and if it had not intermeddled with defendant's property it would not have been hurt, and that the law imposes no duty upon the defendant to make its premises a safe playing ground for children. In the forum of law, as well as of common sense, a child of immature years is expected to

exercise only such care and self-restraint as belongs to childhood, and a reasonable man must be presumed to know this, and the law requires him to govern his actions accordingly. It is a matter of common experience that children of tender years are guided in their actions by childish instincts, and are lacking in that discretion which, in those of more mature years, is ordinarily sufficient to enable them to appreciate and avoid danger: and, in proportion to this lack of judgment on their part, the care which must be observed toward them by others is increased; and it has been held in numerous cases to be an act of negligence to leave unguarded and exposed to the observation of little children dangerous and attractive machinery which they would naturally be tempted to go about or upon, and against the danger of which action their immature judgment interposes no warning or defense. These cases, we think, lay down the true rule. The fact that the turn-table was latched in the way such tables are usually fastened, or according to the usual custom of other railroads, although a matter which the jury had a right to consider in passing upon the question whether defendant exercised ordinary care in the way it maintained the table, was not, of itself, conclusive proof of the fact. Nor is the liability of the defendant affected by the fact that the table was set in motion by the negligent act of other boys * * *.

Judgment and order affirmed.

We concur: BEATTY, C.J.; McFARLAND, J.

———————

Immediately following is a "Sample Brief" of *Barrett*. It features two important changes from our brief for *Kelly*: when we prepared the *Kelly* brief we said repeatedly that different "actors" would write different "scripts." We now give you an illustration of that. You will note that we have three versions of the Issue and four of the Holding. In *Kelly*, we had three each for both but they all tried to give an objective account; they aimed to demonstrate the point that an individual case can support multiple understandings — but the mode, the tone, was non-partisan. Here we do something different: our three versions of the Issue represent how three actors in our little drama — plaintiff, defendant, judge's law clerk — might put the question. When we discussed the jury selection process we said it allows you "to begin subtly to lay out your version of the case."[7] What is true there is doubly true here: a good lawyer will state the issue (or the "question presented," as it is often referred to in appellate filings) in the way that is most favorable to her client.

Take a look at the plaintiff's version of the issue. What does it stress? How does it try to engage the court's sympathy?[8] On what is it trying to focus the court?

Now compare the defendant's statement. What does it stress? What does it omit? What is it trying to appeal to? On what is it trying to focus the court?

Finally, does the clerk provide an honest, objective, non-partisan description of what this is all about?

———————

[7] *See supra* page 25.

[8] *Cf.* Cardozo's "lad of sixteen" in *Hynes, supra* page 91.

Four holdings: we begin with a narrow holding, move to a broader one, to a still broader one, and finally to an impermissibly broad one. Study them closely: experience tells us that you have a seemingly irresistible urge toward a global statement. Resist it! Earlier we said about the "Facts" part of your brief: when in doubt, put it in. Now we say: err on the side of narrower rather than broader statements. First, it is harder to read cases narrowly, and so you need a lot of practice. Second, you cannot really do serious harm by staying closer to the bottom of our inverted pyramid — but you can do serious harm by floating skyward into the wild blue yonder. Third, judges, and other lawyers, know how to, and do, read cases narrowly, and you must be able to keep up with them.

All else in our Sample Brief is self-explanatory.

Sample Brief

Barrett v. Southern Pacific Co., 91 Cal. 296, 27 P. 666 (1891) (3-0) (DeHaven for himself and Beatty, CJ, and McFarland)

Statement of the Case   (boy?)

Negligence action to recover damages for personal injuries sustained by an 8-year-old on defendant railroad's turntable.

Facts

Defendant railroad maintained 72 feet from a public street a turntable which was neither enclosed nor protected by a guard. The table was equipped with a latch and slot, such as was customary in the industry, to prevent it from revolving.

Several families with small children lived within a quarter mile of the table. The children frequently played around or on the table, but were never permitted to do so when observed by defendant's employees.

Plaintiff, then 8 years old, and one of a number of children on the scene, got on the turntable, and while it revolved his leg got caught. It was injured so severely that it had to be amputated.

Procedural History

Defendant moved for a nonsuit.[9] Motion denied. Jury trial. Jury renders verdict for plaintiff. Judgment entered on the verdict.

Defendant moves for a new trial. Motion denied.

---

[9] In 1891 in California a motion for a nonsuit had a particular meaning, which, for present purposes, you need not understand. You should treat a motion for a nonsuit as equivalent to a demurrer, but one that comes at the end of *plaintiff's* case. Compare the "motion for directed verdict" which comes at the end of *plaintiff's and defendant's* case. In all three cases, the moving party is essentially saying, "so what?"

As we noted earlier, modern terminology is quite different. However, you must try to understand the relevant terminology in each and every case you will read in law school or in practice in order to understand older cases.

Defendant appeals from the denial of his motion and from the judgment for the plaintiff.

Outcome

The Supreme Court of California affirms the order denying the motion for a new trial and the judgment for the plaintiff.

Issue

[How the plaintiff might state it.]

Where a young child is seriously injured on a railroad turntable located within easy access of many small children residing in the vicinity, and the railroad knows that such children frequently play on this dangerous, unguarded, and unlocked machinery, which could have been easily and cheaply locked, should the railroad be under a duty of care towards such children, notwithstanding that technically the children are trespassing on defendant's property when serious bodily harm comes to them?

[How the defendant might state it.]

Where a landowner maintains on its premises equipment necessary to the regular and ordinary conduct of his lawful business, and does so in a manner customary in the industry, should it be held liable to trespassers when it has repeatedly and expressly denied such trespassers permission to be on, and evicted them from, the premises?

[Your judge for whom you are clerking has asked you what this case is about.]

Does/should a railroad owe a duty of care to an 8-year-old severely injured on the railroad's turntable, notwithstanding the general rule that landowners owe no duty to trespassers, be they adults or children, where the railroad knew of the presence of children on, and had evicted them from, its premises, and, following industry custom, had not locked the turntable?

Holding

[First version — sticking closely to the facts.]

Where a railroad locates an unenclosed turntable 72 feet from a public street, and within a quarter mile of families with small children, and where the railroad knows that children have played on the turntable, and the railroad could at little cost lock the turntable, the law will impose a duty of care towards such children, and the negligent breach of that duty will subject the railroad to liability where its negligence results in serious bodily harm.

[Second version — broader, but still cautious.]

Where a railroad maintains a turntable and knows or has reason to know that children of young years and immature judgment frequently play around or on the turntable, a duty of care will be imposed and the negligent breach of that duty will result in liability for personal injuries.

[Third version — clearly broader, but still within permissible bounds.]

Where a landowner maintains on his premises dangerous machinery and knows or should know that small children intermeddle with the machinery, yet takes no special precaution to safeguard it, landowner will be under a duty of care to such children for personal injuries, notwithstanding that the children are trespassing.

[Fourth version — an impermissible version.]

Landowners owe a duty of care to trespassing children sustaining injuries on their land.

Reasoning

The court acknowledges the background norm, namely no duty of care is owed to trespassers, as exemplified by the New Hampshire case of *Frost v. Railroad*.

However, it refuses to apply the rule to "children of tender years" who lack judgment to appreciate and avoid danger. Hence others, here the railroad, owe them a duty of care in proportion to this lack of judgment.

It was then for the jury to decide whether the defendant's conduct was negligent under the circumstances of this case, including the fact that the table was latched in the way that such tables are customarily fastened, but could have been easily locked.

Items of special note

The court cites no California cases; it cites a general statement about negligence by Cooley.

NOTES AND QUESTIONS

(1) Before this decision, what was the background norm? What has happened to it?

(2) The court says (following the cite to *Frost v. Railroad Co.*):

> But . . . the rule [that no duty is owed to trespassers] . . . cannot be maintained without a departure from well-settled principles. It is a maxim of the law that one must so use and enjoy his property as to interfere with the comfort and safety of others as little as possible consistent with its proper use. This rule . . . But this principle, as a standard of conduct. . . .

Recall our earlier discussion of rules and standards.[10] Identify the *rules* involved in *Barrett* (and *Frost*). Identify the competing *standards*. Rewrite the passage so that it makes sense.

(3)   The appellant contended that the plaintiff was "a trespasser to whom [it] did

---

[10] *See supra* pages 78–81.

not owe the duty of protection." Was this a description of the world or the assertion of a norm? Does it matter which it was? (You might want to think again about our discussion of the cement factory and your "right" not to have it spew dust on you).[11]

(4) Contrast the precedential value of the following two cases:

In case 1 the child injured on the turntable sues the railroad; the trial court denies the defendant's demurrer and holds a trial. The trial judge denies the defendant's motion for a directed verdict and sends the case to the jury. The jury finds for the defendant. There is no need for, and no purpose to, a motion for a j.n.o.v., or appeal, by the defendant and no appeal is possible by the plaintiff because the judge made no ruling of law against the plaintiff. Case 1 ends in the trial court with a judgment for the defendant by jury verdict.

In case 2 the child is injured on the turntable. The defendant demurs. The trial judge grants the demurrer and dismisses the complaint. The plaintiff appeals. The Supreme Court reverses the grant of demurrer and sends the case back for trial. At trial the jury finds for the defendant (as in case 1). Case 2, in other words, also ends in the trial court with a judgment for the defendant by jury verdict.

PETERS v. BOWMAN
115 Cal. 345, 47 P. 113 (1896)

McFarland, J.

This action was brought by plaintiff to recover damages for the death of his infant son, who was drowned in a pond of water upon a lot of land owned by the defendant, Bowman. The jury returned a verdict for the defendant and the plaintiff appeals from the judgment, and from an order denying his motion for a new trial.

The facts are practically undisputed, and may be stated briefly: Defendant owned the lot in question, and resided on it for several years prior to 1889. It was part of what is known as "Ashbury Heights," in San Francisco. The land sloped toward the west, and on the westerly side fronted on Ashbury Street. It does not appear whether or not it was in a thickly-settled neighborhood. In its natural condition the surface water which came from the lot flowed off through a gully across Ashbury street (over which there was a small bridge), and emptied into a pond a couple of blocks away. At some time prior to 1889 the city of San Francisco graded Ashbury street and threw up an embankment along the street and across the gully, and on the westerly side of said lot, to the height of eight or ten feet. This prevented the flow of surface water from the lot, and on this account, defendant removed his residence, in 1889, to an adjoining county. From that time until 1894, when the boy was drowned, the surface water, being stopped by said embankment, would form during the rainy season a pond, which disappeared during the dry season. Defendant did nothing to create the pond, or to prevent the water from flowing away; and, so far as he is concerned, it may be considered as a natural pond. The lot was not inclosed by a fence or otherwise. After defendant removed his residence, he did not often visit the lot, and did not give permission to or invite

---

[11] See supra pages 13–14.

rules + exceptions

anyone to go upon it; but children did visit it, and play upon the pond, and he must be presumed to have known that fact. He drove children away once, and a policeman did the same several times. The plaintiff knew of the existence of the pond, and knew that his son knew of it, and he "never told him not to go rafting on the pond." The son was over eleven years old, and was "a bright, active boy, an intelligent boy for eleven years, more so than the average boy of that age." He lived with his father, the plaintiff, on Castro Street, "four or five blocks over the hills" southerly from the pond. He had been at the pond often before the day of the accident. He was allowed by his father to run on the streets. On February 16, 1894, he went with two other boys to the pond, and while floating on the pond on a rudely-constructed raft made of railroad ties, and when running along one of the timbers, he fell off, and was drowned. They went onto the pond from the southeasterly side — the side farthest away from Ashbury Street.

Why important?

relevant?

Upon these facts the verdict was right and a verdict for plaintiff would have been unwarranted. The deceased boy was, at the time of the accident which caused his death, a trespasser on the land of defendant and the general rule undoubtedly is that the owner of land is under no duty to keep his premises safe for trespassers. * * * The exceptions to the general rule are instances where the owner maintains on his land something in the nature of a trap or other concealed danger, known to him, and as to which he has given no warning to others and instances where there had been something in the nature of a wanton injury to a trespasser, as where the owner had set spring guns on his premises, by which the trespasser had been shot. There is, also, the instance of an excavation adjoining a public highway, into which a traveler on the highway, where he had the right to be, had accidentally fallen. There are other exceptions not necessary to be here mentioned. And the general rule applies to children as well as to adults, with some exceptions hereinafter noticed. "The rule is that, ordinarily, the owner of premises owes no duty of immunities to trespassers, though the latter be infants." (Whittaker's Smith on Negligence, 2d ed., 67, note, and cases there cited.)

general rule

"trap"

Ditto

Plaintiff seeks to take this case out of the principle above stated by applying to it what is now known as the "Rule of the Turntable Cases." That rule, which is a marked exception to the general principle, has been approved in many of the states, and in others has been repudiated. It must be taken as approved in this state by the decisions of this court in Barrett v. Southern Pac. Co., 91 Cal. 296, 27 Pac. 666, and other cases cited by appellant. * * * But the rule of the Turntable Cases is an exception to the general principle that the owner of land is under no legal duty to keep it in a safe condition for others than those whom he invites there, and that trespassers take the risk of injuries from ordinary visible causes; and it should not be carried beyond the class of cases to which it has been applied. And the cases to which the rule has been applied, so far as our attention has been called to them, are nearly all cases where the owner of land had erected on it dangerous machinery, the consequences of meddling with which are not supposed to be fully comprehended by infant minds. * * *

ditto

why not?

It is not contended by appellant that the rule of the Turntable Cases has ever been applied to facts like those in the case at bar. His contention is that the reasoning and philosophy of the rule ought to extend it to a case like the one at bar. But the same reasoning does not apply to both sets of cases. A body of water —

e.g., 17 yr old

would you have so contended?

either standing, as in ponds and lakes; or running as in rivers and creeks, or ebbing and flowing, as on the shores of seas and bays — is a natural object, incident to all countries which are not deserts. Such a body of water may be found in or close to nearly every city or town in the land; the danger of drowning in it is an apparent open danger, the knowledge of which is common to all; and there is no just view, consistent with recognized rights of property owners, which would compel one owning land upon which such water, or part of it, stands or flows, to fill it up, or surround it with an impenetrable wall. However, general reasoning on the subject is unnecessary, because adjudicated cases have determined the question adversely to appellant's contention. No case has been cited where damages have been successfully recovered for the death of a child drowned in a pond on private premises who had gone there without invitation; while it has been repeatedly held that in such a case no damages can be recovered. It was directly so held in Klix v. Nieman, 68 Wis. 271, 32 N.W. 223; in Overholt v. Vieths, 93 Mo. 422, 6 S.W. 74; in Hargreaves v. Deacon, 25 Mich. 1; in Gillespie v. McGowan, 100 Pa. St. 144; and in the recent case of Richards v. Connell, 45 Neb. 467, 63 N.W. 915. In the last-named case the complaint alleged that the plaintiff's infant son was drowned in a pond on defendant's land in the vicinity of a public school, and the other facts alleged were almost exactly the same as those alleged and proven in the case at bar; but the trial court sustained the demurrer to the complaint on the ground that it did not state a cause of action, and, on appeal, the supreme court of Nebraska affirmed the judgment. The court, in its opinion, after reciting the averments of the complaint, say: "The single question presented by the record is whether the owner of a vacant lot, upon which is situated a pond of water, or a dangerous excavation, is required to fence it, or otherwise insure the safety of strangers, old or young, who may go upon said premises not by his invitation, express or implied, but for the purpose of amusement, or from motives of curiosity. The authorities we find to be in substantial accord, and sustain the proposition that, independent of statute, no such liability exists." * * *

It may be well to notice briefly one or two of the other cases in point. In Klix v. Nieman, supra, the plaintiff's son fell into a pond on defendant's land which had been caused by water collecting in an excavation, and was drowned. The case was very similar to the one at bar, and the supreme court of Wisconsin, in delivering its opinion, says, among other things, as follows: "So the single question presented is: Was it the duty of the defendant to fence or guard this hole or excavation on his lot (which it does not appear he made, or caused to be made), where surface water collected, in order to secure the safety of strangers, young or old, who might go upon or about the pond for play or curiosity? If the defendant was bound to so fence or guard the pond, upon what principle or ground does this obligation rest? There can be no liability unless it was his duty to fence the pond. It surely is not the duty of an owner to guard or fence every dangerous hole or pond or stream of water on his premises, for the protection of persons going upon his land who had no right to go there. No such rule of law is laid down in the books, and it would be unreasonable to so hold." * * * In Gillespie v. McGowan, supra, plaintiff's son, eight years old, had fallen into a cistern on defendant's land which had been abandoned, but had once been used in connection with brickmaking. The court, in delivering its opinion, among other things, say: "* * * Vacant brickyards and open lots exist on all sides of the city. There are streams and pools of water where children may be

who is . . . ?

drowned. There are any quantities of surface where they may be injured. To compel the owners of such property either to inclose it or to fill up their ponds and level the surface, so that trespassers may not be injured, would be an oppressive rule. The law does not require us to enforce any such principle, even where the trespassers are children. We all know that boys of eight years indulge in athletic sports. They fish, shoot, swim, and climb trees. All of these amusements are attended with danger, and accidents frequently occur. It is a part of the boy's nature to trespass, especially where there is tempting fruit; yet I have never heard that it was the duty of the owner of a tree to cut it down because a boy trespasser might possibly fall from its branches. Yet the principle contended for by the plaintiff would bring us to this absurdity, if carried to its logical conclusion. Moreover, it would charge the duty of the protection of children upon every member of the community except their parents."

! ? !

The foregoing are a few of the many authorities which are particularly applicable to the case at bar, and show that in a case like this there can be no recovery. * * *

The judgment and order appealed from are affirmed.

We concur: HENSHAW, J.; TEMPLE, J.

NOTES AND QUESTIONS

(1) The court says it was not contended that the rule of the turntable cases had ever been applied to facts like those in *Peters*. As plaintiff's lawyer, would you have so contended? Make the argument.

(2) The court seems to fear that if it allowed recovery here, owners would next have to cut down their apple trees. This argument is known as the "slippery slope." Why, or when, is the slope slippery? That is, why would a sensible first step lead inescapably to a silly last step? Either later courts should be able to avoid the silly outcome, or that outcome is not so silly after all. Note that those making a slippery slope argument are fundamentally distrustful of later decisionmakers.

Concern over the slippery slope may lead a court to reach the "wrong" outcome in the case before it in order to avoid worse outcomes in the future. Can you justify making today's plaintiff (or defendant, in other circumstances) pay the price for a feared inability of later courts to stop sliding down the slope? Critics of slippery slope arguments characterize the argument as amounting to this: "we ought not to make a sound decision today, for fear of having to draw a sound distinction tomorrow."[12]

the "sub-par" decision

Is the slippery slope argument a variation on the frequent lament: "But where do you draw the line?" On line-drawing, ponder this:

— Comment

---

[12] The comment is attributed to Sir Frederick Maitland. *See* Eugene Volokh, *The Mechanisms of the Slippery Slope*, 116 HARV. L. REV. 1026, 1030 n.7 (2003).

[I]n my mind the best rejoinder to those who have trouble with line-drawing is the comment of John Lowenstein of the Baltimore Orioles: "They should move first base back a step to eliminate all the close plays."[13]

(3) If the court's concern was not the slippery slope, what was it? Consider these possibilities:

(a) The costs of requiring fences or other protective measures would outweigh the benefits.

(b) Boys will be boys, and so protective measures are in any event impossible.

(c) It would be unjust to make the landowner the insurer of trespassers on her land.

(d) It would be unjust to permit parents to externalize the costs of looking after their children.

(e) Right or wrong, "the law" does not allow recovery here.

(4) Given what the court tells us "the law" is, did the case ever have to go to the jury? Suppose the defendant had demurred. How should the trial court have ruled?

(5) Do we need to reformulate the rule of *Barrett* and, if so, how? What do you now know about the *scope* of *Barrett* that you did not know before?

PETERS v. BOWMAN
115 Cal. 345, 47 P. 598 (1897)

In bank. Petition for rehearing. Denied. For original opinion, see 47 Pac. 113.

BEATTY, C.J.

A rehearing of this cause is denied, but the statement contained in the department opinion to the effect that no similar case had been cited in which damages were allowed, requires correction. The case of City of Pekin v. McMahon, 154 Ill. 141, 39 N.E. 484, was noted on the margin of appellant's brief, but escaped attention. There are circumstances which distinguish that case from this, particularly with respect to the culpability of the defendant; but the similarity is sufficient to justify counsel in his claim that his position is supported by a case in point. I can only say that the reasoning of the opinion in that case has failed to convince me, and that the decision stands alone and without other support than may be found in the turntable cases, from which the supreme court of Illinois was unable to distinguish it. I think, however, that there is a distinction which relieves us of the necessity of extending an exceptionally harsh rule of liability to such a case. A turntable is not only a danger specially created by the act of the owner but it is a danger of a different kind to those which exist in the order of nature. A pond, although artificially created, is in nowise different from those natural ponds and

---

[13] Frederick Schauer, *Slippery Slopes*, 99 HARV. L. REV. 361, 380 n.52 (1985) (quoting DETROIT FREE PRESS, Apr. 27, 1984, at F1).

At time, no App. Div. cts. So 3 + panel of t. ct. functions almost like App Div. One App Div t. ct. panels, no more!

streams, which exist everywhere, and which involve the same dangers and present the same appearance and the same attractions to children. A turntable can be rendered absolutely safe, without destroying or materially impairing its usefulness, by simply locking it. A pond cannot be rendered inaccessible to boys by any ordinary means. Certainly no ordinary fence around the lot upon which a pond is situated would answer the purpose; and therefore, to make it safe, it must either be filled or drained, or, in other words, destroyed. But ponds are always useful, and often necessary, and where they do not exist naturally must be created, in order to store water for stock and for domestic purposes, irrigation, etc. Are we to hold that every owner of a pond or reservoir is liable in damages for any child that comes uninvited upon his premises and happens to fall in the water and drown? If so, then upon the same principle must the owner of a fruit tree be held liable for the death or injury of a child who, attracted by the fruit, climbs into the branches, and falls out. But this, we imagine, is an absurdity, for which no one would contend, and it proves that the rule of the Turntable Cases does not rest upon a principle so broad and of such rigid application as counsel supposes. The owner of a thing dangerous and attractive to children is not always and universally liable for an injury to a child tempted by the attraction. His liability bears a relation to the character of the thing, whether natural and common, or artificial and uncommon, to the comparative ease or difficulty of preventing the danger without destroying or impairing the usefulness of the thing; and, in short, to the reasonableness and propriety of his own conduct, in view of all surrounding circumstances and conditions. As to common dangers, existing in the order of nature, it is the duty of parents to guard and warn their children, and, failing to do so, they should not expect to hold others responsible for their own want of care. But, with respect to dangers specially created by the act of the owner, novel in character, attractive and dangerous to children, easily guarded and rendered safe, the rule is, as it ought to be, different; and such is the rule of the turntable cases, of the lumber-pile cases, and others of a similar character.

*** In the Illinois case cited by counsel the city of Pekin was held to have been culpable in excavating a deep pit within the city limits, which afterward filled up with water. It might be granted that that case was well decided, and the principle of the Turntable Cases properly applied, without holding that this defendant is similarly liable. There the existence of a pond in a thickly-peopled quarter was due to the act of the party charged. Here, the existence of the pond was due to the exercise by the city of San Francisco of a power and authority which the defendant could not lawfully resist. By the act of the city, and without any fault on his part, his lot was converted into a pond. He might, it is true, have filled it up; but he was no more bound to do so than if it had been a natural pond, because it was in no respect more of a nuisance than it would have been if it had been there before the city was laid out.

The facts being undisputed, it is the province and the duty of the court to decide, as matter of law, whether a defendant has been guilty of culpable negligence, and I think that it would be most unjust to hold that in this case the defendant has omitted any duty that he owed to the child of plaintiff. ***

Rehearing denied.

this is Calif.!

A

← who usually decides that?

So how come

real crux

of 'care?'

of care?

B

Doesn't it leave room to play? See Traynor

QUESTIONS

(1)   What does "in bank" (or, more commonly, "en banc") mean?

(2)   Does the "correction" undertaken by the court change anything about "the rule" of *Peters* as you understood it after the original opinion? To put it differently, is *Peters II* important or unimportant?

SANCHEZ v. EAST CONTRA COSTA IRRIGATION CO.
205 Cal. 515, 271 P. 1060 (1928)

LANGDON, J.

This is an appeal by the defendant from a judgment in favor of the plaintiff in the sum of $6,000 for the death of the infant son of plaintiff, who was drowned in a syphon at the bottom of an irrigation ditch belonging to the defendant. The defendant owned certain irrigation canals and ditches in Contra Costa County. One of its canals was approximately 10 miles long, and crossed under various roads. In one place it was necessary for this canal to cross a wide arroyo or stream known as Marsh Creek. To cross this creek it was necessary to construct a syphon from the canal on the one side of the creek to the canal on the other side. This syphon ran from the bottom of the irrigation main canal downward under Marsh Creek and came up into the irrigation main canal upon the other side of Marsh Creek. The opening of this syphon in the end of the canal was four feet in diameter, and was unguarded. The defendant company had constructed, within a short distance of the place of the accident, several small houses in which employees of the company, with their families, resided. The roadway leading to these houses ran alongside the side of the canal and along the edge of Marsh Creek; there being nothing but the thickness of a low concrete bulkhead between the canal and the road. The plaintiff was an employee of the company, and lived in one of the said houses with his wife and children. His five year old son, who was drowned, had been playing with other children at the edge of the canal, and attempted to wet his handkerchief in its waters to wipe some blood from an injury he had sustained. He fell into the main canal, which, at the time of the accident, was filled with about 3 feet of water, and then, evidently, slipped into the syphon at the bottom of this 3 feet of water. The water in the canal was muddy and the opening of the syphon could not be seen. The body of the child was recovered from a place some 15 feet down in the syphon. There was no sign of warning to notify passers by of the presence of this large syphon.

Appellant contends that it was not required to guard its canal against the danger of children falling into it, and this is conceded by the plaintiff and respondent. However, this case involves a situation where the defendant has placed upon its property an artificial peril, a concealed danger, without warning to those who were invited by defendant to live close by. The case of Faylor v. Great Eastern Quicksilver Mining Co., 45 Cal. App. 194, 187 P. 101, while presenting a different situation, announces a rule, the reasons for which make it applicable here. In that

case, it was reiterated that the rule of nonliability was not to be applied in "instances where the owner maintains on his land something in the nature of a trap, or other concealed danger, known to him, and as to which he gave no warning to others." * * *

In the instant case, the canal with its shallow water was the bait of the trap. The defendant knew that children lived close by, and the opening to the syphon might have been easily guarded. It is a matter of common knowledge that children playing on the edge of a shallow body of water will be tempted to play in the water and to reach into it, and, while defendant need not have guarded against this open and obvious stream of water, under numerous California decisions, we think a different rule applies where an apparently harmless, shallow stream of water contains a large opening into which anyone might slip, which opening is wholly unguarded and completely concealed from view. If the children had gone swimming in this canal and had slipped into the syphon, a similar legal situation would have been presented. The children assumed the risk of the open, obvious, notorious danger incident to the canal, containing about 3 feet of water; but they did not assume the risk of an unknown, concealed, and unguarded danger. [The present case falls within an] exception to the general rule * * *.

The judgment is affirmed.

We concur: RICHARDS, J.; SHENK, J. — *see p. 142*

see p. 142

NOTES AND QUESTIONS *Cal. App.*

neither we seem to have 3 categories

(1) What authority did the Supreme Court of California cite?

(2) Does this decision follow *Barrett*? Does it follow *Peters*?

(3) The court describes this case as falling within an exception to the general rule. What is the general rule in cases like this (query: *like what?*) and what are the exceptions?

(4) How can there be exceptions to rules? Is not an exception really just a violation (or, more charitably, a suspension) of the rule, and also of the general principle that like cases must be treated alike? If you respond, there are always exceptions to rules, do you recall whether Steffi Graf was permitted to serve three times at Wimbledon to Venus Williams rather than twice when the first serve is not a *let*? Suppose the umpire is convinced that Graf should get three serves to compensate for Williams's advantage in age. This would certainly be an exception to the rule that a player gets two serves. Would it be an exception to or an application of the rule that like cases must be treated alike? Are legal rules different from rules of games and if so, how do they differ?[14] Are there rules for breaking

---

[14] Kenneth I. Winston, *On Treating Like Cases Alike*, 62 CAL. L. REV. 1 (1974), will introduce you to a wealth of literature on questions of this nature. Incidentally, it was said that Ted Williams often got four strikes because his eyes were so good that umpires would give him close calls that they might not have given other hitters.

rules? Are there rules about breaking the rules about breaking the rules?[15]

(5) How does one know whether there still is a general rule or whether there are only exceptions "left?" And if there are only exceptions left, where did the general rule go and when did it leave?

> Is this question reminiscent of the classical Greek paradox of Sorites — the heap?
>
> If the removal of one grain of salt from a heap still leaves a heap, the paradox goes, and so too with the removal of the next grain, and the next, and the one after that, and so on, then it must follow that the removal of *all* the grains still leaves a heap. This is of course absurd, because we all know that heaps and empty spaces are different * * *.[16]

(6) Is there something misleading about setting up what appears to be a dichotomy: rules on one hand, exceptions on the other?

Professor Schauer has written:

> [T]here is no logical distinction between exceptions and what they are exceptions to, their occurrence resulting from the often fortuitous circumstance that the language available to circumscribe a legal rule or principle is broader than the regulatory goals the rule or principle is designed to further. As products of the relationship between legal goals and the language in which law happens to be written, exceptions show how the meaning of a legal rule is related to the meaning of the language that law employs. * * * In important ways exceptions link law to its linguistic and categorical underpinnings, situating law in a world it both reflects and on which it is imposed.
>
> The use (or not) of exceptions can thus tell us more than we have traditionally thought about how law is located in a linguistic and categorical world. But that location is contingent, and consequently what is at some time or place a broad rule with an accompanying exception is at other times a narrow rule having no need for an exception to perform the same prescriptive task.[17]

Can you think of examples that would illuminate Professor Schauer's point? Here is one he uses:

> A good example * * * is the traditional legal prohibition of fornication. Fornication is defined in Webster's Third New International Dictionary as "sexual intercourse other than between a man and his wife." Thus, a statutory or common law prohibition of fornication excludes sexual intercourse between married persons without the necessity of a separate

---

[15] *See* Stewart Macaulay, *Popular Legal Culture: An Introduction*, 98 YALE L.J. 1545, 1556 n.50 (1989), *citing* MARVIN HARRIS, CULTURAL MATERIALISM: THE STRUGGLE FOR A SCIENCE OF CULTURE 274–275 (1980).

[16] Schauer, *supra* note 13, at 378. The paradox goes back to Zeno of Elea, the pre-Socratic philosopher who contrived a famous series of paradoxes around the notion of infinite regress.

[17] Frederick Schauer, *Exceptions*, 58 U. CHI. L. REV. 871, 871–872 (1991).

exception. Were the word "fornication" absent from the language, however, or were the category of "sexual intercourse other than between married persons" absent from the antecedent conceptual apparatus of the society, then we would expect to see the same prohibition couched in terms of a primary prohibition on sexual intercourse with an accompanying exception for sexual intercourse between married persons.[18]

The next two cases, *Copfer v. Golden* and *Wilford v. Little*, must be read together and we postpone all questions and comments until after *Wilford*. Note that both are cases decided by the District Court of Appeal, not the California Supreme Court. They carry correspondingly less authority but are nevertheless important strands in our story.

COPFER v. GOLDEN
135 Cal. App.2d 623, 288 P.2d 90 (1955)

VALLÉE, J.

This is an action for damages for personal injuries sustained by plaintiff while playing on property owned by defendant Vaughn C. Golden. Plaintiff was 6 years of age at the time of the accident. * * * The cause was tried by the court without a jury. * * * Judgment was for plaintiff * * *.

[Defendant owned two adjacent lots. A year or more before the accident defendant moved a building onto the western portion of the two lots, and made it an apartment house. Since 1949, when he bought the two lots, defendant had stored on the eastern portion of the lots materials, machinery, and equipment he used in his business of buying, selling, and moving old buildings. In October 1952 defendant conveyed the western portion of the two lots to his mother and father. The deed was not recorded until May 29, 1953. The court uses the words "the property" to refer *only* to the eastern portion of the two lots.] The accident occurred on May 22, 1953. At that time there was on the property lumber, cement blocks and steps, an old Chevrolet, tires, wheels, pipe, trusses, a hamburger stand for resale, a trailer, a 2-wheeled tubular frame stripped-down trailer, and other material. All of the equipment and material on the property had been moved there by Vaughn and was his property. The tubular part of the stripped-down trailer was a hollow half section of a 12-inch piece of tubing placed over the wheels on each side to make a runway to haul a tractor. Pieces of lumber were tied by wire across the top of the tubular frame trailer and there was some loose lumber on it. Vaughn used it to haul lumber.

Prior to the day of the accident, a number of children lived in the apartment house next to the property in question. That day there were about 13 living there. There was no place for children to play on the west 50 feet of Lots 33 and 34 on which the apartment house was located. They, including plaintiff, played on the east 75 feet and on the equipment which Vaughn kept there. He had observed

---
[18] *Id.* at 878.

them playing on the equipment from time to time and had told them to leave.

Plaintiff, with her parents and younger brothers and sisters, moved into the apartment house in February 1953. On May 22, 1953 plaintiff was severely injured while playing with three other small children on the property in question. There was evidence from which the court could have inferred that she was playing on the tubular frame trailer at the time she fell and was injured on the tubular part of the trailer. * * *

One who maintains upon his property a condition, instrumentality, machine, or other agency which is dangerous to children of tender years by reason of their inability to appreciate the peril therein, and which is one he knows or should know and which he realizes or should realize involves an unreasonable risk of death or serious bodily harm to such children, — is under a duty to exercise reasonable care to protect them against the dangers of the agency. Thus one is negligent in maintaining an agency which he knows or reasonably should know to be dangerous to children of tender years at a place where he knows or reasonably should know such children are likely to resort or to which they are likely to be attracted by the agency unless he exercises reasonable care to guard them against danger which their youth and ignorance prevent them from appreciating. If, to the knowledge of the owner, children of tender years habitually come on his property where a dangerous condition exists to which they are exposed, the duty to exercise reasonable care for their safety arises not because of an implied invitation but because of the owner's knowledge of unconscious exposure to danger which the children do not realize. Children of tender years have no foresight and scarcely any apprehensiveness of danger, a circumstance which those owning instrumentalities with a potential for harm must bear in mind; for it is every individual's duty to use toward others such due care as the situation then and there requires. Civ. Code, § 1714. "The known characteristics of children, including their childish propensities to intermeddle, must be taken into consideration in determining whether ordinary care for the safety of a child has been exercised under particular circumstances." Crane v. Smith, 23 Cal.2d 288, 297, 144 P.2d 356, 361. Of course, if adults or children of such age as to ordinarily be capable of discerning and avoiding danger are injured while trespassing upon the property of another, they may be without remedy; while under similar circumstances children of tender years would be protected.

The Restatement says:

A possessor of land is subject to liability for bodily harm to young children trespassing thereon caused by a structure or other artificial condition which he maintains upon the land, if

(a) the place where the condition is maintained is one upon which the possessor knows or should know that such children are likely to trespass, and

(b) the condition is one of which the possessor knows or should know and which he realizes or should realize as involving an unreasonable risk of death or serious bodily harm to such children, and

(c) the children because of their youth do not discover the condition or realize the risk involved in intermeddling in it or in coming within the area made dangerous by it, and

(d) the utility to the possessor of maintaining the condition is slight as compared to the risk to young children involved therein.

Rest., Torts, § 339. See 65 C.J.S., Negligence, § 28, p. 454. The rule in California is substantially as stated in the Restatement. [Citations omitted].

Dean Prosser says:

who is Prosser?

"Where the trespasser is a child, one important reason for the general rule of non-liability is lacking. Because of his immaturity and lack of judgment, the child is incapable of understanding and appreciating all of the possible dangers which he may encounter in trespassing, and he cannot be expected to assume the risk and look out for himself. While it is true that his parents or guardians are charged with the duty of looking out for him, it is obviously neither customary nor practicable for them to keep him under observation continually, or follow him wherever he may go. If he is to be protected, the person who may do it with the least inconvenience is the one upon whose land he strays, and the interest in unrestricted freedom to make use of the land may be required, within reasonable limits, to give way to the greater social interest in the safety of the child."

would it be desirable?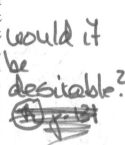

A duty rested on defendant Vaughn C. Golden to protect the young and heedless from themselves and guard them against perils that reasonably could have been foreseen. The trial court was warranted in finding that the circumstances here called the duty into play. The question whether injury to a child legally incapable of negligence will import negligence to the owner or possessor of the injuring instrumentality depends on the circumstances of each case and is peculiarly one for the trier of fact. It was for him to say whether the tubular frame trailer was a dangerous instrumentality of a class which was an unreasonable risk of serious bodily harm to children of tender years upon which they were likely to trespass. The evidence is uncontradicted that defendant Vaughn C. Golden knew that children of tender years, including plaintiff, strayed onto his property and played on the tubular frame trailer and other contrivances and material he kept there. It was for the trial court to say whether the condition was one which he knew or should have known and which he realized or should have realized involved risk of serious bodily harm to children of tender years. It appears to be conceded that plaintiff because of her youth did not realize the risk involved in playing on the tubular frame trailer. It was also for the trier of fact to say whether defendant Vaughn C. Golden should have guarded against injury to the trespassing children. In a word, whether the facts exist which bring the doctrine of injuries to trespassing children into play is generally a question for the trier of fact. * * *

See Beatty on p. 117 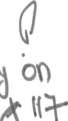 Ⓐ

The judgment in favor of plaintiff and against defendant Vaughn C. Golden is affirmed.

PARKER WOOD, Acting P.J., and ASHBURN, J., pro tem., concur.

WILFORD v. LITTLE
144 Cal. App. 2d 477, 301 P.2d 282 (1956)

FOURT, J.

Plaintiffs commenced an action to recover damages for the death of a minor son who fell into the private swimming pool on defendants' residential property. To an amended complaint the defendants demurred and the same was sustained with leave to amend. No amendment was made and judgment of dismissal was entered. This appeal is from the judgment of dismissal.

A fair résumé of the matters set forth in the amended complaint are as follows: On or about August 31, 1954, the swimming pool in question contained water to a depth of about 9 feet at one end, with a diving board extending over the water. Small children played on the property adjacent to the property of the defendants. The pool and diving board could be seen by the children from the adjacent property and this was known to the defendants. On the date heretofore mentioned Christian McLean Wilford, the four-and-one-half year old son of plaintiffs, and some other small children, were attracted onto the property of the defendants by the diving board and pool. Christian McLean Wilford and one other small boy began to play upon the diving board which was similar to a see-saw or teeter-board in that it had an "up-and-down" motion when jumped upon. The pool was so constructed that it was difficult for a child to hold onto the sides of the pool. The boy and his companions were too young to appreciate the danger involved in playing on the diving board and in the pool. In the course of play the lad fell or jumped from the diving board into the water and drowned. Neither of the plaintiffs knew, nor had reason to know that there was a swimming pool in the neighborhood, or that the property of the defendants was not fenced or enclosed in any manner to keep children or others away from the pool. A fence or other enclosure could have been installed at a relatively small cost. It was then alleged that the defendants were negligent in not properly enclosing the pool and that this negligence resulted in the death of plaintiffs' son to their damage in the sum of $50,000, together with expenses in the sum of $992.06.

It is appellants' contention that California has adopted the rule of law generally referred to as the "Attractive Nuisance Doctrine," or the "Rule of the Turntable Cases," as set forth in the Restatement of the Law of Torts, and cites as authority for such contention the case of Copfer v. Golden, 135 Cal. App.2d 623, 627–628, 288 P.2d 90, and the cases cited therein. It is our opinion, however, that a swimming pool and diving board is not an attractive nuisance as that term is generally used. The California Annotations to the Restatement of the Law of Torts contain the following language (at pages 141–142):

"§ 339. Artificial conditions highly dangerous to trespassing children.

"* * * (b) Ponds or reservoirs: There is no liability for drowning of children in ponds or reservoirs under the attractive nuisance doctrine. * * * * Peters v. Bowman, 1896, 115 Cal. 345, 47 P. 113, 598, 56 Am.St.Rep. 106, is the leading decision. In this case the water collected on a vacant lot by reason of an embankment erected by the city in grading a street. Polk v.

Laurel Hill Cemetery Ass'n, 1918, 37 Cal.App. 624, 174 P. 414, a child of eight drowned in an unguarded reservoir in a cemetery being used as a park. Reardon v. Spring Valley Water Co., 1924, 68 Cal.App. 13, 228 P. 406, a five year old boy drowned after a fall from a rowboat which was allowed to remain unfastened in a negligently guarded reservoir. The court refused to hold that the presence of the boat brought the case within the doctrine.

"(c) 'Siphon' cases: There are several decisions but in only one was the doctrine held applicable. (1) Sanchez v. East Contra Costa Irr. Co., 1928, 205 Cal. 515, 271 P. 1060. In the other two cases there is an obvious effort to pattern after the rules announced in this opinion. Plaintiff's son, aged five, was drowned in a canal when he fell into it after trying to wet his handkerchief. The body was found in a 'siphon' which carried the water under a cross-stream. The court held that defendant had created a concealed danger in the nature of a trap (siphon) to those who lived close by, and one that could easily be guarded. (2) Melendez v. City of Los Angeles, 1937, 8 Cal.2d 741, 68 P.2d 971. The demurrer to the complaint was sustained and on appeal this action of the court was affirmed. The court cited and approved Restatement § 339 as an exception to the rule of nonliability but held the doctrine not applicable. The complaint alleged that plaintiff's two sons were drowned in a pool of water in a storm drain. One son, aged 11, was on a raft and fell into the water and into a deep hole concealed and unknown to him. The other son, aged 13, went to his rescue and was similarly drowned. The decision held that the deep hole was not an artificial contrivance of the possessor of the land and the precedent followed is Beeson v. City of Los Angeles [115 Cal. App. 122, 300 P. 993], infra."

In the recent case of Lake v. Ferrer, 139 Cal. App.2d 114, 293 P.2d 104, hearing denied in the Supreme Court, March 28, 1956, plaintiffs' son of two and one-half years was attracted to the defendant's swimming pool and trespassed upon the defendant's property, fell into the swimming pool and drowned. Plaintiff parents did not know of the pool's existence and had not been told of it. In the Lake case, the plaintiffs relied for authority upon section 339 of the Restatement of Torts and practically all of the cases cited in the instant case, plus several others. It was held that the attractive nuisance doctrine did not apply under allegations considerably stronger than those presented in the instant case. * * *

There are several elements to the doctrine of attractive nuisance in this state. The contrivance must be artificial and uncommon, as well as dangerous * * *.

In Peters v. Bowman, 115 Cal. 345, 355 [47 P. 113, 598, 599] the court said:

"A turntable is not only a danger specially created by the act of the owner but it is a danger of a different kind to those which exist in the order of nature. A pond, although artificially created, is in nowise different from those natural ponds and streams, which exist everywhere, * * *. A pond cannot be rendered inaccessible to boys by any ordinary means. Certainly no ordinary fence around the lot upon which a pond is situated would answer the purpose; and therefore, to make it safe, it must either be filled or drained, or, in other words, destroyed. * * * The owner of a thing

dangerous and attractive to children is not always and universally liable for an injury to a child tempted by the attraction. * * * As to common dangers, existing in the order of nature, it is the duty of parents to guard and warn their children, and, failing to do so, they should not expect to hold others responsible for their own want of care. * * *"

Courts in California have held repeatedly that a body of water, natural or artificial, is not such a thing as may be held to constitute an attractive nuisance. It may be attractive to children but it is also of a common and ordinary nature of that which is to be found anywhere.

Appellants here have advanced an argument very similar to that presented in the case of Meyer v. General Electric Company, 46 Wash.2d 251, 280 P.2d 257. In the Washington case plaintiffs' two year and eight months old child trespassed onto defendant's premises and was drowned when he fell into an artificial ditch on said premises. In reversing a judgment for the plaintiff, the court said, at pages 258–259:

> "This state adheres to the attractive nuisance doctrine. However, our question is: Under what circumstances will a watercourse constitute an attractive nuisance?

> "It is the weight of authority that a *natural* watercourse is not an attractive nuisance, and that an artificial one is not if it has natural characteristics.

> "* * * It was not unnaturally dangerous, had no element of deception or of an inextricable trap, and, in fact, presented no danger by reason of being artificial that was different in any way from that of a natural watercourse. We hold, as a matter of law, that it was not an attractive nuisance. * * *

> "The presence of danger to an unattended infant is not necessarily a test of anything but the need of parental care. An infant is afraid of nothing and in danger of everything when left to his own devices. The primary duty of care is upon the parents of an infant. (Citing case.) Their neglect will not convert a situation admittedly dangerous to an infant into an attractive nuisance which would not be so classed as to older children."

The judgment is affirmed.

WHITE, P.J., concurs.

DORAN, J., dissents.

NOTES AND QUESTIONS

(1) For better or worse (we shall explain "worse" shortly), these cases inject the Restatement of the Law of Torts into the "attractive nuisance" debate. The *Restatement of Torts*, a Torts casebook tells you,

> is a summary of the law of torts that was prepared by Professor Francis Bohlen and was published by the American Law Institute [in 1939]. A newer version, called the Restatement (Second) of Torts, was prepared by

explain

Professors William Prosser and John Wade and was also published by the ALI [in 1965]. The ALI is composed of lawyers, judges, and law professors. The Restatement is not authoritative in the sense that precedent in the relevant jurisdiction would be authoritative. Nevertheless, courts often cite the Restatement and are influenced by it. One pervasive issue is whether courts sometimes neglect careful analysis of problems by deferring too readily to the Restatement.[19]

III

A "hornbook" (do you know why *horn* book?) well-beloved by generations of first-year law students says:

> In this process of weighing interests [in torts cases], and more broadly in ongoing critical evaluation of the development of tort law, the influence of writers upon the courts has been very great. Moreover, within the past half century there has been a very significant attempt at a searching and exhaustive analysis of the entire field in the American Law Institute's Restatement of the Law of Torts, which was begun in 1923, completed in 1939, and more recently revised in the Second Restatement. Some of the most eminent legal scholars have taken part in this work, with the assistance of numerous judges and lawyers.
>
> The form of the Restatement is perhaps unfortunate, in that it seeks to reduce the law to a definite set of black-letter rules or principles, ignoring all contrary authority — since the law of torts in its present stage of development does not lend itself at all readily to such treatment. There is room for suspicion that the courts have tended to cite the Restatement when they are already in agreement with it, and to ignore it when they are not, so that the impressive list of references to it in the cases may be somewhat misleading; and there are those who have disagreed with many of its conclusions, and even denounced the whole project.[20]

?

Why "for worse"? The foregoing excerpts tell you why. "The form of the Restatement is perhaps unfortunate, in that it seeks to reduce the law to a definite set of black-letter rules or principles . . . since the law of torts in its present stage of development does not lend itself at all readily to such treatment." To which we would add, how can a body of "law" dominated by standards of reasonableness applied to the facts of each case largely by juries chosen for only one case ever lend itself to such treatment? And why should that be a desirable goal?

"Why" "worse"? ?

But the crux of the matter, for our purposes, is this: "One pervasive issue is whether the courts sometimes neglect careful analysis of problems by deferring too readily to the Restatement."

CRUX

Whatever may be true for courts, we know it to be true for you. Understandably bewildered by what Cardozo called the "trackless ocean" on which you feel yourself floating, you grab onto the Restatement the way a drowning man or woman might grab onto a piece of driftwood. That is, when given an "attractive nuisance" problem, you do not carefully analyze each and every fact for its relevance to *this*

---

[19] ROBERTSON, POWERS, & ANDERSON, TORTS 15 (1989).

[20] PROSSER AND KEETON ON TORTS 17 (5th ed. 1984).

explain

particular case. Rather, you neatly copy each and every subsection of Section 339: 339(a), 339(b), 339(c), 339(d), then say of each one something like, "Clearly, this applies (or doesn't apply) here and therefore judgment for plaintiff (or defendant)." *It won't do.* You must doggedly grapple with the facts of the cases, not copy the Restatement.

(2) The *Copfer* court says: "The rule in California is substantially as stated in the Restatement." Would you, after *Barrett*, *Peters*, and *Sanchez* (none of them cited in *Copfer*) agree that "the rule" is "substantially" as stated in the Restatement? Make an argument that it is. Make an argument that it is not.

1714

(3) *Copfer* refers to Section 1714 of the California Civil Code, which provides:

Everyone is responsible, not only for the result of his willful acts, but also for an injury occasioned to another by his want of ordinary care or skill in the management of his property or person, except so far as the latter has, willfully or by want of ordinary care, brought the injury upon himself.

The court's paraphrase reads:

It is every individual's duty to use toward others such due care as the situation then and there requires.

NO

Is that a legitimate paraphrase of 1714? If you had read 1714 before you read *Copfer*, would you have thought it was primarily about the duties of potential defendants or about limitations on recovery by potential plaintiffs? Is the moral of the story: don't ever trust anyone to paraphrase a statute? *YES !!!*

NO

Does 1714 embody a rule or a standard? If the latter, can it decide this case without more? Should it make a difference to the decisionmaker that this rule or standard appears in a statute rather than in a prior case?

(4) We now turn to what for us is the most important aspect of these two cases, considered together: in *Copfer*, a 6-year-old who fell from a trailer on defendant's property was allowed to recover after a *trial* by the court sitting without a jury. In *Wilford*, a 4½-year-old who fell off a diving board and drowned was denied relief when the *defendant's demurrer* was sustained. Is there an explanation for this seeming irrationality?

On page 58 we introduced you to the idea that appellate courts are limited in their reviewing function when considering a question of fact but that — within the boundaries of stare decisis — they rule supreme on questions of law. In the one setting they owe deference to the decision "below," in the other they do not.

This leaves these interrelated questions: when is something a question of fact and when is it a question of law? Can a trailer ever be an attractive nuisance — is that a question of fact or a question of law? Can a pool ever be an attractive nuisance — is that a question of fact or a question of law? And who decides which it is going to be?

The answer to the last question and thus implicitly to the first is: the appellate court decides. And when will it call something a question of law? When it thinks the law should keep either (a) *all defendants of this kind* or (b) *this defendant* away from the jury.

[handwritten margin notes: "all Δs", "for failure..."]

In the first instance it will say: "there is no such cause of action; we do not recognize defendant's conduct as giving rise to a legally cognizable claim." (Hence we will sustain the demurrer or, in modern terminology, dismiss for failure to state a claim upon which relief can be granted). In the second instance it says: "Yes, there is such a claim; we do recognize this kind of conduct by a defendant as potentially giving rise to liability, depending on the context in which it took place" (hence the demurrer should have been overruled; the pre-trial motion to dismiss denied). BUT, the court says, "in *this* case, on *these* facts, under *these* circumstances, no reasonable jury, no jury except one that has taken all leave of its senses or has been tampered with, could plausibly find for the plaintiff" — hence the defendant is entitled to a directed verdict.

[handwritten margin note: "this Δ"]

Peters v. Bowman I and *II* held: natural bodies of water or artificial bodies of water with natural characteristics are *as a matter of law* not "attractive nuisances." That is, as a matter of law, the landowner owes no duty even to trespassing children. It reflected a policy about the general undesirability of holding landowners liable for having water on their land; it did not reflect a judgment about this particular landowner under these circumstances.

Peters I had been a jury case. Recall that we asked after the case: did the case have to go to the jury? You should now understand that the answer is *no* and that the trial judge would have been affirmed even if he had granted defendant a directed verdict (motion to dismiss complaint after all evidence has been presented but before the case is sent to the jury). Remember, juries exist to find facts; if water is not an attractive nuisance as a matter of law, and we already know that the case involves a body of water, then there is nothing for the jury to do, for there is no fact that could create liability.

[handwritten margin note: "Peters I"]

But you must also understand this: the result, the outcome in *Peters*, namely judgment for the defendant, could well have been the same even if the court had chosen to recognize such a cause of action; even if it had, in other words, imposed a duty on landowners whose land has a body of water on it (just as it had imposed a duty on landowners who had dangerous machinery on their land). In that event, the plaintiff might[21] have been entitled to go to the jury — but the jury, of course, was free to find that *under these circumstances* (the boy's age, the way in which the "pond" had come about)[22] *this* defendant was not, in the judgment of the community, to be found to have breached his duty.

Most likely that is what the jury thought — after all, it returned a verdict for the defendant.

[handwritten margin note: "V/Δ"]

Had the jury returned a verdict for the plaintiff, what would have happened? The California Supreme Court, we know, did not want to put landowners with bodies of

[handwritten margin note: "What if V/π ?"]

----

[21] Note that we say *might*, not *would*. The reason: even if a duty to use care were imposed, the plaintiff might not introduce enough evidence that defendant breached his duty to support a jury verdict for the plaintiff. In such a case the court directs a verdict for defendant not because defendant had no duty, but rather because plaintiff has not shown breach of that duty.

[22] Perhaps the thought crossed your mind why the plaintiff did not sue the City of San Francisco. The most likely answer is that at that time the city would have been immune against torts claims — a longstanding legal rule now frequently abrogated.

water on their property under a duty, not even to trespassing children. *As a matter of law*, bodies of water could not be, in its view, attractive nuisances. Hence presumably (because you never know) it would have reversed the judgment for the plaintiff, thus telling the trial court, you should not have given this case to the jury, there was nothing for it to do.

As it happened, the Supreme Court did not have to talk about the propriety of giving the case to the jury because *for different reasons* the jury had found for the defendant.

It is important for you to understand this clearly — because we do not want you to fall into the error of thinking: letting a case go to the jury equals a judgment for the plaintiff.

Wilford was treated as a swimming pool case. (An important aside: as the plaintiff's lawyer, would you have argued *Wilford* as a pool case? Was there not a better theory?) The California Supreme Court had "laid down the law" regarding bodies of water. The trial court knew what the law was regarding bodies of water. Hence: demurrer sustained. The District Court of Appeal, too, knew what the law was. It also did not think it was its province to "overrule" the Supreme Court of California. If the no duty rule regarding bodies of water was to be changed, that job properly belonged to the Supreme Court and not to the lower level decisionmaker. Hence: judgment of dismissal affirmed.

Copfer involved a trailer. There were two rules in the system (ignoring *Sanchez* for present purposes): the "no duty for water" rule and the "turntable rule." The latter imposed a duty on landowners who kept certain machinery on their land, but it did not make them liable as a matter of law for any injury occurring on their property.[23] Rather, as *Barrett* said, "the question of defendant's negligence [i.e., whether he breached his duty] in this case was a matter to be decided by the jury in view of all the evidence."[24]

The trial judge in *Copfer* evidently thought trailers were like turntables and unlike bodies of water. Hence he had a trial; because both parties waived a jury trial the judge himself sat as the trier of fact. He found that under the circumstances the defendant had not acted in the manner in which we expect the reasonable and prudent person with machinery on his lot to act; that is, he found that the defendant had breached his duty and hence he gave judgment for the plaintiff.

The District Court of Appeal refused to decide either (a) that trailers were more like bodies of water than they were like turntables or (b) to establish a separate "trailer rule" according to which trailers, in analogy to bodies of water, should be held *not* to be attractive nuisances as *a matter of law*.

Had it done either of these, it would presumably have reversed and told the trial judge: you erred when you thought being injured by falling off a trailer results in a legally cognizable claim. Instead, it was satisfied that under the turntable rule the defendant here had been under a duty and that all the rest was a question of fact.

---

[23] If they were, plaintiffs would be entitled to summary judgments.

[24] *See supra* page 107.

Hence its "standard of review" had to be one of deference to the trier of fact. In exercising this limited reviewing function the court let itself be guided by the Restatement which, in section 339 (a) through (d), identifies factors to look to in judging the defendant's behavior. *But it is worth remembering that all this is already in Barrett:*

> Whether, in any given case, there has been such negligence upon the part of the owner of the property, in the maintenance thereon of dangerous machinery, is a question of fact dependent upon the situation of the property and the attendant circumstances, because upon such facts will depend the degree of care which prudence would suggest as reasonably necessary to guard against injury therefrom.[25]

It seems then, does it not, that we can fault neither court for what it did. But it still may strike you as irrational to let trespassing kids recover, under the appropriate circumstances, when they fall off trailers but not, regardless of the circumstances, when they drown. What produces that irrationality? The answer is probably not to your liking: the source of the trouble is having a per se rule, a nice, firm, orderly, stable, rigid, inflexible (unjust?) rule of law: thou shallst not recover when you drown. To be sure, it saves us time, it saves us trouble, and it spares us from having to deal with those messy facts.

But is it worth it in this context? On one hand we have parents who argue that they should not have to shoulder 100 percent of the burden of looking after their children; that they cannot "fence" their children; that we should not want them to do that; that children need to be curious and need to explore (that's how we get Mac computers and the Polio vaccine). On the other hand we have owners who argue that they are entitled to enjoy their land free from concerns over those who go where they are not invited and not wanted and have no business being; that they should not be expected to fell their trees and fill in the ponds and streams God put on their land; that there is no way to "childproof" against enterprising youngsters short of turning their land into a fort; and that the decision to have children entails the acceptance of responsibility for their well-being and also of the possibility that they will suffer injury or death because life is dangerous.

Does this sort of conflict strike you as best being solved by per se rules? By saying *either*: you own land, there is a body of water on your land, you are under no duty to trespassers, including children, regardless of the circumstances; *or*: you own land, there is a body of water on your land, you are always liable when a child drowns in that body of water, regardless of what you did to safeguard it against children.[26]

If neither leaves you satisfied, if you want to say, can't we decide this *case by case* — then must you not, under our system, treat it as a negligence case and allow the jury to decide case by case whether the defendant fell short of the standard of reasonable and prudent care in the circumstances? And if we do that we reintroduce inconsistency, unpredictability, and perhaps unfairness into the system.

---

[25] *Id.*

 [26] We would call that absolute or strict liability and it is the counterpoint to the *Peters* rule.

Are there other contexts in which you do want rules, in which you do *not* want case by case adjudication? How about procedural rules, "housekeeping" rules, so to speak — would they fall into this category?[27]

(5) We said above that to treat something as a question of law is one mechanism a court can use to keep a case away from the jury. Why would it want to do that? We can come up with different answers in different contexts (the issue is too difficult for the jury to understand, the jury may let itself be swayed by passion, the evidence is too difficult for laypersons to assess, etc.) — but do they at bottom all express a measure of distrust of the jury? Or might courts honestly and impartially think that indeed some questions are questions of fact (e.g., how, where, when) and others questions of law (e.g., what *should* be the rule for cases like this)?[28]

We come now to the pivotal case in the sequence.

KNIGHT v. KAISER
48 Cal.2d 778, 312 P.2d 1089 (1957)

McComb, Justice.

From a judgment predicated upon the sustaining of defendant's demurrer to plaintiff's third amended complaint without leave to amend in an action to recover damages for the death of plaintiff's son, plaintiff appeals.

The amended complaint, in substance, alleged that plaintiff was the natural mother of decedent, Johnny William Bass, Jr., 10 years of age; that defendant owned and maintained premises in Stockton on which it had placed or caused to be placed large piles of sand and gravel and, adjacent thereto, a large conveyor belt; that no fences, guards or railings were placed around these sand and gravel piles or a portion of the conveyor belt; that a road or pathway was close to these objects and children were in the habit of playing upon the sand and gravel piles and the conveyor belt; that defendant knew or should have known the conditions existing involved an unreasonable risk of death or serious bodily harm to children playing on the sand and gravel piles; and that on August 20, 1953, plaintiff's son, while playing upon the premises and digging in one of the sand piles, was asphyxiated when it collapsed upon him.

Plaintiff contends that the facts alleged in the complaint as amended state a cause of action within the "attractive nuisance" doctrine. This contention is untenable.

Where the facts are undisputed, as in the instant case, it is a question of law whether or not the facts alleged fall within the scope of the "attractive nuisance" doctrine.

---

[27] These questions recur in Chapter 5 because Chapter 5 deals with Precedent — that is, with the *rule* that a court must follow its prior decision in a factually similar case — and where we must ask, is that rule more appropriate in some contexts than in others.

[28] The court/jury theme permeates torts and criminal law. Your efforts to understand here will also be amply rewarded in those courses.

[handwritten margin note top: relevant? is that how you would phrase the issue?]

Applying this rule to the admitted facts in the present case, it is conceded that defendant maintained upon its premises large sand and gravel piles and a large conveyor belt; that decedent while playing and digging in one of the sand piles was asphyxiated when it collapsed upon him.

It is the general rule that where a person goes upon the premises of another without invitation, as a bare licensee, and the owner passively acquiesces in his presence, if any injury is sustained by the licensee by reason of a mere defect in the premises the owner is not liable for negligence, for the licensee has assumed the risk himself. * * *

The law is also established that in the absence of circumstances which bring a case under the "attractive nuisance" doctrine, an owner of land owes no other duty to a child trespassing on his premises than he owes to an adult trespasser. (Peters v. Bowman, 115 Cal. 345, 349, 47 P. 113.)

To the general rule there is this exception: If an owner of land maintains thereon what is commonly called an "attractive nuisance," the owner is liable for injuries resulting to a trespassing child.

In view of the foregoing rules and the facts alleged in the complaint, this question is presented: Does a sand pile constitute an "attractive nuisance," i.e., a fact which places liability upon the owner of property for injuries to a trespassing child?

This question must be answered in the negative. It is settled that a body of water, natural or artificial, does not constitute an "attractive nuisance" that will subject the owner to liability for trespassing children who are attracted thereto and are drowned. *[handwritten: 1. "it is not inherently dangerous"?]*

As far as attractiveness to children is concerned, there is no significant difference between a body of water and a sand pile. Pools of water and sand piles duplicate the work of nature and are not uncommon. In fact, a pool of water is far more dangerous than a sand pile, which in and of itself is not dangerous. The *[handwritten: 2]* dangers connected with and inherent in a sand pile are obvious to everyone, even to a child old enough to be permitted by its parents to play unattended.

Sand piles may be attractive to children, but they are also of a common and ordinary nature and are found in numerous places, quite frequently in the child's own backyard. It is common for children to play in sand piles and to dig holes and make excavations in them. They are early instructed by their parents as to the danger of cave-ins. Hence, the owner of private property who maintains thereon a sand pile that merely duplicates the work of nature and to which no new dangers have been added should not be liable to a trespassing child for injuries under the "attractive nuisance" doctrine.

In Restatement of the Law of Torts, volume 2, section 339, page 922, it is said that the duty of the possessor of land "does not extend to those conditions the existence of which is obvious even to children and the risk of which is fully realized by them. This limitation of the possessor's liability to conditions dangerous to children, because of their inability to appreciate their surroundings or to realize the risk involved therein, frees the possessor of land from the danger of liability to

[handwritten margin right: ?! Now do you see you uses & the abuses of the Rest.?]

which he would otherwise be subjected by maintaining on the land the normal, necessary and usual implements which are essential to its normal use but which reckless children can use to their harm in a spirit of bravado or to gratify some other childish desire and with as full a perception of the risks which they are running as though they were adults." (Cf. 28 A.L.R.2d (1953), § 4, p. 200.)

In Anderson v. Reith-Riley Const. Co., 112 Ind. App. 170, 44 N.E.2d 184, defendant removed a large amount of sand from its property, leaving a hole 100 feet long, 50 feet wide and 10 feet deep, with perpendicular walls. Plaintiff's son, nine years of age, was attracted to the hole, where he excavated below the surface and was killed in a cave-in which followed. The court held that defendant was not liable under the "attractive nuisance" doctrine, saying at page 185, 44 N.E.2d:

"Nature has created streams, lakes and pools which attract children. Lurking in their waters is always the danger of drowning. Against this danger children are early instructed so that they are sufficiently presumed to know the danger that if the owner of private property creates an artificial pool on his own property, merely duplicating the work of nature without adding any new danger, and a child, without invitation, ventures on the private property, enters the pool and is drowned, the owner is not liable because of having created an 'attractive nuisance.'

"Nature has created cliffs and embankments which attract children. And here again is always the danger of falling over the cliffs or down the embankments. Against these dangers children are early instructed so that they are sufficiently presumed to know the danger that if the owner of private property by excavating for a basement on his own property, thereby creates an artificial cliff, and a child, without invitation, ventures on the private property and falls into the excavation, the owner is not liable because of having created an 'attractive nuisance.'

"Another common danger in cliffs and embankments is that of cave-ins from excavation below the surface. And it is common for children in play to make such excavations in the sides of cliffs and embankments for the purpose of creating caves, tunnels, etc. So they are early instructed as to the danger of cave-ins and are sufficiently presumed to know the danger that if the owner of private property by excavating on his own property, creates an artificial cliff or embankment, merely duplicating the work of nature without adding any new dangers, and a child, without invitation, ventures on the private property, excavates below the surface and is injured or killed by a resultant cave-in, the owner is not liable because of having created an 'attractive nuisance.' Nor does the rule change with the varying texture of the earth. The danger is the same danger, real and obvious, with only the percentage of probability of the occurrence increased or decreased with the earth's fineness or firmness. * * *"

It is thus evident that the sand pile did not constitute an "attractive nuisance." This conclusion is in accord with the generally accepted rule — to restrict and limit, rather than to extend, the doctrine of "attractive nuisance." It is a doctrine to be applied cautiously and only when the facts come strictly and fully within the rule.

Finally, it is to be noted that if it is conceded that the conveyor belt mentioned in the pleading might constitute an "attractive nuisance," there is no allegation that it caused or contributed to decedent's death. There is a total absence of an allegation of a causal connection between the conveyor belt and his unfortunate death. Under these circumstances, the maintenance of the conveyor belt does not bring the case under the "attractive nuisance" doctrine.

The judgment is affirmed.

SHENK, SCHAUER, and SPENCE, JJ. concur.

TRAYNOR, Justice.

I dissent.

The Civil Code, section 1714, provides: "Every one is responsible, not only for the result of his willful acts, but also for an injury occasioned to another by his want of ordinary care or skill in the management of his property or person, except so far as the latter has, willfully or by want of ordinary care, brought the injury upon himself." Nevertheless, the cases are replete with statements that an occupier of real property owes no such general duty of care to trespassers and bare licensees. With respect to adults we need not pause to determine how many of such statements constitute no more than a determination by the court that the defendant was not negligent at all or that the plaintiff assumed the risk or was guilty of contributory negligence as a matter of law. Clearly the fact that the plaintiff is a trespasser or a bare licensee is relevant to the question what precautions the reasonable man would take to protect him. * * * It cannot be denied, however, that in the case of adult trespassers and licensees the operation of no-duty rules has in many instances resulted in immunity for conduct that unreasonably endangered the plaintiff and was therefore negligent toward him. The dilemma of choosing between such cases and the rule set forth in section 1714 is not now before us. In the case of trespassing children a review of the better considered cases convinces me that it does not exist.

In Barrett v. Southern Pacific Company, 91 Cal. 296, 27 P. 666, this court followed the Supreme Court of the United States in Sioux City & Pacific Railroad Company v. Stout, 21 L.Ed. 745, 17 Wall (U.S.) 657, by solving the problem of the land occupier's liability to trespassing children for dangerous conditions maintained on the premises in terms of ordinary negligence principles. It pointed out that it could not recognize a rule that no duty was owed to trespassing children without departing from well-settled principles.

To recognize such a duty of care toward trespassing children does not impose an unreasonable burden on the defendant, and "it must be kept in mind that it requires nothing of the owner that a man of ordinary care and prudence would not do of his own volition, under like circumstances. Such a man would not willingly take up unreasonable burdens, nor vex himself with intolerable restrictions." Chicago, B. & Q. R. Co. v. Krayenbuhl, 65 Neb. 889, 91 N.W. 880, 882, 59 L.R.A. 920. "The owner of a thing dangerous and attractive to children is not always and universally liable for an injury to a child tempted by the attraction. His liability bears a relation to the character of the thing, whether natural and common, or artificial and uncommon; to the comparative ease or difficulty of preventing the danger without destroying or

impairing the usefulness of the thing; and, in short, *to the reasonableness and propriety of his own conduct, in view of all surrounding circumstances and conditions*. As to common dangers, existing in the order of nature, it is the duty of parents to guard and warn their children, and, failing to do so, they should not expect to hold others responsible for their own want of care. But, with respect to dangers specially created by the act of the owner, novel in character, attractive and dangerous to children, easily guarded and rendered safe, the rule is, as it ought to be, different; and such is the rule of the turntable cases, of the lumber-pile cases, and others of a similar character. But the owner of a thing dangerous and attractive to children is not always culpable, and therefore is not always liable for an injury to a child drawn into danger by the attraction. It is necessary to discriminate between the cases in which culpability does and does not exist." Beatty, C.J., on denial of rehearing in Peters v. Bowman, 115 Cal. 345, 356, 47 P. 113, 598, 599. Italics added.

As Chief Justice Beatty stated such culpability turns on "the reasonableness and propriety of" the defendant's "conduct, in view of all surrounding circumstances and conditions," or, in other words, it is determined by applying familiar negligence standards. [Citations omitted.] Section 339 of the Restatement of Torts has defined these standards by stating four conditions that must be satisfied to impose liability on a possessor of land for injury to trespassing children caused by a structure or other artificial condition on the land. Liability exists if (a) the place where the condition is maintained is one upon which the possessor knows or should know that such children are likely to trespass, and (b) the condition is one of which the possessor knows or should know and which he realizes or should realize as involving an unreasonable risk of death or serious bodily harm to such children, and (c) the children because of their youth do not discover the condition or realize the risk involved in intermeddling in it or in coming within the area made dangerous by it, and (d) the utility to the possessor of maintaining the condition is slight as compared to the risk to young children involved therein." This section was cited with approval in Melendez v. City of Los Angeles, 8 Cal.2d 741, 68 P.2d 971, and has frequently been held to be in accord with the law of this state.

In the present case the allegations of plaintiff's complaint satisfy the foregoing requirements. * * *

Despite the apparent sufficiency of these allegations, the majority opinion holds that the complaint does not state a cause of action on the ground that a sand pile does not constitute an attractive nuisance. This holding necessarily either departs from the general principles governing liability to trespassing children by adopting a special sand-pile rule, or is based on the tacit taking of judicial notice of facts with respect to children and sand piles contrary to those alleged in the complaint. It cannot be justified on either ground. There are no established precedents in this state dealing with sand piles, as there are with respect to bodies of water, that might, under the doctrine of stare decisis, justify adhering to a rigid rule without regard to the facts of the particular case. Precedent-wise we are free to follow the general principles governing liability to trespassing children. In purporting to do so, the majority opinion states that "sand piles duplicate the work of nature and are not uncommon," and that "The dangers connected with and inherent in a sand pile are obvious to everyone, even to a child old enough to be permitted by its parents to play unattended." There is no basis, however, for concluding that every sand pile

[handwritten: what is effect of taking "jud. notice"? Answ: deprives party of having jury decide! No cross-examination]

necessarily duplicates the work of nature or holding as a matter of law that no defendant should reasonably foresee that the dangers connected with and inherent in its sand pile are not obvious to children old enough to be permitted to play unattended. Although Anderson v. Reith-Riley Const. Co., 112 Ind.App. 170, 44 N.E.2d 184, supports the majority's position, the other cases cited in the majority opinion may be explained on their particular facts. Moreover, authority contrary to the Anderson case is not lacking.

[handwritten margin note: See Llewellyn p. 166]

Whether the maintenance of a sand pile can give rise to liability for harm to trespassing children must necessarily turn on the facts of the particular case. Children accustomed to playing in sand piles in their own yards may be totally unfamiliar with the hazards of a large pile maintained for industrial purposes. The very harmlessness of the familiar small pile may lull them into a sense of security. Nor are all children reared in such proximity to natural bluffs, cliffs, caves, and large sand dunes that they may be presumed to be familiar with them or to have been warned of their characteristics by their parents. Thus even if it could be assumed that the sand piles in this case duplicated natural sand piles, we could not judicially notice that plaintiff's child should necessarily have been aware of their hazards. Dean Prosser has pointed out that many "courts have said that the doctrine does not apply to common conditions, or to natural conditions of the land, or that it is limited to latent dangers, or to highly dangerous conditions, or to special and unusual conditions of modern industry; but all such statements appear to be made with reference to the particular case, and to be directed at nothing more than the existence of a recognizable and unreasonable risk of harm to children." (Prosser on Torts, 2d ed., § 76, p. 443.) Professors Harper and James state: "In addition to the probability of trespass, the dangerous condition of the premises must be produced by man, and either created or maintained by the occupier. This requirement stems from the law's reluctance to impose purely affirmative obligations on a man. It is sometimes said that man-made conditions which merely reproduce natural ones stand on the same footing. But if there is to be exemption here it must obviously rest on a different basis. That basis may often be found in the fact that children are likely to appreciate the risks of natural dangers, such as water, fire, or high places, so that these conditions are not highly dangerous to them. But this is not always the case. Some natural conditions have more concealed danger than a turntable, and if a landowner reproduces such a 'natural trap,' liability should not be excluded. Given affirmative arrangement of the premises, the touchstone of liability should be unreasonable probability of harm. All other criteria should be used as guides only, and not erected into rigid rules." (2 Harper and James, Law of Torts, § 27.5, pp. 1452–1453.)

[handwritten margin note: Harper & James]

[handwritten margin note: XXX]

The evil of creating rigid rules is demonstrated by some of the California cases dealing with bodies of water. Since ordinarily it may be presumed that children are aware of the dangers of drowning and since frequently the burden of adequately protecting children from that risk is out of proportion to it, usually the maintenance of a body of water should not give rise to liability. Blindly, however, the rule appropriate for the usual case has been extended to the unusual case unless there was something abnormal about the body of water itself. See, Sanchez v. East Contra Costa Irr. Co., 205 Cal. 515, 271 P. 1060; Long v. Standard Oil Co., supra, 92 Cal.App.2d 455, 207 P.2d 837. Thus recovery has been denied on the pleadings for

[handwritten margin note: "abnormal"]

the death of very young children who could not be presumed to appreciate the danger despite allegations sufficient to justify recovery under general principles and where the facts alleged did not indicate that the burden of protecting such children outweighed the risk to them. Wilford v. Little, 144 Cal.App.2d 477, 301 P.2d 282; Lake v. Ferrer, 139 Cal.App.2d 114, 293 P.2d 104. In nonwater cases, on the other hand, the error of rigid categorization has been recognized and avoided. Woods v. City and County of San Francisco, supra, 148 Cal.App.2d 958, 963–965, 307 P.2d 698; Morse v. Douglas, 107 Cal.App. 196, 200, 290 P. 465; Faylor v. Great Eastern Quicksilver Min. Co., 45 Cal.App. 194, 204, 187 P. 101. This conflict should be resolved by disapproving the former cases. In any event the error of those cases should not be extended. As stated in the Faylor case, "while matching cases is an interesting mental recreation, it is not by matching cases, but by the correct application of sound legal principles, that a case such as this is best determined. . . ." 45 Cal.App. at page 204, 187 P. at page 105. "The naming or labeling of a certain set of facts as being an 'attractive nuisance' case or a 'turntable' case has often led to undesirable conclusions. The inclination is then to find a *stare decisis* pigeonhole or category. The difficulty in such procedure is that too often the result of such a search is the reaching of irreconcilable conclusions. . . . [T]he only proper basis for decision in such cases dealing with personal injuries to children are the customary rules of ordinary negligence cases." Kahn v. James Burton Co., supra, 51 Ill.2d 614, 126 N.E.2d 836, 841.

I would reverse the judgment.

Gibson, C.J., and Carter, J., concur.

Rehearing denied.

———————

NOTES AND QUESTIONS

(1)   Justices McComb and Traynor[29] disagree in any number of ways. Try to pinpoint their disagreements. They involve (at least) three distinct areas: legal doctrine, judicial attitude, and the method or approach for determining liability. With regard to the last of these, consider the following chart:

McComb	Traynor
judge	jury
law	facts
rules	standards

What does this mean and does it help you describe the different methodologies the two justices endorse?

(2)   Justice McComb says: "Where the facts are undisputed, as in the instant case, it is a question of law whether or not the facts alleged fall within the scope of

———————

[29] Justice Traynor ranks as one of the great common-law jurists. It is fair to say that, with help from the New Jersey Supreme Court, the California Supreme Court, under Justice Traynor's tutelage, created much of the law of products liability. Look for his name in your casebooks.

the 'attractive nuisance' doctrine."

Review the many assertions of fact made by Justice McComb in his opinion. Which are "undisputed"? Why are they undisputed? Because of the procedural posture of the case — the trial court's sustaining of a demurrer to the complaint? Are there facts which Justice McComb claims to know that are not contained in the complaint? How does Justice McComb know these facts?

In particular, what does Justice McComb know about Johnny William Bass, Jr.'s knowledge about the dangers of sand piles? Might reasonable people differ about what 10-year-old Johnny knew? If so, why is this fact "undisputed"?

Might a jury rather than a trial judge or an appellate court be the more appropriate agency to determine Johnny's cognitive abilities, knowledge, and maturity?

Does Justice McComb claim to know what was in Johnny's mind because as a judge he knows what is in all children's minds? Does Justice McComb have some special understanding about every ten-year-old in the state of California? Could he? *NO*

(3) Justice Traynor begins by quoting section 1714 of the California Civil Code. And again we must ask: does section 1714 decide this case? Does it decide any particular case? If it postulates a principle or standard, rather than a rule, is it nevertheless helpful? *yes*

(4) Justice Traynor cites *Peters II* (the denial of rehearing) in seeming support *Discuss* of his opinion. Is that not rather problematic, to say the least? Then why does he do it? What is it in *Peters II* that is useful to him here?

but not al= ways (5) Referring to section 339 of the Restatement of Torts, Traynor says it has "frequently been held to be in accord with the law of this state." If so, does that mean that somewhere along the line *Peters* has been quietly overruled? Can courts "quietly," that is, without ever expressly saying so ("sub silentio," as the phrase goes), overrule a case? Is it desirable to do so? Shouldn't a court at least have to say something on this order: "The matter does not appear to [us] now as it appears to have appeared to [us] then?"[30]

In any event, could any of the courts referred to by Justice Traynor have overruled *Peters*? *NO*

(6) On a different occasion, Justice Traynor commented: *Read: Nature of the J.P.*

> A generation ago Mr. Justice Cardozo reflected from experience that the judicial process had recurringly to be creative. For recurringly it happened that a judge failed to find the amiable *ratio decidendi* supposedly awaiting discovery among the reeds of precedent to swaddle a foundling case becomingly and set its cries at rest. Since he could not let it cry forever, he must needs swaddle it with some inventive covering suitable for the occasion and durable enough to serve the future. Every basic precedent

---

[30] Baron Bramwell in Andrews v. Stytrap, 26 L.T. R. (N. S.) 704, 706 (Ex. 1872), quoted in Ruggero J. Aldisert, *Precedent: What It Is and What It Isn't; When Do We Kiss It and When Do We Kill It?*, 17 PEPPERDINE L. REV. 605, 630 (1990). Baron Bramwell was actually speaking in the first person singular.

see Kelly — not entirely
Bart +

was thus once made up out of whole cloth woven by a judge.

There is now wide agreement that a judge can and should participate creatively in the development of the common law. Yet each time he does so, he must reckon with the ancient suspicion that creativeness is a disturbing excess of skill, at odds with circumspection, darkly menacing the stability of the law. Actually, the creative decision is circumspect in the extreme, for it reflects the most careful consideration of all the arguments for a conventional solution and all the circumstances that now render such a solution so unrealistic as to doom its serviceability for future cases. * * *

cf. Weinstein

The real concern is not the remote possibility of too many creative opinions but their continuing scarcity. The growth of the law, far from being unduly accelerated by judicial boldness, is unduly hampered by a judicial lethargy that masks itself as judicial dignity with the tacit approval of an equally lethargic bar.[31]

In his dissent, is Justice Traynor making something "out of whole cloth," and what, exactly, is it?

Dissents

(7) *Knight* is the case we meant when, in discussing briefing, we said the dissent can be more important than the court's opinion. The questions that follow all deal with dissents.

(a) The court's opinion speaks to the parties, to the lawyers in the case, to the legal community and to the community, or parts of it, at large. To whom does the dissenter speak?

According to Cardozo:

The voice of the majority may be that of force triumphant, content with the plaudits of the hour, and recking little of the morrow. The dissenter speaks to the future, and his voice is pitched to a key that will carry through the years. Read some of the great dissents * * * and feel after the cooling time of the better part of a century the glow and fire of a faith that was content to bide its hour. The prophet and martyr do not see the hooting throng. Their eyes are fixed on the eternities.[32]

Justice Rehnquist dissented in *Roe v. Wade* (the 1973 decision holding that the Constitution protects a women's right to choose to have an abortion) and voted to overrule it throughout his remaining 23 years on the bench. Was he a "prophet and martyr" who bravely resisted the "hooting throng" of pro-choice advocates?

On the less exalted plain of "attractive nuisance," to whom was Justice Traynor speaking?

(b) Consider whether dissent is

disastrous because disunity cancels the impact of monolithic solidarity on which the authority of a bench of judges so largely depends. People become

---

[31] Roger Traynor, *Comment on Paper Delivered by Charles D. Breitel*, in Legal Institutions Today and Tomorrow 51–52 (Monrad Paulsen ed., 1959).

[32] Benjamin N. Cardozo, Law and Literature and Other Essays and Addresses 36 (1931).

aware that the answer to the controversy is uncertain, even to those best qualified, and they feel free, unless especially docile, to ignore it if they are reasonably sure that they will not be caught. The reasoning of both sides is usually beyond their comprehension, and is apt to appear as verbiage designed to sustain one side of a dispute that in the end might be decided either way, which is generally the truth.

So said Judge Learned Hand.[33] Would you counter that "monolithic solidarity" might obstruct legal change; that "lawless persons will defy the law whether it is laid down by a court speaking through a 9 to 0 majority or a court speaking through a 5 to 4 majority"; and that judicial controversies *cannot* "generally be decided either way — that is, honestly"?[34]

If you had owned a pool in California at the time and had thought about your potential liability, what significance would you have attached to *Knight's* being a 4 to 3 decision? And to the fact that one of the four was a member of the unanimous three-judge panel in *Sanchez*? (Noticing such a fact is one of the things that Llewellyn meant by "reading.")

(c) If dissent cannot be repressed, should the dissenter at least dissent quietly, without, that is, issuing an opinion?

[W]here significant and deeply held disagreement exists, members of the Court have a responsibility to articulate it. This is why, when I dissent, I always say why I am doing so. Simply to say, "I dissent," I will not do.[35]

Justice Brandeis, on the other hand, often withheld issuing dissenting opinions "replete with the most exquisite detail of citation and the most comprehensive of footnotes."

Brandeis was a great institutional man. He realized that the Court is not the place for solo performances, that random dissents and concurrences weaken the institutional impact of the Court and handicap it in the doing of its fundamental job. Dissents and concurrences need to be saved for major matters if the Court is not to appear indecisive.[36]

(d) Consider Canon 19 of the Canons of Judicial Ethics:

It is of high importance that judges constituting a court of last resort should use effort and self-restraint to promote solidarity of conclusion and the consequent influence of judicial decision. A judge should not yield to pride of opinion, or value more highly his individual reputation than that of the court to which he should be loyal. Except in case of conscientious

---

[33] LEARNED HAND, THE BILL OF RIGHTS 72–73 (1958).

[34] Michael Musmanno, HARVARD LAW SCHOOL RECORD, Mar. 1958. Justice Musmanno, who sat on the Pennsylvania Supreme Court from 1952 to 1968, is a colorful figure whose battle for publication of his dissenting opinions is recounted in Michael A. Musmanno, *Dissenting Opinions*, 60 DICK. L. REV. 139 (1956).

[35] William J. Brennan, Jr., *In Defense of Dissents*, 37 HASTINGS L.J. 427, 435 (1986).

[36] John P. Frank, *Book Review*, 10 J. LEGAL EDUC. 401, 404 (1958) (reviewing Alexander M. Bickel, The Unpublished Opinions of Mr. Justice Brandeis (1957)).

about how no good deed goes unpunished

difference of opinion on fundamental principle, dissenting opinions should be discouraged in courts of last resort.

(e) Finally, we want to highlight this statement by Justice Traynor:

> There are no established precedents in this state dealing with sand piles, as there are with respect to bodies of water, that might, under the doctrine of stare decisis, justify adhering to a rigid rule without regard to the facts of the particular case.

Is this a disingenuous or misleading statement? If so, why? This is a difficult question, demanding that you think about what precedent and stare decisis mean, before you attempt to answer. We will return to it in Chapter 5.

The case about $25.00 ? AND

REYNOLDS v. WILLSON
51 Cal. 2d 94, 331 P.2d 48 (1958)

SHENK, Justice.

j.n.o.v.

This is an appeal by the defendants from an order denying their motion for a judgment notwithstanding the verdict in an action for personal injuries.

2 yo 3 m.

The plaintiff is Keith Reynolds, a boy two years and three months of age at the time of the accident which occurred on January 31, 1953. He is the youngest son of Dr. and Mrs. William J. Reynolds, Jr., who were living at the time with their family of four children at the southeast corner of Wilson Avenue and Buckingham Way in the Fig Garden residential district in the City of Fresno. The defendants, Mr. and Mrs. Melville E. Willson, occupied their residence at the southwest corner of Van Ness Avenue and Buckingham Way. The homes of the two families occupy the full frontage of the block on Buckingham Way between Wilson and Van Ness Avenues with a vacant lot between the houses. The defendants' lot faces on Van Ness Avenue with a frontage of 135 feet, and extends 285 feet on Buckingham Way. Their residence was built in 1930 in what was then a sparsely settled subdivision. The area has since developed into a well occupied section with some 30 families residing in the immediate vicinity. At the time of the accident, approximately 50 or 60 children ranging in age from two years to teenage resided in the neighborhood. An elementary school is located a few blocks away. The defendants had occupied this property since April 1951.

D= 1930 built; 1951 Ds moved in accident 1953

At the rear of their property the defendants maintained a swimming pool. It is about 20 by 40 feet in dimensions and in depth is graduated from about 3 feet on its north side to 9 feet 4 inches on its south side. The shallow portion is toward Buckingham Way with steps leading down from ground level in the northwest corner. A stucco wall extends most of the way around the defendants' property. There is a 10 1/2 foot opening in the wall on the Buckingham Way side in the garage area with gate bolts on each side of the opening but no gate was then maintained. A concrete pavement forms an apron in front of the garage and leads into a walk-way toward the residence and into a walk-way to dressing rooms back of the garage. Buckingham Way is not a through street, is relatively free from traffic and children were accustomed to resort to it for recreation. The swimming

pool was visible therefrom by children and adults through the open gateway. At the time of the accident the cost of installing a gate in the opening in the stucco wall was not more than $25.

The Willsons and the Reynolds were neighborly and invitations to use the swimming pool were extended by the Willsons to the Reynolds and their children. The Reynolds took advantage of the invitation and used the pool on many occasions. Other children in the neighborhood enjoyed a like privilege during the swimming season which ended in September. A general condition, attached by the defendants to the use of the pool, was to the effect that when small children were to use the pool or play in the adjoining area, an adult should be present. The plaintiff was taken to the pool when adults were present during the swimming seasons of 1951 and 1952. On at least one occasion Mrs. Willson observed the plaintiff making his way toward the pool unattended and she returned him to his home.

At the close of the 1952 season the water in the pool was only partially drained. At the close of previous seasons it had been fully drained. Mr. Willson testified that the pool was left in a partially filled condition at the close of the 1952 season in order to prevent his and other children from playing therein and injuring themselves on the concrete surface. At the time of the accident water covered the concrete floor about to the base of the steps at the shallow end of the pool. Near the center of the floor was an abrupt decline to deeper water. In the winter months just prior to the accident the pool, as thus partially filled, had accumulated dirt, decayed leaves from nearby trees, and other decomposed material. Algae and other substances had accumulated and settled on the concrete surface beneath the water, causing it to become slippery when stepped upon.

On the day of the accident Mrs. Reynolds left in the early morning with her three older children for Yosemite Valley. Dr. Reynolds left for his office a little later. The plaintiff child stayed at home in the care of a maid-housekeeper. She put the child down in his room for his nap about 3:30 in the afternoon. When he was supposedly asleep she engaged in a telephone conversation in another room. In about 15 minutes she returned to the boy's room and found him missing. Apparently he had climbed out of a window. She searched the home and neighborhood but failed to find him. Dr. Reynolds returned to his home about 4 p.m. He joined in the search. He entered the defendants' yard through the opening in the wall on Buckingham Way which led to the swimming pool and saw the boy lying face down in the water. He went into the pool to rescue the child. Because of the slippery condition of the bottom, he was unable to carry him to the steps. As soon as possible artificial respiration was administered. Adrenalin was injected directly into the boy's heart. An ambulance was called and upon its arrival oxygen was administered, and the boy was taken to a hospital. He was unconscious for five or six days and at the end of 10 days was paralyzed. Since that time he has made a partial recovery but is afflicted with the symptoms of cerebral palsy and his brain and nervous system are permanently damaged.

The plaintiff, through his father as guardian ad litem, sued for damages on behalf of the child and obtained a verdict in the sum of $50,000. The defendants do not complain of the amount.

(*) i.e., ∏ played it safe w/ trap theory

3 theories

The action was brought apparently on three theories of liability; first, on the theory outlined in section 339 of the Restatement of the Law of Torts * * *.

The second was on the theory that if section 339 is not applicable to the facts of the case or should not be followed, another basis of liability was the physical condition of the pool, maintained as it was at the time of the accident as constituting a peril in the nature of a "trap" as that term has come to be known to the law of this state.

The third theory was that under the facts the defendants owed to the plaintiff the duty of ordinary care as an invitee on the premises.

The action was commenced and the litigation was conducted throughout on behalf of the plaintiff, by allegation, proof, argument to the jury and on appeal, on all three theories, and from the standpoint that the liability of the defendants depended on questions of fact to be determined by the jury.

As noted, the jury returned a verdict in favor of the plaintiff and the only question to be determined on the appeal is whether there is sufficient competent evidence in the record to support the verdict on any of the theories relied upon. * * *

It is contended by the plaintiff that the theory of liability prescribed by section 339 of the Restatement of the Law of Torts * * * is applicable to the facts of the case; that the conditions therein required to impose such liability have been met, and that such a theory is not inconsistent with, but is in conformity with the law of this state.

To meet the requirements of section 339 of the Restatement of the Law of Torts, it appears that the defendants were the possessors of the land; that the swimming pool was a structure artificially constructed thereon; that the plaintiff was an infant of tender years and a trespasser at the time of the accident as contemplated by the section; that the nature of the structure was such that the defendants knew that children were likely to trespass thereon; that the condition in which the pool was maintained at the time was such that the defendants realized or should have realized it involved an unreasonable risk of death or serious bodily harm to children[37]; that because of his youth the plaintiff did not discover the condition of the pool or realize the risk involved in coming within the area made dangerous by it, and that the cost of making it safe against children was slight as compared to the risk to young children trespassing thereon.[38]

the $25 again)

With the limitations placed upon the reviewing court in the consideration of the evidence on an appeal of this sort it must be concluded that the conditions

CRUX OF CASE!

[37] The defendant Melville E. Willson testified that after the close of the 1952 swimming season he realized that the condition in which he had left the pool after the former season was unsatisfactory even for the safety of his own children, so he decided to try to make it safer by partially filling it. This he did in December, the month before the accident happened. It was after the pool had been thus partially filled that the algae accumulated under the shallow water near the steps.

[38] It was in evidence that the aperture in the fence through which the plaintiff gained access to the pool could have been closed or otherwise made safe from entrance by children at an expenditure of about $25.

the crucial paragraph of the case

necessary to establish liability on the theory of section 339 have been met.

The defendants maintain that if this be so and liability thus attaches under their situation the doctrine of attractive nuisance will apply to every possessor of land maintaining a private swimming pool. But such is not the case. It is established in this state that a private swimming pool is not an attractive nuisance as a matter of law. [Citations omitted.] The manner of its maintenance and use may, however, be such as to impose the duty of ordinary care on the possessor toward children of tender years notwithstanding they may technically occupy the position of trespassers at the time. That is the theory of liability imposed by section 339 whether the structure maintained be a swimming pool or some other artificial structure maintained upon his property.

§ 002

still tho'

The plaintiff does not rely solely upon the liability of section 339 but takes the position that the verdict is also sufficiently supported on both of the other two theories. With this we must agree at least as to the second theory.

The second theory is that the possessor of land is liable for the negligent maintenance on his premises of an artificial instrumentality which might constitute a dangerous contrivance in the nature of a "trap" and be encountered by children of tender years incapable of contributory negligence, and who are known by the possessor to enter or would be expected to enter his premises as trespassers. Such a case was Sanchez v. East Contra Costa Irr. Co., 1928, 205 Cal. 515, 271 P. 1060. * * *

"Trap"

In the present case the jury was entitled to find that when in December the defendants partially filled the pool with water nearly to the steps in an endeavor to make it safer for their own children they had in effect made it more attractive to young children such as the plaintiff and that by maintaining the pool in its then condition they were guilty of maintaining a trap as to the plaintiff and responsible to him under the doctrine of ordinary care.

It should be said here, that it is the generally accepted rule as recognized by comment (b) to section 339, that the duty of the possessor does not extend to dangerous conditions on the land which are obvious even to children, such as the usual risks of fire, water, falling from a height and the like (see Prosser on Torts, 2d ed. 1955, 441-442). When however, there are, in addition to the usual risks, concealed dangers not obvious, especially to children, the trap theory may be applied.

like what?

In view of the fact that the order must be affirmed for other reasons, it is unnecessary to determine the extent to which the defendants owed a duty to the plaintiff as an alleged invitee. * * *

[The court proceeded to describe seriatim ten separate California appellate opinions, addressing the difference between obvious dangers and hidden traps.]

Knight v. Kaiser Co., 1957, 48 Cal.2d 778, 312 P.2d 1089, does not preclude the application of section 339 of the Restatement of the Law of Torts to the present case. In that case, the decedent, a boy of ten, was suffocated when one of the defendant's sand piles collapsed on him. The sand was stored on the defendant's private property along with other building material, machinery and supplies. The

Knight

"it was decided on a demurrer. Not "under the facts"..."

discussion in that case emphasizes the obvious nature of the hazard involved in playing or digging in a sand pile. * * * It was held, consistent with section 339 of the Restatement of the Law of Torts, that the hazard of playing in the sand pile is an open and obvious one for which the possessor could not, under the facts of that case, be held liable.

From the foregoing cases and others which might be cited, it is apparent that recovery is granted or denied depending on the facts of each case. Where the elements of section 339 have been fulfilled or the existence of a trap has been sufficiently shown recovery has ordinarily been awarded on the basis of want of ordinary care on the part of the defendant. Where, as in the cases relied on by the defendant, one or more elements of section 339 have failed of proof and no evidence of a trap or other basis of liability proved, recovery has been denied. Recovery in the present case is consistent with the established law of this state.

The order is affirmed.

GIBSON, C.J., and CARTER and TRAYNOR, JJ., concur.

SPENCE, Justice (dissenting).

It has been said that "hard cases make bad law." Such appears to be the situation here; but this case is a hard one only in the sense that a young child has suffered an unfortunate injury. The question involved, however, is whether liability for that unfortunate injury was properly imposed upon the defendant landowners under the circumstances presented by the record. I am of the opinion that such liability was not properly imposed, and that the majority opinion sustains an order which cannot be sustained under the settled law of this state.

The fundamental question presented is whether there was a violation of any duty owed by the defendant landowners toward the trespassing child. This question in turn depends upon the nature and extent of any duty owed by the defendant landowners toward the trespassing child with respect to the condition of the landowners' premises.

The answer to this fundamental question cannot be determined by a mere reference to section 1714 of the Civil Code, which provides in general terms that liability may ordinarily be predicated upon "want of ordinary care." The application of that section is not universal, as it depends upon the relationship of the parties. Traditionally, as will be seen from the authorities hereinafter cited, the duty of a landowner toward a trespasser with respect to the condition of the premises has been held by this court, and practically every other court, to be definitely less than the general duty to exercise ordinary care, which last mentioned duty is owed by the landowner to the business visitor. There is sound reason for this differentiation in the nature of the duty owed, and it is firmly embedded in our law. It is neither an anomaly nor a mere remnant of ancient law. * * *

Heretofore, three members of this court have expressed their dissatisfaction with the settled law of this state on the subject of the duty owed by the landowner to trespassing children. Their views are set forth in the dissenting opinion of Mr. Justice Traynor in Knight v. Kaiser Co., 48 Cal.2d 778, 785–792, 312 P.2d 1089.

XY did π lu k v k "fail of proof"?

They there advocated "disapproving the former cases." 48 Cal.2d at page 792, 312 P.2d at page 1097. While I do not agree that the numerous prior decisions should be disapproved, Mr. Justice Traynor made a forthright approach to the problem in that dissent. The dissenting justices in Knight v. Kaiser Co., supra, have now joined in the opinion prepared by Mr. Justice Shenk. That opinion purports to distinguish, rather than to disapprove, the prior decisions in which liability has been denied, but I am of the opinion that no tenable distinction can be made. In other words, the majority opinion here cannot be reconciled with the prior decisions, and the labored but futile attempt of the majority opinion to bring them into harmony has the unfortunate result of leaving the law in hopeless confusion.

Before discussing the applicable authorities, a brief statement should be made concerning the record in this case. The material facts are not in dispute. With respect to the status of the child, there is no question but that the child was a trespasser. * * *

Condition of pool!!

With respect to the condition of the pool, the exhibits and all the testimony show that the water was clear and that the bottom of the pool, together with the small amount of leaves, silt and algae thereon, was plainly visible. Thus the condition shown involved nothing more than the common, obvious condition which is ordinarily incident to any body of water, natural or artificial.

The situation in this case is therefore controlled by the rules set forth in the numerous cases denying liability for injuries to trespassing children incurred by encountering the common, obvious hazards incident to such bodies of water. * * *

The majority opinion concedes that "It is established in this state that a private swimming pool is not an attractive nuisance as a matter of law." That opinion nevertheless bases its affirmance upon its conclusion that the evidence was sufficient to justify the imposition of liability either (1) under the theory embodied in section 339 of the Restatement of the Law of Torts, or (2) under the so-called "trap" theory. I cannot agree. Where the evidence is uncontradicted, the question of the sufficiency of the evidence to bring the condition within any exception to the general rule limiting the liability of the landowner to trespassers has been treated by the above-mentioned authorities as a question of law for the court. Here the evidence was uncontradicted. There was no showing of any condition presenting anything but the common, obvious danger ordinarily incident to any body of water. It therefore follows as a matter of law under the cited authorities that liability was improperly imposed.

Considering first the so-called "trap" theory, * * * liability has never been imposed in this state under the "trap" theory, or any other theory, for any common, obvious condition incident to a body of water, natural or artificial. On the contrary, liability under the "trap" theory can only be based upon a "hidden danger" (65 C.J.S., Negligence, § 38, pp. 503–504) or a "concealed danger" (35 Cal. Jur.2d, Negligence, § 100, p. 609). * * *

The Sanchez case was later distinguished by this court in Melendez v. City of Los Angeles, supra, 8 Cal.2d 741, 68 P.2d 971, where liability was denied. This court there affirmed a judgment entered following the sustaining of a demurrer without leave to amend on the ground that neither the "attractive nuisance"

doctrine nor the "trap" doctrine was applicable. There it was alleged that the two young boys were drowned in an artificial pool where the "deep hole in this pool was completely concealed by the muddy condition of the water in the pool." This court * * * held the [lower' court's] decision to be consistent with the Sanchez case on the ground that the "concealed hole was not an artificial contrivance or appliance maintained by the owner. . . ." This court further said with respect to the Sanchez case, "In the latter case there was a concealed contrivance which no one would suspect." * * *

Turning now to the consideration of section 339 of the Restatement of the Law of Torts, the majority opinion appears to give that section the force of a legislative enactment nullifying our prior decisions, and extending the exceptions to the general rule to conditions other than those falling within the so-called "attractive nuisance" exception or the "trap" exception, as defined by our decisions. Of course, the Restatement does not have the force of a legislative enactment and in any event, section 339, properly construed, has never heretofore been interpreted by this court as declaring a rule purporting to extend those exceptions. On the contrary, reference has been made to that section in our decisions in which liability has been denied (Knight v. Kaiser Co., supra, 48 Cal.2d 778, 312 P.2d 1089; Melendez v. City of Los Angeles, supra, 8 Cal.2d 741, 68 P.2d 971), and the section has been treated as establishing tests consistent with such decisions. The decisions have further stressed the harshness of any exceptions to the general rule limiting the liability of the landowner to the trespasser and have cautioned against the extension of such exceptions. Heedless of that caution, the majority opinion now has apparently given section 339 its broadest possible interpretation and thereby sanctions the extension of the heretofore well-defined exceptions into ill-defined fields. Any such extension to cover the situation here is obviously inconsistent with our prior decisions as well as with the language employed in the opinions.

The background of section 339, which throws some light upon its proper interpretation, is considered at length in Prosser on Torts, 2d Ed., pp. 432 et seq. * * * Dean Prosser's interpretation of section 339 appears to be in line with the above-mentioned authorities denying liability for injuries sustained by trespassing children in encountering the common, obvious dangers of bodies of water, natural and artificial.

From this historical background, it seems evident that section 339 was intended merely to follow the rules generally adopted by the courts of those jurisdictions, including California, which had theretofore recognized the so-called "attractive nuisance" exception; and to formalize and rationalize that exception. * * *

This court adopted the "attractive nuisance" exception at an early date, but it has not heretofore attempted to interpret section 339 of the Restatement of the Law of Torts or to discuss definitively its relation to our decisions. * * * The opportunity is now presented for this court clearly to define its position, and I think that it should grasp that opportunity. This the majority opinion has failed to do. It states that "the conditions necessary to establish liability on the theory of section 339 have been met"; it makes a futile attempt to distinguish the prior decisions; it declares that "recovery is granted or denied depending on the facts of each case"; and it makes the bald statement that "Recovery in the present case is consistent

with the established law of this state." In my opinion, the majority opinion will serve only to confuse rather than to clarify the settled law in this important field.
* * *

The necessity for clarification by this court of the meaning of section 339 is apparent from a reading of Copfer v. Golden, 135 Cal.App.2d 623, 288 P.2d 90, upon which the District Court of Appeal relied in its opinion in the present case. Reynolds v. Willson, Cal.App., 308 P.2d 464. The Copfer case did not involve a body of water, but its reasoning shows that section 339 was there construed in a manner which would equate its requirements merely with section 1714 of the Civil Code. There the injury to the trespassing child occurred when it fell from a trailer parked on the premises of the owner. There is nothing in that opinion to indicate that the trailer was anything other than a lawful type of trailer presenting only the common, obvious risks which might be presented by any type of trailer upon which a child might see fit to climb. For aught that appears, it was the type of vehicle which could have been lawfully parked upon the streets without incurring liability to children who might have climbed upon and fallen from it. Nevertheless, the court there sustained a judgment imposing liability where the injury occurred when the trespassing child climbed upon and fell from the trailer while parked on the owner's property. In my opinion, the court there placed an erroneous interpretation upon section 339 and further, reached the wrong result on the facts even under its own erroneous interpretation of the section. There was no petition for hearing by this court. I believe that this court should disapprove Copfer v. Golden, supra, and should clearly enunciate this court's interpretation of section 339 for the guidance of the bench and bar. That case and its interpretation of section 339 was made the cornerstone of the opinion of the District Court of Appeal in the present case, when it declared that "The rule in California is stated in Copfer v. Golden, 135 Cal.App.2d 623, 288 P.2d 90, 92." (Reynolds v. Willson, supra, Cal.App., 308 P.2d 464, 468.) It is the only case cited in the briefs or by the District Court of Appeal which has any tendency to support the conclusion reached by the majority, and yet the majority opinion fails expressly to approve or disapprove, or even to mention it.

Of the cases which are cited in the majority opinion, all are in accord with the views expressed in this dissent, and none lend support to the majority. * * *

While this court unquestionably has the power to disapprove prior decisions where it finds compelling reasons for so doing, it likewise has the duty to exercise that power sparingly to the end that the law may possess to a high degree the desirable attributes of certainty and stability. Furthermore, if compelling reasons do appear to this court for disapproving settled rules of law, then this court has the further duty of expressly stating such disapproval and of clearly declaring the new rules which are to replace the old. Those duties cannot be met by declaring in vague terms "that recovery is granted or denied depending on the facts of each case" or by the employment of reasoning which is couched in obscure words and phrases. The bench and bar will be compelled to speculate on the answer to the question: Has this court now departed from the settled law of this state, and if not, what is the effect of the majority opinion? Despite the declaration of the majority that the imposition of liability here is "consistent with the established law of this

state," it fails to sustain that thesis, and it leaves the answer to the above question shrouded in doubt. * * *

In conclusion, it must be remembered that just as happened here, a tragic accident will occasionally occur. But accidents to children resulting from common, obvious conditions are no more unusual when they are trespassing on the land of others without right than they are when playing on their own premises or on public property where they have a right to be. Danger and reasonable risks of harm are present everywhere. Clearly the play apparatus customarily found in public school yards and in public playgrounds, as well as the conditions found around lakes and ponds in public parks, are all "attractive" to children and present dangers and risks of harm at least equal to those presented by any condition which existed on the premises of the defendant landowners. Nevertheless, all such common, obvious dangers have been consistently held to be insufficient to impose liability. I would adhere to the settled rules and reverse the order.

SCHAUER and McCOMB, JJ., concur.

––––––––––

NOTES AND QUESTIONS

(1) "This is an appeal by the defendants from an order denying their motion for a judgment notwithstanding the verdict . . . ," a motion now called the *renewal of a motion for judgment as a matter of law.*[39] Explain what the defendants are arguing.

(2) "As noted, the jury returned a verdict in favor of the plaintiff and *the only question to be determined on the appeal* is whether there is sufficient competent evidence in the record to support the verdict on any of the theories relied upon." Prior to reading this, would you not have thought that "the question to be determined on the appeal is whether landowners who maintain a pool on their premises shall be under a duty of care toward trespassing children (young children?)"?

Explain the difference between these two formulations of "the question to be determined on the appeal."

(3) Justice Shenk's change of mind or heart accounts for the different outcomes in *Knight* and *Reynolds*, decided a year and four months apart. (Do you suppose it was Justice Traynor's dissent in *Knight* that persuaded him? Then again, Justice Shenk voted to let the parents of the drowned child recover in *Sanchez*.) Is it "just" for a legal system to take perhaps even drastic turns in the rules of the game because of one man or one woman?

(4) In California, the Chief Justice assigns the task of writing the court's opinion. Here Chief Justice Gibson apparently chose Justice Shenk. Do you suppose Justice Traynor would have written a different opinion (than the one Justice Shenk wrote) had he been the author? What might Justice Shenk have done then? What

––––––––––

[39] See text accompanying note 41 in Chapter 1.

effect would that have had on the "holding" of the case?

Incidentally, the mechanism for assigning opinions varies from court to court. The California Supreme Court is unusual in having the Chief Justice assign the opinion even if he is in dissent. In the United States Supreme Court, the Chief Justice assigns the opinion if he is in the majority; otherwise the senior Justice who is in the majority makes the assignment. On the New York Court of Appeals, opinion assignments are by lot. Think about why these different approaches might have been adopted. Which makes the most sense?

(5) Do people rely on "the law" — including precedential cases?

> Practically in its application to actual affairs, for most of the laity, the Law, except for a few crude notions of the equity involved in some of its general principles, is all *ex post facto*. When a man marries, or enters into a partnership, or buys a piece of land, or engages in any other transaction, he has the vaguest possible idea of the Law governing the situation, and with our complicated system of Jurisprudence, it is impossible it should be otherwise. If he delayed to make a contract or do an act until he understood exactly all the legal consequences it involved, the contract would never be made or the act done. Now the Law of which a man has no knowledge is the same to him as if it did not exist.[40]

Is it the laity with whom we are concerned?   *The lawyers?*

And see also Cardozo:

> The picture of the bewildered litigant lured into a course of action by the false light of a decision, only to meet ruin when the light is extinguished and the decision overruled, is for the most part a figment of excited brains. The only rules there is ever any thought of changing are those that are invoked by injustice after the event to shelter and intrench itself. In the rarest instances, if ever, would conduct have been different if the rule had been known and the change foreseen. At times the change means the imposition of a bill of costs that might otherwise have been saved. That is a cheap price to pay for the uprooting of an ancient wrong.[41]

Then again:

> The doctrine [that tort liability for injuries suffered by third parties on unsafe leased premises is confined to the lessee and does not extend to the landlord], wise or unwise in its origin, has worked itself by common acquiescence into the tissues of our law. It is too deeply imbedded to be superseded or ignored. Hardly a day goes by in our great centers of population but it is applied by judges and juries in cases great and small. Countless tenants, suing for personal injuries and proving nothing more than the breach of an agreement, have been dismissed without a remedy in adherence to the authority of *Schick v. Fleischhauer* and *Kushes v. Ginsberg*. Countless visitors of tenants and members of a tenant's family

---

[40] JOHN CHIPMAN GRAY, THE NATURE AND SOURCES OF LAW 100 (1921).

[41] BENJAMIN N. CARDOZO, GROWTH OF THE LAW 122 (1924).

have encountered a like fate. If there is no remedy for the tenant, there is none for visitors or relatives present in the tenant's right.[42]

(6) The *Reynolds* decision "stands on more than one leg," as the saying goes. Does being a centipede make a case a stronger, more stable precedent than being a flamingo? Or is the effect just the reverse: the more "legs," the weaker the precedential value of the case?

(7) Justice Shenk says the defendant asserts that Section 339 of the Restatement is not applicable; "that the cases in this state are inconsistent with the declaration of liability and duties stated in that section. *Upon examination it is found that this is not so.*" (Emphasis added.) He then buttresses this latter statement with Peters *v.* Bowman; *Melendez v. City of Los Angeles*; and *Knight v. Kaiser.* In none of these cases (nor in any of the others he discusses) did the plaintiff recover. How, then, can Justice Shenk possibly say "this [the non-applicability of sec. 339] is not so"? Did not Llewellyn tell us: *"no rule can be the ratio decidendi from which the actual judgment * * * does not follow?"* (Emphasis his).

(8) Justice Spence has two separate quarrels with the court: one is over what the substantive rule ought to be in cases of this kind and the other concerns how the majority is going about its business. In which of these is he more convincing and why?

(9) A private swimming pool — is it or is it not an "attractive nuisance"? Could a defendant still prevail in a pool case in which a young child has come to harm on a motion to dismiss for failure to state a claim upon which relief can be granted? After all, Justice Shenk says: "It is established in this state that a private swimming pool is not an attractive nuisance as a matter of law."

GARCIA v. SOOGIAN
52 Cal.2d 107, 338 P.2d 433 (1959)

GIBSON, Chief Justice.

In this action, which was tried by the court sitting without a jury, plaintiff recovered damages for injuries she sustained while playing on defendants' lot, and defendants have appealed.

The accident happened about 8 p.m., when it was getting dark. Plaintiff, who was 12 years and 8 months old, had trespassed on defendants' lot in order to play a form of hide-and-seek with other children. She cut her ankle when, running in pursuit of a playmate, she attempted to jump over a stack of prefabricated building panels containing windows, failed to clear the stack, and landed on top, her foot crashing through the glass. The panels over which she jumped were part of building materials stored on the lot by defendants for the purpose of erecting several prefabricated houses. The materials had been placed about 120 to 150 feet back from the street. The panels with glass, each weighing about 200 pounds, had been stacked in firm, orderly piles which were from 24 to 30 inches high, 8 feet long

---

[42] Cullings v. Goetz, 256 N.Y. 287, 176 N.E. 397, 398 (1931) (Cardozo, J.).

and at least 4 feet wide. Plaintiff's sister, who was one of the children on the lot at the time of the accident, testified that she saw the stacks that evening and that none of them were covered. There was other testimony that at least two of the piles were uncovered. During working hours defendants, who were engaged in building at a nearby site, watched the lot and ordered children away, and, in the absence of defendants, a man who lived in the vicinity did the same on their behalf whenever he saw children on the lot.

The sole question presented on this appeal is whether the judgment is supported by the evidence.

* * * The rule set forth in section 339 [of the Restatement of Torts] has been adopted as the law of this state. Courtell v. McEachen, 51 Cal.2d 448, 334 P.2d 870; Reynolds v. Willson, 51 Cal.2d 94, 331 P.2d 48.

It is apparent that the application of this rule depends upon a number of variable factors. The question of liability must be decided in the light of all the circumstances and not by arbitrarily placing cases in rigid categories on the basis of the type of condition involved without giving due consideration to the effect of all the factors in a particular situation. There is no inflexible rule which would exclude liability in every case involving building materials or buildings under construction, and each such case must be judged on its own facts. * * *

The circumstance that a condition giving rise to injury is common in character does not necessarily exclude liability. Of course, if a dangerous condition is common, children are more likely to be aware of the risk than if the condition is unusual, but it does not follow that common conditions can, under no circumstances, give rise to dangers which are not obvious to children. What is important is not whether conditions are common in character but whether their dangers are fully understood by children. In discussing the duty of care owed by the possessor of land in connection with the ability of children to appreciate the risk presented, the Restatement says, in comment (b) to section 339, that the duty extends to dangerous conditions "which, though observable by adults, are likely not to be observed by children or which contain risks the full extent of which an adult would realize but which are beyond the imperfect realization of children." The duty, of course, does not extend to "those conditions the existence of which is obvious even to children and the risk of which is fully realized by them." Rest., Torts, § 339, comment (b). The further statement in comment (b) that the limitation on the duty operates to remove liability with respect to "the normal, necessary and usual implements which are essential to [the land's] normal use," appears in a sentence which, when taken as a whole, refers only to those situations in which children, knowing the danger of the implements as fully as adults, use them "in a spirit of bravado."[43]

---

[43] The sentence in question reads: "This limitation of the possessor's liability to conditions dangerous to children, because of their inability to appreciate their surroundings or to realize the risk involved therein, frees the possessor of land from the danger of liability to which he would otherwise be subjected by maintaining on the land the normal, necessary and usual implements which are essential to its normal use but which reckless children can use to their harm in a spirit of bravado or to gratify some other childish desire and with as full a perception of the risks which they are running as though they were adults." Rest., Torts, § 339, comment (b).

There is thus no justification for regarding the commonness of a condition as having a decisive significance independent of the obviousness of the risk. Unfortunately, several cases, both in allowing and denying recovery, have used broad language which could be understood as meaning that a common condition can never give rise to liability. Knight v. Kaiser Co., 48 Cal.2d 778, 782, 312 P.2d 1089. Dean Prosser correctly points out: "Many courts have said that the doctrine does not apply to common conditions . . . or that it is limited to . . . special and unusual conditions of modern industry; but all such statements appear to be made with reference to the particular case, and to be directed at nothing more than the existence of a recognizable and unreasonable risk of harm to the child." Prosser on Torts (2d Ed. 1955) 443. See also Reynolds v. Willson, 51 Cal.2d 94, 331 P.2d 48.

A common condition, namely, fire or embers, led to the injuries of the minor plaintiff in the recent case of Courtell v. McEachen, 51 Cal.2d 448, 334 P.2d 870, and we held that, if the condition causing the accident was not obvious to the child, there could be liability under the law applicable to trespassing children. * * * We wish to emphasize that the mere fact that the condition causing an injury is common in character will not prevent recovery by a trespassing child.

With respect to whether the circumstances of this case warrant recovery, it should be kept in mind that a possessor of land is not under a duty to prevent every possibility of harm but only to exercise due care as to those risks which he should realize are unreasonably great and threaten serious bodily harm in a way unlikely to be appreciated by children whose trespass he should foresee. The ability to appreciate danger varies, of course, with the age of the child, and there can be no recovery if the child is of sufficient age and mental capacity to look out for himself under the circumstances presented.

As we have seen, the panels containing windows were heavy and were firmly stacked a considerable distance from the street in such a manner that the glass could be reached only at the top of the piles, 24 to 30 inches from the ground. The chance was slight that a child of plaintiff's age would fail to see the glass or appreciate what risk was presented, and there is no evidence that plaintiff was of less than average intelligence for her age. It may be, as plaintiff in effect testified, that, because it was getting dark, she did not see the glass before jumping, but defendants could not reasonably be required to foresee that there was any substantial likelihood that a normal child of more than 12 would not appreciate the danger of jumping over a large pile of building materials when darkness prevented sufficient perception of the nature of the obstacle. In the light of the undisputed facts now before us, there is no sound basis for concluding that the condition which caused plaintiff's injury should have been recognized as constituting an unreasonably great risk of serious bodily harm which plaintiff was unable to discover or appreciate because of her immaturity. Accordingly, the evidence did not warrant a recovery by plaintiff.

The judgment is reversed.

SHENK, TRAYNOR, and PETERS, JJ., concur.

[If the defendant asked your advice, would you tell him it is quite safe for him to leave his stuff where it is?]

SPENCE, Justice (concurring and dissenting).

I concur in the judgment of reversal, but for the reasons hereinafter stated, I am of the opinion that such reversal should be accompanied with directions to enter judgment in favor of the defendants.

This is another of a series of recent appeals involving the same fundamental question, namely, the nature of the duty owed by the landowner to the trespassing child with respect to the condition of the landowner's premises. While I agree with the majority that "the evidence does not bring the case within the rule set forth in section 339 of the Restatement of Torts," I am further of the opinion that the reversal should be squarely based upon the decisional law of this state involving comparable situations in connection with building materials or with buildings under construction such as Knight v. Kaiser Co., 48 Cal.2d 778, 312 P.2d 1089.

While the reversal ordered by the majority here is entirely consistent with the long line of "former cases," I am of the opinion that such reversal is inconsistent with the majority opinions in Reynolds v. Willson, 51 Cal.2d 94 [331 P.2d 48], and Courtell v. McEachen, 51 Cal.2d 448 [334 P.2d 870]. I discussed the inconsistency of the Reynolds and Courtell opinions with the "former cases" in my dissenting opinion in those cases, and need not repeat that discussion here. Suffice it to say that each of those cases, like the present one, involved only a common, obvious risk rather than some uncommon or concealed risk such as had been previously required to bring the condition within any recognized exception to the general rule which limits the duty owed by the landowner to the trespassing child.

If the well-considered rules established by the "former cases" are to be disregarded upon the ground that they put cases "in rigid categories on the basis of the type of condition involved," then the majority should expressly disapprove those cases, rather than being content with giving them passing reference and leaving to possible conflicting implications the question of whether those cases are being approved or disapproved. However, it should be stated in this connection that a legal principle which is supported by sound reason and abundant authority, should not be disregarded merely because it may impart a fair degree of certainty, or even rigidity, to an important phase of the law. Adherence to well-considered and well-established guiding principles makes for stability in the law while, on the other hand, the jumping from case to case, without following any consistent pattern and without regard for established principles, can only create endless confusion. * * *

But regardless of whether the majority may see fit to approve or disapprove * * * Knight v. Kaiser Co., supra, the position of the majority should be made clear. The existing chaos will only be perpetuated by continuing to quote section 339 of the Restatement of Torts without adequately discussing its relation to the "former cases," and then resting upon the truism that "recovery is granted or denied depending on the facts of each case." Reynolds v. Willson, supra, 51 Cal.2d 94, 106, 331 P.2d 48, 60. Just as the conflict between the two divergent lines of cases and the conflict between the varying constructions placed upon section 339 becomes more apparent with the filing of each decision, so the duty of this court to resolve those conflicts becomes more imperative. Clarification could be easily accomplished by frankly recognizing the conflict and by meeting the issue squarely; but until that

is done, the bench and bar will be compelled to journey on insecure footing over uncertain legal ground in a perplexing situation similar to that described by Justice Learned Hand when he said: "It is quite impossible to establish any rule from the decided cases; we must step from tuft to tuft across the morass." Hutchinson v. Chase & Gilbert, 2 cir., 45 F.2d 139, 142.

For the reasons stated, and for the added reason that there is no suggestion that any further evidence could be adduced which would justify the imposition of liability upon the defendants, I would reverse the judgment with directions to the trial court to enter judgment in favor of the defendants.

SCHAUER and McCOMB, JJ., concur.

QUESTIONS

(1) What did you understand "the law" to be after *Reynolds* and before *Garcia*?

(2) Is it the same now that we have *Garcia*?

(3) All seven justices agreed that the appellant won, but they split 4-3 regarding rationale and, on a narrow point, outcome. What exactly is the difference between the order issued by the court and that which the concurring (and dissenting) justices would have issued?

KING v. LENNEN
53 Cal. 2d 340, 1 Cal. Rptr. 665, 348 P.2d 98 (1959)

GIBSON, Chief Justice. *Demurrer*

Plaintiffs brought this action for damages for the wrongful death of their son, Boyd, who drowned in defendants' swimming pool. A general demurrer to the complaint was sustained without leave to amend, and plaintiffs have appealed from the ensuing judgment. *Reversed*

The allegations of the complaint may be summarized as follows: Defendants' property was located on the northwest corner of an intersection, and they maintained an artificial swimming pool on the premises about 30 feet from one of the streets. Along that street defendants had partially constructed a concrete block wall with an opening four feet wide directly opposite the pool, and facing the other street was a wood rail fence with openings through which children could readily enter. Defendants permitted their cow, two dogs, and three horses to roam freely near the pool. The animals and the pool could be seen by children of tender years who regularly used the streets adjacent to defendants' premises, and, as defendants knew or should have known, such children, attracted by what they saw, habitually entered the premises and played with the animals and in and about the pool. The water in the pool was three and one-half feet deep at the shallow end and nine feet at the deep end. It was dirty and opaque, and its depth could not be ascertained by looking into it. A sharp drop divided the shallow from the deep water, there were no steps, ladders, rails, or other fixtures to assist a person in the

maybe the cow swam in it?

pool to hold on or to climb out, and the walls and bottom of the pool were lined with a slippery plastic material. Boyd, who was one and one-half years old, lived with his parents on the southeast corner of the intersection diagonally across from defendants. During the five months immediately preceding the accident, defendants' teen-age daughter had been employed as a baby sitter by plaintiffs for compensation, and in order to entertain Boyd on these occasions, as defendants knew or should have known, their daughter would bring him to their home and permit him to play with the animals near the pool, with the result that he became attracted to the animals and the pool. Due to the frequency of the babysitting arrangement the relationship was a continuing one, and, by reason of the relationship, Boyd on the date of his death was on the premises at the express invitation of defendants. No adults were present between 6 a.m. and 6 p.m. on weekdays, including the day when at approximately 11 a.m. Boyd's body was found at the bottom of the pool. The pool constituted a dangerous condition and an unreasonable risk of bodily harm to children of tender years, who could not reasonably be expected to realize or appreciate the danger, and Boyd was attracted to the pool without knowledge of the danger. The usefulness of maintaining the pool was slight as compared with the risk involved, and reasonable safeguards could have been provided at small cost.

The rule set forth in section 339 of the Restatement of Torts has been adopted as the law of this state with respect to the liability of a possessor of land for the death of or injury to a child trespasser. * * *

As we explained in Garcia v. Soogian, 52 Cal.2d 107, 110, 338 P.2d 433, 435, the question of liability must be decided in the light of all the circumstances and not by arbitrarily placing cases in rigid categories on the basis of the type of condition involved. We also pointed out in that case that the circumstances that a condition giving rise to injury is common in character does not necessarily exclude liability, that the ability to appreciate danger varies with the age and mental capacity of the child, and that what is important is not whether conditions are common in character but whether their dangers are fully understood by children. In Courtell v. McEachen, 51 Cal.2d 448, 458, 334 P.2d 870, we held that a young trespassing child who was injured by a common condition, namely, fire or embers, might recover under the law applicable to trespassing children and that it was for the trier of fact to determine whether the child was injured by a risk not obvious to her. While a child is more likely to be aware of a dangerous condition which is common than of one which is unusual, see Garcia v. Soogian, it seems obvious that the common nature of a danger, such as that of drowning in a pool, should not bar relief if the child is too young to realize the danger. Even very young children cannot always be kept under the supervision of their parents, and the question whether a parent in a wrongful death case was guilty of contributory negligence in permitting his young child to play unattended near the defendant's property will ordinarily be for the trier of fact.

A number of cases decided before Garcia v. Soogian and Courtell v. McEachen reasoned that the "attractive nuisance" doctrine does not apply unless the dangerous condition is uncommon and different from natural conditions which exist everywhere and that a body of water, natural or artificial, is a common danger and therefore, as a matter of law, will not subject the possessor to liability for the

drowning of a trespassing child, even if that child is too young to appreciate the danger. [Citations omitted.] This reasoning is inconsistent with the Restatement rule, and the cases cited above [inter alia, *Knight* and *Peters*] are disapproved insofar as their language or holdings are contrary to the views expressed herein.

The complaint alleges facts sufficient to meet the requirements enumerated in section 339 of the Restatement and thus states a cause of action. It is specifically alleged that defendants knew or should have that children of tender years habitually entered the premises and played in and about the pool and that defendants knew or should have known that Boyd had frequently been brought to the vicinity of the pool by their daughter with the result that he had become attracted to it. The allegations describing the condition of defendants' pool and the surrounding premises, including the absence of an adequate fence or other safeguards, state facts sufficient to permit a trier of fact to find that defendants should have realized that a serious danger of drowning was presented with respect to any unsupervised child of Boyd's age who might come to the pool. Obviously it could be found that a child of one and one-half years would not understand the risk involved in being near a swimming pool, and it is alleged that Boyd did not know the danger. The last of the requirements set forth in section 339 was also sufficiently covered by the allegations that the utility to defendants of maintaining the condition was slight as compared with the risk to young children and that reasonable safeguards could have been provided at little cost.

The judgment is reversed.

TRAYNOR, PETERS, and WHITE, JJ., concur.

SPENCE, Justice.

I dissent. * * * I would adhere to the settled rules established by the "former cases" and would affirm the judgment.

SCHAUER and MCCOMB, JJ., concur.

——————

NOTES AND QUESTIONS

(1)   Could *King* have been written more narrowly? On the facts described by the Court, was it necessary to "disapprove" *Peters* and *Knight* in order to reverse the lower court's decision? NO

(2)   Is it proper for Justice Spence to continue to dissent? Isn't the law now "settled," and is he not simply being obstreperous?

(3)   Consider:

> This kind of dissent, in which a judge persists in articulating a minority view of the law in case after case presenting the same issue, seeks to do more than simply offer an alternative analysis — that could be done in a single dissent and does not require repetition. Rather, this type of dissent constitutes a statement by the judge as an individual: "Here I draw the line." Of course, as a member of a court, one's general duty is to acquiesce

Brennan

in the rulings of that court and to take up the battle behind the court's new barricades. But it would be a great mistake to confuse this unquestioned duty to obey and respect the law with an imagined obligation to subsume entirely one's own views of constitutional imperatives to the views of the majority. * * * We are a free and vital people because we not only allow, we encourage debate, and because we do not shut down communication as soon as a decision is reached. As law-abiders, we accept the conclusions of our decision-making bodies as binding, but we also know that our right to continue to challenge the wisdom of that result must be accepted by those who disagree with us. So we debate and discuss and contend and always we argue. If we are right, we generally prevail. The process enriches all of us, and it is available to, and employed by, individuals and groups representing all viewpoints and perspectives. * * *

The right to dissent is one of the great and cherished freedoms that we enjoy by reason of the excellent accident of our American births.[44]

(4) Would it be fair to say something like the following: California attractive nuisance law is "settled" in this sense: all landowners owe a duty to all children.[45] But whether they have breached that duty will depend on the particular circumstances of each case. There may be the unusual case in which the circumstances are such that no untainted, reasonable jury could possibly find for the plaintiff. In that event, the court will direct a verdict for the defendant. But in the overwhelming number of cases the jury will have to pass judgment on whether the landowner's conduct measures up to the standard that the community expects from its members; whether in other words, the defendant has acted in the manner of the reasonable and prudent person.

(5) By the time the Supreme Court decides *King*, California attractive nuisance law looks awfully different than it had at the beginning of the case sequence. The cumulative change is profound, but no single decision marks an abrupt break; the change has been incremental. Try to chart the steps of this transformation.

(6) *King* brings our case sequence to a close, but of course it does not mark the end of the evolution of California law. No case ever does or could. What do you suppose comes next? Where is this area of California law headed?

A Contemplative Note

At least as to swimming pools, is the proper level of precaution best left to local ordinances requiring fencing? Should failure to fence and consequent death result in a criminal prosecution to bring the matter forcefully to the attention of pool

---

[44] Brennan, *supra* note 35, at 437–438. Justice Brennan was speaking in the context of the death penalty cases. From January 14, 1957 to July 19, 1990, Justice Brennan filed a total of 2,347 dissents. Included in that number are approximately 1500 "stock dissents" in death penalty cases, a great many of them from denials of certiorari in which Justice Brennan would simply note that he deemed the death penalty unconstitutional in all circumstances. These figures are from Charles G. Curtis, Jr., *The Great Dissenter*, Remarks Delivered at the 1990 Brennan Clerks' Reunion, Oct. 13, 1990. Justice Brennan also wrote a great many opinions *for* the Court.

[45] If you have already studied *Palsgraf* in your Torts class, you will recognize Judge Andrews' dissent in this statement. If you haven't yet, try to recall this discussion when you do.

owners? Compare state statutes that require the removal of doors from discarded refrigerators so that children do not suffocate. Should pool manufacturers and installers be subject to a code that provides for safety?

In short, does the problem of swimming pools push at the limits of what courts can do effectively? Is this an instance where a legislative solution is superior to the case by case development of the common law?[46]

Assignment

Mr. and Mrs. Harrington live in a residential area of Sullivan Harbor, a coastal town in California. They have a dog run, an orchard, and a 20 x 40 foot swimming pool in their backyard (the front of their house faces the ocean). Because the yard is an attraction for children, the Harringtons have erected a six-foot fence to enclose the entire rear portion of their lot.

One of the Harrington's neighbors, Herbert Young, had a five and a half-year old son, an ill-tempered and recalcitrant child named Julius. Young often warned Julius not to go on to other people's property, but Julius was not wont to listen and on occasion joined other children in climbing over the Harrington's fence. Whenever the Harringtons came upon these unwanted visitors, they immediately ordered them off the premises. On one or two occasions they went so far as to call the parents of some of the youngsters to complain.

One fine morning, Mrs. Harrington began to empty the pool in order to clean it. By noon, the pool still contained water at the deep end, but the shallow part had fully drained. Mrs. Harrington covered the exposed portion of the bottom with a cleaning substance. At that moment, she was called into the house to answer the telephone. She returned approximately thirty-five minutes later and discovered Julius' body floating in the deep end of the pool. Attempts to revive him were unsuccessful. Footprints indicated that Julius had probably climbed down the steps into the shallow part of the pool, lost his balance on the surface made slippery by the detergent, and slid into the water.

(1) Young has come to your law firm for advice. A senior partner asks for your opinion. He knows you have just read the nine pertinent cases. He wants you to prepare a written statement (a "memorandum of law") about three pages long, which synthesizes California "attractive nuisance" law. State which cases would support Mr. Young's claim, which would represent obstacles, what arguments to make, and what arguments to expect from the opposing side.

(2) You work in a different law firm. The Harringtons have come for help; they are now the defendants in Mr. Young's suit.

(a) The trial court denied their motion to dismiss for failure to state a claim upon which relief can be granted. The District Court of Appeal affirmed the trial court's decision. The California Supreme Court has agreed to hear the case. A senior partner has asked you to prepare a three-page draft of the brief to be submitted to the Court, asking for a reversal.

---

[46] Judge Weinstein suggested that we raise these questions with you.

(b) The trial court denied their motion for a directed verdict and the jury returned a verdict for Mr. Young. The trial court also denied the Harringtons' motion for a judgment notwithstanding the verdict. They want to know what chances they may have to prevail if they appealed. Your senior partner wants a three-page memo explaining your thinking on the matter.

(3) You are a law clerk to the Chief Justice of the California Supreme Court while the case described in 2(a) above is before the Court. She has asked you to make a tentative decision and to prepare a three-page draft opinion.

Chapter 5

A THEORY OF PRECEDENT

Prologue *Radin* ✓

When the great Omar performed the *tawaf* around the Ka'ba in Mecca, and kissed the black stone there enshrined, he is said to have declared: "I know thou art a stone, powerless to help or hurt, and I would not have kissed thee, if I had not seen the Envoy of God kiss thee." This happened, if it happened at all, some thirteen centuries ago. It was currently believed before that time and it has especially been believed since, that lawyers and judges are very much in the case of the Caliph Omar, that they are principally engaged in doing things they know to be irrational for no better reason than that they have seen some one else do them. And of some lawyers and judges, it can surely be said that they faithfully perform the *tawaf*, that is, they walk around the Ka'ba seven times, doubtless to see whether there is some way of escape. This habit of following the lead of other men, sometimes with obvious reluctance, is a thing with which laymen have from time immemorial reproached lawyers, but only in the Common Law systems has it been openly accepted by lawyers as a rule and given a Latin dress in the famous maxim, *stare decisis et quieta non movere*.[1]

Stare decisis et quieta non movere: "[T]hose things which have been so often adjudged, ought to rest in peace." So Lord Coke.[2]

It is a maxim among these lawyers, that whatever hath been done before, may legally be done again: and therefore they take special care to record all the decisions formerly made against common justice and the general reason of mankind. These, under the name of *precedents*, they produce as authorities, to justify the most iniquitous opinions; and the Judges never fail of directing accordingly.[3]

It is revolting to have no better reason for a rule of law than that so it was laid down in the time of Henry IV.[4]

---

[1] Max Radin, *Case Law and Stare Decisis: Concerning Präjudizienrecht in Amerika*, in Essays on Jurisprudence from the Columbia Law Review 3 (1963). The Latin is generally translated as "to stand by things decided and not to disturb settled points."

[2] Ruggero J. Aldisert, *Precedent: What It Is and What It Isn't; When Do We Kiss It and When Do We Kill It?*, 17 Pepperdine L. Rev. 605, 626 n.54 (1990) (citing Spicer v. Spicer, Cro. Jac. 527, 79 Eng. Rep. 451 (K.B. 1620)).

[3] Jonathan Swift, Gulliver's Travels 296 (1960) (1726).

[4] Oliver Wendell Holmes, Jr., *The Path of the Law*, 10 Harv. L. Rev. 457, 469 (1897), *reprinted in* Collected Legal Papers 167, 187 (1920). See the discussion in Anthony Kronman, *Precedent and Tradition*, 99 Yale L.J. 1029, 1035 (1990).

[I]t is indisputable that *stare decisis* is a basic self-governing principle within the Judicial Branch, which is entrusted with the sensitive and difficult task of fashioning and preserving a jurisprudential system that is not based upon an "arbitrary discretion."[5]

There are no established precedents in this state dealing with sand piles, as there are with respect to bodies of water.[6]

A. INTRODUCTION

The common law is a body of law comprised of precedents. A common law court is formally bound by prior judicial rulings, almost invariably invokes precedent to justify its decisions, and feels obliged to explain away apparently inconsistent prior opinions. But what is precedent and why should courts adhere to it?

Is adherence to precedent an idiocy of a particularly benighted legal system, as Radin and Jonathan Swift suggest?

> But even in those legal systems that have a code, or some other comprehensive and rationally organized statement of principles for their foundation, the rule that judges should respect past decisions interpreting the meaning of these principles is recognized and accorded an important place. Respect for past decisions, for precedent, is not a characteristic of certain legal systems only. It is rather a feature of law in general, and wherever there exists a set of practices and institutions that we believe are entitled to the name of law, the rule of precedent will be at work, influencing, to one degree or another, the conduct of those responsible for administering the practices and institutions in question.[7]

For that matter, do you live your life without recourse to "precedent"?

Why should it be "revolting" that a rule comes to us from the past and that that is its only "reason"? Is the past revolting? Are we similarly revolting since we will, after all, be part of tomorrow's past?

Does precedent parcel the world into innumerable, immutable categories, like sandpiles and bodies of water, each with a rule of its own?

In the pages that follow we pursue primarily, but not exclusively, one man's ideas about these questions. He is Frederick Schauer, a noted scholar and "jurisprude." We chose this approach because here concentration is better than sampling. We chose Professor Schauer because his theorizing is accessible and because he stresses that "reliance on precedent is part of life."[8] To understand his view is to be less mystified:

---

[5] Patterson v. McClean Credit Union, 491 U.S. 164, 172 (1989) (citing THE FEDERALIST No. 78, at 490 (Alexander Hamilton) (H. Lodge ed., 1888)).

[6] Knight v. Kaiser Co., 312 P.2d 1089, 1096 (1957) (Traynor, J., dissenting).

[7] Kronman, *supra* note 4, at 1031–1032.

[8] Frederick Schauer, *Precedent*, 39 STAN. L. REV. 571, 572 (1987). Our goal is for you to gain a basic understanding, omitting many of the more complex philosophical issues. The article is edited accordingly, in some places heavily. You should return to the entire article at a later time.

Professor Schauer's argument is direct and comprehensive, and his article as a whole exemplifies, with admirable clarity, a way of thinking about precedent that is common among contemporary philosophers of law.[9]

B. WHAT IS PRECEDENT?

1. *Precedent as a Rule*

An appeal to precedent is a form of argument, and a form of justification, that is often as persuasive as it is pervasive. The bare skeleton of an appeal to precedent is easily stated: The previous treatment of occurrence X in manner Y constitutes, *solely because of its historical pedigree*, a reason for treating X in manner Y if and when X again occurs. * * *

I want to view precedent as a *rule* of precedent, and not as a nonrule-governed choice by a decisionmaker in an individual case to rely on the prior decisions of others. * * *

A naked argument from precedent thus urges that a decisionmaker give weight to a particular result regardless of whether that decisionmaker believes it to be correct and regardless of whether that decisionmaker believes it valuable in any way to rely on that previous result.[10]

Professor Radin makes the point in a more dramatic fashion:

[T]he rule of precedent is not to be confounded with deference to the authority of the wise and just who have preceded us. If we believe that Coke was infallible, to follow his judgment is not to apply the rule of *stare decisis*, but is a gesture of humility or piety, or an example of inertia. The law has already been discovered by a man better fit to find it out. It is certainly futile to rediscover America or to reinvent the steam engine. If a court follows a previous decision, because a revered master has uttered it, because it is the right decision, because it is logical, because it is just, because it accords with the weight of authority, because it has been generally accepted and acted on, because it secures a beneficial result to the community, that is not application of *stare decisis*. To make the act such an application, the previous decision must be followed because it is a previous decision and for no other reason, and it becomes clear that we cannot be certain that the rule is being followed, unless it is *contre coeur*, just as Kant was undoubtedly right in holding that obedience to the categoric imperative is discernible only when something disagreeable is commanded.[11]

---

[9] Kronman, *supra* note 4, at 1037. For Professor Kronman's own (dissenting) views see *infra* pages 193–95.

[10] Schauer, *supra* note 8, at 571, 575–576.

[11] Radin, *supra* note 1, at 4–5. You should note that the concept of precedent attacked by Professor Radin is a stronger one than the concept defended by Schauer.

Under this reading of "precedent," can we ever know that the rule is being followed because it is the rule? Is a court likely to tell us that it is deciding *contre coeur*? Are there signals it can, and perhaps should, give us?

We return to Professor Schauer:

> Appeals to precedent do not reside exclusively in courts of law. Forms of argument that may be concentrated in the legal system are rarely isolated there, and the argument from precedent is a prime example of the nonexclusivity of what used to be called "legal reasoning." Think of the child who insists that he should not have to wear short pants to school because his older brother was allowed to wear long pants when *he* was seven. Or think of the bureaucrat who responds to the supplicant for special consideration by saying that "we've never done it that way before." In countless instances, out of law as well as in, the fact that something was done before provides, by itself, a reason for doing it that way again.[12]

2.   *What in a Precedent Binds?*

We have seen that a court is bound only by its own prior cases and those from a higher court in the same jurisdiction. In Chapter Four, we saw the California courts relying on, distinguishing, ignoring, or "disapproving" such cases. But what exactly in those cases was *the precedent*? That question repeats the problem of determining the "holding" in briefing a case. What is it that counts: what the prior court *did* or what the prior court *said*?

Consider Llewellyn:

> We turn first to what I may call the orthodox doctrine of precedent. * * * Every case lays down a rule, the rule of the case. The express ratio decidendi is prima facie the rule of the case, since it is the ground upon which the court chose to rest its decision. But a later court can reexamine the case and can invoke the canon that no judge has power to decide what is not before him, can, through examination of the facts or of the procedural issue, narrow the picture of what was actually before the court and can hold that the ruling made requires to be understood as thus restricted. In the extreme form this results in what is known as expressly "confining the case to its particular facts." This rule holds only for redheaded Walpoles in pale magenta Buick cars. And when you find this said of a past case you know that in effect it has been overruled. Only a convention, a somewhat absurd convention, prevents flat overruling in such instances. It seems to be felt as definitely improper to state that the court in a prior case was wrong, peculiarly so if that case was in the same court which is speaking now. It seems to be felt that this would undermine the dogma of the infallibility of courts. So lip service is done to that dogma, while the rule which the prior court laid down is disembowelled. The execution proceeds with due respect, with mandarin courtesy. * * *

[Can you think of any less self-serving reasons for not flatly overruling?]

---

[12] Schauer, *supra* note 8, at 572.

For when you turn to the actual operations of the courts, or, indeed, to the arguments of lawyers, you will find a totally different view of precedent at work beside this first one. That I shall call, to give it a name, the *loose view* of precedent. That is the view that a court has decided, and decided authoritatively, *any* points or all points on which it chose to rest a case, or on which it chose, after due argument, to pass. No matter how broad the statement, no matter how unnecessary on the facts or the procedural issues, if that was the rule the court laid down, then that the court has held. Indeed, this view carries over often into dicta, and even into dicta which are grandly obiter. In its extreme form this results in thinking and arguing exclusively from *language* that is found in past opinions, and in citing and working with that language wholly without reference to the facts of the case which called the language forth.

Now it is obvious that this [relying on the *language* of an opinion] is a device not for cutting past opinions away from judges' feet, but for using them as a springboard when they are found convenient. This is a device for *capitalizing welcome precedents*. And both the lawyers and the judges use it so. And judged by the *practice* of the most respected courts, as of the courts of ordinary stature, this doctrine of precedent is like the other, recognized, legitimate, honorable.

What I wish to sink deep into your minds about the doctrine of precedent, therefore, is that it is two-headed. It is Janus-faced. That it is not one doctrine, nor one line of doctrine, but two, and two which, *applied at the same time to the same precedent, are contradictory of each other*. That there is one doctrine for getting rid of precedents deemed troublesome and one doctrine for making use of precedents that seem helpful. That these two doctrines exist side by side. That the same lawyer in the same brief, the same judge in the same opinion, may be using the one doctrine, the technically strict one, to cut down half the older cases that he deals with, and using the other doctrine, the loose one, for building with the other half. Until you realize this you do not see how it is possible for law to change and to develop, and yet to stand on the past. * * *

Applying this two-faced doctrine of precedent to your work in a case class you get, it seems to me, some such result as this: You read each case from the angle of its *maximum* value as a precedent. * * * Contrariwise, you will also read each case for its *minimum* value as a precedent, to set against the *maximum*. * * * The first question is, how much can this case fairly be made to stand for by a later court to whom the precedent is welcome? * * * The second question is, how much is there in this case that cannot be got around, even by a later court that wishes to avoid it?[13]

---

[13] Karl N. Llewellyn, The Bramble Bush: On Our Law and Its Study 66–67 (Oceana Pubs. 1960; first published 1960).

QUESTIONS

(1) Go back to *Kelly* and to the variation on the actual facts we hypothesized: that is, suppose Gwinnell arrived visibly drunk, the Zaks gave him coffee, which failed to sober him up, and a short while later he drove off, the Zaks having made no attempt to stop him. All else is as in the actual case. Your firm represents the injured party. A senior partner has asked you for a brief memorandum outlining the strongest case for the client. Write the memo, following Llewellyn and using the *language* of *Kelly*.

(2) The senior partner is a cautious woman. Hence she now asks you for a brief memorandum outlining the strongest case *against* your client. Write the memo, following Llewellyn and using the *language* of *Kelly*.

(3) Find examples of the court using Llewellyn's "orthodox" doctrine of precedent in the attractive nuisance series.

(4) Find examples of the court using Llewellyn's "loose view of precedent" in the attractive nuisance series.

Professor Schauer develops the distinction between the words a court used and the decision it made in discussing "the forward looking aspect of precedent":

An argument from precedent seems at first to look backward. The traditional perspective on precedent, both inside and outside of law, has therefore focused on the use of yesterday's precedents in today's decisions. [Most likely, that is how you approached precedent in the attractive nuisance sequence. Eds.] But in an equally if not more important way, an argument from precedent looks forward as well, asking us to view today's decision as precedent for tomorrow's decisionmakers. Today is not only yesterday's tomorrow; it is also tomorrow's yesterday. A system of precedent therefore involves the special responsibility accompanying the power to commit the future before we get there.

Thinking about the effect of today's decision upon tomorrow encourages us to separate the precedential effect of a decision from the canonical language, or authoritative characterization, that may accompany that decision. Looking at precedent only as a backward-looking constraint may produce a distorted preoccupation with the canonical statements of previous decisionmakers. The precedents of the past, especially judicial precedents, come neatly packaged, with selected facts and authoritative language. Dealing with the use of past precedents thus requires dealing with the presence of the previous decisionmaker's *words*. These words may themselves have authoritative force, what Ronald Dworkin calls the "enactment force of precedent," and thus we often find it difficult to disentangle the effect of a past *decision* from the effect caused by its accompanying words. More pervasively, even a previous decisionmaker's noncanonical descriptions channel the way in which the present views those past decisions. So long as the words of the past tell us how to view the deeds of the past, it remains difficult to isolate how much of the effect of a past

decision is attributable to what a past court has *done* rather than to what
it has *said*.[14]

Is it really possible, is it desirable, to disentangle what the court has *done* from
what it has *said*?

Consider:

> The judge founds his conclusions upon a group of facts selected by him
> as material from among a larger mass of facts, some of which might seem
> significant to a layman, but which, to a lawyer, are irrelevant. The judge,
> therefore, reaches a conclusion upon the facts as he sees them. It is on
> these facts that he bases his judgment, and not on any others. It follows
> that our task in analyzing a case is not to state the facts and the conclusion,
> but to state the material facts as seen by the judge and his conclusion based
> on them. It is by his choice of the material facts that the judge creates law.
> A congeries of facts is presented to him; he chooses those which he
> considers material and rejects those which are immaterial, and then bases
> his conclusion upon the material ones. To ignore his choice is to miss the
> whole point of the case. Our system of precedent becomes meaningless if
> we say that we will accept his conclusion but not his view of the facts. His
> conclusion is based on the material facts as he sees them, and we cannot
> add or subtract from them by proving that other facts existed in the case.
> It is, therefore, essential to know what the judge has said about his choice
> of the facts, for what he does has a meaning for us only when considered in
> relation to what he has said.[15]

In *Poethics*, Professor Weisberg says: "Words create law. * * * Words do not
translate the thought of justice, words *are* justice."[16] Not surprisingly, Professor
Weisberg, like Professor Goodhart, albeit for different reasons, rejects the "standard bifurcation":

> The "holding" in a case cannot without some alteration be abstracted
> from the words used to express it. * * *
>
> [O]f course a court has the immediate power to render a decision, and it
> need not even give any reasons justifying it. But we would not think of this
> as an opinion with a "holding." It would be a holding-less, raw act of power
> * * * but our system discourages such procedures except in a small
> category of "easy" cases. Once the judge begins to write, his use of power
> automatically is bound up in the words he uses. * * * [A]ll judges, conscious
> or no of their crafting powers, must match language to outcome, in order to
> produce a coherent result. * * *
>
> In any event, it is the language used in the opinion, and only that
> language, that perfectly constitutes the "doing" — the holding — of the

---

[14] Schauer, *supra* note 8, at 572–573.

[15] Arthur L. Goodhart, *Determining the Ratio Decidendi of a Case*, 40 Yale L.J. 161, 169 (1930).

[16] Richard Weisberg, Poethics 6–8 (1992).

opinion.[17]

But what about the "forward looking aspect of precedent"? Professor Schauer again:

> At the moment when we consider the wisdom of some currently contemplated decision, however, the characterization of that decision is comparatively open. There is no authoritative characterization apart from what we choose to create. In making a decision, we must acknowledge its many possible subsequent characterizations, and thus the many directions in which it might be extended. Yet despite this seeming indeterminacy of the future precedential effect of today's decision, awareness of the future effect of today's decision pervades legal and nonlegal argument. Lawyers and others routinely deploy a battery of metaphors — the slippery slope, the parade of horribles, the floodgates, the foot in the door, and the entering wedge are but a few — to urge decisionmakers to consider the future effect of today's decisions. Undergirding each of these metaphors is the belief that even an uncharacterized precedent can influence the future.
>
> Thus, only the precedents of the past, and not forward-looking precedents, stand before us clothed with generations of characterizations and recharacterizations. When we look at today as a precedent for the future, we remove the distraction of the canonical effect of simultaneous explanatory language, and we can better understand how being constrained by precedent often involves something different from being constrained by specifically formulated normative language.[18]

C.   *CAN* PRECEDENT CONSTRAIN?

1.   *Introduction*

Observers and participants alike have long debated whether and to what extent precedent actually constrains judges. Surely the case sequence in Chapter Four raised such questions for you. Consider the following extended metaphor for common law decisionmaking:

> I want to use literary interpretation as a model for the central method of legal analysis * * *. Suppose that a group of novelists is engaged for a particular project and that they draw lots to determine the order of play. The lowest number writes the opening chapter of a novel, which he or she then sends to the next number who adds a chapter, with the understanding that he is adding a chapter to that novel rather than beginning a new one, and then sends the two chapters to the next number, and so on. Now every novelist but the first has the dual responsibilities of interpreting and creating, because each must read all that has gone before in order to establish, in the interpretivist sense, what the novel so far created is. He or

---

[17] *Id.* at 7–8.

[18] Schauer, *supra* note 8, at 574–575.

she must decide what the characters are "really" like; what motives in fact guide them; what the point or theme of the developing novel is; how far some literary device or figure, consciously or unconsciously used, contributes to these, and whether it should be extended or refined or trimmed or dropped in order to send the novel further in one direction rather than another. * * *

Some novels have in fact been written this way * * * though for a debunking purpose, and certain parlor games for rainy weekends in English country houses have something of the same structure. But in my imaginary exercise the novelists are expected to take their responsibilities seriously and to recognize the duty to create, so far as they can, a single, unified novel rather than, for example, a series of independent short stories with characters bearing the same names. * * *

Deciding hard cases at law is rather like this strange literary exercise. The similarity is most evident when judges consider and decide "common-law" cases; that is, when no statute figures centrally in the legal issue, and the argument turns on which rules or principles of law "underlie" the related decisions of other judges in the past. Each judge is then like a novelist in the chain. He or she must read through what other judges in the past have written not simply to discover what these judges have said, or their state of mind when they said it, but to reach an opinion about what these judges have collectively *done*, in the way that each of our novelists formed an opinion about the collective novel so far written. Any judge forced to decide a law suit will find, if he looks in the appropriate books, records of many arguably similar cases decided over decades or even centuries past by many other judges of different styles and judicial and political philosophies, in periods of different orthodoxies of procedure and judicial convention. * * * He *must* interpret what has gone before because he has a responsibility to advance the enterprise in hand rather than strike out in some new direction of his own. So he must determine, according to his own judgment, what the earlier decisions come to, what the point or theme of the practice so far, taken as a whole, really is.[19]

Does Dworkin's chain novel idea understate the force of precedent? Overstate it? As a descriptive matter? A normative one?

2.   *Categories and Characterizations*

Here is Professor Schauer on the constraining force of precedent:

Rules of Relevance

Reasoning from precedent, whether looking back to the past or ahead to the future, presupposes an ability to identify the relevant precedent. Why

---

[19] Ronald Dworkin, *Law as Interpretation*, 60 Tex. L. Rev. 527, 541–543 (1982). In an omitted footnote, Professor Dworkin discusses the responsibility of the first novelist and whether different places in the chain carry with them different degrees of freedom. (Did the *Barrett* court enjoy more freedom than the *Peters* court?).

does a currently contemplated decision sometimes have a precedent and sometimes not? Such a distinction can exist only if there is some way of identifying a precedent — some way of determining whether a past event is sufficiently similar to the present facts to justify assimilation of the two events. And when we think about the precedential effect in the future of the action we take today, we presuppose that some future events will be descriptively assimilated to today's.

No two events are exactly alike. For a decision to be precedent for another decision does not require that the facts of the earlier and the later cases be absolutely identical. Were that required, nothing would be a precedent for anything else. We must therefore leave the realm of absolute identity. Once we do so, however, it is clear that the relevance of an earlier precedent depends upon how we characterize the facts arising in the earlier case. * * * In order to assess what is a precedent for what, we must engage in some determination of the relevant similarities between the two events. In turn, we must extract this determination from some other organizing standard specifying which similarities are important and which we can safely ignore.

A parent's decision to let a daughter wear high-heeled shoes at the age of thirteen is scarcely precedent when a son then asks to be permitted to wear high-heeled shoes at that age. But a parent's decision to let that daughter stay up until ten o'clock will be relied upon justifiably by the son when he reaches the same age. A judgment finding tort liability based on the ownership of a black dog is precedent for a judgment regarding the owner of a brown dog, but not for a judgment regarding the owner of a black car. This is so only because a principle, or standard, makes dogness relevant in a way that blackness is not. Consider who among Alan Alda, Menachem Begin, and Dave Righetti is most similar to Sandy Koufax. One is the same age, another has the same religion, and a third is employed in the same occupation. The same point about the role of theory in assessing similarity undergirds Holmes' facetious description of the "Vermont justice of the peace before whom a suit was brought by one farmer against another for breaking a churn. The justice took time to consider, and then said that he had looked through the statutes and could find nothing about churns, and gave judgment for the defendant."[20]

Was Justice Traynor, dissenting in *Knight v. Kaiser*, keeping company with Holmes' apocryphal Vermont justice of the peace when he said "there are no established precedents in this state dealing with sand piles, as there are with respect to bodies of water"? Was he deliberately playing the fool, as it were, and if yes, to what end?

We return to Professor Schauer:

It should be clear, therefore, that only the intervention of organizing theory, in the form of *rules of relevance*, allows us to distinguish the precedential from the irrelevant. * * *

---

[20] Schauer, *supra* note 8, at 576–578.

With rule-dependency and context-dependency in mind, let us return to the forward-looking aspect of precedent. What is it to hope or fear that a decision will establish a precedent for some other decision in the future? Imagine a faculty meeting considering a request from a student for an excused absence from an examination in order to attend the funeral of his sister. Invariably someone will object that this case will establish a precedent allowing students to be excused from examinations to attend the funerals of grandparents, aunts, uncles, cousins, nieces, nephews, close friends, and pets. Implicit in this objection is a rule of relevance that treats death as a relevant similarity, "caring" as a relevant similarity, and any distinction between siblings and other meaningful relationships as irrelevant. * * *

A rule of relevance may also be explained as a choice among alternative characterizations. To use the same example, the student's sister is simultaneously a woman, a sibling, a relative, a blood relative, and one with whom the student has a "meaningful relationship." How the relationship is characterized will determine whether later cases will be classed as similar. Thus, one who worries about establishing a precedent, or for that matter one who wants to establish a precedent, has in mind a characterization that the future will give to today's action, some category within which tomorrow's decisionmaker will place today's facts. The issue is one of *assimilation*, how we will group the facts and events of our world. The power of precedent depends upon some assimilation between the event at hand and some other event. * * *

Categories of Decision and Categories of the World

Identifying the central place of a rule of relevance is only the first step. We must still locate the source of the rules enabling us to call something similar to something else. Only by looking to the source can we determine if that source constrains, or if a decisionmaker may classify the black dogs as easily with the black cars as with the dogs of other colors.

The articulated characterization

In seeking to locate the sources of characterization, we can take a large first step by noting the important distinction between decisions containing and those not containing canonical language. At times a decision will be accompanied by an articulated and authoritative characterization of the decision and its underlying facts. This *articulated characterization*, not unlike an articulated and specifically formulated rule, constrains the use of subsequent and inconsistent characterizations. Suppose the faculty grants the request of the student who wishes to attend the funeral of his sister. Suppose further that the grant of the request is accompanied by a written explanation specifying that the excuse was given so that the student could attend the funeral of a member of his immediate family. This characterization of a sister as a member of an immediate family will in subsequent cases constrain (although by no means absolutely) those who desire to characterize this precedent more broadly, such as by characterizing a sister as a relative, or as a close companion. A similar constraint would operate if

the faculty that granted the first excuse attempted to narrow the precedent by denying an excuse in a subsequent case involving a father, mother, or brother.[21]

NOTES AND QUESTIONS

(1)   The decision in *Barrett* was accompanied by an articulated characterization. What was it? Why was not the decisionmaker in *Peters* constrained by *Barrett*? Was it not plausible to assimilate the events in *Peters* to the events in *Barrett*?

(2)   If "turntable" stands in for "black dog," why is not "pond" like "brown *dog*" rather than "black *car*," as it turned out?

(3)   Do you think the decisionmakers in *Barrett*, had they been the decisionmakers in *Peters*, would have assimilated the two events under the heading "duties owed by landowners to small children"? But was not the decisionmaker in *Peters* "the same" as in *Barrett*?

(4)   Did *Peters* narrow the precedent or did it proceed as though *Peters* were "simply" a different case?

(5)   Is expanding a precedent the equivalent of contracting it? Professor Schauer suggests that expansion seems more defensible than contraction.[22] Why would that be so? Professor Schauer tells us: it *is not* a rule of discourse that what we say is all we have to say; it *is* a rule of discourse that we do not "willy-nilly" go back on what we have said. Yet don't we often intentionally say only so much and no more? To the extent a precedent deliberately stopped short of a broader position, it seems just as inconsistent to read it more broadly than it appears on its face as to read it more narrowly.

"Expansion" and "contraction" are not as straightforward as they seem. Was *Peters* an expansion of *Barrett*'s basic rule of nonliability for landowners or a contraction of its "turntable exception"? Did *Sanchez* expand or contract *Peters*?

3.   *Decisions Without Characterizations*

Professor Schauer:

> In classical legal theory, articulated characterizations are often considered mere dicta, but I do not want anything to turn on the questionable distinction between holding and dictum. Whether the characterizing language is treated as holding or dictum, that language cannot absolutely prevent a subsequent interpreter from recharacterizing the first case. But that interpreter must at least confront an argumentative burden not present without an articulated characterization. * * *

---

[21] *Id.* at 578–580.

[22] *Id.* at 580 n.19.

No decision in the real world is completely devoid of characterizations. Even a mere statement of facts is undoubtedly a characterization. Nevertheless, it is heuristically useful to imagine an event and a decision, without an authoritative statement of what the event is an example of. In this case, it appears possible for a subsequent decisionmaker to adopt any rule of relevance at all — or at least so many alternative rules of relevance that precedent appears to impose no constraint. Precedent's forward-looking aspect reveals this open-ended quality, for the forward-looking use of precedent is somewhat closer to the notion of a collection of facts without an authoritative characterization. Prior to a decision, no single authoritative characterization presents itself in the way that it does with a decision already made. Instead, one concerned about what the future might do with today's decision worries that this decision might be taken by the future to constitute a component of any number of categories extending this decision in different directions. In any situation that lacks an articulated characterization, the central problem of precedent remains: Are there constraints on the assessment of similarity when few events are intrinsically similar to others? When there is no authoritative rule of relevance for a particular situation, is it not then illusory to think of the precedent as in any way constraining?[23]

ROBINS DRY DOCK & REPAIR CO. v. FLINT
275 U.S. 303 (1927)

Mr. Justice Holmes delivered the opinion of the Court.

This is a libel by time charterers of the steamship Bjornefjord against the Dry Dock Company to recover for the loss of use of the steamer between August 1 and August 15, 1917. The libelants recovered in both Courts below. 13 Fed. 2d 3. A writ of certiorari was granted by this Court. 273 U.S. 679.

By the terms of the charter party the steamer was to be docked at least once in every six months, and payment of the hire was to be suspended until she was again in proper state for service. In accordance with these terms the vessel was delivered to the petitioner and docked, and while there the propeller was so injured by the petitioner's negligence that a new one had to be put in, thus causing the delay for which this suit is brought. The petitioner seems to have had no notice of the charter party until the delay had begun, but on August 10, 1917, was formally advised by the respondents that they should hold it liable. It settled with the owners on December 7, 1917, and received a release of all their claims.

The present libel "in a cause of contract and damage" seems to have been brought in reliance upon an allegation that the contract for dry docking between the petitioner and the owners "was made for the benefit of the libellants and was incidental to the aforesaid charter party." But it is plain, as stated by the Circuit Court of Appeals, that the libellants, respondents here, were not parties to that contract "or in any respect beneficiaries" and were not entitled to sue for a breach

---

[23] *Id.* at 580–582.

of it "even under the most liberal rules that permit third parties to sue on a contract made for their benefit." 13 F.2d 4. "Before a stranger can avail himself of the exceptional privilege of suing for a breach of an agreement, to which he is not a party, he must, at least show that it was intended for his direct benefit." *German Alliance Insurance Co. v. Home Water Supply Co.*, 226 U.S. 220, 230. Although the respondents still somewhat faintly argue the contrary, this question seems to us to need no more words. * * *

The District Court allowed recovery on the ground that the respondents had a "property right" in the vessel, although it is not argued that there was a demise, and the owners remained in possession. This notion also is repudiated by the Circuit Court of Appeals and rightly. The question is whether the respondents have an interest protected by the law against unintended injuries inflicted upon the vessel by third persons who know nothing of the charter. If they have, it must be worked out through their contract relations with the owners, not on the postulate that they have a right *in rem* against the ship.

Of course the contract of the petitioner with the owners imposed no immediate obligation upon the petitioner to third persons, as we already have said, and whether the petitioner performed it promptly or with negligent delay was the business of the owners and of nobody else. But as there was a tortious damage to a chattel it is sought to connect the claim of the respondents with that in some way. The damage was material to them only as it caused the delay in making the repairs, and that delay would be a wrong to no one except for the petitioner's contract with the owners. The injury to the propeller was no wrong to the respondents but only to those to whom it belonged. But suppose that the respondent's loss flowed directly from that source. Their loss arose only through their contract with the owners — and while intentionally to bring about a breach of contract may give rise to a cause of action, *Angle v. Chicago, St. Paul, Minneapolis & Omaha Ry. Co.*, 151 U.S. 1, no authority need be cited to show that, as a general rule, at least, a tort to the person or property of one man does not make the tortfeasor liable to another merely because the injured person was under a contract with that other, unknown to the doer of the wrong. See *Savings Bank v. Ward*, 100 U.S. 195. The law does not spread its protection so far.

NOTES AND QUESTIONS

(1) Is *Robins Dry Dock* a case without a characterization, one we must treat as "an event and a decision, without an authoritative statement of what the event is an example of"? Is it possible to do so?

(2) You are a subsequent decisionmaker. Articulate rules of relevance that will imbue this case with precedential, constraining force. Do you feel free to "adopt any rule of relevance at all" or are there constraints on your "control over the categories of assimilation"? If so, what are they?

(3) Suppose the Town of Winter Harbor enters into a contract with Seagull, the local water company, to supply water at a certain pressure. A fire breaks out, the Volunteer Fire Department shows up, but because of Seagull's negligence there is

no pressure in the hoses, and several houses burn down. The homeowners bring suit against Seagull. Are the facts plausibly assimilable to *Robins Dry Dock*?

(4) *State of Louisiana ex rel. Guste v. M/V TESTBANK*, 752 F.2d 1019 (5th Cir. 1985) (en banc). As a result of the collision of two boats carrying toxic substances, the United States Coast Guard closed the Mississippi River Gulf Outlet to navigation and suspended all fishing, shrimping, and related activity in the outlet and four hundred square miles of surrounding marsh and waterways. Dozens of maritime tort actions were filed against the ships and their owners by marina and boat rental operators, seafood restaurants, tackle and bait shops, and the like. The plaintiffs had suffered no physical damage to their property. Sitting en banc, a badly divided 5th Circuit held that, under *Robins*, the plaintiffs could not recover for their economic losses in the absence of a physical injury. "Denying recovery for pure economic losses is a pragmatic limitation on the doctrine of foreseeability, a limitation we find to be both workable and useful." The dissenters characterized *Robins* more narrowly, arguing that it "held only that if a defendant's negligence injures party *A*, and the plaintiff suffers loss of expected income or profits because it had a contract with *A*, then the plaintiff has no cause of action based on the defendant's negligence."

Did the majority fairly and accurately characterize *Robins*? Did the dissent? In determining how to characterize *Robins*, must one go outside the opinion itself?

4.   *Categories of Assimilation*

Professor Schauer:

We can now rephrase the problem. For any given decision, are there restraints on the possible categories of assimilation connecting the facts now before us with the facts before a future decisionmaker? Or is the choice of category completely up to the future decisionmaker, who can choose the category that *a posteriori* justifies the decision made on nonprecedential grounds? * * *

The question is not whether there are immutable categories of the world. It is whether the categories used in making a decision are totally within the control of a decisionmaker, or of the decisional environment in which individual decisionmakers operate, or whether categories in some way resist molding by the decisionmakers who use them. * * *

Our nonlegal world inevitably involves and incorporates its own categories of assimilation, its own rules of relevance. Think about why power tools are sold in hardware stores rather than in electrical appliance shops. And think about why we most often group red bicycles with bicycles of other colors rather than with red ties and red meat. Without such classifications our existence would be an undifferentiated sensory bombardment, akin to six radio stations broadcasting on the same frequency.

Many of these larger rules of relevance are implicit in the structure of our language. Despite obvious differences, we refer to both amateur chess and professional football as "games." Despite obvious similarities, we have

a different word for killing deer in the woods in Vermont than we have for killing cows in the stockyards in Omaha. * * *

The temporal and cultural contingency of the rules of life and language is not controversial. But it does not follow from the temporal and cultural contingency of rules of relevance that they are subject to change by a given decisionmaker, or even by a particular decisionmaking institution. That a society may change its collective views about what counts as a "vehicle," or what is "liberal," "fair notice," or "cruel," does not mean that the power to accomplish any of these changes exists in the short run, or inheres in individual or institutional decisionmakers. Take for example the question of the student asking to be excused from an examination in order to attend the funeral of a sibling. Would this establish a precedent with respect to cousins as well as siblings? The question cannot be avoided by noting that a future decisionmaker will have to make that decision. The question is whether there is some preexisting linguistic or social category that will group siblings and cousins together for some purposes, and, if so, what effect the existence of that category would have on the future decisionmaker's decision. * * * If there is no such larger category of assimilation, there may be no risk that the desired decision of today will be grouped tomorrow with a decision that we today see as both undesirable and distinguishable. But if such a category of assimilation exists in the larger consciousness surrounding the particular decisionmaking individual or institution, then there will be significant resistance to any decision that would disregard that category. * * *

Precedent rests on similarity, and some determinations of similarity are incontestable within particular cultures or subcultures. If we can view these similarities as subculturally fixed, or subculturally incontestable, while at the same time recognizing their larger contingency, we can recognize that the rule-dependency and context-contingency of precedent do not force the conclusion that all characterization of a past event are always up for grabs. If the available characterizations constitute a closed and often rather limited set, requiring a decisionmaker to follow some earlier result can substantially affect decisions.[24]

Answer the question: *would* or *would not* excusing a student from an examination, in order to attend the funeral of a "sibling," establish a precedent with respect to "cousins." Explain your answer. What about a student who seeks to be excused because her beloved companion of 14 years, a Golden Retriever named Tom Jones, has to be "put down," as the euphemism goes?

Would the question, or the answer, be different if the faculty had adopted a set of written rules explicitly providing that "students may be excused from exams to attend the funeral of a parent or sibling"?

[24] *Id.* at 582–587.

5. *Do Some Precedents Constrain More Than Others?*

Professor Schauer:

It should be apparent that the extent to which precedent constrains will vary with the size of the assimilating category. In other words, if the conclusions of one case apply to a sweepingly broad set of analogies (and encourage decisionmakers to make such analogies), then the constraints of precedent are likely to be substantial. Not only will a broad set of subsequent decisionmakers feel the impact of the original decision, but the original decisionmaker will feel a greater obligation in making a decision with such broad application. The bigger the group of cases the original decisionmaker is effectively deciding, the more constraining will be the mandate to treat all of those cases alike. Conversely, if the categories of assimilation are comparatively small, the decisionmaker need consider only a few cases beyond the instant case, and the constraints of precedent will be comparatively inconsequential. * * *

A precedential category of "vehicles" will have greater force than smaller categories of "cars," "trucks," and "motorcycles," which in turn will have greater power over the future than categories of "Buicks" or "Toyotas." No precedential rule can begin to capture this question of size. We cannot say that the appropriate categories of decision are just this big, or just this small. Instead, the rules of precedent are likely to resemble rules of language — a series of practices not substantially reducible to specifics. A system in which precedent operates as a comparatively strong constraint will be one in which decisionmakers ignore fine but justifiable differences in the pursuit of large similarities.[25]

QUESTIONS

(1) Rethink the "attractive nuisance" series. Did the California Supreme Court choose "larger" rather than "smaller" categories and did it thus choose a stronger or weaker system of precedent? What, again, about Justice Traynor: sand piles and bodies of water?

(2) In *Garcia* the Court says: "The question of liability must be decided in light of all the circumstances and not by arbitrarily placing cases in rigid categories." In *Reynolds* the Court comments: "[I]t is apparent that recovery is granted or denied depending on the facts of each case." What is the relationship between deciding on a case-by-case basis and deciding according to precedent?

----

[25] *Id.* at 591, 595.

D.   WHY A DOCTRINE OF PRECEDENT?

1.   *Criticisms*

Stare decisis has had its share of detractors. Some you met in our Prologue. Thomas Hobbes was another.

> Hobbes states, reasonably enough, that there is no judge whose interpretations are wholly free from the risk of error. He then asserts, more revealingly, that any judge who has made a mistake is obligated — required, he says, by the laws of nature — to reverse himself should the opportunity to do so subsequently arise. "No man's error becomes his own law," Hobbes writes, "nor obliges him to persist in it. Neither, for the same reason, becomes it a law to other judges, though sworn to follow it." Indeed, Hobbes argues, only the truth should be given any weight in the interpretation of an uncertain or disputed law, no matter how consistently or often the law has been interpreted a particular way in the past. To that extent adjudication is like geometry — the model for Hobbes' new science of politics — where arguments from precedent are quite obviously out of place. In law, as in geometry, Hobbes insists, it is only the dictates of natural reason that are deserving of respect (however liable to error they may be). Against their judgment, the past simply does not count at all. Thus, "though the sentence of the judge [in a given case], be a law to the party pleading, yet it is no law to any judge, that shall succeed him in that office." Each judge must make up his own mind for himself, yielding only to the truth and giving no more deference to the past than a geometer or philosopher would give.[26]

The most vehement detractor of stare decisis was perhaps Jeremy Bentham.[27] But then, he hated the common law in general with a blinding passion:

> It is the judges (as we have seen) that make the common law. Do you know how they make it? Just as a man makes laws for his dog. When your dog does anything you want to break him of, you wait till he does it, and then beat him for it. This is the way you make laws for your dog: and this is the way the judges make law for you and me. They won't tell a man beforehand what it is he *should not do* — they won't so much as allow of his being told: they lie by till he has done something which they say he should not *have done*, and then they hang him for it. What way, then, has any man of coming at this dog-law? Only by watching their proceedings: by observing in what *cases* they have hanged a man, in what *cases* they have sent him to jail, in what *cases* they have seized his goods, and so forth.[28]

---

[26] Kronman, *supra* note 4, at 1034.

[27] The founder of modern utilitarianism, Jeremy Bentham (1748-1832) was a philosopher, political theorist, and jurist. He was also in the grand tradition of English eccentrics: his will stipulated that his skeleton be preserved and clothed, and it remains to this day in a cabinet in the University of London. His most important jurisprudential work is *An Introduction to the Principles of Morals and Legislation* (1789).

[28] 5 JEREMY BENTHAM, THE WORKS OF JEREMY BENTHAM 235 (1843).

As for Bentham's views of precedent in particular, here is Professor Goodhart's discussion:

> His hatred of the common law was such that he imagined that he found in it a deep-laid conspiracy to oppress the people. To him "it was and is the interest of the partnership (the judges and the lawyers) that the law be throughout as irrational as possible." To accomplish this purpose no weapon was so useful as precedent, for "it is acting without reason, to the declared exclusion of reason, and thereby in declared opposition to reason." Therefore, "How should lawyers be otherwise than fond of this brat of their own begetting? Or how should they bear to part with it? It carries in its hand a rule of wax, which they twist about as they please — a hook to lead the people by the nose, and a pair of shears to fleece them with."[29]

Would Bentham have been a more effective advocate had he argued less violently? (Is there perchance a lesson here for you?)

Note, too, that Bentham's conception of the common law is precisely the opposite of Schauer's. To Bentham, the common law provided no precedent and therefore no *ex ante* guidance as to how to act, but only *ex post* decisionmaking and punishment for acts of which judges disapprove.

Is he railing primarily against professionals who exclude "others" from their turf, for instance by developing a language of their own? How though, is stare decisis connected with that?

Consider the following more measured judicial catalogue of some of the costs of adhering to precedent:

> While many consider the principle of binding authority indispensable — perhaps even inevitable — it is important to note that it is not an unalloyed good. While bringing to the law important values such as predictability and consistency, it also (for the very same reason) deprives the law of flexibility and adaptability. A district court bound by circuit authority, for example, has no choice but to follow it, even if convinced that such authority was wrongly decided. Appellate courts often tolerate errors in their caselaw because the rigors of the en banc process make it impossible to correct all errors.
>
> A system of strict binding precedent also suffers from the defect that it gives undue weight to the first case to raise a particular issue. This is especially true in the circuit courts, where the first panel to consider an issue and publish a precedential opinion occupies the field, whether or not the lawyers have done an adequate job of developing and arguing the issue.[30]

Decisions made according to precedent have also been criticized because justice is precluded when one side of the scale is already weighted:

---

[29] Arthur L. Goodhart, *Precedent in English and Continental Law*, 50 L.J. REV. 40, 46 (1934).

[30] Hart v. Massanari, 266 F.3d 1155, 1175 (9th Cir. 2001).

[T]he German for "precedent" is *Präjudiz*. Its primary meaning is "prejudgment" but it also verges on "prejudice." A similar word (praeiudicia) was occasionally used by Roman jurists as a description of prior court decisions; as *préjugés* with the same meaning it appeared in pre-revolutionary France. Whether taken as "prejudgment" or "prejudice" it carries an implication that is distinctly unpleasant; it suggests that minds have been at least partly closed.[31]

But suppose, for the moment, that the doctrine of stare decisis is founded on the idea of treasuring the past, of honoring it, perhaps so that we, in turn, might be honored when we are "past."[32] Must not then our idea of "justice" make room for that reverence and does not then the doctrine of precedent rightly reflect the pull of the past?

Aside from this latter argument, what interaction do you find between precedent on one hand and impartiality, open mindedness and lawfulness (or their opposites) on the other?

Professor Schauer identifies a quite different drawback of a regime based on precedent:

If the future must treat what we do now as presumptively binding, then our current decision must judge not only what is best for now, but also how the current decision will affect the decision of other and future assimilable cases. Thus, the current decisionmaker must also take into account what would be best for some different but assimilable events yet to occur. * * * If the best solution to today's case is identical to the best solution for tomorrow's different but assimilable facts, then there is no problem. But if what is best for today's situation might not be best for a different (but likely to be assimilated) situation, then the need to consider the future as well as the present will result in at least some immediately suboptimal decisions. * * *

[A]lthough in no case can we make a decision that is better than optimal for that case taken in isolation, in some cases we will make decisions that are worse than optimal for that case taken in isolation. It thus becomes plain that adopting a strategy of reliance on precedent is inherently risk averse, in the sense of giving up the possibility of the optimal result in every case in exchange for diminishing the possibility of bad results in some number of cases.

Thus, if the faculty in the case of the student wishing to attend the funeral of a sibling believes that future decisionmakers will assimilate siblings with all other relatives, and if it also believes that in some significant number of nonsibling relative cases it would be wrong to grant the excuse, then the faculty may plausibly deny the request in the present case even though it believes that it would be right to grant the excuse in this case if the case were taken in isolation. When we look at things this

---

[31] JOHN P. DAWSON, THE ORACLES OF THE LAW xv (1968).

[32] See the discussion by Professor Kronman, at *infra* pages 193–95.

way, we see the price of precedent plainly presented. To the extent that a conscientious decisionmaker takes into account the fact that this decision will, within a regime of precedent, substantially control future decisions with respect to similar but assimilable situations, then the conscientious current decisionmaker must partially make those future decisions as well. When this happens, there will be at least some cases in which the best decision within a regime of precedent is nevertheless a suboptimal decision for the case at hand, with each such case being a concrete example of the costs of a system in which precedent matters.[33]

How would you "rule" if you were a member of our hypothetical faculty presented with the present problem?

Professor Schauer suggests that the slippery slope is a particular liability of a system based on precedent. Why, exactly? Couldn't one argue that fixed precedents are precisely what prevent a headlong slide down that slope?

2. *Utilitarian Defenses*

Against this negative barrage, consider the following defenses of basing decisions on precedent. As you consider each, think about whether they apply equally to "vertical" stare decisis (i.e. the obligation of lower courts to follow decisions of higher courts) and "horizontal" stare decisis (i.e. a given court's obligation to stand by its own prior decisions).

(a) Fairness

Among the most common justifications for treating precedent as relevant is the argument from fairness, sometimes couched as an argument from justice. The argument is most commonly expressed in terms of the simple stricture, "Treat like cases alike." To fail to treat similar cases similarly, it is argued, is arbitrary, and consequently unjust or unfair. We achieve fairness by decisionmaking rules designed to achieve consistency across a range of decisions. Where the consistency is among individuals at the same time, we express this decisional rule as "equality." Where the consistency among decisions takes place over time, we call our decisional rule "precedent."

* * * [T]he hard question is what we mean by "alike."

Recall the discussion of the potential *size* of categories of assimilation. From the perspective of the size of the categories involved, the question is not whether like cases should be decided alike, for at that level of abstraction that norm would engender unanimous agreement. Rather, the question is whether the categories of likeness should be large or small. If the categories of likeness, of assimilation, are so small as to enable a decisionmaker to take into account virtually every variation between separate events, then like cases are indeed being decided alike, yet the norm of precedent scarcely constrains. But if relatively large categories act

---

[33] Schauer, *supra* note 8, at 589–591.

to group many slightly different particular cases under general headings of likeness, then the stricture of deciding like cases alike makes reliance on precedent a substantial constraint.

The issue is thus not the sterile question of treating like cases alike. It is instead the more difficult question of whether we should base our decisionmaking norm on relatively large categories of likeness, or by contrast leave a decisionmaker more or less at liberty to consider any possible way in which this particular array of facts might be unique. * * *

Alone, therefore, the argument from fairness, the prescription to treat like cases alike, does not help us choose between a decisional system with a strong precedential constraint and one with virtually no precedential constraint. If we are to find arguments directly addressing the question of precedent, we must look for substantive reasons to choose larger rather than smaller categories of decision.[34]

Can you apply the foregoing to the attractive nuisance sequence? The California Supreme Court did not allow recovery for all of the plaintiff children. Does this mean that the court did or did not treat like cases alike? Does your answer to that question help you "to choose between a decisional system with a strong precedential constraint and one with virtually no precedential constraint"?

(b)   Predictability

The most commonly offered of the substantive reasons for choosing strong over weak precedential constraint is the principle of predictability. * * * The ability to predict what a decisionmaker will do helps us plan our lives, have some degree of repose, and avoid the paralysis of foreseeing only the unknown.

* * * In the language of precedent, following a precedent at a particular time may produce a decision other than the decision deemed optimal on the facts of the particular instance.

* * * But the relationship of these costs [of suboptimal results] to the possible benefits of predictability will vary across different kinds of decisions. When Justice Brandeis noted that "in most matters it is more important that the applicable rule of law be settled than that it be settled right,"[35] he was reminding us of one side of this question. The other side, of course, is that sometimes it is more important that things be settled correctly than that they be settled for the sake of settlement. To take an extreme example, making all capital punishment decisions under a strict precedential rule would satisfy desires for predictability but would also entail putting to death some people who would live if their individual cases were scrutinized carefully. And at the other extreme, many decisions involving the formalities of contracts or real estate transactions are

---

[34] *Id.* at 595–597.

[35] [Ed. Fn.] The quotation is from *Burnet v. Colorado Oil and Gas Co.*, 285 U.S. 393, 406 (1932) (Brandeis, J., dissenting).

decisions in which sacrificing optimality for predictability would involve
negative consequences that are far from catastrophic.

Finally, it is worthwhile adding to the equation some variability in the
value of predictability. Much of what we value about predictability is
psychological. I feel better knowing that the letter carrier will come at the
same time every day, that faculty meetings will not be scheduled on short
notice, and that April brings the opening of the baseball season. Predictability thus often has value even when we cannot quantify it.

Thus, the value of predictability is really a question of balancing
expected gain against expected loss. We ask how important predictability
is for those affected by the decisions, and we then ask whether that amount
of predictability is worth the price of the frequency of suboptimal results
multiplied by the costs of those suboptimal results. But there is no best
answer to this calculation, for the answer will vary with the kinds of
decisions that given decisionmakers are expected to make.[36]

How will "we" (the court? the legal community? the affected community? the
community at large?) find out how important predictability is for those whose
interests are at stake? How do we determine the costs of suboptimal results?

Can we do any better than to accept the first decisionmaker's "hunch" as to the
desirable size of the category?

Professor Schauer's quotation from Justice Brandeis is well-known and others
have expressed a similar view. But surely Schauer is correct that this is not *always*
true. (In fact, Justice Brandeis himself once referred in a speech to "the inexorable
law that nothing is settled until it is settled right."[37]) In the context of "attractive
nuisance," is it more important that the rule be settled or that it be settled right?
Is the answer found in the difference between Justices Traynor and Spence?

An Allegory

In *The Morality of Law*, Professor Fuller tells us about a monarch named Rex:

Rex came to the throne filled with the zeal of a reformer. He considered
that the greatest failure of his predecessors had been in the field of law. For
generations the legal system had known nothing like a basic reform.
Procedures of trial were cumbersome, the rules of law spoke in the archaic
tongue of another age, justice was expensive, the judges were slovenly and
sometimes corrupt. Rex was resolved to remedy all this and to make his
name in history as a great lawgiver. It was his unhappy fate to fail in this
ambition. Indeed, he failed spectacularly, since not only did he not succeed
in introducing the needed reforms, but he never even succeeded in creating
any law at all, good or bad.

His first official act was, however, dramatic and propitious. Since he
needed a clean slate on which to write, he announced to his subjects the

---

[36] Schauer, *supra* note 8, at 597–598.

[37] Louis D. Brandeis, Speech, Boston, Mar. 5, 1913, *quoted in* ALPHEUS T. MASON, BRANDEIS: A FREE
MAN'S LIFE 204 (1946).

immediate repeal of all existing law, of whatever kind. He then set about drafting a new code. Unfortunately, trained as a lonely prince, his education had been very defective. In particular he found himself incapable of making even the simplest generalizations. Though not lacking in confidence when it came to deciding specific controversies, the effort to give articulate reasons for any conclusion strained his capacities to the breaking point.

Becoming aware of his limitations, Rex gave up the project of a code and announced to his subjects that henceforth he would act as a judge in any disputes that might arise among them. In this way under the stimulus of a variety of cases he hoped that his latent powers of generalization might develop and, proceeding case by case, he would gradually work out a system of rules that could be incorporated in a code. Unfortunately the defects in his education were more deep-seated than he had supposed. The venture failed completely. After he had handed down literally hundreds of decisions neither he nor his subjects could detect in those decisions any pattern whatsoever. Such tentatives toward generalization as were to be found in his opinions only compounded the confusion, for they gave false leads to his subjects and threw his own meager powers of judgment off balance in the decision of later cases.[38]

After recounting other misadventures of Rex the lawgiver, Professor Fuller concludes:

Rex's bungling career as legislator and judge illustrates that the attempt to create and maintain a system of legal rules may miscarry in at least eight ways; there are in this enterprise, if you will, eight distinct routes to disaster. The first and most obvious lies in a failure to achieve rules at all, so that every issue must be decided on an ad hoc basis. * * *.[39]

A total failure in any one of these eight directions does not simply result in a bad system of law; it results in something that is not properly called a legal system at all, except perhaps in the Pickwickian sense in which a void contract can still be said to be one kind of contract.[40]

Is California attractive nuisance law the torts equivalent of a void contract, at least in Professor Fuller's view?

(c)   Efficiency

The third standard defense of precedential decisionmaking is that it saves resources.

---

[38] Lon Fuller, The Morality of Law 33–34 (Yale University Press, rev. ed. 1969). This and subsequent excerpts reprinted with permission.

[39] [Ed. Fn.] Can you make a stab at identifying at least one or two of the remaining seven "routes to disaster" for a legal system? In general, they involve ways in which it may be impossible to know or comply with the law.

[40] Fuller, *supra* note 38, at 38–39.

(i) *Judicial Resources.* It is common to hear that courts are busy enough as it is and that it would be intolerably burdensome for them to reinvent the wheel in every case. Here is Justice Cardozo:

> [T]he labor of judges would be increased almost to the breaking point if every past decision could be reopened in every case, and one could not lay one's own course of bricks on the secure foundation of the courses laid by others who had gone before him. Perhaps the constitution of my own court has tended to accentuate this belief. We have had ten judges, of whom only seven sit at a time. It happens again and again, where the question is a close one, that a case which one week is decided one way might be decided another way the next if it were then heard for the first time. The situation would, however, be intolerable if the weekly changes in the composition of the court were accompanied by changes in its rulings. In such circumstances there is nothing to do except to stand by the errors of our brethren of the week before, whether we relish them or not.[41]

If Cardozo has already thought enough about the case at hand to conclude that this week's seven Justices would reach a different result than last week's "mistaken" Justices, is there any gain in efficiency or reduction in judicial workload in his standing by the error?

Professor Schauer has this to say about the efficiency argument:

> If we retain the assumption of assimilability of events more than mere decisional efficiency must be at work. The system of precedent must operate to dampen the variability that would otherwise result from dissimilar decisionmakers. Why should we encourage this process? One possibility is that it might be thought important to create the aura of similarity among decisionmakers even where none may exist. Using a system of precedent to standardize decisions subordinates dissimilarity among decisionmakers, both in appearance and in practice.

> Even more substantially, this subordination of decisional and decisionmaker variance is likely in practice to increase the power of the decisionmaking institution. If internal consistency strengthens external credibility, then minimizing internal inconsistency by standardizing decisions within a decisionmaking environment may generally strengthen that decisionmaking environment as an institution.

> The considerations surrounding the argument from decisionmaking efficiency rest upon a broad notion about the value of stability in decisionmaking distinct from anything about the actual decisions made. It is also apparent that any attempt to stabilize decisionmaking in an unstable world is likely to produce some suboptimal results.[42] The argument from enhanced decisionmaking, then, suggests that the efficiency advantages may justify putting on blinders to the full richness of human experience.

---

[41] BENJAMIN N. CARDOZO, THE NATURE OF THE JUDICIAL PROCESS 149–150 (1921).

[42] [Ed. Fn.] Or, in Cardozo's words, "there is nothing to do except to stand by the errors of our brethren," which seems a particularly virulent form of suboptimality.

This is by no means an implausible argument, but its strength will depend upon many of the same factors discussed in the context of the argument from predictability. Likewise, whether this strength is sufficient to outweigh its costs will vary with those same factors.[43]

(ii) *Other Actors.* A strong system of stare decisis may save more than judicial resources. By enhancing predictability and certainty, it reduces the costs of resolving disputes for the parties as well. Relatively certain outcomes discourage litigation and encourage settlement. Economists have pointed out that litigation will only occur when the parties *disagree* about the likelihood of success; a powerful system of stare decisis makes such disagreement less likely, and so, in theory, should reduce disputes and the costs of resolving them.

(d) Legitimacy

A central tenet of the defense of stare decisis is that adherence to precedent gives legitimacy to the decisionmaking institution. Concern over legitimacy runs as a subtext through arguments from fairness, predictability, and even efficiency. It commingles with a recurrent theme of this book: is there anything that protects the polity from the judicial leviathan? Not surprisingly, legitimacy is a concern much on the minds of Supreme Court Justices.

The following off-the-bench remarks of Justice Powell make the basic point:

> Perhaps the most important and familiar argument for *stare decisis* is one of public legitimacy. The respect given the Court by the public, and by the other branches of government, rests in large part on the knowledge that the Court is not composed of unelected judges free to write their policy views into law. Rather, the Court is a body vested with the duty to exercise the judicial power prescribed by the Constitution. An important aspect of this is the respect the Court shows for its own previous opinions. * * * [E]limination of constitutional *stare decisis* would represent explicit endorsement of the idea that the Constitution is nothing more than what five Justices say it is. This would undermine the rule of law.[44]

The link between stare decisis and judicial legitimacy received a well-known and eloquent expression with regard to the precedential force of *Roe v. Wade.*[45] In

---

[43] Schauer, *supra* note 8, at 600.

[44] Lewis F. Powell, Jr., *Stare Decisis and Judicial Restraint*, 44 Rec. Ass'n Bar 813, 819, 821 (1989). As the last sentence quoted indicates, Justice Powell is discussing precedent in *constitutional* cases in particular. We do the same in presenting excerpts from an abortion case immediately below. The issues of judicial legitimacy are starkest in the constitutional setting because there is no possibility of legislative correction. And among constitutional cases they are starkest in settings such as the debate over whether the Constitution protects a right to abortion. In such "unenumerated fundamental rights" cases, the Court has set aside the decisions of the duly elected representatives of the people on the basis of a constitutional "interpretation" that has a tenuous (for many, an utterly imperceptible) connection with the document itself. But the same questions, if slightly watered down, are present in common law and statutory cases as well, and the asserted link between precedent and legitimacy must be considered in all three settings.

[45] 410 U.S. 113 (1973). *Roe*, in case you have lived in a glass jar, was the decision in which the Supreme Court, in an opinion written by Justice Blackmun, established a constitutional right to abortion.

Planned Parenthood v. Casey, the Supreme Court — defying general expectation, disappointing some, including a couple of Presidents, and elating others — declined to overrule *Roe*, by a vote of 5-4. The excerpt below is from a joint opinion signed, unusually, by *three* Justices: O'Connor, Kennedy, and Souter; the portion reproduced here was also joined by Justices Blackmun and Stevens.

PLANNED PARENTHOOD v. CASEY
505 U.S. 833 (1992)

JUSTICE O'CONNOR, JUSTICE KENNEDY, AND JUSTICE SOUTER * * * delivered [what was in part] the opinion of the Court. * * *

Our analysis would not be complete, however, without explaining why overruling *Roe*'s central holding would not only reach an unjustifiable result under principles of *stare decisis*, but would seriously weaken the Court's capacity to exercise the judicial power and to function as the Supreme Court of a Nation dedicated to the rule of law. To understand why this would be so it is necessary to understand the source of this Court's authority, the conditions necessary for its preservation, and its relationship to the country's understanding of itself as a constitutional Republic.

The root of American governmental power is revealed most clearly in the instance of the power conferred by the Constitution upon the Judiciary of the United States and specifically upon this Court. As Americans of each succeeding generation are rightly told, the Court cannot buy support for its decisions by spending money and, except to a minor degree, it cannot independently coerce obedience to its decrees. The Court's power lies, rather, in its legitimacy, a product of substance and perception that shows itself in the people's acceptance of the Judiciary as fit to determine what the Nation's law means and to declare what it demands.

The underlying substance of this legitimacy is of course the warrant for the Court's decisions in the Constitution and the lesser sources of legal principle on which the Court draws. That substance is expressed in the Court's opinions, and our contemporary understanding is such that a decision without principled justification would be no judicial act at all. But even when justification is furnished by apposite legal principle, something more is required. Because not every conscientious claim of principled justification will be accepted as such, the justification claimed must be beyond dispute. The Court must take care to speak and act in ways that allow people to accept its decisions on the terms the Court claims for them, as grounded truly in principle, not as compromises with social and political pressures having, as such, no bearing on the principled choices that the Court is obliged to make. Thus, the Court's legitimacy depends on making legally principled decisions under circumstances in which their principled character is sufficiently plausible to be accepted by the Nation.

The need for principled action to be perceived as such is implicated to some degree whenever this, or any other appellate court, overrules a prior case. This is not to say, of course, that this Court cannot give a perfectly satisfactory explanation in most cases. People understand that some of the Constitution's language is hard to fathom and that the Court's Justices are sometimes able to

perceive significant facts or to understand principles of law that eluded their predecessors and that justify departures from existing decisions. However upsetting it may be to those most directly affected when one judicially derived rule replaces another, the country can accept some correction of error without necessarily questioning the legitimacy of the Court.

In two circumstances, however, the Court would almost certainly fail to receive the benefit of the doubt in overruling prior cases. There is, first, a point beyond which frequent overruling would overtax the country's belief in the Court's good faith. Despite the variety of reasons that may inform and justify a decision to overrule, we cannot forget that such a decision is usually perceived (and perceived correctly) as, at the least, a statement that a prior decision was wrong. There is a limit to the amount of error that can plausibly be imputed to prior courts. If that limit should be exceeded, disturbance of prior rulings would be taken as evidence that justifiable reexamination of principle had given way to drives for particular results in the short term. The legitimacy of the Court would fade with the frequency of its vacillation.

That first circumstance can be described as hypothetical; the second is to the point here and now. Where, in the performance of its judicial duties, the Court decides a case in such a way as to resolve the sort of intensely divisive controversy reflected in *Roe* and those rare, comparable cases, its decision has a dimension that the resolution of the normal case does not carry. It is the dimension present whenever the Court's interpretation of the Constitution calls the contending sides of a national controversy to end their national division by accepting a common mandate rooted in the Constitution.

The Court is not asked to do this very often, having thus addressed the Nation only twice in our lifetime, in the decisions of *Brown* and *Roe*. But when the Court does act in this way, its decision requires an equally rare precedential force to counter the inevitable efforts to overturn it and to thwart its implementation. Some of those efforts may be mere unprincipled emotional reactions; others may proceed from principles worthy of profound respect. But whatever the premises of opposition may be, only the most convincing justification under accepted standards of precedent could suffice to demonstrate that a later decision overruling the first was anything but a surrender to political pressure, and an unjustified repudiation of the principle on which the Court staked its authority in the first instance. So to overrule under fire in the absence of the most compelling reason to reexamine a watershed decision would subvert the Court's legitimacy beyond any serious question. * * *

The country's loss of confidence in the judiciary would be underscored by an equally certain and equally reasonable condemnation for another failing in overruling unnecessarily and under pressure. Some cost will be paid by anyone who approves or implements a constitutional decision where it is unpopular, or who refuses to work to undermine the decision or to force its reversal. The price may be criticism or ostracism, or it may be violence. An extra price will be paid by those who themselves disapprove of the decision's results when viewed outside of constitutional terms, but who nevertheless struggle to accept it, because they respect the rule of law. To all those who will be so tested by following, the Court

implicitly undertakes to remain steadfast, lest in the end a price be paid for nothing. The promise of constancy, once given, binds its maker for as long as the power to stand by the decision survives and the understanding of the issue has not changed so fundamentally as to render the commitment obsolete. From the obligation of this promise this Court cannot and should not assume any exemption when duty requires it to decide a case in conformance with the Constitution. A willing breach of it would be nothing less than a breach of faith, and no Court that broke its faith with the people could sensibly expect credit for principle in the decision by which it did that. * * *

The Court's concern with legitimacy is not for the sake of the Court but for the sake of the Nation to which it is responsible.

The Court's duty in the present case is clear. In 1973, it confronted the already-divisive issue of governmental power to limit personal choice to undergo abortion, for which it provided a new resolution based on the due process guaranteed by the Fourteenth Amendment. Whether or not a new social consensus is developing on that issue, its divisiveness is no less today than in 1973, and pressure to overrule the decision, like pressure to retain it, has grown only more intense. A decision to overrule *Roe*'s essential holding under the existing circumstances would address error, if error there was, at the cost of both profound and unnecessary damage to the Court's legitimacy, and to the Nation's commitment to the rule of law. It is therefore imperative to adhere to the essence of *Roe*'s original decision, and we do so today.

NOTES AND QUESTIONS

(1) What do you make of the opinion's references to *Roe*'s "central," *Roe*'s "essential" holding? Do the authors mean that *Roe* can be tampered with after all, perhaps significantly, so long as the tampering stops short of overruling? Indeed, in *Casey* the Court upheld a number of restrictions on abortions — for example, a 24-hour waiting period — that it had struck down in prior cases as unconstitutional under *Roe*.

(2) Does the almost anguished discussion of legitimacy reflect a concern over how the Court *actually* operates or only over how it is *perceived* to operate? The joint opinion calls legitimacy "a product of substance and perception." This dual concern is typical. For example, the Court has noted that stare decisis "permits society to presume that bedrock principles are founded in the law rather than in the proclivities of individuals."[46] Does the precise mix of substance and perception matter?

(3) Does the joint opinion reassure you on the question of the judicial leviathan? Or do you feel like exclaiming with Justice Scalia: "The Imperial Judiciary lives"?[47]

---

[46] Vazquez v. Hillery, 474 U.S. 254, 265 (1986).

[47] *Casey*, 505 U.S. at 996 (Scalia, J., dissenting).

It is instructive to compare this Nietzschean vision of us unelected, life-tenured judges — leading a Volk who will be "tested by following," and whose very "belief in themselves" is mystically bound up in their "understanding" of a Court that "speak(s) before all others for their constitutional ideals" — with the somewhat more modest role envisioned for these lawyers by the Founders.

"The judiciary . . . has . . . no direction either of the strength or of the wealth of the society, and can take no active resolution whatever. It may truly be said to have neither FORCE nor WILL but merely judgment. . . ." The Federalist No. 78, pp. 393–394 (G. Wills ed. 1982).[48]

Note that the *Casey* joint opinion concludes that the very breadth and intensity of popular opposition to *Roe* should make the Court *less likely* to overrule it, not more. Is that perhaps exactly backwards? Justice Scalia thought so:

[T]he notion that we would decide a case differently from the way we otherwise would have in order to show that we can stand firm against public disapproval is frightening. It is a bad enough idea, even in the head of someone like me, who believes that the text of the Constitution, and our traditions, say what they say and there is no fiddling with them. But when it is in the mind of a Court that believes the Constitution has an evolving meaning . . . then the notion that the Court must adhere to a decision for as long as the decision faces "great opposition" and the Court is "under fire" acquires a character of almost czarist arrogance. We are offended by these marchers who descend upon us, every year on the anniversary of *Roe*, to protest our saying that the Constitution requires what our society has never thought the Constitution requires. These people who refuse to be "tested by following" must be taught a lesson. We have no Cossacks, but at least we can stubbornly refuse to abandon an erroneous opinion that we might otherwise change — to show how little they intimidate us.

Of course, * * * we have been subjected to what the Court calls "'political pressure'" by both sides of this issue. Maybe today's decision not to overrule *Roe* will be seen as buckling to pressure from that direction. Instead of engaging in the hopeless task of predicting public perception — a job not for lawyers but for political campaign managers — the Justices should do what is legally right by asking two questions: (1) Was *Roe* correctly decided? (2) Has *Roe* succeeded in producing a settled body of law? If the answer to both questions is no, *Roe* should undoubtedly be overruled.

(4)   When Chief Justice John Roberts's nomination was under consideration by the Senate Judiciary Committee, Chairman Arlen Specter created a bit of a tempest among commentators when he coined the term "superprecedent" to refer to *Roe*.[49] *See also* Richmond Medical Center for Women v. Gilmore, 219 F.3d 376, 376 (4th Cir. 2000) ("I understand the Supreme Court to have intended its decision in

[48] *Id.* (alterations in original).

[49] Arlen Specter, *Bringing the Hearings to Order*, N.Y. TIMES, July 24, 2005, § 4, at 12.

Planned Parenthood v. Casey to be a decision of super-stare decisis"). Can there be such a thing as a superprecedent? If so, what factors would create one?

Consider this exchange, between nominee Samuel Alito and Senator Specter during the former's confirmation hearing:

JUDGE ALITO:	Well, I personally would not get into categorizing precedents as superprecedents or super-duper precedents or anything —
SENATOR SPECTER:	You say super-duper?
JUDGE ALITO:	Right.
SENATOR SPECTER:	Good.
JUDGE ALITO:	Any sort of categorization like that sort of reminds me of the size of laundry detergent in the supermarket.
	I agree with the underlying thought that when a precedent is reaffirmed, that strengthens the precedent. And when the Supreme Court says that we are not going to —
SENATOR SPECTER:	How about being reaffirmed 38 times?
JUDGE ALITO:	Well, I think that when a precedent is reaffirmed, each time it's reaffirmed that is a factor that should be taken into account in making the judgment about stare decisis. And when a precedent is reaffirmed on the ground that stare decisis precludes or counsels against re-examination of the merits of the precedent, then I agree that that is a precedent on precedent.[50]

(5)   Does the mere fact that the *Casey* majority was standing by a precedent ensure that the Court's decision was "legitimate," the exercise of judgment rather than will? Wouldn't judicial legitimacy be furthered by ignoring an incorrect precedent rather than perpetuating the error?

In short, *is* there a link between adherence to precedent and judicial legitimacy?

3.   *Burkean "Conservatism"*

The foregoing justifications are all utilitarian or instrumental; they argue that adherence to precedent is a means to certain important systemic goals (including the nonutilitarian goal of fairness to individuals). But such adherence need not be justified only in terms of what it will achieve. In his elegant and moving essay, *Precedent and Tradition*,[51] Professor Kronman offers a different perspective:

> The several different arguments that Schauer offers in defense of precedent all rest, at bottom, on two claims. The first is that respect for past decisions is desirable to the extent that it increases the sum of social

---

[50] Confirmation hearing on the nomination of Samuel A. Alito, Jr. to be an Associate Justice of the Supreme Court of the U.S. before S. Comm. on the Judiciary, 109th Cong. (Jan. 10, 2006).

[51] Kronman, *supra* note 4.

welfare (by enhancing the law's predictability, economizing judicial re
sources, strengthening the prestige of legal institutions, etc.). This first
claim is in essence utilitarian. The second claim is that like cases must be
treated alike if a legal system is to be even minimally fair, so that when a
case is like some other in all relevant respects except for the fact that it
happens to arise at a later moment in time, the later case must be decided
in the same way as the earlier one (a formulation which, as Schauer notes,
leaves open the question of what, in any given situation, makes two cases
relevantly comparable). This second line of defense is not utilitarian, but
deontological. [Deontology is the theory or study of moral obligation.] Its
premise is that people have a right to be treated in the same way as their
equals, including not just contemporaneous equals but also those who
precede and follow them in time.[52]

Against these claims Professor Kronman sets a different one:

> [T]he past deserves to be respected merely because it is the past — not,
> of course, uncritically or unconditionally, but for its own sake nonetheless.
> That is a claim both arguments [utilitarian and deontological] reject * * *.[53]

Yet why should we respect the past solely because it is the past? Drawing for
succor and support on the writings of Edmund Burke,[54] Professor Kronman
answers:

> We are indebted to those who came before us, for it is through their
> efforts that the world of culture we inhabit now exists. But by the same
> token, they are indebted to us, for it is only through our efforts that their
> achievements can be saved from ruin. Our relationship with our predeces-
> sors is therefore one of mutual indebtedness, and so, of course, is our
> relationship with our successors, though the debts in that case are
> reversed. All these debts, moreover, are connected, for the very acts by
> which we satisfy our obligations to the past put the future in debt to us, and
> force us to depend upon the future for the preservation of whatever
> contributions we in turn make to the world of culture during our trustee-
> ship.
>
> The "chain and continuity" of the generations of which Burke speaks is
> therefore a chain of interwoven obligations. In this respect, he says, society
> is founded on "a partnership not only between those who are living, but
> between those who are living, those who are dead, and those who are to be
> born," a "contract" to which the succeeding generations are all parties. This

---

[52] *Id.* at 1038–1039.

[53] *Id.* at 1039.

[54] Edmund Burke (1729-1797), an Anglo-Irish statesman, orator, philosopher, and long-time Whig
Member of Parliament, continues to engage contemporary thinkers. His most famous work is *Reflections
on the Revolution in France.* He is typically regarded as a conservative, albeit one who "supported
Catholic Emancipation in his native Ireland" and "was revered in Revolutionary America for his defense
of the colonists' rights." (A statue of him stands in Washington.) Alan Ryan, *Who Was Edmund Burke,*
N.Y. REVIEW OF BOOKS, Vol. XXXIX, No. 20, Dec. 3, 1992, at 37, reviewing CONOR CRUISE O'BRIEN, THE
GREAT MELODY: A THEMATIC BIOGRAPHY AND COMMENTED ANTHOLOGY OF EDMUND BURKE (1992).

contract is not, of course, one we choose to enter. It is something that a person is born into, like his family, and the benefits he receives from it have already been irrevocably transferred to him by the time he becomes conscious of his own contractual duties: benefits that can no more be disgorged than a person can disgorge the care and nourishment his parents gave him. In that sense Burke's partnership among the generations is only metaphorically a contract, for the duties it imposes on us are entirely a consequence of the temporal position that we happen quite by fate to occupy — of our status, not our will. These duties thus arise, to borrow a phrase that Burke uses in another context, from "a necessity that is not chosen but chooses," unlike the duties we voluntarily assume in most contractual relationships.

But by describing the relationship among the generations as a contract, Burke reminds us that we are not just constrained by the past, but have obligations toward it, in the same way that one partner to a contract of any sort has obligations toward the others. There is, however, no mechanism by which these duties can be enforced. The past cannot enforce its claim against us if we choose to disrespect it. Nor, by the same token, can we enforce the claims we have against our successors and compel them to meet their obligation to conserve the cultural world on whose continued exist-ence our own remembrance depends. Indeed, in the absence of any means of enforcement, the only basis we have for believing our successors will preserve what we have done is our own willingness to carry on the projects of those who came before, despite their inability to compel our collabora-tion. If we have any grounds for believing that the future will honor what we do, it can therefore only be the uncompelled honor we show the past. The partnership among the generations* * *thus depends for the attain-ment of its ends on each generations' treating the achievements of its predecessors as something inherently worthy of respect. It is only on that condition — on the basis of a traditionalism which honors the past for its own sake — that the world of culture can be sustained * * *.

Simone Weil expressed the point perfectly. "The past once destroyed," she wrote, "never returns. The destruction of the past is perhaps the greatest of all crimes. Today the preservation of what little of it remains ought to become almost an obsession." Weil wrote these words in 1943, when the fate of European civilization was in doubt. But we still need the obsession she describes, if our world is to retain its human shape. Indeed, with the earth drawn up into the world of culture and now placed within our trust, we need it on a planetary scale.[55]

---

[55] Kronman, *supra* note 4, at 1067–1068. For a sympathetic but ultimately critical response to Professor Kronman, *see* David Luban, *Legal Traditionalism*, 43 STAN. L. REV. 1035 (1991). Professor Luban would add to the "Preservation Clause" of the intergenerational contract an "Innovation Clause," "in which we offer our descendants the same freedom to break with the past that we ourselves enjoy." *Id.* at 1055.

4.   *Are Courts Constitutionally Required to Adhere to Precedent?*

Apart from a consideration of the pros and cons of stare decisis, we might ask whether following precedent is a legal *requirement*. Could a court simply refuse to be bound by precedent? If following precedent is a requirement of judicial decisionmaking, where does that come from? In the common-law setting, the obligation to adhere to judicial precedents is most obviously imposed by . . . judicial precedents — a rather unsatisfying self-justification. But courts do not materialize out of thin air; the people or the government must create them. And when courts are created, rules are established dictating how they operate and the scope of their authority. Rules of procedure and jurisdiction are the most obvious examples. Such rules might also require (or not) that the court adhere to precedent. One federal court of appeals has found that the United States Constitution requires federal courts to treat their prior decisions as binding authority.

ANASTASOFF v. UNITED STATES
223 F.3d 898, *vacated as moot en banc*, 235 F.3d 1054 (8th Cir. 2000)

RICHARD S. ARNOLD, CIRCUIT JUDGE.

[Like most courts, the U.S. Court of Appeals for the Eight Circuit designates some of its opinions as "unpublished." Unpublished opinions do not appear in the *Federal Reporter*, though they are provided to the parties, are available in the docket kept at the courthouse, and are generally available on-line. Eighth Circuit Rule 28A(i) provides that "[u]npublished opinions are not precedent and parties generally should not cite them."

Anastasoff was seeking a tax refund from the IRS. Her legal theory depended on an interpretation of the relevant statute that the Eighth Circuit had squarely rejected in a previous, *unpublished* decision, *Christie v. United States*. She argued that the court was not bound by its prior decision, since under Rule 28A(i) it was "not precedent."]

Inherent in every judicial decision is a declaration and interpretation of a general principle or rule of law. Marbury v. Madison, 5 U.S. 137 (1803). This declaration of law is authoritative to the extent necessary for the decision, and must be applied in subsequent cases to similarly situated parties. These principles, which form the doctrine of precedent, were well established and well regarded at the time this nation was founded. The Framers of the Constitution considered these principles to derive from the nature of judicial power, and intended that they would limit the judicial power delegated to the courts by Article III of the Constitution.[56] Accordingly, we conclude that 8th Circuit Rule 28A(i), insofar as it would allow us to avoid the precedential effect of our prior decisions, purports to

---

[56] "The judicial Power of the United States, shall be vested in one supreme Court, and in such inferior Courts as the Congress may from time to time ordain and establish." U.S. Const. art. III, § 1, cl. 1.

expand the judicial power beyond the bounds of Article III, and is therefore unconstitutional. * * *

[At the time of the framing,] the doctrine of precedent was not merely well established; it was the historic method of judicial decision-making, and well regarded as a bulwark of judicial independence in past struggles for liberty.

Modern legal scholars tend to justify the authority of precedents on equitable or prudential grounds. By contrast, on the eighteenth-century view (most influentially expounded by Blackstone), the judge's duty to follow precedent derives from the nature of the judicial power itself. As Blackstone defined it, each exercise of the "judicial power" requires judges "to determine the law" arising upon the facts of the case. 3 Blackstone, Commentaries *25. "To determine the law" meant not only choosing the appropriate legal principle but also expounding and interpreting it, so that "the law in that case, being solemnly declared and determined, what before was uncertain, and perhaps indifferent, is now become a permanent rule. . . ." 1 Commentaries *69. In determining the law in one case, judges bind those in subsequent cases because, although the judicial power requires judges "to determine law" in each case, a judge is "sworn to determine, not according to his own judgements, but according to the known laws. [Judges are] not delegated to pronounce a new law, but to maintain and expound the old." Id. The judicial power to determine law is a power only to determine what the law is, not to invent it. Because precedents are the "best and most authoritative" guide of what the law is, the judicial power is limited by them. * * *

The Framers accepted this understanding of judicial power (sometimes referred to as the declaratory theory of adjudication) and the doctrine of precedent implicit in it. * * * [For example, in *Federalist 78*] Hamilton concludes that "to avoid an arbitrary discretion in the courts, it is indispensable that they should be bound down by strict rules and precedents, which serve to define and point out their duty in every particular case that comes before them. . . ."

We do not mean to suggest that the Framers expected or intended the publication (in the sense of being printed in a book) of all opinions. For the Framers, limited publication of judicial decisions was the rule, and they never drew that practice into question. Before the ratification of the Constitution, there was almost no private reporting and no official reporting at all in the American states. As we have seen, however, the Framers did not regard this absence of a reporting system as an impediment to the precedential authority of a judicial decision. Although they lamented the problems associated with the lack of a reporting system and worked to assure more systematic reporting, judges and lawyers of the day recognized the authority of unpublished decisions even when they were established only by memory or by a lawyer's unpublished memorandum.

To summarize, in the late eighteenth century, the doctrine of precedent was well-established in legal practice (despite the absence of a reporting system), regarded as an immemorial custom, and valued for its role in past struggles for liberty. The duty of courts to follow their prior decisions was understood to derive from the nature of the judicial power itself and to separate it from a dangerous union with the legislative power. The statements of the Framers indicate an understanding and acceptance of these principles. We conclude therefore that, as

the Framers intended, the doctrine of precedent limits the "judicial power" delegated to the courts in Article III.

Before concluding, we wish to indicate what this case is not about. It is not about whether opinions should be published, whether that means printed in a book or available in some other accessible form to the public in general. Courts may decide, for one reason or another, that some of their cases are not important enough to take up pages in a printed report. Such decisions may be eminently practical and defensible, but in our view they have nothing to do with the authoritative effect of any court decision. The question presented here is not whether opinions ought to be published, but whether they ought to have precedential effect, whether published or not. We point out, in addition, that "unpublished" in this context has never meant "secret." So far as we are aware, every opinion and every order of any court in this country, at least of any appellate court, is available to the public. You may have to walk into a clerk's office and pay a per-page fee, but you can get the opinion if you want it. Indeed, most appellate courts now make their opinions, whether labeled "published" or not, available to anyone on line. This is true of our Court.

Another point about the practicalities of the matter needs to be made. It is often said among judges that the volume of appeals is so high that it is simply unrealistic to ascribe precedential value to every decision. We do not have time to do a decent enough job, the argument runs, when put in plain language, to justify treating every opinion as a precedent. If this is true, the judicial system is indeed in serious trouble, but the remedy is not to create an underground body of law good for one place and time only. The remedy, instead, is to create enough judgeships to handle the volume, or, if that is not practical, for each judge to take enough time to do a competent job with each case. If this means that backlogs will grow, the price must still be paid. At bottom, rules like our Rule 28A(i) assert that courts have the following power: to choose for themselves, from among all the cases they decide, those that they will follow in the future, and those that they need not. Indeed, some forms of the non-publication rule even forbid citation. Those courts are saying to the bar: "We may have decided this question the opposite way yesterday, but this does not bind us today, and, what's more, you cannot even tell us what we did yesterday." As we have tried to explain in this opinion, such a statement exceeds the judicial power, which is based on reason, not *fiat*.

Finally, lest we be misunderstood, we stress that we are not here creating some rigid doctrine of eternal adherence to precedents. Cases can be overruled. Sometimes they should be. * * * When this occurs, however, there is a burden of justification. The precedent from which we are departing should be stated, and our reasons for rejecting it should be made convincingly clear. In this way, the law grows and changes, but it does so incrementally, in response to the dictates of reason, and not because judges have simply changed their minds.

For these reasons, we must reject Ms. Anastasoff's argument that, under 8th Cir. R. 28A(i), we may ignore our prior decision in *Christie*. Federal courts, in adopting rules, are not free to extend the judicial power of the United States described in Article III of the Constitution. The judicial power of the United States is limited by the doctrine of precedent. Rule 28A(i) allows courts to ignore this

limit. If we mark an opinion as unpublished, Rule 28A(i) provides that is not precedent. Though prior decisions may be well-considered and directly on point, Rule 28A(i) allows us to depart from the law set out in such prior decisions without any reason to differentiate the cases. This discretion is completely inconsistent with the doctrine of precedent * * *. Rule 28A(i) expands the judicial power beyond the limits set by Article III by allowing us complete discretion to determine which judicial decisions will bind us and which will not. Insofar as it limits the precedential effect of our prior decisions, the Rule is therefore unconstitutional.

Ms. Anastasoff's interpretation of § 7502 was directly addressed and rejected in *Christie*. Eighth Cir. R. 28A(i) does not free us from our obligation to follow that decision. Accordingly, we affirm the judgment of the District Court.

NOTES AND QUESTIONS

(1)   The panel decision in *Anastasoff* was vacated as moot, because the IRS ended up giving Ms. Anastasoff the refund she sought, eliminating any actual controversy between them. When a decision is vacated as moot, it is treated as if it had never been issued. In other words, and ironically, *Anastasoff* itself is *not* a precedent and does not bind later courts.

Incidentally, suppose that had not happened. What influence or control would *Anastasoff* have had on (a) the U.S. Supreme Court, (b) the full 8th Circuit, sitting en banc, (c) another panel of the 8th Circuit, (d) a district court within the 8th Circuit, (e) the Supreme Court of Missouri (which is within the 8th Circuit), (f) the Supreme Court of Maine (which is not)?

(2)   The only other court of appeals decision to rule on this issue disagreed with *Anastasoff. Hart v. Massanari*, 266 F.3d 1155 (9th Cir. 2001) (Kozinski, J.).

(3)   All federal courts of appeals designate some opinions as not for publication; they vary significantly with regard to the weight unpublished decisions carry. At the time *Anastasoff* was decided, the 8th Circuit was not alone in prohibiting citation of such opinions, but that was the minority position. And there is variation among the circuits that do allow litigants to cite unpublished opinions: only the D.C. Circuit treats unpublished opinions as binding precedent, just like published opinions; others deem such opinions as persuasive, rather than binding, authority. These distinctions probably matter less in practice than in theory.

(4)   In 2006, the Federal Rules of Civil Procedure were amended to include new Rule 32.1, which provides:

Citation Permitted. A court may not prohibit or restrict the citation of federal judicial opinions, orders, judgments, or other written dispositions that have been:

(i)   designated as "unpublished," "not for publication," "non-precedential," "not precedent," or the like; and

(ii) issued on or after January 1, 2007.

(b) Copies Required. If a party cites a federal judicial opinion, order, judgment, or other written disposition that is not available in a publicly accessible electronic database, the party must file and serve a copy of that opinion, order, judgment, or disposition with the brief or other paper in which it is cited.

Does this rule resolve the split between the 8th and 9th circuits on the issue in *Anastasoff*?

(5) With regard to the merits of *Anastasoff*, are you convinced? Judge Arnold reads a great deal into the phrase "the judicial power," does he not? If that phrase does incorporate the framers' understanding of how courts function, then it would also be necessary to explore exactly what they thought the power of a judicial precedent was; Judge Arnold may be too quick to assume that the framers' views are identical to his own. Is it possible that "the judicial power" includes the power to determine the weight of one's own precedents?

As a practical matter, should unpublished decisions receive the same weight as published opinions? What consequences would flow from treating unpublished opinions as having the same authority as published ones? (You should be aware that the courts of appeals can and often do decide cases with no opinion at all.) Should judges be able to say, when handing down a decision, "This one is not binding"? Will such authority improve or harm judicial decisionmaking?

E. "LIVING LAW" AND THE "DEAD HAND"

The criticisms and defenses of precedent reflect two sides of a balancing act or impossible dialectic. On the one hand, judges (not to mention law students and members of the general citizenry) sing the praises of a "living law." Few wish to be controlled by the "dead hand" of the past: central to the attacks on precedent is the notion that old rules may well be inappropriate in modern situations and that law must be flexible and adaptive. On the other hand, for judges to decide every case anew seems inconsistent with our intuitive sense of what "law" is. As Fuller's allegory suggests, in some sense there is no law at all if every dispute turns not on a pre-existing set of rules but only on the particular judge's assessment of the particular case. And in a democratic system the constraint of precedent seems an important limit against having a (generally unelected) judiciary run amok.

Can this conflict be reconciled? Let us return one last time to Professor Schauer.

Some decisionmaking environments emphasize today — the richness and uniqueness of immediate experience. In those environments we seek the freedom to explore every possible argument or fact that might bear on making the best decision for *this* case, for it is precisely the *thisness* of the case that is most vital. At its extreme, such a system might, and arguably should, deny the relevance of precedent entirely. The virtues of stability would bow to the desire "to get it just right," and in such a framework a past decision would have little if any precedential force. More realistically, perhaps, such a system might still acknowledge precedent, but in small units. For if we see precedents as small units, full of rarely duplicated

particulars, we are likely to find few cases in which the current small unit is like some small unit of the past.

By contrast, other decisional environments focus on yesterday and tomorrow, emphasizing the recurrent rather than the unique elements of the human condition. Here precedent has its greatest role to play, generating a format for decisionmaking that channels decisions toward consideration of a comparatively limited number of factors likely to be repeated over time. In the context of this essay, this would translate into the use of larger categories of assimilation, gathering many conceivably distinguishable particulars within the embrace of the larger categories.

Without a universal answer to the question of whether stability is a good thing, we cannot decide whether decision according to precedent is a good thing. Stability may be unimpeachable in the abstract, but in reality stability comes only by giving up some of our flexibility to explore fully the deepest corners of the events now before us. Whether this price is worth paying will vary with the purposes to be served within a decisional domain, and we get no closer to knowing those purposes by understanding the relationship between stability and categorical size. Still, focusing on this relationship is valuable, because it enables us to see more clearly just how stability is achieved and just what kind of price we must pay to obtain it.[57]

When we "do law," in what "decisional environment" are we?

In his conclusion, Professor Schauer says:

Perhaps we should view legal institutions, including lawyers and law schools, as part of a larger mechanism — call it society — that needs some institutions that are creative, speculative, adaptive, and risk-taking, and other institutions that are cautious, predictable, and risk averse. These latter institutions might act as stabilizers and brakes, rather than as engines and accelerators, and it may be that both forms of institution together constitute, or at least approach, the ideal mix of decisionmaking structures. Within this mix of structures it should be apparent that precedent, as an inherently constraining form of argument, is more suited to some forms of decision than to others. And it should then be apparent why the constraints of precedent have been and perhaps should be reserved not for our institutions of progress, but for our institutions of restraint.[58]

What do you believe should be the function of our legal institutions: "stabilizers and brakes" or "engines and accelerators"; "institutions of progress" or "institutions of restraint"? Would you have a different answer for courts than for legislatures, or the Department of Justice, or law schools? Or is it that "certain

---

[57] Schauer, *supra* note 8, at 601–602.

[58] *Id.* at 604–605. We have omitted that part of Professor Schauer's Conclusion where he returns to what was largely his "project" in the article: "the rejection of the view that a theory of law must identify some form of thinking or decisionmaking unique to legal institutions." *Id.* at 603. That project is not, at this point, your concern.

institutions may contain several such decisional domains working in parallel"?[59]

Professor Schauer cites Equity and Administrative Law as two "ideals of rule-free and precedent-free decisionmaking, focusing on the richness of this case without taking on the burdens of the last case or the next case * * *."[60]

If "courts may at times rely on something close to the theoretical ideal of a system of equity, while at other times they rely more on a rule — or precedent-based approach,"[61] by what standards or principles do we in a given case judge whether their reliance on one or the other was appropriate? (Does this question echo one we raised earlier: how do we decide whether it is better that the rule be settled than that it be settled right?)

Think once more of the California Supreme Court. In what sort of decisionmaking environment did the story of *Barrett* to *King v. Lennen* take place?

If it makes sense to ask whether a single judge is stabilizer and brake or engine and accelerator, what was Justice Traynor?

Epilogue

Perhaps you think that "precedent" is Much Ado About Too Little: because appellate cases "present us exclusively with situations existing at the margins of rules and precedent" and hence there will be many cases "in which decisional constraints are inoperative and few in which they are effective,"[62] and because in any event a court can "disapprove" (or just plain overrule) prior cases.

The case that follows shows you one context in which the question of precedent quite literally determines life or death.

BUTLER v. MCKELLAR
494 U.S. 407 (1990)

CHIEF JUSTICE REHNQUIST delivered the opinion of the Court.

Petitioner Horace Butler was convicted and sentenced to death for the murder of Pamela Lane. After his conviction became final on direct appeal, Butler collaterally attacked his conviction by way of a petition for federal habeas corpus. Butler relied on our decision in *Arizona v. Roberson*, 486 U.S. 675 (1988), decided after his conviction became final on direct appeal. We have held, however, that a new decision generally is not applicable in cases on collateral review unless the decision was dictated by precedent existing at the time the petitioner's conviction became final. We hold that our ruling in *Roberson* was not so dictated and that Butler's claim is not within either of two narrow exceptions to the general rule.

---

[59] *Id.* at 603.

[60] *Id.* at 604.

[61] *Id.* at 603.

[62] *Id.* at 588 n.38.

Pamela Lane, a clerk at a convenience store near Charleston, South Carolina, was last seen alive when she left work riding a moped late in the evening of July 17, 1980. The next day several fishermen discovered Lane's body near a bridge, and the following day a local minister found Lane's moped submerged in a pond behind his church.

Petitioner Butler was arrested six weeks later on an unrelated assault and battery charge and placed in the Charleston County Jail. After invoking his Fifth Amendment right to counsel, Butler retained counsel who appeared with him at a bond hearing on August 31, 1980. He was unable to make bond, however, and was returned to the county jail. Butler's attorney would later contend in state collateral relief proceedings that after the bond hearing, he had told the police officers not to question Butler further. The officers testified that they remembered no such instruction.

Early in the morning of September 1, 1980, Butler was taken from the jail to the Charleston County Police station. He was then informed for the first time that he was a suspect in Lane's murder. After receiving Miranda warnings, Butler indicated that he understood his rights and signed two "waiver of rights" forms. The police then interrogated Butler about the murder. Butler did not request his attorney's presence at any time during the interrogation.

Butler offered two explanations for Lane's death. First, he claimed that a friend, one White, killed Lane and then sought Butler's help in disposing of the moped. When his interrogators evidenced skepticism over this statement, Butler tried again. He said that he had come upon Lane in his car and had motioned her over to the side of the road. She then voluntarily accompanied him in a drive to a nearby wooded area where the two engaged in consensual sex. Afterwards Lane threatened to accuse Butler of rape when she realized she would be late getting home. Butler maintained that he panicked, shot Lane with a handgun, and dumped her body off a bridge. In this version of the story, Butler asserted that White helped him dispose of the moped. Butler later took the police to the locations of the various events culminating in Lane's death.

The State indicted Butler and brought him to trial on a charge of first-degree murder. The trial court denied Butler's motion to suppress the statements given to police, and the statements were introduced into evidence. The jury found Butler guilty and, in a separate proceeding, sentenced him to death concluding that he committed the murder during the commission of a rape. The Supreme Court of South Carolina upheld Butler's conviction on direct appeal, *State v. Butler*, 277 S. C. 452, 290 S. E. 2d 1, and we denied certiorari. *Butler v. South Carolina*, 459 U.S. 932 (1982). Subsequently, Butler unsuccessfully petitioned for collateral relief in the State's courts, see *Butler v. State*, 286 S. C. 441, 334 S. E. 2d 813 (1985), and we again denied certiorari. *Butler v. South Carolina*, 474 U.S. 1094 (1986).

In May 1986, Butler filed this petition for federal habeas relief pursuant to 28 U.S.C. § 2254. As characterized by the District Court, one question raised in the petition was "whether police had the right to initiate questioning about the murder knowing petitioner had retained an attorney for the assault charge." App. 119. The District Court dismissed the petition on respondents' motion for summary judgment.

On appeal to the United States Court of Appeals for the Fourth Circuit, see *Butler v. Aiken*, 846 F.2d 255 (1988), Butler argued that *Edwards v. Arizona*, 451 U.S. 477 (1981), requires the police, during continuous custody, to refrain from all further questioning once an accused invokes his right to counsel on any offense. * * *

The court concluded that Butler's statements were preceded by appropriate warnings and a voluntary waiver of Fifth Amendment protections. * * *

On the same day the court denied Butler's rehearing petitions, we handed down our decision in *Roberson*. We held in *Roberson* that the Fifth Amendment bars police-initiated interrogation following a suspect's request for counsel in the context of a separate investigation. On Butler's motion for reconsideration, the original Fourth Circuit panel considered Butler's new contention that *Roberson* requires suppression of his statements taken in the separate investigation of Lane's murder. Although the panel conceded that the substance of its prior conclusion "was cast into immediate and serious doubt" by our subsequent decision in *Roberson*, it nevertheless determined that Butler was not entitled to the retroactive benefit of *Roberson*. According to the panel, the *Edwards-Roberson* limitations on police interrogation are only tangentially related to the truth-finding function. 864 F.2d, at 25. They are viewed most accurately as part of the prophylactic protection of the Fifth Amendment right to counsel created to be "guidelines" for the law enforcement profession * * *. The interrogation of Butler, while unquestionably contrary to present "guidelines," was conducted in strict accordance with established law at the time. The panel, therefore, denied Butler's petition for rehearing. A majority of the Circuit judges denied, over a dissent, Butler's petition for a rehearing en banc. We granted certiorari, 490 U.S. 1045 (1989), and now affirm.

Last Term in *Penry v. Lynaugh*, 492 U.S. 302 (1989), we held that in both capital and noncapital cases, "new rules will not be applied or announced in cases on collateral review unless they fall into one of two exceptions." * * * [W]e reiterated that, in general, a case announces a "new rule" when it breaks new ground or imposes a new obligation on the States or the Federal Government. Put differently, and, indeed, more meaningfully for the majority of cases, a decision announces a new rule " 'if the result was not dictated by precedent existing at the time the defendant's conviction became final.' "

A new decision that explicitly overrules an earlier holding obviously "breaks new ground" or "imposes a new obligation." In the vast majority of cases, however, where the new decision is reached by an extension of the reasoning of previous cases, the inquiry will be more difficult. * * *

Butler contends that *Roberson* did not establish a new rule and is, therefore, available to support his habeas petition. Butler argues that *Roberson* was merely an application of Edwards to a slightly different set of facts. * * * In support of his position, Butler points out that the majority had said that Roberson's case was directly controlled by *Edwards*. * * * According to [Butler's] counsel, the opinion in Roberson showed that the Court believed Roberson's case to be within the "logical compass" of *Edwards*. * * *

But the fact that a court says that its decision is within the "logical compass" of an earlier decision, or indeed that it is "controlled" by a prior decision, is not conclusive for purposes of deciding whether the current decision is a "new rule" * * *. Courts frequently view their decisions as being "controlled" or "governed" by prior opinions even when aware of reasonable contrary conclusions reached by other courts. In *Roberson*, for instance, the Court found *Edwards* controlling but acknowledged a significant difference of opinion on the part of several lower courts that had considered the question previously. That the outcome in *Roberson* was susceptible to debate among reasonable minds is evidenced further by the differing positions taken by the judges of the Courts of Appeals for the Fourth and Seventh Circuits noted previously. It would not have been an illogical or even a grudging application of *Edwards* to decide that it did not extend to the facts of *Roberson*. We hold, therefore, that *Roberson* announced a "new rule."

The question remains whether the new rule in *Roberson* nevertheless comes within one of the two recognized exceptions under which a new rule is available on collateral review. [The court concluded that it did not.] * * *

The judgment of the Court of Appeals is therefore

Affirmed.

JUSTICE BRENNAN, * * * dissenting. * * *

The Court's exceedingly broad definition of "new rule" — and conversely its narrow definition of "prevailing" law — betrays a vision of adjudication fundamentally at odds with any this Court has previously recognized. * * * As every first-year law student learns, adjudication according to prevailing law means far more than obeying precedent by perfunctorily applying holdings in previous cases to virtually *identical* fact patterns. Rather, such adjudication requires a judge to evaluate both the content of previously enunciated legal rules and the breadth of their application. A judge must thereby discern whether the principles applied to specific fact patterns in prior cases fairly extend to govern *analogous* factual patterns. In Justice Harlan's view, adjudication according to prevailing law demands that a court exhibit "conceptual faithfulness" to the principles underlying prior precedents, not just "decisional obedience" to precise holdings based upon their unique factual patterns.

NOTES

(1)   Chief Justice Rehnquist frequently inveighed against what he regarded as the abuse of habeas corpus in the form of multiple petitions. In 1963 Justice Brennan, who abhorred the death penalty and considered it unconstitutional in all circumstances, wrote the opinion in *Fay v. Noia*, 372 U.S. 391 (1963), a case that opened the federal courthouse doors to thousands of state prisoners bringing *habeas corpus* petitions.

(2)   Recall Cardozo: "Deep below consciousness are other forces, the likes and the dislikes, the predilections and the prejudices, the complex of instincts and

emotions and habits and convictions, which make the man [and woman] whether * * * litigant or judge."

PLANNED PARENTHOOD v. CASEY
505 U.S. 833 (1992)

Justice Blackmun, concurring in part [and] dissenting in part. * * *

In one sense the Court's approach is worlds apart from that of The Chief Justice and Justice Scalia. And yet, in another sense, the distance between the two approaches is short — the distance is but a single vote.

I am 83 years old. I cannot remain on this Court forever, and when I do step down, the confirmation process for my successor well may focus on the issue before us today. That, I regret, may be exactly where the choice between the two worlds will be made.[63]

---

[63] [Ed. Fn.] "Single vote," because the Chief Justice and Justices White, Scalia, and Thomas had voted to overrule *Roe*. The Court's membership has changed since — only four of the Justices who participated in *Casey* were still on the Court at the start of the 2009 Term — but a single vote (presently Justice Kennedy's) continued to dictate outcomes in the Court's abortion cases. *See, e.g.*, Gonzales v. Carhart, 550 U.S. 124 (2007) (5-4) (upholding federal ban on "partial birth abortion").

Chapter 6

WHAT JUDGES DO — A CODA

A. INTRODUCTION

In *Precedent*, Professor Schauer said that in appellate cases the "system presents us exclusively with situations existing at the margins of rule and precedent." If this is true for appellate courts generally (as you saw in the attractive nuisance sequence), it must be doubly true for the United States Supreme Court. (Why?) How, then, if you were a Supreme Court Justice (or a lawyer arguing before the Court), would you navigate on Cardozo's "trackless ocean," if trackless it be? That is the question we now want to revisit.

Our vehicle will be what Justice Brennan has called "the most haunting jurisprudential problem * * * one that may be the lawyer's equivalent of the physicist's hunt for the quark."[1] It arises from these simple words in the Fifth Amendment to the United States Constitution:

> [N]or shall private property be taken for public use without just compensation.

Why choose such a daunting topic? Because it probably is the apogee of what Cardozo must have meant by his metaphor.

B. PENNSYLVANIA COAL V. MAHON

General propositions do not decide concrete cases.

> — Oliver Wendell Holmes[2]

---

[1] San Diego Gas & Electric Co. v. San Diego 450 U.S. 621, 649 n.15 (1980) (Brennan, J., dissenting) (quoting CHARLES M. HAAR, LAND USE PLANNING 766 (3d ed. 1976)).

Quarks are thought to be a truly fundamental constituent of matter. Particles such as the proton and neutron, once believed to be indivisible, are composed of several quarks. While there is much indirect experimental evidence of quarks, no one has isolated a single quark. Current theory suggests that isolating the quark is impossible in principle. This "active evasion" arises from a property unique to quarks — as the separation between quarks increases, the attractive force between them also increases (contrast electric, magnetic, and gravitational forces). The term "quark" comes from a line in *Finnegans Wake*, "Three quarks for Muster Mark."

[2] Lochner v. New York, 198 U.S. 45, 76 (1905) (Holmes, J., dissenting).

PENNSYLVANIA COAL CO. v. MAHON
260 U.S. 393 (1922)

Mr. Justice Holmes delivered the opinion of the Court.

This is a bill in equity brought by the defendants in error to prevent the Pennsylvania Coal Company from mining under their property in such way as to remove the supports and cause a subsidence of the surface and of their house. The bill sets out a deed executed by the Coal Company in 1878, under which the plaintiffs claim. The deed conveys the surface, but in express terms reserves the right to remove all the coal under the same, and the grantee takes the premises with the risk, and waives all claim for damages that may arise from mining out the coal. But the plaintiffs say that whatever may have been the Coal Company's rights, they were taken away by an Act of Pennsylvania, approved May 27, 1921, P.L. 1198, commonly known there as the Kohler Act. The Court of Common Pleas found that if not restrained the defendant would cause the damage to prevent which the bill was brought, but denied an injunction, holding that the statute if applied to this case would be unconstitutional. On appeal the Supreme Court of the State agreed that the defendant had contract and property rights protected by the Constitution of the United States, but held that the statute was a legitimate exercise of the police power and directed a decree for the plaintiffs. A writ of error was granted bringing the case to this Court.

The statute forbids the mining of anthracite coal in such way as to cause the subsidence of, among other things, any structure used as a human habitation, with certain exceptions, including among them land where the surface is owned by the owner of the underlying coal and is distant more than one hundred and fifty feet from any improved property belonging to any other person. As applied to this case the statute is admitted to destroy previously existing rights of property and contract. The question is whether the police power can be stretched so far.

Government hardly could go on if to some extent values incident to property could not be diminished without paying for every such change in the general law. As long recognized, some values are enjoyed under an implied limitation and must yield to the police power. But obviously the implied limitation must have its limits, or the contract and due process clauses are gone. One fact for consideration in determining such limits is the extent of the diminution. When it reaches a certain magnitude, in most if not in all cases there must be an exercise of eminent domain and compensation to sustain the act. So the question depends upon the particular facts. The greatest weight is given to the judgment of the legislature, but it always is open to interested parties to contend that the legislature has gone beyond its constitutional power.

This is the case of a single private house. No doubt there is a public interest even in this, as there is in every purchase and sale and in all that happens within the commonwealth. Some existing rights may be modified even in such a case. *Rideout v. Knox*, 148 Mass. 368. But usually in ordinary private affairs the public interest does not warrant much of this kind of interference. A source of damage to such a house is not a public nuisance even if similar damage is inflicted on others in

different places. The damage is not common or public. *Wesson v. Washburn Iron Co.*, 13 Allen 95, 103. The extent of the public interest is shown by the statute to be limited, since the statute ordinarily does not apply to land when the surface is owned by the owner of the coal. Furthermore, it is not justified as a protection of personal safety. That could be provided for by notice. Indeed the very foundation of this bill is that the defendant gave timely notice of its intent to mine under the house. On the other hand the extent of the taking is great. It purports to abolish what is recognized in Pennsylvania as an estate in land — a very valuable estate — and what is declared by the Court below to be a contract hitherto binding the plaintiffs. If we were called upon to deal with the plaintiffs' position alone, we should think it clear that the statute does not disclose a public interest sufficient to warrant so extensive a destruction of the defendant's constitutionally protected rights.

But the case has been treated as one in which the general validity of the act should be discussed. The Attorney General of the State, the City of Scranton, and the representatives of other extensive interests were allowed to take part in the argument below and have submitted their contentions here. It seems, therefore, to be our duty to go farther in the statement of our opinion, in order that it may be known at once, and that further suits should not be brought in vain.

It is our opinion that the act cannot be sustained as an exercise of the police power, so far as it affects the mining of coal under streets or cities in places where the right to mine such coal has been reserved. As said in a Pennsylvania case, "For practical purposes, the right to coal consists in the right to mine it." *Commonwealth v. Clearview Coal Co.*, 256 Pa. St. 328, 331. What makes the right to mine coal valuable is that it can be exercised with profit. To make it commercially impracticable to mine certain coal has very nearly the same effect for constitutional purposes as appropriating or destroying it. This we think that we are warranted in assuming that the statute does.

It is true that in *Plymouth Coal Co. v. Pennsylvania*, 232 U.S. 531, it was held competent for the legislature to require a pillar of coal to be left along the line of adjoining property, that, with the pillar on the other side of the line, would be a barrier sufficient for the safety of the employees of either mine in case the other should be abandoned and allowed to fill with water. But that was a requirement for the safety of employees invited into the mine, and secured an average reciprocity of advantage that has been recognized as a justification of various laws.

The rights of the public in a street purchased or laid out by eminent domain are those that it has paid for. If in any case its representatives have been so short sighted as to acquire only surface rights without the right of support, we see no more authority for supplying the latter without compensation than there was for taking the right of way in the first place and refusing to pay for it because the public wanted it very much. The protection of private property in the Fifth Amendment presupposes that it is wanted for public use, but provides that it shall not be taken for such use without compensation. * * * When this seemingly absolute protection is found to be qualified by the police power, the natural tendency of human nature is to extend the qualification more and more until at last

private property disappears. But that cannot be accomplished in this way under the Constitution of the United States.

The general rule at least is, that while property may be regulated to a certain extent, if regulation goes too far it will be recognized as a taking. It may be doubted how far exceptional cases, like the blowing up of a house to stop a conflagration, go — and if they go beyond the general rule, whether they do not stand as much upon tradition as upon principle. * * * In general it is not plain that a man's misfortunes or necessities will justify his shifting the damages to his neighbor's shoulders. We are in danger of forgetting that a strong public desire to improve the public condition is not enough to warrant achieving the desire by a shorter cut than the constitutional way of paying for the change. As we already have said, this is a question of degree — and therefore cannot be disposed of by general propositions. But we regard this as going beyond any of the cases decided by this Court. * * *

We assume, of course, that the statute was passed upon the conviction that an exigency existed that would warrant it, and we assume that an exigency exists that would warrant the exercise of eminent domain. But the question at bottom is upon whom the loss of the changes desired should fall. So far as private persons or communities have seen fit to take the risk of acquiring only surface rights, we cannot see that the fact that their risk has become a danger warrants the giving to them greater rights than they bought.

Decree reversed.

MR. JUSTICE BRANDEIS, dissenting.

The Kohler Act prohibits, under certain conditions, the mining of anthracite coal within the limits of a city in such a manner or to such an extent "as to cause the . . . subsidence of any dwelling or other structure used as a human habitation, or any factory, store, or other industrial or mercantile establishment in which human labor is employed." Coal in place is land; and the right of the owner to use his land is not absolute. He may not so use it as to create a public nuisance; and uses, once harmless, may, owing to changed conditions, seriously threaten the public welfare. Whenever they do, the legislature has power to prohibit such uses without paying compensation; and the power to prohibit extends alike to the manner, the character and the purpose of the use. Are we justified in declaring that the Legislature of Pennsylvania has, in restricting the right to mine anthracite, exercised this power so arbitrarily as to violate the Fourteenth Amendment?[3]

---

[3] [Ed. Fn.] This reference to the 14th Amendment should perplex you; until this point you thought this was a 5th Amendment case. The explanation is in some ways no less perplexing. The Bill of Rights (i.e., the first 10 Amendments to the Constitution) originally applied only to the *federal* government, not the states. As far as the United States Constitution was concerned, then, Pennsylvania could freely take Pennsylvania Coal's property without compensation (or make a law abridging the freedom of speech, or conduct unreasonable warrantless searches, etc.). Over the years, however, the Supreme Court has held that almost every provision in the Bill of Rights does apply to the states exactly as it applies to the federal government. (The Court first held the 5th Amendment applicable to the states in Chicago, B. & J.R. v. Chicago, 166 U.S. 226 (1897)). Under a historically controversial but now well-settled approach, the Court has held that these protections are "incorporated" in the 14th Amendment, which forbids any state to deprive a person of life, liberty, or property without due process of law. Ultimately what counts

Every restriction upon the use of property imposed in the exercise of the police power deprives the owner of some right theretofore enjoyed, and is, in that sense, an abridgment by the State of rights in property without making compensation. But restriction imposed to protect the public health, safety or morals from dangers threatened is not a taking. The restriction here in question is merely the prohibition of a noxious use. The property so restricted remains in the possession of its owner. The State does not appropriate it or make any use of it. The State merely prevents the owner from making a use which interferes with paramount rights of the public. Whenever the use prohibited ceases to be noxious, — as it may because of further change in local or social conditions, — the restriction will have to be removed and the owner will again be free to enjoy his property as heretofore.

The restriction upon the use of this property can not, of course, be lawfully imposed, unless its purpose is to protect the public. But the purpose of a restriction does not cease to be public, because incidentally some private persons may thereby receive gratuitously valuable special benefits. * * * Furthermore, a restriction, though imposed for a public purpose, will not be lawful, unless the restriction is an appropriate means to the public end. But to keep coal in place is surely an appropriate means of preventing subsidence of the surface; and ordinarily it is the only available means. Restriction upon use does not become inappropriate as a means, merely because it deprives the owner of the only use to which the property can then be profitably put. The liquor and the oleomargarine cases settled that. *Mugler v. Kansas*, 123 U.S. 623, 668, 669; *Powell v. Pennsylvania*, 127 U.S. 678, 682. Nor is a restriction imposed through exercise of the police power inappropriate as a means, merely because the same end might be effected through exercise of the power of eminent domain, or otherwise at public expense. * * * If by mining anthracite coal the owner would necessarily unloose poisonous gasses, I suppose no one would doubt the power of the State to prevent the mining, without buying his coal fields. And why may not the State, likewise, without paying compensation, prohibit one from digging so deep or excavating so near the surface, as to expose the community to like dangers? In the latter case, as in the former, carrying on the business would be a public nuisance.

It is said that one fact for consideration in determining whether the limits of the police power have been exceeded is the extent of the resulting diminution in value; and that here the restriction destroys existing rights of property and contract. But values are relative. If we are to consider the value of the coal kept in place by the restriction, we should compare it with the value of all other parts of the land. That is, with the value not of the coal alone, but with the value of the whole property. The rights of an owner as against the public are not increased by dividing the interests in his property into surface and subsoil. The sum of the rights in the parts can not be greater than the rights in the whole. The estate of an owner in land is grandiloquently described as extending *ab orco usque ad coelum*. But I suppose no one would contend that by selling his interest above one hundred feet from the surface he could prevent the State from limiting, by the police power, the height of

---

in this case is the 5th Amendment. But strictly speaking the constitutional provision at issue is the 14th Amendment; the Court's conclusion is that Pennsylvania has deprived Penn Coal of property without due process *in that* it took the company's property for public use without just compensation in violation of the 5th Amendment.

structures in a city. And why should a sale of underground rights bar the State's power? For aught that appears the value of the coal kept in place by the restriction may be negligible as compared with the value of the whole property, or even as compared with that part of it which is represented by the coal remaining in place and which may be extracted despite the statute. Ordinarily a police regulation, general in operation, will not be held void as to a particular property, although proof is offered that owing to conditions peculiar to it the restriction could not reasonably be applied. But even if the particular facts are to govern, the statute should, in my opinion, be upheld in this case. For the defendant has failed to adduce any evidence from which it appears that to restrict its mining operations was an unreasonable exercise of the police power. Where the surface and the coal belong to the same person, self-interest would ordinarily prevent mining to such an extent as to cause a subsidence. It was, doubtless, for this reason that the legislature, estimating the degrees of danger, deemed statutory restriction unnecessary for the public safety under such conditions.

C. NOTE ON THE JURISPRUDENCE OF "TAKINGS"

The following is meant to locate you, *in a rudimentary way*, on the legal landscape. Warning: do not make a foray into the relevant literature — you will drown in it, and it is not necessary for our purposes!

As an incident of sovereignty, "the government" (federal, state, local) has the power to "condemn" private property. We call this the power of eminent domain. The 5th Amendment prescribes that it be exercised only for a "public use" and upon payment of "just compensation."

Example: the government condemns land for a highway, a military base, a dam, an urban renewal project, etc. In doing so, officials appropriating the property must observe certain procedures to meet the requirements of due process. The cases may involve difficult questions of, what is a "public use," and, what is "just compensation." They do not involve the question: has there been a taking — there clearly has been, for title to the land now resides in the government.

Pennsylvania Coal is *not* this type of case.

As an incident of sovereignty, the state also holds the power to act, in a traditional formulation, for the "health, safety, morals, and general welfare" of its citizens. This "police power" allows the state to curtail our actions and to "regulate" our property without any obligation to provide compensation.[4]

Pennsylvania Coal involves a challenge to the exercise of the police power. The court holds that such exercises can compromise private ownership ("property") to such a degree as to amount to a taking.

---

[4] As you will learn in Constitutional Law, the federal government possesses the power of eminent domain. It does not have a general "police power." Legislation concerning the public weal must be based on particular grants of authority in the Constitution. The overwhelming majority of federal legislation rests on Congress's power to regulate interstate commerce, U.S. CONST. art. I, § 8, cl. 3, which has been read expansively by the courts.

Where is the boundary between these two great powers? Where *should* it be, for the question is normative. If the Court calls the governmental action a "regulation," whatever losses it inflicts on a citizen will have to be borne by her without compensation. If the Court calls the governmental action a "regulatory taking," the regulation is struck down as unconstitutional and the sovereign entity must now decide whether to proceed with its project by way of eminent domain and the payment of compensation.

Much governmental regulatory activity redistributes wealth. What the Kohler Act "takes" from the coal companies, it gives to the surface owners. If that is so, when *should* the Court say that a regulation "takes property" within the meaning of the 5th Amendment?

This problem of "regulatory takings" is what Justice Brennan compared to the search for the quark, and *Pennsylvania Coal* stands at the beginning of the modern history of the problem. It is the most famous case in the canon — perhaps because Justice Holmes wrote for the Court and Justice Brandeis dissented. It has been said, "The Court has made no important doctrinal advance" since then;[5] and that Justice Holmes' opinion is "both the most important and most mysterious writing in takings law."[6]

It is our paradigmatic case of the trackless ocean because of the issues at stake:

> The fascination of the eminent domain clause is that it poses the question how political and economic processes which permit redistributions that are widely perceived as necessary can be controlled in a world that recognizes and gives great respect to property rights.[7]

Or, more starkly: are a popular democracy and private property compatible institutions? Or finally, how do we lead "the good life"?

From where is your lodestar to come? From the constitutional text? From "precedent"? From reverence for the past *qua* past?

Here, incidentally, is what Justice Holmes said privately about the key "precedent" (*Mugler v. Kansas*) at issue in *Pennsylvania Coal*:

> I fear that I am out of accord for the moment with my public-minded friends in another way. Frankfurter generally writes to me about any important opinions of mine and he has been silent as to the one I sent you in which Brandeis dissented [*Mahon*]; probably feeling an unnecessary delicacy about saying that he disagrees. Of course, I understand the possibility of thinking otherwise — I could not fail to, even if Brandeis had agreed. But nevertheless when the premises are a little more emphasized, as they should have been by me, I confess to feeling as much confidence as I often do. I always have thought that old Harlan's decision in *Mugler* v. *Kansas* was pretty fishy.[8]

---

[5] Bruce Ackerman, Private Property and the Constitution 236 n.9 (1977).

[6] *Id.* at 156.

[7] Joseph Sax, *Takings*, 53 U. Chi. L. Rev. 279, 293 (1986) (book review).

[8] Letter from Oliver Wendell Holmes, Jr. to Harold Laski (Jan. 13, 1923), *in* 2 Holmes-Laski Letters

Justice Holmes's confident account of the case seems at odds with our suggestion that the substantive issue is as insoluble as any in law. But this reveals more about Holmes than about regulatory takings. Holmes was rarely stymied; as he once wrote to a friend, "I have long said there is no such thing as a hard case. I am frightened weekly but always when you walk up to the lion and lay hold the hide comes off and the same old donkey of a question of law is underneath."[9]

What do you suppose were the premises Justice Holmes had in mind which he wished he had "a little more emphasized"?

D.   IN SEARCH OF LODESTARS: ECONOMICS

Justice Holmes once observed that the future belonged to "the master of economics."[10] That suggests that mastery of economics may lay tracks in our metaphorical ocean, may perhaps help, in particular and especially, to undo the riddle of regulatory takings, ripe with questions over government-mandated attempts to redistribute wealth.

Consider then:

> Pennsylvania is a state with extensive coal resources located under its land, and the question, which should delight any economic analyst, is how does the owner of the land maximize the joint value of two inconsistent uses, that of the surface and the mineral rights below. The Pennsylvania landowners did not await the growth of economic theory in order to reach their own conclusion on the question. In the years between 1890 and 1920, a large number of landowners sold the mineral rights to coal companies in standard transactions whereby the surface owners expressly took the risk of cave-ins and subsidence from mining operations. The sales of the mineral rights made perfectly good sense because the companies had far greater expertise in mining coal than did the surface owners. It was therefore possible to find some price greater than the value of the coal to landowners, but less than its value to the coal companies. The transfer of the mineral rights therefore left both sides better off than they were before the deal took place.

> Yet, it may be asked, why did the original owners retain the surface rights? If these had been transferred, then the coal owners would not have

---

473 (Mark DeWolfe Howe ed., 1963). *Mugler* upheld legislation that prohibited the manufacture of alcoholic beverages, thereby rendering the plaintiff's brewery suddenly valueless. "Old Harlan" is John Marshall Harlan, who was on the Court from 1877 to 1911, and is generally referred to as "the first Justice Harlan" to distinguish him from his grandson, the "second" Justice Harlan, who served from 1955 to 1971. "Frankfurter" is Felix Frankfurter, Harvard Law Professor and a member of the Court from 1939 to 1962.

[9] Letter from Oliver Wendell Holmes, Jr. to Frederick Pollock (Dec. 11, 1909), *in* 1 HOLMES-POLLOCK LETTERS 155, 156 (Mark DeWolfe Howe ed., 1941). Someone once observed that in a humility contest Holmes would have finished tied for last place with Charles DeGaulle. Is profound self-confidence a virtue or a vice in a judge?

[10] As well as "the man of statistics." Oliver Wendell Holmes, Jr., *The Path of the Law, in* COLLECTED LEGAL PAPERS 187 (1920).

had to worry about the danger of lawsuits from cave-in or subsidence, and they surely could have drawn up simpler deeds without the divided ownership of the land. Yet there are drawbacks to this solution as well. The coal companies would have had to increase the purchase price paid to the original owners, when there is no reason to think that the surface rights were worth more to the coal companies than to the people already using them. Unlike the purchase of the mineral rights, the purchase of the surface rights only would move resources from higher to lower value uses.

Once the original landowners retained the surface rights, it became necessary to anticipate conflicts that might arise from the inconsistent use of surface and mining rights. The most evident conflict concerns that over cave-in and subsidence * * *.

The risk of subsidence of surface lands is neither remote nor improbable. It is the ordinary stuff of coal mining. The parties therefore did direct their attention to this question, and by explicit terms agreed that the risk of subsidence should fall on the surface owner. The logic behind this choice must have been as follows. It makes no sense to avoid the conflict of interest by having the coal companies acquire the surface as well as the mineral rights, for then the interim use value of the land before subsidence (which itself need never come) is lost to both sides. Since by their joint subjective evaluations the right to mine is more valuable to the companies than the right to the fully protected surface is to the landowner, then the surface owner should take the risk of failure, while retaining the benefit of the use of the land until the subsidence occurred. This result was achieved by having the surface owner sign over the support rights, the so-called "third" or support estate, to the mineral company. * * * The transaction costs between the parties were low, so that rights and duties, including the risk of loss, were allocated to maximize the joint value of the whole. Whatever the surface owner lost in the value of the support rights, he gained by an appropriate upward adjustment of the sale price of the mineral rights to the coal company. There were too many transactions on identical terms for everyone to have gotten the economics wrong.

As a case of private bargaining, then, the transaction between the coal companies and the surface owners proved to be quite stable. At any relevant time, individual surface owners could have reacquired by purchase the support rights for their land from the coal companies. The paperwork was simple enough, but undoing the original deal did not make economic sense, if only because the coal companies rightly would demand a very high price to surrender support rights under one piece of land which could well limit their capacity to work large tracts of coal under adjacent parcels. Once acquired, therefore, the title to the mineral and the support rights tended to remain in place — at least insofar as private markets were concerned.

* * * This assignment of property rights, while stable in private economic markets, need not prove stable in political markets, however, where very different decision rules operate, especially when there are no

constitutional constraints on legislative behavior. While no surface owner may be prepared to pay the coal companies what it takes to recover the support rights, many surface owners may well be quite willing to invest the smaller sums needed to persuade the legislatures to pass laws that will prevent the coal companies from mining in ways that cause damage or subsidence to coal properties. These opportunities are always present because the distribution of votes and political influence is not the same as the distribution of property rights, if only because the coal companies do not vote, and their shareholders may well reside out of state. Coal companies (or for that matter, their unions) are never without their political clout, but clout is not the same as invincibility. In principle there is no reason to think that the landowners must necessarily fail. Their relative political power could be, and indeed has proved, quite sufficient to get the legislature to move to upset the distribution of property rights between coal companies and surface owners that the contracts between them had mandated.[11]

Professor Epstein's first point is that coal companies and landowners all over Pennsylvania had struck deals, in arm's length bargaining, that maximized the economic well-being of both, and that had, by way of "the invisible hand," led to efficient allocations of resources.

Suppose you share the assumption of freely negotiated deals. How does it help you to decide *Penn Coal*? Would not your reasoning have to go something like this: I believe in free markets — or at least, I believe that this country is committed to a market economy. Therefore, I will approve government regulations designed to help the market to function (e.g., anti-trust regulations), but I will disapprove regulations that interfere with the market (e.g., rent control) or that try to upset freely negotiated wealth allocations (*Penn Coal*).

Set aside the question: what do we do with regulations that fail to fall neatly into either category (what, for instance, is pollution legislation?). Even within the narrower framework set forth above, what legitimizes economics generally and the economics of free markets in particular as a mode of constitutional analysis?

In your search for guidance, are you merely elevating your personal economic theory into constitutional doctrine? Are you rewriting the police power to mean: power to act for the health, safety, morals, and general welfare unless it violates principles of laissez faire? Is that too steep a price to pay for such guidance as these principles may give you?

E. IN SEARCH OF LODESTARS: POLITICS

Professor Epstein's second point goes to the integrity of the political process that led to the passage of the Kohler Act. Treating "political markets" as much the same as "economic markets," he describes the landowners as having in essence bought

---

[11] Richard Epstein, *Takings: Descent and Resurrection*, 1987 Sup. Ct. Rev. 1, 5–8. For an extraordinarily full exposition of the background of *Penn Coal* see Carol Rose, Mahon *Reconstructed: Why The Takings Issue Is Still A Muddle*, 57 S. Cal. L. Rev. 561 (1984).

the legislation. For him, the Act represents the successful exercise of political clout, enabling the surface owners to acquire protection for far less than it would have cost them in a private transaction.[12]

(1) Suppose, again, that you share this view of the political provenance of the regulation before you.

What guidance does that give you? Is it your role to "go behind" the legislative enactment, as it were? The 5th Amendment seems only to say that the state *cannot* do certain things; does it matter why the state *does* something? From the point of view of the coal company, why should it matter whether the Pennsylvania legislature responded to political pressures or sincerely pursued its view of the public interest?

(2) If the legislative background is relevant, what aspects is it legitimate for you to look for in your quest for guidance?

(a) Suppose you discovered that the legislation was passed only as a result of logrolling by two key legislators. Should that be your concern? And so what? Why should a mere two traded votes contaminate the outcome?

If today's logrolling worked in favor of the Mahons, might not tomorrow's logrolling work in favor of coal companies? Will not every interest in the political market place get a slice of the pie in the long run?[13]

(b) Or suppose you found or "knew" that one opponent outspent the other. Should it matter?

(c) Or suppose you found out or suspected that five key legislators had been "bought" by the homeowners?

(3) Would it matter to you whether you thought the legislation represented the successful exercise of power by the few against the many or by the many against the few? Should it matter?

(4) Does anything in Justice Holmes' opinion hint at his having been troubled by the provenance of the Kohler Act? Was *that* one of the premises he wished he had "a little more emphasized"? If not, was that because he was singularly naive about

---

[12] Epstein's point is not that bribery must have taken place (although that is one way that legislation can be purchased), but rather that a mutually beneficial exchange occurred in which both the legislators and the beneficiaries of the legislation gave the other something of value, if only political support. This analysis is an application of "public choice theory." Public choice theorists apply economic principles in non-market settings, particularly in the study of public institutions. The approach is the opposite of what one learns in high school civics classes; it is deeply cynical about both politics and human nature. For the public choice theorist, legislative activity has nothing to do with the pursuit of the public good, which does not really exist and could not be discerned or attained by a legislature even if it did, or with the battle between different ideologies, which are irrelevant to legislative decisionmaking. The legislative process is simply and entirely a bidding war between competing interest groups.

[13] Rose, *supra* note 11, at 583. *But see id.* at 584 n.117 (critiquing logrolling) (citing JAMES BUCHANAN & GORDON TULLOCK, THE CALCULUS OF CONSENT: LOGICAL FOUNDATIONS OF CONSTITUTIONAL DEMOCRACY 131–145 (1962)). The Buchanan and Tullock book is one of the groundbreaking works of public choice theory and the centerpiece of the work that won Buchanan the Nobel Prize for Economics in 1986. *See also supra* note 12.

the realities of the political arena or because he thought it inappropriate to look for guidance in this particular place?

F. IN SEARCH OF LODESTARS: "PROPERTY"

Justice Holmes says:

> When this seemingly absolute protection [of property] is found to be qualified by the police power, the natural tendency of human nature is to extend the qualification more and more until at last private property disappears. But that cannot be accomplished in this way under the Constitution of the United States.[14]

What is so important about private property that the Constitution saw fit to protect it? For that matter, is not "property" a legal construct, a label for a bundle of rights that courts will (or will not) enforce? If so, what does a constitutional "right to property" mean? And how is human nature implicated in the need for the protection of property?

> The principle that the state necessarily owes compensation when it takes private property was not generally accepted in either colonial or revolutionary America. Uncompensated takings were frequent and found justification first in appeals to the crown and later in republicanism, the ideology of the Revolution. * * *

> ### Republican Ideology and the Right to Property

> The failure to establish this safeguard [i.e., compensation] for property rights was consistent with central tenets of republicanism, the reigning ideology of 1776. At the center of republican thought lay a belief in a common good and a conception of society as an organic whole. The state's proper role consisted in large part of fostering virtue, of making the individual unselfishly devote himself to the common good. Individual rights played no more than a secondary role in republican thought. * * *

> The role of property in this school of thought was complex. Ownership of a certain amount of property — such as a farm or a workshop — was necessary for participation in the polity. A man dependent on others for his livelihood did what they wanted him to do. He lacked the independence necessary to pursue the common good. At the same time, the possession and pursuit of property could corrupt and lead the individual to place personal before public interest. Celebrations of self-denial and denunciations of commerce, of luxury, and of speculation were common elements in republican rhetoric. Many republican thinkers pilloried great wealth: Wealth encouraged greed in its possessors and enabled them to wield undue power. Moreover, the monopolization of possessions by a few denied to others the minimum of property that they needed to be full participants in the republican polity.

---

[14] *Pennsylvania Coal*, 260 U.S. at 415.

Drawing on these premises, a major strand of republican thought held that the state could abridge the property right in order to promote common interests. Thus, in framing the Declaration of Independence's list of inalienable rights, Jefferson did not use the standard Lockean-liberal formulation of "life, liberty, and property." Because he did not consider property an inalienable right, he employed instead the phrase "life, liberty and the pursuit of happiness." * * *

Faith in Legislatures

The fact that the first state constitutions lacked just compensation clauses is only in part attributable to republican conceptions of property and of rights. It is also evidence of the faith in legislatures that was a central tenet of republican thought. * * *

The Shift from Republicanism to Liberalism

* * * Faith in legislatures and belief in the existence of a community of interests among citizens had developed at a time when local legislatures opposed crown officials and defended the common causes of the colonists. Once the state legislatures came to rule in their own right, however, social divisions that had been masked during the struggle with royal governors were exposed. Revolutionary legislatures confiscated the land of loyalists; through stay laws and the issuance of paper money, they aided debtors at the expense of creditors.

As legislatures began to take actions with such redistributive consequences, many individuals reexamined and rejected the republican orthodoxy. Loss of faith in legislatures was common, but the critique of republicanism went beyond attacks on legislatures. When the diversity of economic interests manifested itself in political struggle, many rejected the idea that a readily discernible common good existed. Republicans stressed the harmony in American society and the role of self-denial and austerity in promoting public welfare. The emerging non-republican school of thought, to which such politicians as John Adams, Benjamin Lincoln, James Madison, and Theophilus Parsons belonged, emphasized societal tensions and the benefits to be derived from self-interest.

Non-republicans had a more expansive view than republicans of which rights could not be undermined by the state. They sought to create a large sphere within which the individual could exercise privileges and enjoy immunities free from state interference. Their focus on individual rights and their essentially atomistic view of society characterized these non-republicans as liberal thinkers.

III. The Fifth Amendment

The just compensation clause of the Fifth Amendment reflected the liberalism of its author, James Madison, who in synthesizing revolutionary era trends gave them substance and coherence* * * * The ideology underlying the clause ran counter to the republicanism espoused by the Anti-Federalists, the opponents of the Constitution. In the years after

ratification of the Constitution, however, Madisonian liberalism came to dominate American legal and political thought. * * *

Madison was a liberal. The ideas of a readily discernible common interest and of property rights subject to government abridgment were alien to him. For Madison, society was characterized by conflicts among interest groups, and those conflicts were often over property. "[T]he most common and durable source of factions," he wrote, "has been the various and unequal distribution of property. Those who hold, and those who are without property, have ever formed distinct interests in society."

Although Madison did not believe property was a natural right — it depended for its existence on positive law — its protection was of critical importance. The diversity of interests that possession of property occasioned prevented tyranny, and the acquisition of property was a necessary by-product of the freedom of action he deemed an essential part of liberty. "Government," he wrote, "is instituted no less for protection of the property, than of the persons of individuals."[15]

And see Professor Michelman:

Property as Paradigm

It seems that through the republic's first century and a half, property — security of legally justified possession and material expectation — was the paradigm of the constitutionally protected private sphere. * * *

At least three reasons can be suggested for this original focus on property as an especially urgent or attractive object of constitutional protection as private right. First, property seems to have been, above all others, the realm of affairs in which it was feared that factional interest would overcome civic empathy and enlightened deliberation, propelling government toward exploitative and unjust action in the absence of special controls. * * * A redistributively inclined majority would always be ready to violate a minority's proprietary interests and rights.

Second, property seems to have lent itself especially well to the notion of a categorical separation of law from politics — the notion of a law "above" politics — on which the otherwise mysterious idea of a self-limiting popular sovereign power crucially depended. * * * Property, with its long history of common-law elucidation and its naturalistic imagery of clearly demarcated "closes," was Atlantic legal culture's very model of a private sphere rightfully guarded against human encroachment by a higher law.

Third, * * * security of property holding was considered a matter not just of private self-interest but of general *political* concern. Property was, to be sure, one primary mode of private liberty and self-realization, but it was more: a claim going to the heart of the prospects for successful republican self-government. In the ancient and early modern republican

---

[15] William Michael Treanor, *The Origins and Original Significance of the Just Compensation Clause of the Fifth Amendment*, 94 Yale L.J. 694, 694, 699–701, 704–705, 708–710 (1985).

traditions of which the founding generation were still in some measure partaking, an unquestionably secure base of material support was viewed as indispensable if one's independence and competence as a participant in public affairs was to be guaranteed. Material security was thought necessary to ensure the authenticity and reliability of one's politically expressed judgment regarding what course of policy would best conduce to the rights and other interests of the governed. The person whose material security became a matter of doubt or contingency — either because the person had no property and thus depended for livelihood on the grace of others or because the person relied on a form of property, such as public office, pension, or public debt, that was constantly up for grabs in the conduct of government itself — would too likely act in public councils either as the tool of his patron or as the tool of his own particular, immediate and possibly delusive material interest. Either way, that person would not be reliably acting in the more systemic or longer-run interest of either national prosperity or common liberty, including the person's own. In the traditional republican diction, that person was not "independent" but "corrupt." In short, the *distribution* of secure property endowments was regarded as a matter of constitutive political concern, an essential factor in any scheme of popular sovereignty valued as a medium of the people's self-determination or self-protection regarding both general welfare and individual liberty.[16]

(1) Does this help you to decide *Pennsylvania Coal*?

(2) Suppose you were presented with this argument:

Rights under a political constitution are political rights; and so what one primarily has a right to is the maintenance of the conditions of one's fair and effective participation in the constituted order, as an individual no less entitled than others to the respect and concern of the community, and also no more entitled than they to any particular outcomes save those that affect the conditions of continued effective participation. Loss — even great loss — of the economic value of one's property holdings does not as such violate those conditions. What does, perhaps, violate them is exposure to sudden changes in the major elements and crucial determinants of one's established position in the world, as one has come reasonably to understand that position * * *.[17]

Property would then be regarded as:

an indispensable ingredient in the constitution of the individual as a participant in the life of the society, including not least the society's processes for collectively regulating the conditions of an ineluctably social existence.[18]

---

[16] Frank Michelman, *Possession vs. Distribution in the Constitutional Idea of Property*, 72 Iowa L. Rev. 1319, 1327–1329 (1987).

[17] Frank Michelman, *Mr. Justice Brennan: A Property Teacher's Appreciation*, 15 Harv. C.R.-C.L. L. Rev. 296, 305–306 (1980).

[18] *Id.* at 304.

This is Professor Michelman's interpretation of what he believes to be "the makings of an illuminating answer [by Justice Brennan] to the problem of how to understand the notion of constitutionally guaranteed property rights within a regime of popular democracy."

How should, under this perspective, *Pennsylvania Coal* have been decided?

(3) Does this help?

> If at one level the judicial opinion is a ratiocination on deliberate social ordering by law, at another level it may record a certain social common sense regarding people's capacities for leading good lives together, a sense that is common to the judicial author's own era, culture, and professional circle.[19]

Or this?

> Takings doctrine is generated not by any abstract methodological or theoretical concern, but by the pictures that judges have in their heads about the participants in the public land-use planning arena, pictures about who is empowered, who is unempowered and how those who enjoy a power monopoly have used that power to their strategic advantage. Takings doctrine is shaped by striking pictures and powerful metaphors that communicate basic assumptions, about who holds power and how those who hold power use it. These pictures, or narratives, are shaped by underlying political visions, that is, belief structures about how society is and ought to be organized.[20]

Did the Holmes-Brandeis disagreement represent two different ratiocinations or did it represent two different conceptions of the good life?

Was the difference caused "simply" by the fact that Holmes was a "liberal" and Brandeis a "civic republican"?

What is *your* conception of people's capacities "for leading good lives together"? What pictures do *you* have in your head, what "belief structures about how society is and ought to be organized"?

For example, do you think that participation in the affairs of the body politic is the best that life has to offer? Or do you believe that your deepest happiness will come from the private realm, the web of your personal connections to family, to friends, to nature, whatever?

Or do you in fact have "*two* faces, one a communicative consensus-seeking, politically active, reasonable face, in the sense of 'reasonable' that is opposed to fanatical, the other a private and autonomous, perhaps detached and secretive, uncompromising face of a person pursuing his own distinctive good, perhaps guided in this by a comprehensive rationality"?[21]

---

[19] Frank Michelman, *Dunwody Distinguished Lecture in Law, Conceptions of Democracy in American Constitutional Argument: Voting Rights*, 41 Fla. L. Rev. 443, 444 (1989).

[20] Gregory S. Alexander, *Takings, Narratives, and Power*, 88 Colum. L. Rev. 1752, 1753 (1988).

[21] Stuart Hampshire, *Liberalism: The New Twist*, N.Y. Rev. Books, Aug. 12 1993, at 43, 44 (reviewing

What do these questions — and your answers — have to do with the 5th Amendment, *Pennsylvania Coal*, and "Property"?

G.   IN SEARCH OF LODESTARS: "A LAW OF RULES"

If decisions derive from "social common sense regarding people's capacities for leading good lives together" or from "pictures that judges have in their heads" is there room left for The Rule of Law? Should there be? Or should we adopt a "less reverential stance towards the rule of law than that to which we are inured?"[22]

After *Penn Coal*, is the ocean any less trackless? Has the court offered any meaningful guidance to governments or property owners, or is the existence of a taking left to standardless judicial discretion? In another famous "takings" case, *Penn Central Transportation Co.* v. *New York City*[23] (upholding the constitutionality of "landmark" legislation and the designation of New York City's Grand Central Station as a landmark), Justice Brennan said:

> [T]his Court, quite simply, has been unable to develop any "set formula" for determining when "justice and fairness" require that economic injuries caused by public action be compensated by the government, rather than remain disproportionately concentrated on a few persons.[24]

All that can be said is that

> In engaging in these essentially ad hoc, factual inquiries, the Court's decisions have identified several factors that have significance.[25]

Does the adoption of a so-called "balancing test" for each case reflect a "less reverential stance towards the rule of law" or is it, "quite simply," the abnegation of the rule of law?

In any event, why should clear rules be important? In *The Rule of Law as a Law of Rules*,[26] Justice Scalia gives six reasons:[27]

1) Consistency and the appearance of consistency: "When a case is accorded a different disposition from an earlier one, it is important, if the system of justice is to be respected, not only that the later case *be* different, but that it *be seen to be so.*

2) Uniformity among the lower courts. Under a balancing test "it is not *we* [the Supreme Court] who will be 'closing in on the law,'" but rather the various lower courts.

John Rawls, Political Liberalism) (emphasis added).

[22] Michelman, *supra* note 17, at 1337.

[23] 438 U.S. 107 (1987).

[24] *Id.* at 124.

[25] *Id.* at 124.

[26] Antonin Scalia, *The Rule of Law as a Law of Rules*, 56 U. CHI. L. REV. 1175 (1989).

[27] The following summary of Scalia's argument is taken from Kathleen Sullivan, *The Supreme Court, 1991 Term — Foreword: The Justices of Rules and Standards*, 106 HARV. L. REV. 22, 65 (1992). Quotations are from Justice Scalia; bracketed material is Professor Sullivan's.

3) Predictability, or the avoidance of uncertainty. "Rudimentary justice requires that those subject to the law must have the means of knowing what it prescribes."

4) Judicial restraint "Only by announcing rules do we hedge ourselves in" to the "governing principle."

5) Judicial armor against popular disapproval. "The chances that frail men and women [judges] will stand up to their unpleasant duty [to countermand the popular will] are greatly increased if they can stand behind the solid shield of a firm, clear principle enunciated in earlier cases."

6) Keeping matters of law separate from matters of fact. A judge using a balancing test "begins to resemble a finder of fact more than a determiner of law" and "(t)o reach such a stage is, in a way, a regrettable concession of defeat — an acknowledgment that we have passed the point where 'law,' properly speaking, has any further application."

Professor Sullivan comments:

The first three justifications for rules track traditional definitions of the rule of law and resemble traditional fairness or utility arguments for rules. The last three arguments for rules focus on the judicial role, the separation of powers, and the distinction between law and politics. Justice Scalia treats the choice of rules over standards as essential to maintaining the distinctiveness of the judicial craft and the legitimacy of courts in a democracy. He takes it as given that the Supreme Court, both through its outcomes and its modes of analysis, can " 'make' law" in interpreting the Constitution, but, having admitted as much, he is anxious to reduce the reality or appearance of personal discretion in judging and argues that rules are just the thing to do the trick.[28]

Against this, consider Professor Margaret Jane Radin's defense of case-by-case balancing:

But is anything wrong with "essentially ad hoc factual inquiries?" That is simply one way of expressing a pragmatic approach to decision making. Pragmatism is essentially particularist, essentially context-bound and holistic; each decision is an all-things-considered intuitive weighing. Pragmatism is indeed "essentially" ad hoc. There is a great philosophical tradition of pragmatism, currently enjoying a renaissance, and there is much to recommend a view that legal decision making and legal practice is best understood as pragmatic. Yet pragmatism is much feared because of its particularism, because of its wholehearted embrace of the contextuality of everything.

The fear of "essentially ad hoc" inquiries — the fear of pragmatism — is a fear of *arbitrariness*. How can we achieve consistency — or at least perceived consistency — and how can we achieve fairness by deciding like cases alike, unless some general rule by force of its own formulation can

---

[28] *Id.* at 65–66.

carve out a whole category of cases that we can be sure fall together under the rule? How can we give citizens notice of what they may or may not do under the law if we cannot lay down hard-and-fast rules?

When put this way, we can see that the dialectic in takings jurisprudence * * * is simply an instance of what has been called the dialectic of rules and standards. In this dialectic, the "rule" pole is associated with conceptualism and per se rules and the "standards" pole is associated with pragmatism and balancing tests. When we put the problem this way, we can also see * * * that deeply at work in takings jurisprudence — as indeed in all jurisprudence — is the question whether pragmatism and balancing tests can be faithful to the ideal of the Rule of Law. All of the questions of consistency and like treatment under the law, and the pre-existence and knowability of law necessary for notice and compliance, reflect the elements of the ideal of the Rule of Law. * * *

The model of rules is a conservative interpretation of the Rule of Law, or at least congenial to conservatives, because it ties in so well with the Hobbesian view of politics. If majority rule is a shifting coalition of rent seekers, then democratic government is a Leviathan to be restrained. But if majoritarian bargains can be dissolved by unelected judges whose decisions do not even represent fulfillment of interest-group bargaining, then judges are even more in need of restraint than legislatures. * * * The only way the conservative can see to tie judges down this way is to employ formal rules with self-evident applications. In other words, unless law consists of rules that tie judges' hands, government is unjustified.

One who accepts a Hobbesian model of politics requiring law as the model of rules also accepts an underlying Hobbesian model of human nature. In this model of human nature, limitless self-interest and the consequent urgent need for self-defense require the most expansive possible notion of private property, indeed, the classical liberal conception of property. Nothing will get produced unless people are guaranteed the permanent internalization of the benefits of their labor; nobody will restrain herself from predation against others unless all are restrained from predation against her. * * *

We can now understand more clearly why neoconservatives think that if takings jurisprudence cannot be reduced to formal rules * * * it must violate the Rule of Law. Nevertheless, I think instead that this is a field in which pragmatic judgment under a standard — an explicit balancing approach — is better. The pragmatic ethical issue defies reduction to formal rules. When the Court's takings jurisprudence has not been conclusory, it has usually attempted to address in a practical way an underlying issue of political and moral theory: is it appropriate to make this particular person bear the cost of this particular government action for the benefit of this particular community? Such is the burden of the *Penn Central* multi-factor balancing test * * *.[29]

---

[29] Margaret Radin, *The Liberal Conception of Property: Cross Currents in the Jurisprudence of*

Is belief in the Rule of Law the same as formalism and mechanical ("self-evident") application of rules to cases?

Is "ad hoc" the same as "an explicit balancing approach?" Is balancing necessarily incompatible with The Rule of Law? Is it the balancing per se that is worrisome (to some) or is it the fear that, deliberately or otherwise, the wrong things will be balanced? For instance, describe the different ways in which you could first identify and then balance what is at stake in *Penn Coal*. Are those choices outcome-determinative? On what "pragmatic judgments" did you base your choices?

Against Professor Radin's stance, consider that of Professor Herbert Wechsler, in his classic piece, *Toward Neutral Principles of Constitutional Law*:[30]

> Are there, indeed, any criteria that both the Supreme Court and those who undertake to praise or to condemn its judgements are morally and intellectually obligated to support?
>
> * * * The man who simply lets his judgment turn on the immediate result may not, however, realize that his position implies that the courts are free to function as a naked power organ, that it is an empty affirmation to regard them, as ambivalently he so often does, as courts of law. If he may know he disapproves of a decision when all he knows is that it has sustained a claim put forward by a labor union or a taxpayer, a Negro or a segregationist, a corporation or a Communist — he acquiesces in the proposition that a man of different sympathy but equal information may no less properly conclude that he approves. * * *
>
> I now add that whether you are tolerant, perhaps more tolerant than I, of the *ad hoc* in politics, with principle reduced to a manipulative tool, are you not also ready to agree that something else is called for from the courts? I put it to you that the main constituent of the judicial process is precisely that it must be genuinely principled, resting with respect to every step that is involved in reaching judgment on analysis and reasons quite transcending the immediate result that is achieved. To be sure, the courts decide, or should decide, only the case they have before them. But must they not decide on grounds of adequate neutrality and generality, tested not only by the instant application but by others that the principles imply? Is it not the very essence of judicial method to insist upon attending to such other cases, preferably those involving an opposing interest, in evaluating any principle avowed?

Takings, 88 Colum. L. Rev. 1667, 1680–1684 (1988). Note that "classical liberal" here also means "neo-conservative." For an accessible introduction to the "rule of law" debate in its current form, *see* Margaret Radin, *Reconsidering The Rule of Law*, 69 B.U. L. Rev. 781 (1989). Note also that Professor Radin's own thinking with regard to takings shifted shifted somewhat after she published *The Liberal Conception of Property*. For a (somewhat dense) statement of her later views, *see* Margaret Radin & Frank Michelman, *Pragmatics and Post-Structuralist Legal Practice*, 139 U. Pa. L. Rev. 1019 (1991).

[30] Herbert Wechsler, *Toward Neutral Principles of Constitutional Law*, 73 Harv. L. Rev. 1, 11–12, 15 (1959). "Neutral Principles," as it is known, was delivered on April 7, 1959, as the Oliver Wendell Holmes Lecture at the Harvard Law School.

Does *Penn Coal* embody a neutral principle? What is it?

Does invocation of neutral principles in itself "tell us anything useful about the appropriate content of those principles or how the Court should derive the values they embody"?[31] Professor Ely uses two examples: "Freedom of speech is guaranteed to Republicans" and "Legislatures can do whatever they want." Identify the problems he meant to exemplify.

H.   IN SEARCH OF LODESTARS: "DEMOCRACY"

(1) Regulations have redistributive impact: the Kohler Act made surface owners richer and coal companies poorer; the landmark designation of Grand Central Station enriched the citizens of New York at the expense of a single entity, Penn Central.

What should judges do when faced with majoritarian redistributions of wealth — assuming a rough consensus exists that to redistribute from the better off to the less well off is necessary as well as ethical. Should the Court accept this consensus as binding or should it come to its own conclusions about the politics, the ethics, the morality of redistribution?

(2) If it accepts the consensus, should it, nevertheless, undertake an independent appraisal of whether the redistributive impact indeed flows in the "right" direction — since presumably no consensus exists about the appropriateness of redistributing from the less well-off to the better off?

(3) What should the Court do if it felt that although it is desirable in the short run to uphold landmark designations (for instance), in the long run such action would impoverish the entire community — because people might no longer build buildings remotely in danger of being designated "landmarks"?

(4) Would taking any action other than bowing to the consensus threaten the dissolution of "majoritarian bargains * * * by unelected judges whose decisions do not even represent fulfillment of interest-group bargaining?"[32]

(5) Is the juxtaposition of a bargaining majoritarian *us* and an unelected judicial elite, *them*, too facile?

> [T]he lawmaker to whom the nasty old undemocratic Supreme Court is supposed to yield so reverently because of his greater democratic virtues is the entire mass of majoritarian-antimajoritarian, elected-appointed, special interest-general interest, responsible-irresponsible elements that make up American national politics. If we are off on a democratic quest, the dragon begins to look better and better and St. George worse and worse.[33]

---

[31] John Hart Ely, Democracy and Distrust: A Theory of Judicial Review 55 (1980).

[32] *See* Radin, *supra* note 29, at 1682. Cass R. Sunstein, *Interest Groups in American Public Law*, 38 Stan. L. Rev. 29 (1985), will introduce you to the debate over interest groups.

[33] Martin Shapiro, Freedom of Speech: The Supreme Court and Judicial Review 32 (1966).

In *The Vanishing Constitution*,[34] Professor Chemerinsky says:

> If majority rule is defined as government decisions accurately reflecting the preferences of the citizens, there is reason to doubt whether any government institution is majoritarian.[35] Thus, a more realistic definition of majority rule is needed and a wide variety of forms of electoral accountability and popular responsiveness can be deemed to be more or less majoritarian. Majority rule is not a unitary concept, but a continuum of arrangements ranging from constant direct democracy to officials who are only indirectly electorally accountable. The House of Representatives, the Senate, the President, cabinet agencies, independent agencies, and federal judges all occupy various points on this continuum; exact placement of any institution or office is likely to be a matter of some disagreement.
>
> The fact that federal judges are chosen by the President, approved by the Senate, and subject to impeachment is enough to place them on the continuum, albeit at a different place than the House, Senate, or President. Presidential appointments assure that the Court's ideology, over time, will reflect the general sentiments of the majority in society. In fact, the composition of the Rehnquist Court is largely a result of Republican victories in all but one presidential election in the last twenty years. The Senate's rejection of almost twenty percent of nominees for the Supreme Court in American history has served as another majoritarian influence. This is not to imply that the Court reflects popular opinion or to lessen the importance of its independence from the electoral process. The judiciary is — and was meant to be — more insulated from direct popular pressures. Nor is it to say that the institutions are identical or that the differences in electoral accountability are irrelevant. Analysis cannot be based on the simple conclusion that executives and legislatures are majoritarian and courts are not. This dichotomy is misleading and establishes a great presumption against judicial review.

In any event, is the Court not a constitutive part of the democracy created by the Founders? What, then, is the significance of the Court being "non-elected"? Does being "non-elected" make the Court "undemocratic"? Is review of governmental action by a non-elected body "anti" or "counter" majoritarian? Is democracy the same as majority rule?[36]

---

[34] Erwin Chemerinsky, *The Supreme Court 1988 Term — Foreword: The Vanishing Constitution*, 103 Harv. L. Rev. 43, 82–83 (1989).

[35] [Ed. Fn.] Dean Chemerinsky is referring to social choice theorists who have shown "why multi-member bodies cannot accurately aggregate preferences." *Id.* at 79.

[36] Make it a point, before you leave law school, to read Alexander Bickel, The Least Dangerous Branch (2d ed. 1980), a classic treatment of judicial review. It will equip you to comment meaningfully on these issues far better than you can now.

I. A (SOMEWHAT LENGTHY) EPILOGUE

KEYSTONE BITUMINOUS COAL ASSOCIATION v. DEBENEDICTIS
480 U.S. 470 (1987)

Justice STEVENS delivered the opinion of the Court.

In *Pennsylvania Coal Co. v. Mahon,* * * * the Court reviewed the constitutionality of a Pennsylvania statute that admittedly destroyed "previously existing rights of property and contract." * * *

In that case the "particular facts" led the Court to hold that the Pennsylvania Legislature had gone beyond its constitutional powers when it enacted a statute prohibiting the mining of anthracite coal in a manner that would cause the subsidence of land on which certain structures were located.

Now, 65 years later, we address a different set of "particular facts," involving the Pennsylvania Legislature's 1966 conclusion that the Commonwealth's existing mine subsidence legislation had failed to protect the public interest in safety, land conservation, preservation of affected municipalities' tax bases, and land development in the Commonwealth. Based on detailed findings, the legislature enacted the Bituminous Mine Subsidence and Land Conservation Act ("Subsidence Act" or "Act"), Pa. Stat. Ann., Tit. 52, § 1406.1 et seq. (Purdon Supp. 1986). Petitioners contend, relying heavily on our decision in *Pennsylvania Coal,* that §§ 4 and 6 of the Subsidence Act and certain implementing regulations violate the Takings Clause, and that § 6 of the Act violates the Contracts Clause of the Federal Constitution. The District Court and the Court of Appeals concluded that *Pennsylvania Coal* does not control for several reasons and that our subsequent cases make it clear that neither § 4 nor § 6 is unconstitutional on its face. We agree.

I

* * * Pennsylvania's Subsidence Act authorizes the Pennsylvania Department of Environmental Resources (DER) to implement and enforce a comprehensive program to prevent or minimize subsidence and to regulate its consequences. Section 4 of the Subsidence Act * * * prohibits mining that causes subsidence damage to three categories of structures that were in place on April 17, 1966: public buildings and noncommercial buildings generally used by the public; dwellings used for human habitation; and cemeteries. Since 1966 the DER has applied a formula that generally requires 50% of the coal beneath structures protected by § 4 to be kept in place as a means of providing surface support. Section 6 of the Subsidence Act, * * * authorizes the DER to revoke a mining permit if the removal of coal causes damage to a structure or area protected by § 4 and the operator has not within six months either repaired the damage, satisfied any claim arising therefrom, or deposited a sum equal to the reasonable cost of repair with the DER as security.

II

In 1982, petitioners filed a civil rights action in the United States District Court for the Western District of Pennsylvania seeking to enjoin officials of the DER from enforcing the Subsidence Act and its implementing regulations. The petitioners are an association of coal mine operators, and four corporations that are engaged, either directly or through affiliates, in underground mining of bituminous coal in western Pennsylvania. The members of the association and the corporate petitioners own, lease, or otherwise control substantial coal reserves beneath the surface of property affected by the Subsidence Act. The defendants in the action, respondents here, are the Secretary of the DER, the Chief of DER's Division of Mine Subsidence, and the Chief of the DER's Section on Mine Subsidence Regulation.

The complaint alleges that Pennsylvania recognized three separate estates in land: The mineral estate; the surface estate; and the "support estate." Beginning well over 100 years ago, land owners began severing title to underground coal and the right of surface support while retaining or conveying away ownership of the surface estate. It is stipulated that approximately 90% of the coal that is or will be mined by petitioners in western Pennsylvania was severed from the surface in the period between 1890 and 1920. * * *

III

Petitioners assert that disposition of their takings claim calls for no more than a straightforward application of the Court's decision in *Pennsylvania Coal Co. v. Mahon.* Although there are some obvious similarities between the cases, we agree with the Court of Appeals and the District Court that the similarities are far less significant than the differences, and that *Pennsylvania Coal* does not control this case. * * *

In his opinion for the Court, Justice Holmes first characteristically decided the specific case at hand in a single, terse paragraph:

This is the case of a single private house * * *.

Then — uncharacteristically — Justice Holmes provided the parties with an advisory opinion discussing "the general validity of the Act."[37] In the advisory portion of the Court's opinion, Justice Holmes rested on two propositions, both critical to the Court's decision. First, because it served only private interests, not health or safety, the Kohler Act could not be "sustained as an exercise of the police power." *Id.*, at 414. Second, the statute made it "commercially impracticable" to mine "certain coal" in the areas affected by the Kohler Act.[38]

---

[37] "But the case has been treated as one in which the general validity of the act should be discussed. The Attorney General of the State, the City of Scranton, and the representatives of other extensive interests were allowed to take part in the argument below and have submitted their contentions here. It seems, therefore, to be our duty to go farther in the statement of our opinion, in order that it may be known at once, and that further suits should not be brought in vain." 260 U.S., at 414.

[38] "What makes the right to mine coal valuable is that it can be exercised with profit. To make it commercially impracticable to mine certain coal has very nearly the same effect for constitutional

The holdings and assumptions of the Court in *Pennsylvania Coal* provide obvious and necessary reasons for distinguishing *Pennsylvania Coal* from the case before us today. The two factors that the Court considered relevant, have become integral parts of our takings analysis. We have held that land use regulation can effect a taking if it "does not substantially advance legitimate state interests, * * * or denies an owner economically viable use of his land." * * * Application of these tests to petitioners' challenge demonstrates that they have not satisfied their burden of showing that the Subsidence Act constitutes a taking. First, unlike the Kohler Act, the character of the governmental action involved here leans heavily against finding a taking; the Commonwealth of Pennsylvania has acted to arrest what it perceives to be a significant threat to the common welfare. Second, there is no record in this case to support a finding, similar to the one the Court made in *Pennsylvania Coal*, that the Subsidence Act makes it impossible for petitioners to profitably engage in their business, or that there has been undue interference with their investment-backed expectations.

The Public Purpose

Unlike the Kohler Act, which was passed upon in *Pennsylvania Coal*, the Subsidence Act does not merely involve a balancing of the private economic interests of coal companies against the private interests of the surface owners. The Pennsylvania Legislature specifically found that important public interests are served by enforcing a policy that is designed to minimize subsidence in certain areas. Section 2 of the Subsidence Act provides:

> "This act shall be deemed to be an exercise of the police powers of the Commonwealth for the protection of the health, safety and general welfare of the people of the Commonwealth, by providing for the conservation of surface land areas which may be affected in the mining of bituminous coal by methods other than "open pit" or "strip" mining, to aid in the protection of the safety of the public, to enhance the value of such lands for taxation, to aid in the preservation of surface water drainage and public water supplies and generally to improve the use and enjoyment of such lands and to maintain primary jurisdiction over surface coal mining in Pennsylvania.'
> Pa. Stat. Ann., Tit. 52, § 1406.2 (Purdon Supp. 1986).

The District Court and the Court of Appeals were both convinced that the legislative purposes set forth in the statute were genuine, substantial, and legitimate, and we have no reason to conclude otherwise.

None of the indicia of a statute enacted solely for the benefit of private parties identified in Justice Holmes' opinion are present here. First, Justice Holmes explained that the Kohler Act was a "private benefit" statute since it "ordinarily does not apply to land when the surface is owned by the owner of the coal." 260 U.S., at 414, 43 S. Ct. at 159. The Subsidence Act, by contrast, has no such exception. The

---

purposes as appropriating or destroying it. This we think that we are warranted in assuming that the statute does." *Id.*, at 414–415.

This assumption was not unreasonable in view of the fact that the Kohler Act may be read to prohibit mining that causes any subsidence — not just subsidence that results in damage to surface structures. The record in this case indicates that subsidence will almost always occur eventually.

current surface owner may only waive the protection of the Act if the DER consents. See 25 Pa. Code § 89.145(b) (1983). Moreover, the Court was forced to reject the Commonwealth's safety justification for the Kohler Act because it found that the Commonwealth's interest in safety could as easily have been accomplished through a notice requirement to landowners. The Subsidence Act, by contrast, is designed to accomplish a number of widely varying interests, with reference to which petitioners have not suggested alternative methods through which the Commonwealth could proceed. * * *

Thus, the Subsidence Act differs from the Kohler Act in critical and dispositive respects. With regard to the Kohler Act, the Court believed that the Commonwealth had acted only to ensure against damage to some private landowners' homes. Justice Holmes stated that if the private individuals needed support for their structures, they should not have "take[n] the risk of acquiring only surface rights." 260 U.S., at 416. Here, by contrast, the Commonwealth is acting to protect the public interest in health, the environment, and the fiscal integrity of the area. That private individuals erred in taking a risk cannot estop the Commonwealth from exercising its police power to abate activity akin to a public nuisance. The Subsidence Act is a prime example that "circumstances may so change in time as to clothe with such a [public] interest what at other times * * * would be a matter of purely private concern." *Bloch v. Hirsh*, 256 U.S. 135, 155 (1921). * * *

Chief Justice REHNQUIST, with whom Justice POWELL, Justice O'CONNOR, and Justice SCALIA join, dissenting. * * *

I

In apparent recognition of the obstacles presented by *Pennsylvania Coal* to the decision it reaches, the Court attempts to undermine the authority of Justice Holmes' opinion as to the validity of the Kohler Act, labeling it "uncharacteristically advisory." I would not so readily dismiss the precedential value of this opinion. There is, to be sure, some language in the case suggesting that it could have been decided simply by addressing the particular application of the Kohler Act at issue in the case. * * * The Court, however, found that the validity of the Act itself was properly drawn into question. * * * The Court's implication to the contrary is particularly disturbing in this context, because the holding in *Pennsylvania Coal* today discounted by the Court has for 65 years been the foundation of our "regulatory takings" jurisprudence. See *Penn Central Transportation Co. v. New York City*, 438 U.S. 104, 127 (1978); D. Hagman & J. Juergensmeyer, Urban Planning and Land Development Control Law 319 (2d ed. 1986) ("Pennsylvania Coal was a monumental decision which remains a vital element in contemporary takings law"). We have, for example, frequently relied on the admonition that "if regulation goes too far it will be recognized as a taking." Thus even were I willing to assume that the opinion in *Pennsylvania Coal* standing alone is reasonably subject to an interpretation that renders more than half the discussion "advisory," I would have no doubt that our repeated reliance on that opinion establishes it as a cornerstone of the jurisprudence of the Fifth Amendment's Just Compensation Clause.

I accordingly approach this case with greater deference to the language as well as the holding of *Pennsylvania Coal* than does the Court. Admittedly, questions arising under the Just Compensation Clause rest on ad hoc factual inquiries, and must be decided on the facts and circumstances in each case. Examination of the relevant factors presented here convinces me that the differences between them and those in *Pennsylvania Coal* verge on the trivial.

NOTES AND QUESTIONS

(1) Are these two cases "the same" or are they different? Explain. Is *Pennsylvania Coal* "overruled?"

Scholars have found the distinction drawn by Justice Stevens "unconvincing,"[39] even "incredible."[40] Professor Michelman spoke of "Justice Stevens's amazing reconstruction [of *Penn Coal*] * * * chiefly by recasting as advisory dicta what generations of sophisticated lawyers and judges have regarded (although not without some puzzlement) as gospel holding."[41]

Does Chief Justice Rehnquist's dissent mean that *dicta* (is an "advisory opinion" the same as dicta?) treated by the Court as *holding* long enough and frequently enough can turn into at least "cornerstone," if not "precedent?" Does it mean that at least in the Supreme Court distinctions between dicta and holding disappear? That it is after all more important what the court *said* than what it *did*?

(2) Is there a justification for what Justice Stevens (and those Justices who agreed with him) did? What is it? By what charts did he sail the trackless ocean? By what charts would you have navigated, had you been a member of the *Keystone* Court? Could you write *your* opinion in *Keystone*?

Assignment

Consider all you learned in the course of studying Part I about precedent and the judicial process. Write an essay defending Justice Stevens's "handling" of *Pennsylvania Coal*. Write an essay criticizing Justice Stevens's handling of *Pennsylvania Coal*.

Postscript

In nearly all the important transactions of life, indeed in all transactions whatever which have relation to the future, we have to take a leap in the dark. * * * When we are to take any important resolution, to adopt a profession, to make an offer of marriage, to enter upon a speculation, to write a book — to do anything, in a word, which involves important

---

[39] Joseph L. Sax, *Property Rights in the Supreme Court: A Status Report*, 7 UCLA JOURNAL ENVTL. L. & POLICY 139, 145 (1988).

[40] Epstein, *supr* a note 11, at 14.

[41] Frank I. Michelman, *Takings*, 1987, 88 COLUM. L. REV. 1600, 1600 n.2(i) (1988). Apparently the matter also escaped the notice of Justice Brandeis.

consequences — we have to act for the best, and in nearly every case act upon very imperfect evidence.

The one talent which is worth all other talents put together in all human affairs is the talent of judging right upon imperfect materials, the talent if you please of guessing right. * * * All that can be said about it is, that to see things as they are, without exaggeration or passion, is essential to it; but how can we see things as they are? Simply by opening our eyes and looking with whatever power we may have.[42]

---

[42] JAMES FITZJAMES STEPHEN, LIBERTY, EQUALITY, FRATERNITY: AND THREE BRIEF ESSAYS 269–270 (R.J. White ed., 1967). Sir James Fitzjames Stephen (1829-1894) was an eminent legal historian and jurist and older brother of Virginia Woolf's father, Leslie Stephen.

Introduction to Part II

IN THE DOMAIN OF STATUTES

For Cardozo, statutory construction was an acquired taste. He preferred common law subtleties, having great skill in bending them to modern uses. But he came to realize that problems of statutory construction had their own exciting subtleties and gave ample employment to philosophic and literary talents.

— Justice Felix Frankfurter[1]

Much more than you probably yet realize, the work of lawyers and judges occurs outside the domain of the common law. Over the 20th century, and particularly in its second half, American law metamorphosed from a system dominated by the common law to one dominated by laws promulgated by legislatures — that is, by statutes.

For example, if, today, a property owner were to ask you whether to fence in a swimming pool, you would be committing malpractice if all you did was read common-law cases concerning potential tort liability. You would also need to investigate whether the state, city, county, or even federal legislature had promulgated "laws" bearing on the subject. Most likely you would find something like this:

(a) No person in possession of land within the County of San Bernardino, [California,] either as owner, purchaser under contract, lessee, tenant, licensee or otherwise, upon which is situated a swimming pool or other out-of-doors body of water designed, constructed and used for swimming, dipping or immersion purposes by men, women or children, having a depth in excess of eighteen (18) inches, shall fail to maintain on the lot or premises upon which such pool or body of water is located and completely surround

---

[1] Felix Frankfurter, *Some Reflections on the Reading of Statutes*, 47 Colum. L. Rev. 527, 532 (1947).

ing such pool or body of water, a fence or wall not less than four (4) feet in height, with openings, holes or gaps therein no larger than four (4) inches in any dimension except for doors or gates; provided, however, that if a picket fence is erected or maintained the opening or spaces between the pickets shall not exceed four (4) inches; provided, further, that a dwelling house or accessory building may be used as a part of such enclosure.

(b) All gates or doors opening through such enclosure shall be equipped with a self-closing and self-latching device designed to keep, and capable of keeping, such door or gate securely closed at all times when not in actual use; provided, however, that the door of any dwelling occupied by human beings and forming any part of the enclosure hereinabove required need not be so equipped.[2]

What is the *justification* (or *explanation*) for this ordinance? One might have thought that common-law liability sufficed to deal with the problem of dangerous swimming pools by providing compensation for injured parties and (thereby) creating incentives for the appropriate level of care by pool owners. If so, then the ordinance is redundant at best, and more likely disruptive and inefficient. Does its existence reflect a legislative judgment that the common law *fails* to produce the appropriate amount of care? Alternatively, does it suggest the existence of a powerful fence-builders' lobby? Is the swimming pool problem more amenable to legislative than to judicial solutions?

What would make it so?

What is the *legal effect* of this ordinance? Most obviously, a pool-owner who violates it may be subject to enforcement by the government, which could lead to a fine or, depending on the penalties provided for in the ordinance, prison. The relevance of a statute or ordinance to a private civil suit for damages is more complicated. For example, would compliance with the ordinance be a defense in a negligence suit? Would failure to comply in itself establish that the defendant was negligent? Does the legislative decision to regulate pool safety displace the common law altogether, meaning that no suits can be brought at all?

What is the *meaning* of this ordinance? No piece of legislation is utterly clear in every case; it will almost always require "interpretation." Our ordinance looks complete and detailed, but cases will inevitably arise in which its meaning is debatable. For example, would it violate the ordinance to prop the gate open? Is a property owner who rents the premises to someone else still responsible for maintaining the fence? Would it be a violation if the owner maintained a fence, but the fence gave way when a seven-year old tried to climb over it? Would the Willsons be in violation of this ordinance, if indeed there was less than 18" of water in their pool?

These questions — about justification, effect, and meaning — can be asked about any piece of legislation. The first two will receive little direct attention in these

[2] San Bernardino, Cal., Ordinance No. 804, *quoted in* Grant v. Hipsher, 64 Cal. Rptr. 892, 896 (Cal. Ct. App. 1967).

materials; it is the third issue, the interpretation of statutes, which is the main focus of Part II.

Before we start, a word about the differences between statutory and common-law cases. Two stand out. First, in statutory cases the court confronts an authoritative text.

> Lawyers and judges find the definition of a proposition of common law in inferences and trends of policy indicated by doctrinal analysis and holdings in a succession of precedents; it inheres in the common law process that boundaries and specifications have no single definitive expression. The special character of legislation is the presence of a formally defined text, providing the authoritative base and framework within which all who would resort to the statute must operate.[3]

Although common-law judging also typically involves "texts" in the form of prior opinions, these lack the binding force of a statutory text. In interpreting a common-law precedent, what the court *did* is as important as what it *said*, if not more so; later courts may reject or ignore language in earlier opinions as dicta, or carelessly put, or incomplete. These strategies are not so readily available to a court reading a statute, where what the legislature said *is* what it did. The dominant role of text in statutory cases introduces a set of interpretive and linguistic problems that are absent or at least much less pronounced in common law cases.

The second basic difference is that in statutory cases lawmaking is not just the product of courts and litigants. Legislatures are now added to the brew (and, as we shall see in Chapter 13, administrative agencies as well). The presence of these additional players makes for complicated questions of authority, legitimacy, and deference to other decisionmakers.

The most important premise underlying statutory cases is this: *statutes are binding statements of law*. One can imagine a different system, but in the system we have, legislatures can modify legal rules adopted by courts but courts cannot alter, amend, or ignore legislation. This is the principle of "legislative supremacy." Legislatures are not unconstrained, of course; they are bound by the Constitution. And courts interpret the Constitution and will set aside statutes that are inconsistent with the Constitution — this power of "judicial review," dates back, at the federal level, to the famous case of *Marbury v. Madison*.[4] But as long as they are within constitutional boundaries, statutes trump other sources of law.

> [T]he argument for deference to statutes is [usually] cast in terms of democratic theory. American society, it is argued, is committed to the concept of majority rule. Because of this commitment, judges — like other governmental actors — should follow the will of the majority. The adoption of a statute reflects this will, so under democratic theory the statute should supersede the common law and control the actions of judges, who do not represent the majority. * * *

---

[3] JAMES WILLARD HURST, DEALING WITH STATUTES 48–49 (1982).

[4] 1 Cranch (5 U.S.) 137 (1803).

[Another] explanation for the doctrine of legislative supremacy is simply that it reflects a deeply-embedded premise of the American political system. The premise is that, within constitutional limits, the legislature (however constituted) has authority to prescribe rules of law that, until changed legislatively, bind all other governmental actors within the system. * * * To challenge this premise is to attack one of the most basic political axioms of the governmental structure.[5]

At a sufficiently broad level of generality, legislative supremacy is undisputed. At that level of generality, however, it ducks two hard questions. First, how much room for judicial policymaking does the judiciary's subordinate position allow? Second, once we identify the proper judicial task, what are the appropriate tools by which it is accomplished? These are the central questions for Part II.

---

[5] Earl M. Maltz, *Statutory Interpretation and Legislative Power: The Case for a Modified Intentionalist Approach*, 63 Tul. L. Rev. 1, 7–9 (1988).

Chapter 7

STATUTES V. THE COMMON LAW

This chapter introduces you to statutes and their interaction with and difference from common law precedents. The "v." in the chapter heading has two meanings. First, we will consider how statutes and the common law are adversaries, or at least competitors, in the legal system. The second idea behind the "v." is comparative; this chapter should start you thinking about how statutory and common-law judging differ.

[handwritten: ✓ ✓ Slayer loses manslaughter]

A. A COMMON LAW RULE

[handwritten: Not a statutory case]

FILMORE v. METROPOLITAN LIFE INSURANCE CO.
82 Ohio St. 208, 92 N.E. 26 (1910)

[handwritten: after Deem: 1892]

The plaintiff in error, Elmer G. Filmore, as the beneficiary under a policy of life insurance issued to Emma Filmore, his wife, by defendant in error, The Metropolitan Life Insurance Company, brought suit against said company in the court of common pleas of Clark county, Ohio, to recover the sum of two hundred and thirty-nine dollars, with interest thereon from September 3, 1906, which sum he alleged in his petition was due him as such beneficiary under the policy of insurance so issued by said company. For answer to plaintiff's petition, the insurance company pleaded two defenses, the first of which was a general denial, and the second was in the words and figures following, to-wit:

[handwritten: $239⁰⁰]

> For a second cause of defense to the petition, this defendant says that on the 3rd day of September, 1906, the said plaintiff murdered his said wife, Emma Filmore, in the city of Springfield, county of Clark, state of Ohio; that on the 25th day of October, 1906, he was indicted by the grand jury of said county for manslaughter on account of the killing of his said wife, and on the 31st day of December, 1906, he was convicted of said crime, and on February 25, 1907, he was sentenced by the court of common pleas to six years' hard labor in the Ohio Penitentiary, at Columbus, Ohio, where the said plaintiff is now confined. Defendant says that, plaintiff having caused the death of the said assured, as herein set forth, he is estopped from asserting any claim as beneficiary under said policy. Defendant, having fully answered, prays to be hence dismissed with its costs.

To this defense a demurrer was interposed by the plaintiff, Elmer G. Filmore, on the ground that the facts therein stated were insufficient in law to constitute a defense. This demurrer was overruled by the court of common pleas, and, the plaintiff not desiring to plead further, judgment was entered dismissing his petition. This judgment of dismissal was subsequently affirmed by the circuit court, and the

plaintiff in error now asks that this judgment of affirmance be reversed by this court.

The sole question here presented is as to the legal sufficiency, against a general demurrer, of this second defense as pleaded in defendant's answer. It is conceded by counsel for plaintiff in error to be the well settled and established rule of law that a beneficiary under a policy of life insurance is without right to recover thereon where the death of the insured has been intentionally caused by the act of such beneficiary, but it is contended in the present case that the second defense of defendant's answer is lacking in essential allegation, and is fatally defective, because it contains no direct or sufficient averment that the killing of the assured by Elmer G. Filmore, the beneficiary under said policy, was an intentional killing. That such objection is purely technical, and in the present case wholly without merit, is apparent, we think, from a consideration of the character and legal effect of the matter pleaded and the allegations made in said second defense. [The defendant's statement that Elmer had "murdered" his wife sufficed as an allegation of an intentional and unlawful killing.] * * * [A]s said by Mr. Justice Field in N. Y. Mut. Life Ins. Co. v. Armstrong, 117 U.S., 600: "It would be a reproach to the jurisprudence of the country if one could recover insurance money payable on the death of a party whose life he had feloniously taken. As well might he recover insurance money upon a building that he had willfully fired." In the case of Schreiner v. High Court of Illinois Catholic Order of Foresters, 35 Ill. App., 576, cited and relied upon by counsel for plaintiff in error as supporting their contention in the present case, the court also clearly recognizes the principle, applicable to all contracts of insurance, that the insured or beneficiary cannot under such contract receive indemnity for a loss that he himself has intentionally brought about; the second paragraph of the syllabus in that case being as follows: "There can be no recovery in an action founded upon intentional wrong. The beneficiary in an insurance policy cannot recover, where the death of assured has been intentionally caused by his act." * * *

Judgment affirmed.

NOTES AND QUESTIONS

(1) What is the holding of *Filmore*? Note that the insurance company stated that Elmer had *murdered* Emma, but he was actually convicted of *manslaughter,* a less serious crime. Both murder and manslaughter have precise, varying, and multiple definitions. But, very loosely, the basic distinction is between an intentional and an unintentional killing. Do the details of the slaying matter, or is it enough that Elmer killed Emma? Can you think of circumstances in which a slayer should not be barred from recovering under the victim's life insurance policy?

(2) Is *Filmore* correctly decided? Why should a killer forfeit the victim's life insurance benefits?

(3) Suppose you are a trial judge in the state of Ohio with the following case before you. Mrs. X is dead. Under her will, all of her property goes to Mr. X. However, the reason Mrs. X is dead is that Mr. X killed her. The X children, who

would receive the estate were it not to go to Mr. X, sue, arguing that Mr. X cannot take under the will given the fact that he murdered the deceased. There are no Ohio cases about murderous devisees.[1] *Filmore* is the closest thing you can find. With *Filmore* as precedent, how would you rule and why?

In deciding this case, you would do what common law judges do all the time: reason by analogy in light of prior cases and their underlying principles. With an eye on the justification for the court-created rule applied in *Filmore*, you must decide upon "rules of relevance" to determine whether wills and life insurance policies are similar or different, whether they can be assimilated into a single larger category. Is a murdering devisee "like" a murdering insurance beneficiary?

B.   THE STATUTORY COMPLICATION

When these cases come up in the real world — and they come up rather more often than one might have hoped — there is always an added complication. The state legislature has had something to say about "descent," that is, about the passing of property from a decedent to the heirs. Assume that in our hypothetical the Ohio legislature has enacted no law specifically addressing the rights of murdering devisees. However, it has provided that (1) a person can direct the disposition of property at her death by will, subject only to certain specific limitations and requirements of formality, and (2) if a person dies without a will, her property passes to her closest surviving relative(s), i.e. to her spouse, or if there is no surviving spouse to her children or their descendants, or if there are none to the parents, and so on.

Are these statutes of any relevance to the case of Mr. X?

DEEM v. MILLIKIN
6 Ohio Cir. Ct. 357 (1892)

[Caroline Sharkey, a widow, died on January 11, 1889 without a will. Under the Ohio statute of descents, her son, Elmer Sharkey, was her sole heir. To secure certain debts, Elmer then mortgaged property his mother had owned. This is a suit between the lenders, who contended that they held a security interest in the property to cover Elmer's debts, and Caroline Sharkey's siblings, who argued that Elmer had not inherited, and therefore could not mortgage, his mother's property. As for Elmer, he is not participating in the suit for the simple reason that he was hanged on December 19, 1890, having been convicted of murdering his mother.

The lower court ruled that Elmer had inherited his mother's entire estate and therefore the mortgages were valid.]

The judgment under review is unquestionably right if the terms used in the statute of descents should, in all cases, receive their plain and natural meaning.

---

[1] A note on terminology. A person who takes property under the will of a deceased person (a "decedent") is a "devisee"; a gift by will is a "devise." Where the decedent has no will (is "intestate"), statutory or common law rules dictate where the property goes. In these circumstances, the recipient is not a "devisee" (there has been no devise), but an "heir." The latter term is also often used more broadly to indicate anyone who receives a decedent's property, whether by statute or by will.

meaning? Do you necessarily believe this?

Mrs. Sharkey died intestate and [owning] the lands in controversy. There is neither condition nor exception in the statute which provides that they should descend to her son. * * *

a frequently invoked "saying"

The statute of descents * * * is a legislative declaration of a rule of public policy. * * * [C]ourts should be guided by the maxim "*index animi sermo* [language indicates intention]," and the interpretation should be consistent with the language employed. Knowledge of the settled maxims and principles of statutory interpretation is imputed to the legislature. To the end that there may be certainty and uniformity in legal administration it must be assumed that statutes are enacted with a view to their interpretation according to such maxims and principles. When they are regarded, the legislative intent is ascertained. When they are ignored, interpretation becomes legislation in disguise. The well considered cases warrant the pertinent conclusions that when the legislature, not transcending the limits of its power, speaks in clear language upon a question of policy, it becomes the judicial tribunals to remain silent. [To do otherwise would be] the manifest assertion of a wisdom believed to be superior to that of the legislature upon a question of policy. Chief Justice REDFIELD, in *In re Powers*, observed: "It is scarcely necessary, we trust, at this late day, to say that the judicial tribunals of the state have no concern with the policy of legislation."

Affirmed.

NOTES AND QUESTIONS

(1) The Ohio Supreme Court affirmed without opinion, adopting the reasoning of the court below. 53 Ohio St. 668, 44 N.E. 1134 (1895).

(2) Was this the necessary result? Are you confident that the court effectively carried out the legislature's will? Did the legislature leave no room for a common law resolution?

(3) Do you understand why the *Filmore* court did not even cite *Deem*? Are the two decisions consistent?

Other courts, in cases much like *Deem*, have reached the opposite result. The following is the best-known such case.

RIGGS v. PALMER
115 N.Y. 506, 22 N.E. 188 (1889)

slayer loses

EARL, J.

devisee

On the 13th day of August 1880, Francis B. Palmer made his last will and testament, in which he gave small legacies to his two daughters, Mrs. Riggs and Mrs. Preston, the plaintiffs in this action, and the remainder of his estate to his grandson, the defendant, Elmer E. Palmer. * * * At the date of the will, and, subsequently, to the death of the testator, Elmer lived with him as a member of his family, and at his death was sixteen years old. He knew of the provisions made in

his favor in the will, and, that he might prevent his grandfather from revoking such provisions, which he had manifested some intention to do, and to obtain the speedy enjoyment and immediate possession of his property, he willfully murdered him by poisoning him. He now claims the property, and the sole question for our determination is, can he have it? — *Elmer*

The defendants say that the testator is dead; that his will was made in due form and has been admitted to probate, and that, therefore, it must have effect according to the letter of the law. It is quite true that statutes regulating the making, proof and effect of wills, and the devolution of property, if literally construed, and if their force and effect can in no way and under no circumstances be controlled or modified, give this property to the murderer.

The purpose of those statutes was to enable testators to dispose of their estates to the objects of their bounty at death, and to carry into effect their final wishes legally expressed; and in considering and giving effect to them this purpose must be kept in view. It was the intention of the law-makers that the donees in a will should have the property given to them. But it never could have been their intention that a donee who murdered the testator to make the will operative should have any benefit under it. If such a case had been present to their minds, and it had been supposed necessary to make some provision of law to meet it, it cannot be doubted that they would have provided for it. It is a familiar canon of construction that a thing which is within the intention of the makers of a statute is as much within the statute as if it were within the letter; and a thing which is within the letter of the statute is not within the statute, unless it be within the intention of the makers. * * *

There was a statute in Bologna that whoever drew blood in the streets should be severely punished, and yet it was held not to apply to the case of a barber who opened a vein in the street. It is commanded in the Decalogue that no work shall be done upon the Sabbath, and yet, giving the command a rational interpretation founded upon its design, the Infallible Judge held that it did not prohibit works of necessity, charity or benevolence on that day.

What could be more unreasonable than to suppose that it was the legislative intention in the general laws passed for the orderly, peaceable and just devolution of property, that they should have operation in favor of one who murdered his ancestor that he might speedily come into the possession of his estate? Such an intention is inconceivable. We need not, therefore, be much troubled by the general language contained in the laws.

Besides, all laws as well as all contracts may be controlled in their operation and effect by general, fundamental maxims of the common law. No one shall be permitted to profit by his own fraud, or to take advantage of his own wrong, or to found any claim upon his own iniquity, or to acquire property by his own crime. These maxims are dictated by public policy, have their foundation in universal law administered in all civilized countries, and have nowhere been superseded by statutes. * * *

My view of this case does not inflict upon Elmer any greater or other punishment for his crime than the law specifies. It takes from him no property, but

simply holds that he shall not acquire property by his crime, and thus be rewarded for its commission. * * *

All concur with EARL, J., except GRAY, J., who reads dissenting opinion, and DANFORTH, J., concurring.

Judgment in accordance with the prevailing opinion.

GRAY, J. (dissenting). This appeal presents an extraordinary state of facts, and the case, in respect of them, I believe, is without precedent in this state.

The respondent, a lad of sixteen years of age, being aware of the provisions in his grandfather's will, which constituted him the residuary legatee of the testator's estate, caused his death by poison in 1882. For this crime he was tried and was convicted of murder in the second degree, and at the time of the commencement of this action he was serving out his sentence in the state reformatory. This action was brought by two of the children of the testator for the purpose of having those provisions of the will in the respondent's favor canceled and annulled.

* * * [I]f I believed that the decision of the question could be affected by considerations of an equitable nature, I should not hesitate to assent to views which commend themselves to the conscience. But the matter does not lie within the domain of conscience. We are bound by the rigid rules of law, which have been established by the legislature, and within the limits of which the determination of this question is confined. The question we are dealing with is, whether a testamentary disposition can be altered, or a will revoked, after the testator's death, through an appeal to the courts, when the legislature has, by its enactments, prescribed exactly when and how wills may be made, altered and revoked, and, apparently, as it seems to me, when they have been fully complied with, has left no room for the exercise of an equitable jurisdiction by courts over such matters. * * * The capacity and the power of the individual to dispose of his property after death, and the mode by which that power can be exercised, are matters of which the legislature has assumed the entire control, and has undertaken to regulate with comprehensive particularity. * * *

I concede that rules of law, which annul testamentary provision made for the benefit of those who have become unworthy of them, may be based on principles of equity and of natural justice. It is quite reasonable to suppose that a testator would revoke or alter his will, where his mind has been so angered and changed as to make him unwilling to have his will executed as it stood. But these principles only suggest sufficient reasons for the enactment of laws to meet such cases.

* * * [T]o concede appellants' views would involve the imposition of an additional punishment or penalty upon the respondent. What power or warrant have the courts to add to the respondent's penalties by depriving him of property? The law has punished him for his crime, and we may not say that it was an insufficient punishment. In the trial and punishment of the respondent the law has vindicated itself for the outrage which he committed, and further judicial utterance upon the subject of punishment or deprivation of rights is barred. We may not * * * "enhance the pains, penalties and forfeitures provided by law for the punishment of crime."

NOTES AND QUESTIONS

(1)   An aside: Judge Gray refers to Elmer as "a lad of sixteen." This may have rung a bell; Cardozo begins his opinion in *Hynes* using the same phrase to refer to the innocent youthful victim, Harvey Hynes. *See supra* page 91. Although Judge Gray was not the stylist that Cardozo was, his use of the phrase not only recalls *Hynes*, it is used to the same end — to elicit the reader's sympathy and conjure up a vision of innocent childish fun. Of course, Judge Gray has rather an uphill battle in that regard.[2]

(2)   Can you distinguish *Riggs* and *Deem* on the facts?

(3)   The *Riggs* court states that for Elmer to take under the will would be an "offense against public policy." Is this an appropriate consideration for the court? *Deem* says that judges must avoid evaluating "the policy of legislation." In invoking public policy, does *Riggs* run afoul of that admonition?

(4)   Suppose a statute prescribes that an unmarried intestate's estate goes to her "children." Mary Smith dies, survived by her two sons. One is a devoted, attentive, upstanding Boy Scout, the other a good-for-nothing, prodigal lout. Could a court say that the good son inherits the entire estate?[3] If not, why exactly does the bad son lose his share if he actually kills his mother?

(5)   Consider whether the *Riggs* court was simply following this ancient instruction from William Blackstone:

> [I]f there arise out of [acts of parliament] collaterally any absurd consequences, manifestly contradictory to common reason, they are, with regard to those collateral consequences, void. * * * [T]he judges are in decency to conclude that this consequence was not foreseen by the parliament, and therefore they are at liberty to expound the statute by equity, and only quoad hoc disregard it. Thus if an act of parliament gives a man power to try all causes, that arise within his manor of Dale; yet, if a cause should arise in which he himself is a party, the act is construed not to extend to that; because it is unreasonable that any man should determine his own quarrel.[4]

---

[2] Although for us, in these materials, the *Riggs* dissent "recalls" *Hynes*, the case itself preceded *Hynes* by almost half a century. Cardozo was familiar with *Riggs*; he devoted a few pages to it in *The Nature of the Judicial Process*. *See* NJP at 40–43. It is the purest speculation, but it is at least possible that, consciously or not, Gray's description of the wretched Elmer Palmer contributed to Cardozo's of Harvey Hynes.

[3] For example, in Cheatle v. Cheatle, 662 A.2d 1362 (D.C. 1995), the will left all to the decedent's sister; the decedent's brother challenged the bequest arguing that the sister, who lived with and cared for the decedent during the last decade of his life, had mistreated him and hastened his death. In the sort of finding of fact you do not hear every day, the trial court determined that the sister was "selfish, angry, resentful, indignant, bitter, self-centered, spiteful, vindictive, paranoid and stingy," and that her "benign neglect" of her brother had shortened his life. But her general poor conduct and character defects did not stand in the way of her taking the bequest.

[4] WILLIAM BLACKSTONE, COMMENTARIES ON THE LAWS OF ENGLAND *91 (1765).

What general principle, if any, equivalent to the proposition that "no man should determine his own quarrel," justifies the result in *Riggs*? Can you think of a general principle to support the result in *Deem*?

(6) Suppose the blanket rule that an intestate's estate goes to her children was not set out in the Ohio Code, as was the case in *Deem*, but instead arose out of a series of common law decisions. Would *Deem* have come out the same way? After all, "the law" — the substantive standard — would be no different. Yet presumably the court would be free to narrow broad statements about children taking their parents' estate found in the opinions of those prior cases. It could, assuming that *Filmore* or a similar case is "on the books," equate a murdering heir with a murdering life insurance beneficiary, not with an innocent heir. Should the courts have the same freedom to "fine-tune" statutory requirements? Is that in essence what the court in *Riggs* did?

(7) One important lesson from *Deem* and *Riggs* is that it seems unwise to name a child Elmer (or to marry an Elmer, see *Filmore*). What other conclusions do you draw? In particular, what do the two decisions teach you about the relation between courts and legislatures? Which is more consistent with the principle of legislative supremacy? What makes the court in *Deem* so cautious, what is it worried about?

C. THE LEGISLATIVE RESPONSE

In 1932 Ohio adopted a so-called "slayer statute," thereby "overruling" *Deem v. Millikin* legislatively. The statute is at issue in the following case.

WADSWORTH v. SIEK
23 Ohio Misc. 112, 254 N.E.2d 738, 50 Ohio Op.2d 507 (1970)

[Rosaline Siek made out her will on May 19, 1967, dividing her estate between her mother, brother, and nieces and nephews. In September she married John Siek. Not long thereafter, he beat her to death. Siek was indicted for first degree murder but pled guilty to the lesser offense of manslaughter in the first degree. He was convicted and sentenced to prison.

Like every state, Ohio has legislatively guaranteed a surviving spouse at least some share of the decedent's estate, even if the will gives him or her nothing. Seeking to avoid having to make any such payment, the executor of the estate brought this declaratory judgment action, asking the court to rule that Siek's manslaughter conviction precluded his receiving any of his wife's estate.]

Our starting point logically, though not chronologically, is Section 2105.19, [of the Ohio] Revised Code, the pertinent part of which reads:

> No person finally adjudged guilty * * * of murder in the first or second degree, shall inherit or take any part of the real or personal estate of the person killed. * * * With respect to inheritance from or participation under the will of the person killed, such person shall be considered as though he had preceded in death the person killed. * * *

Prior to the adoption of the statute, Ohio case law permitted a murderer to inherit from his victim. The basic case is *Deem v. Millikin* * * *.

Siek was not adjudged guilty of murder, but only of first degree manslaughter. That he was indicted for murder in the first degree is immaterial under the statute.

In the absence of a statutory provision precluding defendant Siek from inheriting, Ohio case law will govern. As we have seen, this case law allows even a murderer to inherit.

There appear to be no Ohio cases dealing directly with the effect of the statute on a person adjudged guilty of manslaughter; but there are Ohio cases holding or stating that the statute means what it says, i.e., that the person must be adjudged guilty of murder in the first or second degree in order to be precluded from inheriting.

The cases outside Ohio hold that under a statute like ours, a person convicted of manslaughter is not precluded from inheriting from the estate of his victim. By contrast, consider a statute providing that any person who shall kill another shall be precluded from inheriting from his victim.

I have considered the possibility of holding that Section 2105.19, Revised Code, indicates a change in policy by the legislature, whereby no felonious killer, in any degree, shall be permitted to inherit from his victim. But such a decision would be directly contrary to the provisions of the statute. Had the legislature wished to include a person adjudged guilty of manslaughter, it could easily have done so, and it may do so in the future by amending the statute.

Whether the omission by the legislature was intentional or inadvertent, the fact is that manslaughter was omitted, and this Court has no right to "amend" the statute by adding it.

First degree manslaughter, although a felony, is much less serious than murder. It lacks the deliberate and premeditated malice of first degree murder and the malice of second degree murder. It consists of voluntary manslaughter, which is an unlawful and intentional killing under the influence of a sudden passion or heat of blood produced by an adequate provocation; or involuntary manslaughter, which is an unintentional killing while in the commission of an unlawful act.

We have no right to regard defendant John J. Siek as a murderer. He has been convicted only of manslaughter in the first degree. Whether the manslaughter was voluntary or involuntary is not a matter of record. Despite the tragic circumstances of this case, I must conclude that under the present law of Ohio, defendant John J. Siek is entitled to one half of his wife's net estate.

QUESTIONS *No obviously right answer!*

(1) Is it accurate to say that the legislature decided that a *manslaughterer* *should* inherit, or did it decide only that a *murderer* should *not*?

Problem in all these cases: the answer isn't clear!

(2) The reasoning and approach in *Wadsworth* seems generally consistent with *Deem v. Millikin*. In which, if either, is the inference from legislative silence stronger?

NOTE ON STATUTES AND PRECEDENTS

Suppose the rule of § 2105.19 were contained in common-law precedents rather than in a statute. That is, in several prior cases, Ohio courts have held that persons found guilty of first or second degree murder could not inherit or take any part of the estate of the person they had killed. The manslaughter case has not come up. Now *Wadsworth* arises. How is the question different in this setting than in the actual case? Can a court reason analogically from a statute the way it does from a common law precedent? The possibility seems not to have crossed the court's mind in *Wadsworth*. Why not?

One possible answer is this. In the common law, judges are free, indeed expected, to determine the appropriate categories of assimilation. Turntables and pools, for example, might be assimilated into the same broader category of attractive nuisances. In statutory cases, in contrast, the statute itself defines the category of assimilation, which judges cannot broaden. Does this make sense?

Suppose *Barrett v. Southern Pacific Co.* had been based on a statute making railroads liable for the negligent maintenance of turntables. Now *Knight v. Kaiser* (the sand pile case) arises. Could or should the court "simply" "follow" *Barrett*?

In Chapter 5, Professor Schauer referred, borrowing from Ronald Dworkin, to "the enactment force" of a common law precedent.[5] Did you understand what he meant? Do you now? Here is a fuller excerpt from Dworkin:

> Statutory interpretation * * * depends upon the availability of a canonical form of words, however vague or unspecific, that set limits to the political decisions that the statute may be taken to have made. * * * [In contrast, most judicial opinions] do not contain any special propositions taken to be a canonical form of the rule that the case lays down. * * * [E]ven important opinions rarely attempt that legislative sort of draftsmanship. They cite reasons, in the form of precedents and principles, to justify a decision, but it is the decision, not some new and stated rule of law, that these precedents and principles are taken to justify. Sometimes a judge will acknowledge openly that it lies to later cases to determine the full effect of the case he has decided.
>
> Of course, [a judge] might well decide that when he does find, in an earlier case, a canonical form of words, he will use his techniques of statutory interpretation to decide whether the rule composed of those words embraces a novel case. He might well acknowledge what could be called an enactment force of precedent. He will nevertheless find that when a precedent does have enactment force, its influence on later cases is not taken to be limited to that force. Judges and lawyers do not think that the

---

[5] *See supra* page 168.

force of precedents is exhausted, as a statute would be, by the linguistic limits of some particular phrase. [The precedent also has a "gravitational" force; it affects the result in cases to which the opinion's language does not squarely apply.] * * *

The gravitational force of precedent cannot be captured by any theory that takes the full force of precedent to be its enactment force as a piece of legislation. But the inadequacy of that approach suggests a superior theory. The gravitational force of a precedent may be explained by appeal, not to the wisdom of enforcing enactments, but to the fairness of treating like cases alike. * * * This general explanation of the gravitational force of precedent accounts for the feature that defeated the enactment theory, which is that the force of a precedent escapes the language of its opinion.[6]

Does the distinction between "enactment" force and "gravitational" force accurately describe the different judicial treatment of statutes and common-law precedents?

———

In 1975 the Ohio legislature amended the statute at issue in *Wadsworth v. Siek* in three respects: (1) the offenses mentioned were changed from "murder in the first or second degree," to offenses contained in "section 2903.01, 2903.02, or 2903.03 of the Revised Code" (these sections forbid, respectively, murder in the first degree, murder in the second degree, and voluntary manslaughter); (2) the law was changed to apply to one who was "convicted" or pleads guilty to one of these offenses; and (3) the sanction was changed from one prohibiting a person to "inherit or take any part of the real or personal estate of the person killed," to one providing that no person "shall in any way benefit by the death," and specifically disentitling the slayer to "all money, insurance proceeds, or other property or benefits payable or distributable in respect of the decedent's death."

In light of the legislature's change, extending § 2105.19 to manslaughter, would you say that *Siek* was wrongly decided? Would your answer be different if the amendment had come just one year after *Siek* rather than five?

Suppose Wadsworth thinks the amendment shows that his case was wrongly decided. Relying on the new statute, he brings a new suit to recover the portion of the estate that went to John Siek as a result of the decision in *Wadsworth v. Siek*. Apart from the fact that the suit would be barred by *res judicata*, does the new statute even apply to John Siek?

By amending the statute to include manslaughter the Ohio legislature seems now to have covered the waterfront. Or has it? Suppose the slayer is acquitted because crucial evidence was suppressed, or is never prosecuted, or kills himself immediately after killing the victim. Then in a civil trial over the inheritance the court finds that he was indeed the slayer. In all these situations, the slayer has committed the crime, but has not been *convicted*. Should the statute apply? Do you think the Ohio courts would apply it?

———

[6] Ronald Dworkin, Taking Rights Seriously 110–113 (1978).

slayer loses
~~tokes~~
no criminal trial!

Consider the following decision.

life ins. policy

SHRADER v. EQUITABLE LIFE ASSURANCE SOCIETY
20 Ohio St. 3d 41, 485 N.E.2d 1031, 20 Ohio B. Rep. 343 (1985)

[In 1981 Jean Shrader was strangled to death in a parking garage in downtown Columbus, Ohio. No one was ever arrested for, charged with, or convicted of the crime. Equitable Life held two life insurance policies on Jean Shrader, each of which named her husband as the primary beneficiary and her parents as the secondary beneficiary. Husband and parents both sought the proceeds; the former brought this suit to obtain them. The insurance company deposited the funds with the court and left the two claimants to fight the matter out between them. The key issue at trial concerned whether the husband had killed his wife. The trial court concluded that he had and that he was therefore ineligible to receive the proceeds of the policy. The court of appeals reversed, holding that the identity of the killer had to be established in a criminal proceeding. The case is now before the Ohio Supreme Court.]

I   *substantive issue*

The first issue in this case is whether R.C. 2105.19, dealing with persons prohibited from benefiting from the death of another, is applicable in this case. * * *

2105.19 not applicable

It is undisputed that John Shrader has never been convicted of, or pled guilty to, any of the homicides enumerated in the above provision. Indeed, he has never been charged with any criminal homicide offense. Since Shrader is presumed innocent of any criminal violation until his guilt is established by proof beyond any reasonable doubt, he cannot be said to be a "guilty person." Since R.C. 2105.19 only operates to prevent certain criminals from reaping the fruits of their crimes, and since John Shrader does not fall into that category of persons, the statute is not applicable in this case.

Shrader argues that R.C. 2105.19 provides the exclusive method for disqualifying a beneficiary from receiving life insurance proceeds. A familiar principle of statutory construction, however, is that a statute should not be construed to impair pre-existing law in the absence of an explicit legislative statement to the contrary. All that R.C. 2105.19(A) does or purports to do is to eliminate the necessity to prove that the beneficiary of a policy of life insurance committed such an act, when the beneficiary has been convicted of or has pled guilty to one of the specifically enumerated homicide offenses. There is no indication that the General Assembly or any case law intended or requires that the statute be construed to be the exclusive method to determine whether a person should be barred from recovering as a beneficiary under a policy of insurance on the life of a decedent alleged to have been killed by the beneficiary. Thus we find Shrader's argument regarding the statute unpersuasive.

II

The second issue in this case is whether the common law will bar a beneficiary of a life insurance policy from receiving the proceeds of that policy when the beneficiary intentionally and feloniously caused the death of the insured.

* * * [Under *Filmore v. Metropolitan Life Ins. Co.*, among other cases,] the common law bars a beneficiary of a life insurance policy from receiving the proceeds of that policy when the beneficiary intentionally and feloniously caused the death of the insured.

III

The third issue in this case is whether the identity of one who intentionally and feloniously causes the death of another can be established in a civil proceeding thereby preventing the wrongdoer from receiving the proceeds of the deceased's life insurance policy.

* * * Is it reasonable to say that because there has been no criminal conviction in such cases that those seeking to prove the identity of an alleged wrongdoer are precluded in a civil proceeding from doing so because there has been no criminal conviction? We think such a proposition is neither reasonable nor proper.

* * * [T]he concept that no one should be allowed to profit from his own wrongful conduct is a civil concept, and the civil courts are, therefore, a proper forum to determine the identity of one who has been alleged to have caused, intentionally and feloniously, the death of another and if that person is the beneficiary of the proceeds of insurance held on the life of a decedent, then to deprive such person of the proceeds and thereby prevent ill-begotten gain.

NOTES AND QUESTIONS

(1)   Is the result or method of this case consistent with those in the prior Ohio cases? Did the court show adequate deference to the legislature? One Ohio law professor concluded that *Siek*, which was an example of "rigid formalism," was "devitalized" by *Shrader*.[7] Was it? Can you synthesize these cases?

(2)   *Shrader* was followed in *In re Estate of Cotton*, 104 Ohio App. 3d 368, 662 N.E.2d 63 (1995). There, a husband killed his wife; a criminal prosecution resulted in his pleading guilty to involuntary manslaughter. In a subsequent civil suit over the victim's estate, the court concluded that, notwithstanding the plea, the husband had in fact "intentionally and feloniously" killed his wife. Relying on *Shrader*, the court ruled that section 2105.19 was not the exclusive mechanism for disqualifying a devisee. "Although defendant was not convicted of any of the offenses specified in R.C. 2105.19(A), and thus is not barred by the terms of that statute from benefitting from his wife's death, [the administrator of the estate] may assume the burden

---

[7] Addison E. Dewey, *Civil Murder Trials: Macabre Reflections of Our Violent Society*, 19 Cap. U. L. Rev. 897, 925 (1990).

under common law to prove that defendant intentionally and feloniously killed decedent, and thus is barred under common-law principles from receiving under her last will and testament." Are the two settings the same? Could *Shrader* be distinguished?

(3) Suppose a state court holds that at common law a murderer/beneficiary *can* recover on the victim's life insurance policy. The legislature then passes a law forbidding a murderer/devisee to take under the victim's will. Now the life insurance case arises again. Does the statute have any bearing on the case?

Many years ago — at a time when courts and lawyers viewed statutes with "indifference, if not contempt" — Roscoe Pound suggested four possible ways in which courts might treat legislative innovation:

> (1) They might receive it fully into the body of the law as affording not only a rule to be applied but a principle from which to reason, and hold it, as a later and more direct expression of the general will, of superior authority to judge-made rules on the same general subject; and so reason from it by analogy in preference to them. (2) They might receive it fully into the body of the law to be reasoned from by analogy the same as any other rule of law, regarding it, however, as of equal or co-ordinate authority in this respect with judge-made rules upon the same general subject. (3) They might refuse to receive it fully into the body of the law and give effect to it directly only; refusing to reason from it by analogy but giving it, nevertheless, a liberal interpretation to cover the whole field it was intended to cover. (4) They might not only refuse to reason from it by analogy and apply it directly only, but also give to it a strict and narrow interpretation, holding it down rigidly to those cases which it covers expressly.[8]

Apply each of these approaches to the hypothetical.

(4) Go back and review the cases in this section. Which of Pound's four categories do they reflect? In light of these cases, can you describe how statutes and the common law interact?

Assignment

You are a trial judge in Ohio. You have before you a will contest between A and B. A was the husband of the decedent, who left her entire estate to him in what is indisputably a valid will. B is Mrs. A's brother and would inherit the estate if it did not go to A. The evidence established the following facts. Mrs. A had a debilitating illness, was unable to care for herself, and had no hope of recovery. She repeatedly requested her husband to help her commit suicide. After many months of refusing to do so, Mr. A reluctantly agreed. He obtained sleeping pills, mixed them in a drink, and, after informing her of what he was doing, held it to his wife's lips as she drank. Mrs. A died, and Mr. A was convicted of murder.

Does Mr. A take under his wife's will?

---

[8] Roscoe Pound, *Common Law and Legislation*, 21 HARV. L. REV. 383, 385 (1908).

Chapter 8

THEORIES OF STATUTORY INTERPRETATION

Since the mid-1980s, the debate has raged among at least three schools of statutory interpretation theory: the old intentionalism, the old Holy Trinity Church purposivism, and the new textualism. The Supreme Court remains up for grabs. For every case that seems to be a victory of textualism, another can be found that reflects more conventional intentionalist methodologies, and the purpose approach is not dead, either. For the first time in a long while, perhaps the first time ever, the Justices are frequently debating statutory interpretation methodologies at a level of theory that far transcends the details of the case at hand, and that implicates the very question of the Court's interpretive role in a democracy.

— **Philip P. Frickey**[1]

Over the last quarter-century, law professors and judges have been engaged in heady debates over theories of statutory interpretation. As the quote from Professor Frickey implies, the debates have been pitched and complex. A great deal is at stake. It is impossible to interpret a statute without a theory, and the choice of theory is critical to the outcomes of actual cases. On the other hand, as the quote from Professor Molot indicates, there has emerged from this debate, if not unanimity, a moderately strong consensus that holds among most contemporary judges.

It will help you to think in terms of two basic models of the judicial role in statutory cases: "agency" and "partnership."[2] In the first, courts are the agents (sometimes, for emphasis, "faithful agents") of legislatures, obediently carrying out their instructions with little or no independent judgment or discretion. This is the mainstream view, and it rests on the constitutional allocation of policymaking to the legislative branch. To say that courts should be faithful agents only leads to a separate question: *how* do judges best fulfill that role? Here the central, though not the only, disagreement is over when and to what extent to look beyond the statutory text itself. Should a judge try to discern and pursue the legislature's intent or purpose? If so, how does the judge determine what those were?

---

[1] Philip P. Frickey, *From the Big Sleep to the Big Heat: The Revival of Theory in Statutory Interpretation*, 77 MINN. L. REV. 241, 256 (1992).

[2] Other labels are of course possible. For example, Reed Dickerson aims at a similar distinction in identifying the "cognitive function" of ascertaining or extracting meaning, on the one hand, and the "creative function" of assigning or adding meaning to the statute, on the other. *See* REED DICKERSON, THE INTERPRETATION AND APPLICATION OF STATUTES 13–33 (1975).

Under the second model, that of partnership, courts are lawmakers in their own right, working with the legislature to produce a coherent and sound legal regime. These are not really two separate categories; they are tendencies or points along a continuum. The basic question is the extent to which the court's task is, on the one hand, to discern or execute a decision made by the legislature or, on the other, to play a lawmaking role itself, supplementing, elaborating, refining, or even correcting the legislature's handiwork.

It is a commonplace that, apart from constitutional issues, judges are subordinate to legislatures in the making of public policy. If this subordinate role means anything at all, it must somehow constrain judges who interpret statutes from implementing their own notions of public policy. Although this much is clear, the extent of the constraint is far from obvious. At the one extreme, judges may be free to implement virtually any policies they want; at the other, they may be forbidden even to consider their own views of public policy in deciding statutory issues.[3]

One other taxonomy may be helpful to keep in mind. Professor William Popkin divides approaches to statutory interpretation into three. A "writer-based" approach focuses on the will or intent of the legislature. A "reader-based" approach gives greater rein to the views of the court. A "text-based" approach rejects any extrinsic aids to interpretation, including indications of legislative intent or broader considerations of principle or policy, and looks exclusively to the words of the statute.[4]

These debates arise at all because of an inescapable fact: words *always* require interpretation. The reader must choose among possible meanings. Often, the task will be straightforward, and virtually everyone will agree on the "correct" interpretation. But that does not mean that no interpretation has occurred. Consider the following classic, though prosaic, example, first offered in 1830 by the once-famous Francis Lieber, who was to become the second member of the faculty of the Columbia Law School:

> Suppose a housekeeper says to a domestic: "fetch some soupmeat," accompanying the act with giving some money to the latter; he will be unable to execute the order without interpretation, however easy and, consequently, rapid the performance of the process may be. Common sense and good faith tell the domestic, that the housekeeper's meaning was this: 1. He should go immediately, or as soon as his other occupations are finished; or, if he be directed to do so in the evening, that he should go the next day at the usual hour; 2. that the money handed him by the housekeeper is intended to pay for the meat thus ordered, and not as a present to him 3. that he should buy such meat and of such parts of the animal, as, to his knowledge, has commonly been used in the house he stays at, for making soups; 4. that he buy the best meat he can obtain, for a fair

---

[3] Daniel A. Farber, *Statutory Interpretation and Legislative Supremacy*, 78 GEO. L.J. 281, 281–282 (1989).

[4] William D. Popkin, *Law-Making Responsibility and Statutory Interpretation*, 68 IND. L.J. 865 (1993).

price 5. that he go to that butcher who usually provides the family, with whom the domestic resides, with meat, or to some convenient stall, and not to any unnecessarily distant place; 6. that he return the rest of the money; 7. that he bring home the meat in good faith, neither adding any thing disagreeable nor injurious; 8. that he fetch the meat for the use of the family and not for himself. Suppose, on the other hand, the housekeeper, afraid of being misunderstood, had mentioned these eight specifications, she would not have obtained her object, if it were to exclude all possibility of misunderstanding. For, the various specifications would have required new ones. Where would be the end? We are constrained then, always, to leave a considerable part of our meaning to be found out by interpretation, which, in many cases must necessarily cause greater or less obscurity with regard to the exact meaning, which our words were intended to convey.[5]

We will invoke this example repeatedly in what follows. However, domestics and soupmeat both being much rarer than they once were, we will update Lieber's hypothetical: assume instead that I ask you to "go buy a quart of milk."

A. COURTS AS AGENTS OF THE LEGISLATURE

1. Traditional Intentionalism

On the standard account, affirmed by countless judicial opinions, the touchstone of statutory interpretation is legislative intent. As the Supreme Court said early in its history and has been repeating ever since: "In construing these laws, it has been truly stated to be the duty of the court to effect the intention of the legislature."[6] Or, as Judge Patricia Wald wrote: "When a statute comes before me to be interpreted, I want first and foremost to get the interpretation right. By that, I mean simply this: *I want to advance rather than impede or frustrate the will of Congress*."[7] State courts, too, repeat the same refrain: "When presented with an issue of statutory interpretation, the court's primary consideration 'is to ascertain and give effect to the intention of the Legislature.' "[8] The leading early treatise on statutes stated flatly: "The intent of a statute is the law" and "[t]o find out the intent [is] the object of all interpretation."[9]

The task of the court is thus to determine what the legislature "had in mind" when it used the language at issue. This approach is modeled on the way in which we think about ambiguities in communication between individuals. I ask you to buy me a quart of milk. You are not sure if I mean whole milk, skim milk, or buttermilk.

[5] Francis Lieber, Legal and Political Hermeneutics 17–19 (3d ed. 1880), *reprinted in* 16 Cardozo L. Rev. 1883, 1904 (1995). For a very helpful application of contemporary debates to this example, *see* William N. Eskridge, *"Fetch Some Soupmeat"*, 16 Cardozo L. Rev. 2209 (1995).

[6] Schooner Paulina's Cargo v. United States, 11 U.S. (7 Cranch) 52, 60 (1812).

[7] Patricia M. Wald, *The Sizzling Sleeper: The Use of Legislative History in Construing Statutes in the 1988-89 Term of the United States Supreme Court*, 39 Am. U. L. Rev. 277, 301 (1990) (emphasis in original).

[8] Long v. State of New York, 7 NY3d 269, 273 (2006) (citations omitted).

[9] J.G. Sutherland, Statutes and Statutory Construction 309, 311 (1891).

So you ask. I say, "Oh, I *meant* skim milk." You assumed that when I used the vague term "milk" I had in mind something like a picture of a container, on which I was conscious of the words "whole milk," or "skim milk," or "buttermilk." In answering your question, I specify the picture that was in my conscious mind when I spoke, what I "intended" "milk" to mean, and thus what my somewhat vague instructions actually meant (or, what is synonymous, what I meant by my somewhat vague instructions).

A court cannot ask the legislature directly what it meant. But it implicitly asks that question of the enacting legislature when it interprets the statute.

The cases you read in Chapter 7 generally took, or purported to take, this *intentionalist* approach. The courts described their function as carrying out legislative intent, disagreeing only over what the intent was and how to discern it. For example, *Deem* invoked the principle that the words are the best indicator of intent, and hewed to the literal language because by doing so "the legislative intent is ascertained."

It is no accident that this understanding of the court's role in a statutory case has long dominated the scene. It sounds right; it fits with our basic constitutional commitments and intuitions about policymaking in a democracy. The legislature is the (primary) lawmaking body; the executive implements statutes and courts apply statutes in resolving disputes, but the decision as to what the law should be, outside of constitutional questions, lies with the legislature. Indeed, in a system of legislative supremacy, what options could the courts possibly have other than to effectuate the legislature's will?

> By requiring adherence to the views of the enacting legislature, [intentionalism] attempts to impose constraints on the judge. This is the main attraction of [intentionalism]: it claims to curb policymaking by an un-elected, life-tenured judiciary. Unless the pedigree of the result can be tied to the enacting legislature, the judge is free to roam the legal-societal landscape and render pure policy decisions. According to [intentionalism], such a judicial role cannot be reconciled with our democratic form of government.[10]

Note that identifying the proper judicial *role* (the end) is not the same as identifying the *tools or techniques* (the means) by which that role is best fulfilled. If you accept the traditional mission, you still have to decide *how* courts should figure out what the legislature's intent was. But means and ends are closely related; certain approaches will incline judges toward certain tools. In particular, intentionalism tends to lead judges beyond exclusive reliance on statutory text and to an examination of "legislative history," i.e. the circumstances and materials surrounding and produced during the legislative process that produced the statute in question.

> [E]xamination of circumstances preceding enactment may give interpreters a clearer understanding of how the legislature would have wanted

---

[10] Nicholas S. Zeppos, *The Use of Authority in Statutory Interpretation: An Empirical Analysis*, 70 TEXAS L. REV. 1073, 1079–1080 (1992).

the particular statutory question resolved. Getting closer to what the legislature actually intended is thought to serve the goal of legislative supremacy better. Unlike textualism, which sees the words of the statute as "law," intentionalism locates statutory law beyond, or behind, the statutory language. The actual words used by the legislature may be strong evidence of its intent, but they are merely windows on the legislative intent (or purpose) that is the law. * * *

Some intentionalists are heady archeologists. They would scrutinize the legislative materials to see if the legislature actually considered and expressed an opinion on the question under review.[11]

The "legislative materials" relied on by the intentionalist include the transcripts of hearings and of congressional debates, reports written by congressional committees, amendments made and amendments rejected, and statements of the drafters and/or sponsors. As we shall see in Chapter 12, judicial use of these materials is controversial. For now, the key point is that the essential justification for consulting them is the belief that they shed light on legislative intent:

> [W]hy do American judges (and therefore lawyers) consult legislative history so avidly? One reason is the belief that it improves their access to actual legislative intent. * * * Another reason is that many courts feel a higher fidelity to legislative intent than they do to [statutes themselves, even though statutes are] the official, constitutional vehicles for expressing that intent.[12]

Accordingly, the intentionalist inquiry is not unlimited. As Cass Sunstein has observed:

> As agents, courts should say what the statute means, and in that process *language, history, and structure* are relevant; but background norms, policy considerations, or general principles are immaterial. Above all, those who accept the agency view would bar courts from undertaking value-laden inquiries into (for example) appropriate institutional arrangements, or statutory function and failure, as part of the process of interpretation. The judicial task is one of discerning and applying a judgment made by others, most notably the legislature.[13]

2. *Doubts About the Focus on Legislative Intent*

Despite its prominence, the focus on legislative intent in statutory cases has long been under attack. To some extent, the objections are purely practical: legislative intent may be difficult to discern. Still, that alone is not a reason *not* to make the search, and does not undercut the claim that the court should respect legislative intent, at least to the extent it can be determined.

---

[11] T. Alexander Aleinikoff, *Updating Statutory Interpretation*, 87 Mich. L. Rev. 20, 23–24 (1988).

[12] Dickerson, *supra* note 2, at 137.

[13] Cass R. Sunstein, After the Rights Revolution 112 (1990) (emphasis added).

But what if the search for intent is so difficult because the thing being searched for is not there? Legislative intent may be like the Loch Ness Monster: for years many have believed (generally against their better judgment) that it exists, and some claim even to have glimpsed it, but in reality there just is no such thing. If there is no "legislative intent," then the whole theory of intentionalism must be wrong.

(a)   Fictional Intent

It is a longstanding objection that the idea of legislative intent is largely fictional. A legislature cannot think of everything. Moreover, its many members are unlikely each to understand a bill in exactly the same way; after all, to quote the title of a well-known article, "Congress is a they, not an it."[14] For example, it seems highly unlikely that the legislators who voted for the statute at issue in *Deem v. Milliken* ever thought about its application to slayers, or that if they had each would have had the same understanding of its application in that setting.

Such doubts were strenuously expressed by the legal realists in the early 20th century. Just as the realists attacked the idea that judges were apolitical dispute resolvers who found rather than made the law in common law cases, so they attacked traditional views of statutory interpretation, denying that a statute can have a "plain meaning" or a legislature an "intent." The classic statement of exasperation with the judicial preoccupation with legislative intent comes from Max Radin.

It has frequently been declared that the most approved method is to discover the intent of the legislator. Did the legislator * * * have a series of pictures in mind, one of which was this particular [case]? On this transparent and absurd fiction it ought not to be necessary to dwell. * * * A legislature certainly has no intention whatever in connection with words which some two or three men drafted, which a considerable number rejected, and in regard to which many of the approving majority might have had, and often demonstrably did have, different ideas and beliefs.

That the intention of the legislature is undiscoverable in any real sense is almost an immediate inference from a statement of the proposition. The chances that of several hundred men each will have exactly the same determinate situations in mind as possible reductions of a given determinable [i.e. the general principle set out in the statute], are infinitesimally small. The chance is still smaller that a given * * * litigated issue * * * will not only be within the minds of all these men but will be certain to be selected by all of them as the present limit to which the determinable should be narrowed. In an extreme case, it might be that we could learn all that was in the mind of the draftsman, or of a committee of half a dozen men who completely approved of every word. But when this draft is submitted to the legislature and at once accepted without a dissentient voice and without debate, what have we then learned of the intentions of the four or

---

[14] Kenneth A. Shepsle, *Congress Is a "They," Not an "It": Legislative Intent as Oxymoron*, 12 INT'L REV. L. & ECON. 239 (1992).

five hundred approvers? Even if the contents of the minds of the legislature were uniform, we have no means of knowing that content except by the external utterances or behavior of these hundreds of men, and in almost every case the only external act is the extremely ambiguous one of acquiescence, which may be motivated in literally hundreds of ways, and which by itself indicates little or nothing of the pictures which the statutory descriptions imply. It is not impossible that this knowledge could be obtained. But how probable it is, even venturesome mathematicians will scarcely undertake to compute.[15]

Is Radin's objection that intent is (a) irrelevant, (b) undiscoverable, or (c) nonexistent? Does it matter? Is his critique overstated? Radin seems to treat the legislature's "intentions" and "motivations" synonymously. Is there a difference?

(b)   Public Choice

The claim that intentionalism is incoherent is particularly strong in "public choice" scholarship.[16] Ambrose Bierce captured the essence of public choice theory, long before such a school existed, when he defined politics thus: "A strife of interests masquerading as a contest of principles. The conduct of public affairs for private advantage."[17]

Public choice scholarship applies principles of market economics to explain institutional and political behavior and decisionmaking. The public choice approach assumes that people are "egoistic, rational utility maximizers" in political as well as economic arenas. Under the public choice vision of legislation, many, if not most, important public problems are not resolved by the legislature. Even when the legislature does act on an important issue, the resulting statute "tends to represent compromise because the process of accommodating conflicts of group interest is one of deliberation and consent . . . What may be called public policy is the equilibrium reached in [the political] struggle at any given moment." The legislature is a political battlefield; most of its activity is no more purposive than the expedient accommodation of special interest pressures. "It is hard to imagine a more effective way of saying that Congress has no mind or force of its own than the prognosis of public choice theory."[18]

On this view, the vote of any given legislator is based on nothing other than self-interest. It is the result of interest group pressure (which in turn is powerful only because of its bearing on the legislator's chances for reelection), and reflects strategic choices and logrolling (I'll vote for your provision if you vote for mine)

---

[15] Max Radin, *Statutory Interpretation*, 43 HARV. L. REV. 863, 869–871 (1920). Compare Radin's equally exasperated view of stare decisis at *supra* page 165.

[16] For a readable and helpful summary of the public choice literature as applied to statutory interpretation, *see* DANIEL FARBER & PHILIP P. FRICKEY, PUBLIC CHOICE: A CRITICAL INTRODUCTION 88–115 (1991).

[17] AMBROSE BIERCE, THE DEVIL'S DICTIONARY 101 (1911). In a similar vein: "Lighthouse, n. A tall building on the seashore in which the government maintains a lamp and the friend of a politician." *Id.* at 78.

[18] William N. Eskridge, Jr. & Philip P. Frickey, *Legislation Scholarship and Pedagogy in the Post-Legal Process Era*, 48 U. PITT. L. REV. 691, 703 (1987).

rather than any sincere pursuit of sound policy or the public interest. Legislation is an incoherent compromise, negotiated by or on behalf of private interest groups. In the words of Judge Frank Easterbrook, "Legislation is compromise. Compromises have no spirit; they just are."[19] Its language is simply whatever it took to get a majority on board, and "legislative intent" does not exist.

This disheartening view of the political process is buttressed by the work of Nobel laureate Kenneth Arrow on the impossibility of aggregating preferences. Arrow demonstrated that, making certain assumptions, it is impossible to design a voting system that will reliably produce results that reflect majority preferences. In particular, outcomes depend on the order in which alternatives are considered, which gives enormous power to whoever controls the agenda. "Arrow's theorem" and related work further undercuts the meaningfulness of viewing statutes as the reflection of a particular design or intent.

Whether the pessimistic view of the legislative process offered by public choice scholars is accurate is a matter of debate. Certainly most legislators would deny it (as public choice theory would predict). Former Judge Abner Mikva, who sat on the U.S. Court of Appeals for the D.C. Circuit after many years in the Illinois Legislature and the U.S. House of Representatives, has argued that public choice theory is exaggerated past the point of usefulness:

> I have found it hard to read or to profit from the "public choice" literature. The politicians and other people I have known in public life just do not fit the "rent-seeking" egoist model that the public choice theorists offer. Perhaps I am still one of those naive citizens who believe that politics is on the square, that majorities in effect make policy in this country, and that out of the clash of partisan debate and frequent elections "good" public policy decisions emerge. Not even my five terms in the Illinois state legislature — that last vestige of democracy in the "raw" — nor my five terms in the United States Congress, prepared me for the villains of the public choice literature. * * *
>
> My chief objection to the use of the public choice analysis is that it claims to be scientific and therefore infallible. By contrast, most defenders of the public interest model acknowledge that it is as much a goal as it is an analysis. The public choice theorists, adopting the economists' lingo, start equations by saying "everything else being equal"; but of course nothing else *is* equal in the political arena, and as such the models just aren't very useful. In fact, the claims for accuracy despite the lack of real empirical data put the public choice theorists in the league of the blind man who felt the trunk of the elephant and proclaimed the animal to be a tree.[20]

Needless to say, we cannot determine the validity of public choice theory here. But if it is valid, traditional intentionalist models of statutory interpretation collapse.

---

[19] Frank H. Easterbrook, *Text, History, and Structure in Statutory Interpretation*, 17 Harv. J.L. & Pub. Pol'y 61, 68 (1994).

[20] Abner J. Mikva, *Foreword*, 74 Va. L. Rev. 167, 167, 169–170, 176–177 (1988).

3. Agents of a Principal without Intent

In light of the powerful criticisms just outlined, few theorists are now willing to describe statutory interpretation as merely the search for legislative intent. Many scholars and judges have instead tried to articulate theories of statutory interpretation that respect the agency model's view of the judiciary as a subordinate, non-policymaking branch but also acknowledge that the notion of a legislative intent is fictional. These efforts go in two basic directions: one broadens the judicial inquiry, the other narrows it. Both still portray the judiciary as subordinate to the policymaking authority of the legislature, but move away from the preoccupation with "legislative intent."

(a) Broadening Intentionalism

Even if it is fruitless to seek an intent with regard to the specific question of statutory meaning any given case presents, the court might still defer to legislative authority by (i) determining what the legislature *would* have decided if it *had* thought about the issue, and/or (ii) determining what resolution is most consistent with the broad purposes underlying the statute.

(i) "Imaginative Reconstruction".

P. 455

As is so often the case, Aristotle anticipated us:

> Law is always a general statement, yet there are cases which it is not possible to cover in a general statement. * * * [I]t is then right, where the lawgiver's pronouncement because of its absoluteness is defective and erroneous, to rectify the defect by deciding as the lawgiver would himself decide if he were present on that occasion, and would have enacted if he had been cognizant of the case in question.[21]

Consider the following guidelines offered by Judge Richard Posner.

> I suggest a two-part approach. First, the judge should try to put himself in the shoes of the enacting legislators and figure out how they would have wanted the statute applied to the case before him. This is the method of imaginative reconstruction. If it fails, as occasionally it will, either because the necessary information is lacking or because the legislators had failed to agree on essential premises, then the judge must decide what attribution of meaning to the statute will yield the most reasonable result in the case at hand — always bearing in mind that what seems reasonable to the judge may not have seemed reasonable to the legislators, and that it is their conception of reasonableness, to the extent known, rather than the judge's, that should guide decision.
>
> [This approach requires rather challenging historical reconstruction.] And it invites the criticism that judges do not have the requisite imagination and that what they will do in practice is to assume that the legislators were people just like themselves, with the result that statutory construc

---

[21] ARISTOTLE, NICOMACHEAN ETHICS V.x.4–6.

tion will consist of the judge voting his own preferences and ascribing them to legislators. But the irresponsible judge will twist any approach to yield the outcomes that he desires, and the stupid judge will do the same thing unconsciously.

The judge who follows the suggested approach will not only consider the language, structure, and history of the statute, but also study the values and attitudes, as far as they can be known today, of the period when the legislation was enacted. It would be a mistake to ascribe to legislators of the 1930s or the 1960s and early 1970s the skepticism regarding the size of government and the efficiency of regulation that is widespread today, or to impute to the Congress of the 1920s current ideas of conflict of interest. The judge's job is not to keep a statute up to date in the sense of making it reflect contemporary values, but to imagine as best he can how the legislators who enacted the statute would have wanted it applied to situations they did not foresee. * * *

If the lines of compromise are not clear, if the judge's scrupulous search for the legislative will does not turn up anything, the second part of my approach ("reasonable result") comes into play — provided the case is at least within the statute's domain. If someone was shortchanged on the purchase of a bag of oranges and brought suit against the seller under the federal securities laws, arguing that the court should read "security" to include an orange because fraud is a bad thing, he would receive short shrift. The securities laws do not authorize the courts to deal with a sale of oranges. But if the case involves something that is or may be a security, and the judge is simply very uncertain whether the statute was meant to apply, he cannot just dismiss the case out of hand; it is within the scope of the legislative delegation to him. He must decide the case, even though on the basis of considerations that cannot be laid at Congress's door. These might be considerations of judicial administrability — what interpretation of the statute will provide greater predictability, require less judicial fact-finding, and otherwise reduce the cost and frequency of litigation under the statute? Or they might be considerations drawn from some broadly based conception of the public interest. It is always possible, of course, to refer these considerations back to Congress — to say that Congress would have wanted the courts, in cases where they could not figure out what interpretation would advance the substantive objectives of the statute, to adopt the "better" one; or to say * * * that legislators should be presumed reasonable until shown otherwise. But these methods of imputing congressional intent are artificial; and it is not healthy for a judge to conceal from himself that he is being creative.[22]

How would Posner have you go about deciding what type of milk to buy? First, you should put yourself in my shoes. If you knew what milk I usually bought, or what prompted me to ask for milk, or for whom I was buying it, or whether I had invested in a particular dairy, you might be able imaginatively to reconstruct my answer to the question of what type to buy. Absent such information, you must

---

[22] Richard A. Posner, The Federal Courts: Crisis and Reform 286–287, 289–290 (1985).

p. 242 — the murdered grandfather

determine the most "reasonable" action, which will require some information, or some assumptions, with regard to the purpose for which I want the milk, or some independent judgment on your part as to what makes good milk, or an evaluation of what is available.

The opinion in *Riggs* includes a heavy dose of Posner; indeed, Posner has written approvingly of *Riggs*,[23] a case in which, he says, imaginative reconstruction "works splendidly."[24] For example, the following excerpt from *Riggs* is pure imaginative reconstruction:

> It was the intention of the law-makers that the donees in a will should have the property given to them. But it never could have been their intention that a donee who murdered the testator to make the will operative should have any benefit under it. If such a case had been present to their minds, and it had been supposed necessary to make some provision of law to meet it, it cannot be doubted that they would have provided for it.

Ⓐ *p. 243*

Note that Posner is still very much seeking to be, at least as far as possible, the faithful agent of the legislature. Indeed, his proposed modifications to traditional interpretive methods are aimed at greater faithfulness. Does he believe in such a thing as legislative intent, or would he agree that legislatures don't have intents, only results? His archeology is at least challenging; is it impossible? Can we *ever* say with any confidence what the legislature would have done?

Not really

Professor Einer Elhauge defends a variation on imaginative reconstruction, arguing that when confronted with unsolvable statutory ambiguity a judge should "maximize political satisfaction." By this Elhauge means adopting the interpretation that accords with the preferences of the *current* legislature, not the enacting legislature. He argues that an *enacting* legislature would actually prefer such an approach, because while it dilutes the legislature's future influence, it increases its current influence. Elhauge also argues that what should guide the court is not the general sentiments of the current legislature (or the public), but, more narrowly, the *enactable* preferences. So, for example, if a majority of Congress supports and would actually vote for reading A, but the current president would veto such legislation, the preferences are not *enactable* and do not control. (Note one obvious objection to this approach is whether courts can in fact meaningfully assess what the current Congress's enactable preferences *are*.) Elhauge's argument is too lengthy and complex to summarize here, but the essential proposition is a straightforward one that is borrowed from the private law setting. Basic principles of the law of agency hold that where the express instructions of the principal give out, the agent is expected to act consistently with the principal's current preferences.[25]

Ⓐ *p. 287M*

---

[23] Richard A. Posner, The Problems of Jurisprudence 106–107 (1990).

[24] *Id.* at 273.

[25] *See generally* Einer Elhauge, Statutory Default Rules: How to Interpret Unclear Legislation (2008).

(ii) *Purposivism*

Let us distinguish "intent" from "purpose." The two are often lumped together, but careful users mean different things by them. We will use "intent" to refer to what the legislature meant, the specific understanding it had in mind; we will use "purpose" to refer to what it is the legislature ultimately sought to accomplish. In Reed Dickerson's words, intent is "immediate," purpose "ulterior."[26] The distinction, like most distinctions, can become slippery, but intent is about means, and purpose is about ends.

Consider the milk purchase. My *intent* was that you purchase whole, or skim, or buttermilk. My *purpose* may have been to feed a baby that is just switching from formula, in which case whole milk is most appropriate; or to maintain a healthy diet for myself because I am on a recent health kick (a month ago I would have asked for Coca Cola), in which case skim milk would be appropriate; or to make my famous buttermilk cornbread, in which case buttermilk is appropriate. (*How* you know what my purpose is of course another matter.)

The following excerpt from Justice Frankfurter argues for judicial consideration of statutory purpose as opposed to legislative intent:

> You may have observed that I have not yet used the word "intention." All these years I have avoided speaking of the "legislative intent" and I shall continue to be on my guard against using it. * * * Legislation has an aim; it seeks to obviate some mischief, to supply an inadequacy, to effect a change of policy, to formulate a plan of government. That aim, that policy is not drawn, like nitrogen, out of the air; it is evinced in the language of the statute, as read in the light of other external manifestations of purpose. That is what the judge must seek and effectuate, and he ought not to be led off the trail by tests that have overtones of subjective design. We are not concerned with anything subjective. We do not delve into the mind of legislators or their draftsmen, or committee members.[27]

A focus on legislative purpose has a long history and many supporters. (Judge Learned Hand once described statutory interpretation as *nothing but* "proliferating a purpose."[28]) It reached its fullest flowering in the work of two Harvard law professors, Henry Hart and Albert Sacks, in the 1950s. Hart and Sacks's *The Legal Process* is surely the most famous *un*published book in law.[29] These teaching materials were put together as a tentative edition in 1958 and used at the Harvard Law School and elsewhere around that time.

Hart and Sacks began with a particular view of law: "[L]aw is a doing of something, a purposive activity, a continuous striving to solve the basic problems of

Hard +
Sachs

---

[26] DICKERSON, *supra* note 2, at 285.

[27] Felix Frankfurter, *Some Reflections on the Reading of Statutes*, 47 COLUM. L. REV. 527, 538–539 (1947).

[28] Brooklyn Nat'l Corp. v. Commissioner, 157 F.2d 450, 451 (2d Cir. 1946).

[29] Although famous as an unpublished book, *The Legal Process* was ultimately published. Hart and Sacks never saw it in print, but Foundation Press published their opus, with an introduction by William Eskridge and Philip Frickey, in 1994.

xx use the spouse hypo?

social living";[30] it is an "on-going, functioning, purposive process."[31] This leads to a particular view of statutes: "Every statute must be conclusively presumed to be a purposive act. The idea of a statute without an intelligible purpose is foreign to the idea of law and inadmissible."[32] This assumption about statutes has a corollary assumption about legislatures. "[U]nless the contrary unmistakably appears, [the reader should assume] that the legislature was made up of reasonable persons pursuing reasonable purposes reasonably."[33] Faced with an ambiguous statute, the task is to carefully consider the context of the statute in order to "[d]ecide what purpose ought to be attributed to the statute."[34] (Note how active and strong the interpreter's role seems to be in determining the purpose.) The proper interpretation is the one most consistent with that purpose. For Hart and Sacks, purpose seems to drive interpretation even more than text; the words, in historical context, limit the meanings the statute can bear, but they are equally or more important as guides to the statute's purpose.

What is the difference between "imaginative reconstruction" and "attribution of purpose"? Judge Posner sees the central divergence as follows:

> Hart and Sacks appear to be suggesting that the judge should ignore interest groups, popular ignorance and prejudice, and anything else that deflects legislators from the single-minded pursuit of the public interest as the judge would conceive it. But this approach risks attributing to legislation not the purposes reasonably inferable from the legislation itself but the judge's own conception of the public interest. When Hart and Sacks were writing — in the wake of the New Deal — the legislative process was widely regarded as progressive and public-spirited. Today there is less agreement that the motives behind most legislation are benign, and this should make the judge wary about too readily assuming a congruence between his conception of the public interest and the latent purposes of the statutes he is called on to interpret.

> A related characteristic of * * * Hart and Sacks is a reluctance to recognize that statutes often are the product of compromise between opposing groups and that a compromise is unlikely to embody a single consistent purpose. Of course, as I pointed out earlier, it is hard for judges, limited as they are to the formal materials of the legislative process, to identify the existence of compromise. But where the lines of compromise are discernible, the judge's duty is to follow them, to implement not the purposes of one group of legislators but the compromise itself.[35]

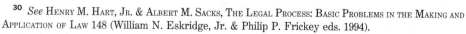

---

[30] *See* Henry M. Hart, Jr. & Albert M. Sacks, The Legal Process: Basic Problems in the Making and Application of Law 148 (William N. Eskridge, Jr. & Philip P. Frickey eds. 1994).

[31] *Id.* at cxxxvii.

[32] *Id.* at 1124.

[33] *Id.* at 1378.

[34] *Id.* at 1374.

[35] Posner, *supra* note 22, at 288–289.

(b) Narrowing Intentionalism — Herein of "The New Textualism"

Judge Posner is strongly influenced by the public choice view of the legislative process. His project is to define an honest intentionalism that is consistent with it. In contrast, the Hart and Sacks approach assumes the inaccuracy of the public choice model. Subscribers to public choice may have their doubts about Posner, but must find Hart and Sacks preposterous.

> If, as public choice theory asserts, legislation is the product of compromises among groups, then attributing a purpose to a statute either may improperly privilege the interests of one group over another (thereby undermining the bargain) or may impute a purpose where none (other than the desire to reach agreement) existed.[36]

The alternative response to the defects of intentionalism, then, is not to broaden but to narrow the judicial inquiry — to abandon intentionalism and purposivism in favor of a (nearly) exclusive focus on the statutory text. If the search for intent behind the words is doomed, the most obvious strategy for the faithful agent would be simply to follow the law as written. This approach is called *textualism*. Instead of attempting to adhere to the *subjective intent* of the legislature, the court would adhere to the *objective meaning* of the statutory text. Justice Antonin Scalia, the most visible and influential judicial textualist, argues that the judge's task is "not to enter the minds of the Members of Congress — who need have nothing in mind in order for their votes to be both lawful and effective — but rather to give fair and reasonable meaning to the text of the United States Code."[37] Or, to quote Justice Scalia again, "[i]t is the law that governs, not the intent of the lawgiver."[38] Thus, you do not ask me what I *meant* by "milk," indeed you do not care. Instead you ask what the average person means when she refers to milk, without any qualifying adjective. What is the ordinary meaning of the word "milk"?

Of course, the answer to that question is quite unclear. Many words have multiple meanings, and if by "ordinary" meaning we mean "most common," textualism will produce absurd and unacceptable results. Textualists turn frequently to dictionaries, but a dictionary alone is no more sufficient for the textualist judge than for the tourist who does not know the local language. When textualists speak of a term's ordinary meaning, what they mean (and this always implicit and often explicit) is its meaning *in context*.

> [I]t is now well settled that textual interpretation must account for the text in its social and linguistic context. Even the strictest modern textualists properly emphasize that language is a social construct. They ask how

---

[36] Aleinikoff, *supra* note 11, at 28.

[37] Pennsylvania v. Union Gas Co., 491 U.S. 1, 30 (1989).

[38] ANTONIN SCALIA, A MATTER OF INTERPRETATION: FEDERAL COURTS AND THE LAW 17 (1998). This short book, which also includes commentaries by leading academics, is an accessible, straightforward, and consistently interesting (for some, enraging) statement of Justice Scalia's views on constitutional and statutory interpretation. It is usefully compared with another brief book by one of Justice Scalia's colleagues, STEPHEN BREYER, ACTIVE LIBERTY (2005), though the latter is somewhat more focused on constitutional interpretation.

a reasonable person, conversant with the relevant social and linguistic conventions, would read the text in context. This approach recognizes that the literal or dictionary definitions of words will often fail to account for settled nuances or background conventions that qualify the literal meaning of language and, in particular, of legal language.[39]

In its strongest version, textualism forbids reference to anything but statutory text in any and all cases. (The "statutory text" may include related provisions of the same Act and even other statutes that use the term in question.) One might say that it makes the judge the agent not of the legislature but of *the statute.* This idea is captured in a famous passage from Justice Holmes:

> [A statute] does not disclose one meaning conclusively according to the laws of language. Thereupon we ask, not what this man meant, but what those words would mean in the mouth of a normal speaker of English, using them in the circumstances in which they were used. * * * But the normal speaker of English is merely a special variety, a literary form, so to speak, of our old friend the prudent man. He is external to the particular writer, and a reference to him as the criterion is simply another instance of the externality of the law. * * * We do not inquire what the legislature meant; we ask only what the statute means.[40]

Wadsworth v. Siek displayed a strong strain of textualism, particularly in the following passage:

> [To hold that] no felonious killer, *in any degree,* shall be permitted to inherit from his victim * * * would be directly contrary to the provisions of the statute. Had the legislature wished to include a person adjudged guilty of manslaughter, it could easily have done so, and it may do so in the future by amending the statute.

> Whether the omission by the legislature was intentional or inadvertent, the fact is that manslaughter *was* omitted, and this Court has no right to "amend" the statute by adding it.

What are the justifications for focusing so exclusively on text? Much of the argument is not that text is so illuminating, but that other sources of interpretation are so harmful and illegitimate. First, only the statutory text undergoes the full, constitutionally required procedures for lawmaking, including a vote by both houses and presentment to the President. Second, materials other than text — in particular, "legislative history" — are inaccurate indicators of the intent of the legislature as a whole and infinitely manipulable. Third, textualists are strongly influenced by the public choice view of the legislative process, under which arguments about intent are often incoherent and arguments from purpose fictional and misleading. Finally, resort to any interpretive guide other than the statutory text is an opportunity for judges to read their own policy preferences into the statute. (In this desire to cabin judicial discretion, statutory textualists have much

---

[39] John F. Manning, *The Absurdity Doctrine,* 116 HARV. L. REV. 2387, 2392–2393 (2003).

[40] Oliver Wendell Holmes, *The Theory of Legal Interpretation,* 12 HARV. L. REV. 417, 417–419 (1899), *reprinted in* COLLECTED LEGAL PAPERS 204, 207 (1920).

in common with constitutional originalists; indeed, the two generally go hand in hand.) So, for Justice Scalia, "legislative intent" is a "handy cover for judicial intent," and reliance on statutory purpose is "an invitation to judicial lawmaking."[41]

Do these justifications hold up? With regard to the last, consider whether textualism might actually *increase* judicial discretion. Justice Stevens has so argued:

> [T]he "minimalist" judge "who holds that the purpose of the statute may be learned only from its language" has more discretion than the judge "who will seek guidance from every reliable source." A method of statutory interpretation that is deliberately uninformed, and hence unconstrained, may produce a result that is consistent with a court's own view of how things should be, but it may also defeat the very purpose for which a provision was enacted.[42]

Textualism may further legislative intent; the *Deem* court even had a Latin maxim so asserting (*index animi sermo* [language indicates intention]). But modern textualists do not justify their method on that ground and will acknowledge that in some cases textualism will simply implement an unintentional mistake. Textualism's central claimed virtue is more negative: it prevents furthering mere *judicial* intent. The textualist's central fear is that judges will impose their own views of sound policy under the guise of having discovered a subtly hidden legislative intent in the legislative history or purpose.

Textualism has proven enormously influential. The period from, say, 1985 to 2005 saw a significant decline in judicial reliance on legislative history (particularly in the federal courts, where such reliance had been most extensive) and a significant increase in the seriousness with which judges have grappled with statutory text. At the same time, textualists have avoided more extreme versions, or parodies, of their approach. The result is that there may be less to remaining debates than meets the eye.

> Textualism has outlived its utility as an intellectual movement. * * * Textualists have been so successful discrediting strong purposivism, and distinguishing their new brand of "modern textualism" from the older, more extreme "plain meaning" school, that they no longer can identify, let alone conquer, any remaining territory between textualism's adherents and nonadherents. Leading textualists may proceed today as if their quest is still worth pursuing, but in so doing they overlook a strong consensus on the interpretive enterprise that dwarfs any differences that remain. * * * It is time for us to put the textualism-purposivism debate behind us, acknowledge areas of agreement as well as disagreement, stop talking past one another, and engage in a more productive dialogue regarding the narrow differences that remain.[43]

---

[41] SCALIA, *supra* note 38, at 18, 21.

[42] Circuit City Stores, Inc. v. Adams, 532 U.S. 105, 133 (2001) (Stevens, J., dissenting) (quoting AHARON BARAK, JUDICIAL DISCRETION 62 (Yadin Kaufmann. trans. 1989)).

[43] Jonathan T. Molot, *The Rise and Fall of Textualism*, 106 COLUM. L. REV. 1, 2 (2006).

B. COURTS AND LEGISLATURES AS LAWMAKING PARTNERS

You might take yet another approach to my request for milk. Given the vagueness in my choice of words, you might base the decision on some principle completely independent of *my* aims or desires and independent of the word I chose. For example, you might choose skim milk because it is healthiest, and you (or society in general) consider healthy eating a virtue. That is not the choice you would have made 50 years ago, of course; had we been living then you would have chosen whole milk for the same reason. Or you might choose whole milk because you think it tastes better. You are now not simply carrying out my command; we are making the decision together (though sequentially). I have narrowed the possibilities — you would not be free to bring back orange juice — but within the boundaries of the language I used, *you* are deciding what to do.

Some commentators suggest such an approach to the interpretation of statutes. The traditional model of statutory interpretation is "archeological": "statutory meaning [i]s determined on the date of the statute's enactment" and "the interpreter's task [i]s essentially a factual inquiry: a judge uncovers and describes an already fixed past." But one might also adopt a "nautical" approach, in which the legislature launches the statutory ship but the courts chart the voyage.[44]

1. *Independent Judicial Judgment*

Recall the analogy made by Ronald Dworkin between common-law decisionmaking based on judicial precedents and the chain novel. Dworkin has applied the metaphor to statutory interpretation. His model judge, Hercules,

> will use much the same techniques of interpretation to read statutes that he uses to decide common-law cases * * *. He will treat Congress as an author earlier than himself in the chain of law, though an author with special powers and responsibilities different from his own, and he will see his own role as fundamentally the creative one of a partner continuing to develop, in what he believes is the best way, the statutory scheme Congress began. He will ask himself which reading of the act * * * shows the political history including and surrounding that statute in the better light. His view of how the statute should be read will in part depend on what certain congressmen said when debating it. But it will also depend on the best answer to political questions * * *. He must rely on his own judgment in answering these questions, of course, not because he thinks his opinions are automatically right, but because no one can properly answer any question except by relying at the deepest level on what he himself believes.[45]

The so-called "new legal process" theorists contend that statutory interpretation must be a creative act. They are at least implicitly unfazed by the possibility of judicial policymaking that drives, or at least is reckoned with by, the various "agency" theories.

---

[44] Aleinikoff, *supra* note 11, at 21–22.

[45] RONALD DWORKIN, LAW'S EMPIRE 313–314 (1986).

[M]any [legal scholars] remain committed to the ideal of a legal process that seeks law reform and justice. These progressive scholars have responded to the challenge in a variety of ways; the directions they have taken have created a "new" legal process which self-consciously pursues substantive as well as procedural justice. Although responses to the attacks on legal process vary greatly, they have several common themes. One is anti-pluralist: legislation must be more than the accommodation of exogenously defined interests; lawmaking is a process of value creation that should be informed by theories of justice and fairness. Another theme is that legislation too often fails to achieve this aspiration, and, thus, creative lawmaking by courts and agencies is needed to ensure rationality and justice in law. A final theme is the importance of dialogue or conversation as the means by which innovative judicial lawmaking can be validated in a democratic polity and by which the rule of law can best be defended against charges of unfairness or illegitimacy.

* * * [These] scholars are willing to abandon the notion that all political choices must be made by the majoritarian legislature. Certain critical "public values" simply cannot be bargained away, and much of the process of political norm-creation must or should occur in the courts. * * * Like longstanding legal process work, this body of scholarship analyzes or defends the legitimacy of judicial lawmaking. Unlike prior legal process work, new legal process scholarship proceeds in wide-ranging new directions, based upon a more open pessimism about the rationality of the legislative process. * * *

[N]ew legal process theorists * * * explicitly emphasize the demands of substantive justice and the evolutive rather than formal nature of legitimacy. * * * [For example,] Ronald Dworkin has dealt with the problem of aging statutes, and he argues that judges can advance progressive social policy without imposing their own values onto statutes. * * * [For Dworkin,] "integrity in legislation" requires lawmakers to try to make the total set of laws morally coherent. * * * The courts' role is to interpret authoritative statements of law (the Constitution, statutes, common law precedents) in light of the underlying principles of the community. Thus, in the "hard cases" of statutory interpretation, the best interpretation is the one that is most consonant with the underlying values of society and makes the statute the best statute it can be (within the limitations imposed by the language).[46]

Of the cases in Chapter 7, *Riggs* shows the strongest tendency toward this approach. The court rejects a literal reading of the text, invokes a general principle of reasonableness, and asserts that all statutes "may be controlled in their operation and effect by general, fundamental maxims of the common law" — a "universal law administered in all civilized countries." Note that on this account the judge is still not simply making it up, or imposing her own, particular preferences; rather, she is pursuing right answers in light of prevailing societal values. Whether such an

---

[46] Eskridge & Frickey, *supra* note 18, at 717, 720–722.

approach is legitimate, or even viable, will depend in large measure on whether you believe that such answers exist and, if they do, that judges are in a position to discern them.

2. *Dynamic Statutory Interpretation*

the young statute again

p. 263

Responsiveness to the needs and values of society will mean that statutory meaning can change and develop; courts should not blindly enforce the legislative deals of the past but should adapt the legislation to contemporary needs and conditions. The idea of "dynamic statutory interpretation" is endorsed by and closely associated with Professor William Eskridge. Note that this approach goes beyond Professor Elhauge's argument that statutory ambiguity should be resolved by reference to the enactable preferences of the *current* legislature,[47] although that obviously has an element of dynamism. The idea is that even "clear" statutory meaning can change with time (and absent legislative amendment). Eskridge's theory is both descriptive and normative; he concludes both that in the real world judges *do* update older statutes (although they rarely acknowledge it) and that they *should.* The descriptive proposition is not very controversial; there is consensus that judges do update statutes, and most commentators agree that their doing so is, at least to some extent, unavoidable and inevitable. The normative prong of Eskridge's theory is more controversial. Eskridge explains:

> The static vision of statutory interpretation prescribed by traditional doctrine is strikingly outdated. In practice, it imposes unrealistic burdens on judges, asking them to extract textual meaning that makes sense in the present from historical materials whose sense is often impossible to recreate faithfully. As doctrine, it is intellectually antediluvian, in light of recent developments in the philosophy of interpretation. Interpretation is not static, but dynamic. Interpretation is not an archeological discovery, but a dialectical creation. Interpretation is not mere exegesis to pinpoint historical meaning, but hermeneutics to apply that meaning to current problems and circumstances.
>
> The dialectic of statutory interpretation is the process of understanding a text created in the past and applying it to a present problem. This process cannot be described simply as the recreation of past events and past expectations, for the "best" interpretation of a statute is typically the one that is most consonant with our current "web of beliefs" and policies surrounding the statute. That is, statutory interpretation involves the present-day interpreter's understanding and reconciliation of three different perspectives, no one of which will always control. These three perspectives relate to (1) the statutory text, which is the formal focus of interpretation and a constraint on the range of interpretive options available (textual perspective); (2) the original legislative expectations surrounding the statute's creation, including compromises reached (historical perspective); and (3) the subsequent evolution of the statute and its present context, especially the ways in which the societal and legal

---

[47] *See supra* page _____ .

environment of the statute has materially changed over time (evolutive perspective).

Under dynamic statutory interpretation, the textual perspective is critical in many cases. The traditional understanding of the "rule of law" requires that statutes enacted by the majoritarian legislature be given effect, and that citizens have reasonable notice of the legal rules that govern their behavior. When the statutory text clearly answers the interpretive question, therefore, it normally will be the most important consideration. Exceptions, however, do exist because an apparently clear text can be rendered ambiguous by a demonstration of contrary legislative expectations or highly unreasonable consequences. The historical perspective is the next most important interpretive consideration; given the traditional assumptions that the legislature is the supreme lawmaking body in a democracy, the historical expectations of the enacting legislature are entitled to deference. Hence, when a clear text and supportive legislative history suggest the same answer, they typically will control.

The dynamic model, however, views the evolutive perspective as most important when the statutory text is not clear and the original legislative expectations have been overtaken by subsequent changes in society and law. In such cases, the pull of text and history will be slight, and the interpreter will find current policies and societal conditions most important. The hardest cases, obviously, are those in which a clear text or strong historical evidence or both, are inconsistent with compelling current values and policies.[48]

3. *Legislative Supremacy*

The fundamental question about invoking the evolutive or partnership perspective is whether doing so flouts the principle of legislative supremacy. For many, it is self-evidently inconsistent with this basic principle of the separation of powers, under which all legislature authority lies with Congress. Several writers have sought to square dynamic interpretation with legislative supremacy by arguing that the *enacting legislature itself* might well prefer such an interpretive methodology. If the legislature would prefer courts to read statutes dynamically, a court doing so is being a faithful agent after all. William Eskridge has made that argument.[49] The following is a slightly different version offered by Daniel Farber.

Perhaps the most obvious understanding of legislative supremacy is that courts must follow legislative directives: "Judges must be honest agents of the political branches. They carry out decisions they do not make." Hence, the "judges' role is to decipher and enforce" the statute. This is a "strong," or "formalist," conception of legislative supremacy. The strong conception views the supremacy principle as an all-encompassing prescription of the

---

[48] William N. Eskridge, Jr., *Dynamic Statutory Interpretation*, 135 U. Pa. L. Rev. 1479, 1482–1483 (1987). Eskridge developed and refined the ideas from this seminal article in a 1994 book of the same title.

[49] William N. Eskridge, Jr., *Spinning Legislative Supremacy*, 78 Geo. L.J. 319 (1988).

judicial role in statutory cases rather than as a mere constraint on judicial behavior. * * *

Judges have been compared to military officers attempting to obey unclear orders from headquarters.[50] This military analogy suggests some of the difficulties with the strong conception of supremacy. Within the confines of his orders, even a subordinate officer is expected to exercise his discretion in accordance with sound military judgement. In the absence of orders, the officer is not expected to sit on his hands regardless of circumstances. Again, the agency model can be misleading if oversimplified. The captain must follow the general's orders, but to do so the captain may have to interpret an occasionally unclear order in light of his primary allegiance to the United States Army. Similarly, legislative supremacy does not prescribe statutory interpretation that may result in the elimination of judicial policymaking. This is not to say, of course, that statutory interpretation is an exercise in raw policymaking, but only that on occasion, the judiciary may properly consider nonlegislative sources of public policy. * * *

Under the weak conception of legislative supremacy, a judge may not contravene statutory directives. Thus, unlike the strong conception, the weak conception views supremacy as a constraint on judicial action, rather than as a complete specification of the judicial role in statutory cases.

The military analogy is helpful in clarifying the nature of this constraint. We cannot readily specify just what it means to tell an officer to follow orders, because to do so would require a complete philosophical account of interpretation. Inverting the prescription may be more useful: whatever else an officer may do, he cannot *disobey* lawful orders.

One advantage of the weak conception is that it demands relatively little consensus about what sources of public policy, if any, a judge may bring to bear in interpreting statutes. It does not assume that statutes are determinate in the sense of having a single correct interpretation. It assumes only that methods of interpretation are not completely "up for grabs," and that a statute's language and legislative history together preclude at least some interpretations. * * *

When the statutory command is unclear, the supremacy principle does not preclude courts from bringing contemporary values to bear. But when

---

[50] Judge Posner, who originated the military analogy, explains that "[i]n our system of government the framers of statutes and constitutions are the superiors of the judges. The framers communicate orders to the judges through legislative texts. . . . If the orders are clear, the judges must obey them." Richard A. Posner, *Legal Formalism, Legal Realism, and the Interpretation of Statutes and the Constitution*, 37 CASE WESTERN RES. L. REV. 179, 189 (1986-1987). [Ed. Note: Professor Eskridge has offered a similar analogy, comparing judges to "diplomats acting upon orders from their national foreign service. These diplomats must often apply ambiguous or outdated communiqués to unforeseen situations, which they do in a creative way, not strictly constrained by their orders. But they are, at bottom, agents in a common enterprise, and their freedom of interpretation is bounded by the mandates of their orders, which are not necessarily consistent or coherent over time, or even at any one time." Eskridge, *supra* note 48, at 1554.].

the statutory language and legislative history make the statute's meaning unmistakable, such "interpretation" is more in the nature of a partial repeal. * * *

A rational legislator might, however, favor a rule that would allow courts to disregard statutory directives under other circumstances. Our hypothetical military officer, for example, might not want his order carried out if unforeseen circumstances make the order obviously futile or counterproductive. For instance, it would hardly be an act of insubordination to disregard an order to shell a hill, if in the meantime the hill had been taken by friendly forces. Similarly, the legislature might not appreciate having its intended beneficiaries wiped out by the courts' "friendly fire."[51]

CONCLUDING NOTE

We have not asked many questions in this chapter. One big one — the biggest of all — is implicit, however: Which approach to statutory interpretation is correct?

One possibility is that all of them are. To be sure, they are to a large extent mutually exclusive. Yet examples of all of each can be found in decided cases; often several appear side by side in the same opinion. Perhaps the search for a *single* all-purpose theory of statutory interpretation is mistaken.

In the next chapter, we turn to a case that draws on several (though not all) of the theories we have reviewed here. Consider whether the opinion is stronger or weaker as a result of its eclectic approach.

Assignment

Review the *Shrader* case that concludes Chapter 7. How would that case be decided under each of the theories of statutory interpretation discussed above?

---

[51] Farber, *supra* note 3, at 284–285, 287–288, 309–310.

Chapter 9

SOURCES OF STATUTORY INTERPRETATION

CHURCH OF THE HOLY TRINITY v. UNITED STATES
143 U.S. 457 (1892)

9-zero

MR. JUSTICE BREWER delivered the opinion of the court.

Plaintiff in error is a corporation, duly organized and incorporated as a religious society under the laws of the State of New York. E. Walpole Warren was, prior to September, 1887, an alien residing in England. In that month the plaintiff in error made a contract with him, by which he was to remove to the city of New York and enter into its service as rector and pastor; and in pursuance of such contract, Warren did so remove and enter upon such service. It is claimed by the United States that this contract on the part of the plaintiff in error was forbidden by the act of February 26, 1885, * * * [which provides, in relevant part]:

> "[I]t shall be unlawful for any person, company, partnership, or corpo-
> ration, in any manner whatsoever, to prepay the transportation, or in any
> way assist or encourage the importation or migration of any alien or aliens,
> any foreigner or foreigners, into the United States, * * * under contract or
> agreement, parol or special, express or implied, made previous to the
> importation or migration of such alien or aliens, foreigner or foreigners, to
> perform labor or service of any kind in the United States * * *."

It must be conceded that the act of the corporation is within the letter of this section, for the relation of rector to his church is one of service, and implies labor on the one side with compensation on the other. Not only are the general words labor and service both used, but also, as it were to guard against any narrow interpretation and emphasize a breadth of meaning, to them is added "of any kind;" and, further, as noticed by the Circuit Judge in his opinion, the fifth section, which makes specific exceptions, among them professional actors, artists, lecturers, singers and domestic servants,[1] strengthens the idea that every other kind of labor

---

[1] [Ed. Fn.] Section five of the Act provides, in part:

> [N]othing in this act shall be so construed as to prevent * * * any person, or persons, partnership, or corporation from engaging, under contract or agreement, skilled workmen in foreign countries to perform labor in the United States in or upon any new industry not at present established in the United States; *Provided,* That skilled labor for that purpose cannot be otherwise obtained; nor shall the provisions of this act apply to professional actors, artists, lecturers, or singers, nor to persons employed strictly as personal or domestic servants;

and service was intended to be reached by the first section. While there is great force to this reasoning, we cannot think Congress intended to denounce with penalties a transaction like that in the present case. It is a familiar rule, that a thing may be within the letter of the statute and yet not within the statute, because not within its spirit, nor within the intention of its makers. This has been often asserted, and the reports are full of cases illustrating its application. This is not the substitution of the will of the judge for that of the legislator, for frequently words of general meaning are used in a statute, words broad enough to include an act in question, and yet a consideration of the whole legislation, or of the circumstances surrounding its enactment, or of the absurd results which follow from giving such broad meaning to the words, makes it unreasonable to believe that the legislator intended to include the particular act. * * * In *United States v. Kirby*, 7 Wall. 482, 486, the defendants were indicted for the violation of an act of Congress, providing "that if any person shall knowingly and wilfully obstruct or retard the passage of the mail, or of any driver or carrier, or of any horse or carriage carrying the same, he shall, upon conviction, for every such offence pay a fine not exceeding one hundred dollars." The specific charge was that the defendants knowingly and wilfully retarded the passage of one Farris, a carrier of the mail, while engaged in the performance of his duty, and also in like manner retarded the steamboat General Buell, at that time engaged in carrying the mail. To this indictment the defendants pleaded specially that Farris had been indicted for murder by a court of competent authority in Kentucky; that a bench warrant had been issued and placed in the hands of the defendant Kirby, the sheriff of the county, commanding him to arrest Farris and bring him before the court to answer to the indictment; and that in obedience to this warrant, he and the other defendants, as his posse, entered upon the steamboat General Buell and arrested Farris, and used only such force as was necessary to accomplish that arrest. The question as to the sufficiency of this plea was certified to this court, and it was held that the arrest of Farris upon the warrant from the state court was not an obstruction of the mail, or the retarding of the passage of a carrier of the mail, within the meaning of the act. In its opinion the court says: "All laws should receive a sensible construction. General terms should be so limited in their application as not to lead to injustice, oppression or an absurd consequence. It will always, therefore, be presumed that the legislature intended exceptions to its language which would avoid results of this character. The reason of the law in such cases should prevail over its letter. The common sense of man approves the judgment mentioned by Puffendorf, that the Bolognian law which enacted 'that whoever drew blood in the streets should be punished with the utmost severity,' did not extend to the surgeon who opened the vein of a person that fell down in the street in a fit. The same common sense accepts the ruling, cited by Plowden, that the statute of 1st Edward II., which enacts that a prisoner who breaks prison shall be guilty of felony, does not extend to a prisoner who breaks out when the prison is on fire, 'for he is not to be hanged because he would not stay to be burnt.' And we think that a like common sense will sanction the ruling we make, that the act of Congress which punishes the obstruction or retarding of the passage of the mail, or of its carrier, does not apply to a case of temporary detention of the

----

Provided, That nothing in this act shall be construed as prohibiting any individual from assisting any member of his family or any relative or personal friend, to migrate from any foreign country to the United States, for the purpose of settlement here.

mail caused by the arrest of the carrier upon an indictment for murder."

Among other things which may be considered in determining the intent of the legislature is the title of the act. We do not mean that it may be used to add to or take from the body of the statute, but it may help to interpret its meaning. * * * Now, the title of this act is, "An act to prohibit the importation and migration of foreigners and aliens under contract or agreement to perform labor in the United States, its Territories and the District of Columbia." Obviously the thought expressed in this reaches only to the work of the manual laborer, as distinguished from that of the professional man. No one reading such a title would suppose that Congress had in its mind any purpose of staying the coming into this country of ministers of the gospel, or, indeed, of any class whose toil is that of the brain. The common understanding of the terms labor and laborers does not include preaching and preachers; and it is to be assumed that words and phrases are used in their ordinary meaning. So whatever of light is thrown upon the statute by the language of the title indicates an exclusion from its penal provisions of all contracts for the employment of ministers, rectors and pastors.

Again, another guide to the meaning of a statute is found in the evil which it is designed to remedy; and for this the court properly looks at contemporaneous events, the situation as it existed, and as it was pressed upon the attention of the legislative body. The situation which called for this statute was briefly but fully stated by Mr. Justice Brown when, as District Judge, he decided the case of *United States v. Craig*, 28 Fed. Rep. 795, 798: "The motives and history of the act are matters of common knowledge. It had become the practice for large capitalists in this country to contract with their agents abroad for the shipment of great numbers of an ignorant and servile class of foreign laborers, under contracts, by which the employer agreed, upon the one hand, to prepay their passage, while, upon the other hand, the laborers agreed to work after their arrival for a certain time at a low rate of wages. The effect of this was to break down the labor market, and to reduce other laborers engaged in like occupations to the level of the assisted immigrant. The evil finally became so flagrant that an appeal was made to Congress for relief by the passage of the act in question, the design of which was to raise the standard of foreign immigrants, and to discountenance the migration of those who had not sufficient means in their own hands, or those of their friends, to pay their passage."

It appears, also, from the petitions, and in the testimony presented before the committees of Congress, that it was this cheap unskilled labor which was making the trouble, and the influx of which Congress sought to prevent. It was never suggested that we had in this country a surplus of brain toilers, and, least of all, that the market for the services of Christian ministers was depressed by foreign competition. Those were matters to which the attention of Congress, or of the people, was not directed. So far, then, as the evil which was sought to be remedied interprets the statute, it also guides to an exclusion of this contract from the penalties of the act.

A singular circumstance, throwing light upon the intent of Congress, is found in this extract from the report of the Senate Committee on Education and Labor, recommending the passage of the bill: "The general facts and considerations which induce the committee to recommend the passage of this bill are set forth in the

Handwritten margin notes: "but it didn't anyway!", "House", "te", "the House again", "should this be the end?", "But beyond..."

Report of the Committee of the House. The committee report the bill back without
amendment, although there are certain features thereof which might well be
changed or modified, in the hope that the bill may not fail of passage during the
present session. Especially would the committee have otherwise recommended
amendments, substituting for the expression 'labor and service,' whenever it occurs
in the body of the bill, the words 'manual labor' or 'manual service,' as sufficiently
broad to accomplish the purposes of the bill, and that such amendments would
remove objections which a sharp and perhaps unfriendly criticism may urge to the
proposed legislation. The committee, however, believing that the bill in its present
form will be construed as including only those whose labor or service is manual in
character, and being very desirous that the bill become a law before the adjournment, have reported the bill without change." And, referring back to the report of
the Committee of the House, there appears this language: "It seeks to restrain and
prohibit the immigration or importation of laborers who would have never seen our
shores but for the inducements and allurements of men whose only object is to
obtain labor at the lowest possible rate, regardless of the social and material
well-being of our own citizens and regardless of the evil consequences which result
to American laborers from such immigration. This class of immigrants care nothing
about our institutions, and in many instances never even heard of them; they are
men whose passage is paid by the importers; they come here under contract to labor
for a certain number of years; they are ignorant of our social condition, and that
they may remain so they are isolated and prevented from coming into contact with
Americans. They are generally from the lowest social stratum, and live upon the
coarsest food and in hovels of a character before unknown to American workmen.
They, as a rule, do not become citizens, and are certainly not a desirable acquisition
to the body politic. The inevitable tendency of their presence among us is to degrade
American labor, and to reduce it to the level of the imported pauper labor." Page
5359, Congressional Record, 48th Congress.

We find, therefore, that the title of the act, the evil which was intended to be
remedied, the circumstances surrounding the appeal to Congress, the reports of the
committee of each house, all concur in affirming that the intent of Congress was
simply to stay the influx of this cheap unskilled labor.

But beyond all these matters no purpose of action against religion can be
imputed to any legislation, state or national, because this is a religious people. This
is historically true. From the discovery of this continent to the present hour, there
is a single voice making this affirmation. The commission to Christopher Columbus,
prior to his sail westward, is from "Ferdinand and Isabella, by the grace of God,
King and Queen of Castile," etc., and recites that "it is hoped that by God's
assistance some of the continents and islands in the ocean will be discovered," etc.
The first colonial grant, that made to Sir Walter Raleigh in 1584, was from
"Elizabeth, by the grace of God, of England, Fraunce and Ireland, queene, defender
of the faith," etc.; and the grant authorizing him to enact statutes for the
government of the proposed colony provided that "they be not against the true
Christian faith now professed in the Church of England." The first charter of
Virginia, granted by King James I in 1606, after reciting the application of certain
parties for a charter, commenced the grant in these words: "We, greatly commend-
ing, and graciously accepting of, their Desires for the Furtherance of so noble a

Work, which may, by the Providence of Almighty God, hereafter tend to the Glory of his Divine Majesty, in propagating of Christian Religion to such People, as yet live in Darkness and miserable Ignorance of the true Knowledge and Worship of God, and may in time bring the Infidels and Savages, living in those parts, to human Civility, and to a settled and quiet Government; DO, by these our Letters-Patents, graciously accept of, and agree to, their humble and well-intended Desires."

[Justice Brewer continues in this vein at considerable length, identifying numerous examples of the invocation of God in public discourse.]

There is no dissonance in these declarations. There is a universal language pervading them all, having one meaning; they affirm and reaffirm that this is a religious nation. These are not individual sayings, declarations of private persons: they are organic utterances; they speak the voice of the entire people. While because of a general recognition of this truth the question has seldom been presented to the courts, yet we find that in *Updegraph v. The Commonwealth*, 11 S. & R. 394, 400, it was decided that, "Christianity, general Christianity, is, and always has been, a part of the common law of Pennsylvania; . . . not Christianity with an established church, and tithes, and spiritual courts; but Christianity with liberty of conscience to all men." And in *The People v. Ruggles*, 8 Johns. 290, 294, 295, Chancellor Kent, the great commentator on American law, speaking as Chief Justice of the Supreme Court of New York, said: "The people of this State, in common with the people of this country, profess the general doctrines of Christianity, as the rule of their faith and practice; and to scandalize the author of these doctrines is not only, in a religious point of view, extremely impious, but, even in respect to the obligations due to society, is a gross violation of decency and good order." * * *

If we pass beyond these matters to a view of American life as expressed by its laws, its business, its customs and its society, we find everywhere a clear recognition of the same truth. Among other matters note the following: The form of oath universally prevailing, concluding with an appeal to the Almighty; the custom of opening sessions of all deliberative bodies and most conventions with prayer; the prefatory words of all wills, "In the name of God, amen;" the laws respecting the observance of the Sabbath, with the general cessation of all secular business, and the closing of courts, legislatures, and other similar public assemblies on that day; the churches and church organizations which abound in every city, town and hamlet; the multitude of charitable organizations existing everywhere under Christian auspices; the gigantic missionary associations, with general support, and aiming to establish Christian missions in every quarter of the globe. These, and many other matters which might be noticed, add a volume of unofficial declarations to the mass of organic utterances that this is a Christian nation. In the face of all these, shall it be believed that a Congress of the United States intended to make it a misdemeanor for a church of this country to contract for the services of a Christian minister residing in another nation?

Suppose in the Congress that passed this act some member had offered a bill which in terms declared that, if any Roman Catholic church in this country should contract with Cardinal Manning to come to this country and enter into its service as pastor and priest; or any Episcopal church should enter into a like contract with

Canon Farrar; or any Baptist church should make similar arrangements with Rev. Mr. Spurgeon; or any Jewish synagogue with some eminent Rabbi, such contract should be adjudged unlawful and void, and the church making it be subject to prosecution and punishment, can it be believed that it would have received a minute of approving thought or a single vote? Yet it is contended that such was in effect the meaning of this statute. The construction invoked cannot be accepted as correct. It is a case where there was presented a definite evil, in view of which the legislature used general terms with the purpose of reaching all phases of that evil, and thereafter, unexpectedly, it is developed that the general language thus employed is broad enough to reach cases and acts which the whole history and life of the country affirm could not have been intentionally legislated against. It is the duty of the courts, under those circumstances, to say that, however broad the language of the statute may be, the act, although within the letter, is not within the intention of the legislature, and therefore cannot be within the statute.

The judgment will be reversed, and the case remanded for further proceedings in accordance with this opinion.

BACKGROUND NOTE

This case has its roots in the efforts of one John S. Kennedy to hire an English gardener. The gardener was deported because he had been brought to this country in violation of the Act at issue in *Holy Trinity*. Apparently feeling much abused, and noticing an announcement in the newspaper of Reverend Warren's new appointment, on September 22, 1887, Kennedy fired off the following letter to the chief customs official in New York:

DEAR SIR: I desire to call your attention to the fact that the Rev. Mr. Warren, an English gentleman and an alien, has been called to the pastorate of the Church of the Holy Trinity in this city, and I am informed he is expected to arrive on or about Saturday next.

Under the act of Congress * * * he cannot be allowed to land on his arrival without directly violating both the letter and spirit of that law, and * * * he should be returned to England in the same manner and for the same reasons as other parties have recently been returned.

In calling your attention to this matter I desire distinctly to say that I have nothing whatever against Mr. Warren * * * and my only object in serving this notification upon you is in order to make this a test case, and by enforcing a most obnoxious and unreasonable law I hope thereby it will lead to its total abrogation.[2]

Kennedy's letter prompted the following editorial in the *New York Times*:

---

[2] Letter from John S. Kennedy to Daniel Magone, Collector of U.S. Customs, New York, Sept. 22, 1887, *in Importing a Rector. Does Mr. Warren's Engagement Conflict with the Law?*, N.Y. TIMES, Sept. 25, 1887, p. 2.

Mr. Warren had already landed when *Mr. Kennedy's* letter was delivered to the Collector, and will in a week or two begin his unholy work of undermining our institutions by performing the "contract labor" for the performance of which he was imported. The duty of the Collector would have been much simplified if he had received the letter before the arrival of the gentleman who may be described, in his relation to the law, as a "coolie" clergyman. In that case Mr. *Magone* would have needed merely to notify the master of the *Adriatic* that in Mr. *Warren* he had been conveying a pernicious and unlawful immigrant, a kind of human dynamite, and to warn that astonished skipper to take back the dangerous exile whence he came. Now it will be necessary for him to resort to some more complicated process in order to rid the Republic of Mr. *Warren*.

Nevertheless, it seems clear that the emigration of a foreign clergyman to this country, under a call from an American parish, is a violation of the law, and we must applaud the purpose of Mr. *Kennedy* to enforce the law in a case where its enforcement will be a riotous travesty upon sense and justice. The law is no respecter of parsons, and what is sauce for the agricultural and manufacturing goose must be sauce also for the theological gander. * * *

There are exceptions to the statute, but Mr. *Warren* is not entitled to the benefit of any of them. Opera singers may come in under contracts, and actors and lecturers and domestic servants, but there is no mention of clergymen. An astute lawyer might endeavor to smuggle the new Rector of the Church of the Holy Trinity under the clause which permits the admission of "skilled workmen, in or upon any industry not at present established in the United States, provided that skilled labor for that purpose cannot be otherwise obtained." * * * [I]f it can be shown that there is anything peculiar in Mr. *Warren's* theology, and that it is not now inculcated from the American pulpit, he might come in as the practitioner of a new industry. Congress has no objection to heresiarchs any more than to Anarchists or dynamiters, so long as they do not compete with talent native or already established.

Seriously, nothing could be better adapted to show the complete absurdity of the law than this proposition to use it against a man who is in all senses a welcome and valuable citizen. For the terms of the law do apparently exclude Mr. *Warren*, while they do not exclude the hundreds of Neapolitan paupers and criminals on board the *Alesia*, who are detained at present because they have brought cholera to the country, but are not detained when they bring only idleness and crime. If such a contrast cannot induce Congress to revise the outrageous statute invoked by Mr. *Kennedy* the case for its revision is hopeless.[3]

A history of the Holy Trinity Church notes that "a controversy * * * raged when [Warren] first came to the United States," and the episode caused "a prolonged

---

[3] *A "Coolie" Clergyman*, N.Y. Times, Sept. 25, 1887, p. 4.

public furor."[4] As for the final outcome:

> [The Supreme Court] reversed because Dr. Warren was classified as a "public speaker." The final decision annoyed Dr. Warren more than anything else in the whole affair, for he had hoped to be the cause of the defeat of a law he regarded as unfair. Furthermore, he objected to this classification of public speaker, feeling that the Ministry is more than that.
>
> With the exception of the slur on the Ministry, which he felt was represented in the final verdict of the Courts, Dr. Warren himself had little personal concern with the Kennedy suit, for it was aimed at the Trustees of the Holy Trinity in particular and the contract labor law in general. But the novelty of the case was enough to bring the name of Warren to the attention of New Yorkers. His effective preaching and leadership at Holy Trinity sustained the initial interest * * *.[5]

NO

Is this description of the Supreme Court's opinion accurate? When the decision came down, the *Times*'s brief account was headlined: "Pastors Are Not Laborers."[6] Is that description of the holding accurate?   *NO*

THE SOURCES OF INTERPRETATION

Holy Trinity presented a specific and clear question of law: whether the entry of Reverend Warren under a contract of employment with the Holy Trinity Church violated the Foreign Contract Labor Act. If the Church had come to you in advance to ask whether it could hire Reverend Warren where would you have looked for an answer? Where did Justice Brewer look? Consider the following catalogue:

1. *Text*

It is a commonplace that statutory interpretation must begin with the words of the statute. Justice Brewer's *opinion* does so. Do you think Justice Brewer *himself* began with the words of the statute when he was considering this case?

Justice Brewer basically concedes that the words are against him. Perhaps not surprisingly, then, he does not dwell on them. Did he give in too soon? Construct an argument, based solely on the text of the statute, to support the Court's result.

Alternatively, is the text even more strongly against him than Justice Brewer cares to acknowledge? Construct an argument, again based solely on the text of the statute, against the Court's result.

---

[4] James Elliott Lindsley, A History of Saint James' Church in the City of New York 1810–1960, at 59–60 (1960). In an interview, Lindsley offered a different take on Warren's reaction, saying that Warren "was always irritated by the implication that he was not a 'worker,' since ministers work as hard as anyone." Carol Chomsky, *Unlocking the Mysteries of* Holy Trinity: *Spirit, Letter, and History in Statutory Interpretation*, 100 Colum. L. Rev. 901, 921 n.99 (2000).

[5] Lindsley, *supra* note 4, at 60–61.

[6] *Pastors Are Not Laborers, The Rev. Mr. Warren Came Here Legitimately*, N.Y. Times, Mar. 1, 1892, at 9.

With regard to both these arguments, of what relevance is the list of exceptions in § 5, which, as Justice Brewer notes with seeming dismay, seems not to include Ministers of the Gospel?

Brewer does not mention § 4 of the Act. That provision made it a crime for the master of any ship to "knowingly bring within the United States . . . any alien laborer, mechanic or artisan" who had contracted to perform "labor or service in the United States." Does this section support or undermine the Court's result? (Hint: your answer will largely depend on whether you think § 1 and § 4 should be read *in pari materia*; that is, whether they should be construed together because they cover the same subject.)

2. *Beyond Text*

Most of the opinion is an effort to accumulate sufficiently weighty considerations that run counter to the apparent meaning of the text to justify ignoring that meaning. Thus, the proposition for which *Holy Trinity* is generally cited is that "a thing may be within the letter of the statute and yet not within the statute, because not within its spirit, nor within the intention of its makers." Is this approach to statutory construction (or statutory *re* construction?) defensible, or is it the usurpation of the legislative function? Justice Scalia would say the latter. Indeed, he *has* said the latter. Dissenting in *Zuni Public School District No. 89 v. Department of Education*, 550 U.S. 81, 116 (2007), he argued that the statutory text directly contradicted the majority's result. "How then, if the text is so clear, are respondents managing to win this case? The answer can only be the return of that miraculous redeemer of lost causes, *Church of the Holy Trinity*."

The central problem of statutory interpretation, Justice Frankfurter once wrote, is figuring out "the extent to which extraneous documentation and external circumstances may be allowed to infiltrate the text on the theory that they were part of it, written in ink discernible to the judicial eye."[7] In *Holy Trinity* the Court moves increasingly further away from the actual words to more distant considerations. Is there a point at which it goes too far?

3. *Title*

Justice Brewer begins by invoking the Act's title, which suggests a narrower application in that it refers only to those under contract "to perform *labor*." Convincing?

Rarely if ever does statutory interpretation turn on an Act's title, but the standard rule is essentially as described by Justice Brewer: the title is relevant to the interpretation of the statute but not dispositive.

In *Bellew v. Dedeaux*, 240 Miss. 79 (1961), a criminal statute provided that someone found guilty of concealing an escaped prisoner "shall be fined not less than one hundred dollars ($100.00) nor more than five hundred dollars ($500.00) or by imprisonment in the penitentiary not to exceed five (5) years." The defendant

---

[7] Felix Frankfurter, *Some Reflections on the Reading of Statutes*, 47 Colum. L. Rev. 527, 529 (1947).

argued that he could not be sentenced to prison because the only punishment authorized by the statute was a *fine*. The court disagreed. In light of the nonsensical reference to being "fined * * * by imprisonment," it relied primarily on the statute's title: "An Act to make it a felony for any person to conceal or harbor any prisoner." Since a felony is by definition a crime subject to punishment by imprisonment for more than one year, the title revealed that the legislature intended to provide for imprisonment for this crime.

Is the reliance on the title in *Holy Trinity* the same as in *Bellew*? Can the title trump the actual words of the statute? Do you imagine that legislators focus less, equally, or more on the title of a bill or on its actual provisions?

Compare the treatment of the Act's title by the District Court in *Holy Trinity*:

> If it were permissible to narrow the provisions of the act to correspond with the purport of the title, and restrain its operation to cases in which the alien is assisted to come here under contract "to perform labor," there might be room for interpretation; and the restricted meaning might possibly be given to the word "labor" which signifies the manual work of the laborer, as distinguished from the work of the skilled artisan, or the professional man. But no rule in the construction of statutes is more familiar than the one to the effect that the title cannot be used to extend or restrain positive provisions in the body of the act.[8]

4. *Purpose*

Central to the Court's method is the interpretation of the statute in light of "the evil to be remedied." This part of the opinion recalls Hart and Sacks, although Justice Brewer relies on evidence of actual purpose rather than "attributing" the purpose that a reasonable legislator would have been pursuing.

What was the particular problem on which Congress was focused? Would excluding Reverend Warren help remedy this problem? Might brain toilers have posed the same threat as unskilled laborers to Americans seeking employment?

Legislators almost always have a particular model before them, a specific, paradigmatic situation to which the legislation is a response. But this does not mean that they aim only at that situation and at none of its cousins when adopting a remedy. Given the breadth of the statutory language, is it not possible that Congress, though spurred to action by the influx of unskilled workers, said, in essence, "While we're at it, let's get rid of foreign competition across the board"?

It seems most likely that no one in Congress paused to think about the labor situation with regard to ministers. Assuming this to be so, is the Court's reliance on purpose pure fiction? Would it make more sense to say not that Congress intended to allow foreign ministers into American churches, but only that *if* Congress had thought about the question, that is what it would have done? Or does this confuse purpose and intent?

---

[8] United States v. Rector of the Church of the Holy Trinity, 36 F. 303, 304 (S.D.N.Y. 1888).

Consider the following objections to judicial invocation of legislative purpose. Are they compelling as applied to *Holy Trinity*?

(a) It simply is not the court's job to interpret a statute in light of what it *= Scalia* perceives to be the legislature's purpose. If the words of the statute seem inconsistent with the purpose, that just means the legislature did not do a very good job in writing the statute. It is not up to the court to rewrite it; that remains the legislature's task. In any event, the best indicator of the legislature's purpose is what it actually did, i.e. the words it used in the statute.

In an oft-cited passage, the Court defended the *Holy Trinity* approach against *American Trucking* this criticism:

> There is, of course, no more persuasive evidence of the purpose of a statute than the words by which the legislature undertook to give expression to its wishes. Often these words are sufficient in and of themselves to determine the purpose of the legislation. In such cases we have followed their plain meaning. When that meaning has led to absurd or futile results, however, this Court has looked beyond the words to the purpose of the act. Frequently, however, even when the plain meaning did not produce absurd results but merely an unreasonable one "plainly at variance with the policy of the legislation as a whole" this Court has followed that purpose, rather than the literal words. When aid to construction of the meaning of words, as used in the statute, is available, there certainly can be no "rule of law" which forbids its use, however clear the words may appear on "superficial examination."[9]

The foregoing more or less describes the methodology of *Holy Trinity*. Does it make sense? Or is it self-indulgent gibberish — simply a statement that we are bound by the words Congress has chosen except when we choose not to be — revealing only that the Court wants to have its cake and eat it too (which, being the Supreme Court, it can)?

(b) Emphasizing the legislative purpose is one-sided and will cause courts to expand statutory programs beyond what the legislature desired or enacted. Yes, purpose is important; but the legislature has always made a determination to go only so far and no further in pursuing a particular purpose. Where the legislature *stopped* is just as important as where it was *headed*. The text indicates that stopping point. A court errs if it reads the statute to do *everything* conceivable to further the relevant purpose.

This critique is most obviously relevant when a court reads a statute more broadly than its language might support rather than more narrowly, as was the case in *Holy Trinity*. But can you criticize the Brewer opinion along these lines? We will return to this idea in Chapter 11.

(c) Purpose is theoretically relevant, but is simply too hard to determine. Not having been present for the enactment, a later interpreter can never reconstruct the legislature's actual purpose. The malleability of the historical and legislative record invites judges to latch on to what seems to *them* a good purpose and to

[9] United States v. American Trucking Ass'ns, 310 U.S. 534, 543–544 (1940).

advance their own policies under the banner of advancing Congress's. As Justice Kennedy has complained about *Holy Trinity*-style inquiries into the "spirit" of the statute: "The problem with spirits is that they tend to reflect less the views of the world whence they come than the views of those who seek their advice."[10]

How did the *Holy Trinity* Court discern Congress's purpose? Are you confident that it fairly describes Congress's *actual* purpose? Or did it merely identify what Justice Brewer thought *should have been* Congress's purpose?

(d) Reliance on legislative purpose is doomed from the start because there is no such thing. Different legislators no doubt had different purposes in mind — some may have had more than one — and they are likely to have been conflicting. Max Radin's debunking of the whole idea of legislative intent applies equally to the fiction of legislative "purpose."

(e) Even if there is such a thing as an identifiable statutory purpose, a court is not equipped — by training, available tools, or democratic mandate — to determine what construction of a particular provision will best further it. Deciding how best to advance a particular purpose is a quintessentially legislative task. For example, the *purpose* of a rent control ordinance is to ensure a reasonable stock of affordable housing; the court cannot decide what construction of such an ordinance will best achieve that goal without making tremendously controversial policy decisions as to which it lacks expertise, information, and authority.

In the Foreign Contract Labor Act, for example, Congress may have thought a blanket exclusion was the most effective *means* to achieve its narrower *end*:

> The breadth of the statutory text, the use of generic terms, and the repeated choice of alternative phrasing suggest that Congress may have intended to cast a wide net to prevent evasion of its policy, at the expense of including some situations that Congress would not regulate on their own merits.[11]

If so, the Court misread the statute even though it correctly identified Congress's purpose.

5.   *Historical and Legislative Context*

The Court also refers to "the circumstances surrounding the appeal to Congress." In part, this is simply a reference to purpose, to "the evil to be remedied." But the context may also give clues as to what exactly the legislature was thinking when it passed the statute and/or what sort of coalitions and deals underlie it.

Long ago, Chief Justice Taney counseled against consideration of what the legislature *said* that its intent was, but distinguished, and endorsed, consideration of the social and political circumstances surrounding passage of a law:

---

[10] Public Citizen v. United States Department of Justice, 491 U.S. 440, 473 (1989) (Kennedy, J., concurring in the judgment).

[11] JAMES WILLARD HURST, DEALING WITH STATUTES 52–53 (1982).

In expounding this law, the judgment of the court cannot, in any degree, be influenced by the construction placed upon it by individual members of Congress in the debate which took place on its passage, nor by the motives or reasons assigned by them for supporting or opposing amendments that were offered. The law as it passed is the will of the majority of both houses, and the only mode in which that will is spoken is in the act itself; and we must gather their intention from the language there used, comparing it, when any ambiguity exists, with the laws upon the same subject, and looking, if necessary, to the public history of the times in which it was passed.[12]

Consider whether the following background information about "the public history of the times" has any bearing on the meaning of the Contract Labor Act.

For the first three-quarters of the nineteenth century, immigration into the United States was essentially uncontrolled. In 1875, Congress forbade the importation of prostitutes and alien convicts, and in 1882 it excluded idiots, convicts, and those obviously unable to care for themselves. The more significant immigration legislation in 1882 was the Chinese Exclusion Act. The outcome of a lengthy battle over cheap Chinese labor (referred to as "coolies," hence the *New York Times* reference to Reverend Warren as a "coolie" clergyman), the Chinese Exclusion Act suspended Chinese labor immigration for ten years (a period that was later extended). In 1885, during the middle of an economic depression (surely no coincidence), Congress enacted the Foreign Contract Labor Act, at issue in *Holy Trinity*, which it tightened by amendments in 1887 and 1888.

The new restrictions on immigration owed a good deal to the rise of organized labor. Indeed, John Kennedy (the frustrated seeker of an English gardener) complained that the "law is nothing better than a sop to the Knights of Labor."[13] Kennedy's reference is to the most important early labor organization, the Order of the Knights of Labor, founded in 1869, which

> was an attempt to unite workers into one big union under centralized control. Its professed object was to escape from the wage system through producers' co-operation, popular education, and the *union of all workers by hand or brain.* * * * [T]he order first became powerful in 1884 by winning a railroad strike in the Southwest. Capital met labor on equal terms, for the first time in America, when the financier Jay Gould conferred with the Knights' executive board and conceded their demands. The Knights were largely responsible for a congressional act of 1885 which forbade the importation of contract labor.[14]

Labor leaders were closely involved in drafting the legislation. As Senator Blair, a key supporter of the bill and the chair of the relevant Senate committee, stated on the Senate floor in objecting to efforts to amend the bill:

---

[12] Aldridge v. Williams, 44 U.S. 9, 24 (1844).

[13] *Mr. Kennedy in Earnest*, N.Y. TIMES, Sept. 27, 1887, at 4.

[14] 3 SAMUEL ELIOT MORISON, THE OXFORD HISTORY OF THE AMERICAN PEOPLE 81–82 (1972) (emphasis added).

The bill was not framed by children and babes, but by the men whose interests it undertakes to guard and conserve. By their leading and most intellectual representatives they came before the committee of the House of Representatives, as they did before our committee, asking for this bill, which they had studied, and which embodied the ideas and propositions which they thought necessary to remedy the public evils of which they complain.[15]

Labor representatives were not shy about making their feelings known, as the following comment from one of the Act's Senate opponents indicates:

I could very conveniently allow this matter to go along and yield to the pressure that is brought to bear upon me by these hundreds and hundreds of labor unions, if I chose to do so and if I thought it was exactly what my duty is as a Senator; but I do not.[16]

Are the role and views of the Knights of Labor relevant to the interpretation of the statute? A realistic view of the political process might support saying so, since Congress is trying to please the most important stakeholders, or special interests. On the other hand, the Supreme Court has viewed such arguments dubiously. *See, e.g., Circuit City Stores v. Adams*, 532 U.S. 105, 120 (2001) ("We ought not attribute to Congress an official purpose based on the motives of a particular group that lobbied for or against a certain proposal — even assuming the precise intent of the group can be determined, a point doubtful both as a general rule and in the instant case. It is for the Congress, not the courts, to consult political forces and then decide how best to resolve conflicts in the course of writing the objective embodiments of law we know as statutes.").

The foregoing concerns the legislative and political context *at the time of enactment.* Does, or should, the legislative and political context *at the time of the judicial decision* influence statutory interpretation? When *Holy Trinity* was decided, the United States was on the verge of a crushing depression. Economic conditions had begun to look ominous. The major parties in the 1892 election both favored additional restrictions on immigration. Do you think these factors had, or should have had, any bearing on the proper enforcement and interpretation of the Contract Labor Act?

6.   *Legislative History*

The process of enacting legislation is long and tortuous and, in the federal government at least, leaves a paper trail. (In most states, such materials are sketchier; the process is essentially the same as at the federal level, but the participants do not keep much of a record.) Lawyers and judges alike generally turn to a statute's legislative history to cast light on the statute itself. The relevance of legislative history to statutory construction is a matter of considerable dispute. Few judges have foresworn its use altogether, but courts rely on — or, to

---

[15] 16 CONG. REC. 1622 (1885).

[16] 16 CONG. REC. 1632 (1885) (remarks of Senator Morgan).

be precise, cite (which is not necessarily the same thing) — legislative history far less than they did a generation ago.

The *Holy Trinity* Court relied on hearings testimony and the House Report to determine the background and purpose of the Act. But it also found what a litigator would view as a smoking gun: a directly relevant discussion in the Senate Report. The Senate Report goes directly to legislative intent as opposed to purpose. This case is the first instance in which the United States Supreme Court placed such reliance on the legislative record. Unusual for its time, this reliance on the report presaged modern trends.

Committee reports are usually treated as the most persuasive pieces of legislative history. They set out the understanding of the legislation of those most intimately acquainted with it, who may well have had a hand in drafting it, and on whom the other members of Congress rely. Articulate exactly why the Senate Report supports Justice Brewer's argument. Suppose you represented the United States in this case. How would you have argued against the value or relevance of the Report? Does the Report's explanation for leaving the poorly drafted statute intact ring true?

What does the Senate Report tell us about what the *House* thought about the scope of the Act? There is a strong argument that in this case the House Report (which, to be sure, is also helpful to the Court) should carry more weight than the Senate Report. Do you see why?

An opponent of the use of legislative history might object as follows:

> This reliance on a single sentence in the Report exhibits everything that is wrong with the judicial overreliance on legislative history. First, it creates all the wrong incentives for Congress. If the Committee really wanted a narrower statute it should have amended the bill so to provide. The Court let the Senate off the hook and only encouraged sloppy drafting in the future. Second, what the Senate actually *passed* was the statute; it never voted on the report. For all the Court knew most of the Senate was happy with the broad language of the bill. Third, it is entirely likely that the Committee's explanation for why it did not amend the House version of the bill is pure smoke. An equally plausible explanation is that it knew that an amendment did not have the votes. In that circumstance the Committee (more precisely, an unelected staffer under the sway of a lobbyist) did the politically expedient thing; it left the actual bill alone but attached this (unvoted upon) rider for the courts to discover later. In essence, it *did* amend the bill, but without having to put the amendment to a vote. In short, it is at least possible here that the Court had the wool pulled over its eyes. Instead of enforcing the duly enacted statute, approved by a majority of Congress and the President, which is its constitutionally assigned task, the Court rewrote the statute according to the instructions of a subterranean, closet Senate.

Even accepting the Senate Report at face value, should it be dispositive? Suppose you could show (through, for example, comments made on the floor of the Senate during debate on the bill), that the Committee's worst fears had been

realized and that many Senators did view the legislation as reaching non-manual labor. What's more, that is why they voted *for* it. Whose views should control the interpretation of the statute?

Consider the following exchange on the floor of the Senate during debate on the bill. Senator Blair was a primary supporter of the bill; Senator Morgan its primary opponent.

Mr. MORGAN:	[This is] vicious legislation * * * in that, even in the admission of people into this country, it discriminates in favor of professional actors, lecturers, or singers. It makes an express exception and provision for professional actors, lecturers, and singers, leaving out all the other classes of professional men. * * * Personal or domestic servants are excepted; that is to say, a gentleman who has got the money can come here and bring his personal or domestic servants with him from abroad; but if he happens to be a lawyer, an artist, a painter, an engraver, a sculptor, a great author, or what not, and he comes under employment to write for a newspaper, or to write books, or to paint pictures, as we are informed that a recent Secretary of State sent abroad for an artist to paint his picture, he comes under the general provisions of the bill.
Mr. BLAIR:	The Senator will observe that it is only the importation of such people under contract to labor that is prohibited.
Mr. MORGAN:	Of course; I understand.
Mr. BLAIR:	If that class of people are liable to become the subject-matter of such importation, then the bill applies to them. Perhaps the bill ought to be further amended.
Mr. MORGAN:	People who can instruct us in morals and religion and in every species of elevation by lectures and by acting plays in the theaters and by singing are not prohibited. * * * Let them come and act and sing and play as much as they please for the enlightenment of humanity on this side of the Atlantic Ocean. * * * Now, I shall propose when we get to it to put an amendment in there. I want to associate with the lecturers and singers and actors, painters, sculptors, engravers, or other artists, farmers, farm laborers, gardeners, orchardists, herders, farriers, druggists and druggists' clerks, shopkeepers, clerks, book-keepers, or any person having special skill in any business, art, trade, or profession.[17]

A few days later, when the Senate was considering amendments, it added "artists" to the list of exempted professions. Senator Morgan then moved to add

---

[17] 16 CONG. REC. 1632–1633 (1885).

"artisans" to the list as well; his motion was defeated.[18] The Senate then passed the bill by a vote of 50–9, with Senator Morgan among the nays.

Does the Blair/Morgan exchange and the later amendment illuminate the statute's meaning? Construct an argument based on these bits of legislative history to support the Court's result. Construct such an argument against the Court's result.[19]

7. *Later Amendments*

In 1891 — that is, after the events that gave rise to the *Holy Trinity* litigation but before the Supreme Court's decision — Congress amended the statute. Among a number of changes, it added an explicit exemption for "ministers of any religious denomination." (Interestingly, when first introduced, in 1889, the amendment would have exempted "ministers of the gospel"; this phrase was considered too narrow because it would have covered only Christian ministers.) The amendment was not mentioned in the briefs or the opinion in *Holy Trinity*. Should it have any bearing on the decision?

The 1891 amendments explicitly provided that they did *not* apply to pending cases. How does that bear on the relevance of the 1891 exception for ministers to *Holy Trinity*?

Ⓐ p.473

8. *Public Policy and the Nature of Things*

Perhaps what counts most for Justice Brewer is none of the foregoing but rather that this is a religious — more particularly, a Christian — nation. He is quite frank about his unwillingness to read a statute of the United States Congress inconsistently with that premise.

(a) Is this judicial legislation or judicial deference? The answer depends in part on what exactly Justice Brewer is doing. One description of his method is that he is simply saying that Congress, being composed of reasonable people, could not possibly have wanted to exclude ministers. A less deferential version, not usually explicit in judicial opinions, is that he refuses to apply the statute because doing so would just be wrong, period; it would conflict with the Court's (or universal) views of sound policy. Which of these better describes Justice Brewer's method? Is either version an acceptable role for the judiciary?

Cass Sunstein suggests that the opinion can be read in three different ways:

1. General language will not be taken to produce an outcome that would, in context be taken as absurd by those who enacted it, at least if there is no affirmative evidence that this result was intended by the legislature. * * *

---

[18] *Id.* at 1837.

[19] For lengthy reviews of the legislative history, reaching conflicting conclusions, compare Adrian Vermeule, *Legislative History and the Limits of Judicial Competence: The Untold Story of* Holy Trinity Church, 50 STAN. L. REV. 1833 (1998) (concluding that Justice Brewer misread the legislative history) with Chomsky, *supra* note 4 (concluding that Justice Brewer was correct that Congress did not intend to exclude someone such as Reverend Warren).

On this view, *Holy Trinity* is a rerun of the famous case of Riggs v. Palmer
* * *.

2. General language will not be taken to produce an outcome that was
clearly not intended by the enacting legislature, as those intentions are
revealed by context, including legislative history. * * *

3. General language will not be taken to depart from long-standing social
understandings and practices, at least or especially if the departure would
raise serious constitutional doubts. * * * On this view, the background
tradition of religious liberty thus operates as a "clear statement" principle,
one that requires Congress to speak unambiguously if it wishes to intrude
on that tradition. Congress will not be taken to have barred a church from
paying for the transportation of a rector unless there is affirmative
evidence that Congress intended to do precisely that.[20]

Which of these accounts is the most descriptively accurate? The most normatively appealing?

(b) Consider Justice Kennedy's criticism:

I should pause for a moment to recall the unhappy genesis of [the *Holy
Trinity* approach] and its unwelcome potential. * * * The central support
for the Court's ultimate conclusion that Congress did not intend the law to
cover Christian ministers is its lengthy review of the "mass of organic
utterances" establishing that "this is a Christian nation," * * *. I should
think the potential of this doctrine to allow judges to substitute their
personal predilections for the will of the Congress is so self-evident from
the case which spawned it as to require no further discussion of its
susceptibility to abuse.[21]

Justice Kennedy did not observe, though it might support his argument about
"personal predilections," that Justice Brewer was the son of Christian missionaries
and generally fond of the "Christian nation" theme.

[Justice Brewer's mother] grew up in the impoverished home of an
austere New England pastor. Her father was convinced of the majesty and
immutability of the Biblical law and reality of hell; the nine Field children
were faced with the glories of perseverance and personal frugality. She
ended these formative years abruptly in 1829 when her head was turned by
a Reverend Josiah Brewer, fresh from divinity training at Yale. The
nuptials were barely spoken when the couple * * * was headed for the
Mediterranean Sea to staff a school for women recently established by the
Ladies Greek Association of New Haven. Eight years later (June 20, 1837)
in Smyrna, Asia Minor, David Josiah was born. There he spent his early
years, developing an abiding concern for missions and the rights of women,

---

[20] CASS R. SUNSTEIN, ONE CASE AT TIME: JUDICIAL MINIMALISM ON THE SUPREME COURT 219–220 (1999).

[21] Public Citizen v. United States Department of Justice, 491 U.S. 440, 473–474 (1989) (Kennedy, J.,
concurring in the judgment).

and maturing in the Christian virtues.[22] * * *

[Justice Brewer] saw character to lie at the base of the nation's strength, doubly so because of the democratic nature of the Republic. Countless times he repeated the assertion that this was a Christian nation — in pamphlet, speech, and court decision. * * * [While rejecting an active political role, Justice Brewer was quick] to advocate from the public platform causes dear to his heart. The reduction of arms, international arbitration, women's suffrage, Philippine independence (to prevent our "Anglo-Saxon stock" from being "submerged"), high professional standards at the bar, and "Christian citizenship" won frequent platform support from him. He was throughout his life an active member of the Congregational Church, both at the local and national level. On the day of his death he was Vice President of the American Missionary Association.[23]

Justice Brewer's own Christian faith was deep and abiding. In a 1904 address delivered in Boston's Old South Church, he noted the impossibility of a human judge ever having the level of understanding necessary to render true justice, but found reassurance in the idea of ultimate justice in the hereafter:

[T]he answer which has come out of my long experience on the bench is that somewhere and some time all the failures of human justice will be made good. Through the light of the judicial glass I have seen the splendid vision of immortality. * * * So out of my judicial experience, and looking through the glass of my life-work, I have learned to see in the cross the visible symbol of faultless justice, and in the resurrection of Christ the prophecy and truth of its final triumph.[24]

Does this information about Justice Brewer affect your view of the result in *Holy Trinity*? Of the method of the opinion? Of its style? Can Justice Brewer's approach be justified notwithstanding its correspondence to his religious faith in this particular case?

If you were the Chief Justice, would you have assigned Justice Brewer the opinion?

(c) The method of *Holy Trinity* has found favor with modern commentators who are not at all sympathetic to its particular "Christian nation" theme. Professors William Eskridge and Philip Frickey, two of the most important contemporary

---

[22] [Ed. Fn.] Lack of financial support forced Josiah Brewer to abandon his foreign missionary work. He then became chaplain of the St. Francis Prison in Wethersfield, Connecticut. Arnold M. Paul, *David J. Brewer, in* II THE JUSTICES OF THE UNITED STATES SUPREME COURT 1789-1969: THEIR LIVES AND MAJOR OPINIONS at 1515 (Leon Friedman & Fred L. Israel eds., 1969).

[23] Robert E. Gamer, *Justice Brewer and Substantive Due Process: A Conservative Court Revisited,* 18 VAND. L. REV. 615, 617–620 (1965).

[24] David J. Brewer, *The Religion of a Jurist,* THE OUTLOOK, June 24, 1905, at 533, 534–536. This speech was one of many. Though Brewer is now largely forgotten, while on the bench he was the Justice most familiar to the American public, largely as a result of "his love of public speaking and his willingness to go almost anywhere to address an audience." J. Gordon Hylton, *The Perils of Popularity: David Josiah Brewer and the Politics of Judicial Reputation,* 62 VAND. L. REV. 567, 571 (2009).

writers on statutory interpretation, largely endorse *Holy Trinity* as an example of their preferred style of interpretation, what they call "practical reason":

> *Holy Trinity Church* is a classic critique of naive textualism. When generalized, the critique illustrates the operation of our practical reasoning model. According to the model, the text of the statute powerfully supports the government's position, creating a strong presumption for that interpretation. But the apparent meaning of the text becomes less clear when we consider the statute's purpose and legislative history, and test that meaning against background social values. This evidence suggested an alternative reading to the Court, one that emphasized the value of religious freedom, and the Court's faith in this as a "Christian nation." The values of textualism seem little impaired by this reading, and the Court appears admirably sensitive to legislative expectations. The Court's opinion may be more persuasive because it weaves different arguments together to present powerful reasons for rethinking the apparent meaning of the bare text.[25]

Noting Justice Kennedy's criticism, Eskridge and Frickey counter that the Court did not simply substitute its values for those enacted by Congress. Its holding is supported by a "much richer combination of arguments * * *. The opinion's unfortunate genuflections toward Christianity should not obscure its central message."[26]

(d) If societal values *do* count, which should prevail: those prevalent at the time of the statute's enactment or those prevalent now? If this statute had remained on the books unchanged and the *Holy Trinity* situation arose today, might the Supreme Court reach a different result by invoking contemporary values rather than historical ones? If so, what values would be relevant? Is the United States less a Christian nation, or less a religious nation, now than a century ago?

A CONCLUDING NOTE ON THE SOURCES OF STATUTORY INTERPRETATION

The *Holy Trinity* Court is typical in not finding any of the sources to which it turns dispositive. Courts often, and litigators almost always, review all of these various clues as to statutory meaning without relying on any one alone. One might conceive of this process as a sort of football game. The ball begins on the 50-yard line, then moves in one direction or the other as different sources are consulted until finally it is in an end zone.

Holy Trinity is somewhat less typical in that it is fairly candid in acknowledging a conflict between different sources of statutory meaning. Not infrequently, a court discovers that text, purpose, history, and policy all point toward a single meaning, while the dissent finds that they all point toward the opposite single meaning. Does that mean that there is *no* constraining force in these sources of statutory interpretation?

[25] William N. Eskridge, Jr. & Philip P. Frickey, *Statutory Interpretation as Practical Reasoning*, 42 STAN. L. REV. 321, 361–362 (1990).

[26] *Id.* at 362 n.151.

Finally, we asked before whether the whole of Justice Brewer's argument is greater than the sum of its parts. One lesson of *Holy Trinity* might be that the very strength of the opinion is its reliance on a variety of sources and, implicitly, a variety of theoretical approaches.

Assignment — Text, Interpretation, and Religion Revisited

Since the earliest days of the republic, though with varying formulations, the selective service law has exempted conscientious objectors from military service. Here is § 6(j) of the Selective Service Act of 1948:

> Nothing contained in this title shall be construed to require any person to be subject to combatant training and service in the armed forces of the United States who, by reason of religious training and belief, is conscientiously opposed to participation in war in any form. Religious training and belief in this connection means an individual's belief in a relation to a Supreme Being involving duties superior to those arising from any human relation, but does not include essentially political, sociological, or philosophical views or a merely personal moral code.

It is the height of the Vietnam War. The Selective Service produces a form to be signed by those seeking "C.O." status under this provision. Tracking the statute, the form states, "I am, by reason of my religious training and belief, conscientiously opposed to participation in war in any form." Elliott Ashton Welsh II, who is seeking C.O. status, is given the form and crosses out "my religious training and" before signing it. On being questioned, he states that he has deep moral opposition to war but agnostic religious views. Is Welsh eligible for the exemption?

These are the facts of *Welsh v. United States,* 398 U.S. 333 (1970). Welsh was convicted of failing to submit to induction and sentenced to three years in prison; the lower courts rejected his defense that he qualified as a conscientious objector. In the Supreme Court, a plurality of four Justices (Black, who wrote the opinion, Douglas, Brennan and Marshall) concluded that the statute was not limited to those whose opposition to war is prompted by orthodox or parochial religious beliefs. A registrant's conscientious objection to all war is "religious" if it stems from the registrant's moral, ethical, or religious beliefs about what is right and wrong and these beliefs are held with the strength of traditional religious convictions. There was no dispute over the sincerity or depth of conviction of Welsh's views. For these Justices, what counted was whether the registrant's beliefs are, "in his own scheme of things," religious. "[T]he central consideration in determining whether the registrant's beliefs are religious is whether these beliefs play the role of a religion and function as a religion in the registrant's life." Therefore, "[i]f an individual deeply and sincerely holds beliefs that are purely ethical or moral in source and content but that nevertheless impose upon him a duty of conscience to refrain from participating in any war at any time" he qualifies for the exemption.

Justice Harlan rejected this reading as more than the words of the statute could bear:

> [I]t is one thing to give words a meaning not necessarily envisioned by Congress so as to adapt them to circumstances also uncontemplated by the

legislature in order to achieve the legislative policy; it is a wholly different matter to define words so as to change policy. The limits of this Court's mandate to stretch concededly elastic congressional language are fixed in all cases by the context of its usage and legislative history, if available, that are the best guides to congressional *purpose* and the lengths to which Congress enacted a policy. The prevailing opinion today snubs both guidelines for it is apparent from a textual analysis of § 6(j) and the legislative history that the words of this section, as used and understood by Congress, fall short of enacting the broad policy of exempting from military service all individuals who in good faith oppose all war.

Reviewing the legislative history as well, Harlan concluded that Congress had extended the exemption only to members of "conventional religions that usually have an organized and formal structure and dogma and a cohesive group identity" who had theistic beliefs in opposition to war. This interpretation posed a new problem, however: so read, the statute violated the First Amendment to the Constitution, which forbids Congress to make laws "respecting the establishment of a religion." What, then, to do in this case? Noting the long history of the conscientious objector statute, Justice Harlan concluded that the court should extend it to people in Welsh's position rather than striking it altogether:

> When a policy has roots so deeply embedded in history, there is a compelling reason for a court to hazard the necessary statutory repairs if they can be made within the administrative framework of the statute and without impairing other legislative goals, even though they entail, not simply eliminating an offending section, but rather building upon it. Thus I am prepared to accept the prevailing opinion's conscientious objector test, not as a reflection of congressional statutory intent but as patchwork of judicial making that cures the defect of underinclusion in § 6(j) and can be administered by local [draft] boards in the usual course of business. Like the prevailing opinion, I also conclude that petitioner's beliefs are held with the required intensity and consequently vote to reverse the judgment of conviction.

Justice White, joined by Chief Justice Burger and Justice Stewart, dissented. They agreed with Justice Harlan that the statute simply would not bear the reading given by the plurality but disagreed that it would violate the Establishment Clause to deny the exemption to nonbelievers. Accordingly, they would have upheld the conviction.

(1) Which of the three opinions would Justice Brewer have joined? Plausible arguments can be made for each.

(2) Which opinion would you have joined?

Chapter 10

READING STATUTORY TEXTS

The legislature is like a composer. It cannot help itself: It must leave interpretation to others . . . .

— **Jerome Frank**[1]

A. THE PRIMACY OF THE TEXT

Professor (later Justice) Felix Frankfurter, echoing the real estate broker's assessment of the three most important characteristics of a piece of property (location, location, location), "developed his threefold imperative to law students: (1) Read the statute; (2) read the statute, (3) read the statute!"[2] Law students, and lawyers, too often focus on what judges say about a statute rather than, simply, what the statute itself says. This chapter is devoted to reading the actual texts of statutes.

Coming to grips with statutory texts is not always an unmitigated delight. Percy Bysse Shelley once said, a trifle grandiosely, that "poets are the unacknowledged legislators of the world"; no one has ever suggested that legislators are the unacknowledged poets.[3] Like poems, however, statutes repay the most careful reading.

As we saw in Chapter 8, and will see again in Chapter 12, a significant dispute exists as to whether the text of a statute should be the *exclusive* basis for judicial interpretation. But even the flightiest theorists begin with the text, and all arguments about statutory meaning occur within boundaries imposed by the text.

---

[1] Jerome Frank, *Words and Music: Some Remarks on Statutory Interpretation*, 47 COLUM. L. REV. 1259, 1264 (1947).

[2] Henry J. Friendly, *Mr. Justice Frankfurter and the Reading of Statutes*, in BENCHMARKS 196, 202 (1967).

[3] The United States government does have the post of "Poetry Consultant to the Library of Congress." Since 1986, the post has been combined with the position of poet laureate. When Robert Frost was poetry consultant in the late 1950s, he reportedly held a press conference after 6 weeks on the job to lament (presumably with tongue firmly in cheek) that Congress had not consulted him even once in that time. Sad but true, few statutes read as if they were drafted in consultation with the poet laureate.

On the other hand, the Senate debate on the Foreign Contract Labor Act of 1885, a statute you know well, contains the following remarkable entry:

Mr. BLAIR: I should like to have a verbal transposition made of the words "service or labor" in the sixth line of the second section, so as to read "labor or service." That would be altogether more poetic, while the other phrase savors rather of blank verse. * * *

The amendment was agreed to.

16 Cong. Rec. 1839 (1885).

Indeed, in the real world (as opposed to the world of law school casebooks) most statutory questions are resolved simply by reading the statute, however tedious or difficult that task may be. Even when the statutory text does not provide a definitive answer, it *always* excludes some possibilities.

So we begin this chapter with six statutory problems, which you should solve relying solely on the relevant text. The first two are not straightforward, but each has a determinate right answer. The others are more uncertain. Answers to the first two can be found in Appendix F; for the other four, you're on your own.

1. *The Internal Revenue Code*

The Internal Revenue Code imposes a tax on "income from whatever source derived." Section 83 of the Code provides:

> (a) If, in connection with the performance of services, property is transferred to any person other than the person for whom such services are performed, the excess of —
>
>> (1) the fair market value of such property * * * at the first time the rights of the person having the beneficial interest in such property are transferable or are not subject to a substantial risk of forfeiture, whichever occurs earlier, over
>>
>> (2) the amount (if any) paid for such property,
>
> shall be included in the gross income of the person who performed such services in the first taxable year in which the rights of the person having the beneficial interest in such property are * * * not subject to a substantial risk of forfeiture * * *.
>
> (c)(1) The rights of a person in property are subject to a substantial risk of forfeiture if such person's rights to full enjoyment of such property are conditioned upon the future performance of substantial services by any individual.

Internal Revenue Service regulations, which for our purposes you may treat as if they were part of the statute, provide: "In computing the gain or loss from the subsequent sale or exchange of such property, its basis shall be the amount paid for the property increased by the amount included in gross income under § 83." Section 1001(a) of the Code provides that "[t]he gain from the sale or other disposition of property shall be the excess of the amount realized therefrom over the * * * basis."

In 2001, Jane Smith signs an employment contract with a new employer, Super Electronics, Inc. Super is a start-up company whose sole product (still in the developmental stage) is a robot nanny that it believes will make the human model obsolete. Smith is a child psychologist and computer programmer who will design the robot's personality, and all recognize that her role is instrumental to the success or failure of the product. Upon signing the employment contract, and pursuant thereto, Super gives 100 shares of Super stock to Smith's son. The gift is conditional; the stock must be returned to the company if Smith resigns within three years after signing the contract. Thereafter, it belongs to her son irrevocably.

Smith stays with Super, which prospers. Though worth only $5/share in 2001, the stock is worth $500/share in 2004. By 2007, its value has risen to $700/share, at which point Smith's son sells it.

Under § 83, and in light of the foregoing transactions, how much money is included in whose income when?

2.　*Building an Incinerator*

The fact that statutes do sometimes contain determinate answers does not mean those answers are easily found. Much modern legislation is gruesomely complex, full of interminable sentences and obscure cross-references. It is possible to make sense of these statutes, but it requires patience and determination. Our next problem, which arises under the Federal Clean Air Act, will give you a taste of, though perhaps not a taste for, this kind of legal work.

The Clean Air Act is one of the most complex, difficult, and, at over 700 pages, lengthy regulatory statutes. As you answer this question, remember that we have already done a great deal of the work for you by pulling out all (and only) the relevant provisions from this morass.

§ 111. Standards of performance for new stationary sources

(a) Definitions

For purposes of this section:

(1) The term "standard of performance" means a standard for emissions of air pollutants which reflects the degree of emission limitation achievable through the application of the best system of emission reduction which (taking into account the cost of achieving such reduction and any nonair quality health and environmental impact and energy requirements) the Administrator [of the Environmental Protection Agency] determines has been adequately demonstrated.

(2) The term "new source" means any stationary source, the construction or modification of which is commenced after the publication of regulations (or, if earlier, proposed regulations) prescribing a standard of performance under this section which will be applicable to such source.

(b) List of categories of stationary sources; standards of performance

(1)(A) The Administrator shall * * * publish (and from time to time thereafter shall revise) a list of categories of stationary sources. He shall include a category of sources in such list if in his judgment it causes, or contributes significantly to, air pollution which may reasonably be anticipated to endanger public health or welfare.

(B) Within one year after the inclusion of a category of stationary sources in a list under subparagraph (A), the Administrator shall publish proposed regulations, establishing Federal standards of performance for new sources within such category. The Administrator shall afford

interested persons an opportunity for written comment on such proposed regulations. After considering such comments, he shall promulgate, within one year after such publication, such standards with such modifications as he deems appropriate.

§ 165. Preconstruction requirements

(a) Major emitting facilities on which construction is commenced

No major emitting facility * * * may be constructed * * * unless —

(1) a permit has been issued for such proposed facility in accordance with this part setting forth emission limitations for such facility which conform to the requirements of this part; * * *

(4) the proposed facility is subject to the best available control technology for each pollutant [that is regulated under the Clean Air Act] emitted from, or which results from, such facility * * *.

§ 169. Definitions

(1) The term "major emitting facility" means any of the following stationary sources of air pollutants which emit, or operating at full capacity would emit, one hundred tons per year or more of any air pollutant from the following types of stationary sources: fossil-fuel fired steam electric plants of more than two hundred and fifty million British thermal units per hour heat input, coal cleaning plants (thermal dryers), kraft pulp mills, Portland Cement plants, primary zinc smelters, iron and steel mill plants, primary aluminum ore reduction plants, primary copper smelters, municipal incinerators capable of charging more than fifty tons of refuse per day, hydrofluoric, sulfuric, and nitric acid plants, petroleum refineries, lime plants, phosphate rock processing plants, coke oven batteries, sulfur recovery plants, carbon black plants (furnace process), primary lead smelters, fuel conversion plants, sintering plants, secondary metal production facilities, chemical process plants, fossil-fuel boilers of more than two hundred and fifty million British thermal units per hour heat input, petroleum storage and transfer facilities with a capacity exceeding three hundred thousand barrels, taconite ore processing facilities, glass fiber processing plants, charcoal production facilities. Such term also includes any other source which operating at full capacity would emit two hundred and fifty tons per year or more of any air pollutant. * * *

(3) The term "best available control technology" means an emission limitation based on the maximum degree of reduction of each pollutant [regulated under the Clean Air Act] emitted from or which results from any major emitting facility, which the permitting authority, on a case-by-case basis, taking into account energy, environmental, and economic impacts and other costs, determines is achievable for such facility through application of production processes and available methods, systems, and techniques. In no event shall application of "best available control technology" result in emissions of any pollutants which

will exceed the emissions allowed by any applicable standard established pursuant to section 111.

Assume the following. In 1985, pursuant to § 111, the EPA Administrator issued a New Source Performance Standard ("NSPS") limiting emissions of particulate matter from municipal incinerators. That NSPS reflected then-current technology, but it is now quite obsolete. Two months ago, EPA proposed a revision to the 1985 regulation. Reflecting recent technological improvements, operational in engineering labs but as yet untested in the field, the new standard would be much more stringent than the existing one.

Six months ago New City began construction of an incinerator that will burn 40 tons of garbage a day. Without pollution controls, the incinerator will emit 1000 tons of particulate matter (in essence, smoke) each year. (For purposes of this problem, assume that particulate matter is the only pollutant emitted by incinerators.) Adhering to the 1985 NSPS would require it to hold its particulate emissions to 500 tons per year. With a modern "baghouse" of a sort now quite common on new incinerators, it could hold its particulate emissions to 100 tons per year. Were it to use the cutting edge equipment reflected in EPA's proposed NSPS, it could probably reduce particulate emissions to about 75 tons per year. Needless to say, the greater the level of control, the higher its cost.

New City does not want to spend any more for pollution control than it absolutely has to. How many tons of particulates will its incinerator be allowed to emit? Why are the other answers wrong?

    A. 1000 tons

    B. 500 tons

    C. 249 tons

    D. 100 tons

    E. 75 tons

3.　*A Violent Felony*

Federal law makes it a crime, punishable by up to 10 years in prison, for anyone who has been convicted of a felony (i.e., a crime punishable by more than a year in prison) to possess a firearm. 18 U.S.C. § 922(g)(1). Separately, the Armed Career Criminal Act imposes an additional, mandatory 15-year prison term on anyone convicted under § 922(g) who has three or more prior convictions for committing "a violent felony." 18 U.S.C. § 924(e)(1). The Act defines "violent felony" as any crime punishable by more than one year's imprisonment that

(i) has as an element the use, attempted use, or threatened use of physical force against the person of another; or

(ii) is burglary, arson, or extortion, involves use of explosives, or otherwise involves conduct that presents a serious potential risk of physical injury to another.

18 U.S.C. § 924(e)(2)(B).

Larry Begay is convicted of felony possession of a firearm under 922(g)(1). It turns out that Begay has eight prior convictions in New Mexico for driving under the influence. DUI is not a felony in New Mexico, at least not the first time. However, the fourth (and any subsequent) conviction for DUI is a felony under state law.

Is Begay subject to the 15-year mandatory sentence enhancement under § 924(e)(2)(B) — that is, does he have three or more convictions for a violent felony?

4. *The Case of the Suspended Teacher*

While employed as a junior high school teacher, Simon Unzueta was arrested and charged with simple possession and use of cocaine. The school district suspended Unzueta from his teaching position without pay. See Education Code §§ 44940(e), 44940.5(b), (c).

The criminal prosecution against Unzueta did not proceed. Instead, Unzueta was "diverted" under a California program for defendants who are charged with first-time possession of drugs, have not yet gone to trial, and are found to be suitable for treatment and rehabilitation at the local level. After two years, during which time he held various odd jobs, Unzueta successfully completed the drug treatment program. The criminal charges were dismissed. See Penal Code § 1000.3. Unzueta was then rehired by the school district.

Unzueta now sues seeking $40,000 in back pay, representing the wages he lost as a result of the suspension, plus interest. The school district argues that he is not entitled to back pay at all, and that if he is, he is not entitled to interest and the award should by offset by the $30,000 Unzueta earned in other employment during this period.

The relevant statutory provisions are as follows:

Education Code § 44940(b): "[Simple possession and use of cocaine is] an optional leave of absence offense."

Education Code § 44940(e): "Whenever any certificated employee of a school district is charged with an optional leave of absence offense as defined in subdivision (b), the governing board of the school district may immediately place the employee upon compulsory leave in accordance with the procedure in this section and Section 44940.5."

Education Code § 44940.5(b): "Any employee placed upon compulsory leave of absence * * * shall continue to be paid his or her regular salary during the period of his or her compulsory leave of absence if and during that time he or she furnishes to the school district a suitable bond * * * as a guarantee that the employee will repay to the school district the amount of salary so paid to him or her during the period of the compulsory leave of absence in case the employee is convicted."

Education Code § 44940.5(c): "If the employee does not elect to furnish bond * * * and if the employee is acquitted of the offense, or the charges against him or her are dismissed, the school district shall pay to the

employee his or her full compensation for the period of the compulsory leave of absence upon his or her return to service in the school district."

Penal Code § 1000.3: "If the divertee has performed satisfactorily * * * the criminal charges shall be dismissed."

Penal Code § 1000.5: "Upon successful completion of a diversion program the arrest upon which the diversion was based shall be deemed to have never occurred. The divertee may indicate in response to any question concerning his prior criminal record that he was not arrested or diverted for such offense. A record pertaining to an arrest resulting in successful completion of a diversion program shall not, without the divertee's consent, be used in any way which could result in the denial of any employment, benefit, license, or certificate."

What result? *See* Unzueta v. Ocean View School Dist., 6 Cal. App. 4th 1689, 8 Cal. Rptr. 2d 614 (1992).

5. *"Using a Gun"*

William Wilson is in deep trouble. He has been convicted of five separate crimes growing out of the flurry of criminal activity described below:

While visiting a friend on a U.S. Army base Wilson saw a high-powered pistol lying on a countertop. When he was left alone in his friend's room, Wilson grabbed the pistol, stuck it in his jacket pocket, and walked off.

On his way out the now-emboldened Wilson accosted a soldier. Grabbing him from behind, Wilson snarled, "Don't move, I've got a gun," and ordered the victim to hand over his wallet, which Wilson took before running away.

Several soldiers saw the incident and ran after Wilson. Realizing that he was being pursued, Wilson pulled out the gun, waving it menacingly in the air. His chastened pursuers abandoned the chase.

Wilson, who it turns out is a drug dealer, then went to his lab. Some customers arrived. With the gun still hidden in his pocket, Wilson negotiated and transacted a sale of methamphetamine, which is a controlled substance.

Wilson's next appointment was with Watson, a potential supplier of Ephedrine, which is used to manufacture methamphetamine. Watson wanted to satisfy himself that he wasn't dealing with an amateur. Having learned that Watson was interested in guns, Wilson decided to impress him by displaying his expertise not merely with drugs, but with illegal weapons as well. Wilson showed him the pistol, explained how it worked, and showed off the silencer with which it was equipped. Wilson's dog-and-pony show was a hit; Watson was fascinated by the gun. But when he asked Wilson how much he wanted for it, Wilson said it wasn't for sale — unless he agreed to supply Ephedrine, in which case Wilson would give him the gun and silencer for free. The supplier agreed, exchanging a large quantity of Ephedrine for the gun, the silencer, and some cash.

As a result of these five escapades, Wilson is tried and convicted of larceny (the theft of the gun), robbery (the mugging), assault (waving his gun at the pursuers),

sale of a controlled substance (the sale of the methamphetamine), and possession of a controlled substance with intent to distribute (the purchase and possession of ephedrine).

Section 924(c) of title 18 of the U.S. Code provides:

(1) Whoever, during and in relation to any crime of violence or drug trafficking crime * * * uses * * * a firearm, shall, in addition to the punishment provided for such crime of violence or drug trafficking crime, be sentenced to imprisonment for five years, and if the firearm is a short-barreled rifle [or] short-barreled shotgun to imprisonment for ten years, and if the firearm is a machinegun, or a destructive device, or is equipped with a firearm silencer or firearm muffler, to imprisonment for thirty years.

(2) For purposes of this subsection, the term "drug trafficking crime" means any felony punishable under the Controlled Substances Act.

(3) For purposes of this subsection the term "crime of violence" means an offense that is a felony and —

(A) has as an element the use, attempted use, or threatened use of physical force against the person or property of another, or

(B) that by its nature, involves a substantial risk that physical force against the person or property of another may be used in the course of committing the offense.

(a) Is Wilson subject to the five-year enhancement because he "used a firearm" during any (all?) of the crimes for which he was convicted?

(b) Suppose you conclude that Wilson did "use a firearm" in relation to the purchase of the ephedrine. Did Watson?

(c) In fact, the statute applies somewhat more broadly, referring to "whoever, during and in relation to any crime of violence or drug trafficking crime . . . uses *or carries* a firearm. . . ." Does this change any of your answers?

6.   *Using a House*

Revealing some deep intra-familial tensions, Dewey Jones tossed a Molotov cocktail through a window of the Fort Wayne, Indiana home of his cousin. The ensuing fire caused no injuries, but it severely damaged the home. The home was an ordinary residence, not used in any trade or business.

Jones has clearly committed arson, which in these circumstances is punishable by up to 10 years in prison under Indiana law. However, he is not prosecuted by the state; instead, he is prosecuted by the feds, who charge him with violating 18 U.S.C. § 844(i), which provides:

Whoever maliciously damages or destroys, or attempts to damage or destroy, by means of fire or an explosive, any building, vehicle, or other real or personal property used in interstate or foreign commerce or in any activity affecting interstate or foreign commerce shall be imprisoned for

not less than 5 years and not more than 20 years, fined under this title, or both.

Jones is convicted and sentenced to 35 years in prison. He appeals, arguing that his activity was not covered by the statute because the building he damaged was not "used in interstate or foreign commerce or in any activity affecting interstate or foreign commerce."

The Government argues that the residence was "used" in at least three "activities affecting commerce." First, the homeowner "used" the dwelling as collateral to obtain and secure a mortgage from an Oklahoma bank; the bank, in turn, "used" the property as security for the home loan. Second, the homeowner "used" the residence to obtain a casualty insurance policy from a Wisconsin insurer. That policy, the Government points out, safeguarded the interests of the home-owner and the mortgagee. Third, the homeowner "used" the dwelling to receive natural gas from sources outside Indiana.

Assume the facts relied on in the government's argument are true. What result?

B. STATUTORY UNCERTAINTY

The problems in Part A were difficult in different, and typical, ways — in part the statutes were just complex and confusing, in part they used words that were terms of art, in part they just did not seem to address the situation at hand, in part they used words that were unclear. In this section we focus on the last of these.

1. *Why Aren't Statutes Clearer?*

Statutory language will never clearly resolve all disputes arising under them.

The challenges of language. Learned Hand wrote:

> Law has always been unintelligible, and I might say that perhaps it ought to be. And I will tell you why, because I don't want to deal in paradoxes. It ought to be unintelligible because it ought to be in words — and words are utterly inadequate to deal with the fantastically multiform occasions which come up in human life.[4]

Legislation struggles against the inescapable inadequacy of words. As usual, Holmes provides the striking aphorism: "A word is not a crystal, transparent and unchanged, it is the skin of a living thought."[5]

> Certain of the draftsman's difficulties are not unique to legislative work but arise in connection with the preparation of all legal documents. The draftsman must express his understanding and purpose in words, and words are notoriously imperfect symbols for the communication of ideas. Justice Cardozo was speaking for our entire word-bound profession when he began his little classic, *The Paradoxes of Legal Science*, with the

---

[4] Learned Hand, *Thou Shalt Not Ration Justice*, 9 BRIEF CASE, No. 4, at 3, 4 (1951) (quoted in THE OXFORD DICTIONARY OF AMERICAN LEGAL QUOTATIONS 426 (Fred R. Shapiro ed., 1993)).

[5] Towne v. Eisner, 245 U.S. 418, 425 (1918).

mournful exclamation, "They do things better with logarithms." What makes the legislative draftsman's job more trying than the task of the draftsman of a contract or a will is that the words of the statute must communicate the intention to at least three crucial classes of readers; the legislators who are to examine the bill to decide whether it is in accordance with their specifications, the lawyers who must make use of the statute in counseling and litigation, and the judges who will give the statute its final and authoritative interpretation. One does not have to be an expert in semantics to know that words rarely mean the same thing to all men or at all times. An intent that seems "plainly" expressed to the legislative experts on a standing committee may be ambiguous to affected persons and their lawyers and quite unintelligible to judges with no special knowledge or experience in the field of regulation.[6]

Unanticipated situations. The second source of uncertainty is that statutes will often be applied in unanticipated situations. Knowing this, legislatures try to be comprehensive, covering any and all situations. Common law courts make no such effort (or when they do, we treat it as ill-advised dicta). Think back to the attractive nuisance cases and recall Llewellyn's statement that no case can be understood standing on its own since its meaning only begins to appear once it has been applied in the next case. A common law decision resolves only the particular case; the general rule is gleaned from the sum of particular cases. To overgeneralize, common law reasoning is from the particular to the general, it is inductive; statutory decisionmaking moves from the general to the particular, it is deductive. For such a system to function perfectly, whoever lays down the general rule must be able to anticipate every conceivable situation in which it might be applied. To date, such an omniscient legislature has yet to be elected.

Unforeseen cases account for the great majority of the instances of statutory uncertainty. The problem here is that the typical drive for legislative action originates not in a desire for an over-all codification of the law but in some felt necessity for a better way of dealing with some specific situation or group of situations. The draftsman must make effective provision for the specific needs which are urged upon him, but he must write the statute in the form of a proposition of general applicability. * * * [This] leaves to the draftsman of statutes the hard task of formulating a general rule that adequately takes care of the specific situations before the legislature without including in its apparent scope unthought-of cases somewhat similar in fact content but distinguishable on policy grounds.

Case-minded judges and lawyers might be a little less caustic in their comments on the ambiguity of statutes if they were to reflect that the problem of uncertainty in relation to the unthought-of case arises also in the use of case precedents. * * * Th[e] immemorial common law distinction between *holding* and *dictum* is based on a recognition that even the finest judge is at his best only when dealing with the facts of the case at hand, the issues on which he has had the benefit of argument of counsel. The same is true of the statute-law maker and his technical drafting assistants. If the

[6] Harry W. Jones, *Some Causes of Uncertainty in Statutes*, 36 A.B.A. J. 321, 321 (1950).

draftsman is respectably skilled and careful, he will make unmistakably clear provision for the specific situations called to his attention at committee hearings and in other ways. If he is at all imaginative, he will anticipate and take care of other situations within the reach of reasonable anticipation. But human foresight is limited and the variety of fact-situations endless. Every generally worded statute, sooner or later, will fail to provide a certain direction as to the handling of those inevitable legislative nuisances, the cases nobody thought of.[7]

Assignment

The challenges of legislative draftsmanship are beyond the scope of this course. But consider one brief problem.

Suppose a teacher, enamored of the genius of the common law, has the students in her class watch as, just before lunch, she makes a peanut butter and jelly sandwich on white bread. She then says: "For your homework tonight, do what I just did. Bring in your project tomorrow." Like a common law court, she has produced a result; it is up to the students, the later interpreters, to determine the meaning and scope of that result. The next day, Jane brings in a bologna sandwich on rye; John a roasted chicken; Joan a piece of cake; Jim a cream cheese and anchovy sandwich. The teacher flunks them all. Indignantly, Jane protests that what the teacher had done was "make a sandwich," John that she had "made lunch," Joan, who loves peanut butter, that she had "made something delicious," Jim, who hates it, that she had "made something disgusting." Who is right and who is wrong? Or are they all right (wrong)?

Dismayed, the teacher attempts the legislative approach. She drafts instructions for the homework project. The instructions are headed "How to make a peanut butter and jelly sandwich." Attempt to draft such instructions. Can you come up with something foolproof? If so, what shared understandings between reader and writer were necessary to this success? Give your instructions to a friend and ask him to follow them. Do you get what you had in mind? Give your instructions to an enemy (or someone who hates peanut butter and absolutely does not want to end up with a peanut butter and jelly sandwich). Same result?

The Legislative Process. Compounding the inherent difficulty of drafting is the fact that the reality of the legislative process hardly lends itself to careful, precise, definitive statutes. First, time pressures can be intense. Committee staffers themselves identify the need to draft in a hurry — it's always an emergency on Capitol Hill — as a central cause of a lack of statutory clarity.[8]

---

[7] Jones, *supra* note 6, at 321–322.

[8] Victoria F. Nourse & Jane S. Schacter, *The Politics of Legislative Drafting: A Congressional Case Study*, 77 N.Y.U.L. Rev. 575, 594–595 (2002).

Congress is also more than capable of intentional vagueness and ambiguity. Opaque or empty generality may be essential to agreement. The broader the language, the more likely it is that a majority will accept it. As Edward Levi wrote long ago: "Controversy does not help. Agreement is then possible only through escape to a higher level of discourse with greater ambiguity. This is one element which makes compromise possible."[9] Or, in the practical phrasing of a Senate staffer: "We know that if we answer a certain question, we will lose one side or the other."[10]

As a practical matter, vague and standardless statutes essentially delegate authority to the courts or to an administrative agency, leaving it to them to work out the regulatory details, if not the whole legislative scheme. For example, the core requirement of the Individuals with Disabilities Education Act is that public school districts receiving federal funds provide all children, regardless of disability, a "free appropriate public education."[11] In imposing such a requirement, what has Congress actually decided, if anything? (One federal judge (in dissent) concluded that the Act is so empty that it does not "amount to legislation by Congress" and therefore is unenforceable.[12]) It has been the Department of Education and the courts that have actually determined the meaning of "appropriate."

What forces lead to such empty promulgations?

Commentators more sympathetic to delegations point to the comparative advantage agencies have with regard to technical and complex problems of implementation. They also argue that Congress simply [lacks the time and expertise to] enact the volumes of specific directives found in the Code of Federal Regulations and agency manuals. In addition, reforms within Congress that have weakened the role of party leaders and committee chairs may have created significant obstacles to firm policy-making by this group decisionmaker.

Commentators less sympathetic to delegation tend to focus on legislators' personal failings. John Hart Ely, for example, stresses that standard-less delegations allow members of Congress to take credit and avoid blame. Professor Ely wrote that "it is simply easier, and it pays more visible political dividends, to play errand-boy-cum-ombudsman than to play one's part in a genuinely legislative process." Public choice theorists have recently been the most prominent of these critics. They ascribe vague and standardless legislation to the legislators' purely self-interested pursuit of power and re-election. The ambiguous statute is a method of avoiding

---

[9] EDWARD H. LEVI, AN INTRODUCTION TO LEGAL REASONING 31 (1949).

[10] Nourse & Schacter, *supra* note 8, at 596.

[11] 20 U.S.C. § 1412(a)(1)(A) (2006).

[12] Georgia Ass'n of Retarded Citizens v. McDaniel, 716 F.2d 1565, 1582 (11th Cir. 1983) (Hill, J., dissenting) (objecting that the law merely identifies a real problem and announces that it should receive an appropriate solution), *cert. denied*, 469 U.S. 1228 (1985). Is the command in this statute any less specific or helpful than the common law's general mandate that people act reasonably, use due care, and exercise the caution that the circumstances require?

ideologically-based voter disapproval.[13]

Group authorship. Legislation is the product of group authorship both in the abstract sense that it emerges from a large collegial body and in the practical sense that many individuals write the text that is compiled in the final product. Individual legislators (or, more likely, their staff), numerous lobbyists, committee staffers, officials from the White House or administrative agencies — all may have written one section or another of a bill. Drafting by committee is bound to produce some inconsistencies and incoherency. Paul Shupack offers a revealing metaphor for some of these difficulties:

> A bronze fountain in front of the Library of Congress facing the Capitol stands as a warning against [the defects of collective legislative drafting].

> The fountain's subject is Neptune with two assistants. The figures are cast in the best Roman-Renaissance revival style. Neptune is cast as a mature nude male, while his assistants are portrayed as young men. Curiously, while Neptune and the young man to his right are wearing fig leaves, the young man to Neptune's left has exposed genitals. Since the fig leaf embodies prudery, its appearance on only two of the three figures is problematic. Because prudery admits of no compromise, the moral shielding must be complete to have any effect at all. Prudery, therefore, cannot explain the presence of only two fig leaves.

> We are taught that politics is the art of the possible. In democratic politics, it is against the rules of the game for one party or faction to attempt to achieve total victory, if for no other reason than the fear that another might take advantage of some future victory in the same way. But, as these figures demonstrate, some issues by their very nature cannot be compromised. If exposed genitals corrupt morals, then it is hard to imagine what moral purpose is served by covering two sets, after leaving one set exposed. Yet, the figures have the appearance of a compromise cast in bronze. Did some turn-of-the-century Comstock[14] gain satisfaction from preventing the cumulative immorality that would have attended all three figures being totally nude? We shall never know. What we do know is that the solution to a problem reached by collective processes is often unsupportable on any logical grounds. Symbolic victories often combine with utter defeats in substance. To expect legislation to have complete internal consistency is to hope for the impossible. The missing fig leaf stands for this

---

[13] Michael Herz, *Judicial Textualism Meets Congressional Micromanagement: A Potential Collision in Clean Air Act Interpretation*, 16 HARV. ENVTL. L. REV. 175, 176 nn. 4–5 (1992).

[14] [Ed. Fn.] Anthony Comstock was a "purity crusader" of the late nineteenth and early twentieth centuries. As an energetic private citizen, he induced and assisted in the prosecution of large numbers of people for selling obscene materials and contraceptives. He is best remembered as the driving force behind the Comstock Act of 1873, which forbade the interstate mailing or transport of "obscene, lewd or lascivious" items, including all devices or information pertaining to "preventing contraception and producing abortion." The Act created the position of special agent within the Post Office to enforce its provisions; two days after it became law the Postmaster General appointed Comstock to the post. Comstock remained as special agent, pursuing his duties with enthusiasm and vigor, until his death in 1915. On Comstock *see generally* David M. Rabban, *The Free Speech League, the ACLU, and Changing Conceptions of Free Speech in American History*, 45 STAN. L. REV. 47, 55–70 (1992).

essential truth about the legislative process.[15]

2. *Vagueness*

REGINA v. OJIBWAY
8 Crim. L.Q. 137 (1965)

Blue, J.:

This is an appeal by the Crown by way of a stated case from a decision of the magistrate acquitting the accused of a charge under the Small Birds Act, R.S.O., 1960, c.724, s.2. The facts are not in dispute. Fred Ojibway, an Indian, was riding his pony through Queen's Park on January 2, 1965. Being impoverished, and having been forced to pledge his saddle, he substituted a downy pillow in lieu of the said saddle. On this particular day the accused's misfortune was further heightened by the circumstance of his pony breaking its right foreleg. In accord with current Indian custom, the accused then shot the pony to relieve it of its awkwardness.

The accused was then charged with having breached the Small Birds Act, s.2 of which states:

> 2. Anyone maiming, injuring or killing small birds is guilty of an offence and subject to a fine not in excess of two hundred dollars.

The learned magistrate acquitted the accused, holding, in fact, that he had killed his horse and not a small bird. With respect, I cannot agree.

In light of the definition section my course is quite clear. Section 1 defines "bird" as "a two legged animal covered with feathers". There can be no doubt that this case is covered by this section.

Counsel for the accused made several ingenious arguments to which, in fairness, I must address myself. He submitted that the evidence of the expert clearly concluded that the animal in question was a pony and not a bird, but this is not the issue. We are not interested in whether the animal in question is a bird or not in fact, but whether it is one in law. Statutory interpretation has forced many a horse to eat birdseed for the rest of its life.

Counsel also contended that the neighing noise emitted by the animal could not possibly be produced by a bird. With respect, the sounds emitted by an animal are irrelevant to its nature, for a bird is no less a bird because it is silent.

Counsel for the accused also argued that since there was evidence to show accused had ridden the animal, this pointed to the fact that it could not be a bird but was actually a pony. Obviously, this avoids the issue. The issue is not whether the animal was ridden or not, but whether it was shot or not, for to ride a pony or a bird is of no offense at all. I believe that counsel now sees his mistake.

---

[15] Paul Shupack, *Confusion in Policy and Language in the Uniform Fraudulent Transfer Act*, 9 Cardozo L. Rev. 811, 811–812 (1987).

Counsel contends that the iron shoes found on the animal decisively disqualify it from being a bird. I must inform counsel, however, that how an animal dresses is of no concern to this court.

Counsel relied on the decision in *Re Chicadee*, where he contends that in similar circumstances the accused was acquitted. However, this is a horse of a different colour. A close reading of that case indicates that the animal in question there was not a small bird, but, in fact, a midget of a much larger species. Therefore, that case is inapplicable to our facts.

Counsel finally submits that the word "small" in the title Small Birds Act refers not to "Birds" but to "Act," making it The Small Act relating to Birds. With respect, counsel did not do his homework very well, for the Large Birds Act, R.S.O., 1960, c.725, is just as small. If pressed, I need only refer to the Small Loans Act, R.S.O., 1960, c.727, which is twice as large as the Large Birds Act.

It remains then to state my reason for judgment which, simply, is as follows: Different things may take on the same meaning for different purposes. For the purpose of The Small Birds Act, all two legged, feather-covered animals are birds. This, of course, does not imply that only two legged animals qualify, for the legislative intent is to make two legs merely the minimum requirement. The statute therefore contemplated multi-legged animals with feathers as well. Counsel submits that having regard to the purpose of the statute only small animals "naturally covered" with feathers could have been contemplated. However, had this been the intention of the legislature, I am certain that the phrase "naturally covered" would have been expressly inserted just as "Long" was inserted in the Longshoreman's Act.

Therefore, a horse with feathers on its back must be deemed for the purposes of this Act to be a bird, and *a fortiori*, a pony with feathers on its back is a small bird.

Counsel posed the following rhetorical question: If the pillow had been removed prior to the shooting, would the animal still be a bird? To this let me answer rhetorically: Is a bird any less of a bird without its feathers?

QUESTIONS

(1) Why is this not a perfectly reasonable approach to statutory construction?

(2) If you think a pony cannot be a "small bird," could it qualify as a "non-motorized vehicle"?

Rider Says "Whoa" to Drunk Charges

A man charged with drunken driving says he doesn't think his horse should be considered a non-motorized vehicle under the law. "She's got a mind of her own," Mark A. Whitt said of his trusty 2-year-old filly, Mable. "I don't think a vehicle has a mind." Kentucky amended its drunken-driving law in 1991 to include drivers of non-motorized vehicles. Officials say the Pike County case might be the first involving a horse. If convicted, Whitt,

20, could be fined $20 to $100. He says he has ridden Mable home safely
after drinking at clubs before. "I've even passed out in the saddle before,"
he said. "She knows the way home."[16]

If you represented Mark Whitt, how would you defend him against drunken
driving charges? Is it relevant that, unlike Mable, a vehicle doesn't have a mind? Is
it just as goofy to deem a horse a nonmotorized vehicle as it is to deem a pony a
small bird?

(3)   The Kentucky statute under which Whitt was charged reads: "No person
under the influence of intoxicating beverages or any substance which may impair
one's driving ability shall operate a vehicle that is not a motor vehicle anywhere in
this state." K.R.S. Ann. § 189.520(1). " 'Vehicle' includes all agencies for the
transportation of persons or property over or upon the public highways of this
Commonwealth and all vehicles passing over or upon the highways, [with exemptions for construction equipment and trains not relevant here]. 'Motor vehicle'
includes all vehicles as defined above which are propelled otherwise than by
muscular power." *Id.* § 189.010(18). Does the actual text change your answers to the
previous questions?

"NO VEHICLES IN THE PARK"

Consider, sticking with vehicles, this provision: "No vehicles may be taken into
the park." Professor H.L.A. Hart first offered this hypothetical statute in the
1950s[17] and it has been a law professors' favorite ever since. Hart used this
hypothetical to illustrate that words have *some* determinate meaning, that there are
cases in which the statute indisputably applies or indisputably does not apply.

If we are to communicate with each other at all, and if, as in the most
elementary form of law, we are to express our intentions that a certain type
of behavior be regulated by rules, then the general words we use — like
"vehicle" in the case I consider — must have some standard instance in
which no doubts are felt about its application. There must be a core of
settled meaning, but there will be, as well, a penumbra of debatable cases
in which words are neither obviously applicable nor obviously ruled out.
These cases will each have some features in common with the standard
case; they will lack others or be accompanied by features not present in the
standard case. * * *

[Hart argued that in the zone of "core" meaning, a judge would simply
apply the term in the statute. In the penumbral cases, however, such an
approach will not work.] A judge has to apply a rule to a concrete case —
perhaps the rule that one may not take a stolen "vehicle" across state lines,
and in this case an airplane has been taken. * * * He ignores, or is blind to,
the fact that he is in the area of the penumbra and is not dealing with a
standard case. * * * He [therefore] either takes the meaning that the word
most obviously suggests in its ordinary nonlegal context to ordinary men,

---

[16] St. Petersburg Times, Oct. 18, 1992, at 17A.

[17] *See* H.L.A. Hart, The Concept of Law 121–132 (1961); H.L.A. Hart, *Positivism and the Separation
of Law and Morals*, 71 Harv. L. Rev. 593, 607 (1958).

or one which the word has been given in some other legal context, or, still worse, he thinks of a standard case and then arbitrarily identifies certain features in it — for example, in the case of a vehicle, (1) normally used on land, (2) capable of carrying a human person, (3) capable of being self-propelled — and treats these three as always necessary and always sufficient conditions for the use in all contexts of the word "vehicle," irrespective of the social consequences of giving it this interpretation. This choice, not "logic," would force the judge to include a toy motor car (if electrically propelled) and to exclude bicycles and the airplane. In all this there is possibly great stupidity * * *.[18]

NOTES AND QUESTIONS

(1)   Can you link Hart's criticisms of a particular style of legal reasoning with Justice Traynor's dissent in *Knight v. Kaiser*? When Justice Traynor argues that precedents concerning bodies of water have no bearing on cases involving sand piles, is he pursuing just the mistaken approach lamented by Hart? On the other hand, when Traynor inveighs against the formalism of the majority, is he siding with Hart's criticism?

(2)   Was *Ojibway* in the penumbra, statute obviously applicable, or statute obviously ruled out category? What about Mable, the non-motorized vehicle?

(3)   Would it violate the prohibition on vehicles to bring any of the following into the park?

(a) A war memorial which includes a military jeep placed on a pedestal[19]

(b) A riding lawnmower[20]

(c) A motorized wheelchair[21]

---

[18]   Hart, *Positivism, supra* note 17, at 607, 610–611.

[19]   This example, as famous as Hart's statute, is from Lon L. Fuller, *Positivism and Fidelity to Law — A Reply to Professor Hart*, 71 HARV. L. REV. 630, 663 (1958).

[20]   Compare the following case. The Florida no-fault auto insurance law requires payment of benefits to any Florida resident injured by an automobile "while not an occupant of a self-propelled vehicle." Thus a pedestrian who is hit by a car is covered, someone in another car is not. In Miller v. Allstate Insurance Co., 560 So. 2d 393 (Fla. Dist. Ct. App. 1990), the court held that a city maintenance worker struck by a car while riding a lawnmower along the side of the road could not recover benefits because he was "the occupant of a self-propelled vehicle."

The statute had formerly referred to the occupants of "motor vehicles." Applying that language, the same court had held that a bus passenger *was* entitled to benefits, because a bus was *not* a motor vehicle. State Farm v. Butler, 340 So. 2d 1185 (Fla. Dist. Ct. App. 1976).

[21]   The dissent in *Miller v. Allstate* reads, in full: "In my judgment a lawn mower, with or without a detachable seat, is not a motor vehicle, any more than is an electric wheelchair or similar device. There is nothing about this equipment or its design to indicate otherwise." *Miller*, 60 So. 2d at 395 (Stone, J., dissenting).

From time to time intoxicated wheelchair users are charged with driving under the influence. We are not aware of any actual convictions on this theory. *See, e.g.,* Duane Bourne, *Judge Tosses Out*

(d) A nonmotorized wheelchair

(e) A motorized bar stool[22]

(f) A bicycle[23]

(g) A baby stroller

(h) A child's wagon[24]

(i) H.L.A. Hart's *The Concept of Law*[25]

(4)   In considering the application of the ordinance in these different situations, did you rely *solely* on your (mental) definition of "vehicle," or were other considerations relevant? Did you avoid the pitfalls identified by Hart?

According to Hart, the interpreter should decide these sort of "penumbral" cases by looking to "social consequences" and "aims, purposes, and policies." Subsequent disagreement with Hart has not been about whether reference to statutory purpose or policy is necessary to decide the penumbral cases. Rather, the usual objection is that such reference to purpose *also* underlies application of the statute to the core case. Consider Fuller's war memorial (item (a) above); surely a functioning jeep is within the core meaning of "vehicle," yet just as surely no court would apply the statute to forbid the war memorial. Why not? Here is a snippet of Lon Fuller's response to Hart:

DUI-Wheelchair Case, St. Petersburg Times (Jan. 4, 2005) at 1B.

[22] Consider the following news item:

> Authorities in Ohio say a man has been charged with drunken driving after crashing his motorized bar stool.
>
> Police in Newark, 30 miles east of Columbus, say that when they responded to a report of a crash with injuries on March 4, they found a man who had wrecked a bar stool powered by a deconstructed lawn mower.
>
> Kile Wygle, 28, was hospitalized for minor injuries. Police say he was charged with operating a vehicle while intoxicated after he told an officer at the hospital that he had consumed 15 beers. Wygle told police his motorized bar stool can go up to 38 mph.
>
> Wygle has pleaded not guilty and has requested a jury trial.

Chicago Daily Law Bulletin, Mar. 31, 2009.

[23] In Johnson v. Railway Express Agency, 131 F.2d 1009 (7th Cir. 1942), the court found that the following provision did not apply to bicycles: "All vehicles, including animal-drawn vehicles * * * shall * * * be equipped with" front and rear lights. "Vehicle" was defined as "[e]very device in, upon, or by which any person or property is or may be transported or drawn upon a highway, except devices moved by human power, or used exclusively upon stationary rails or tracks." *See also* Geiger v. President of Perkiomen & R. Turnpike Road, 31 A. 918 (Pa. 1895) (bicycle a vehicle under statute requiring payment of toll for use of turnpike); Richardson v. Town of Danvers, 57 N.E. 688 (Mass. 1900) (bicycle not a "carriage" for purposes of 1786 statute requiring towns to maintain streets "so that the same may be reasonably safe and convenient for travelers, with their horses, teams, and carriages at all seasons of the year").

[24] *Compare* Jermane v. Forfar, 240 P.2d 351 (Cal. 1952) (child lying on four-wheel scooter, propelling it with his foot, was not "the driver of a vehicle") *with* Hattie v. Shaheen, 174 N.E. 20 (Ohio 1930) (child who rode coaster wagon out into street was "operator of a vehicle").

[25] *See* Anthony D'Amato, *Can Legislatures Constrain Judicial Interpretation of Statutes?*, 75 Va. L. Rev. 561, 596–597 n.93 (1989) (noting that a book is a vehicle for ideas).

In [Hart's] illustration of the "vehicle," although he tells us this word has a core of meaning that in all contexts defines unequivocally a range of objects embraced by it, he never tells us what these objects might be. If the rule excluding vehicles from parks seems easy to apply in some cases, I submit this is because we can see clearly enough what the rule "is aiming at in general" so that we know there is no need to worry about the difference between Fords and Cadillacs. If in some cases we seem to be able to apply the rule without asking what its purpose is, this is not because we can treat a directive arrangement as if it had no purpose. It is rather because, for example, whether the rule be intended to preserve quiet in the park, or to save carefree strollers from injury, we know, "without thinking," that a noisy automobile must be excluded.[26]

How do we know "without thinking" when allowing a particular vehicle into the park is inconsistent with the statutory purpose? How is that purpose revealed? What are the possible purposes of this statute? Review items (a)–(i), above, and as to each one try to articulate a plausible underlying purpose that would allow it into the park and one that would keep it out.

(5) *McBoyle v. United States*.[27] A federal statute made it a crime to transport a stolen motor vehicle across state lines. The statute provided that: "The term 'motor vehicle' shall include an automobile, automobile truck, automobile wagon, motorcycle, or any other self-propelled vehicle not designed for running on rails." McBoyle was convicted under this provision for bringing a stolen airplane from Illinois to Oklahoma. In an opinion by Justice Holmes, the Court unanimously held that an airplane was not a motor vehicle and reversed the conviction.

Was *McBoyle* correctly decided? Would Hart think so? Would Fuller? Does the statutory definition make the case easier or harder?

In its current form, the statute at issue in *McBoyle* reads: "Whoever transports in interstate or foreign commerce a motor vehicle, vessel, or aircraft, knowing the same to have been stolen, shall be fined * * * or imprisoned not more than 10 years, or both." 18 U.S.C. § 2312. Someone on the Hill seems to be reading Supreme Court cases. Is there a lesson in that?

(6) *United States v. Reid*.[28] The USA PATRIOT Act, passed in the wake of the 9/11 attacks, punished anyone who "willfully wrecks, derails, sets fire to, or disables a mass transportation vehicle . . . [or] attempts, threatens, or conspires to do any of the aforesaid acts." The provision did not define "vehicle." It defined "mass transportation" by cross-reference to another provision, under which "mass transportation" is "transportation by a conveyance that provides regular and continuing general or special transportation to the public." In December 2001, Richard Reid, a passenger on a commercial flight from Paris to Miami, unsuccessfully attempted to ignite an explosive device contained in his shoes. In one count of a multi-count indictment, Reid was charged with violating this section. He argued that an airplane

---

[26] Fuller, *supra* note 19, at 663.

[27] 283 U.S. 25 (1931).

[28] 206 F. Supp.2d 132 (D. Mass. 2002).

is not a "vehicle" and therefore this section could not apply to his conduct. The District Court agreed. It relied on *McBoyle*. It also cited "The Dictionary Act," which provides generally applicable definitions for a number of terms in the U.S. Code, including "vehicle," which "includes every description of carriage or other artificial contrivance used, or capable of being used, as a means of transportation on land." 1 U.S.C. § 4. The court found that the usage of the term "vehicle" (as opposed to "vessel" and "aircraft") is consistent with this limitation throughout the U.S. Code.

The specific provision at issue in *Reid* has since been repealed and replaced; the current version defines "vehicle" to mean "any carriage or other contrivance used, or capable of being used, as a means of transportation on land, on water, or through the air." 18 U.S.C. § 1992(d)(16).

NOTE ON VAGUENESS AND DELEGATION

Recall the Individuals with Disabilities Education Act and its requirement that children receive a "free appropriate education." Such a statute is far "vaguer" than the provisions we have been dealing with thus far. Such open-ended, broadly worded statutes amount to a legislative invitation to create a sort of common law. A prominent example is the basic antitrust law, the Sherman Act of 1890. The Act forbids agreements that "restrain trade or commerce," but gives no indication of what those are. The statute cannot be read literally, since *every* agreement "restrains trade" in the sense that it precludes ("restrains") a later, different transaction. When A agrees to sell 100 widgets to B for $15, A is restrained from selling those widgets to C. Thus, the law reflects a basic preference for open competition and hostility toward monopolies, but provides the judiciary with little more guidance than that. As a result, the court in a Sherman Act case is not really "interpreting" the statute; it is developing a common law of antitrust. A century after the Act was passed, the statutory text is practically (in both senses of the term) irrelevant; "antitrust law" consists of the body of caselaw. And the particular rules arising from the cases have shifted and developed over the years without congressional involvement.

With statutes such as the Sherman Act, "the only thing one can know for certain about Congress's intent is that Congress wanted the courts to work out the relevant details."[29] Should there be limits on Congress's ability to cede legislative authority to other actors? Would it be preferable for Congress to hand over such discretionary policymaking to a specialized administrative agency rather than a court?

3. *Ambiguity*

The foregoing problems involved a *vague* term; the boundaries of the category "vehicle" were uncertain. A different kind of uncertainty arises from *ambiguous* terms. Ambiguity and vagueness are not the same thing. A word is ambiguous

---

[29] Margaret H. Lemos, *The Other Delegate: Judicially Administered Statutes and the Nondelegation Doctrine*, 81 S. Cal. L. Rev. 405, 431 (2008).

when it has more than one possible meaning; each is clear, but we do not know which applies. For example, in denying that he is mad, Hamlet asserts that he can tell a "hawk from a handsaw." That should not be hard, and one is inclined to think that Hamlet must indeed be mad precisely because he thinks the ability to distinguish a bird from a saw proves otherwise. In Shakespeare's day, however, a "handsaw" was a kind of bird. If that is how it is being used here, it suggests an ability to make a much finer distinction. "Handsaw" is not vague; it is ambiguous. Either of its two meanings is easy to apply here; the problem is choosing between them.

The following case involves such a problem. Perhaps when you were in elementary school some know-it-all was fond of saying, "You know, a tomato is really a fruit, not a vegetable." Little did you know that the Supreme Court had weighed in on this important question.

NIX v. HEDDEN
149 U.S. 304, Treas. Dec. 14045 (1893)

[A federal statute imposed a 10% import duty on "Vegetables, in their natural state, or in salt or brine, not specially enumerated or provided for in this act." In contrast, the "free list" included "Fruits, green, ripe or dried, not specially enumerated or provided for in this act." Petitioner imported tomatoes. The government required payment of the 10% duty. This is a suit against the tax collector for a refund.]

At the trial, the plaintiff's counsel, after reading in evidence definitions of the words "fruit" and "vegetables" from Webster's Dictionary, Worcester's Dictionary and the Imperial Dictionary, called two witnesses, who had been for thirty years in the business of selling fruit and vegetables, and asked them, after hearing these definitions, to say whether these words had "any special meaning in trade or commerce, different from those read."

One of the witnesses answered as follows: "Well, it does not classify all things there, but they are correct as far as they go. It does not take all kinds of fruit or vegetables; it takes a portion of them. I think the words 'fruit' and 'vegetable' have the same meaning in trade to-day that they had on March 1, 1883 [the date the Tariff Act was enacted]. I understand that the term 'fruit' is applied in trade only to such plants or parts of plants as contain the seeds. There are more vegetables than those in the enumeration given in Webster's Dictionary under the term 'vegetable,' as 'cabbage, cauliflower, turnips, potatoes, peas, beans, and the like,' probably covered by the words 'and the like.'"

The other witness testified: "I don't think the term 'fruit' or the term 'vegetables' had, in March, 1883, and prior thereto, any special meaning in trade and commerce in this country, different from that which I have read here from the dictionaries."

The plaintiff's counsel then read in evidence from the same dictionaries the definitions of the word "tomato."

The defendant's counsel then read in evidence from Webster's Dictionary the definitions of the words "pea," "egg plant," "cucumber," "squash" and "pepper."

The plaintiff then read in evidence from Webster's and Worcester's dictionaries the definitions of "potato," "turnip," "parsnip," "cauliflower," "cabbage," "carrot" and "bean."

No other evidence was offered by either party. [The District Court directed a verdict for the defendant.] * * *

Mr. Justice Gray, after stating the case, delivered the opinion of the court.

The single question in this case is whether tomatoes, considered as provisions, are to be classed as "vegetables" or as "fruit," within the meaning of the Tariff Act of 1883.

The only witnesses called at the trial testified that neither "vegetables" nor "fruit" had any special meaning in trade or commerce, different from that given in the dictionaries * * *.

The passages cited from the dictionaries define the word "fruit" as the seed of plants, or that part of plants which contains the seed, and especially the juicy, pulpy products of certain plants, covering and containing the seed. These definitions have no tendency to show that tomatoes are "fruit," as distinguished from "vegetables," in common speech, or within the meaning of the Tariff Act.

There being no evidence that the words "fruit" and "vegetables" have acquired any special meaning in trade or commerce, they must receive their ordinary meaning. Of that meaning the court is bound to take judicial notice, as it does in regard to all words in our own tongue; and upon such a question dictionaries are admitted, not as evidence, but only as aids to the memory and understanding of the court.

Botanically speaking, tomatoes are the fruit of a vine, just as are cucumbers, squashes, beans and peas. But in the common language of the people, whether sellers or consumers of provisions, all these are vegetables, which are grown in kitchen gardens, and which, whether eaten cooked or raw, are, like potatoes, carrots, parsnips, turnips, beets, cauliflower, cabbage, celery and lettuce, usually served at dinner in, with or after the soup, fish or meats which constitute the principal part of the repast, and not, like fruits generally, as dessert. * * *

NOTES AND QUESTIONS

(1)   Here are some definitions from Webster's New International Dictionary (2d ed. 1934).

> **Fruit:** 1. Any product of plant growth useful to man or animals, as grain, vegetables, cotton, etc.; — commonly in *pl.* 2. The edible, more or less succulent, product of a perennial or woody plant, consisting of the ripened seeds and adjacent tissues, or of the latter alone. In popular usage there is no exact distinction between a *fruit* and a *vegetable*, except where the latter consists of the stem, leaves, or root of the plant.

> **Vegetable:** A plant; specif., in common usage, a herbaceous plant cultivated for food, as the cabbage, potato, bean, etc.; also, the edible part or parts of such plants, as prepared for market or table.

> **Tomato: a** A south American perennial herb * * * of the nightshade family, widely cultivated for its fruit. **b** Its large rounded pulpy berry which is red or yellow when ripe.

> **Eggplant: a** A widely cultivated herb * * *, allied to the potato. **b** The large smooth ovoid fruit of this plant, used as a vegetable.

(At least one of your authors thinks the definition of "eggplant," though confounding on first reading, is the most helpful. Why?)

(2) *Is* a tomato a vegetable? The dictionary, the botanist, a federal agency,[30] importers, members of the general public all may have different answers. *Nix* says the general rule is that, absent some clear indication that a term is being used in a technical sense or as a term of art, the common usage carries the day. What are the justifications for this approach?

(3) *McBoyle*, the airplane-is-not-a-vehicle case, is often cited as an example of the Court sticking to the ordinary meaning of a word. Justice Holmes there observed that "in everyday speech 'vehicle' calls up the picture of a thing moving on land."[31]

(4) The Court's approach in *Nix* could be described as highly formal and rests on a limited set of considerations. If the dictionary is all the evidence that is required to decide the case, is tomato then within the "core" meaning of "vegetable"? Is there any other information you would like to have to decide the case? Would Hart see *Nix* as an example of the sort of error he criticizes in the excerpt above or, to the contrary, would he agree with both the method and the result? Would Fuller?

(5) An earlier, less well-known court-room battle over a similar question is wonderfully described in D. Graham Burnett's *Trying Leviathan.*[32] The 1818 case of *Maurice v. Judd* concerned whether a whale is a fish. If so, whale oil was subject to inspection as "fish oil." As in *Nix v. Hedden*, the lay understanding (here, that a whale *is* a fish) triumphed over the scientific.

---

[30] In 1981 the Department of Health and Human Services proposed that ketchup should count as a "vegetable" for purposes of a requirement that school lunches include two servings of vegetables. If ketchup is a vegetable, then *a fortiori*, as lawyers say, tomatoes must be. Leaving no stone unturned in their search for enlightenment, your authors have explored this path, but run into a dead end. It turns out that the specific provision in question requires "2 or more servings of vegetables or fruit or both." Thus, they leave the particular classification of tomato unresolved. (By the way, the ketchup-as-a-vegetable proposal was abandoned. On the other hand, peanut butter counts as "meat.").

[31] *McBoyle*, 283 U.S. at 26.

[32] D. Graham Burnett, Trying Leviathan: The Nineteenth-Century New York Court Case That Put the Whale on Trial and Challenged the Order of Nature (2007).

UNIVERSITY OF UTAH HOSPITAL v. BETHKE
101 Idaho 245, 611 P.2d 1030 (1980)

[The University of Utah Hospital and Medical Center sought reimbursement of $20,000 in medical expenses from Minidoka County, Idaho, for the treatment of two infants who were residents of Minidoka County but had been transferred to and treated at the Medical Center. An Idaho statute requires the county to pick up the tab for hospital expenses incurred by the "medically indigent." It had been previously determined that the children were medically indigent.] [T]he sole issue [is] whether the definition of "hospital" in I.C. § 31-3502(2) limits payment for necessary medical care and treatment to only those hospitals located in Idaho. * * *

I.C. § 31-3502(2) defines "hospital" as:

"[A] facility licensed as such in Idaho providing community service for in-patient, medical and/or surgical care of acute illness or injury and/or obstetrics, and excluding state institutions."

However, a literal reading of the above statute does not limit hospitals to only those facilities located in Idaho. The words "as such" indicate an exemplary use of the phrase as it applies to "facility." "As" means "like, similar to, of the same kind, in the same manner, in the manner in which." *Black's Law Dictionary* 104 (5th ed. 1979). "Such" means "of that kind . . . alike, similar, of the like kind." *Black's Law Dictionary, supra* at 1284. Clearly, the phrase "as such" is exemplary, not exclusive, so that it applies to hospitals licensed like those licensed in Idaho.

Had the legislature intended the statute to apply only to Idaho hospitals, the term "as such" was not necessary to the statute and constitutes mere surplusage. This Court is required to give effect to every word, clause and sentence of a statute, where possible. * * * We therefore decline to hold that the term "as such" was mere surplusage and thus, we construe the statute as applying to all hospitals, including appellant.

SHEPARD, Justice, dissenting. * * *

The majority opinion unequivocally states that there is only one interpretation of the statutory phrase, " 'hospital' means a facility licensed as such in Idaho." I must disagree and not even very respectfully. In my judgment, the very best position that the majority can assert is that the statutory phrase is subject to more than one interpretation. Even assuming that the majority's interpretation could, by some stretch of the imagination, be correct, I cannot believe it would be the preferred interpretation. In my linguistic judgment, "as such" refers back to the antecedent noun "hospital." In my opinion, and contrary to the assertion of the majority, "in Idaho" is a distinct prepositional phrase separate and apart from "as such." If the legislature had intended that the term "hospital" was to mean any licensed hospital regardless of whether located in or out of Idaho, it could merely have defined "hospital" as "a facility licensed as such" and not utilized the phrase "in Idaho." Alternatively, the legislature could have completely and clearly defined "hospital" as meaning any facility so licensed by any state and wherever located. * * *

I cannot join the majority in its syntactic hopscotch, but would approve the district court's statutory construction and affirm its judgment.

NOTES AND QUESTIONS

(1)   Is the majority's result "syntactic hopscotch" or the faithful adherence to the rules of English usage?

(2)   Whenever a court (or an advocate) asserts that something is "clearly" or "obviously" so, you should assume that it is not, otherwise the adverb would be unnecessary. Is "as such" "clearly," as the court says, "exemplary"? Does *Black's Law Dictionary* help?

(3)   The majority invokes the familiar principle that statutes should be read to avoid "surplusage": every word must be given meaning, every word must do some work. How sound is this principle? Aren't lawyers famous for surplusage? Does the majority employ this approach correctly? Make the argument that the majority's reading of the statute creates its own surplusage.

4.   *Punctuation and Grammatical Uncertainty*

Like any reader, courts rely on rules of grammar or punctuation to determine statutory meaning. Like any writer, however, legislatures often create ambiguity through grammatical carelessness. Consider whether the courts in the following three examples reached the correct result.

(a) *Young v. Community Nutrition Institute*, 476 U.S. 974 (1986). A public interest organization sued the Commissioner of the Federal Food and Drug Administration seeking to compel him to limit the permissible amount of aflatoxin, a carcinogen produced by a fungal mold, in the food supply. Though potentially harmful, aflatoxin is naturally and unavoidably present in some food. The relevant statute provided that when a toxic substance is inescapably present in food, the Commissioner "shall promulgate regulations limiting the quantity therein or thereon *to such extent as he finds necessary* for the protection of public health."

The Commissioner had not issued aflatoxin regulations. Did the statute require him to do so? What exactly is the argument that he must; what is the argument that he need not; and what is the grammatical ambiguity in the quoted language that gives rise to this uncertainty?

In the actual case, a majority of the Court threw up its hands and concluded that the statute was impossibly unclear. Under the doctrine of deference to administrative interpretations (on which more in Chapter 15) it simply accepted the agency's view. Justice Stevens, the sole dissenter, argued that "[t]o one versed in the English language, the meaning of this provision is readily apparent." (This seems a rather demeaning jibe at his colleagues.) He concluded that the statute required the Secretary to regulate the permissible amount of aflatoxin.

The problem in *Community Nutrition Institute* could have been resolved by invoking the rule — sometimes grandly referred to as the "doctrine of the last

antecedent" — that qualifying or limiting words or phrases refer to the immediately preceding word or phrase. That approach supports Justice Stevens. Should the Court have relied on this grammatical rule?

(b) *Petition of Smith*, 986 P.2d 131 (Washington 1999). A Washington state law provides:

> [A]n offender committed to a correctional facility operated by the department, may be reduced by earned early release time in accordance with procedures that shall be developed and promulgated by the correctional agency having jurisdiction in which the offender is confined. * * * In the case of an offender convicted of a serious violent offense or a sex offense that is a class A felony, the aggregate earned early release time may not exceed fifteen percent of the sentence. In no other case shall the aggregate earned early release time exceed one-third of the total sentence.

Derek Gronquist is convicted of attempted kidnapping; under Washington law, attempted kidnapping is a serious violent offense; it is also a class B felony. Is he subject to the 15% cap on early release time, or the 1/3 cap? The Washington Supreme Court held the latter.

(c) *Stark v. Advanced Magnetics, Inc.*, 119 F.3d 1551 (Fed. Cir. 1997). The federal Patent Act gives the Commissioner of Patents certain authority to correct errors in the name of the inventor that are discovered after a patent has been issued. It provides:

> Whenever through error a person is named in an issued patent as the inventor, or through error an inventor is not named in an issued patent and such error arose without any deceptive intention on his part, the Commissioner may * * * issue[] a certificate correcting such error.

35 U.S.C. § 256.

This provision identifies two sorts of errors: "misjoinder," which is when someone who is not the inventor is named as the inventor, and "nonjoinder," which when someone who is the inventor is not named at all. The Commissioner can correct both. The question is, can he do so if the error resulted from deception? Clearly, he can correct nonjoinder only if "such error arose without any deceptive intention on [the inventor's] part. But does the quoted language also apply to misjoinder? A careful reading, with particular attention paid to the use of commas, suggests that it does not, i.e. that misjoinder can be corrected whether or not the error arose with deceptive intention. And, indeed, so the court in *Stark* held.

The plot thickens a bit, however, when one looks at another provision of the Act. This provision applies to exactly the same errors, but when they are discovered when a patent application is pending, rather than after the patent has been issued. It is almost identical to § 256:

> Whenever through error a person is named in an application for patent as the inventor, or through error an inventor is not named in an application, and such error arose without any deceptive intention on his part, the Commissioner may permit the application to be amended accordingly, under such terms as he prescribes.

35 U.S.C. § 116. Same statute, same sort of errors, same apparent approach, identical wording, *mutatis mutandis* — and one extra comma. Under § 116, must it be shown (unlike under § 256) that misjoinder was not deceptive? The *Stark* court held that it must. Is one little comma a sufficient basis for reading the two provisions differently? Do you think Congress really intended different results under the two provisions, or did someone just forget to put in a comma (in 256) or mistakenly include one (in 116)? The court acknowledged that pertinent legislative history suggested that Congress expected the two sections "to be interpreted in a uniform manner," but concluded that the text trumped all and that if the inconsistency was a problem, it was one Congress could solve.

5. *Context*

Words always appear in a context. "A provision that may seem ambiguous in isolation is often clarified by the remainder of the statutory scheme — because the same terminology is used elsewhere in a context that makes its meaning clear, or because only one of the permissible meanings produces a substantive effect that is compatible with the rest of the law." *United Savings Ass'n v. Timbers of Inwood Forest Assocs.*, 484 U.S. 365, 371 (1988). Interpretation almost always looks beyond the specific operative term to other textual clues such as the use of the term in other provisions or the structure of the statute. The majority and dissent make several different "contextual" arguments in the following decision.

UNITED STATES v. RESSAM
553 U.S. 272 (2008)

[After respondent gave false information on his customs form while attempting to enter the United States from Canada, a search of his car revealed explosives that he intended to detonate in this country. He was convicted of making a false statement to a customs official, which is a felony under 18 U.S.C. § 1001. He was also convicted under 18 U.S.C. § 844(h), which provides:

Whoever-

(1) uses fire or an explosive to commit any felony which may be prosecuted in a court of the United States, or

(2) carries an explosive during the commission of any felony which may be prosecuted in a court of the United States, * * *

shall, in addition to the punishment provided for such felony, be sentenced to imprisonment for 10 years.

The Court of Appeals set aside the latter conviction because it read the word "during" in § 844(h)(2) to include a requirement that the explosive be carried "in relation to" the underlying felony.]

Justice STEVENS delivered the opinion of the Court.

I

The most natural reading of the relevant statutory text provides a sufficient basis for reversal. * * * It is undisputed that the items hidden in respondent's car were "explosives." It is also undisputed that respondent was "carr[ying]" those explosives when he knowingly made false statements to a customs official, and that those statements violated § 1001.

There is no need to consult dictionary definitions of the word "during" in order to arrive at the conclusion that respondent engaged in the precise conduct described in § 844(h)(2). The term "during" denotes a temporal link; that is surely the most natural reading of the word as used in the statute. Because respondent's carrying of the explosives was contemporaneous with his violation of § 1001, he carried them "during" that violation.

II

The history of the statute we construe today further supports our conclusion that Congress did not intend to require the Government to establish a relationship between the explosive carried and the underlying felony. [Section 844(h)(2) was modeled on a provision of the Gun Control Act, 18 U.S.C. § 924(c), which made it a crime unlawfully to carry a firearm during the commission of any felony. The two provisions as originally enacted were essentially identical. Congress later amended the firearms provision by deleting the word "unlawfully" and adding the phrase "and in relation to" immediately after the word "during." Legislative history suggested, and the Ninth Circuit had held, that this was not intended to be a substantive change but, rather, that it was a clarifying amendment to make clear a condition already implicit in the term "during." Relying on that previous gloss on the firearms statute, the Court of Appeals in this case concluded that the term "during" in § 844(h)(2) also included an implicit "in relation to" requirement.] Whatever the merits of the argument that § 924(c) as originally enacted contained a relational requirement, the subsequent changes to both statutes convince us that the Government's reading of § 844(h) as presently written is correct.

III

In 1988, Congress enacted the "Explosives Offenses Amendments," which modified the text of § 844(h). Those amendments increased the penalties for violating the provision; they also deleted the word "unlawfully." Unlike its earlier amendment to the firearm statute, however, Congress did not also insert the words "and in relation to" after the word "during." While it is possible that this omission was inadvertent, that possibility seems remote given the stark difference that was thereby introduced into the otherwise similar texts of 18 U.S.C. §§ 844(h) and 924(c).

Even if the similarity of the original texts of the two statutes might have supported an inference that both included an implicit relationship requirement, their current difference virtually commands the opposite inference. While the two provisions were initially identical, Congress' replacement of the word "unlawfully" in the firearm statute with the phrase "and in relation to," coupled with the deletion

of the word "unlawfully" without any similar replacement in the explosives statute, convinces us that Congress did not intend to introduce a relational requirement into the explosives provision, but rather intended us to accept the more straightforward reading of § 844(h). Since respondent was carrying explosives when he violated § 1001, he was carrying them "during" the commission of that felony. The statute as presently written requires nothing further.

Justice BREYER, dissenting. * * *

My problem with the Court's interpretation is that it would permit conviction of any individual who legally carries explosives at the time that he engages in a totally unrelated felony. * * * [T]he Court's opinion brings within the statute's scope (and would impose an additional mandatory 10-year prison term upon), for example, a farmer lawfully transporting a load of fertilizer who intentionally mails an unauthorized lottery ticket to a friend, a hunter lawfully carrying gunpowder for shotgun shells who buys snacks with a counterfeit $20 bill, a truckdriver lawfully transporting diesel fuel who lies to a customs official about the value of presents he bought in Canada for his family, or an accountant who engaged in a 6-year-long conspiracy to commit tax evasion and who, one day during that conspiracy, bought gas for his lawnmower. In such instances the lawful carrying of an "explosive" has *nothing whatsoever* to do with the unlawful felonies. I cannot imagine why Congress would have wanted the presence of totally irrelevant, lawful behavior to trigger an additional 10-year mandatory prison term.

The statute's language does not demand such an interpretation. I agree with the majority that the word "during" requires a "temporal link." But a statement that uses the word "during" may or may not imply *other* limitations as well, depending upon the context in which the statement is made. Thus, when I tell a friend from Puerto Rico, "I wear gloves during Washington's winter," he does not think I mean baseball mitts. Rather, I imply (and he understands) a relation or link between the gloves and the winter. When I say to a group of lawyers, "I take notes during oral argument," I imply (and they understand) that the notes bear a relation to the law being argued. But when I say, "I called my brother during the day," I do not imply any particular relation (other than a temporal relation) between the day and the phone call. Context makes the difference.

Here, the statute's context makes clear that the statutory statement does not cover a "carr[ying]" of explosives that is totally unrelated to the "felony." The lengthy mandatory minimum sentence is evidence of what the statute's legislative history separately indicates, namely that Congress sought to criminalize and impose harsh penalties in respect to the "intentional *misuse* of explosives," see H.R. Rep. No. 91-1549, p. 38 (1970). A person who *lawfully* carries explosives while committing some other felony does not even arguably "misuse" those explosives unless the carrying has something to do with the other felony. Nor in the absence of some such relationship is there any obvious reason to impose an additional mandatory 10-year sentence on a person who *unlawfully* carries explosives while committing some other felony. * * *

I recognize that the language of the firearms statute now differs from the language of the explosives statute in an important way. * * * The words "in relation to" do not appear in the explosives statute. But neither did those words appear in

the pre-1984 version of the firearms statute * * * [in which] the Ninth Circuit nonetheless found an implicit relational requirement. And the fact that these words now appear in the firearms statute but not the explosives statute cannot make the determinative difference. * * *

The absence of the words "in relation to" here must lead us to ask (but it does not answer) the question: Did Congress intend something different in respect to the explosives statute? There are strong reasons for thinking it did not. Congress, after all, amended the explosives statute in response to the Department of Justice's express request to "bring" the explosives statute "in line with" the firearms statute. See 131 Cong. Rec. 14166 (1985); see also 134 Cong. Rec. 32700 (1988) (statement of Sen. Biden) (noting that the purpose of amending the explosives statute was to "bring it in line with similar amendments [previously] adopted . . . with respect to the parallel offense of using or carrying a firearm during the commission of federal offenses"). Congress accordingly increased the mandatory minimum punishment to five years and struck the word "unlawfully." If Congress, in neglecting to add the words "in relation to," sought to create a meaningful distinction between the explosives and firearms statutes, one would think that someone somewhere would have mentioned this objective. * * *

At the same time one can explain the absence of the words "in relation to" in less damaging ways. The legislative drafters of the explosives amendment may have assumed that prior judicial interpretation made the words "in relation to" unnecessary. Or, as the majority recognizes, the omission of the language may reflect simple drafting inadvertence. * * *

No more here than elsewhere in life can words alone explain every nuance of their intended application. Context matters. And if judges are to give meaningful effect to the intent of the enacting legislature, they must interpret statutory text with reference to the statute's purpose and its history.

NOTES AND QUESTIONS

(a) *Silence.* One common type of contextual clue might be termed "meaningful silence." If Congress includes particular language in one section of a statute but omits it in another section of the same Act, it is generally presumed that the difference in wording was intentional and meaningful. Thus, language that might be confusing read in isolation is clarified by being read in context. The usual formulation is, "When Congress wanted to do such and such, it knew how to do so." For example, the Coal Industry Retiree Health Benefit Act of 1992 required two types of businesses to make payments to support health plans for retired coal miners: "signatory operators," who were coal operators who had actually signed pension agreements with workers, and "related persons," companies that had enjoyed statutorily specified forms of business affiliation with signatory operators. The Act explicitly imposed liability for retiree health plans on successors in interest to "related persons" but said nothing about imposing liability on successors to "signatory operators." In *Barnhart v. Sigmon Coal Co.,* 534 U.S. 438 (2002), the Supreme Court held that Sigmon, which was the successor in interest to

a signatory operator, was not liable. "[W]here Congress wanted to provide successor liability in the * * * Act, it did so explicitly." *Id.* at 452. We will see another example of this very standard argument in the next chapter in *West Virginia University Hospitals v. Casey.*

This argument is at the heart of the majority opinion in *Ressam.* Justice Breyer works hard to overcome the usual presumption. Does he succeed? Is it realistic to assume that Congress really does consciously make small changes in the language of similar provisions? Perhaps the opposite approach would be more realistic; we could presume that when Congress has two provisions that are similar in nature and purpose, they should be read identically notwithstanding minor differences in wording, since Congress is likely to take similar approaches to similar problems. Is that Justice Breyer's presumption? (Might it be significant that Justice Breyer was the one member of the Court in *Ressam* who actually worked for Congress at one point in his career?)

(b) *Application.* A second type of contextual clue is derived from considering to what the term in question is applied. Looking a word up in the dictionary is insufficient; one must see how it is actually used. Justice Breyer's dissent in *Ressam* emphasizes this sort of contextualism. He does not disagree with Justice Stevens that "during" generally means "while the other thing is taking place," but argues that *in context* it involves more than simultaneity. Were you convinced?

Whether or not Justice Breyer is correct about the statute at issue in *Ressam,* his general point is important and generally acknowledged. This is why *textualism* is not the same as *literalism* and why textualists do more than just look up words in a dictionary. A leading textualist law professor explains, using an example that will be familiar:

> [R]easonable users may give words a contextual gloss that reflects ordinary usage, but that is not found in dictionaries, which have a limited capacity to record all of the subtleties of usage. As Justice Scalia recently put it, "the acid test of whether a word can reasonably bear a particular meaning is whether you could use the word in that sense at a cocktail party without having people look at you funny." Consider, for example, a statute that imposes sentence enhancement when a person "during and in relation to any crime of violence or drug trafficking crime * * * uses * * * a firearm." In *Smith v. United States,* the Court relied on the broad dictionary definition of "use" to hold that a defendant "used" a gun, within the meaning of the statute, when he traded it for illegal narcotics. In dissent, Justice Scalia invoked the "fundamental principle of statutory construction (and, indeed, of language itself) that the meaning of a word cannot be determined in isolation, but must be drawn from the context in which it is used." Reading the crucial term in the context of the surrounding sentence, Justice Scalia reasoned that the defendant had not "used" a firearm in the sense of the statute:

>> To use an instrumentality ordinarily means to use it for its intended purpose. When someone asks, "Do you use a cane?," he is not inquiring whether you have your grandfather's silver-handled walking stick on display in the hall; he wants to know whether you walk with a cane.

Similarly, to speak of "using a firearm" is to speak of using it for its distinctive purpose, i.e., as a weapon.

* * * If the meaning of words is a function of the way speakers use them in context, it follows that the identical words may have different meanings when used in different contexts. Hence, a literal approach will more often pick up meanings that make little sense of the context in which the legislature used statutory words. More precisely, if legislators use words to achieve some end, a literal approach will yield results that bear little relation to those apparent ends. In *Smith*, for example, a literal interpretation of "using a firearm" would require a substantial sentence enhancement for using a non-functioning antique musket as a doorstop in a drug den. And [those who believe judges should look to statutory purpose] would argue that their approach is necessary to narrow the statutory meaning to more sensible boundaries. A more contextual approach to textualism alleviates much of this necessity. Focusing on the contextual gloss put upon "using a firearm" in the context of committing a crime, the *Smith* dissent arrived at a more plausible conclusion — that penalties were to be enhanced only for brandishing a gun in connection with drug trafficking. While this facet of textualism cannot solve all perceived mismatches between contextual meaning and apparent background purpose, it certainly alleviates the standard concern that textualism * * * "makes a fortress out of the dictionary."[33]

(c) *Clues from other provisions.* The Federal Bankruptcy Code — which is an enormously complex statute, ridiculously simplified for present purposes — allows a debtor to obtain a "fresh start." By "going into bankruptcy," a person can shed all debts at the cost of giving up most assets. The debtor is allowed to keep certain property that the Code exempts from the reach of creditors. 11 U.S.C. § 522(d).

Say an auto mechanic has filed for bankruptcy. He owns a pick-up truck that he uses in his work, carrying tools and parts to his garage or to disabled vehicles. He argues that the truck is exempt under § 522(d)(6) and therefore need not be turned over to pay his debts.

(i) Subsection (d)(6) exempts "the debtor's aggregate interest in * * * tools of the trade of the debtor." Does this apply to the pick-up?

(ii) To quote more fully, the subsection exempts "the debtor's aggregate interest in implements, professional books, or tools, of the trade of the debtor." How does the reference to these other items affect your understanding of whether the truck is a tool of the trade?

(iii) To quote more fully, the Code exempts "the debtor's aggregate interest, not to exceed $2,025 in value, in implements, professional books, or tools of the trade of the debtor." Does the monetary cap affect your answer?

(iv) Subsection (d)(2) exempts "The debtor's interest, not to exceed $3,225 in value, in one motor vehicle." Is this relevant to the scope of subsection (d)(6)?

---

[33] John F. Manning, *Textualism and the Equity of the Statute*, 101 Colum. L. Rev. 1, 109–111 (2001).

As we added provisions to the statute, the initial provision remained unaltered — the question remained whether the truck could be a "tool of the trade." But our understanding of that phrase stems not just from reading this single provision in isolation, but by examining the full statute of which it is a part. With each additional piece of information about the statute, the argument for exempting the truck became weaker.

 ## 6. *Canons of Construction*

One technique for handling statutory ambiguity is to turn to the so-called "canons of construction." These are interpretive principles, rules of thumb as to textual meaning. In general, canons are not found in the statute but are invoked by judges on their own. The principle offered in *Nix*, for example, that words should receive their ordinary meaning, is a canon of construction. Many canons have the added dignity (or pomposity) that comes with being in Latin. In this section, we will see a few representative canons in action and try to assess their effect. This is far from a comprehensive survey of the canons, which are numerous.

(a)   Invoking Canons

There is no shortage of canons or of judicial citations to them. For as long as anyone alive can remember, however, observers have been suspicious as to whether the canons actually control — or even affect — interpretation. The following case should do nothing to put such suspicions to rest.

UNITED STATES v. SCRIMGEOUR
636 F.2d 1019 (5th Cir. 1981)

The Government appeals from the district court's dismissal of a five-count indictment charging William Scrimgeour with knowingly making false material declarations before a grand jury * * *.

Scrimgeour made material declarations under oath before a grand jury and subsequently reappeared and admitted those declarations to be false. * * *

The district court dismissed the perjury indictment on the basis of 18 U.S.C.A. § 1623(d), which provides that a person who recants or admits that he has made false declarations shall not be prosecuted for those declarations, "if, at the time the admission is made, the declaration has not substantially affected the proceeding, or it has not become manifest that such falsity has been or will be exposed." The district court held that "or" must be read in the disjunctive and not in the conjunctive, i.e., if either of the two conditions of Section 1623(d) is satisfied, recantation bars prosecution. [The Court of Appeals disagreed.] * * *

We must keep in mind several basic principles that relate to the construction of criminal statutes: A federal criminal statute should be construed narrowly in order to encompass only that conduct that Congress so intended to criminalize. Dunn v. United States, 442 U.S. 100, 112 (1979); United States v. Dudley, 581 F.2d 1193, 1197 (5th Cir. 1978). Although a criminal statute must be strictly construed, it must not be construed so strictly as to defeat the clear intention of the legislature. Barrett v. United States, 423 U.S. 212, 218 (1976); Huddleston v. United States,

415 U.S. 814, 831 (1974); United States v. Cook, 384 U.S. 257, 262–63 (1966). "The principle of strict construction 'does not mean that every criminal statute must be given the narrowest possible meaning in complete disregard of the purpose of the legislature.'" United States v. Levy, 579 F.2d 1332, 1337 (5th Cir. 1980), cert. denied, 440 U.S. 920 (1979), quoting United States v. Bramblett, 348 U.S. 503, 510 (1955).

A basic canon of statutory construction is that words should be interpreted as taking their ordinary and plain meaning. E.g., Perrin v. United States, 444 U.S. 37, 42 (1980). Although in interpretation of statutory language reference should first be made to the plain and literal meaning of the words, the overriding duty of a court is to give effect to the intent of the legislature. Flora v. United States, 357 U.S. 63, 65 (1958); United States v. Second National Bank of North Miami, 502 F.2d 535, 539 (5th Cir. 1974), cert. denied, 421 U.S. 912 (1975). A statute should ordinarily be interpreted according to its plain language, unless a clear contrary legislative intention is shown. United States v. Apfelbaum, 445 U.S. 115, 121 (1980). Although words should ordinarily be given their plain and ordinary meaning, that meaning must be in accord with the intent of the legislature. United States v. Cook, supra, 384 U.S. at 262–63; United States v. Mississippi Valley Co., 364 U.S. 520, 550 (1961); Rainwater v. United States, 356 U.S. 590, 593 (1958); United States v. Corbett, 215 U.S. 233, 242 (1909); United States v. Bryant, 563 F.2d 1227, 1230 (5th Cir. 1977), cert. denied, 435 U.S. 972 (1978). A court must construe a federal statute so as to give effect to the intent of Congress. Train v. Colorado Public Interest Research Group, Inc., 426 U.S. 1, 9–10 (1976); Philbrook v. Glodgett, 421 U.S. 707, 713 (1975); United States v. American Trucking Assns., 310 U.S. 534, 542 (1940); Johnson v. Southern Pacific Co., 196 U.S. 1, 18 (1904); Craig v. Finch, 425 F.2d 1005, 1008 (5th Cir. 1970).

"A criminal statute should be fairly construed in accordance with the legislative purpose behind its enactment." United States v. Levy, supra, 579 F.2d at 1337, citing United States v. Turley, 352 U.S. 407, (1957). See Hattaway v. United States, 304 F.2d 5, 8–9 (5th Cir. 1962). Criminal statutes are not to be interpreted in such a manner as to defeat or disregard the legislative purpose. See United States v. Culbert, 435 U.S. 371, 379 (1978); Barrett v. United States, 423 U.S. 212, 218 (1976); United States v. Corbett, supra, 215 U.S. at 242. * * *

The strict construction principle governing interpretation of criminal statutes "cannot provide a substitute for common sense, precedent and legislative history." United States v. Standard Oil Co., 384 U.S. 224, 225 (1966). The canon that penal statutes should be strictly construed "is not an inexorable command to override common sense and evident statutory purpose." United States v. Cook, supra, 384 U.S. at 262, quoting United States v. Brown, 33 U.S. 18, 25 (1948).

Although as a general rule the use of a disjunctive in a statute indicates that alternatives were intended, Quindlen v. Prudential Insurance Co. of America, 482 F.2d 876, 878 (5th Cir. 1973), where a strict grammatical construction of the word "or" would frustrate legislative intent, "or" has been read to mean "and." De Sylva v. Ballantine, 351 U.S. 570 (1956). The Supreme Court has stated that "[c]anons of construction ordinarily suggest that terms connected by a disjunctive be given

separate meanings, unless the context dictates otherwise. . . ." Reiter v. Sonotone Corp., 442 U.S. 330, 339 (1979).

The recantation provision of Section 1623(d) is an exception to the remaining subsections of Section 1623. The rule of strict construction also applies to exceptions or provisions of a criminal statute which exempt conduct otherwise within a statute and the exception is to be strictly construed against the defendant seeking to invoke its protection. United States v. Scharton, 285 U.S. 518, 521–22 (1932); Moore, supra, 613 F.2d at 1044–45. See United States v. An Article of Drug . . . "Bentex Ulcerine," 469 F.2d 875, 878 (5th Cir. 1972), cert. denied, 412 U.S. 938 (1973). The defendant must show that he is within an exception. McKelvey v. United States, 260 U.S. 353, 356–57 (1922); Green, Moore & Co. v. United States, 19 F.2d 130, 131 (5th Cir.), cert. denied, 275 U.S. 549 (1927).

The conjunctive reading of Section 1623(d) comports with accepted principles of statutory construction and is supported by the underlying congressional intent. We have determined that Congress did not intend to allow a perjurer to avoid prosecution by merely recanting before his perjury adversely affected a grand jury proceeding, even after his perjury had already been exposed. Therefore, we hold that recantation bars prosecution only when the defendant has satisfied both conditions of Section 1623(d).

Do you suppose Justice Scalia had opinions like *Scrimgeour* in mind when he wrote:

> Every judge, and indeed perhaps every lawyer, acquires over the years an intense dislike for certain oft-repeated statements that he is condemned to read, again and again, in the reported cases. It gets to be a kind of Chinese water torture: one's intelligence strapped down helplessly by the bonds of *stare decisis*, which require these cases to be read, and trickled upon, time after time, by certain ritual errors. It is usually impossible to cry out, even in a dissent, for these statements typically have little actual impact upon the decision of the case. They are part of its atmospherics, or of its overarching philosophy; it is fruitless to complain about the weather, and unlawyerlike to discuss philosophy rather than the holdings of the cases.[34]

The *Scrimgeour* opinion is actually somewhat more substantial than our edited version makes it appear. But are the excerpted portions of *any* value? Do the many canons cited by the court, each backed up by compendious case-law citations, guide it to its conclusion? Or are the canons rendered meaningless by (1) their vagueness, (2) their qualifiedness, and (3) the apparent existence of a canon for every possible proposition, including many that completely undercut one another?

---

[34] Antonin Scalia, *Assorted Canards of Contemporary Legal Analysis*, 40 CASE W. RES. L. REV. 581, 581 (1989).

This last characteristic is the subject of a famous critique of canonical interpretation by Karl Llewellyn.[35] In two columns, headed "thrust" and "parry," Llewellyn laid out 28 pairs of contradicting canons. For example: "A statute cannot go beyond its text" (thrust), but "To effect its purpose a statute may be implemented beyond its text" (parry). Or, "Statutes in derogation of the common law will not be extended by construction" (thrust) but "Such acts will be liberally construed if their nature is remedial" (parry). Since most statutes are *both* in derogation of the common law (that is why the legislature deemed it necessary to pass a statute) and remedial (in that they cure, or remedy, the state of affairs that prompted their passage), these two canons will fight to a draw in the majority of statutory cases. (One of the defects of *Scrimgeour* is that unintentionally it reads a bit like Llewellyn's thrust and parry.) Llewellyn's debunking suggested that the canons were meaningless boilerplate added after-the-fact to justify a result reached on other grounds, which grounds were now camouflaged by the canons.

[I]n the years following Llewellyn's work, it was conceivable that the outdated reliance on maxims would soon give way to a more enlightened approach to statutory interpretation.

This optimism did not prove warranted. * * *

Indeed, there is reason to believe that the maxims are making something of a comeback. Over the past decade, the Supreme Court has edged steadily away from reliance on legislative history in favor of plain meaning. Moreover, the Court increasingly is willing to defer to statutory language even when the results appear misguided as a matter of social policy — thus undermining, although not entirely repudiating, the doctrine that a matter may be within the letter of a statute yet not be within its spirit. All this enhanced attention to text creates a potentially fertile ground for a revival of the maxims.[36]

(b) Types of Canons

The canons fall into two general categories. One set of canons are "linguistic." These reflect basic rules of grammar or usage; they rest on assumptions about how speakers use words and, in theory, steer the interpreter toward a reading consistent with legislative intent. For example, Justice Holmes could have, but did not, invoke a linguistic canon in *McBoyle*, the is-an-airplane-a-vehicle case. The canon is *"ejusdem generis,"* which holds that a general term following a list of specific items should be interpreted in light of the specific items. Do you see how that canon supports the Court's holding? The Court in *Ressam*, the carrying explosives during a felony case, is implicitly relying on a canon, *viz.* the principle that every word in a statute must have some meaning ("no surplusage"). If "during" meant "in relation to," then the latter phrase would be surplusage in § 924(c), so "during" must mean something else.

[35] Karl N. Llewellyn, *Remarks on the Theory of Appellate Decision and the Rules or Canons about How Statutes are to be Construed*, 3 VAND. L. REV. 395 (1950).

[36] Geoffrey P. Miller, *Pragmatics and the Maxims of Interpretation*, 1990 WIS. L. REV. 1179, 1180–1181.

The second category of canons consists of general substantive principles. Think back to *Riggs v. Palmer* and the principle that no one should benefit from his own wrong. The substantive canons include such propositions as: remedial statutes are to be broadly construed, penal statutes should be construed strictly, i.e. in favor of the defendant ("the rule of lenity"), ambiguous provisions for benefits to members of the Armed Services are to be construed in the beneficiaries' favor, statutes are presumed to apply prospectively only, statutes will be interpreted to avoid doubts as to their constitutionality, etc. Such canons are not neutral principles of English usage; they are frank policy or value choices that direct courts toward particular substantive outcomes. Where might courts legitimately discover such interpretive principles?

Which type of canon would you expect to be more controversial? The linguistic canons at least in theory help identify legislative intent; they are aids to the court operating as faithful agent. The substantive canons, in contrast, do not necessarily help the court determine what the legislature intended; instead, they point the court to, or justify, a particular substantive outcome in the face of uncertainty.

(c)   A Linguistic Canon — *Expressio Unius*

Black's Law Dictionary defines "expressio unius est exclusio alterius" as follows: "A canon of construction holding that to express or include one thing implies the exclusion of the other, or the alternative." It's common sense, isn't it? When Mom says that Sue and Bobbie can watch TV, that means that Joey and Jill can't.

We have already spent a good deal of time with a case where the canon would seem to apply: *Holy Trinity*. Recall that the statute specified certain classes of persons who were exempt from its prohibition. This expression of some (such as actors) would seem to exclude others (such as ministers). In *Holy Trinity*, however, the Court rejected the result suggested by the canon. Compare *United States v. Brockamp*, 519 U.S. 347 (1997). A taxpayer who pays more than she owes can request a refund, but the Internal Revenue Code imposes a time limit:

> Claim for credit or refund of an overpayment of any tax imposed by this title in respect of which tax the taxpayer is required to file a return shall be filed by the taxpayer within 3 years from the time the return was filed or 2 years from the time the tax was paid, whichever of such periods expires the later. * * * No credit or refund shall be allowed or made after the expiration of the period of limitation prescribed * * * unless a claim for * * * refund is filed * * * within such period.

26 U.S.C. §§ 6511(a), (b)(1). In *Brockamp*, several taxpayers had paid taxes they did not owe but missed the deadline for requesting a refund. They explained that they had missed the deadline through no fault of their own but because of a mental disability (senility in one case, alcoholism in the other), and that the familiar general principle of "equitable tolling" should be applied to excuse the delay and allow them to file a late refund request. The court unanimously rejected this argument. A key part of its reasoning was that § 6511 did contain *some* exceptions to the deadline, but not this one:

In addition, § 6511 sets forth explicit exceptions to its basic time limits, and those very specific exceptions do not include "equitable tolling." See § 6511(d) (establishing special time limit rules for refunds related to operating losses, credit carrybacks, foreign taxes, self-employment taxes, worthless securities, and bad debts) * * *. Section 6511's detail, its technical language, the iteration of the limitations in both procedural and substantive forms, and the explicit listing of exceptions, taken together, indicate to us that Congress did not intend courts to read other unmentioned, open-ended, "equitable" exceptions into the statute that it wrote.

NOTE ON THE LIMITS OF *EXPRESSIO UNIUS*

As you see, sometimes courts follow the *expressio unius* canon and sometimes they don't. Judges frequently assert that it is only a guide rather than an inexorable command. The question, of course, is when it should be adhered to and when not.

(i) Is silence to be expected?

Suppose a statute forbids anyone under eighteen to drive a vehicle on the public streets. The *expressio unius* canon would suggest, uncontroversially, that a 16-year old remains free to drive a tractor on a private farm:

> When a legislature expressly provides a particular bit of information, it creates a "conversational" setting between the legislature and its audience — courts and citizens — in which other information of the same type is expected to be conveyed. By virtue of banning drivers under eighteen from the public streets, the legislature has made a statement about the locations where the statute applies. Since the legislature is obviously capable of stating other areas in which the statute applies, the fact that it did not do so gives rise to the implicature that it did not intend the statute to apply in settings other than in those expressly mentioned. * * *

> Consider also the closely related (perhaps identical) principle of the negative pregnant. If a reporter were to file a news report that "Imelda Marcos owns twenty-five pairs of shoes," this would not be inconsistent, as a logical matter, with the proposition that Imelda Marcos owns two thousand pairs of shoes. But aside from the fact that the report is not news (lots of people own twenty-five pairs of shoes), the statement represents a flouting [of an important convention] * * * because it provides less information than would be expected by readers of the report (we expect to be told the total number of shoes, not just a partial count). Similarly, regarding legislation, if a statute says, "All cats born on or after January 1, 1989, shall be vaccinated for feline leukemia," this is not inconsistent logically with the proposition that cats born *before* January 1, 1989, shall be vaccinated; yet any reader would understand intuitively that construing the statute to cover this second class of cats would flout a standard convention of interpretation. If your cat is born before January 1, 1989, and you do not

vaccinate, you are in the clear as far as the law is concerned * * *.[37]

Where do our expectations, or intuitions, about whether silence would be expected come from? In part, they come from the text of the statute itself. That is why the negative inference in *Wadsworth v. Siek* (slayer statute does not apply to manslaughterer) was stronger than that in *Deem v. Millikin* (murderer inherits under general statutes of descent).

(ii) Is the canon realistic?

A second concern is whether the canon rests on an unrealistic understanding of the legislative process. It is a common objection that the legislature's failure to address something is far more likely to reflect inadvertence, an inability to agree, or a delegation to the courts or an agency than a purposeful omission.

> Most canons of statutory construction go wrong not because they misconceive the nature of judicial interpretation or of the legislative or political process but because they impute omniscience to Congress. Omniscience is always an unrealistic assumption, and particularly so when one is dealing with the legislative process. The basic reason why statutes are so frequently ambiguous in application is not that they are poorly drafted — though many are — and not that the legislators failed to agree on just what they wanted to accomplish in the statute — though often they do fail — but that a statute necessarily is drafted in advance of, and with imperfect appreciation for the problems that will be encountered in, its application. * * * The canon *expressio unius est exclusio alterius* is * * * based on the assumption of legislative omniscience, because it would make sense only if all omissions in legislative drafting were deliberate.[38]

Does this criticism justify the Court's rejection of the *expressio unius* canon in *Holy Trinity*? Should *no* court ever adhere to it? Should we banish it from the legal vocabulary?

A good deal of political science seems to underscore this criticism of the canon's unrealistic assumptions. For example, Professor Popkin suggests that an interest-group based view of the political process argues against the canon.

> [P]olitical groups seeking a benefit do not care much about how a statute might be interpreted without an express provision. They want an express statement on which they can rely, regardless of whether the best interpretation of the statute would have provided the benefit in any event. In other words, expressly helping person X may say nothing about whether persons X, Y and Z are already helped under the statute. Person X may just have the legislature's ear.[39]

---

[37] Miller, *supra* note 36, at 1196.

[38] Richard A. Posner, *Statutory Interpretation — In the Classroom and in the Courtroom*, 50 U. Chi. L. Rev. 800, 811, 813 (1983).

[39] William D. Popkin, Materials on Legislation: Political Language and the Political Process 223–224 (5th ed. 2009).

Yet perhaps this view of the political process supports something like *expressio unius*. Consider Judge Easterbrook's endorsement of the Supreme Court's decision in *Block v. Community Nutrition Institute*.[40] The case arose under a 1937 law that keeps milk prices high by allowing producers to fix prices in the form of "marketing agreements" under the Secretary's general supervision. The question in the case was whether milk consumers could sue the Secretary of Agriculture over a decision limiting the availability of powdered milk.

The Court unanimously enforced the bargain of 1937 and dismissed the suit. It characterized the Act as what it is: "a cooperative venture among the Secretary, handlers [i.e., middlemen], and producers the principal purposes of which are to raise the price of agricultural products and to establish an orderly system for marketing them." It tracked down the compromises and noticed that "[n]owhere in the Act . . . is there an express provision for participation by consumers in any proceeding. In a complex scheme of this type, the omission of such a provision is sufficient reason to believe that Congress intended to foreclose consumer participation in the regulatory process." * * *

This is not a simplistic "expressio unius est exclusio alterius" approach. The Court does not presume an omniscient legislature that anticipates all problems or provides all solutions. [Its] approach is based, rather, on a sound appreciation of the difference between interest-group and public-interest legislation. Interest-group legislation requires adherence to the terms of the compromise. The court cannot "improve" on a pact that has no content other than the exact bargain among the competing interests, because the pact has no purpose. Recognition of the way in which economic legislation comes to be thus turns out to have the most fundamental implications for how the Justices approach their functions.[41]

What exactly is the difference between the "simplistic" approach Easterbrook derides and what he sees as the more sophisticated approach taken by the Court in this case? Can Easterbrook's endorsement of this opinion be generalized into an endorsement of the expressio unius canon? If you reject Easterbrook's public choice premises, is that implicitly a rejection of the expressio unius canon?

Are Popkin and Easterbrook operating from the same premises? Who is right? Both, perhaps?

(d) A Substantive Canon — The Presumption Against Interference with State Governmental Operations

Suppose the Court adopted the following rationale in *Nix v. Hedden*, the is-a-tomato-a-fruit case. The statute itself being unclear, we should read it in light of the fundamental American commitment to the free market. In doubtful cases, then, tariffs do not apply. Therefore, for purposes of this statute, tomatoes are fruits. If

---

[40] 467 U.S. 340 (1984).

[41] Frank H. Easterbrook, *The Supreme Court, 1984 Term — Foreword: The Court and the Economic System*, 98 HARV. L. REV. 4, 50–51 (1984).

Congress wants to tax their importation, it can do so, but it must do so more clearly.

That argument has (at least) two problematic steps. The first is the premise that the statute is ambiguous. Is it really so unclear that the court should resort to some sort of background principle, or would the court be inventing an ambiguity to reach the result it prefers? Second, where does the Court find the substantive principle in light of which it interprets the statute — and how does it know it has the right one? Perhaps the statute should be read in light of a basic commitment not to the free market but to protectionism, which is also a longstanding principle of economic policy for this and other countries.

Bear these two questions in mind as you read the following case. The case involves a "clear statement rule." These are canons that establish a strong presumption that Congress has or has not done something; Congress can trump the presumption, but it must do so through language that is crystal clear.

GREGORY v. ASHCROFT
501 U.S. 452 (1991)

JUSTICE O'CONNOR delivered the opinion of the Court. * * *

[The Age Discrimination in Employment Act (ADEA) forbids employment discrimination on the basis of age. The Act protects all employees, including state employees, subject to certain exceptions. The following are not "employees" under the Act, and therefore not protected by it:

> any person elected to public office in any State or political subdivision of any State by the qualified voters thereof, or any person chosen by such officer to be on such officer's personal staff, or an appointee on the policymaking level or an immediate adviser with respect to the exercise of the constitutional or legal powers of the office.

29 U.S.C. § 630(f).

The Missouri Constitution provides that all judges must retire at the age of 70. A group of appointed Missouri judges challenged this provision under the ADEA. If the judges are "employees" under the Act, they win; it is well-settled that the Act forbids a policy of mandatory retirement. The state argued, however, that appointed judges are exempted by § 630(f). The lower courts held that judges are not "employees" under the Act.]

As every schoolchild learns, our Constitution establishes a system of dual sovereignty between the States and the Federal Government. * * *

This federalist structure of joint sovereigns preserves to the people numerous advantages. It assures a decentralized government that will be more sensitive to the diverse needs of a heterogeneous society; it increases opportunity for citizen involvement in democratic processes; it allows for more innovation and experimentation in government; and it makes government more responsive by putting the States in competition for a mobile citizenry.

Perhaps the principal benefit of the federalist system is a check on abuses of government power. * * *

The present case concerns a state constitutional provision through which the people of Missouri establish a qualification for those who sit as their judges. This provision goes beyond an area traditionally regulated by the States; it is a decision of the most fundamental sort for a sovereign entity. Through the structure of its government, and the character of those who exercise government authority, a State defines itself as a sovereign. "It is obviously essential to the independence of the States, and to their peace and tranquility, that their power to prescribe the qualifications of their own officers . . . should be exclusive, and free from external interference, except so far as plainly provided by the Constitution of the United States."

Congressional interference with this decision of the people of Missouri, defining their constitutional officers, would upset the usual constitutional balance of federal and state powers. For this reason, "it is incumbent upon the federal courts to be certain of Congress' intent before finding that federal law overrides" this balance. We explained recently:

"If Congress intends to alter the 'usual constitutional balance between the States and the Federal Government,' it must make its intention to do so 'unmistakably clear in the language of the statute.' * * *"

This plain statement rule is nothing more than an acknowledgement that the States retain substantial sovereign powers under our constitutional scheme, powers with which Congress does not readily interfere. * * *

Governor Ashcroft contends that the § 630(f) exclusion of certain public officials also excludes judges, like petitioners, who are appointed to office by the Governor * * *. First, he argues, these judges are selected by an elected official and, because they make policy, are "[a]ppointees on the policymaking level."

Petitioners counter that judges merely resolve factual disputes and decide questions of law; they do not make policy. * * *

"[A]ppointee at the policymaking level," particularly in the context of the other exceptions that surround it, is an odd way for Congress to exclude judges; a plain statement that judges are not "employees" would seem the most efficient phrasing. But in this case we are not looking for a plain statement that judges are excluded. We will not read the ADEA to cover state judges unless Congress has made it clear that judges are included. This does not mean that the Act must mention judges explicitly, though it does not. Rather, it must be plain to anyone reading the Act that it covers judges. In the context of a statute that plainly excludes most important state public officials, "appointee on the policymaking level" is sufficiently broad that we cannot conclude that the statute plainly covers appointed state judges. Therefore, it does not.

Justice WHITE, with whom Justice STEVENS joins, concurring in part, dissenting in part, and concurring in the judgment.

* * * [T]he majority * * * imposes upon Congress a "plain statement" requirement. The majority claims to derive this requirement from the plain

statement approach developed [in prior cases]. The issue in those cases, however, was whether Congress intended a particular statute to extend to the States at all. * * * In the present case, by contrast, Congress has expressly extended the coverage of the ADEA to the States and their employees. Its intention to regulate age discrimination by States is thus "unmistakably clear in the language of the statute." The only dispute is over the precise details of the statute's application. We have never extended the plain statement approach that far, and the majority offers no compelling reason for doing so.

* * * The vagueness of the majority's rule undoubtedly will lead States to assert that various federal statutes no longer apply to a wide variety of State activities if Congress has not expressly referred to those activities in the statute. Congress, in turn, will be forced to draft long and detailed lists of which particular state functions it meant to regulate.

The imposition of such a burden on Congress is particularly out of place in the context of the ADEA. Congress already has stated that all "individuals employed by any employer" are protected by the ADEA unless they are expressly excluded by one of the exceptions in the definition of "employee." The majority, however, turns the statute on its head, holding that state judges are not protected by the ADEA because "Congress has [not] made it clear that judges are included." *Cf. EEOC v. Wyoming*, 460 U.S. 226 (1983), where we held that state game wardens are covered by the ADEA, even though such employees are not expressly included within the ADEA's scope.

NOTES AND QUESTIONS

(1)   Where does the majority's clear statement rule come from?

(2)   Suppose that, the presumption in favor of state governmental autonomy aside, the usual tools of construction indicate that (although the matter is not crystal clear) the ADEA does apply to judges. Given that, was the case correctly decided?

(3)   Is it realistic to expect Congress to have expressly applied the ADEA to judges? Going forward, after and in light of the decision in *Gregory*, is it realistic to expect Congress to legislate with the necessary specificity to overcome the presumption? If not, is that good or bad?

(4)   The Americans with Disabilities Act prohibits discrimination on the basis of disability. Title II of the Act provides: "[N]o qualified individual with a disability shall, by reason of such disability, be excluded from participation in or be denied the benefits of the services, programs, or activities of a public entity, or be subjected to discrimination by any such entity." The statutory definition of "public entity" includes "any department, agency, special purpose district, or other instrumentality of a State or States or local government." Is an inmate in a state prison covered by the statute? *See* Pennsylvania Dep't of Corrections v. Yeskey, 524 U.S. 206 (1998).

(5)   A central question about substantive canons is whether they amount to judicial lawmaking. With which, if any, of the following assessments do you agree?

(a) In applying substantive canons, judges are simply furthering their own preferred policies. Rather than adhering to the legislative command, judges are, with unusual frankness, making policy themselves.

(b) Yes, substantive canons amount to judicial policymaking, but that is inevitable. When all other things are equal, as they sometimes are in statutory cases, the court has to rely on *something*. Indeed, it shows relatively greater restraint for courts to adhere to a limited and known set of substantive values than for them to apply private whim while pretending to follow legislative commands.

(c) Substantive canons are not judicial legislation. First, they do not originate with the judges themselves, but are drawn from other sources, such as the constitution and the common law. Second, legislatures are presumed to act with knowledge of the canons; the passage of ambiguous statutes is an implicit endorsement of the canons and a delegation to the courts to apply them. Third, judicial reliance on substantive principles does not intrude on legislative authority because the legislature remains completely free to legislate around or in contradiction of the canons.

CONCLUDING NOTE ON CANONICAL INTERPRETATION

Debate about the content and efficacy of interpretive canons continues; indeed it is more heated now than it has been for some time. In particular, many scholars look to substantive canons as a way for "public values" to influence statutory interpretation in a systematic and principled way. The most thorough defense of canonical interpretation comes from Professor Cass Sunstein. Sunstein argues that a properly developed set of interpretive principles would bring candor, clarity, openness, certainty, rationality, and justice to statutory interpretation.[42] While not all share his confidence, debate over, and judicial invocation of, interpretive canons will be with us for some time.

C.   IGNORING UNAMBIGUOUS MEANING

The cases we have looked at so far in this chapter have involved unclear language; the court was forced to choose one of several plausible meanings. Now we turn to the opposite problem: when, if ever, should a court *ignore unambiguous* meaning?

UNITED STATES v. LOCKE
471 U.S. 84 (1985)

[Section 314(a) of the Federal Land Policy and Management Act of 1976 requires all persons holding mining claims on federal land to file an annual notice of claim with the Bureau of Land Management (BLM) "prior to December 31." Section 314(c) of the Act provides that failure to comply with this requirement "shall be deemed conclusively to constitute an abandonment of the mining claim * * * by the owner." The appellees filed their 1980 notice on December 31. The

---

[42] *See* CASS R. SUNSTEIN, AFTER THE RIGHTS REVOLUTION 147–192 (1990).

government thereupon took their claim, which was valued at several million dollars, on the ground that the filing was late. In an opinion by Justice Marshall, the Court upheld the government's action.] * * *

Before the District Court, appellees asserted that the § 314(a) requirement of a filing "prior to December 31 of each year" should be construed to require a filing "on or before December 31." Thus, appellees argued, their December 31 filing had in fact complied with the statute, and the BLM had acted ultra vires in voiding their claims.

* * * It is clear to us that the plain language of the statute simply cannot sustain the gloss appellees would put on it. As even counsel for appellees conceded at oral argument, § 314(a) "is a statement that Congress wanted it filed by December 30th. I think that is a clear statement. . . ." While we will not allow a literal reading of a statute to produce a result "demonstrably at odds with the intentions of its drafters," with respect to filing deadlines a literal reading of Congress' words is generally the only proper reading of those words. To attempt to decide whether some date other than the one set out in the statute is the date actually "intended" by Congress is to set sail on an aimless journey, for the purpose of a filing deadline would be just as well served by nearly any date a court might choose as by the date Congress has in fact set out in the statute. "Actual purpose is sometimes unknown," and such is the case with filing deadlines; as might be expected, nothing in the legislative history suggests why Congress chose December 30 over December 31, or over September 1 (the end of the assessment year for mining claims, 30 U. S. C. § 28), as the last day on which the required filings could be made. But "[d]eadlines are inherently arbitrary," while fixed dates "are often essential to accomplish necessary results." Faced with the inherent arbitrariness of filing deadlines, we must, at least in a civil case, apply by its terms the date fixed by the statute. * * *

[W]e are not insensitive to the problems posed by congressional reliance on the words "prior to December 31." But the fact that Congress might have acted with greater clarity or foresight does not give courts a carte blanche to redraft statutes in an effort to achieve that which Congress is perceived to have failed to do. "There is a basic difference between filling a gap left by Congress' silence and rewriting rules that Congress has affirmatively and specifically enacted." Nor is the Judiciary licensed to attempt to soften the clear import of Congress' chosen words whenever a court believes those words lead to a harsh result. On the contrary, deference to the supremacy of the Legislature, as well as recognition that Congressmen typically vote on the language of a bill, generally requires us to assume that "the legislative purpose is expressed by the ordinary meaning of the words used." * * * The phrase "prior to" may be clumsy, but its meaning is clear. Under these circumstances, we are obligated to apply the "prior to December 31" language by its terms. * * *

[T]he District Court held that, even if the statute required a filing on or before December 30, appellees had "substantially complied" by filing on December 31. We cannot accept this view of the statute.

The notion that a filing deadline can be complied with by filing sometime after the deadline falls due is, to say the least, a surprising notion, and it is a notion

without limiting principle. If 1-day late filings are acceptable, 10-day late filings might be equally acceptable, and so on in a cascade of exceptions that would engulf the rule erected by the filing deadline; yet regardless of where the cutoff line is set, some individuals will always fall just on the other side of it. Filing deadlines, like statutes of limitations, necessarily operate harshly and arbitrarily with respect to individuals who fall just on the other side of them, but if the concept of a filing deadline is to have any content, the deadline must be enforced. "Any less rigid standard would risk encouraging a lax attitude toward filing dates." A filing deadline cannot be complied with, substantially or otherwise, by filing late — even by one day.

STEVENS, J., dissenting. * * * The statutory scheme requires periodic filings on a calendar-year basis. The end of the calendar year is, of course, correctly described either as "prior to the close of business on December 31," or "on or before December 31," but it is surely understandable that the author of § 314 might inadvertently use the words "prior to December 31" when he meant to refer to the end of the calendar year. As the facts of this case demonstrate, the scrivener's error is one that can be made in good faith. The risk of such an error is, of course, the greatest when the reference is to the end of the calendar year. That it was in fact an error seems rather clear to me because no one has suggested any rational basis for omitting just one day from the period in which an annual filing may be made, and I would not presume that Congress deliberately created a trap for the unwary by such an omission.

NOTES AND QUESTIONS

(1)   The Court is correct that "prior to December 31" is crystal clear, isn't it? Is *Locke* an example of the Court doing what Justice Holmes said its job was — not to "do justice" but to "play the game according to the rules"? Or did it misunderstand the rules?

(2)   Do you think that Justice Marshall would have so relentlessly applied a statute that provided amnesty for illegal aliens if they applied "prior to December 31st" to a bedraggled petitioner who emerged *on* December 31st? January 10th? Assume he would have been more solicitous toward such a litigant. Would such divergent results be unjustifiably inconsistent, or appropriately cognizant of differing circumstances? If the latter, is it not for Congress and not the courts to take such considerations into account?

(3)   Consider the following formal argument for adhering to the plain import of the statutory text, as the *Locke* Court did:

> [I]f we insist that the audience is responsible for what the legislator meant rather than for what he said, we must concede that either (a) the statute consists of the string of words actually on the rolls, in which case that statute (*i.e.*, that string of words) is not binding, or (b) the statute is

binding but consists of a different string of words from that on the rolls.[43]

Neither (a) nor (b) seems acceptable; statutes are binding, and they are found in statute books. Are these really the only two choices?

(4)   Consider the following arguments for ignoring plain meaning. Each has been relied on by courts at one time or another; all three can be found in *Holy Trinity*. Think about whether each of these (a) makes sense and (b) would justify a different result in *Locke*.

(a) *Absurd Results*. Even committed textualists generally concede that a judge should not follow the literal meaning of statutory language in such circumstances. *See, e.g., Public Citizen v. United States Dep't of Justice*, 491 U.S. 440, 470–71 (Kennedy, J., concurring) ("Where the plain language of the statue would lead to 'patently absurd consequences,' that 'Congress could not *possibly* have intended,' we need not apply the language" literally.). Back in 1819, Chief Justice Marshall wrote that judges could ignore text when "the absurdity and injustice of applying the provision to the case, would be so monstrous, that all mankind would, without hesitation, unite in rejecting the application." *Sturges v. Crowninshield*, 17 U.S. (4 Wheat.) 122, 203 (1819).

The absurdity doctrine poses two sorts of problems. One is theoretical. What is the justification for such an exception? The parenthetical quotation from *Public Citizen* sounds in intentionalism; and that is the standard view. But how can we be at all certain of what Congress intended once we ignore the words it used? On the other hand, if we are to be textualists, can the absurdity doctrine be squared with the view that only the text is "law"? For some, permission to ignore absurd results makes textualism more palatable. But others have argued that resort to the absurd results canon is especially problematic for textualists; once one accepts some deviation from text, then it's all just a matter of degree, and textualism's basic claim collapses. Indeed, justifying a departure from text as "absurd" is arguably *worse* than relying on other extrinsic sources. "If textualists object to strong intentionalism in general, the absurdity doctrine is particularly problematic because it permits judges to alter clear statutory language based on vaguely defined social values, rather than sources (such as legislative history) that are more immediately linked to the legislative process."[44]

The second problem concerning the absurdity doctrine is intensely practical: How absurd is absurd enough? What's absurd to one judge will be merely odd to another and perhaps plausible to a third. Was the strict reading of the statute in *Locke* "patently absurd"? Justice Breyer gives a laundry list of silly prosecutions that are possible under the majority's holding in *Ressam, supra* page 323; should this have swayed the Court?

(b) *Legislative Intent*. In some circumstances, the apparent meaning of the statutory text may be inconsistent with actual legislative intent, as best as it can be discerned. How one can discern legislative intent other than by reading the statute is the subject of Chapter 12. But what do you think the court's job is, to follow text

---

[43]   Gerald C. MacCallum, Jr., *Legislative Intent*, 75 Yale L.J. 754, 762–763 (1966).

[44]   John F. Manning, *The Absurdity Doctrine*, 116 Harv. L. Rev. 2387, 2392 (2003).

or follow intent? Judicial admonitions such as the following are not uncommon:

> If Congress enacted into law something different from what it intended, then it should amend the statute to conform it to its intent. "It is beyond our province to rescue Congress from its drafting errors, and to provide for what we might think . . . is the preferred result." This allows both of our branches to adhere to our respected, and respective, constitutional roles. In the meantime, we must determine intent from the statute before us.[45]

On the other hand, Judge Posner has written that *Locke* was wrongly decided because it really does conflict with legislative intent.

> [I]t seems highly likely that when Congress said "prior to December 31" it meant "by December 31." The end of the year is a common deadline, and no explanation of why Congress might have wanted to set the deadline in this statute a day earlier, thereby creating a trap for valuable property rights, has ever been suggested. * * *

> Reading "prior to December 31" literally was a wooden, unimaginative response to the legislative command, like that of the assistant in MacCallum's example who, when told to fetch all the ashtrays he could find, ripped some off the walls.[46] That was a case where the command was (to the outsider to the culture in which it was given) incomplete. *Locke* is a case where the command was garbled. We encounter such cases frequently in everyday life. Suppose I ask my secretary to call Z and tell him I must cancel our lunch date today — I have been called out of town suddenly. The secretary notices that on my calendar I have marked lunch with Y, not Z, but it is too late to check back with me, because I have left the office and cannot be reached. Is it not plain that the secretary should call Y, even though there was no semantic or internal ambiguity in my instruction? And is not *Locke* a similar case? Well, you may say, statutes are not casual commands; surely if Congress had meant *by* December 31 it would have said so. But it is not unusual for statutes to contain inexplicable typographical or logical errors. Statutory drafting is often a rushed and careless process.[47]

Suppose you are convinced that, as Judge Posner argues, Congress *meant* to require a filing before the end of the year. Does Justice Marshall assert otherwise? Does that mean that the case was wrongly decided? Recall Justice Holmes's famous aphorism: "We do not inquire what the legislature meant; we ask only what the statute means."[48] Can Holmes's approach be defended?

What considerations could justify adhering to the plain language of the statute even though it seems to conflict with legislative intent?

---

[45] Lamie v. United States Trustee, 540 U.S. 526, 542 (2004).

[46] [Ed. Fn.] The reference is to MacCallum, *supra* note 43, at 771–775.

[47] Richard A. Posner, The Problems of Jurisprudence 267–268 (1990).

[48] Oliver Wendell Holmes, Jr., *The Theory of Legal Interpretation*, 12 Harv. L. Rev. 417, 419 (1899). For a fuller excerpt, *see supra* page 267.

Consider the following defense of *Locke*:

[The dissent makes the] assertion that the "text [of the statute] cannot possibly reflect the actual intent of Congress." If this assertion was correct and relevant, either the statute was simply not binding or the statute *was* binding but consisted of a different string of words from that in the statute books (*i.e.*, it actually said "on or before December 31" or "prior to the close of business on December 31"). In some cases, it may be proper to suggest that unstated words are implicit in statutory language — *if* the context is strong enough to imply them — but to read a statute as if "actual intent" could alter the string of words in the statute denies the force of law to validly enacted legislation. Moreover, when the "actual intent" of Congress is divined solely from the assumption that Congress could not have meant what it said, judges deny to the statute the force of law based largely on what their own intent would have been.[49]

[I]n one sense, the intent of the legislature is probably best understood as requiring that claims be filed "on or before" December 31. * * * [But] the Senators and Representatives voted for the *wrong language*. If asked the meaning of the statutory language that they adopted, most legislators would probably agree that a claim filed on December 31 was too late. Moreover, and perhaps more to the point, a private citizen reading the statute could have only that understanding. Admittedly, in *Locke* itself, no private rights would have been lost had the Court ruled in favor of the claim. However, each time a court ignores the plain meaning of a statute, confidence in statutory language generally is undermined. Thus, the Supreme Court was correct in holding that a claim filed on December 31 was not timely.[50]

Do you agree that a citizen could only have read the statute in the way the Court did?

(c) *Background norms.* A court might reject apparent textual meaning because it conflicts with important background norms.

Judge Posner again:

A normal English speaker does not interpret a message merely by consulting the dictionary definitions of each word (assume these definitions are stored in his brain) and the relevant grammatical and syntactical principles. He does not ignore what I have called external ambiguity. He consults the totality of his relevant experience, which in my example of the direction to cancel a lunch date includes what is written on my calendar; * * * in *Locke* includes other passages in the statute, social practices with regard to deadlines, and arguably a background norm against setting traps

---

[49] UNITED STATES DEP'T OF JUSTICE, OFFICE OF LEGAL POLICY, USING AND MISUSING LEGISLATIVE HISTORY 24 (1989).

[50] Earl M. Maltz, *Statutory Interpretation and Legislative Power: The Case for a Modified Intentionalist Approach*, 63 TUL. L. REV. 1, 23 (1988).

for the unwary * * *.[51]

Is reliance on "background norms" defensible? Would it lead to a different result in *Locke*?

UNITED STATES v. WELLS FARGO BANK
485 U.S. 351 (1988)

BRENNAN, J., delivered the opinion of the [unanimous] Court.

In the late 1930's, the Nation faced a severe housing shortage. To meet that crisis, Congress enacted the Housing Act of 1937, 50 Stat. 888 et seq., which was designed to stimulate local financing of housing projects by empowering state and local housing authorities to issue tax-free obligations, termed "Projects Notes." [Section 5(e) of the Act provides that Projects Notes are "exempt from all taxation imposed by the United States."] For almost 50 years after the Act's passage, it was generally assumed that this exempted the Notes from federal income tax, but not from federal estate tax. However, in 1984, [a Federal District Court ruled that Project Notes were also exempt from federal estate taxes. The appellees, executors of estates who had paid estate taxes on Project Notes, sought refunds, which were denied by the Commissioner of Internal Revenue. Appellees thereupon filed this suit.]

* * * Well before the Housing Act was passed, an exemption of property from all taxation had an understood meaning: the property was exempt from direct taxation, but certain privileges of ownership, such as the right to transfer the property, could be taxed. Underlying this doctrine is the distinction between an excise tax, which is levied upon the use or transfer of property even though it might be measured by the property's value, and a tax levied upon the property itself. The former has historically been permitted even where the latter has been constitutionally or statutorily forbidden. The estate tax is a form of excise tax. Consistent with this understanding, on the rare occasions when Congress has exempted property from estate taxation it has generally adverted explicitly to that tax, rather than generically to "all taxation." Placed in context, then, § 5(e) does not stand for appellees' proposition that Project Notes were intended to be exempt from estate taxes; it stands for exactly the opposite.

Appellees attempt to bolster their contrary view with various indicia of an alleged congressional intent. Although these considerations were found compelling in *Haffner*, we conclude, as did the Tax Court in Estate of Egger v. Commissioner, 89 T. C. 726 (1987), that the factors appellees rely upon, whether considered alone or in combination, are insufficient to demonstrate that Congress intended to exempt Project Notes from estate taxation in contravention of the understood meaning of § 5(e), a demonstration which must be unambiguous under the principle disfavoring implied tax exemptions.

* * * [Appellees pointed out that in a separate section, the Housing Act expressly exempted certain obligations from "all taxation (except surtaxes, estate,

---

[51] POSNER, *supra* note 47, at 268–269.

inheritance, and gift taxes)."] The familiar argument goes that Congress knew how to limit the scope of the exemption when it wanted to do so; its decision not to include limiting language in § 5(e), in light of an express limitation in § 20(b), demonstrates an intent to exempt Project Notes from estate tax. [The Court had an explanation, not worth going into here, as to why express reference was necessary in the other provision and not in § 5(e). In addition, it stated,] [w]e cannot attribute to Congress an intent to break new ground in tax law by cleverly hiding an estate tax exemption, discernable only by comparing two unrelated provisions of the Housing Act. Nor would it make sense for Congress to legislate in such a bizarre fashion. If Congress really wanted to create an especially broad tax exemption for Project Notes, as appellees assert, one would expect it to do so notoriously enough to attract investors, not surreptitiously enough to evade detection for half a century.

Appellees' second indicator of congressional intent is a statement made by Senator Walsh during the floor debate. In the midst of a lengthy speech, he stated: "Obligations, including interest thereon, issued by public housing agencies, . . . are to be exempt from all taxation now or hereafter imposed by the United States. In other words, the bill gives the public housing agencies the right to issue tax-exempt bonds, which means they are free from income tax, surtax, estate, gift and inheritance taxes." 81 Cong. Rec. 8085 (1937). If, as appears from the statement's structure, the Senator intended to offer a definition of "tax-exempt bonds," then we must conclude that he misspoke, for as we have already demonstrated, tax-exempt bonds were presumed to be exempt only from direct taxes. Even if, as appellees assert, the Senator intended to refer solely to Project Notes, we do not deem his statement compelling in this case. The relevant passage comes in the middle of a long speech, and no similar expression is to be found in any other legislative debate or document. This short, isolated comment simply cannot overcome the understood meaning of § 5(e) and the presumption against implied tax exemptions.

Appellees also assert that Congress' intent can be discerned by reference to a rejected administration housing proposal, which contained in its analogue to § 5(e) an express statement that Project Notes would be subject to estate taxes. We are unpersuaded by appellees' contention that the Finance Committee's decision not to include a similar express reference to the estate tax indicates a desire to exempt Project Notes from that tax. Equally plausible is that the Committee omitted the express exception as unnecessary. Further, neither the administration, the Finance Committee, nor even a single Senator considered this difference worthy of comment, although numerous other variations between the two proposals received attention. * * *

NOTES AND QUESTIONS

(1) Did the Court in this case rely on one of the three rationales for trumping apparent textual meaning identified above (plain meaning absurd, contrary to legislative intent, or inconsistent with a background norm)?

(2) Recall the distinction Judge Hutcheson drew between "the judgment or decision, the solution itself" as opposed to "the apologia for that decision; the decree as opposed to the logomachy."[52] Do you think the tension between decree and logomachy is greater in common law adjudication or in statutory cases?

(3) Compare the unflinching adherence to plain meaning in *Locke* with its rejection in *Wells Fargo*. Can you reconcile the two? In which did the Court better fulfill its role? Or were the approaches, though different, nonetheless each appropriate (or inappropriate) to the task at hand?

Assignment

While serving a five-year sentence for burglary and conspiracy to commit burglary, Green was injured by a machine at a car wash where he was working as part of a work-release program. Green sued the machine's manufacturer, the Bock Laundry Machine Company. You are the trial judge.

Green has testified at the trial concerning the circumstances of the accident. Bock now seeks to introduce evidence of Green's criminal convictions in order to "impeach" his testimony, that is, to attack his credibility and suggest that the jury should not believe him. Green objects that such evidence would be unduly prejudicial and therefore is inadmissible.

The legislature has enacted rules of evidence that control what is admissible and what is not. Three rules may apply here:

> 402. All relevant evidence is admissible, except as otherwise provided by the Constitution of the United States or by these rules. Evidence which is not relevant is not admissible.

> 403. Although relevant, evidence may be excluded if its probative value is substantially outweighed by the danger of unfair prejudice, confusion of the issues, or misleading the jury, or by considerations of undue delay, waste of time, or needless presentation of cumulative evidence.

> 609. For the purpose of attacking the credibility of a witness, evidence that the witness has been convicted of a crime shall be admitted if elicited from the witness or established by public record during cross-examination but only if the crime (1) was punishable by death or imprisonment in excess of one year under the law under which the witness was convicted, and the court determines that the probative value of admitting this evidence outweighs its prejudicial effect to the defendant, or (2) involved dishonesty or false statement, regardless of the punishment.

Is evidence of Green's convictions admissible?

---

[52] *See supra* page 83.

Chapter 11

STATUTORY PURPOSE

[T]he most universal and effectual way of discovering the true meaning of a law, when the words are dubious, is by considering the reason and spirit of it; or the cause which moved the legislator to enact it. For when this reason ceases, the law itself ought likewise to cease with it.

— **William Blackstone[1]**

[I]t is one of the surest indexes of a mature and developed jurisprudence not to make a fortress out of the dictionary; but to remember that statutes always have some purpose or object to accomplish, whose sympathetic and imaginative discovery is the surest guide to their meaning.

— **Learned Hand[2]**

HEYDON'S CASE
3 Coke 7a, 76 Eng. Rep. 637 (Court of Exchequer 1584)

[F]or the sure and true interpretation of all statutes in general (be they penal or beneficial, restrictive or enlarging of the common law), four things are to be discerned and considered:

1st. What was the common law before making of the Act.

2nd. What was the mischief and defect for which the common law did not provide.

3rd. What remedy the Parliament hath resolved and appointed to cure the disease of the commonwealth.

---

[1] WILLIAM BLACKSTONE, COMMENTARIES ON THE LAWS OF ENGLAND *61 (1765).

[2] Cabell v. Markham, 148 F.2d 737, 739 (2d Cir.), *aff'd*, 326 U.S. 404 (1945). On the other hand:

> True, there is often no surer way to misconceive the meaning of a statute or any other writing than to construe it verbally; indeed, interpretation is the art of proliferating a purpose which is meant to cover many occasions [so] that it shall be best realized upon the occasion in question. However, although there are no certain guides, the colloquial meaning of the words is itself one of the best tests of purpose, and situations of which *Markham v. Cabell* is the last example are the exception. * * * [T]his is not a situation in which it would be proper not to follow the literal meaning of the words.

Brooklyn National Corp. v. Commissioner, 157 F.2d 450, 451 (2d Cir. 1946) (L. Hand, J.).

And, 4th. The true reason of the remedy; and then the office of all the Judges is always to make such construction as shall suppress the mischief, and advance the remedy, and to suppress subtle inventions and evasions for the continuance of the mischief, and *pro privato commodo*, and to add force and life to the cure and remedy, according to the true intent of the makers of the Act, *pro bono publico*.

As the classic, oft-cited statements from Blackstone and from *Heydon's Case* show, reference to legislative purpose "for the sure and true interpretation" of a statute has a lengthy pedigree. This is not surprising; it reflects a basic conviction that law should make sense. When we considered the "no vehicles in the park" ordinance, we found it rather challenging to apply without some understanding of its purpose (or, put differently, fairly easy to apply *because of* an understanding of its purpose). Courts often invoke the legislation's larger purpose when adopting a less than obvious reading of the text; *Holy Trinity* is one of innumerable examples.

Karl Llewellyn wrote (in the article in which he trashed the canons of interpretation): "If a statute is to make sense, it must be read in the light of some assumed purpose. A statute merely declaring a rule, with no purpose or objective, is nonsense."[3] Justice Breyer echoes this thought: "[M]eaning in law depends upon an understanding of purpose. Law's words, however technical they may sound, are not magic formulas; they must be read in light of their purposes, if we are to avoid essentially arbitrary applications and harmful results."[4] Yet Justice Breyer said this in a dissent, which suggests that not everyone necessarily agrees. Indeed, although purposivism has a lengthy and impressive pedigree, it has come under significant attack in the last few decades. The rise of the new textualism has inflicted serious blows. In this chapter we consider whether and to what extent judges should rely on legislative purpose when interpreting statutes.

The principal cases in this chapter involve requests by the winning party in a civil rights action for the loser to pay the winner's attorneys fees and other costs of litigation. In general, the "American rule" — so-called because it is almost unique to this country — is that each party in a lawsuit bears its own expenses. At times, federal courts have ordered losing defendants to cover the costs of the plaintiffs' lawyers in cases where the plaintiff had acted as a "private attorney general," enforcing laws such as the pollution statutes that benefitted the public in general. The Supreme Court brought a halt to this practice in *Alyeska Pipeline Service Co. v. Wilderness Society*, 421 U.S. 240 (1975). But *Alyeska* says nothing about Congress's ability make exceptions to the American rule, and in hundreds of individual settings it has done so. One study found that between 1887 and 2004, and increasingly after *Alyeska*, Congress enacted 245 separate statutes providing that losing defendants, though usually not losing plaintiffs, pay the other side's attorney's fees.[5] The underlying idea comes from Economics 101: the higher the expected return on lawsuits, the more lawsuits will be brought. The "totally

[3] Karl N. Llewellyn, *Remarks on the Theory of Appellate Decision and the Rule or Canons About How Statutes Are to be Construed*, 3 VAND. L. REV. 395, 400 (1950).

[4] Behrens v. Pelletier, 516 U.S. 299, 324 (1996) (Breyer, J., dissenting).

[5] SEAN FARHANG, THE LITIGATION STATE: PUBLIC REGULATION AND PRIVATE LAWSUITS IN THE U.S. (2010).

unambiguous"[6] purpose of fee-shifting statutes is universally understood to be a desire to promote certain types of litigation. If ever one can speak confidently and meaningfully about statutory purpose, it is here.

> The legislative histories of [fee-shifting] statutes * * * are replete with statements by legislators and witnesses that optimal enforcement of the relevant statutes depends on private litigation, and that some form of inducement is necessary in order to facilitate suit. Congress * * * use[s] fee shifts and damage enhancements in an effort to ensure that particular individuals or groups have the ability and incentive to enforce federal legislation. Not surprisingly, the legislators who support litigation incentives tend to be the same legislators who champion the policies embodied in the relevant bill. Legislators vote for such procedural mechanisms in the belief that they will help promote the substance of the statute.[7]

In the cases that follow, the courts show varying degrees of reliance on arguments from purpose in interpreting fee-shifting positions.

CHRISTIANSBURG GARMENT CO. v. EEOC
434 U.S. 412 (1978)

MR. JUSTICE STEWART delivered the opinion of the Court.

Section 706(k) of Title VII of the Civil Rights Act of 1964 provides:

> "In any action or proceeding under this title the court, in its discretion, may allow the prevailing party . . . a reasonable attorney's fee. . . ."

The question in this case is under what circumstances an attorney's fee should be allowed when the defendant is the prevailing party in a Title VII action * * *. [The Equal Employment Opportunity Commission sued Christiansburg Garment Co. alleging that it had discriminated against an employee on the basis of race. The District Court granted summary judgment to the defendant for technical reasons without considering the merits of the underlying claim of discrimination. It denied the defendant's request for attorney's fees.]

It may be taken as established [by our prior decisions], as the parties in this case both acknowledge, that under § 706(k) of Title VII a prevailing plaintiff ordinarily is to be awarded attorney's fees in all but special circumstances. The question in the case before us is what standard should inform a district court's discretion in deciding whether to award attorney's fees to a successful defendant in a Title VII action. * * *

Relying on what it terms "the plain meaning of the statute," the company argues that the language of § 706(k) admits of only one interpretation: "A prevailing defendant is entitled to an award of attorney's fees on the same basis as a prevailing plaintiff." But the permissive and discretionary language of the statute does not

---

[6] *Id.* at 90.

[7] Margaret Lemos, *Do Litigation Incentives Work? How Attorneys' Fee Shifts and Damage Enhancements Affect Litigants and the Law* at 9–10 (2009).

even invite, let alone require, such a mechanical construction. The terms of § 706(k) provide no indication whatever of the circumstances under which either a plaintiff or a defendant should be entitled to attorney's fees. And a moment's reflection reveals that there are at least two strong equitable considerations counseling an attorney's fee award to a prevailing Title VII plaintiff that are wholly absent in the case of a prevailing Title VII defendant.

First, * * * the plaintiff is the chosen instrument of Congress to vindicate "a policy that Congress considered of the highest priority." Second, when a district court awards counsel fees to a prevailing plaintiff, it is awarding them against a violator of federal law. As the Court of Appeals clearly perceived, "these policy considerations which support the award of fees to a prevailing plaintiff are not present in the case of a prevailing defendant." A successful defendant seeking counsel fees under § 706(k) must rely on quite different equitable considerations.

But if the company's position is untenable, the Commission's argument [that Congress intended to permit the award of attorney's fees to a prevailing defendant only in a situation where the plaintiff was motivated by bad faith in bringing the action] also misses the mark. * * * [I]f that had been the intent of Congress, no statutory provision would have been necessary, for it has long been established that even under the American common-law rule attorney's fees may be awarded against a party who has proceeded in bad faith.

Furthermore, while it was certainly the policy of Congress that Title VII plaintiffs should vindicate "a policy that Congress considered of the highest priority," it is equally certain that Congress entrusted the ultimate effectuation of that policy to the adversary judicial process. A fair adversary process presupposes both a vigorous prosecution and a vigorous defense. It cannot be lightly assumed that in enacting § 706(k), Congress intended to distort that process by giving the private plaintiff substantial incentives to sue, while foreclosing to the defendant the possibility of recovering his expenses in resisting even a groundless action unless he can show that it was brought in bad faith.

The sparse legislative history of § 706(k) reveals little more than the barest outlines of a proper accommodation of the competing considerations we have discussed. The only specific reference to § 706(k) in the legislative debates indicates that the fee provision was included to "make it easier for a plaintiff of limited means to bring a meritorious suit." During the Senate floor discussions of the almost identical attorney's fee provision of Title II, however, several Senators explained that its allowance of awards to defendants would serve "to deter the bringing of lawsuits without foundation," "to discourage frivolous suits," and "to diminish the likelihood of unjustified suits being brought." If anything can be gleaned from these fragments of legislative history, it is that while Congress wanted to clear the way for suits to be brought under the Act, it also wanted to protect defendants from burdensome litigation having no legal or factual basis. * * *

[The two Courts of Appeals to have] consider[ed] what criteria should govern the award of attorney's fees to a prevailing Title VII defendant have found that * * * such awards should be permitted "not routinely, not simply because he succeeds, but only where the action brought is found to be unreasonable, frivolous, meritless or vexatious."

To the extent that abstract words can deal with concrete cases, we think that the concept embodied in the language adopted by these two Courts of Appeals is correct. We would qualify their words only by pointing out that the term "meritless" is to be understood as meaning groundless or without foundation, rather than simply that the plaintiff has ultimately lost his case, and that the term "vexatious" in no way implies that the plaintiff's subjective bad faith is a necessary prerequisite to a fee award against him. In sum, a district court may in its discretion award attorney's fees to a prevailing defendant in a Title VII case upon a finding that the plaintiff's action was frivolous, unreasonable, or without foundation, even though not brought in subjective bad faith. * * *

That § 706(k) allows fee awards only to prevailing private plaintiffs should assure that this statutory provision will not in itself operate as an incentive to the bringing of claims that have little chance of success. To take the further step of assessing attorney's fees against plaintiffs simply because they do not finally prevail would substantially add to the risks inhering in most litigation and would undercut the efforts of Congress to promote the vigorous enforcement of the provisions of Title VII. Hence, a plaintiff should not be assessed his opponent's attorney's fees unless a court finds that his claim was frivolous, unreasonable, or groundless, or that the plaintiff continued to litigate after it clearly became so. And, needless to say, if a plaintiff is found to have brought or continued such a claim in bad faith, there will be an even stronger basis for charging him with the attorney's fees incurred by the defense. * * *

[The Court affirmed the decisions below, which had been consistent with the standards it laid out.]

NOTES AND QUESTIONS

(1)   Does the text of the statute provide any basis for the Court's asymmetrical standards for plaintiffs and defendants?

(2)   Are the Court's asymmetrical standards for fee recovery by plaintiffs and defendants sensible? Do they reflect a reasonable balance of competing considerations and create an appropriate set of incentives for potential employment discrimination plaintiffs?

(3)   Is this opinion an example of textualism, intentionalism, purposivism, or something else altogether?

(4)   The federal Copyright Act provides: "In any civil action under this title, the court in its discretion may allow the recovery of full costs by or against any party other than the United States or an officer thereof. Except as otherwise provided by this title, the court may also award a reasonable attorney's fee to the prevailing party as part of the costs." Does the dual standard articulated in *Christiansburg* apply under this provision? The Supreme Court has held that it does not — prevailing plaintiffs and prevailing defendants are treated identically. *Fogerty v. Fantasy Inc.*, 510 U.S. 517 (1994). Are the two cases consistent?

The next two cases arise under 42 U.S.C. § 1988, adopted in 1976 in the wake of *Alyeska*, which provides that in a civil rights case a court "in its discretion, may allow the prevailing party, other than the United States, a reasonable attorney's fee as part of the costs." In both, the trial court awards fees to a victorious civil rights plaintiff. The question is whether that award should include reimbursement for the cost of expert witnesses. When these cases arose, the Supreme Court had already held that § 1988 applies to paralegals' fees. *Missouri v. Jenkins*, 491 U.S. 274 (1989).

FRIEDRICH v. CITY OF CHICAGO
888 F.2d 511 (7th Cir. 1989)

POSNER, Circuit Judge. * * *

[The district court awarded plaintiffs $42,000 for attorney's fees, expenses, and expert witness fees under § 1988.]

The Supreme Court and this court have rejected the strongest argument against the district court's result, the argument from the statute's "plain language." The fee statute authorizes the award of a reasonable attorney's fee, and an expert witness or consultant is not an attorney. But neither is a paralegal, yet paralegal fees may be awarded. An attorney's travel expense or long-distance telephone expense is not an attorney's fee, yet is awardable too. * * *

The defendants argue that a paralegal is more like an attorney than is an economist, a psychiatrist, a police commissioner (one of the experts here), or a sociologist (the other — William Whyte, of *Organization Man* fame). That may be, but it does not touch the question whether the fee statute is to be read literally. A sheep is more like a goat than it is like an ostrich; but if a statute regulating sheep had been applied to goats, an attempted application to ostriches could not be defeated simply by pointing out that an ostrich is not a sheep. If "attorney" in the fee statute can mean something different from attorney, and "fee" something different from fee, then maybe one of the other things "attorney's fee" can mean is the fee paid an expert witness or consultant.

* * * [J]udges realize in their heart of hearts that the superficial clarity to which they are referring when they call the meaning of a statute "plain" is treacherous footing for interpretation. They know that statutes are purposive utterances and that language is a slippery medium in which to encode a purpose. They know that legislatures, including the Congress of the United States, often legislate in haste, without considering fully the potential application of their words to novel settings. The presence of haste here is suggested by the fact that the civil rights fees statute was passed on the last day of the Ninety-Fourth Congress.

When a court can figure out what Congress probably was driving at and how its goal can be achieved, it is not usurpation — it is interpretation in a sense that has been orthodox since Aristotle — for the court to complete (not enlarge) the statute by reading it to bring about the end that the legislators would have specified had they thought about it more clearly or used a more perspicuous form of words. That

is what the Supreme Court did in the *Jenkins* case. * * * Noting that the fee statute had been enacted in order to overrule *Alyeska* with respect to civil rights cases, the Court in *Jenkins* asked whether an award of paralegal fees would serve the statutory purpose, and concluded that it would. Paralegals provide a low-cost substitute for work that would otherwise be performed by the attorney himself. The substitute is part of the attorney's work product. If fees for the services of paralegals could not be shifted to the losing party, as attorney's fees can be, there would be an incentive to substitute attorney time for paralegal time. So even defendants would be made worse off in the long run; they would be paying for the same work but at a higher rate. A nonliteral interpretation was necessary to make sense of the statute.

Much the same argument can be made for the shifting of experts' fees. Experts are not only hired to testify; sometimes they are hired, also or instead, to educate counsel in a technical matter germane to the suit. The time so spent by the expert is a substitute for lawyer time, just as paralegal time is, for if prohibited (or deterred by the cost) from hiring an expert the lawyer would attempt to educate himself about the expert's area of expertise. To forbid the shifting of the expert's fee would encourage underspecialization and inefficient trial preparation, just as to forbid shifting the cost of paralegals would encourage lawyers to do paralegals' work. There is thus no basis for distinguishing *Jenkins* from the present case so far as time spent by these experts in educating the plaintiffs' lawyer is concerned * * * and so we think the district judge must have been right at least in part. If so, this is a reason for thinking he was right in whole, for it is difficult to separate time spent by an expert in educating the lawyer from time spent in preparing to testify. Sometimes it is impossible; the same time may serve both purposes.

Time actually spent on the stand, however, is not easily conceived of as a substitute for lawyer time or lawyer work product. And such time is easily separated out from the other time spent by an expert on a case, though usually it is just the tip of the iceberg; in this case, so far as we can determine, less than ten percent of the money paid the experts was for time actually testifying. But the Court in *Jenkins* did not insist on a relation of substitution for paralegal fees to be shifted, and of course paralegals do not just do at lower cost what lawyers do. In part because they are cheaper, they do things that lawyers would not consider worth their while to do. They expand the scope of trial preparation. And so it is with experts. * * *

The question what a statute means is only in part a function of what the legislators thought it meant. The scope of legislation is not circumscribed by the conscious thoughts of the legislators. Nor does the answer to an interpretive question turn on how the statute might be read by someone utterly ignorant of its background or by the same someone reading with the same literalism statements in the legislative history. "Clarity depends on context, which legislative history may illuminate." We ask what meaning would be obvious to one familiar with the circumstances of enactment, including, here, the judicial history that provides the backdrop of the statute. We ask whether we can be confident that if someone had told Congress in the deliberations leading up to enactment that it had neglected to say anything about the shifting of expert-witness fees, Congress would have added language making clear to the most literal-minded that such fees could be shifted.

We think it would have, and one reason is simply that we are given and can think of no reason against such shifting — especially given our earlier point that expert fees for advice and consultation can be shifted along with paralegal and other incidental expenses normally incurred in litigation. There would be a reason if the civil rights fees statute had been a hard-fought compromise between those who wanted judges to have the broad equitable authority they had exercised before *Alyeska* and those who wanted no inroads made on *Alyeska*, for then the court's duty would be to give effect to the compromise, not to give proponents a victory that had eluded them in the legislative arena. But there is no indication of compromise on any issue relevant to this case, and the defendants do not argue it. All the evidence is to the contrary. Recognizing that most civil rights suits were not lucrative for the plaintiffs' lawyers, Congress wanted to make losing defendants bear the expenses of suit beyond the usual items taxable as costs. Why exclude expert-witness fees? Why in particular exclude those fees when they are incurred for testimony and its preparation but not when they are incurred for advice and consultation?

QUESTIONS

(1)   Judge Posner dodges the plain meaning argument by noting that other courts had already gone beyond the statute's plain meaning. Suppose that had not happened; if this were the first case to arise under § 1988, should it have come out the same way? Even if prior courts had abandoned the plain meaning, is that a reason to compound the error (if error it is)?

(2)   What was the "purpose" of § 1988? Is this result consistent with that purpose? Would § 1988 not serve its purpose if the court had reached the opposite result?

(3)   Go back and have a look at the critique of judicial reliance on statutory purpose in the Notes after *Holy Trinity* on pages 285–86. Do those criticisms apply to Judge Posner's opinion?

WEST VIRGINIA UNIVERSITY HOSPITALS, INC. v. CASEY
499 U.S. 83 (1991)

Justice SCALIA delivered the opinion of the Court. * * *

[The district court awarded successful civil rights plaintiffs over $100,000 in expert witness fees pursuant to 42 U.S.C. § 1988.]

The record of statutory usage demonstrates convincingly that attorney's fees and expert fees are regarded as separate elements of litigation cost. While some fee-shifting provisions, like § 1988, refer only to "attorney's fees," see, e.g., Civil Rights Act of 1964, 42 U.S.C. § 2000e-5(k), many others explicitly shift expert witness fees as well as attorney's fees. In 1976, just over a week prior to the enactment of § 1988, Congress passed those provisions of the Toxic Substances Control Act which provide that a prevailing party may recover "the costs of suit

and reasonable fees for attorneys *and expert witnesses*." (Emphasis added.) [Justice Scalia offered numerous similar examples.] * * * At least 34 statutes in 10 different titles of the U.S. Code explicitly shift attorney's fees and expert witness fees. * * *

We think this statutory usage shows beyond question that attorney's fees and expert fees are distinct items of expense. If, as WVUH argues, the one includes the other, dozens of statutes referring to the two separately become an inexplicable exercise in redundancy.

[The Court then reviewed, at some length, pre-1976 practice with regard to the award of fees for attorneys and for expert witnesses. It concluded] that at the time this provision was enacted neither statutory nor judicial usage regarded the phrase "attorney's fees" as embracing fees for experts' services. * * *

WVUH further argues that the congressional purpose in enacting § 1988 must prevail over the ordinary meaning of the statutory terms. It quotes, for example, the House Committee Report to the effect that "the judicial remedy [must be] full and complete," and the Senate Committee Report to the effect that "[c]itizens must have the opportunity to recover what it costs them to vindicate [civil] rights in court." As we have observed before, however, the purpose of a statute includes not only what it sets out to change, but also what it resolves to leave alone. The best evidence of that purpose is the statutory text adopted by both Houses of Congress and submitted to the President. Where that contains a phrase that is unambiguous — that has a clearly accepted meaning in both legislative and judicial practice — we do not permit it to be expanded or contracted by the statements of individual legislators or committees during the course of the enactment process. Congress could easily have shifted "attorney's fees and expert witness fees," or "reasonable litigation expenses," as it did in contemporaneous statutes; it chose instead to enact more restrictive language, and we are bound by that restriction. * * *

WVUH's last contention is that, even if Congress plainly did not include expert fees in the fee-shifting provisions of § 1988, it would have done so had it thought about it. Most of the pre-§ 1988 statutes that explicitly shifted expert fees dealt with environmental litigation, where the necessity of expert advice was readily apparent; and when Congress later enacted the [Equal Access to Justice Act, which authorizes an award of fees against the federal government and is in that sense] the federal counterpart of § 1988, it explicitly included expert fees. Thus, the argument runs, the 94th Congress simply forgot; it is our duty to ask how they would have decided had they actually considered the question. See *Friedrich v. City of Chicago*, 888 F.2d 511, 514 (CA7 1989) (awarding expert fees under § 1988 because a court should "complete . . . the statute by reading it to bring about the end that the legislators would have specified had they thought about it more clearly").

This argument profoundly mistakes our role. * * * [I]t is not our function to eliminate clearly expressed inconsistency of policy, and to treat alike subjects that different Congresses have chosen to treat differently. The facile attribution of congressional "forgetfulness" cannot justify such a usurpation. Where what is at issue is not a contradictory disposition within the same enactment, but merely a difference between the more parsimonious policy of an earlier enactment and the

more generous policy of a later one, there is no more basis for saying that the earlier Congress forgot than for saying that the earlier Congress felt differently. In such circumstances, the attribution of forgetfulness rests in reality upon the judge's assessment that the later statute contains the better disposition. But that is not for judges to prescribe. We thus reject this last argument for the same reason that Justice Brandeis, writing for the Court, once rejected a similar (though less explicit) argument by the United States:

> "[The statute's] language is plain and unambiguous. What the Government asks is not a construction of a statute, but, in effect, an enlargement of it by the court, so that what was omitted, presumably by inadvertence, may be included within its scope. To supply omissions transcends the judicial function." * * *

Justice MARSHALL, dissenting.

As Justice STEVENS demonstrates, the Court uses the implements of literalism to wound, rather than to minister to, congressional intent in this case. That is a dangerous usurpation of congressional power when any statute is involved. It is troubling for special reasons, however, when the statute at issue is clearly designed to give access to the federal courts to persons and groups attempting to vindicate vital civil rights.

Justice STEVENS, with whom Justice MARSHALL and Justice BLACKMUN join, dissenting.

In *Jenkins*, we interpreted the award of "a reasonable attorney's fee" to cover charges for paralegals and law clerks, even though a paralegal or law clerk is not an attorney. Similarly, the federal courts routinely allow an attorney's travel expenses or long-distance telephone calls to be awarded, even though they are not literally part of an "attorney's fee," * * *. To allow reimbursement of these other categories of expenses, and yet not to include expert witness fees, is both arbitrary and contrary to the broad remedial purpose that inspired the fee-shifting provision of § 1988. * * *

[Justice Stevens detailed the background of § 1988, stressing Congress's goal of ensuring access to the courts for civil rights plaintiffs.] This Court's determination today that petitioner must assume the cost of $ 104,133.00 in expert witness fees is at war with the congressional purpose of making the prevailing party whole. * * *

In the domain of statutory interpretation, Congress is the master. It obviously has the power to correct our mistakes, but we do the country a disservice when we needlessly ignore persuasive evidence of Congress' actual purpose and require it "to take the time to revisit the matter" and to restate its purpose in more precise English whenever its work product suffers from an omission or inadvertent error. * * *

The Court concludes its opinion with the suggestion that disagreement with its textual analysis could only be based on the dissenters' preference for a "better" statute. It overlooks the possibility that a different view may be more faithful to Congress' command. The fact that Congress has consistently provided for the inclusion of expert witness fees in fee-shifting statutes when it considered the

matter is a weak reed on which to rest the conclusion that the omission of such a provision represents a deliberate decision to forbid such awards.

NOTES AND QUESTIONS

(1)   In the fall of 1991, Congress passed the Civil Rights Act of 1991, Pub. L. 102-166, which "overruled," in whole or in part, 12 different Supreme Court decisions, including *West Virginia University Hospitals*. As amended in 1991, the statute now provides for including expert witness fees in attorney's fees awards, but only in certain kinds of civil rights cases. *See* 42 U.S.C. § 1988(c) ("In awarding an attorney's fee under subsection (b) of this section in any action or proceeding to enforce a provision of section 1981 or 1981a of this title, the court, in its discretion, may include expert fees as part of the attorney's fee."). *West Virginia University Hospitals* was brought under 42 U.S.C. § 1983, not 1981 or 1981a, and thus the same result would be reached under the amended statute. Does that say anything about the correctness of the decision?

(2)   Is the Supreme Court's result consistent with the statute's purpose?

(3)   "Purpose" might be invoked in two ways to support awarding expert witness fees. One is to say, with Justice Stevens, that doing so will further Congress's goals. The other is to say, as Judge Posner does at the end of his opinion in *Friedrich*, that no conceivable purpose supports *denying* such an award:

> Congress has specifically provided civil rights plaintiffs with the ability to recover attorney's fees to vindicate rights that have special societal importance. Why, then, would it single out civil rights plaintiffs and deny them expert witness fee recovery while allowing such recovery by plaintiffs in antitrust, securities, and other categories of cases? * * *

> Noting that this reading of Section 1988 "prevents . . . accommodation" with the provision and the corpus juris of which it is a part, Justice Scalia seems content to state that "different Congresses have chosen to treat [different fee situations] differently." He may be correct, but the crucial question is *why might this be so*? If an interpreter cannot come up with a plausible explanation for such disparate treatment, then it seems sensible to us that the statute ought to be construed in another manner — in a way that furthers some purpose that plausibly might be ascribed to the overall statutory structure and rationally connected to the world in which it operates.[8]

Should Justice Scalia have explained why Congress would treat civil rights plaintiffs differently from other successful litigants with respect to expert witness fees? Must judges always identify "some purpose that plausible might be ascribed to the statute" to support their interpretation?

---

[8] T. Alexander Aleinikoff & Theodore M. Shaw, *The Costs of Incoherence: A Comment on Plain Meaning*, West Virginia University Hospitals, Inc. v. Casey, *and Due Process of Statutory Interpretation*, 45 VAND. L. REV. 687, 696, 705 (1992).

(4)   Section 307(f) of the Clean Air Act provides: "In any judicial proceeding under this section, the court may award costs of litigation (including reasonable attorney and expert witness fees) whenever it determines that such award is appropriate." Suppose an environmental group sues the Environmental Protection Agency under § 307, challenging the legality of an EPA regulation. The court *upholds* the regulation. Could it still award fees to the environmental group? *See* Ruckelshaus v. Sierra Club, 463 U.S. 680 (1983).

(5)   It is not entirely clear that fee-shifting statutes actually work. For example, empirical studies indicate little or no meaningful difference in filing rates for civil rights actions before and after enactment of § 1988. If it could be shown that fee-shifting does not increase the number of "desirable" lawsuits, should that affect the analysis in any of the foregoing cases?

(6)   Consider the following syllogism with regard to the no-vehicles-in-the-park rule. The purpose of the ordinance was to preserve quiet, tranquility, and safety in the park. Rugby games are loud, boisterous, and lead to frequent injury. Therefore, rugby in the park is forbidden by the ordinance. Surely that goes too far, but why exactly?

If that example strikes you as extreme and too violative of the statutory language, what about good old Mable? Would it be proper for a court to hold that riding a horse in the park violates the ordinance, given its purposes?

(7)   Here is some advice from the Supreme Court:

[N]o legislation pursues its purposes at all costs. Deciding what competing values will or will not be sacrificed to the achievement of a particular objective is the very essence of legislative choice — and it frustrates rather than effectuates legislative intent simplistically to assume that *whatever* furthers the statute's primary objective must be the law.[9]

[Although legislation always results] from an experience of evils, * * * its general language should not * * * be necessarily confined to the form that evil had theretofore taken. * * * [A] principle to be vital must be capable of wider application than the mischief which gave it birth.[10]

Helpful with regard to rugby or horseback riding?

(8)   And some advice from Judge Easterbrook:

In deciding how to address a subject, the legislature * * * must choose between a rule and a standard. Rules * * * are easy to administer but are inevitably both too narrow in some situations (all rules have loopholes) and overbroad in others. Standards * * * could in principle match the outcome more closely to the legislative objective, but standards are difficult to administer and create errors of their own. Courts cannot ascertain intent or good faith without hearings; the principal evidence would be oral and correspondingly difficult to evaluate. Rules have lower administrative costs

---

[9]   Rodriguez v. United States, 480 U.S. 522, 525–526 (1987) (per curiam).

[10]   Weems v. United States, 217 U.S. 349, 373 (1910).

and will be preferable unless they increase the error costs (the sum of false positives and false negatives) by more than the savings in administrative costs. Whether to choose a rule or a standard is a legislative decision. Judges ought not turn a rule into a standard; that amounts to little more than disagreement with a legislative choice. Boosting the level of generality by attempting to discern and enforce legislative "purposes" or "goals" instead of the enacted language is just a means to turn rules into standards. [When the legislature] creates a bright line, * * * we must enforce it that way.[11]

Apply this description of what is going on in purposive interpretation to the example of a judge who holds that a rugby game counts as a "vehicle." Does this critique apply to Judge Posner's opinion in *Friedrich*? Justice Brewer's in *Holy Trinity*?

NOTE ON DETERMINING, OR ATTRIBUTING, PURPOSE

We have so far assumed that courts are able to discern the purpose behind legislation, and that the only problem is deciding how much weight that purpose should carry. Many would quarrel with that assumption.

First, statutes are not the product of a single lawmaker but of a large collegial body. Might not individual legislators have different, even conflicting, purposes in mind? Suppose only a portion (a majority? a majority of the majority? a few dozen?) of the legislators had a particular purpose in mind — can that be "the" purpose of the Act? A good deal of political science views the legislative process as a struggle among competing interest groups with very different goals, which hammer out a compromise that has no necessary policy coherence. If that is right, invocations of legislative purpose are simply fictions.

Second, how does a court discover legislative purpose? Where did the courts look in *Holy Trinity* and *Friedrich*? Where did Justice Stevens look in *West Virginia University Hospitals*?

Courts often assert that purpose can be inferred from the words of the statute. One example is the opinion from Learned Hand in footnote one, above. Is this reasoning uselessly circular (the meaning of the words reveals the purpose, and the purpose reveals the meaning of the words)? Or might each illuminate the other?

Hart and Sacks offer the following guidance:

A formally enacted statement of purpose in a statute should be accepted by the court if it appears to have been designed to serve as a guide to interpretation, is consistent with the words and context of the statute, and is relevant to the question of meaning at issue.

In all other situations, the purpose of a statute has in some degree to be inferred. * * *

---

[11] Jaskolski v. Daniels, 427 F.3d 456, 461–462 (7th Cir. 2005).

In determining the more immediate purpose which ought to be attributed to a statute, and to any subordinate provision of it which may be involved, a court should try to put itself in imagination in the position of the legislature which enacted the measure.

The court, however, should not do this in the mood of a cynical political observer, taking account of all the short-run currents of political expedience that swirl around any legislative session.

It should assume, unless the contrary unmistakably appears, that the legislature was made up of reasonable persons pursuing reasonable purposes reasonably.

It should presume conclusively that these persons, whether or not entertaining concepts of reasonableness shared by the court, were trying responsibly and in good faith to discharge their constitutional powers and duties.

The court should then proceed to do, in substance, just what Lord Coke said it should do in *Heydon's Case*. The gist of this approach is to infer purpose by comparing the new law with the old. Why would reasonable men, confronted with the law as it was, have enacted this new law to replace it? * * *

The whole context of a statute may be examined in aid of its interpretation, and should be whenever substantial doubt about its meaning exists in the interpreter's mind, or is suggested to him. * * *

The internal legislative history of the measure (that is, its history from the filing of the bill to enactment) may be examined, if this was reduced to writing officially and contemporaneously. But in the use which is made of this material two closely related limitations should be scrupulously observed.

First. The history should be examined for the light it throws on *general purpose.* Evidence of specific intention with respect to particular applications is competent only to the extent that the particular applications illuminate the general purpose and are consistent with other evidence of it.

Second. Effect should not be given to evidence from the internal legislative history if the result would be to contradict a purpose otherwise indicated and to yield an interpretation disadvantageous to private persons who had no reasonable means of access to the history. * * *

The court's last resort, when doubt about the immediate purpose of a statute remains, is to resort to an appropriate presumption drawn from some general policy of the law.

This is likely to be its only resort when the question concerns more nearly ultimate policy, or the mode of fitting the statute into the general fabric of the law.[12]

---

[12] HENRY M. HART, JR. & ALBERT M. SACKS, THE LEGAL PROCESS: BASIC PROBLEMS IN THE MAKING AND

NOTE ON PURPOSE AND THE PROPER JUDICIAL ROLE

In the two principal cases, Judge Posner and Justice Scalia are unusually explicit in their discussions of the role of the courts. Who has the better of their disagreement as to whether judicial reliance on purpose usurps the legislative role?

Consider also Justice Kennedy's criticism, taken from another decision, of the use of purpose to trump text:

> Unable to show that an application of [the statute in question] according the plain meaning of its terms would be absurd, the Court turns instead to the task of demonstrating that a straightforward reading of the statute would be inconsistent with the congressional purposes that lay behind its passage. To the student of statutory construction, this move is a familiar one. It is * * * the classic *Holy Trinity* argument. "[A] thing may be within the letter of the statute and yet not within the statute, because not within its spirit, nor within the intention of its makers." I cannot embrace this principle. Where it is clear that the unambiguous language of a statute embraces certain conduct, and it would not be patently absurd to apply the statute to such conduct, it does not foster a democratic exegesis for this Court to rummage through unauthoritative materials to consult the spirit of the legislation in order to discover an alternative interpretation of the statute with which the Court is more comfortable. * * * The problem with spirits is that they tend to reflect less the views of the world whence they come than the views of those who seek their advice.[13]

Ultimately, this attack becomes an argument that the *Holy Trinity* approach is undemocratic in that it substitutes the preferences of the (unelected) judiciary for those of the (elected) legislature. Yet if the court is truly pursuing *congressional* goals, how isn't that democratic? Might it be *un*democratic for the court to hew blindly to the narrow meaning of the text, ignoring Congress's overall purpose? Consider the following observations by Justice Stevens, concurring in a case in which the majority had relied heavily on statutory purpose and the dissent, written by Justice Scalia, had objected that the decision was "nothing other than the elevation of judge-supposed legislative intent over clear statutory text."

> [Justice Scalia] correctly observes that a judicial decision that departs from statutory text may represent "policy-driven interpretation." As long as that driving policy is faithful to the intent of Congress (or, as in this case, aims only to give effect to such intent) — which it must be if it is to override a strict interpretation of the text — the decision is also a correct performance of the judicial function. Justice Scalia's argument today rests on the incorrect premise that ever policy-driven interpretation implements a judge's personal view of sound policy, rather than a faithful attempt to carry out the will of the legislature. Quite the contrary is true of the work of the judges with whom I have worked for many years. If we presume that our judges are intellectually honest — and I do — there is no reason to fear

---

APPLICATION OF LAW 1377–1380 (William N. Eskridge, Jr. & Philip P. Frickey eds. 1994).

[13] Public Citizen v. United States Department of Justice, 491 U.S. 440, 472–473 (1989) (Kennedy, J., concurring in the judgment).

"policy-driven interpretations" of Acts of Congress.[14]

Bear the foregoing concerns in mind in considering one last example of purposive interpretation. This is an opinion by Justice Holmes, who is not generally known for taking a purposivist approach, writing for a 4-3 majority of the Massachusetts Supreme Judicial Court. The language in question is actually from the state Constitution, not a statute, but for present purposes you need not worry about whether that makes a difference.

IN RE HOUSE BILL NO. 1,291
178 Mass. 605, 60 N.E. 129 (1901)

[The Massachusetts Constitution requires that certain public officials "shall be chosen by written vote." The question before the Court in this advisory opinion was whether it was permissible to use voting machines, which would record all votes on a single strip of paper, or without the use of paper at all.]

[HOLMES, J. I]t is not so important to consider what picture the framers of the constitution had in their minds as what benefits they sought to secure, or evils to prevent, — what they were thinking against in their affirmative requirement of writing, and what they would have prohibited if they had put the clause in a negative form. * * * No doubt the picture in the minds of those who used the words was that of a piece of paper with the names of the candidates voted for written upon it in manuscript, but the thing which they meant to stop was oral or hand voting, and the benefits which they meant to secure were the greater certainty and permanence of a material record of each voter's act and the relative privacy incident to doing that act in silence. They did not require the signature of the voter, or any means of identifying his vote as his after it had been cast. It was settled by *Henshaw v. Foster* that they did not require manuscript. In our opinion, they did not require a separate piece of paper for each voter. That is to say, by requiring writing they did not prevent the legislature from authorizing several voters to use a single ballot if the voters all signed it, or in some way sufficiently indicated that a single paper expressed the act and choice of each. It seems to use that the object and even the words of the constitution in requiring "written votes" are satisfied when the voter makes a change in a material object, — for instance, by causing a wheel to revolve a fixed distance, — if the material object changed is so connected with or related to a written or printed name purporting to be the name of a candidate for office that, by the understanding of all, the making of the change expresses a vote for the candidate whose name is thus connected with the device.

NOTES AND QUESTIONS

(1) Pulling a lever, or punching a card, just is not a "written vote," is it? The dissenters certainly didn't think so. Does Justice Holmes think otherwise, or does he not care?

---

[14] Zuni Public School District No. 89 v. Dep't of Education, 550 U.S. 81, 105 (2007).

(2) One of Justice Holmes's best-known statements about interpretation is: "We do not inquire what the legislature meant; we ask only what the statute means." Is this opinion consistent with that admonition?

(3) This opinion might be seen as an example of "imaginative reconstruction," that is, Holmes asks what the enactors of the written vote requirement would have said had they been asked about the propriety of voting machines. Does the opinion give you confidence in the imaginative reconstruction approach?

(4) In this setting, the reliance on statutory purposive leads to a sort "dynamic interpretation." By focusing on purpose rather than text, or purpose rather than intent — in short, the legislator's goal rather than the picture in the heads of the legislators — Holmes allows the written vote requirement to evolve, to have its meaning altered in light of changing times. We will return to the question of changing statutory meaning in Chapter 14.

Assignment

The central provision of the Age Discrimination in Employment Act (ADEA), to which you were introduced through *Gregory v. Ashcroft*, the state judges case excerpted in Chapter 10, reads:

(a) It shall be unlawful for an employer —

(1) to fail or refuse to hire or to discharge any individual or otherwise discriminate against any individual with respect to his compensation, terms, conditions, or privileges of employment, because of such individual's age; [or]

(2) to limit, segregate, or classify his employees in any way which would deprive or tend to deprive any individual of employment opportunities or otherwise adversely affect his status as an employee, because of such individual's age * * *.

29 U.S.C. § 623(a). This provision has an important qualifier: "The prohibitions in this chapter shall be limited to individuals who are at least 40 years of age." *Id.* § 631(a). (When originally passed in 1967, the Act applied only to those who were at least 40 but not over 65; in 1978 Congress changed the upper limit to 70; in 1986 it eliminated the upper limit altogether.)

The Act begins with the following "Congressional statement of findings and purpose":

(a) The Congress hereby finds and declares that —

(1) in the face of rising productivity and affluence, older workers find themselves disadvantaged in their efforts to retain employment, and especially to regain employment when displaced from jobs;

(2) the setting of arbitrary age limits regardless of potential for job performance has become a common practice, and certain otherwise desirable practices may work to the disadvantage of older persons;

(3) the incidence of unemployment, especially long-term unemployment with resultant deterioration of skill, morale, and employer acceptability is, relative to the younger ages, high among older workers; their numbers are great and growing; and their employment problems grave;

(4) the existence in industries affecting commerce, of arbitrary discrimination in employment because of age, burdens commerce and the free flow of goods in commerce.

(b) It is therefore the purpose of this chapter to promote employment of older persons based on their ability rather than age; to prohibit arbitrary age discrimination in employment; to help employers and workers find ways of meeting problems arising from the impact of age on employment.

29 U.S.C. § 621. As these findings suggest, the legislative history of the Act is entirely devoted to the problems faced by older workers and expressions of concern over the stereotype that older workers are less productive and competent than younger ones.

General Dynamics, Inc. has long provided heath care coverage for its retired former employees. However, these costs have become increasingly burdensome. After bargaining with the union representing current workers, General Dynamics changes its pension plan to eliminate health coverage for retirees. However, it keeps the old plan in place for (a) everyone who has already retired and (b) for all current employees age 50 and over. Dennis Cline is a 45-year-old General Dynamics employee. Cline sues, arguing that this change discriminates against him on the basis of his age (to be precise, on the basis of his youth) in violation of the ADEA.

Does the Act apply to this sort of age-based distinction? Is consideration of statutory purpose irrelevant, helpful, or necessary to answering that question?

Chapter 12

LEGISLATIVE HISTORY

"I'll let you write the statute if you let me write the committee report."

— **Congressman Jack Brooks (D-TX)**[1]

"[W]e are a Government of laws, not of committee reports."

— **Justice Antonin Scalia**[2]

A. INTRODUCTION

Courts often invoke legislative history in statutory cases. The range of possible materials is enormous: the pre-enactment historical and legal background, testimony of both private and governmental witnesses at legislative hearings, analysis of bills by legislative counsel or concerned executive agencies, acceptance or rejection of proposed amendments, comments made during markup, committee reports, conference reports, statements of both proponents and opponents during debate on the floor (including planned colloquies and remarks that were subsequently revised or amended), statements made by the President when vetoing or signing legislation, changes made by Congress in a new version of a vetoed bill, and subsequent statements by legislators or the President about their understanding of now-enacted legislation — all these and more have been referenced in opinions from the federal courts. (State courts turn to legislative history much less often than their federal counterparts, largely because most state legislatures maintain only a sketchy record of their proceedings.) In this chapter we explore how courts rely on legislative history in interpreting statutes and whether they should do so.

One note at the outset. Legislative history is a tool, not an interpretative approach in itself. It might be employed under almost any of the theories of statutory interpretation we have studied. For example, a judge might turn to such materials in search of the subjective legislative intent, or to divine the overall legislative purpose, or to "imaginatively reconstruct" how the legislature would have answered a particular question, or to determine whether a word was used according to its ordinary or technical meaning. That said, in practice reference to legislative materials is most commonly associated with the theory that courts should interpret statutes according to legislative intent. Courts consult the record of a bill's consideration and passage in the hope that it will reveal *what Congress meant.*

---

[1] Quoted in Arthur Maass, Congress and the Common Good 139 (1983).

[2] Wisconsin Public Intervenor v. Mortier, 501 U.S. 597, 621 (1991) (Scalia, J., concurring).

To get you thinking about the usefulness of legislative history, suppose that during debate on the Loser Pays Act (set out in Appendix E) Representative X stands up and says, "I shall vote against this bill because it goes too far in allowing for recovery of expert witness fees by the prevailing party." The bill passes. You are now the judge in a case in which the winner seeks to recover its expert witness fees under the Loser Pays Act. It points to X's comment to show that the statutory reference to "attorneys' fees" covers expert witness fees.

Which of the following positions makes sense to you?

(a) X's views are relevant because they indicate the general understanding of the bill (assuming no one contradicted him).

(b) X's views are relevant because others will have relied on his description in formulating their own views.

(c) X's views are relevant but barely; what 1/535ths of Congress thinks about a piece of legislation is virtually beside the point.

(d) X's views are irrelevant, because he voted against the bill; the only "intent" that matters is that of those who voted for it.

(e) X's views are irrelevant because they reveal nothing; we have no way of knowing whether those who voted for the legislation did so because they agreed with X's interpretation or because they disagreed with it.

(f) X's views are irrelevant because there is every reason to doubt his sincerity. Opponents to legislation will often overstate its effect, exaggerating to make others hesitate about their support.

(g) X's views are irrelevant because they are not law. No one, not even X, voted on his interpretation, they voted only on the bill itself. All that matters is what the statute says.

B. USING LEGISLATIVE HISTORY

1. *The Plain Meaning Rule*

In theory, judicial reference to legislative history is governed by "the plain meaning rule":

> If the words are plain, they give meaning to the act, and it is neither the duty nor the privilege of the courts to enter speculative fields in search of a different meaning.
>
> * * [W]hen words are free from doubt they must be taken as the final expression of the legislative intent, and are not to be added to or subtracted from by considerations drawn from titles or designating names or reports accompanying their introduction, or from any extraneous source. In other words, the language being plain, and not leading to absurd or wholly impracticable consequences, it is the sole evidence of the ultimate legisla

tive intent.[3]

Like the parol evidence rule in contract law, the plain meaning rule rests on the belief that the actual words agreed to are the best evidence of meaning and intent. Is this right? Is there any harm in just checking to see whether the apparently "plain" meaning is confirmed by extrinsic materials? No text is *utterly* "plain"; how does a judge know when the threshold of ambiguity allowing resort to legislative history has been crossed? Justice Stevens has rejected the plain meaning rule:

> In recent years the Court has suggested that we should only look at legislative history for the purpose of resolving textual ambiguities or to avoid absurdities. It would be wiser to acknowledge that it is always appropriate to consider all available evidence of Congress's true intent when interpreting its work product.[4]

> Because ambiguity is apparently in the eye of the beholder, I remain convinced that it is unwise to treat the ambiguity *vel non* of a statute as determinative of whether legislative history is consulted.[5]

Judicial adherence to the plain meaning rule ebbs and flows. A pair of enterprising (and patient) scholars reviewed all the Supreme Court's statutory decisions from 1938 to 1979, counting references to legislative history. They found a steady increase, with 1970 being the critical year in which the Court relied on legislative history in more cases than it did not.[6] By the early 1980s Judge Patricia Wald was able to write that "although the Court still refers to the 'plain meaning' rule, the rule has effectively been laid to rest. No occasion for statutory construction now exists when the Court will *not* look at legislative history."[7]

That statement is no longer true. To be more precise, it is impossible to say whether the justices *look at* legislative history less than they once did, but it is clear that Supreme Court opinions *cite* legislative history far less than was the case, say, in the 1970s and early 1980s.[8] This shift is often labeled "the Scalia effect." As we shall see, Justice Scalia, who joined the Court in 1987, has been a ferocious and influential opponent of judicial reliance on legislative history. A significant portion of the decline simply reflects the fact that Justices Scalia and Thomas virtually never invoke legislative history. But other justices as well, including longtime members of the Court, also have relied on legislative history less than in years past.

---

[3] Caminetti v. United States, 242 U.S. 470, 490 (1917).

[4] Koons Buick Pontiac GMC, Inc. v. Nigh, 543 U.S. 50, 65 (2004) (Stevens, J., concurring).

[5] Exxon Mobil Corp. v. Allapattah Servs., Inc., 545 U.S. 546, 572 (2005) (Stevens, J., dissenting).

[6] *See* Jorge L. Carro & Andrew R. Brann, *Use of Legislative Histories by the United States Supreme Court: A Statistical Analysis*, 9 J. Legis. 282 (1982).

[7] Patricia M. Wald, *Some Observations on the Use of Legislative History in the 1981 Supreme Court Term*, 68 Iowa L. Rev. 195, 195 (1983) (emphasis original).

[8] *See* James J. Brudney & Corey Ditslear, *The decline and fall of legislative history? Patterns of Supreme Court reliance in the Burger and Rehnquist eras*, 89 Judicature 220 (Jan.–Feb. 2006).

2. *A Hierarchy of Legislative Sources*

Not all pieces of legislative history are created equal. Committee reports are generally seen as especially important and persuasive. Next in rank are statements made on the floor by the sponsor of the bill or the floor manager. Statements by other supporters carry less weight; statements by opponents carry very little and are often rejected as simply irrelevant. Statements made at hearings are also treated with varying degrees of respect. The concerns of a particular witness — say a private citizen testifying about her experiences with health maintenance organizations — may have only the most limited light to cast on the meaning of the legislation finally adopted. On the other hand, the description of current conditions by certain witnesses might help define statutory purpose. The Court in *Holy Trinity* invoked hearings testimony in this way. And the hearings may include statements by the sponsor or drafter (for example, an executive branch official appearing as a witness) that carry particular weight.

Why are committee reports the weightiest type of legislative history? After all, the report is actually written not by legislators but by staffmembers, with heavy input from lobbyists and interest groups; neither the committee nor the full house votes on the language of the report; the committee is only a tiny minority of the total membership of Congress; the report reflects, even in theory, the views of only those members of the committee who supported the bill.

The usual justifications are as follows:

(a) Expertise. Committee reports represent the "collective understanding of those Congressmen involved in drafting and studying proposed legislation,"[9] those who have developed the greatest expertise about the statutory proposal and the problem it is designed to remedy.

(b) Care. Committee reports "presumably are well considered and carefully prepared."[10]

(c) Delegation. To a large extent the other members of Congress have essentially delegated the legislative task to committees. That is where the real work on the formulation, consideration, and refinement of the legislation takes place. In a practical sense, the committee is the legislature.

(d) Congressional reliance. Although Congress votes on the language of the bill, not on the report, in practice Members often place considerable reliance on the report. Indeed, in some cases they may read the report rather than the bill. For example, when the Clean Air Act Amendments of 1990 came out of conference, the legislative language was over 800 pages long (or, as Senator Moynihan observed on the Senate floor, over 4" thick), and the accompanying explanation from the conferees only 40 double-spaced pages. It seems likely that if busy Senators looked at either prior to casting their votes, they turned to the report rather than the bill.

Are you convinced?

---

[9] Zuber v. Allen, 396 U.S. 168, 186 (1969), quoted with approval in Garcia v. United States, 469 U.S. 70, 76 (1984).

[10] Schwegmann Bros. v. Calvert Distillers Corp., 341 U.S. 384, 395 (1951) (Jackson, J., concurring).

Incidentally, the Conference Report, if there is one, is usually deemed especially weighty. Do you see why?

How does the following description of Committee reports, co-authored by a former Congressman and a Hill insider, affect your view of their appropriate use by courts:

> Each report, by rule, must contain certain items: the actual wording of the bill, showing by the use of italics and brackets the precise changes occasioned by the bill in existing law * * *; a summary of the alterations of existing law; the impact of the legislation on the budget and federal regulations; a full discussion of the merits of the legislation; and a recording of the roll-call vote. The report, however, is relatively insignificant for purposes of floor action. At best, it serves to educate the legislative assistants of non committee members. However, its public relations value is considerable. Because the report is generally written by proponents of the legislation, neither the problems nor the opposition's viewpoint is highlighted. The problems are sometimes described in minority reports, but these are not always written.

> Staff members use the language in a report as a significant bargaining tool. An interest group is sometimes content to get its language into the report, knowing that somewhere down the line it can point to the language in a court challenge or in an agency proceeding. Because report language is so callously used to assuage important members and interest groups, it often contains conflicting statements or statements that are as vague as the legislation itself. To get a true understanding of the controversial aspects of legislation, transcripts of the debate at the * * * mark-up and the floor debate are far more useful.[11] Rare is the report that is read by a congressman or a senator or that has actually persuaded someone to support legislation.[12]

If the committee report is generally the *weightiest* item of legislative history, the *weakest* is a statement by an individual legislator after a bill has been passed. For example, the issue in *Environmental Defense Fund v. City of Chicago*[13] was whether toxic ash from waste-to-energy incinerators had to be handled as a hazardous waste. The defendants argued that a provision of a 1984 statute exempted ash from the hazardous waste laws. In arguing for a narrower reading of the exemption, the plaintiffs relied on two letters. The first, dated October 2, 1987, was from Representative James Florio to the Administrator of the EPA; the second, also dated October 2, 1987, was from six U.S. Senators to the Administrator. Both letters set out their authors' view that the 1984 legislation did not exempt waste-to-energy facilities from otherwise applicable hazardous waste laws and

---

[11] [Ed. Fn.] Note that with only rare exceptions a transcript is not kept of markups. Some observers view the decisions made at the markup as the most important for understanding legislation; the participants' comments and the flow of accepted and, more important, rejected changes are revealing. Calls for keeping a transcript of markups are not uncommon. Wald, *supra* note 7, at 202.

[12] ABNER J. MIKVA & PATTI B. SARIS, THE AMERICAN CONGRESS: THE FIRST BRANCH 216 (1983).

[13] 948 F.2d 345 (7th Cir. 1991), *rev'd* 506 U.S. 982 (1992).

urged the Administrator so to interpret the statute. The court was not interested: "post-enactment statements, such as we have here, bear no necessary relationship to the forces at work at the time of enactment: the preferences of the enacting legislator and his or her constituency and the impact of pressure groups."[14] While adopting the plaintiffs' reading of the statute, the court's opinion relied on the letters not at all.

QUESTION

What justifies the quite different judicial receptions of committee reports on the one hand and a post-enactment letter from key legislators on the other?

3.   *Legislative History in Practice*

(a)   Air Quality Standards

Under the Clean Air Act, the EPA Administrator is to promulgate Air Quality Standards for certain common and harmful air pollutants. The standards must be set at levels that will "protect the public health." 42 U.S.C. § 7409(b)(1). What is that? Should the standards ensure no adverse health effects for the average healthy adult, the average child, asthmatics, hospital patients with lung ailments? How the "public" is defined will have tremendous impact on the stringency of the actual standards.

As it turns out, the Senate Report addressed exactly this issue:

> In requiring that national ambient air quality standards be established at a level necessary to protect the health of persons, the Committee recognizes that such standards will not necessarily provide for the quality of air required to protect those individuals who are otherwise dependent on a controlled internal environment such as patients in intensive care units or newborn infants in nurseries. However, the Committee emphasizes that included among those persons whose health should be protected by the ambient standard are particularly sensitive citizens such as bronchial asthmatics and emphysematics who in the normal course of daily activity are exposed to the ambient environment. In establishing an ambient standard necessary to protect the health of these persons, reference would be made to a representative sample of persons comprising the sensitive group rather than to a single person in such a group.[15]

Relying on this passage, EPA has taken the position (upheld in the courts) that an ambient standard should be set at the level where the most sensitive group, but not the most sensitive individual, would have no adverse health effects as a result of exposure to the pollutant.

---

[14] *Id.* at 351.

[15] S. Rep. No. 91-1196, at 10 (1970).

QUESTIONS

(1)   Is such reliance on the report appropriate? If not, how *should* the agency determine the meaning of "the public health" and what does that phrase mean?

(2)   If it knew whose health must be protected, why didn't Congress include a definition of "public health," corresponding to the language in the report, in the statute itself?

(b)   Liability for Hazardous Waste Cleanup

The Comprehensive Environmental Response, Compensation, and Liability Act (CERCLA or Superfund) imposes sweeping liabilities for the costs of cleaning up old hazardous waste sites. If hazardous wastes leak from a site, "the owner and operator [among others] * * * shall be liable for all costs of removal or remedial actions incurred by the United States Government or a State." 42 U.S.C. § 9607(a). In *New York v. Shore Realty Corp.*, 759 F.2d 1032 (2d Cir. 1985), the state had incurred "removal costs" at a hazardous waste site and was suing the owner, Shore Realty Corp. ("Shore"), for reimbursement. Shore argued that it was not liable because all the wastes had been placed at the site before Shore purchased it; thus, it had in no way contributed to the problem. It contended that it was not liable for a problem it had not caused.

To support its reading of the statute, Shore pointed to an exchange between Representatives Al Gore (yes, that Al Gore) and David Stockman on the floor of the House during debate on CERCLA. Stockman, who opposed the legislation, objected that it would lead to enormous liabilities "triggered by nothing more than a decision of a [government bureaucrat] that some landfill * * * needed to be cleaned up" and that a given company "contributed a few hundred pounds of waste to that site 30 years ago." Gore, who strongly supported the legislation, repeatedly insisted that this would not happen because "[p]roof of causation must occur. One must prove the damage was caused by the defendant." 126 Cong. Rec. 26,786–87 (1980).

The court concluded that the statute did not include a causation requirement and that Shore was liable.

> Our interpretation draws further support from the legislative history. Congress specifically rejected including a causation requirement in section 9607(a). The early House version imposed liability only upon "any person who caused or contributed to the release or threatened release [of a hazardous substance]." The compromise version, to which the House later agreed, imposed liability on classes of persons [including owners] without reference to whether they caused or contributed to the release or threat of release. Thus, the remarks of Representatives Stockman and Gore describing the House version containing the causation language, on which Shore relies, are inapposite.

The court continued in a footnote:

Indeed, an opponent of the bill, Representative Broyhill, argued that one of the defects of the bill was that the owner of a facility could be held "strictly liable . . . entirely on the basis of having been found to be an owner. . . . There is no language requiring any causal connection with a release of a hazardous substance." There is, to be sure, a contrary statement from Senator Helms: "The Government can sue a defendant under the bill only for those costs and damages that it can prove were caused by the defendant's conduct." Senator Helms, who opposed the legislation, appears to have been fighting a rearguard action by that remark.

NOTES AND QUESTIONS

(1)   The court's central legislative history argument is based not on what anyone *said* but on what the House *did*. What was that, and how does it cast light on the issue in *Shore Realty*?

(2)   The court takes the flatly contradictory statements of Broyhill and Helms and somehow makes them both support its result. How does it do that? Are you convinced? Can you recharacterize both comments to support the opposite result?

(3)   The usual rule is that statements by opponents of legislation carry less weight than statements by supporters. Why?

(4)   Representative Gore was a proponent of the bill and sponsor of relevant amendments. How can the court simply dismiss his description of CERCLA's provisions as "inapposite"? Consider the following admonition from Professor Otto Hetzel:

> [S]ome courts fail to be sufficiently discerning in their use of legislative history, using it in seeking legislative intent without due regard for its relative weight. Each of the types of legislative history bears evaluation and a determination of the proper weight to be accorded it. Such consideration includes the need to determine what happened on the floor of the legislature when the measure was considered. Should floor changes make reference to affected provisions in the committee report invalid? To what extent do reports in one House have significance in the other? How should "bulleted" floor testimony be evaluated for these purposes? These questions must be examined before the legislative history can be properly utilized in interpreting a statute.
>
> Other significant factors in evaluating various aspects of legislative history relate to identifying the status of the legislator whose floor comments are referenced. [Sponsors and party leaders carry special weight; opponents little or none.] * * * While one might assume that these evaluative doctrines are generally understood, they are so frequently ignored in the search for legislative history favorable to a preferred interpretation as to belie that assumption.

[An example of such carelessness is to rely on statements in a bill's legislative history made *before* the critical provision was added.] Obviously, many of the statements made before the insertion of that particular provision become irrelevant once that provision was added.[16]

Is the *Shore Realty* court's treatment of the Gore/Stockman exchange an example of a court doing what Hetzel urges or what he objects to?

Would Hetzel require judges to evaluate legislative history with the depth and subtlety of a political scientist? That is, would he require the impossible?

(5)   With regard to Professor Hetzel's reference to "bulleted floor testimony": Members of Congress are allowed to "revise and extend" their remarks for publication in the *Congressional Record*. Until 1978, the *Record* did not indicate in any way whether its contents had actually been delivered on the floor. Hence the following entry in the middle of a House debate:

> Mr. Speaker, having received unanimous consent to extend my remarks in the RECORD, I would like to indicate that I am not actually speaking these words. * * * As a matter of fact, I am back in my office typing this out on my own hot little typewriter. * * * Such is the pretense of the House that it would have been easy to just quietly include these remarks in the RECORD, issue a brave press release, and convince thousands of cheering constituents that I was in there fighting every step of the way, influencing the course of history in the heat of debate.[17]

In 1978 both houses began to indicate subsequently added statements with a bullet and, on the House side, a different typeface. This eliminated the most fictionalized versions of congressional proceedings. However, it remains the practice to give members a transcript of their remarks, prior to publication in the *Record*, so that any "transcription errors" can be corrected. As long as they are editing a statement actually made, as opposed to adding a whole new statement, it is impossible to tell whether or how the words in the publication differ from the words actually spoken on the floor. In theory, the *Record* is supposed to be "substantially a verbatim report of proceedings," 44 U.S.C. § 901, but in reality the gap between what was said and what gets printed can still be meaningful.

(c)   *Gregory v. Ashcroft*

You read excerpts from this case in Chapter 10. The question is whether appointed state judges are "employees" under the Age Discrimination in Employment Act (ADEA). The Act's definition of "employee" *excludes*

> any person elected to public office in any State or political subdivision of any State by the qualified voters thereof, or any person chosen by such officer to be on such officer's personal staff, or an *appointee on the*

---

[16] Otto J. Hetzel, *Instilling Legislative Interpretation Skills in the Classroom and the Courtroom*, 48 U. Pitt. L. Rev. 663, 684–685 & n.70 (1987).

[17] 117 Cong. Rec. 36,506 (1971) (statement of Rep. Heckler).

policymaking level or an immediate adviser with respect to the exercise of the constitutional or legal powers of the office.

29 U.S.C. § 630(f) (emphasis added).

The lower courts held that judges are not "employees" because they are not "on the policymaking level." The Supreme Court affirmed. As we saw in Chapter 10, the majority ruled against the judges without a definitive interpretation of the statute. It held only that if Congress wishes to regulate judicial selection and retention, it must do so explicitly. However, the concurrence (by Justice White) and the dissent (by Justice Blackmun) did join issue over the meaning of the statute. Part of their disagreement involved dueling legislative histories.

The first problem in turning to the legislative history of § 630(f) is that there is none. The section was added to the ADEA in 1974, with virtually no discussion or explanation in the legislative record. There is, however, a fuller record with regard to § 630(f)'s counterpart in Title VII of the Civil Rights Act of 1964, from which § 630(f) was copied verbatim. (Title VII forbids discrimination in employment on the basis of race, sex, religion, or national origin.) Justices White and Blackmun turn to the legislative history of § 630(f)'s counterpart in Title VII. Their assumption is that that history shows what the provision means in Title VII, and that it must mean the same thing in the ADEA.

The background to the discussion in the opinions below is this. The original version of Title VII (and of the ADEA) applied only to private employers. In 1972, Congress extended Title VII to state employees as well. The original version of this bill did so across the board. Many felt that was going too far, however, and the bill was amended to exclude some state officials. The discussion quoted by Justices White and Blackmun are from the Senate's debate about the scope of that amendment. Justice White argues that Congress clearly wanted to exclude judges from the coverage of Title VII (and therefore the ADEA). Justice Blackmun argues that Congress was not even thinking about judges; for him the key lesson of the legislative history is that the excluded groups consist solely of high-ranking nonjudicial officials such as cabinet members.

GREGORY v. ASHCROFT
501 U.S. 452 (1991)

Justice WHITE, with whom Justice STEVENS joins, concurring in part, dissenting in part, and concurring in the judgment. * * *

There is little legislative history discussing the definition of "employee" in the ADEA, so petitioners point to the legislative history of the identical definition in Title VII. If anything, that history tends to confirm that the "appointee[s] on the policymaking level" exception was designed to exclude from the coverage of the ADEA all high-level appointments throughout state government structures, including judicial appointments.

For example, during the debates concerning the proposed extension of Title VII to the States, Senator Ervin repeatedly expressed his concern that the (unamended) definition of "employee" would be construed to reach those "persons

who exercise the legislative, executive, *and judicial* powers of the States and political subdivisions of the States." 118 Cong. Rec. 1838 (1972) (emphasis added). Indeed, he expressly complained that "[t]here is not even an exception in the [unamended] bill to the effect that the EEOC will not have jurisdiction over . . . State judges, whether they are elected or appointed to office." *Id.*, at 1677. Also relevant is Senator Taft's comment that, in order to respond to Senator Ervin's concerns, he was willing to agree to an exception not only for elected officials, but also for "those at the top decisionmaking levels in the executive and judicial branch as well." *Id.*, at 1838.

The definition of "employee" subsequently was modified to exclude the four categories of employees [identified in the final statute.] The Conference Committee that added the "appointee[s] on the policymaking level" exception made clear the separate nature of that exception:

> "It is the intention of the conferees to exempt elected officials and members of their personal staffs, and persons appointed by such elected officials as advisors *or* to policymaking positions *at the highest levels* of the departments or agencies of State or local governments, such as cabinet officers, and persons with comparable responsibilities at the local level." H. R. Conf. Rep. No. 92-899, pp. 15–16 (1972) (emphasis added).

The italicized "or" in that statement indicates, contrary to petitioners' argument, that appointed officials need not be advisers to be covered by the exception. Rather, it appears that "Congress intended two categories: policymakers, who need not be advisers; and advisers, who need not be policymakers." *EEOC v. Massachusetts*, 858 F.2d 52, 56 (CA1 1988). This reading is confirmed by a statement by one of the House Managers, Representative Erlenborn, who explained that "in the conference, an additional qualification was added, exempting those people appointed by officials at the State and local level in policymaking positions." 118 Cong. Rec., at 7567. * * *

Justice BLACKMUN, with whom Justice MARSHALL joins, dissenting.

* * * The evidence of Congress' intent in enacting the policymaking exclusion supports [a] narrow reading. As noted by Justice WHITE, there is little in the legislative history of § 630(f) itself to aid our interpretive endeavor. Because Title VII of the Civil Rights Act of 1964 contains language identical to that in the ADEA's policymaking exclusion, however, we accord substantial weight to the legislative history of the cognate Title VII provision in construing § 630(f).

When Congress decided to amend Title VII to include States and local governments as employers, the original bill did not contain any employee exclusion. As Justice WHITE notes, the absence of a provision excluding certain state employees was a matter of concern for Senator Ervin, who commented that the bill, as reported, did not contain a provision "to the effect that the EEOC will not have jurisdiction over . . . State judges, whether they are elected or appointed to office. . . ." 118 Cong. Rec. 1677 (1972). Because this floor comment refers to appointed judges, Justice WHITE concludes that the later amendment containing the exclusion of "an appointee on the policymaking level" was drafted in "response to

the concerns raised by Senator Ervin and others," and therefore should be read to include judges.

Even if the only legislative history available was the above-quoted statement of Senator Ervin and the final amendment containing the policymaking exclusion, I would be reluctant to accept Justice WHITE's analysis. It would be odd to conclude that the general exclusion of those "on the policymaking level" was added in response to Senator Ervin's very specific concern about appointed judges. Surely, if Congress had desired to exclude judges — and was responding to a specific complaint that judges would be within the jurisdiction of the EEOC — it would have chosen far clearer language to accomplish this end. In any case, a more detailed look at the genesis of the policymaking exclusion seriously undermines the suggestion that it was intended to include appointed judges.

After commenting on the absence of an employee exclusion, Senator Ervin proposed the following amendment:

"[T]he term 'employee' as set forth in the original act of 1964 and as modified in the pending bill shall not include any person elected to public office in any State or political subdivision of any State by the qualified voters thereof, or any person chosen by such person to advise him in respect to the exercise of the constitutional or legal powers of his office." 118 Cong. Rec. 4483 (1972).

Noticeably absent from this proposed amendment is any reference to those on the policymaking level or to judges. Senator Williams then suggested expanding the proposed amendment to include the personal staff of the elected individual, leading Senators Williams and Ervin to engage in the following discussion about the purpose of the amendment:

"Mr. WILLIAMS: . . . . First, State and local governments are now included under the bill as employers. The amendment would provide, for the purposes of the bill and for the basic law, that an elected individual is not an employee and, therefore, the law could not cover him. The next point is that the elected official would, in his position as an employer, not be covered and would be exempt in the employment of certain individuals.

". . . [B]asically the purpose of the amendment . . . [is] to exempt from coverage those who are chosen by the Governor or the mayor or the county supervisor, whatever the elected official is, and who are in a close personal relationship and an immediate relationship with him. Those who are his first line of advisers. Is that basically the purpose of the Senator's amendment?

"Mr. ERVIN: I would say to my good friend from New Jersey that that is the purpose of the amendment." *Id.* at 4492–4493.

Following this exchange, Senator Ervin's amendment was expanded to exclude "any person chosen by such officer to be a personal assistant." *Id.,* at 4493. The Senate adopted these amendments, voting to exclude both personal staff members and immediate advisers from the scope of Title VII.

The policymaker exclusion appears to have arisen from Senator Javits' concern that the exclusion for advisers would sweep too broadly, including hundreds of functionaries such as "lawyers, . . . stenographers, subpena servers, researchers, and so forth." *Id.*, at 4097. Senator Javits asked "to have overnight to check into what would be the status of that rather large group of employees," noting that he "realize[d] that . . . Senator [Ervin was] . . . seeking to confine it to the higher officials in a policymaking or policy advising capacity." *Ibid.* In an effort to clarify his point, Senator Javits later stated:

> "The other thing, the immediate advisers, I was thinking more in terms of a cabinet, of a Governor who would call his commissioners a cabinet, or he may have a cabinet composed of three or four executive officials, or five or six, who would do the main and important things. That is what I would define these things expressly to mean." *Id.*, at 4493.

Although Senator Ervin assured Senator Javits that the exclusion of personal staff and advisers affected only the classes of employees that Senator Javits had mentioned, *ibid.*, the Conference Committee eventually adopted a specific exclusion of an "appointee on the policymaking level" as well as the exclusion of personal staff and immediate advisers contained in the Senate bill. In explaining the scope of the exclusion, the conferees stated:

> "It is the intention of the conferees to exempt elected officials and members of their personal staffs, and persons appointed by such officials as advisors or to policymaking positions at the highest levels of the departments or agencies of State or local governments, such as cabinet officers, and persons with comparable responsibilities at the local level. It is the conferees['] intent that this exemption shall be construed narrowly." S. Conf. Rep. No. 92-681, pp. 15–16 (1972).

The foregoing history decisively refutes the argument that the policymaker exclusion was added in response to Senator Ervin's concern that appointed state judges would be protected by Title VII. Senator Ervin's own proposed amendment did not exclude those on the policymaking level. Indeed, Senator Ervin indicated that all of the policymakers he sought to have excluded from the coverage of Title VII were encompassed in the exclusion of personal staff and immediate advisers. It is obvious that judges are neither staff nor immediate advisers of any elected official. The only indication as to whom Congress understood to be "appointee[s] on the policymaking level" is Senator Javits' reference to members of the Governor's cabinet, echoed in the Conference Committee's use of "cabinet officers" as an example of the type of appointee at the policymaking level excluded from Title VII's definition of "employee." When combined with the Conference Committee's exhortation that the exclusion be construed narrowly, this evidence indicates that Congress did *not* intend appointed state judges to be excluded from the reach of Title VII or the ADEA.

NOTES AND QUESTIONS

(1)   Both opinions treat the legislative history of § 630(f)'s identically worded counterpart in Title VII as relevant to the meaning of § 630(f). This approach assumes that the two provisions must mean the same thing, so any clues as to the meaning of the Title VII provision are also relevant to the ADEA provision. Is this sensible? When in 1972 Congress incorporated the *language* of that provision did it also incorporate its *history*? Could exactly the same provision mean two different things in two different places in the U.S. Code?

(2)   Do you understand exactly what each of the sources invoked by Justices White and Blackmun is? Did you notice whether all the quoted floor statements occurred during the same debate?

(3)   Senator Ervin comments explicitly on the issue in this case. Why isn't this dispositive? What is the difference between Senator Ervin's statement and, for example, the Senate Report's discussion of the meaning of "the public health" in the Clean Air Act?

(4)   In the end, Senator Ervin voted against the bill, notwithstanding his success in getting it amended.[18] Does or should that affect White's or Blackmun's analysis?

(5)   Where does each Justice stretch a bit (too much?) in drawing inferences as to statutory meaning? Who has the better of this argument?

(6)   Note the colloquy between Senators Ervin and Williams. Does it sound off-the-cuff? If it was scripted, would that affect its weight? Judge Abner Mikva says it should:

> [F]requently the process of "making legislative history" is abused. In fact, that very term used to offend me when I was in Congress. Nothing made me squirm more than when some lawyer, who ought to have known better, would get up for the purpose of "making legislative history," saying, "watch me, I'm making history" — and then proceed to read a speech that had been prepared for him before he got to the floor.
>
> Even more offensive is the *pas de deux* that frequently occurs on the floor. Two members will rise and engage in a colloquy for the purpose of "making legislative history." Frequently, however, the colloquy is written by just one of the members, not both. It is handed to the other actor and the two of them read it like a grade B radio script. And that is the material that judges later will solemnly pore over, under the guise of "studying the legislative history." This, of course, is ridiculous. The problem is that judges don't know as much as they ought to know about the legislative process. Judges, who are educable, ought to be able to learn about how the process works, just as congressmen ought to be able to learn about how the judicial review process works. With more interchange than now occurs, these two branches ought to be able to agree on common rules of behavior so that when a judge talks about debate, he is talking about real debate and

---

[18] 118 Cong. Rec. 4944 (1972).

not the phenomenon I have just described.[19]

Why should a scripted exchange (which after all has been carefully thought through) count less than spontaneous remarks made in the heat of debate? Given the traditionally heavy judicial reliance on legislative history, might Judge Mikva's hesitations extend to other materials besides the scripted colloquy?

(7)   Should remarks not actually spoken in the legislative chamber carry any weight? If not, what about remarks spoken on the floor but in the presence of, say, only a dozen other legislators? (Which is often a pretty good turnout; just watch C-Span sometime.) What assumptions about why floor debate is relevant to statutory interpretation in the first place underlie Judge Mikva's comments?

C.   THE ASSAULT ON JUDICIAL RELIANCE ON LEGISLATIVE HISTORY

Consider the following objections to the use of legislative history in interpreting statutes. As you do so, apply them to the cases in the previous section. How powerful are these objections as applied to the opinions you have read?

1.   *Constitutional Illegitimacy*

Says Justice Scalia:

The greatest defect of legislative history is its illegitimacy. We are governed by laws, not by the intentions of legislators. As the Court said in 1844: "The law as it passed is the will of the majority of both houses, *and the only mode in which that will is spoken is in the act itself. . . .*"[20]

This view is shared by Judge Easterbrook:

Statutes are law, not evidence of law. References to "intent" in judicial opinions do not imply that legislators' motives and beliefs, as opposed to their public acts, establish the norms to which all others must conform. "Original meaning" rather than "intent" frequently captures the interpretive task more precisely, reminding us that it is the work of the political branches (the "meaning") rather than of the courts that matters, and that their work acquires its meaning when enacted ("originally"). Revisionist history may be revelatory; revisionist judging is simply unfaithful to the enterprise. * * *

An opinion poll revealing the wishes of Congress would not translate to legal rules. Desires become rules only after clearing procedural hurdles, designed to encourage deliberation and expose proposals (and arguments) to public view and recorded vote. Resort to "intent" as a device to short-circuit these has no more force than the opinion poll — less, because the legislative history is written by the staff of a single committee and not

---

[19]   Abner J. Mikva, *A Reply to Judge Starr's Observations*, 1987 Duke L.J. 380, 384.

[20]   Conroy v. Aniskoff, 507 U.S. 511, 519 (1993) (Scalia, J., concurring), quoting Aldridge v. Williams, 3 How. 9, 24 (1845) (emphasis added).

subject to a vote or veto. The Constitution establishes a complex of procedures, including presidential approval (or support by two-thirds of each house). It would demean the constitutionally prescribed method of legislating to suppose that its elaborate apparatus for deliberation on, amending, and approving a text is just a way to create some *evidence* about the law, while the *real* source of legal rules is the mental processes of legislators.[21]

This is at bottom a constitutional argument. Article I, section 7 of the Constitution lays out mandatory procedures for passage of legislation. In particular, laws must be approved by both houses of Congress and presented to the President. Only something that has been through this process is law. Legislative history has not been through this process, and so is no more law than is a bill that was passed by the House but failed in the Senate.

Can one accept Judge Easterbrook's point — that legislative history is not law — without rejecting all judicial reliance on that history? The Justices in cases such as *Holy Trinity* and *Gregory v. Ashcroft* would not say that they were turning to the legislative history because that was where they would find binding legal rules; but that they were searching for illumination as to what the binding legal rule meant. Did they read the Committee Reports as if they were statutes?

2.   *Inaccurate Evidence of Members' Actual Views*

In *Blanchard v. Bergeron* the Court had to decide how attorney's fees should be calculated for purposes of 42 U.S.C. § 1988. The majority bolstered its interpretation of the statute by noting that it was consistent with the holdings of three district court cases decided before the statute had passed and cited approvingly in a Committee Report. Justice Scalia was unimpressed:

> That the Court should refer to the citation of three District Court cases in a document issued by a single committee of a single house as the action *of Congress* displays the level of unreality that our unrestrained use of legislative history has attained. I am confident that only a small proportion of the Members of Congress read either one of the Committee Reports in question, even if (as is not always the case) the Reports happened to have been published before the vote. * * * As anyone familiar with modern-day drafting of congressional committee reports is well aware, the references to the cases were inserted, at best by a committee staff member on his or her own initiative, and at worst by a committee staff member at the suggestion of a lawyer-lobbyist; and the purpose of those references was not primarily to inform the Members * * * what the bill meant * * * but rather to influence judicial construction. What a heady feeling it must be for a young staffer, to know that his or her citation of obscure district court cases can transform them into the law of the land, thereafter dutifully to be observed by the Supreme Court itself.[22]

---

[21] *In re* Sinclair, 870 F.2d 1340, 1343–1344 (7th Cir. 1989).

[22] Blanchard v. Bergeron, 489 U.S. 87, 98–99 (1989) (Scalia, J., concurring).

As an example of the phenomenon that Justice Scalia is describing, here is a former House committee staffer:

> I once wrote an 828-page report on Food Stamps in 1977 in which I successfully tried to imagine all the possible lawsuits that would be brought in the next three years and resolve them and the district court judges were stupid enough to follow me almost every single time. It was totally illegitimate, the chairman hadn't read it, the committee members wouldn't read it — I even put some recipes in there for food stamp recipients which people did notice because you flip the book and say "what the heck is this?".

Justice Scalia presented a fuller attack on the self-consciousness of the committee report in a speech before he was appointed to the high court:

> Ironically but understandably enough, the more the courts have relied upon committee reports in recent years, the less reliable they have become. In earlier days, when their sole purpose was to inform the members of Congress who were to vote upon the committee's bill, it was not as absurd (though still absurd enough) to pretend that those members had read and agreed with the report. But nowadays, when it is universally known and expected that judges will resort to the reports as authoritative expressions of "legislative intent" on the details they address, affecting the courts rather than informing the Congress has become the primary purpose of the exercise. In all of their ever-increasing, profuse detail, it is less that the courts refer to them because they exist, than that they exist because the courts refer to them.[23]

When Justice Scalia says that reports have become less "reliable," what does he mean? Legislative history from earlier times does *what* more reliably?

Justice Scalia's argument in *Blanchard* and in the speech calls for a realistic view of the legislative process. Yet realism might also argue *for* reference to committee reports. Learned Hand thought it did:

> It is of course true that members who vote upon a bill do not all know, probably very few of them know, what has taken place in committee. On the most rigid theory possibly we ought to assume that they accept the words just as the words read, without any background of amendment or other evidence as to their meaning. But courts have come to treat the facts more really; they recognize that while members deliberately express their personal position upon the general purposes of the legislation, as to the details of its articulation they accept the work of the committees; so much they delegate because legislation could not go on in any other way.[24]

Similarly, could the self-consciousness of so much legislative history be an argument *for* judicial reliance on it? For years the courts have told Congress that they will pay attention to legislative history in general and committee reports in

---

[23] Address by Judge Antonin Scalia, Speech on Use of Legislative History (delivered at various law schools between fall 1985 and spring 1986), *quoted in* William N. Eskridge, Jr. & Philip P. Frickey, *Legislative Intent and Public Choice*, 74 Va. L. Rev. 423, 443 n.65 (1988).

[24] SEC v. Collier, 76 F.2d 939, 941 (2d Cir. 1935).

particular. It is in response to that message that Congress has developed "conventions by which much of the elaboration of statutes — references to judicial decisions ratified or overruled, purposes to be fulfilled, specific issues thought to be resolved — has been put in committee reports rather than in the statutes themselves, where most of it would be cumbersome and out-of-place anyway."[25] Against this background, would it amount to the unfair con game of "bait and switch" for the courts now to defeat congressional expectations by adopting a pure textualist approach?[26]

3.   *Indeterminacy*

Critics of the use of legislative history doubt that consultation of legislative history provides any answers other than those that the investigator seeks; invocation of legislative intent is merely "a handy cover for judicial intent." Concurring in *Conroy v. Aniskoff*, 507 U.S. 511 (1993), Justice Scalia sought to make this point by amassing legislative history *against* the majority's result, even though he agreed with it.

> [N]ot the least of the defects of legislative history is its indeterminacy. If one were to search for an interpretive technique that, *on the whole*, was more likely to confuse than to clarify, one could hardly find a more promising candidate than legislative history. And the present case nicely proves that point.
>
> Judge Harold Leventhal used to describe the use of legislative history as the equivalent of entering a crowded cocktail party and looking over the heads of the guests for one's friends. If I may pursue that metaphor: The legislative history of § 205 of the Soldiers' and Sailors' Civil Relief Act contains a variety of diverse personages, a selected few of whom — its "friends" — the Court has introduced to us in support of its result. But there are many other faces in the crowd, most of which, I think, are set against today's result.

After laying out a number of aspects of the legislative history that went *against* the result he considered correct, Justice Scalia concluded:

> After reading th[is] legislative history, one might well conclude that the result reached by the Court today, though faithful to law, betrays the congressional intent. * * *
>
> I confess that I have not personally investigated the entire legislative history * * *. The excerpts I have examined and quoted were unearthed by a hapless law clerk to whom I assigned the task. The other Justices have, in the aggregate, many more law clerks than I, and it is quite possible that if they all were unleashed upon this enterprise they would discover * * * many faces friendly to the Court's holding. Whether they would or not makes no difference to me — and evidently makes no difference to the Court, which gives lipservice to legislative history but does not trouble to

---

[25] William N. Eskridge, Jr., *The New Textualism*, 37 UCLA L. Rev. 621, 683 (1990).

[26] *See id.*

set forth and discuss the foregoing material * * *. In my view, that is as it should be, except for the lipservice. The language of the statute is entirely clear, and if that is not what Congress meant then Congress has made a mistake and Congress will have to correct it. We should not pretend to care about legislative intent (as opposed to the meaning of the law), lest we impose upon the practicing bar and their clients obligations that we do not ourselves take seriously.[27]

The objection that legislative history is infinitely manipulable is a common one. Legislative history is so diffuse and extensive, it is argued, that at least a morsel can be found in support of almost any interpretation, making its use redundant at best and pernicious at worst. This is a hard charge to evaluate without having read a bunch of cases. The standoff in *Gregory* should suggest to you that this objection is at least not wholly fanciful.

Of course, the fact that legislative history is somewhat indeterminate does not necessarily mean that it is *more* indeterminate than a textual approach. Justice Stevens, arguably the strongest proponent of reliance on purpose and history among the current Justices, has repeatedly argued that consulting legislative history *narrows* rather than expands judicial discretion. For example:

> [Justice Scalia] correctly observes that a judicial decision that departs from statutory text may represent "policy-driven interpretation." As long as that driving policy is faithful to the intent of Congress (or, as in this case, aims only to give effect to such intent) — which it must be if it is to override a strict interpretation of the text — the decision is also a correct performance of the judicial function. Justice Scalia's argument today rests on the incorrect premise that every policy-driven interpretation implements a judge's personal view of sound policy, rather than a faithful attempt to carry out the will of the legislature. Quite the contrary is true of the work of the judges with whom I have worked for many years. If we presume that our judges are intellectually honest — and I do — there is no reason to fear "policy-driven interpretations" of Acts of Congress. * * *

> This happens to be a case in which the legislative history is pellucidly clear and the statute difficult to fathom. Moreover, it is a case in which I cannot imagine anyone accusing any member of the Court of voting one way or the other because of that Justice's own policy preferences.

> Given the clarity of the evidence of Congress' "intention on the precise question at issue," I would affirm the judgment of the Court of Appeals even if I thought that petitioners' literal reading of the statutory text was correct. The only "policy" by which I have been driven is that which the Court has endorsed on repeated occasions regarding the importance of remaining faithful to Congress's intent.[28]

---

[27] 507 U.S. at 519, 526–528.

[28] Zuni Public School District No. 89 v. Department of Education, 550 U.S. 81, 105–107 (2007) (Stevens, J., concurring).

4. *Unavailability and Cost*

One of the eight "routes to disaster" travelled by Rex, Lon Fuller's floundering lawgiver, who failed to create a system that could even be called law, was the failure to publicize, or at least make available to the affected party, the rules that party is expected to observe.[29] A law that is promulgated and then kept in a sealed box is no law at all. Does extensive reliance on legislative history create such secret law? Should the principle that law must be accessible at least impose an obligation on courts to rely only on such history as is readily available?

Even if historical legislative materials can be tracked down, is doing so (a) worth the effort or (b) fair to those without unlimited legal resources? Consider Justice Scalia's objections to an opinion in which the majority invoked legislative history to confirm its reading of the text:

> [T]he Court feels compelled to demonstrate that its holding is consonant with legislative history, including some dating back to 1917 — *a full quarter century* before the provision at issue was enacted. That is not merely a waste of research time and ink; it is a false and disruptive lesson in the law. It says to the bar that even an "unambiguous [and] unequivocal" statute can never be dispositive; that, presumably under penalty of malpractice liability, the oracles of legislative history, far into the dimmy past, must always be consulted. This undermines the clarity of law, and condemns litigants (who, unlike us, must pay for it out of their own pockets) to subsidizing historical research by lawyers.[30]

On the other hand, if legislative history merely explains the meaning of a statute, and in some sense of ultimate truth the meaning resides *in the statute*, why should the general availability of these materials matter? What does matter is reaching the correct reading of the statute. Furthermore, in practice most legislative history is almost as available, at least to the trained legal researcher, as the statutes themselves, and without huge additional expenses of time or effort. And even if citizens are wholly unaware of legislative history, are they any more aware of statutory texts? It may be no more of a fiction to assume familiarity with legislative history than to assume familiarity with the statutes themselves. Finally, with regard to *unclear* statutes use of legislative history may make it easier rather than harder for citizens to plan their conduct.

NOTES AND QUESTIONS

(1) Textualist judges are sometimes willing to consult legislative history for particular, limited purposes — for example, to see if there is any indication that Congress intended a bizarre result that the literal words suggest, or to learn something of the context within which a term was used so as better to understand its meaning at the time the statute was passed. It is thus a slight exaggeration to

---

[29] Lon L. Fuller, The Morality of Law 39, 49–51 (1964); *see supra* pages 185–86.

[30] Conroy v. Aniskoff, 507 U.S. 511, 518–519 (1993) (Scalia, J., concurring).

say that Justice Scalia and his followers would forbid any recourse to legislative history whatsoever. Still, as you have seen, the textualist position is sharply at odds with what had been the widely accepted approach of the federal courts in statutory cases.

(2)   Has the Scalia camp made its case? Apply each of the specific objections described above to the courts' use of legislative history in *Holy Trinity*, *Gregory*, and *Shore Realty*.

(3)   The real question is not whether reliance on legislative history has its pitfalls, but whether the alternatives are any better. Does a strong version of textualism also have its pitfalls? Would it be preferable to decide the cases in this chapter without recourse to legislative history? In what way(s)?

NOTE ON LEGISLATIVE HISTORY AND "DEMOCRATIC EXEGESIS"

One recurrent point of emphasis in the attack on the use of legislative history is that it is undemocratic. Textualists claim that a central virtue of a focus on text is that it empowers the ruled as opposed to the rulers (either legislative or judicial). By forcing the legislature to express its intent on the face of the statute, textualism facilitates public monitoring and thus congressional accountability. Writes Justice Scalia:

> It should not be possible, or at least should not be easy, to be sure of obtaining a particular result in this Court without making that result apparent on the face of the bill which both Houses consider and vote upon, which the President approves, and which, if it becomes law, the people must obey. I think we have an obligation to conduct our exegesis in a fashion which fosters that democratic process.[31]

Furthermore, the argument runs, by reducing judicial power (by reducing the opportunity for judicial policymaking under the guise of interpretation), textualism necessarily increases the power of the democratically accountable branches. The supposed predictability of the textualist method provides Congress with "a sure means by which it may work the people's will."[32] In contrast, "it does not foster a democratic exegesis for this Court to rummage through unauthoritative materials" in search of the interpretation it likes better than the one apparent on the face of the statute.[33]

The question of what interpretive method best promotes democratic governance is not so clear, however. Some observers insist that "[t]he lesson of history is that for judges to restrict themselves to language risks displacing, not defending, a 'democratic exegesis.' "[34] More than half a century ago, James Landis took judges

---

[31]   United States v. Taylor, 487 U.S. 326, 345–346 (1988) (Scalia, J., concurring).

[32]   Chisom v. Roemer, 501 U.S. 380, 417 (1991) (Scalia, J., dissenting). The case is set out at pages 443–49 *infra*.

[33]   Public Citizen v. United States Dep't of Justice, 491 U.S. 440, 473 (1989) (Kennedy, J., concurring).

[34]   Peter L. Strauss, *When the Judge is not the Primary Official with Responsibility to Read: Agency*

to task for failing to look behind statutory language on precisely these grounds. Responding to Max Radin's attack on the preoccupation with legislative intent, Landis wrote:

> Legislative history * * * affords in many instances accurate and compelling guides to legislative meaning. * * * The real difficulty is twofold: that strong judges prefer to override the intent of the legislature in order to make law according to their own views, and that barbaric rules of interpretation [forbidding reference to legislative history] too often exclude the opportunity to get at legislative meaning in a realistic fashion. The latter, originating at a time when records of legislative assemblies were not in existence, deserve no adherence in these days of carefully kept journals, debates, and reports. Unfortunately they persist with that tenaciousness characteristic of outworn legal rules. Strong judges are always with us; no science of interpretation can ever hope to curb their propensities. But the effort should be to restrain their tendencies, not to give them free rein[.] * * *

> The real problems [in statutory interpretation] arise where the meaning of the legislature is not discoverable. Here the gravest sins are perpetrated in the name of the intent of the legislature. Judges are rarely willing to admit their role as actual lawgivers, and such admissions as are wrung from their unwilling lips lie in the field of common and not statute law. To condone in these instances the practice of talking in terms of the intent of the legislature, as if the legislature had attributed a particular meaning to certain words, when it is apparent that the intent is that of the judge, is to condone atavistic practices too reminiscent of the medicine man. No compromise can be had on this issue.

> A statute rarely stands alone. * * * [I]t is the culmination often of long legislative processes, too rarely understood by the mere lawyer, and too rarely studied to have been lifted from the contempt bred of ignorance. Such material frequently affords a guide to the intent of the legislature conceived of in terms of purpose. * * *

> The use of extrinsic aids to statutory interpretation thus has real and not illusory significance. Hopeful developments toward a science of statutory interpretation must be in the direction of devising means of properly evaluating the effectiveness to be given such extrinsic aids. Of course, guessing will not thereby be eliminated; but what science, natural or otherwise, has eliminated the necessity for guesswork? Nevertheless the emphasis must lie upon the honest effort of courts to give effect to the legislature's aims, even though their perception be perforce through a glass darkly.[35]

Modern-day judges who turn to legislative history also seek to wrap themselves in the mantle of democratic authority. For example:

Interpretation and the Problem of Legislative History, 66 CHI.-KENT L. REV. 321, 346 (1990).

[35] James M. Landis, *A Note on "Statutory Interpretation"*, 43 HARV. L. REV. 886, 889–891, 893 (1930).

Having [reached a conclusion based on the statutory text,] Justice Kennedy refuses to consult [the] legislative history — which he later denounces, with surprising hyperbole, as "unauthoritative materials," * * * — because this result would not, in his estimation, be "absurd." * * * [T]his Court has never adopted so strict a standard for reviewing committee reports, floor debates, and other nonstatutory indications of congressional intent, *and we explicitly reject that standard today* * * *. Nor does it strike us as in any way "unhealthy," or undemocratic, to use all available materials in ascertaining the intent of our elected representatives, rather than read their enactments as requiring what may seem a disturbingly unlikely result, provided only that the result is not "absurd." Indeed, the sounder and more democratic course, the course that strives for allegiance to Congress' desires in all cases, not just those where Congress' statutory directive is plainly sensible or borders on the lunatic, is the traditional approach we reaffirm today.[36]

Who has the better of this argument? Does reliance on legislative history increase or decrease judicial discretion? Increase or decrease congressional control? Increase or decrease transparency and popular control of government institutions?

Assignment

The basic federal prohibition on counterfeit coins dates back to 1806. Its key provision, 18 U.S.C. § 485, was amended in minor ways over the years, but remained essentially unchanged for a century and a half. Here is one early version:

Every person who falsely makes, forges, or counterfeits * * * any coin or bars in resemblance or similitude of the gold or silver coins or bars which have been, or hereafter may be, coined or stamped at the mints and assay-offices of the United States, or in resemblance or similitude of any foreign gold or silver coin which by law is, or hereafter may be, current in the United States, or are in actual use and circulation as money within the United States, or who passes, utters, publishes, or sells * * * or has in his possession any such false, forged or counterfeited coin or bars, knowing the same to be false, forged or counterfeited, with intent to defraud any body politic or corporate, or any other person or persons whatsoever, shall be punished by a fine of not more than five thousand dollars, and by imprisonment at hard labor not more than ten years.

In 1965, Congress enacted the Coinage Act. According to the Senate and House Reports, the purpose of this Act was to authorize the minting and use of non-silver coins in order to conserve the nation's silver supply. *See* S. Rep. No. 317, 89th Cong., 1st Sess. 1 (1965); H. Rep. No. 509, 89th Cong., 1st Sess. 1 (1965), 1965 U.S. Code Cong. & Admin. News 2299. Previously, dimes, quarters, and coins of larger denominations had been solid silver; after the Coinage Act they became "sandwiches," with a non-silver center.

---

[36] Public Citizen v. United States Dep't of Justice, 491 U.S. 440, 453–454 n.9 (1989).

The Coinage Act amended § 485 to read as follows:

Whoever falsely makes, forges, or counterfeits any coin or bar in resemblance or similitude of any coin of a denomination higher than 5 cents or any gold or silver bar coined or stamped at any mint or assay office of the United States, or in resemblance or similitude of any foreign gold or silver coin current in the United States or in actual use and circulation as money within the United States; or

Whoever passes, utters, publishes, sells, possesses, or brings into the United States any false, forged, or counterfeit coin or bar, knowing the same to be false, forged, or counterfeit, with intent to defraud any body politic or corporate, or any person, or attempts the commission of any offense described in this paragraph-

Shall be fined not more than $ 5,000 or imprisoned not more than fifteen years, or both.

The legislative history with regard to the change to § 485 is sparse. The House Report stated:

Section 485 of title 18 of the United States Code makes it a felony to counterfeit silver coins. * * * [T]he bill amends it to cover coins of any denomination in excess of 5 cents, thus covering coins of the same denomination as existing law, but describing them in terms which make their composition irrelevant.

The Senate Report is similar:

[The bill] would make necessary changes in the counterfeiting laws to assure they will be applicable to the new coins in the same terms as they were applicable to the present subsidiary coins. As in the case of current coins, the counterfeiting of the new coins will carry penalties of a fine of $ 5,000 or 15 years' imprisonment, or both.

Margaret Richards is charged with violating § 485. The indictment alleges that she possessed with intent to defraud counterfeit Krugerrands, which are gold coins used as currency in South Africa but not in the United States.

Does possession of counterfeit Krugerrands violate the statute?

Chapter 13

STATUTES IN THE ADMINISTRATIVE STATE

The implementation and interpretation of statutes is not solely a function of *judicial* elaboration. Often equally important is the interpretation of a statute by the administrative agency charged with its implementation. The functions, powers, procedures, and control of agencies are topics for courses in constitutional and administrative law and are well beyond the scope of this one. Nevertheless, we cannot ignore agencies while discussing statutes. Where there is an agency, there is a statute; and almost as frequently (and more to our point), where there is a statute, there is an agency.

A. INTRODUCING ADMINISTRATIVE AGENCIES

The United States Constitution creates the posts of President, Vice President, Member of Congress, and Justice of the Supreme Court. Currently, that comes to 546 government employees. Add "such inferior Courts as Congress may from time to time ordain and establish," and you are in the neighborhood of 1500. Yet the civilian workforce of the U.S. Government is over 2 million. Who are all these people? The huge majority work for administrative agencies — they form the notorious federal bureaucracy. The Constitution does refer to "Officers of the United States," "inferior officers," and "heads of departments," anticipating the development of some sort of federal bureaucracy whose principal officers will be appointed by the President. But the bureaucracy is not established by the Constitution; it is created by Congress, through, and in order to implement, statutes.

Particularly since the New Deal, we have been living in "the administrative state." Most contacts that an individual, or a firm, has with the government are with an agency. The IRS is an agency; so is the Department of Motor Vehicles. It is an agency that takes the legislature's often general language and translates it into specific requirements; it is an agency that grants licenses and permits and decides whether a violation has occurred; it is an agency that inspects regulated entities to ensure compliance. In short, day-to-day government is in the hands of agencies.

Agencies are creatures of statute, created by Congress, with all, but only, the powers Congress gives them. (Our discussion in this chapter focuses exclusively on the federal government. For the most part, however, state systems are similar.) Many questions of administrative law therefore involve disputes as to the scope of agency authority, and those disputes, in turn, almost always involve a statute.

Congress generally creates federal agencies of two basic types. *Executive agencies* are squarely within the executive branch; headed by a single political appointee who serves at the President's pleasure, these include the cabinet

departments (state, defense, health and human services, etc.) as well as a few free-standing entities such as the Environmental Protection Agency. The leadership of executive agencies turns over completely with each new presidential administration. *Independent agencies* generally take the form of multi-member, bi-partisan commissions. The commissioners serve lengthy, staggered terms generally corresponding in years to the number of spots on the commission. For example, the Federal Communications Commission has five members, each serving a five-year term; terms are staggered, so, absent resignations, one spot opens up each year. Commissioners have a sort of tenure; they can be fired by the President, but only for "neglect of duty, malfeasance, or good cause shown," or similar such language. The National Labor Relations Board, the Federal Communications Commission, and the Securities and Exchange Commission, among others, are independent agencies. The general functions of the executive and independent agencies are essentially the same; as their names suggest, they differ in their independence from executive control.

Historically, Congress tended to create independent agencies; many of the independent agencies date back to the New Deal. The agencies established in the 1970s and thereafter, by contrast, have tended to be executive agencies. There are many possible explanations for this shift, but one has to do with changes in prevailing theories about governance. The independent agency model rests on the idea that there is a science of governing; the way to ensure good decisionmaking is to hire experts and keep the politicians out of their hair. The executive agency model, in contrast, reflects doubts that there are right answers to policy questions and sees preference and politics as legitimating rather than corrupting forces in government decisionmaking.

The Clean Air Act problem in Chapter 10 gave you a hint of the importance of agencies. If you read the provisions carefully, you saw that they give the Environmental Protection Agency two important roles. First, it must write "regulations." Section 111, for example, has no regulatory effect by itself; it requires EPA to develop "new source performance standards" (NSPSs). Private parties cannot "comply" with § 111; there is nothing in it with which to comply. Rather, they must comply with EPA's regulations *issued pursuant to* § 111; it is the regulations that impose legal obligations on private parties.

Most federal regulations are produced through "notice and comment rulemaking," the basic procedures for which are set out in the Administrative Procedure Act, which, as its name implies, is a generally applicable set of default procedures for agency action.[1] The agency first issues a proposed rule for public comment, publishing it the *Federal Register*, a daily governmental publication, and on line. All interested parties can then submit comments. When issuing a final rule, the agency must consider and respond to these comments. The final regulation along with a generally lengthy explanation must be published in the *Federal Register*. Increasingly, rulemaking is moving on line. The federal government maintains a central

---

[1] The APA, which was enacted in 1946, is found at 5 U.S.C. §§ 551–706. It sets out procedures for rulemaking and adjudication, and also provides the mechanisms and standards for judicial review of agency action. The Freedom of Information Act, adopted in 1966 and amended several times since, is formally an amendment to the APA and is found at 5 U.S.C. § 552.

ized online rulemaking docket management system, found at www.regulations.gov. It is worth having a look at. Any person can use it to review and comment on proposed rules.

Final regulations are also collected in the Code of Federal Regulations (the "CFR"), the regulatory counterpart to the U.S. Code. Agency regulations are subject to judicial review; courts will set aside regulations that are inconsistent with the statute, procedurally invalid, or "arbitrary, capricious, or an abuse of discretion."[2] Unless set aside by a court, however, regulations are binding statements of law that private parties must obey.

The second role played by EPA and implicit in the incinerator problem is issuing permits to new sources of air pollution. To obtain a permit, an applicant must show, at a trial-type hearing, that it has satisfied numerous statutory and regulatory requirements. Thus, while writing regulations is essentially *legislative* in nature, issuing permits (or ruling on applications for disability or veterans benefits, or issuing drivers licenses, or imposing fines for violating regulatory requirements) is essentially *adjudicatory* in nature. Like a court, the agency must find facts regarding a particular party, interpret the relevant law, and apply the law to the facts to reach a result. In doing this, the agency holds a trial-type hearing, often presided over by an "administrative law judge" (ALJ), with witnesses, lawyers, and exhibits.

Agencies also have a third role: inspections and enforcement. If an incinerator, for example, were to violate the New Source Performance Standard promulgated by EPA, or operate without a required permit, or exceed the emission limits set out in its permit, enforcement would likely involve an EPA inspection, an EPA citation, and an EPA fine, all without any judicial involvement. In many circumstances, under environmental and other statutes, the agency will conduct a formal adjudication to determine whether the statute or regulation has been violated and, if so, what fine to impose. Alternatively, it may sue the violator in court.

Agencies are understood to be in the executive branch. But as we have just seen, they perform functions that are typical of the work of each of the branches. They have a *legislative* function in promulgating regulations. Depending on the detail in the underlying statute, regulations may just flesh out the details; often, though, it is the agency that is making the critical policy decisions pursuant to a broad delegation from Congress. Agencies have a *judicial* function in adjudicating (a) applications for permits or licenses and (b) alleged violations of statutes, regulations, or permits. And they have an *executive* function in inspecting, policing compliance, and bringing enforcement actions either before the agency or in court.

B. AGENCY INTERPRETATIONS

In each of these functions agencies are called on to interpret the statutes under which they operate. Again, consider Section 111 of the Clean Air Act. It requires the EPA Administrator to publish a list of "categories of stationary sources," including a category on the list "if in his judgment it causes, or contributes significantly to, air

---

[2] 5 U.S.C. § 706 (2006).

pollution which may reasonably be anticipated to endanger public health or welfare." It must then promulgate new source performance standards for facilities in each category, setting

> a standard for emissions of air pollutants which reflects the degree of emission limitation achievable through the application of the best system of emission reduction which (taking into account the cost of achieving such reduction and any non-air quality health and environmental impact and energy requirements) the Administrator determines has been adequately demonstrated.

Developing an NSPS thus requires EPA to make a number of interpretive calls: is a device "adequately demonstrated" if it has been used on other types of plants but not on the ones that are the subject of the NSPS; what counts as an "air pollutant" (a question to which we will return); does air pollution "endanger" public health if the science supports only a suspected rather than an established link between the pollutant and disease; what exactly is a "new" source; should the costs of pollution control equipment be weighed against its benefits; etc., etc., etc.

In adjudications, too, the agency is explaining and refining its understanding of the statute. The National Labor Relations Board, for example, operates under extremely general and vague statutes regulating collective bargaining and union affairs and it issues virtually no regulations. It develops and refines a sort of common law of labor relations through its decisions in individual adjudications over alleged violations of the labor laws. To those trying to comply with the law, NLRB precedents are just as important as judicial decisions.

Interpretation in, or through, enforcement is less formal and will not concern us here. Still, its practical importance should not be underestimated. Consider the laws against jaywalking or adultery. In the real world, the nonenforcement of these provisions is their most salient feature; it is a de facto interpretation that we might say "reads into" the law an exception for jaywalkers. To the regulated community, an agency's enforcement policy under a particular statute is as important as its interpretation of the statute's language.

As a general rule, when an agency does something, it is, once final, subject to review in the courts. The Administrative Procedure Act (the "constitution of administrative law") provides:

> To the extent necessary to decision and when presented, the reviewing court shall decide all relevant questions of law, interpret constitutional and statutory provisions, and determine the meaning or applicability of the terms of an agency action. The reviewing court shall —
>
> > (1) compel agency action unlawfully withheld or unreasonably delayed; and
> >
> > (2) hold unlawful and set aside agency action, findings, and conclusions found to be —
> >
> > > (A) arbitrary, capricious, an abuse of discretion, or otherwise not in accordance with law;

(B) contrary to constitutional right, power, privilege, or immunity;

(C) in excess of statutory jurisdiction, authority, or limitations, or short of statutory right;

(D) without observance of procedure required by law;

(E) unsupported by substantial evidence in a case subject to sections 556 and 557 of this title or otherwise reviewed on the record of an agency hearing provided by statute; or

(F) unwarranted by the facts to the extent that the facts are subject to trial de novo by the reviewing court.

5 U.S.C. § 706. To paraphrase: a court can set aside agency action that is nuts (or, as the courts have put it, not the result of "reasoned decisionmaking"), is unconstitutional, violated required procedures, rests on dubious findings of fact, or, most important for present purposes, is inconsistent with a relevant statute. This last category looms largest.

The cases in this chapter each arise after an agency has taken a position about the meaning of a statute. The first, *Skidmore*, is not an example of direct review of the agency decision; it is a private lawsuit that involves an issue as to which the agency has expressed an opinion, and the question is whether that opinion should carry weight with a court. The second two cases, *Chevron* and *Massachusetts v. EPA*, are examples of direct challenges to agency decisions — the promulgation of a regulation in one, the refusal to promulgate a regulation in the other.

C.   DEFERENCE TO AGENCY INTERPRETATIONS

Courts often state that they must defer to the interpretation of a statute given by the agency charged with implementing it. The key questions are why and how much.

SKIDMORE v. SWIFT & CO.
323 U.S. 134 (1944)

Mr. Justice Jackson delivered the opinion of the Court.

Seven employees of the Swift and Company packing plant at Fort Worth, Texas, brought an action under the Fair Labor Standards Act [which requires employers to pay time and a half for overtime] to recover overtime, liquidated damages, and attorneys' fees, totaling approximately $77,000. [The employees were firefighters. Their regular employment was during the day. However, they also agreed to spend three or four nights a week on the company premises or close by in case of fire. The dispute was whether the time spent hanging around in this way was "working time" for purposes of the Act.] * * *

[N]o principle of law found either in the statute or in Court decisions precludes waiting time from also being working time. We have not attempted to, and we cannot, lay down a legal formula to resolve cases so varied in their facts as are the

many situations in which employment involves waiting time. * * * Facts may show that the employee was engaged to wait, or they may show that he waited to be engaged. His compensation may cover both waiting and task, or only performance of the task itself. Living quarters may in some situations be furnished as a facility of the task and in another as a part of its compensation. The law does not impose an arrangement upon the parties. It imposes upon the courts the task of finding what the arrangement was. * * *

Congress * * * create[d] the office of Administrator, impose[d] upon him a variety of duties, endow[ed] him with powers to inform himself of conditions in industries and employments subject to the Act, and put on him the duties of bringing injunction actions to restrain violations. Pursuit of his duties has accumulated a considerable experience in the problems of ascertaining working time in employments involving periods of inactivity and a knowledge of the customs prevailing in reference to their solution. From these he is obliged to reach conclusions as to conduct without the law, so that he should seek injunctions to stop it, and that within the law, so that he has no call to interfere. He has set forth his views of the application of the Act under different circumstances in an interpretative bulletin and in informal rulings. They provide a practical guide to employers and employees as to how the office representing the public interest in its enforcement will seek to apply it.

* * * [T]he conclusion of the Administrator, as expressed in the brief amicus curiae, is that the general tests which he has suggested point to the exclusion of sleeping and eating time of these employees from the workweek and the inclusion of all other on-call time * * *.

There is no statutory provision as to what, if any, deference courts should pay to the Administrator's conclusions. * * * They do not constitute an interpretation of the Act or a standard for judging factual situations which binds a district court's processes, as an authoritative pronouncement of a higher court might do. But the Administrator's policies are made in pursuance of official duty, based upon more specialized experience and broader investigations and information than is likely to come to a judge in a particular case. * * * The fact that the Administrator's policies and standards are not reached by trial in adversary form does not mean that they are not entitled to respect. * * *

We consider that the rulings, interpretations and opinions of the Administrator under this Act, while not controlling upon the courts by reason of their authority, do constitute a body of experience and informed judgment to which courts and litigants may properly resort for guidance. The weight of such a judgment in a particular case will depend upon the thoroughness evident in its consideration, the validity of its reasoning, its consistency with earlier and later pronouncements, and all those factors which give it power to persuade, if lacking power to control.

* * * [I]n this case, although the District Court referred to the Administrator's Bulletin, its evaluation and inquiry were apparently restricted by its notion that waiting time may not be work, an understanding of the law which we hold to be erroneous. Accordingly, the judgment is reversed and the cause remanded for further proceedings consistent herewith.

CHEVRON U.S.A. INC. v. NRDC
467 U.S. 837 (1984)

JUSTICE STEVENS delivered the opinion of the Court.

[The Natural Resources Defense Council, a non-profit environmental advocacy organization, sued EPA, challenging the validity of certain EPA regulations under the Clean Air Act. Chevron U.S.A., which liked the regulations, intervened on EPA's side. When NRDC won in the Court of Appeals, Chevron filed the first petition for certiorari; hence the case name. Although not mentioned in the caption (which gives only the first party on each side), EPA is also a petitioner in this action.]

In the Clean Air Act Amendments of 1977 Congress enacted certain requirements applicable to States that had not achieved the national air quality standards established by the Environmental Protection Agency (EPA) pursuant to earlier legislation. The amended Clean Air Act required these "nonattainment" States to establish a permit program regulating "new or modified major stationary sources" of air pollution. Generally, a permit may not be issued for a new or modified major stationary source unless several stringent conditions are met. The EPA regulation promulgated to implement this permit requirement allows a State to adopt a plantwide definition of the term "stationary source." Under this definition, an existing plant that contains several pollution-emitting devices may install or modify one piece of equipment without meeting the permit conditions if the alteration will not increase the total emissions from the plant [i.e., if it makes offsetting emission reductions elsewhere in the plant]. The question presented by these cases is whether EPA's decision to allow States to treat all of the pollution-emitting devices within the same industrial grouping as though they were encased within a single "bubble" is based on a reasonable construction of the statutory term "stationary source." * * *

When a court reviews an agency's construction of the statute which it administers, it is confronted with two questions. First, always, is the question whether Congress has directly spoken to the precise question at issue. If the intent of Congress is clear, that is the end of the matter; for the court, as well as the agency, must give effect to the unambiguously expressed intent of Congress.[3] If, however, the court determines Congress has not directly addressed the precise question at issue, the court does not simply impose its own construction on the statute, as would be necessary in the absence of an administrative interpretation. Rather, if the statute is silent or ambiguous with respect to the specific issue, the question for the court is whether the agency's answer is based on a permissible construction of the statute.[4] * * *

---

[3] The judiciary is the final authority on issues of statutory construction and must reject administrative constructions which are contrary to clear congressional intent. If a court, employing traditional tools of statutory construction, ascertains that Congress had an intention on the precise question at issue, that intention is the law and must be given effect.

[4] The court need not conclude that the agency construction was the only one it permissibly could have

We have long recognized that considerable weight should be accorded to an executive department's construction of a statutory scheme it is entrusted to administer, and the principle of deference to administrative interpretations

> "has been consistently followed by this Court whenever decision as to the meaning or reach of a statute has involved reconciling conflicting policies, and a full understanding of the force of the statutory policy in the given situation has depended upon more than ordinary knowledge respecting the matters subjected to agency regulations.

> ". . . If this choice represents a reasonable accommodation of conflicting policies that were committed to the agency's care by the statute, we should not disturb it unless it appears from the statute or its legislative history that the accommodation is not one that Congress would have sanctioned."

In light of these well-settled principles it is clear that the Court of Appeals misconceived the nature of its role in reviewing the regulations at issue. Once it determined, after its own examination of the legislation, that Congress did not actually have an intent regarding the applicability of the bubble concept to the permit program, the question before it was not whether in its view the concept is "inappropriate" in the general context of a program designed to improve air quality, but whether the Administrator's view that it is appropriate in the context of this particular program is a reasonable one. Based on the examination of the legislation and its history which follows, we agree with the Court of Appeals that Congress did not have a specific intention on the applicability of the bubble concept in these cases, and conclude that the EPA's use of that concept here is a reasonable policy choice for the agency to make.

[Parsing the statutory language and reviewing the legislative history, the Court concluded that Congress had not resolved or even thought about the bubble concept.]

The arguments over policy that are advanced in the parties' briefs create the impression that respondents are now waging in a judicial forum a specific policy battle which they ultimately lost in the agency and in the 32 jurisdictions opting for the "bubble concept," but one which was never waged in the Congress. Such policy arguments are more properly addressed to legislators or administrators, not to judges.

* * * [T]he Administrator's interpretation represents a reasonable accommodation of manifestly competing interests and is entitled to deference: the regulatory scheme is technical and complex, the agency considered the matter in a detailed and reasoned fashion, and the decision involves reconciling conflicting policies. Congress intended to accommodate both interests [i.e., both environmental protection and economic growth], but did not do so itself on the level of specificity presented by these cases. Perhaps that body consciously desired the Administrator to strike the balance at this level, thinking that those with great expertise and charged with responsibility for administering the provision would be in a better position to do so;

---

adopted to uphold the construction, or even the reading the court would have reached if the question initially had arisen in a judicial proceeding.

perhaps it simply did not consider the question at this level; and perhaps Congress was unable to forge a coalition on either side of the question, and those on each side decided to take their chances with the scheme devised by the agency. For judicial purposes, it matters not which of these things occurred.

Judges are not experts in the field, and are not part of either political branch of the Government. Courts must, in some cases, reconcile competing political interests, but not on the basis of the judges' personal policy preferences. In contrast, an agency to which Congress has delegated policymaking responsibilities may, within the limits of that delegation, properly rely upon the incumbent administration's views of wise policy to inform its judgments. While agencies are not directly accountable to the people, the Chief Executive is, and it is entirely appropriate for this political branch of the Government to make such policy choices — resolving the competing interests which Congress itself either inadvertently did not resolve, or intentionally left to be resolved by the agency charged with the administration of the statute in light of everyday realities.

When a challenge to an agency construction of a statutory provision, fairly conceptualized, really centers on the wisdom of the agency's policy, rather than whether it is a reasonable choice within a gap left open by Congress, the challenge must fail. In such a case, federal judges — who have no constituency — have a duty to respect legitimate policy choices made by those who do. The responsibilities for assessing the wisdom of such policy choices and resolving the struggle between competing views of the public interest are not judicial ones: "Our Constitution vests such responsibilities in the political branches." TVA v. Hill, 437 U.S. 153, 195 (1978).
* * *

NOTES AND QUESTIONS

(1) *Chevron* has provoked endless citation and commentary. Indeed, it is said to be the single most-cited decision in the history of the Supreme Court. Its precise reach and meaning remain controversial. A strong reading would seem to displace the judiciary from its traditional role of "saying what the law is," leaving it merely the mechanical task of enforcing unambiguous statutes. Real authority would lie with the agencies. Does it go that far? Is the level of deference and the room for judicial interpretation the same in *Skidmore* and *Chevron*?

(2) Both these decisions require courts to give weight to the agency's interpretation of the statute. Do they do so for the same reasons? What is the agency's advantage over a court — what does it know, or what skills does it have, that the court lacks that justify deference?

(3) Note the factors identified by the *Skidmore* Court in the penultimate paragraph, which is the best-known and most cited part of the opinion. Why should the weight of an agency interpretation vary according to these factors? Are these factors relevant under *Chevron*?

(4) Is the attack on the use of legislative history reviewed in Chapter 12 equally applicable when an agency rather than a court is the interpreter?

(5)   *Chevron* directs the reviewing court to proceed in two steps. Try to articulate exactly what happens in each step. Step one involves standard statutory interpretation; indeed, the court is supposed to rely on "the traditional tools of statutory construction." Courts and commentators are divided as to what is going on in step two. Does it also involve an inquiry into statutory meaning? If so, how, if at all, is it different from step one? Or does it involve a consideration of the reasonableness of the agency's position on the merits? If so, then it doesn't seem to be about "interpretation" at all.

(6)   One recurrent question concerns when *Chevron* applies, an inquiry sometimes referred to as "*Chevron* step zero" (i.e. the step before step one and step two). *Chevron* does not kick in every time an agency expresses a view on the meaning of a statute. But when exactly it does apply is unclear. It is settled that *Chevron* applies to agency interpretations that are expressed in (a) a regulation issued through notice-and-comment procedures and having the force of law or (b) result from so-called "formal adjudication" (i.e. agency adjudications that involve full trial-type procedures). But consider the following situations:

> *Interpretations of statutes that apply to multiple agencies.* Courts do not extend *Chevron* deference to agency interpretations of statutes that no single agency is charged with administering, such as the Administrative Procedure Act or the Freedom of Information Act.[5] What does this reveal about the justifications underlying *Chevron?*

> *Litigating positions. Chevron* also does not apply to agency interpretations that represent merely the agency's litigating posture and are developed after the decision being challenged.[6]

> *Agency manuals, guidance documents, policy statements, and the like.* Agencies often explain their views on a particular statute in informal documents that are intended to provide information and guidance to regulated entities without being legally binding on either the agency or private parties. Such documents are not issued pursuant to a notice-and-comment process. The key case here is *United States v. Mead Corp.*, 533 U.S. 218 (2001). The Customs Service had classified a "day planner" manufactured by Mead as a "diary" under the tariff schedule; it was therefore subject to an import tax. Mead took the position that its planner, which was a three-ring binder with pages having room for notes of daily schedules, addresses, and a calendar, was not a "diary." The Customs Service took this decision in a "ruling letter." The Service issues thousands of ruling letters every year, without notice and comment, to state its official position regarding the tariff classification of specific imports. The Service's regulations provide that a ruling letter is to be "applied only with respect to transactions involving articles identical to the" item covered by the letter and "is subject of modification or revocation without notice to any person, except the person to whom the letter was addressed." They are not subject to notice and comment; they may be published, but need only be made

---

[5] *See, e.g.*, Metro. Stevedore Co. v. Rambo, 521 U.S. 121, 137 n.9 (1997).

[6] *See, e.g.*, Bowen v. Georgetown Univ. Hosp., 488 U.S. 204, 212 (1988).

"available for public inspection." The Court's decision focused on indicia, or lack thereof, that Congress would have wanted courts to defer:

> We hold that administrative implementation of a particular statutory provision qualifies for *Chevron* deference when it appears that Congress delegated authority to the agency generally to make rules carrying the force of law, and that the agency interpretation claiming deference was promulgated in the exercise of that authority. Delegation of such authority may be shown in a variety of ways, as by an agency's power to engage in adjudication or notice-and-comment rulemaking, or by some other indication of a comparable congressional intent. The Customs ruling at issue here fails to qualify, although the possibility that it deserves some deference under *Skidmore* leads us to vacate and remand.

The absence of notice and comment procedures was important less for its own sake than as an indication that Congress did not intend the agency statements to carry the force of law. But the Court was careful to explain that "[t]he fact that the tariff classification here was not a product of * * * [a] formal process [such as notice and comment rulemaking or formal adjudication] does not alone * * * bar the application of *Chevron*."

(7)   An empirical study of 1,014 Supreme Court cases over more than two decades by William Eskridge and Lauren Baer made the following findings:

> Based upon our data, we conclude that there has not been a *Chevron* "revolution" at the Supreme Court level. * * * Indeed, from the time it was handed down until the end of the 2005 term, *Chevron* was applied in only 8.3% of Supreme Court cases evaluating agency statutory interpretations. * * * [D]uring this time frame, the Court employed a *continuum* of deference regimes. This continuum is more complicated than the literature or even the Court's own opinions suggest, and it is a continuum in which *Chevron* plays a modest role. Indeed, our most striking finding is that in the majority of cases — 53.6% of them — the Court does not apply any deference regime at all. Instead, it relies on ad hoc judicial reasoning of the sort that typifies the Court's methodology in regular statutory interpretation cases.

> We * * * examine[d] * * * the application of *Chevron* in depth. To our surprise, we found that the Court usually does not apply *Chevron* to cases that are, according to *Mead* and other opinions, *Chevron*-eligible. Moreover, in analyzing how Chevron is applied in the cases where it is invoked by the Court, we found little doctrinal consistency. There is some indication that while congressional delegation is not a solid predictor of when the Court will invoke *Chevron*, it is correlated with, and may influence, the agency's chances of prevailing once *Chevron* has been invoked. And there is clear evidence that where *Chevron* is invoked, legislative history remains relevant to the two-step inquiry. However, explanations for why the Court chose to invoke *Chevron* when it did, and how the Court applied *Chevron* once invoked, were not apparent from the data.

* * * Are there factors that predict (1) when particular deference regimes will be invoked, and (2) when the agency is more likely to win? As to the first question, our data offer little to latch onto; there is no clear guide as to when the Court will invoke particular deference regimes, and why. As to the second question, our data were somewhat more helpful. Based upon the academic literature, we expected to find that high agency win rates would be positively associated with (1) the application of *Chevron* or *Seminole Rock* [or *Auer*] deference; (2) an open, legitimate process such as notice-and-comment rulemaking or formal adjudication; and (3) the absence of a plain statutory meaning (which leaves more room for agency discretion). We found some positive correlation with the first two factors, but none with the third. Based upon our own experience, we expected to find that high agency win rates would also be positively associated with (1) statutory subject matter and comparative agency expertise; and (2) agency consistency in adhering to the interpretation over time. Both hypotheses bore out. As a separate point, we also found (3) a strong association between judicial ideology and the likelihood of liberal or conservative agency interpretations prevailing, with liberal justices more likely to support liberal agency interpretations, and conservative justices more likely to support conservative agency interpretations.[7]

(8) Perhaps the whole *Chevron* approach is an inherently inadequate mechanism for achieving a consistent, coherent system of judicial deference. Would it make more sense to replace the whole thing with a straightforward voting rule — for example, that an agency interpretation would be upheld unless a 3-judge panel unanimously disagreed, or the Supreme Court rejected it by a vote of at least 6-3? That argument is made in Jacob Gersen & Adrian Vermeule, Chevron *as a Voting Rule*, 116 YALE L.J. 676 (2007).

D. AN AGENCY (IN)ACTION

MASSACHUSETTS v. EPA
549 U.S. 497 (2007)

[In October 1999 a group of private organizations petitioned the Environmental Protection Agency (EPA) to regulate the emissions of four greenhouse gases (GHGs), including carbon dioxide, under § 202(a)(1) of the Clean Air Act, 42 U.S.C. § 7521(a)(1). That section provides that the Administrator of the EPA "shall by regulation prescribe . . . standards applicable to the emission of any air pollutant from any class . . . of new motor vehicles . . . which in [the EPA Administrator's] judgment causes, or contributes to, air pollution . . . reasonably . . . anticipated to endanger public health or welfare." The Act defines "air pollutant" to mean "any air pollution agent or combination of such agents, including any physical, chemical . . . substance or matter which is emitted into or otherwise enters the ambient

---

[7] William N. Eskridge, Jr. & Lauren E. Baer, *The Continuum of Deference: Supreme Court Treatment of Agency Statutory Interpretations from* Chevron *to* Hamdan, 96 GEO. L.J. 1083, 1090–1091 (2008).

air." 42 U.S.C. § 7602(g). The rulemaking petition argued that EPA's own statements indicated that the statutory standard had been met — that in the Administrator's judgment GHG emissions from new motor vehicles did cause air pollution reasonably anticipated to endanger public health or welfare — and that therefore the Administrator had a duty to promulgate standards limiting those emissions.

EPA denied the petition. Its reasons for doing so were numerous. One set of conclusions were legal in nature. First, EPA found that the Clean Air Act does not authorize it to issue mandatory regulations to address global climate change. EPA General Counsels had taken conflicting positions on whether carbon dioxide was an "air pollutant" under the Act; with the more recent opinion concluding that it did not. Although the actual definition of air pollutant was broad, numerous contextual clues suggested that Congress had not intended to give EPA authority to regulate CO_2: "(1) no CAA provision specifically authorizes global climate change regulation, (2) the only CAA provision specifically mentioning CO_2 authorizes only 'nonregulatory' measures, (3) the codified CAA provisions related to global climate change expressly preclude the use of those provisions to authorize regulation, (4) a Senate committee proposal to include motor vehicle CO_2 standards in the 1990 CAA amendments failed, (5) Federal statutes expressly addressing global climate change do not authorize regulation, and (6) numerous congressional actions suggest that Congress has yet to decide that such regulation is warranted." Climate change was so important and its regulation so significant that Congress would never have given it authority to regulate in this area without saying so explicitly.

Even if the Administrator found that GHG emissions from motor vehicles threatened health or welfare, that would not *require* her to issue the standards sought by the petition. "An important issue before the Administrator is whether, given motor vehicles' relative contribution to a problem, it makes sense to regulate them. In the case of some types of air pollution, motor vehicles may be one of many contributors, and it may make sense to control other contributors instead of, or in tandem with, motor vehicles. The discretionary nature of the Administrator's section 202(a)(1) authority allows her to consider these important policy issues."

EPA's second set of conclusions were more policy-based. "EPA disagrees with the regulatory approach urged by petitioners. . . . We do not believe . . . that it would be either effective or appropriate for EPA to establish GHG standards for motor vehicles at this time."

The petitioners, now joined by intervenor Massachusetts and other state and local governments, sought review in the U.S. Court of Appeals for the D.C. Circuit, which denied the petition.]

Justice STEVENS delivered the opinion of the Court.

A well-documented rise in global temperatures has coincided with a significant increase in the concentration of carbon dioxide in the atmosphere. Respected scientists believe the two trends are related. For when carbon dioxide is released into the atmosphere, it acts like the ceiling of a greenhouse, trapping solar energy and retarding the escape of reflected heat. It is therefore a species — the most

important species — of a "greenhouse gas."

Calling global warming "the most pressing environmental challenge of our time," a group of States, local governments, and private organizations, alleged in a petition for certiorari that the Environmental Protection Agency (EPA) has abdicated its responsibility under the Clean Air Act to regulate the emissions of four greenhouse gases, including carbon dioxide. Specifically, petitioners asked us to answer two questions concerning the meaning of § 202(a)(1) of the Act: whether EPA has the statutory authority to regulate greenhouse gas emissions from new motor vehicles; and if so, whether its stated reasons for refusing to do so are consistent with the statute. * * *

I

Section 202(a)(1) of the Clean Air Act, 42 U.S.C. § 7521(a)(1), provides:

The [EPA] Administrator shall by regulation prescribe (and from time to time revise) in accordance with the provisions of this section, standards applicable to the emission of any air pollutant from any class or classes of new motor vehicles or new motor vehicle engines, which in his judgment cause, or contribute to, air pollution which may reasonably be anticipated to endanger public health or welfare. . . .

The Act defines "air pollutant" to include "any air pollution agent or combination of such agents, including any physical, chemical, biological, radioactive . . . substance or matter which is emitted into or otherwise enters the ambient air." § 7602(g). "Welfare" is also defined broadly: among other things, it includes "effects on . . . weather . . . and climate." § 7602(h).

When Congress enacted these provisions, the study of climate change was in its infancy. In 1959, shortly after the U.S. Weather Bureau began monitoring atmospheric carbon dioxide levels, an observatory in Mauna Loa, Hawaii, recorded a mean level of 316 parts per million. This was well above the highest carbon dioxide concentration — no more than 300 parts per million — revealed in the 420,000-year-old ice-core record. By the time Congress drafted § 202(a)(1) in 1970, carbon dioxide levels had reached 325 parts per million.

In the late 1970's, the Federal Government began devoting serious attention to the possibility that carbon dioxide emissions associated with human activity could provoke climate change. In 1978, Congress enacted the National Climate Program Act, which required the President to establish a program to "assist the Nation and the world to understand and respond to natural and man-induced climate processes and their implications." President Carter, in turn, asked the National Research Council, the working arm of the National Academy of Sciences, to investigate the subject. The Council's response was unequivocal: "If carbon dioxide continues to increase, the study group finds no reason to doubt that climate changes will result and no reason to believe that these changes will be negligible. . . . A wait-and-see policy may mean waiting until it is too late."

Congress next addressed the issue in 1987, when it enacted the Global Climate Protection Act. Finding that "manmade pollution — the release of carbon dioxide, chlorofluorocarbons, methane, and other trace gases into the atmosphere — may be

producing a long-term and substantial increase in the average temperature on Earth," § 1102(1), 101 Stat. 1408, Congress directed EPA to propose to Congress a "coordinated national policy on global climate change," § 1103(b), and ordered the Secretary of State to work "through the channels of multilateral diplomacy" and coordinate diplomatic efforts to combat global warming, § 1103(c). Congress emphasized that "ongoing pollution and deforestation may be contributing now to an irreversible process" and that "necessary actions must be identified and implemented in time to protect the climate." § 1102(4). * * *

VI

On the merits, the first question is whether § 202(a)(1) of the Clean Air Act authorizes EPA to regulate greenhouse gas emissions from new motor vehicles in the event that it forms a "judgment" that such emissions contribute to climate change. We have little trouble concluding that it does. In relevant part, § 202(a)(1) provides that EPA "shall by regulation prescribe . . . standards applicable to the emission of any air pollutant from any class or classes of new motor vehicles or new motor vehicle engines, which in [the Administrator's] judgment cause, or contribute to, air pollution which may reasonably be anticipated to endanger public health or welfare." 42 U.S.C. § 7521(a)(1). Because EPA believes that Congress did not intend it to regulate substances that contribute to climate change, the agency maintains that carbon dioxide is not an "air pollutant" within the meaning of the provision.

The statutory text forecloses EPA's reading. The Clean Air Act's sweeping definition of "air pollutant" includes "*any* air pollution agent or combination of such agents, including *any* physical, chemical . . . substance or matter which is emitted into or otherwise enters the ambient air. . . ." § 7602(g) (emphasis added). On its face, the definition embraces all airborne compounds of whatever stripe, and underscores that intent through the repeated use of the word "any." Carbon dioxide, methane, nitrous oxide, and hydrofluorocarbons are without a doubt "physical [and] chemical . . . substances which [are] emitted into . . . the ambient air." The statute is unambiguous.

Rather than relying on statutory text, EPA invokes postenactment congressional actions and deliberations it views as tantamount to a congressional command to refrain from regulating greenhouse gas emissions. Even if such postenactment legislative history could shed light on the meaning of an otherwise-unambiguous statute, EPA never identifies any action remotely suggesting that Congress meant to curtail its power to treat greenhouse gases as air pollutants. That subsequent Congresses have eschewed enacting binding emissions limitations to combat global warming tells us nothing about what Congress meant when it amended § 202(a)(1) in 1970 and 1977. And unlike EPA, we have no difficulty reconciling Congress' various efforts to promote interagency collaboration and research to better understand climate change with the agency's pre-existing mandate to regulate "any air pollutant" that may endanger the public welfare. Collaboration and research do not conflict with any thoughtful regulatory effort; they complement it.

EPA's reliance on *Brown & Williamson Tobacco Corp.* is similarly misplaced. In holding that tobacco products are not "drugs" or "devices" subject to Food and

Drug Administration (FDA) regulation pursuant to the Food, Drug and Cosmetic Act (FDCA), we found critical at least two considerations that have no counterpart in this case.

First, we thought it unlikely that Congress meant to ban tobacco products, which the FDCA would have required had such products been classified as "drugs" or "devices." Here, in contrast, EPA jurisdiction would lead to no such extreme measures. EPA would only *regulate* emissions, and even then, it would have to delay any action "to permit the development and application of the requisite technology, giving appropriate consideration to the cost of compliance," § 7521(a)(2). However much a ban on tobacco products clashed with the "common sense" intuition that Congress never meant to remove those products from circulation, *Brown & Williamson*, there is nothing counterintuitive to the notion that EPA can curtail the emission of substances that are putting the global climate out of kilter.

Second, in *Brown & Williamson* we pointed to an unbroken series of congressional enactments that made sense only if adopted "against the backdrop of the FDA's consistent and repeated statements that it lacked authority under the FDCA to regulate tobacco." We can point to no such enactments here: EPA has not identified any congressional action that conflicts in any way with the regulation of greenhouse gases from new motor vehicles. Even if it had, Congress could not have acted against a regulatory "backdrop" of disclaimers of regulatory authority. Prior to the order that provoked this litigation, EPA had never disavowed the authority to regulate greenhouse gases, and in 1998 it in fact affirmed that it *had* such authority. There is no reason, much less a compelling reason, to accept EPA's invitation to read ambiguity into a clear statute. * * *

VII

The alternative basis for EPA's decision — that even if it does have statutory authority to regulate greenhouse gases, it would be unwise to do so at this time — rests on reasoning divorced from the statutory text. While the statute does condition the exercise of EPA's authority on its formation of a "judgment," 42 U.S.C. § 7521(a)(1), that judgment must relate to whether an air pollutant "causes, or contributes to, air pollution which may reasonably be anticipated to endanger public health or welfare," ibid. Put another way, the use of the word "judgment" is not a roving license to ignore the statutory text. It is but a direction to exercise discretion within defined statutory limits.

If EPA makes a finding of endangerment, the Clean Air Act requires the agency to regulate emissions of the deleterious pollutant from new motor vehicles. * * *

EPA has refused to comply with this clear statutory command. Instead, it has offered a laundry list of reasons not to regulate. * * *

Although we have neither the expertise nor the authority to evaluate these policy judgments, it is evident they have nothing to do with whether greenhouse gas emissions contribute to climate change. * * * The statutory question is whether sufficient information exists to make an endangerment finding.

In short, EPA has offered no reasoned explanation for its refusal to decide whether greenhouse gases cause or contribute to climate change. We need not and do not reach the question whether on remand EPA must make an endangerment finding, or whether policy concerns can inform EPA's actions in the event that it makes such a finding. We hold only that EPA must ground its reasons for action or inaction in the statute.

[A dissent by Chief Justice Roberts, joined by Justices Scalia, Thomas, and Alito, arguing that the petitioners lacked standing, is omitted.]

Justice SCALIA, with whom THE CHIEF JUSTICE, Justice THOMAS, and Justice ALITO join, dissenting.

I

A

I am willing to assume, for the sake of argument, that the Administrator's discretion in this regard is not entirely unbounded — that if he has no reasonable basis for deferring judgment he must grasp the nettle at once. * * * When the Administrator *makes* a judgment whether to regulate greenhouse gases, that judgment must relate to whether they are air pollutants that "cause, or contribute to, air pollution which may reasonably be anticipated to endanger public health or welfare." But the statute says *nothing at all* about the reasons for which the Administrator may *defer* making a judgment — the permissible reasons for deciding not to grapple with the issue at the present time. Thus, the various "policy" rationales that the Court criticizes are not "divorced from the statutory text," except in the sense that the statutory text is silent, as texts are often silent about permissible reasons for the exercise of agency discretion. The reasons the EPA gave are surely considerations executive agencies *regularly* take into account (and *ought* to take into account) when deciding whether to consider entering a new field: the impact such entry would have on other Executive Branch programs and on foreign policy. There is no basis in law for the Court's imposed limitation.

EPA's interpretation of the discretion conferred by the statutory reference to "its judgment" is not only reasonable, it is the most natural reading of the text. The Court nowhere explains why this interpretation is incorrect, let alone why it is not entitled to deference under *Chevron*. As the Administrator acted within the law in declining to make a "judgment" for the policy reasons above set forth, I would uphold the decision to deny the rulemaking petition on that ground alone. * * *

II

A

Even before reaching its discussion of the word "judgment," the Court makes another significant error when it concludes that "§ 202(a)(1) of the Clean Air Act *authorizes* EPA to regulate greenhouse gas emissions from new motor vehicles in the event that it forms a 'judgment' that such emissions contribute to climate

change." For such authorization, the Court relies on what it calls "the Clean Air Act's capacious definition of 'air pollutant.' "

"Air pollutant" is defined by the Act as "any air pollution agent or combination of such agents, including any physical, chemical, . . . substance or matter which is emitted into or otherwise enters the ambient air." 42 U.S.C. § 7602(g). The Court is correct that "carbon dioxide, methane, nitrous oxide, and hydrofluorocarbons," fit within the second half of that definition: They are "physical, chemical, . . . substances or matter which [are] emitted into or otherwise enter the ambient air." But the Court mistakenly believes this to be the end of the analysis. In order to be an "air pollutant" under the Act's definition, the "substance or matter [being] emitted into . . . the ambient air" must also meet the *first* half of the definition — namely, it must be an "air pollution agent or combination of such agents." The Court simply pretends this half of the definition does not exist.

The word "including" can indeed indicate that what follows will be an "illustrative" sampling of the general category that precedes the word. Often, however, the examples standing alone are broader than the general category, and must be viewed as limited in light of that category. The Government provides a helpful (and unanswered) example: "The phrase 'any American automobile, including any truck or minivan,' would not naturally be construed to encompass a foreign-manufactured [truck or] minivan." The general principle enunciated — that the speaker is talking about *American* automobiles — carries forward to the illustrative examples (trucks and minivans), and limits them accordingly, even though in isolation they are broader. . . . In short, the word "including" does not require the Court's (or the petitioners') result. It is perfectly reasonable to view the definition of "air pollutant" in its entirety: An air pollutant *can* be "any physical, chemical, . . . substance or matter which is emitted into or otherwise enters the ambient air," but only if it retains the general characteristic of being an "air pollution agent or combination of such agents." This is precisely the conclusion EPA reached: "[A] substance does not meet the CAA definition of 'air pollutant' simply because it is a 'physical, chemical, . . . substance or matter which is emitted into or otherwise enters the ambient air.' It must also be an 'air pollution agent.' " Once again, in the face of textual ambiguity, the Court's application of *Chevron* deference to EPA's interpretation of the word "including" is nowhere to be found. Evidently, the Court defers only to those reasonable interpretations that it favors.

B

Unlike "air pollutants," the term "air pollution" is not itself defined by the CAA; thus, once again we must accept EPA's interpretation of that ambiguous term, provided its interpretation is a "permissible construction of the statute." *Chevron*. In this case, the petition for rulemaking asked EPA for "regulation of [greenhouse gas] emissions from motor vehicles to reduce the risk of global climate change." Thus, in deciding whether it had authority to regulate, EPA had to determine whether the concentration of greenhouse gases assertedly responsible for "global climate change" qualifies as "air pollution." EPA began with the commonsense observation that the "problems associated with atmospheric concentrations of CO_2," bear little resemblance to what would naturally be termed "air pollution":

EPA's prior use of the CAA's general regulatory provisions provides an important context. Since the inception of the Act, EPA has used these provisions to address air pollution problems that occur primarily at ground level or near the surface of the earth. For example, national ambient air quality standards (NAAQS) established under CAA section 109 address concentrations of substances in the ambient air and the related public health and welfare problems. This has meant setting NAAQS for concentrations of ozone, carbon monoxide, particulate matter and other substances in the air near the surface of the earth, not higher in the atmosphere. . . . CO_2, by contrast, is fairly consistent in concentration throughout the world's atmosphere up to approximately the lower stratosphere.

In other words, regulating the buildup of CO_2 and other greenhouse gases in the upper reaches of the atmosphere, which is alleged to be causing global climate change, is not akin to regulating the concentration of some substance that is *polluting* the *air*.

We need look no further than the dictionary for confirmation that this interpretation of "air pollution" is eminently reasonable. In the end, EPA concluded that since "CAA authorization to regulate is generally based on a finding that an air pollutant causes or contributes to air pollution" the concentrations of CO_2 and other greenhouse gases allegedly affecting the global climate are beyond the scope of CAA's authorization to regulate. "The term 'air pollution' as used in the regulatory provisions cannot be interpreted to encompass global climate change." Once again, the Court utterly fails to explain why this interpretation is incorrect, let alone so unreasonable as to be unworthy of *Chevron* deference.

* * *

The Court's alarm over global warming may or may not be justified, but it ought not distort the outcome of this litigation. This is a straightforward administrative-law case, in which Congress has passed a malleable statute giving broad discretion, not to us but to an executive agency. No matter how important the underlying policy issues at stake, this Court has no business substituting its own desired outcome for the reasoned judgment of the responsible agency.

NOTES AND QUESTIONS

(1) First, consider this as a *Chevron* decision. Is the denial of a rulemaking petition the sort of agency decision to which *Chevron* applies? Assuming the answer is yes, should the Court have been more deferential? The majority treated the issue as arising within step one; that is, the statute was sufficiently clear that the Court could resolve the case on its own, using "the traditional tools of statutory construction," without moving to step two, in which it would uphold any reasonable interpretation. Is the statute unambiguous? Assuming *Chevron* does not apply, is this a *Skidmore* case?

(2) Now, forget *Chevron*. As a garden-variety statutory interpretation decision, who has the better of the textual disagreement argument between Justice Stevens and Justice Scalia?

(3) In its briefs in *Massachusetts v. EPA*, the government relied heavily on *FDA v. Brown & Williamson Tobacco Corp.*, 529 U.S. 120 (2000). EPA's General Counsel had placed even greater emphasis on that decision in concluding that EPA lacked the authority to regulate GHGs. That case involved the FDA's promulgation of regulations aimed at preventing teenagers from smoking cigarettes. The critical issue was whether the FDA had authority to regulate cigarettes under the Food, Drug, and Cosmetic Act (FDCA). The FDCA gives the FDA authority to regulate "drugs," "devices," and "combination products." On their face, the statutory definitions of those terms seemed to fit nicotine and cigarettes. However, for decades the general understanding, consistently urged by FDA itself, had been that the FDA lacked jurisdiction over tobacco. The regulations thus reflected a novel legal position. The Supreme Court rejected this new position by a vote of 5 to 4; Justice Kennedy is the only justice to have been in the majority in both *Massachusetts v. EPA* and *Brown & Williamson*. Critical to the Court's reasoning was the fact that over the years Congress has enacted half a dozen pieces of legislation concerning cigarettes; these statutes clearly reflect a considered decision to go only so far in restricting their sale and were adopted against the background of the FDA's statements that it lacked authority to regulate. This extensive body of legislation indicates not merely congressional acquiescence in but congressional "ratification" of the FDA's position that it could not regulate cigarettes. Does Justice Stevens adequately distinguish *Brown & Williamson*?

(4) The *Chevron* doctrine is about who gets to decide. Note that the underlying issues in both cases were of enormous practical and economic significance. The majority in *Brown & Williamson* emphasizes that deciding whether or not to regulate cigarettes is not an interstitial, subsidiary, gap-filling sort of question. Rather, it is a central and important policy decision; the sort of thing, says the majority, one would expect Congress to decide for itself rather than delegate to an agency through ambiguity or carelessness. In *Massachusetts v. EPA*, a different five-Justice majority also insisted on respect for congressional decisionmaking authority. Consider whether the Court ruled as it did, at least in part, because it thought that in both cases the administration had exceeded its democratic mandate.

Assignment

Reread the Assignment at the end of Chapter 11. Now add the following to the background circumstances.

The Equal Employment Opportunity Commission (EEOC) is a five-member independent federal agency charged with implementing and enforcing the employment discrimination laws, including the ADEA. It has authority to investigate, adjudicate, and litigate alleged violations, and any employee who believes he or she has been discriminated against on the basis of age must file a charge with the EEOC before proceeding against the employer in court. (In fiscal year 2008, the EEOC received approximately 25,000 charges of age discrimination.) The Commission generally tries to resolve the matter informally; if that fails, it can proceed against the employer through an administrative proceeding, sue the employer in federal court, or drop the matter. If, but only if, the Commission decides not to proceed, the employee can sue the employer.

The EEOC also has authority to issue regulations. The ADEA provides:

> [T]he Equal Employment Opportunity Commission may issue such rules and regulations as it may consider necessary or appropriate for carrying out this chapter, and may establish such reasonable exemptions to and from any or all provisions of this chapter as it may find necessary and proper in the public interest.

29 U.S.C. § 628.

Scenario 1

Cline files a charge with the EEOC. The Commission agrees that the Act prohibits an employer from favoring older over younger workers, and concludes that General Dynamics violated the Act. Its informal efforts to resolve the matter fail. It decides not to pursue the matter further. Cline files suit.

What deference, if any, does the court owe to the EEOC's conclusion that the ADEA protects both younger and older workers? Would your answer change if the EEOC filed an amicus brief taking the same position? If the EEOC itself sued the employer on Cline's behalf?

Scenario 2

In 1981, after notice and comment, the EEOC issued the following "interpretative regulation":

> It is unlawful in situations where this Act applies, for an employer to discriminate in hiring or in any other way by giving preference because of age between individuals 40 and over. Thus, if two people apply for the same position, and one is 42 and the other 52, the employer may not lawfully turn down either one on the basis of age, but must make such decision on the basis of some other factor.

In at least one adjudication, the EEOC relied on that regulation in holding that an employer could not use "earliest date of birth" as a tie-breaker when determining seniority for allocating particular desirable job assignments.

What deference, if any, does the court owe to the EEOC's position that the ADEA prohibits an employer from favoring older over younger workers?

Chapter 14

STABILITY AND CHANGE IN STATUTORY LAW

In the introduction to the case sequence in Chapter 4 we said:

> On the practical level, you will learn how to read cases against one another: how to read the first case, standing by itself; how to read the next case in relation to the preceding case; to read the third in light of the prior two, the fourth against the prior three, etc. — all the time articulating and rearticulating, shaping and reshaping "the rule of law" evolving under the court's jurisprudence.

In this chapter, we ask whether courts ought similarly to "shape and reshape" *statutory* rules. Can a statute's meaning evolve through the course of judicial interpretation, or is it frozen in place as of its enactment unless and until amended by the legislature?

A. *STARE DECISIS* IN STATUTORY CASES

A common law court sometimes refines, or redefines, a legal principle by simply overruling a prior decision. How does the strength of judicial precedent in a statutory case compare to its strength in a common law case? There are three possibilities: (a) a precedent is a precedent is a precedent, (b) a court is freer to overrule a statutory precedent than a common law precedent, or (c) statutory precedents are especially strong and should be overruled in only the most extraordinary circumstances. Which of these approaches seems correct to you?

PATTERSON v. MCLEAN CREDIT UNION
491 U.S. 164 (1989)

JUSTICE KENNEDY delivered the opinion of the Court.

Petitioner Brenda Patterson, a black woman, was employed by respondent McLean Credit Union as a teller and a file coordinator, commencing in May 1972.

In July 1982, she was laid off. After the termination, petitioner commenced this action in the United States District Court for the Middle District of North Carolina. She alleged that respondent, in violation of 42 U.S.C. § 1981,[1] had

---

[1] [Ed. Fn.] This section, part of § 1 of the 1866 Civil Rights Act, provides:

Equal rights under the law. All persons within the jurisdiction of the United States shall have the same right in every State and Territory to make and enforce contracts, to sue, be parties, give evidence, and to the full and equal benefit of all laws and proceedings for the security of persons and property as is enjoyed by white citizens, and shall be subject to like

harassed her, failed to promote her to an intermediate accounting clerk position, and then discharged her, all because of her race. * * *

We granted certiorari to decide whether petitioner's claim of racial harassment in her employment is actionable under § 1981 * * *. After oral argument * * * we requested the parties to brief and argue an additional question:

> "Whether or not the interpretation of 42 U.S.C. § 1981 adopted by this Court in *Runyon v. McCrary*, 427 U.S. 160 (1976), should be reconsidered."

In *Runyon*, the Court considered whether § 1981 prohibits private schools from excluding children who are qualified for admission, solely on the basis of race. We held that § 1981 did prohibit such conduct, noting that it was already well established in prior decisions that § 1981 "prohibits racial discrimination in the making and enforcement of private contracts." The arguments about whether *Runyon* was decided correctly in light of the language and history of the statute were examined and discussed with great care in our decision. It was recognized at the time that a strong case could be made for the view that the statute does not reach private conduct, but that view did not prevail. Some Members of this Court believe that *Runyon* was decided incorrectly, and others consider it correct on its own footing, but the question before us is whether it ought now to be overturned. We conclude after reargument that *Runyon* should not be overruled, and we now reaffirm that § 1981 prohibits racial discrimination in the making and enforcement of private contracts.

The Court has said often and with great emphasis that "the doctrine of *stare decisis* is of fundamental importance to the rule of law." Although we have cautioned that "*stare decisis* is a principle of policy and not a mechanical formula of adherence to the latest decision," it is indisputable that *stare decisis* is a basic self-governing principle within the Judicial Branch, which is entrusted with the sensitive and difficult task of fashioning and preserving a jurisprudential system that is not based upon "an arbitrary discretion." The Federalist, No. 78, p. 490 (H. Lodge ed. 1888) (A. Hamilton).

Our precedents are not sacrosanct, for we have overruled prior decisions where the necessity and propriety of doing so has been established. * * * [T]he burden borne by the party advocating the abandonment of an established precedent is greater where the Court is asked to overrule a point of statutory construction. Considerations of *stare decisis* have special force in the area of statutory interpretation, for here, unlike in the context of constitutional interpretation, the legislative power is implicated, and Congress remains free to alter what we have done.

We conclude, upon direct consideration of the issue, that no special justification has been shown for overruling *Runyon*. In cases where statutory precedents have been overruled, the primary reason for the Court's shift in position has been the intervening development of the law, through either the growth of judicial doctrine or further action taken by Congress. Where such changes have removed or weakened the conceptual underpinnings from the prior decision, or where the later law has rendered the decision irreconcilable with competing legal doctrines or

---

punishment, pains, penalties, taxes, licenses, and exactions of every kind, and to no other.

policies, the Court has not hesitated to overrule an earlier decision. Our decision in *Runyon* has not been undermined by subsequent changes or development in the law.

Another traditional justification for overruling a prior case is that a precedent may be a positive detriment to coherence and consistency in the law, either because of inherent confusion created by an unworkable decision, or because the decision poses a direct obstacle to the realization of important objectives embodied in other laws. In this regard, we do not find *Runyon* to be unworkable or confusing. * * *

Finally, it has sometimes been said that a precedent becomes more vulnerable as it becomes outdated and after being " 'tested by experience, has been found to be inconsistent with the sense of justice or with the social welfare.' " *Runyon*, 427 U.S., at 191 (STEVENS, J., concurring), quoting B. Cardozo, The Nature of the Judicial Process 149 (1921). Whatever the effect of this consideration may be in statutory cases, it offers no support for overruling *Runyon*. In recent decades, state and federal legislation has been enacted to prohibit private racial discrimination in many aspects of our society. Whether *Runyon*'s interpretation of § 1981 as prohibiting racial discrimination in the making and enforcement of private contracts is right or wrong as an original matter, it is certain that it is not inconsistent with the prevailing sense of justice in this country. To the contrary, *Runyon* is entirely consistent with our society's deep commitment to the eradication of discrimination based on a person's race or the color of his or her skin. See *Bob Jones University v. United States*, 461 U.S. 574, 593 (1983) ("[E]very pronouncement of this Court and myriad Acts of Congress and Executive Orders attest a firm national policy to prohibit racial segregation and discrimination"); see also *Brown v. Board of Education*, 347 U.S. 483 (1954).[2]

We decline to overrule *Runyon* and acknowledge that its holding remains the governing law in this area. * * *

---

[2] Justice BRENNAN chides us for ignoring what he considers "two very obvious reasons" for adhering to *Runyon*. First, he argues at length that *Runyon* was correct as an initial matter. As we have said, however, it is unnecessary for us to address this issue because we agree that, whether or not *Runyon* was correct as an initial matter, there is no special justification for departing here from the rule of *stare decisis*.

Justice BRENNAN objects also to the fact that our *stare decisis* analysis places no reliance on the fact that Congress itself has not overturned the interpretation of § 1981 contained in *Runyon*, and in effect has ratified our decision in that case. This is no oversight on our part. As we reaffirm today, considerations of *stare decisis* have added force in statutory cases because Congress may alter what we have done by amending the statute. In constitutional cases, by contrast, Congress lacks this option, and an incorrect or outdated precedent may be overturned only by our own reconsideration or by constitutional amendment. It does not follow, however, that Congress' failure to overturn a statutory precedent is reason for this Court to adhere to it. It is "impossible to assert with any degree of assurance that congressional failure to act represents" affirmative congressional approval of the Court's statutory interpretation. Congress may legislate, moreover, only through the passage of a bill which is approved by both Houses and signed by the President. Congressional inaction cannot amend a duly enacted statute. We think also that the materials relied upon by Justice BRENNAN as "more positive signs of Congress' views," which are the *failure* of an amendment to a *different statute* offered *before* our decision in *Runyon*, and the passage of an attorney's fee statute having nothing to do with our holding in *Runyon*, demonstrate well the danger of placing undue reliance on the concept of congressional "ratification."

Justice Brennan, with whom Justice Marshall and Justice Blackmun join, and with whom Justice Stevens joins [in part], concurring in the judgment in part and dissenting in part. * * *

Even were there doubts as to the correctness of *Runyon*, Congress has in effect ratified our interpretation of § 1981, a fact to which the Court pays no attention. We have justified our practice of according special weight to statutory precedents by reference to Congress' ability to correct our interpretations when we have erred. To be sure, the absence of legislative correction is by no means in all cases determinative, for where our prior interpretation of a statute was plainly a mistake, we are reluctant to " 'place on the shoulders of Congress the burden of the Court's own error.' " Where our prior interpretation of congressional intent was plausible, however — which is the very least that can be said for our construction of § 1981 in *Runyon* — we have often taken Congress' subsequent inaction as probative to varying degrees, depending upon the circumstances, of its acquiescence. Given the frequency with which Congress has in recent years acted to overturn this Court's mistaken interpretations of civil rights statutes, [here Justice Brennan gives five examples of amendments to the civil rights laws that overrode Supreme Court decisions,] its failure to enact legislation to overturn *Runyon* appears at least to some extent indicative of a congressional belief that *Runyon* was correctly decided. * * *

There is no cause, though, to consider the precise weight to attach to the fact that Congress has not overturned or otherwise undermined *Runyon*. For in this case we have more positive signs of Congress' views. Congress has considered and rejected an amendment that would have rendered § 1981 unavailable in most cases as a remedy for private employment discrimination, which is evidence of congressional acquiescence * * *.

After the Court's decision in *Jones v. Alfred H. Mayer Co.*, Congress enacted the Equal Employment Opportunity Act of 1972, amending Title VII of the Civil Rights Act of 1964. During Congress' consideration of this legislation — by which time there had been ample indication that § 1981 was being interpreted to apply to private acts of employment discrimination — it was suggested that Title VII rendered redundant the availability of a remedy for employment discrimination under provisions derived from the Civil Rights Act of 1866. Some concluded that Title VII should be made, with limited exceptions, the exclusive remedy for such discrimination. See H. R. Rep. No. 92-238, pp. 66–67 (1971) (minority views). Senator Hruska proposed an amendment to that effect. 118 Cong. Rec. 3172 (1972). [Debate on the amendment revealed that opponents and proponents alike under-stood § 1981 to apply to private discrimination actions.] * * *

The Hruska amendment failed to win passage on a tied vote, *id.*, at 3373, and the Senate later defeated a motion to reconsider the amendment by a vote of 50 to 37, *id.*, at 3964–3965. Though the House initially adopted a similar amendment, 117 Cong. Rec. 31973, 32111 (1971), it eventually agreed with the Senate that Title VII should not preclude other remedies for employment discrimination, see H. R. Conf. Rep. No. 92-899 (1972). Thus, Congress in 1972 assumed that § 1981 reached private discrimination, and declined to alter its availability as an alternative to those remedies provided by Title VII. * * * "[T]here could hardly be a clearer indication

of congressional agreement with the view that § 1981 *does* reach private acts of racial discrimination."

Events since our decision in *Runyon* confirm Congress' approval of our interpretation of § 1981. [For example, the committee reports concerning the Civil Rights Attorney's Fees Awards Act of 1976, 42 U.S.C. § 1988 (at issue in the *West Virginia University Hospitals* case in Chapter 11), indicate the expectation that § 1988 would make fees available for private employment discrimination actions under § 1981.]

NOTES AND QUESTIONS

(1) *Background and subsequent developments.* The portion of § 1 of the 1866 Civil Rights Act that is codified at 42 U.S.C. § 1981 is quoted in footnote 1, above. The portion codified in § 1982 grants all citizens the same right "to inherit, purchase, lease, sell, hold, and convey real and personal property" that is enjoyed by white citizens. For a century after their enactment, these provisions were understood not to apply to relations between private parties. In *Jones v. Alfred H. Mayer Co.*, however, the Court held that § 1982 forbade a property owner's refusal to sell to blacks. As the *Patterson* Court recounts, *Runyon v. McCrary* then held, largely in reliance on *Jones*, that § 1981 applies to private school admissions policies.

Two years after *Patterson*, Congress codified its result, amending § 1981 expressly to provide that "[t]he rights protected by this section are protected against nongovernmental discrimination and impairment under color of state law." 42 U.S.C. § 1981(c).

(2) *Merits.* After deciding not to overrule *Runyon*, the *Patterson* Court went on to rule that most of Patterson's claims, including all those relating to racial harassment, were not actionable under § 1981. Focusing on § 1981's reference to the right "to make and enforce contracts," it distinguished a racially-based refusal to enter into — to "make" — a contract, which was actionable, from post-formation conduct within the contractual relationship, which was outside the statute's domain. (The Court did allow Patterson to proceed on her claim that the employer had refused to promote her because of her race.) Justice Brennan complained in dissent that "[w]hat the Court declines to snatch away with one hand, it takes with the other."

(3) *Standing by erroneous decisions.* The Court clearly had doubts about the correctness of *Runyon*. Two Justices (White and Rehnquist) had dissented in *Runyon* itself; the Court had expressly ordered the parties in *Patterson* to brief the question of overruling even though neither had raised it; and only three Justices (Brennan, Marshall, and Blackmun) were willing to come right out in *Patterson* and say that *Runyon* was right. Yet in the end all nine Justices voted to stand by the precedent. Assuming that at least five Justices considered *Runyon* incorrect, should they have overruled it?

Consider Justice Stevens's concurrence in *Runyon*:

For me the problem in th[is] case[] is whether to follow a line of authority which I firmly believe to have been incorrectly decided.

Jones v. Alfred H. Mayer Co., 392 U.S. 409, and its progeny have unequivocally held that § 1 of the Civil Rights Act of 1866 prohibits private racial discrimination. There is no doubt in my mind that that construction of the statute would have amazed the legislators who voted for it. * * * [Moreover,] it is extremely unlikely that reliance upon *Jones* has been so extensive that this Court is foreclosed from overruling it. There are, however, opposing arguments of greater force.

The first is the interest in stability and orderly development of the law. * * * [Second,] even if *Jones* did not accurately reflect the sentiments of the Reconstruction Congress, it surely accords with the prevailing sense of justice today.

The policy of the Nation as formulated by the Congress in recent years has moved constantly in the direction of eliminating racial segregation in all sectors of society. This Court has given a sympathetic and liberal construction to such legislation. For the Court now to overrule *Jones* would be a significant step backwards, with effects that would not have arisen from a correct decision in the first instance. Such a step would be so clearly contrary to my understanding of the mores of today that I think the Court is entirely correct in adhering to *Jones*.[3]

Is Justice Stevens following the approach of Justice Brewer in *Holy Trinity*? Is he going even further?

(4) *Relative weight of precedents.* In Chapter 5, we identified five justifications for a system of binding precedent under the common law: fairness, predictability, efficiency, judicial legitimacy, and respect for the past. Are these equally, less, or more powerful with regard to statutory precedents?

Courts frequently assert that stare decisis is especially strong in statutory cases. What justifies the special force of statutory precedents? *Patterson* states that statutory precedents are weightier than *constitutional* precedents. Do the reasons it gives also apply in comparing statutory and common law precedents? Why is it silent as to the weight of common law precedents?

(5) *Legislative silence.* One central disagreement among the Justices in *Patterson* concerns the meaningfulness of legislative silence in the face of a statutory precedent. One might consider such silence as indicating ratification, or endorsement, or acquiescence, or ignorance, or nothing at all. The majority says that Justice Brennan's opinion "demonstrate[s] well the danger of placing undue reliance on the concept of congressional 'ratification.' " What exactly is the danger?

Consider the following objections to inferring congressional endorsement of, or acquiescence in, a judicial ruling:[4]

---

[3] Runyon v. McCrary, 427 U.S. 160, 189–192 (1976) (Stevens, J., concurring).

[4] For a fuller exposition of these criticisms, *see* Lawrence C. Marshall, *"Let Congress Do It": The Case for an Absolute Rule of Statutory Stare Decisis*, 88 MICH. L. REV. 177, 186–196 (1989); William N.

(a) Realistically, legislative inaction is more likely to indicate ignorance than agreement. Judge Abner Mikva has said: "While it is true * * * that a majority of the members of Congress are lawyers, they have not kept up-to-date on recent legal developments. In fact, most Supreme Court opinions never come to the attention of Congress."[5]

In response to this objection, judges relying on legislative inaction often look for specific evidence that the legislature *was* aware of a particular decision and still left it untouched. Justice Brennan spent a good deal of time doing just that in *Patterson*. Does he succeed? Would a barrage of ultimately unsuccessful efforts to override a decision, by proving legislative awareness, reassure you that the legislature approved of that decision?

What would complete legislative agreement with a judicial decision look like?

(b) Even if the legislature is aware of the judicial interpretation, its inaction will generally result from inertia or the presence of more pressing concerns. The legislature's inability to get to the problem is a reason *for* the courts to correct their own error instead of perpetuating it.

For example, the following is from a West Virginia Supreme Court decision overruling a long line of prior cases. Those cases had held that the time limits in the state workers' compensation statute were "jurisdictional"; that is, failure to file a claim within the time limit was a flat bar to any recovery. In concluding that some late filings were permissible after all, the court said:

> We are not persuaded that legislative acquiescence in our "jurisdictional" rule can be taken as an expression of legislative intent. The failure of harried legislatures awash in statutes to modify or explain statutory details is as likely the result of inattention or overwork as it is of implicit legislative approval. In this context, pavid reluctance to forge legal principles where the expression of the legislature's will is unclear, obsolete, or nonexistent, is inappropriate for a court. Furthermore the alternative — an attempt to attract the legislature's attention by sacrificing these appellants on the altar of judicial deference — is distasteful to us. If the legislature does intend to have strict time limitations, they can amend the statutes to express that intent explicitly, as the Virginia Legislature has done.[6]

(c) Even if the absence of legislative correction *does* reflect some sort of acquiescence, it may not be acquiescence in the specific holding of the prior case. First, holdings are not always crystal clear, and the legislature's interpretation of the prior ruling may differ from the court's. Second, the legislature may be acquiescing not in the particular ruling, but in the general principle that courts ought to have relatively free interpretive rein, at least on this topic. Both of these become reasons for overruling rather than standing by a mistaken precedent.

Eskridge, Jr., *Overruling Statutory Precedents*, 76 Geo. L.J. 1361, 1402–1409 (1988).

[5] Abner J. Mikva, *How Well Does Congress Support and Defend the Constitution?*, 61 N.C.L. Rev. 587, 609 (1983).

[6] Bailey v. State Workmen's Compensation Commissioner, 296 S.E.2d 901, 907 (W. Va. 1982).

(d) Even if legislative silence means that the legislature completely agrees with the decision and believes it reflects what the law should be, the views of the *current* legislature are irrelevant. Courts must adhere to the views of the *enacting* legislature. If the current legislature disagrees with a prior legislature, it must pass new legislation. If the court believes its precedent is wrong, then to stick by it because the *current* legislature is content amounts to a statutory amendment without the constitutionally required procedures. The fact that Congress is on board is small consolation given that (1) the constitutionally required formalities have not been observed, (2) Congress might not actually pass such an amendment, and (3) the President has been excluded from the process.

Justice Scalia made this point in *West Virginia University Hospitals, Inc. v. Pennsylvania:*[7]

> "Only time will tell," [the dissent] says, "whether the Court * * * has correctly interpreted the will of Congress." The implication is that today's holding will be proved wrong if Congress amends the law to conform with [the] dissent. We think not. The "will of Congress" we look to is not a will evolving from Session to Session, but a will expressed and fixed in a particular enactment. Otherwise, we would speak not of "interpreting" the law but of "intuiting" or "predicting" it. Our role is to say what the law, as hitherto enacted, *is*; not to forecast what the law, as amended, *will be*.

Professor Elhauge, whose prescriptions were briefly summarized in Chapter 8, takes exactly the opposite position, arguing that when faced with statutory ambiguity courts interpret the statute to reflect the enactable preferences of the current, not the enacting, Congress.[8]

Who is correct?

Note that soon after the Supreme Court's decision in *West Virginia University Hospitals*, Congress did amend section 1988, authorizing an award of expert witness fees in some but not all civil rights cases. Civil Rights Act of 1991, Pub. L. 102-166, § 113(a), codified at 42 U.S.C. § 1988(c).

(6) *An important aside on ways of arguing about statutes.* These four arguments against taking legislative silence as approval illustrate a dichotomy that pervades discussions about statutory meaning. The first three all attack the inference of legislative endorsement as counterfactual. A realistic view of the legislative process, the argument goes, shows the inference to be pure fiction. The fourth argument is altogether different: it rests on a *theory* of legislative authority. The first three arguments are descriptive; the fourth normative. It dismisses the legislative ratification idea "for failure to state a claim" rather than by directed verdict, so to speak. We saw the same two types of argument in the attack on legislative history discussed in Chapter 12, and it will be useful to keep them separate in your own mind.

(7) *Legislative silence and common-law decisions.* Let us return to the

---

[7]   499 U.S. 83, 101–102 n.7 (1991). Fuller excerpts from this case are set out in Chapter 9.

[8]   *See generally* EINER ELHAUGE, STATUTORY DEFAULT RULES: HOW TO INTERPRET UNCLEAR LEGISLATION (2008); *see supra* page 263.

question of common-law precedents. State legislatures are always free to alter common law doctrines.[9] If the legislature has left untouched a line of common-law decisions — say, about the attractive nuisance doctrine — is that an implicit endorsement, suggesting that the judiciary should also leave the precedents untouched? Should our list of reasons in Chapter 5 for respecting precedents have included the possibility of legislative correction?

B. CHANGING STATUTORY MEANING

An unstated premise of the prior section was that a given statute has a single, fixed meaning. The stare decisis issue arises because today's court concludes that yesterday's court mistook that meaning. But there is another possible argument for abandoning a statutory precedent: the prior decision was correct *at the time it was decided,* but the meaning of the statute has changed. If statutory meaning can evolve, that is a reason for a milder rule of stare decisis. It would also, of course, have implications for statutory interpretation in general.

The traditional understanding is that statutory meaning cannot develop in the manner of the common law; to the extent changed circumstances render a statute awkward or obsolete, it is for the legislature to correct the situation, not the courts.

> Despite the established nonoriginalist elements in common law and constitutional adjudication, something rubs us the wrong way about [such] models of statutory interpretation. The legislature did something back then, our intuitions tell us, and until they act again it is not up to the courts (or any interpreter) to update the law. To update is to usurp the legislature's job, to violate important notions of legislative supremacy and separation of powers, to undermine the rule of law.[10]

There is no shortage of judicial citations for this proposition. As we saw in Chapter 8, however, some have argued that statutes might be read "dynamically" — their meaning can change as the surrounding circumstances and attitudes change.

The following case concerns a provision that you have encountered before: § 1714 of the California Civil Code, which was lurking in the background of the attractive nuisance cases in Chapter 4.

---

[9] And from time to time they do so quite directly. For example, *Hynes v. N.Y. Central R.R.,* which we read in Chapter 3, was the result of legislative intervention. Common law courts had devised the rule that a person was liable for damages caused by an intentional or negligent injury to another, but if the harm was so severe as to cause the victim's *death* then there was no remedy. The logical plaintiff, after all, was not available. This rule was changed in all 50 states, but not by the judiciary; statutes created a cause of action for "wrongful death" that could be brought by the victim's survivors.

[10] T. Alexander Aleinikoff, *Updating Statutory Interpretation,* 87 MICH. L. REV. 20, 56 (1988).

LI v. YELLOW CAB CO.
13 Cal. 3d 804, 119 Cal. Rptr. 858, 532 P.2d 1226 (1975) (In Bank)

SULLIVAN, JUSTICE.

[Plaintiff was injured when her car collided with a taxi. She sued the driver of the taxi and his employer. Ruling for the defendants, the trial court found that both drivers had failed to exercise due care and that plaintiff's contributory negligence barred any recovery.]

In this case we address the grave and recurrent question whether we should judicially declare no longer applicable in California courts the doctrine of contributory negligence, which bars all recovery when the plaintiff's negligent conduct has contributed as a legal cause in any degree to the harm suffered by him, and hold that it must give way to a system of comparative negligence, which assesses liability in direct proportion to fault. * * *

It is unnecessary for us to catalogue the enormous amount of critical comment that has been directed over the years against the "all-or-nothing" approach of the doctrine of contributory negligence. The essence of that criticism has been constant and clear: the doctrine is inequitable in its operation because it fails to distribute responsibility in proportion to fault. Against this have been raised several arguments in justification, but none have proved even remotely adequate to the task. The basic objection to the doctrine — grounded in the primal concept that in a system in which liability is based on fault, the extent of fault should govern the extent of liability — remains irresistible to reason and all intelligent notions of fairness. [These concerns are exacerbated by the fact that practical experience has shown that juries often, but inconsistently, employ a sort of de facto comparative negligence doctrine, finding for the plaintiff but reducing the award in light of plaintiff's fault.] * * *

It is in view of these theoretical and practical considerations that to this date 25 states have abrogated the "all or nothing" rule of contributory negligence and have enacted in its place general apportionment *statutes* calculated in one manner or another to assess liability in proportion to fault. In 1973 these states were joined by Florida, which effected the same result by *judicial* decision. We are likewise persuaded that logic, practical experience, and fundamental justice counsel against the retention of the doctrine rendering contributory negligence a complete bar to recovery — and that it should be replaced in this state by a system under which liability for damage will be borne by those whose negligence caused it in direct proportion to their respective fault. * * *

It is urged [, however,] that any change in the law of contributory negligence must be made by the Legislature, not by this court. Although the doctrine of contributory negligence is of judicial origin * * * the enactment of section 1714 of the Civil Code in 1872 codified the doctrine as it stood at that date and, the argument continues, rendered it invulnerable to attack in the courts except on constitutional grounds. Subsequent cases of this court, it is pointed out, have unanimously affirmed that — barring the appearance of some constitutional infirmity — the "all-or-nothing" rule is the law of this state and shall remain so

until the Legislature directs otherwise. The fundamental constitutional doctrine of separation of powers, the argument concludes, requires judicial abstention.

[The court began by noting that the Civil Code is broadly worded and incomplete and itself states that it is to be liberally construed. The code thus leaves generous room for judicial flexibility — flexibility that the courts had exercised in other areas.] * * * It is with these general precepts in mind that we turn to a specific consideration of section 1714. That section * * * provides in relevant part as follows: "Everyone is responsible, not only for the result of his willful acts, but also for an injury occasioned to another by his want of ordinary care or skill in the management of his property or person, *except so far as the latter has, willfully or by want of ordinary care, brought the injury upon himself.*" (Italics added.)

The present-day reader of the foregoing language is immediately struck by the fact that it seems to provide in specific terms for a rule of *comparative* rather than *contributory* negligence — i.e., for a rule whereby plaintiff's recovery is to be diminished *to the extent* that his own actions have been responsible for his injuries. The use of the compound conjunction "except so far as" — rather than some other conjunction setting up a wholly disqualifying condition — clearly seems to indicate an intention on the part of the Legislature to adopt a system other than one wherein contributory fault on the part of the plaintiff would operate to *bar* recovery. Thus it could be argued — as indeed it has been argued with great vigor by plaintiff and the amici curiae who support her position — that no *change* in the law is necessary in this case at all. Rather, it is asserted, all that is here required is a recognition by this court that section 1714 announced a rule of comparative negligence in this state in 1872 and a determination to brush aside all of the misguided decisions which have concluded otherwise up to the present day. * * *

[Careful examination of the legislative history, however,] establishes conclusively that the intention of the Legislature in enacting section 1714 of the Civil Code was to state the basic rule of negligence together with the defense of contributory negligence modified by the emerging doctrine of last clear chance [under which a negligent plaintiff can still recover if the defendant had, but did not exercise, the "last clear chance" to avoid the accident]. It remains to determine whether by so doing the Legislature intended to restrict the courts from further development of these concepts according to evolving standards of duty, causation, and liability.

This question must be answered in the negative. As we have explained above, the peculiar nature of the 1872 Civil Code as an avowed *continuation* of the common law has rendered it particularly flexible and adaptable in its response to changing circumstances and conditions. To reiterate the words of Professor Van Alstyne, "[the code's] incompleteness, both in scope and detail [,] have provided ample room for judicial development of important new systems of rules, frequently built upon Code foundations." * * * [W]e do not believe that the general language of section 1714 dealing with defensive considerations should be construed so as to stifle the orderly evolution of such considerations in light of emerging techniques and concepts. On the contrary we conclude that the rule of liberal construction made applicable to the code by its own terms together with the code's peculiar character as a continuation of the common law permit if not require that section

1714 be interpreted so as to give dynamic expression to the fundamental precepts which it summarizes.

The aforementioned precepts are basically two. The first is that one whose negligence has caused damage to another should be liable therefor. The second is that one whose negligence has contributed to his own injury should not be permitted to cast the burden of liability upon another. The problem facing the Legislature in 1872 was how to accommodate these twin precepts in a manner consonant with the then progress of the common law and yet allow for the incorporation of future developments. The manner chosen sought to insure that the harsh accommodation wrought by the New York rule — i.e., *barring* recovery to one guilty of *any* negligence — would not take root in this state. Rather the Legislature wished to encourage a more humane rule — one holding out the hope of recovery to the negligent plaintiff in some circumstances.

The resources of the common law at that time (in 1872) did not include techniques for the apportionment of damages strictly according to fault * * *. They did, however, include the nascent doctrine of last clear chance which, while it too was burdened by an "all-or-nothing" approach, at least to some extent avoided the often unconscionable results which could and did occur under the old rule precluding recovery when *any* negligence on the part of the plaintiff contributed in *any* degree to the harm suffered by him. Accordingly the Legislature sought to include the concept of last clear chance in its formulation of a rule of responsibility. We are convinced, however, as we have indicated, that in so doing the Legislature in no way intended to thwart future judicial progress toward the humane goal which it had embraced. Therefore, and for all of the foregoing reasons, we hold that section 1714 of the Civil Code was not intended to and does not preclude present judicial action in furtherance of the purposes underlying it. * * *

CLARK, J. (dissenting.)

I dissent.

For over a century this court has consistently and unanimously held that Civil Code section 1714 codifies the defense of contributory negligence. Suddenly — after 103 years — the court declares section 1714 shall provide for comparative negligence instead. In my view, this action constitutes a gross departure from established judicial rules and role.

First, the majority's decision deviates from settled rules of statutory construction. A cardinal rule of construction is to effect the intent of the Legislature. The majority concedes "the intention of the Legislature in enacting section 1714 of the Civil Code was to state the basic rule of negligence together with the defense of contributory negligence modified by the emerging doctrine of last clear chance." Yet the majority refuses to honor this acknowledged intention — violating established principle.

The majority decision also departs significantly from the recognized limitation upon judicial action — encroaching on the powers constitutionally entrusted to the Legislature. The power to enact and amend our statutes is vested exclusively in the Legislature. "This court may not usurp the legislative function to change the statutory law which has been uniformly construed by a long line of judicial

decisions." The majority's altering the meaning of section 1714, notwithstanding the original intent of the framers and the century-old judicial interpretation of the statute, represents no less than amendment by judicial fiat. Although the Legislature intended the courts to develop the working details of the defense of contributory negligence enacted in section 1714, no basis exists — either in history or in logic — to conclude the Legislature intended to authorize judicial repudiation of the basic defense itself at any point we might decide the doctrine no longer serves us.

I dispute the need for judicial — instead of legislative — action in this area. The majority is clearly correct in its observation that our society has changed significantly during the 103-year existence of section 1714. But this social change has been neither recent nor traumatic, and the criticisms leveled by the majority at the present operation of contributory negligence are not new. I cannot conclude our society's evolution has now rendered the normal legislative process inadequate. * * *

By abolishing this century old doctrine today, the majority seriously erodes our constitutional function. We are again guilty of judicial chauvinism.

NOTES AND QUESTIONS

(1)   *Text.* Simply on the basis of the statute's text, is *Li* correctly decided?

(2)   *Purpose.* What are the purposes of § 1714? Is the Court's result consistent with (or compelled by) those purposes?

(3)   *Statutory evolution?* Does the court conclude that it had misread the statute for the preceding century, or that the statute's meaning has somehow changed? How could it have changed? The court does not even pretend that its result is consistent with the intent or understanding of the enacting legislature; to the contrary, it is at pains to demonstrate that the enactors imposed a rule of contributory negligence. Given the clarity of that conclusion, is there any way to justify the court's result? Is this a statutory case or a common law case? Is there any way in which *Li* is consistent with legislative intent?

(4)   *Statutory obliteration?* Writing soon after *Li* was decided, Professor Maurice Rosenberg observed that despite the proliferation of statutes judges "manage to keep open at least these trails to active creativity: invalidation, interpretation, and obliteration." Invalidation, i.e., declaring a statute unconstitutional, is a topic for another course. As for interpretation, Rosenberg observes that sometimes courts reach a "happy ending" by discovering hidden meanings in the legislative history, sometimes by ignoring legislative history in favor of plain meaning. Finally, there is "obliteration," of which *Li v. Yellow Cab Company* is a "prime example." Concludes Rosenberg: "Obsequies for judicial creativity, assertedly brought on by statutory suffocation, are premature."[11]

---

[11] Maurice Rosenberg, *Anything Legislatures Can Do, Courts Can Do Better?*, 62 A.B.A.J. 587, 587 (1976).

Did the California Supreme Court improperly "obliterate" § 1714?

SAINT FRANCIS COLLEGE v. AL-KHAZRAJI
481 U.S. 604 (1987)

[Respondent, a United States citizen born in Iraq, was a professor at Saint Francis College, which denied him tenure. He filed this suit under 42 U.S.C. § 1981, the text of which is set out in note 1, *supra*, claiming that the college had discriminated against him on the basis of race.]

Although § 1981 does not itself use the word "race," the Court has construed the section to forbid all "racial" discrimination in the making of private as well as public contracts. *Runyon v. McCrary*, 427 U.S. 160, 168, 174–175 (1976). * * * The issue is whether respondent has alleged *racial* discrimination within the meaning of § 1981. * * *

Petitioner's submission [that respondent is Caucasian and that § 1981 does not apply to discrimination by one Caucasian against another] rests on the assumption that all those who might be deemed Caucasians today were thought to be of the same race when § 1981 became law in the 19th century; and it may be that a variety of ethnic groups, including Arabs, are now considered to be within the Caucasian race. The understanding of "race" in the 19th century, however, was different. Plainly, all those who might be deemed Caucasian today were not thought to be of the same race at the time § 1981 became law.

In the middle years of the 19th century, dictionaries commonly referred to race as a "continued series of descendants from a parent who is called the *stock*," [and similar references to a common ancestor.] * * * It was not until the 20th century that dictionaries began referring to the Caucasian, Mongolian, and Negro races, or to race as involving divisions of mankind based upon different physical characteristics. * * *

Encyclopedias of the 19th century also described race in terms of ethnic groups, which is a narrower concept of race than petitioners urge. * * * The Ninth edition of the Encyclopedia Britannica also referred to Arabs, Jews, and other ethnic groups such as Germans, Hungarians, and Greeks as separate races.

These dictionary and encyclopedic sources are somewhat diverse, but it is clear that they do not support the claim that for the purposes of § 1981, Arabs, Englishmen, Germans, and certain other ethnic groups are to be considered a single race. * * * The [congressional] debates are replete with references to the Scandinavian races, as well as the Chinese, Latin, Spanish, and Anglo-Saxon races. Jews, Mexicans, blacks, and Mongolians were similarly categorized. Gypsies were referred to as a race. Likewise, the Germans * * *.

Based on the history of § 1981, we have little trouble in concluding that Congress intended to protect from discrimination identifiable classes of persons who are subjected to intentional discrimination solely because of their ancestry or ethnic characteristics. Such discrimination is racial discrimination that Congress intended § 1981 to forbid, whether or not it would be classified as racial in terms of modern scientific theory. * * * If respondent on remand can prove that he was subjected to intentional discrimination based on the fact that he was born an Arab

* * * he will have made out a case under § 1981.

NOTES AND QUESTIONS

(1)   Shaare Tefila. Another case decided the same day, *Shaare Tefila Congregation v. Cobb*, 481 U.S. 615 (1987), held that Jewish plaintiffs could sue white defendants under 42 U.S.C. § 1982. (Section 1982 was the provision at issue in *Patterson*; both it and § 1981 were part of § 1 of the 1866 Civil Rights Act.) "[T]he question before us is not whether Jews are considered to be a separate race by today's standards, but whether, at the time § 1982 was adopted, Jews * * * were among the peoples then considered to be distinct races and hence within the protection of the statute."

(2)   *Archeology.* In neither of these unanimous decisions did the Court explain *why* the 19th century understanding of "race" must control the 20th century interpretation of the statute. One might have thought that if there was any setting where we would want to abandon 19th-century attitudes and assumptions it would be with regard to race. In what ways was the result in these cases consistent with contemporary mores and in what ways inconsistent?

What differences in the legal setting might explain the different approaches by the U.S. Supreme Court in these cases and the California Supreme Court in *Li*?

(3)   Jones *and* Runyon. As best you can tell, is the Court's approach here consistent with that in *Jones* and *Runyon*? Although the Court in those cases invoked legislative intent, it adopted readings of §§ 1981 and 1982 that were different from what everyone had understood the statute to mean for over a century. In particular, reconsider Justice Stevens's concurrence in *Runyon*. There he seems to endorse a dynamic reading of § 1981 in light of contemporary mores. Should he therefore have dissented in *St. Francis College*?

(4)   Whereas § 1982 refers (albeit implicitly) only to racial discrimination, Title VII of the Civil Rights Act of 1964 forbids discrimination in employment on the basis of race, sex, religion, or national origin. Argue that Title VII's longer list of impermissible bases of employment decisions supports the result in *St. Francis*. Argue that it weakens that result.

(5)   *The famous problem of women jurors.* States usually draw jurors from lists of voters. The relevant statutes long predate women's suffrage, which arrived only with the adoption of the Nineteenth Amendment to the Constitution in 1917. Suppose a 19th century statute provides that jurors are to be drawn from lists of qualified "electors." After the ratification of the 19th Amendment, are women not only voters but jurors as well?

This problem divided state courts in the early 1920s. In *Commonwealth v. Maxwell*, 271 Pa. 378, 114 A. 825 (1921), the Pennsylvania Supreme Court held that the term "elector" was a general term that included new classes of electors as they were granted the right to vote. Women were indisputably "electors" and therefore were eligible for jury service. In *People ex rel. Fyfe v. Barnett*, 319 Ill. 403, 150 N.E. 290 (1925), the Illinois Supreme Court reached the opposite conclusion. It reasoned

that women were not within the statute because " 'electors,' in the statute here in question, meant male persons, only, to the legislators who used it."

Both courts claimed to be following the legislature's intent. Exactly what intent does each invoke? Does one seem more plausible to you than the other?

If you think that *Maxwell* is right and *Fyfe* wrong (that is, you think that after the 19th Amendment women could serve as jurors because they were "electors" within the meaning of the jury statutes), must you conclude that *St. Francis College* is wrong? Did not the *Fyfe* court proceed in exactly the same way as the Supreme Court, reading an old statute with an old dictionary?

If a court ruled today that women are not "electors" and therefore are not eligible for jury service, the decision would surely provoke an immediate legislative response. The overwhelming consensus today is that women should serve on juries. Is the certainty of a legislative override a reason for or against having the courts update the statute to fit the times?

BOB JONES UNIVERSITY v. UNITED STATES
461 U.S. 574 (1983)

CHIEF JUSTICE BURGER delivered the opinion of the Court. * * *

Until 1970, the Internal Revenue Service granted tax-exempt status to private schools, without regard to their racial admissions policies, under § 501(c)(3) of the Internal Revenue Code, 26 U.S.C. § 501(c)(3),[12] and granted charitable deductions for contributions to such schools under § 170 of the Code, 26 U.S.C. § 170.[13] * * *

In Revenue Ruling 71-447, the IRS formalized the [new] policy, first announced in 1970, that § 170 and § 501(c)(3) embrace the common-law "charity" concept. Under that view, to qualify for a tax exemption pursuant to § 501(c)(3), an institution must show, first, that it falls within one of the eight categories expressly set forth in that section, and second, that its activity is not contrary to settled public policy. [Invoking the "national policy to discourage racial discrimination in education," the IRS ruled that a private "school not having a racially nondiscriminatory policy as to students is not 'charitable' within the common law

---

[12] Section 501(c)(3) lists the following organizations, which, pursuant to § 501(a), are exempt from taxation unless denied tax exemptions under other specified sections of the Code:

"Corporations, and any community chest, fund, or foundation, organized and operated exclusively for religious, charitable, scientific, testing for public safety, literary, or educational purposes, or to foster national or international amateur sports competition (but only if no part of its activities involve the provision of athletic facilities or equipment), or for the prevention of cruelty to children or animals, no part of the net earnings of which inures to the benefit of any private shareholder or individual, no substantial part of the activities of which is carrying on propaganda, or otherwise attempting, to influence legislation . . . , and which does not participate in, or intervene in (including the publishing or distributing of statements), any political campaign on behalf of any candidate for public office." (Emphasis added.)

[13] Section 170(a) allows deductions for certain "charitable contributions." Section 170(c)(2)(B) [tracks the language of § 501(c)(3),] includ[ing] within the definition of "charitable contribution" a contribution or gift to or for the use of a corporation "organized and operated exclusively for religious, charitable, scientific, literary, or educational purposes. . . ."

concepts reflected in sections 170 and 501(c)(3) of the Code." Petitioners are two private schools, with racially discriminatory admissions and student life policies, seeking tax-exempt status.] * * *

Section 501(c)(3) * * * must be analyzed and construed within the framework of the Internal Revenue Code and against the background of the congressional purposes. Such an examination reveals unmistakable evidence that, underlying all relevant parts of the Code, is the intent that entitlement to tax exemption depends on meeting certain common-law standards of charity — namely, that an institution seeking tax-exempt status must serve a public purpose and not be contrary to established public policy.

This "charitable" concept appears explicitly in § 170 of the Code. That section contains a list of organizations virtually identical to that contained in § 501(c)(3). It is apparent that Congress intended that list to have the same meaning in both sections.[14] In § 170, Congress used the list of organizations in defining the term "charitable contributions." On its face, therefore, § 170 reveals that Congress' intention was to provide tax benefits to organizations serving charitable purposes. The form of § 170 simply makes plain what common sense and history tell us: in enacting both § 170 and § 501(c)(3), Congress sought to provide tax benefits to charitable organizations, to encourage the development of private institutions that serve a useful public purpose or supplement or take the place of public institutions of the same kind.

Tax exemptions for certain institutions thought beneficial to the social order of the country as a whole, or to a particular community, are deeply rooted in our history, as in that of England. The origins of such exemptions lie in the special privileges that have long been extended to charitable trusts.

More than a century ago, [well before the federal income tax existed,] this Court announced the caveat that is critical in this case:

"[It] has now become an established principle of American law, that courts of chancery will sustain and protect . . . a gift . . . to public charitable uses, *provided the same is consistent with local laws and public policy. . . ." Perin v. Carey*, 24 How. 465, 501 (1861) (emphasis added).

Soon after that, in 1877, the Court commented:

"A charitable use, *where neither law nor public policy forbids*, may be applied to almost any thing *that tends to promote the well-doing and well-being of social man." Ould v. Washington Hospital for Foundlings*, 95 U.S. 303, 311 (emphasis added).

* * * These statements clearly reveal the legal background against which Congress enacted the first charitable exemption statute in 1894: charities were to be

---

[14] The predecessor of § 170 originally was enacted in 1917, whereas the predecessor of § 501(c)(3) dates back to the income tax law of 1894. There are minor differences between the lists of organizations in the two sections. Nevertheless, the two sections are closely related; both seek to achieve the same basic goal of encouraging the development of certain organizations through the grant of tax benefits. The language of the two sections is in most respects identical, and the Commissioner and the courts consistently have applied many of the same standards in interpreting those sections.

given preferential treatment because they provide a benefit to society. * * *

When the Government grants exemptions or allows deductions all taxpayers are affected; the very fact of the exemption or deduction for the donor means that other taxpayers can be said to be indirect and vicarious "donors." Charitable exemptions are justified on the basis that the exempt entity confers a public benefit — a benefit which the society or the community may not itself choose or be able to provide, or which supplements and advances the work of public institutions already supported by tax revenues. History buttresses logic to make clear that, to warrant exemption under § 501(c)(3), an institution must fall within a category specified in that section and must demonstrably serve and be in harmony with the public interest. The institution's purpose must not be so at odds with the common community conscience as to undermine any public benefit that might otherwise be conferred.

We are bound to approach these questions with full awareness that determinations of public benefit and public policy are sensitive matters with serious implications for the institutions affected; a declaration that a given institution is not "charitable" should be made only where there can be no doubt that the activity involved is contrary to a fundamental public policy. But there can no longer be any doubt that racial discrimination in education violates deeply and widely accepted views of elementary justice. Prior to 1954, public education in many places still was conducted under the pall of *Plessy v. Ferguson*, 163 U.S. 537 (1896); racial segregation in primary and secondary education prevailed in many parts of the country.[15] This Court's decision in *Brown v. Board of Education*, 347 U.S. 483 (1954), signaled an end to that era. Over the past quarter of a century, every pronouncement of this Court and myriad Acts of Congress and Executive Orders attest a firm national policy to prohibit racial segregation and discrimination in public education.

An unbroken line of cases following *Brown v. Board of Education* establishes beyond doubt this Court's view that racial discrimination in education violates a most fundamental national public policy, as well as rights of individuals. [The Court then describes numerous examples of legislative and executive action demonstrating a commitment "to the fundamental policy of eradicating racial discrimination." Congress has prohibited racial discrimination in public education, voting rights, housing, public accommodations, and private employment; the President has prohibited racial discrimination in federal hiring, in the military, and in activities receiving federal funds.]

Few social or political issues in our history have been more vigorously debated and more extensively ventilated than the issue of racial discrimination, particularly in education. Given the stress and anguish of the history of efforts to escape from the shackles of the "separate but equal" doctrine of *Plessy v. Ferguson*, 163 U.S. 537 (1896), it cannot be said that educational institutions that, for whatever reasons, practice racial discrimination, are institutions exercising "beneficial and stabilizing influences in community life," or should be encouraged by having all taxpayers

---

[15] In 1894, when the first charitable exemption provision was enacted, racially segregated educational institutions would not have been regarded as against public policy. Yet contemporary standards must be considered in determining whether given activities provide a public benefit and are entitled to the charitable tax exemption.

share in their support by way of special tax status.

There can thus be no question that the interpretation of § 170 and § 501(c)(3) announced by the IRS in 1970 was correct. That it may be seen as belated does not undermine its soundness. It would be wholly incompatible with the concepts underlying tax exemption to grant the benefit of tax-exempt status to racially discriminatory educational entities * * *.

[The Court goes on to conclude that the IRS had the authority to reverse its prior policy by regulation and without statutory amendment. The opinion ends by emphasizing Congress's failure to modify the IRS rulings, notwithstanding great controversy and the introduction of 13 separate bills to do so.]

The judgments of the Court of Appeals are, accordingly,

Affirmed.

JUSTICE REHNQUIST, dissenting.

The Court points out that there is a strong national policy in this country against racial discrimination. To the extent that the Court states that Congress in furtherance of this policy could deny tax-exempt status to educational institutions that promote racial discrimination, I readily agree. But, unlike the Court, I am convinced that Congress simply has failed to take this action and, as this Court has said over and over again, regardless of our view on the propriety of Congress' failure to legislate we are not constitutionally empowered to act for it.

In approaching this statutory construction question the Court quite adeptly avoids the statute it is construing. This I am sure is no accident, for there is nothing in the language of § 501(c)(3) that supports the result obtained by the Court. [Justice Rehnquist here sets out the full text of § 501(c)(3).] With undeniable clarity, Congress has explicitly defined the requirements for § 501(c)(3) status. An entity must be (1) a corporation, or community chest, fund, or foundation, (2) organized for one of the eight enumerated purposes, (3) operated on a nonprofit basis, and (4) free from involvement in lobbying activities and political campaigns. Nowhere is there to be found some additional, undefined public policy requirement.

The Court first seeks refuge from the obvious reading of § 501(c)(3) by turning to § 170 of the Internal Revenue Code * * *. The Court seizes the words "charitable contribution" [in § 170(a)] and with little discussion concludes that "[o]n its face, therefore, § 170 reveals that Congress' intention was to provide tax benefits to organizations serving charitable purposes," intimating that this implies some unspecified common-law charitable trust requirement.

The Court would have been well advised to look to subsection (c) where * * * Congress has defined a "charitable contribution" [in language that] * * * simply tracks the requirements set forth in § 501(c)(3). Since § 170 is no more than a mirror of § 501(c)(3) and, as the Court points out, § 170 followed § 501(c)(3) by more than two decades, it is at best of little usefulness in finding the meaning of § 501(c)(3).

Making a more fruitful inquiry, the Court next turns to the legislative history of § 501(c)(3) * * *. I think that the legislative history of § 501(c)(3) unmistakably makes clear that *Congress has decided* what organizations are serving a public

purpose and providing a public benefit within the meaning of § 501(c)(3) and has clearly set forth in § 501(c)(3) the characteristics of such organizations. In fact, there are few examples which better illustrate Congress' effort to define and redefine the requirements of a legislative Act.

[Justice Rehnquist reviews the numerous amendments and revisions to § 501(c)(3) and its predecessors since 1894.]

One way to read the opinion handed down by the Court today leads to the conclusion that this long and arduous refining process of § 501(c)(3) was certainly a waste of time, for when enacting the original 1894 statute Congress intended to adopt a common-law term of art, and intended that this term of art carry with it all of the common-law baggage which defines it. Such a view, however, leads also to the unsupportable idea that Congress has spent almost a century adding illustrations simply to clarify an already defined common-law term. * * *

I have no disagreement with the Court's finding that there is a strong national policy in this country opposed to racial discrimination. I agree with the Court that Congress has the power to further this policy by denying § 501(c)(3) status to organizations that practice racial discrimination. But as of yet Congress has failed to do so. Whatever the reasons for the failure, this Court should not legislate for Congress.

NOTES AND QUESTIONS

(1) *Text.* Assess the following argument: The Code says that to qualify for exempt status an organization need be *either* charitable *or* educational. The petitioners were indisputably educational institutions. That suffices. End of case.

(2) *Legislative inaction.* We have edited out an extensive discussion of legislative acquiescence through inaction. The argument parallels that in *Patterson,* although here the action in which Congress is said to have acquiesced is an agency regulation rather than a judicial decision. Should that make any difference? Note that, as Justice Rehnquist points out, prior to 1970 Congress had acquiesced in the *opposite* rule for decades. Should *that* acquiescence count? Or is more recent acquiescence more relevant? (Recall Einer Elhauge's theory, described in Chapter 8, that courts should defer to the enactable preferences of the *current* Congress.)

The legislative inaction question is complicated by the fact that in January 1982, after the Supreme Court had decided to hear this case but before it was argued, the Reagan administration announced that it would abandon the prevailing IRS interpretation; it had concluded that racially discriminatory schools *were* charities within the meaning of §§ 170 and 501(c)(3). Thus, the government lawyers ended up arguing *for* the petitioners and *against* "the United States." The Court appointed an attorney to argue for respondent.

For the nearly a year and a half that the case was pending in the Supreme Court following the administration's change of position, Congress did nothing. What inferences can one draw from that congressional inaction? Scholars have dis

agreed.[16]

(3) *Changing times.* Is *Bob Jones* a case in which contemporary policy dictated one clear answer, the statute dictated another, and the Court opted to follow policy? Professor Sunstein argues that such a question improperly separates "contemporary policy" on the one hand from "the statute" on the other. He endorses *Bob Jones* as appropriate dynamic interpretation:

> There is no doubt that if th[e] question had been put to the Congress that initially enacted the relevant provision of the Code, it would have answered that there was no such requirement [that tax-exempt institutions not discriminate on the basis of race]. Institutions that discriminated on the basis of race were common at that time, and they were not thought to violate public policy. But if the enacting Congress were brought forward to the present, and informed of the changing developments of law and policy, it would in all likelihood have concluded that the deduction was impermissible. Perhaps the public policy exception should be taken to embody a general principle capable of change over time.[17]

Note also footnote 15 in the majority's opinion. What changed, the statute's meaning or the circumstances in which it was applied?

(4) *Limits on statutory change.* Suppose you accept that to some extent, and in certain circumstances, courts should reinterpret statutes to have meanings foreign to their enactors but consistent with modern conditions. What limits, if any, should there be on such judicial creativity? Does your answer depend on your expectations as to whether the legislature or the judiciary, as constituted now or in the future, will produce outcomes more to your liking?

At the least, both the ease and appropriateness of such an approach are likely to vary with the specificity of the statute. Grant Gilmore pointed out that "the more tightly a statute was drafted originally, the more difficult it becomes to adjust the statute to changing conditions without legislative revision."[18] Could the San Bernardino pool fence ordinance be interpreted dynamically, readjusted in light of changing times (or changing fencing technology)?

What factors besides textual specificity will make dynamic interpretation more or less appropriate in individual instances?

---

[16] *See* ELHAUGE, *supra* note 8, at 75–77 (arguing that the Court's decision did reflect a current enactable congressional preference, and that the administration's new position reflected a new interpretation of existing law, not a policy preference); Elizabeth Garrett, *Book Review*, 122 HARV. L. REV. 2104, 2134–2135 (2009) (reviewing Elhauge) (concluding that it is impossible to tell what Congress's preferences were); Mayer Freed & Daniel D. Polsby, *Race, Religion, and Public Policy: Bob Jones University v. United States*, 1983 SUP. CT. REV. 1, 9–10 (suggesting that Congress would have left the new interpretation untouched, approving by acquiescence).

[17] CASS R. SUNSTEIN, AFTER THE RIGHTS REVOLUTION 126–127 (1990).

[18] GRANT GILMORE, THE AGES OF AMERICAN LAW 96 (1977).

C. "DESUETUDE" — HEREIN OF STATUTORY OBSOLESCENCE

The Roman jurist Julian wrote that "statutes may be abrogated not only by a vote of the legislator, but also by desuetude with the tacit consent of all."[19] This idea surfaces occasionally but rarely in American law, usually with regard to ancient and anachronistic criminal statutes. The boldest call for an aggressive judicial stance toward older statutes has come from the former dean of the Yale Law School, Guido Calabresi, now a judge on the U.S. Court of Appeals for the Second Circuit. In a 1982 book, *A Common Law for the Age of Statutes*, Calabresi argued that courts should simply declare obsolete statutes defunct and strike them from the statute books.

Calabresi would model a court's treatment of outmoded statutes on its treatment of outmoded common law precedents. Like an old common law case, an old statute has little to support it other than the fact that it has gone unrepealed by the legislature. That it once commanded majoritarian support is irrelevant if that support has disappeared. When a statute (1) no longer "fits into the overall legal landscape," (2) no longer enjoys majoritarian support, and (3) remains on the books because of paralyzing legislative inertia, rather than because of legislative approval, it merits no more respect than an obsolete common law precedent. And just as courts have always "updated" the common law, so they should "update" the statute books. Calabresi cautions that "[t]he court must * * * do the best it can to avoid following the requirements of the legal landscape when that would conflict with powerful legislative desires." But where no such desire is evident, the judiciary should bring statutory law into line with contemporary social and legal realities. If a court misjudges in rewriting a statute, it will at least draw the legislature's attention. It is then up to the legislature to reenact the statute, let the new judicial version stand, or impose a third rule.

Consider whether the following case would have been an appropriate case for application of Calabresi's approach.

FRANKLIN v. HILL
444 S.E.2d 778 (Ga. 1994)

[Section 51-1-16 of the Georgia Code provides: "The seduction of a daughter, unmarried and living with her parent, whether followed by pregnancy or not, shall give a right of action to the father or to the mother if the father is dead, or absent permanently, or refuses to bring an action." Nancy Franklin sued her daughter's former high school teacher under this provision. The majority held that the statute was unconstitutional because it discriminated on the basis of sex. We set out only the concurring opinion.]

Sears-Collins, Justice, concurring.

I write separately to urge a new method for reviewing the validity of statutes that focuses not on the application of traditional constitutional and interpretive

---

[19] Digest 3.32.1, quoted in Arthur E. Bonfield, *The Abrogation of Penal Statutes by Nonenforcement*, 49 Iowa L. Rev. 389, 395 (1964).

principles but rather on what, in many cases, would be the less strained approach of examining whether the statute has become obsolete since its enactment. In this case, I believe that § 51-1-16, which was enacted in 1863, has become hopelessly obsolete in the last 131 years and therefore may not be enforced.

Obviously, courts should be reluctant to declare statutes void as obsolete. However, that power is justified in rare instances. Certainly, in this case, where the constitutionality of the statute is doubtful, where the statute is woefully out of step with current legal and societal standards, and where the statute has been rarely used, the court should not hesitate to declare the statute void so as to give our General Assembly the opportunity to reexamine the statute in its entirety.

Turning to § 51-1-16, we have held that it applies in cases in which the child

is led astray and her morals destroyed, uprooted and extirpated, her social standing damaged, and she is thereby rendered an unfit associate for other children in the family and a debased member of society.

In discussing the damages due for the seduction, we have stated that it is the jury's duty to compensate the father

for the dishonor and disgrace thus cast upon his family; for this atrocious invasion of his household peace. There is nothing like it, since the entrance of Sin and Death into this lower world. Money can not redress a parent who is wronged beyond the possibility of redress; can not minister to a mind thus diseased. * * *

Further, the rationale in placing the action in the father, or the mother if the father is dead or permanently absent, is that

[b]efore the child attains the age of twenty-one, the law gives the father dominion over her; and after [age 21], the law presumes the contract, when the daughter is so situated as to render service to the father, or is under his control; and this it does for the wisest and most benevolent of purposes, to preserve his domestic peace, by guarding from the spoiler the purity and innocence of his child. * * *

The statute is based on outdated notions of a parent having dominion and control of his or her daughter, including an adult daughter, and in fact harkens back to times when parents, particularly fathers, had property interests in the bodies of their children. * * * Moreover, the statute even applies to adult daughters who are living at home. Certainly, today, an adult daughter who is living at home is not under the dominion and control of her father, and if she has a consensual sexual relationship, it does not bring the " 'dishonor and disgrace' " upon her parents that it might have brought in 1863. By perpetuating the idea that an adult daughter who lives at home is under the control of her parents and the idea that, when she engages in a consensual sexual relationship, that relationship immeasurably damages her parents, the statute fails to recognize the long sought after freedom and independence which has been achieved by women.

Further, the statute runs contrary to modern notions that actions should be brought in the name of the real party in interest. If the seduction of a daughter truly

creates harm, then it clearly harms the daughter, who then should be the party having the right of action.* * *

Further, the statute does not fit within the framework of current constitutional law because it discriminates against the parents of male children by only providing a cause of action for the seduction of a daughter, and because it gives preferential treatment to fathers by permitting them, if they are living and present, to bring the action to the exclusion of mothers. Such gender-based classifications are out of touch with today's constitutional standards. * * *

The final factor in deciding that the statute should be declared obsolete is that the statute has largely fallen into disuse. Indeed, the statute has seen negligible use since its enactment in 1863, and since 1932, the only reported cases of its use are the present case and [one other 1993 decision]. Although disuse might not be a decisive factor in holding this, or any, statute obsolete, the fact that the statute has seldom been used in 131 years and not at all in about 60 years sends a signal that the statute is not being relied on by the general public and is thus a factor to consider in determining whether to force a reconsideration of the law by the people's representatives.

Because § 51-1-16 is based on outdated legal and societal notions and has a significant history of disuse, the statute should be repealed as being obsolete, thus forcing the General Assembly to reexamine the tort of seduction in view of modern day concepts. Thus, in addition to the reasons given in the majority opinion, I would affirm the trial court's judgment on the ground that the statute is obsolete.

NOTES AND QUESTIONS

(1) Commentators have criticized Calabresi on two basic grounds. First, they contend that he asks too much of judges.

> [T]he key feature of Calabresi's proposal [is] the extraordinary intellectual expectations he has for his judges. In assessing prevailing legal principles, the judge must be a scholar of considerable breadth and an astute political analyst. Most of all, he must be a subtle interpreter of a complex "text": the [entire] legal landscape . . .[20]

Second, it is argued that even if judges were up to the task Calabresi sets them, it would be inappropriate, if not unconstitutional, to revise the legislature's work in this way.

> Our legislative process is designed so that laws will outlive the political coalitions that enact them. It is not at all clear that a democratic system could function otherwise. What is clear is that pure majoritarianism has never been our system of government. It is a basic institutional require-ment of our system of government that the legitimacy of a statute be

---

[20] Robert Weisberg, *The Calabresian Judicial Artist: Statutes and the New Legal Process*, 35 STAN. L. REV. 213, 225–226 (1983).

independent of the current state of public opinion. Thus, it would be a mistake to add a proviso to the supremacy principle that "courts must enforce statutes, unless the latest Gallup poll shows that a statute has clearly lost majority support."[21]

Does the concurrence in *Franklin v. Hill* bear out or undercut these objections?

(2)   Under Calabresi's approach, which (if any) of the statutes in this section should the courts have set aside as obsolete? (Or did they?)

(3)   What differences are there between Calabresi's approach and "dynamic statutory interpretation"? Are the foregoing objections equally applicable to any interpretive method that tries to do more than simply follow the words as written and/or the intent of the enacting legislature?

(4)   Calabresi's proposal for judicially administered statutory euthanasia has attracted considerable academic attention but not much enthusiasm and almost no judicial endorsements. Would you endorse it?

Assignment

In 1950, Congress began to consider a total overhaul of the Immigration and Nationalization Act, the basic law governing immigration into the country. Traditionally, one of the many grounds for excluding those seeking entry into this country was "mental disease." Among many other recommended changes, the Senate Judiciary Committee proposed that this provision be amended specifically to exclude "homosexuals and other sex perverts."

In 1952, Congress enacted extensive amendments to the Act. It did not explicitly refer to "homosexuals and other sex perverts." Instead, the exclusion referred to "aliens afflicted with psychopathic personality, epilepsy, or a mental defect." The Senate Report explained that "[t]he Public Health Service has advised that the provision for the exclusion of aliens afflicted with psychopathic personality or a mental defect * * * is sufficiently broad to provide for the exclusion of homosexuals and sex perverts. This change in nomenclature is not to be construed in any way as modifying the intent to exclude all aliens who are sexual deviates."

In 1967, in *Boutilier v. INS*, 387 U.S. 118 (1967), the Supreme Court ruled that the phrase "psychopathic personality" in the 1952 provision included homosexuals. The Court found that Congress had used "psychopathic personality" as a "term of art" to "effectuate its purpose to exclude from entry all homosexuals and other sex perverts." "[T]he test here is what Congress intended, not what differing psychiatrists may think. It was not laying down a clinical test, but an exclusionary standard which it declared to be inclusive of those having homosexual and perverted characteristics."

(1) Were *Boutilier* to arise today — same facts, same statute — would or should it be decided the same way?

---

[21] Daniel A. Farber, *Statutory Interpretation and Legislative Supremacy*, 78 Geo. L.J. 281, 308–309 (1989).

(2) Prior to *Boutilier*, the Ninth Circuit had held that "psychopathic personality" did not include gay men and lesbians. In response, Congress amended § 212(a)(4) in 1965 to exclude: "Aliens afflicted with psychopathic personality, or sexual deviation, or a mental defect." The Senate Report quoted the 1952 report, described the holding of the 9th Circuit case, and stated: "To resolve any doubt the committee has specifically included the term 'sexual deviation' as a ground of exclusion in this bill." *Boutilier* arose under the pre-1965 provision and the Court therefore did not consider the added phrase. Does the fact of the 1965 amendment change your answer to the first question? For conflicting results under the amended statute, see *In re Longstaff*, 716 F.2d 1439 (5th Cir. 1983) (homosexuality sufficient basis for excluding an alien), *cert. denied*, 467 U.S. 1219 (1984); *Hill v. INS*, 714 F.2d 1470 (9th Cir. 1983) (because the Surgeon General had concluded that "current medical standards classify homosexuality as simply a form of sexual behavior," rather than a psychopathic disorder, homosexuality could no longer be the basis of exclusion).

(3) In 1990, Congress amended the Act once again. An alien may now be excluded on health-related grounds only if she has a communicable disease of public health significance, has a physical or mental disorder and behavior associated with it that poses a threat to property, safety, or welfare, had such a disorder that is likely to recur, or is a drug abuser. What result were *Boutilier* to arise under the current statute?

Chapter 15

SUMMARY AND CONCLUSION:
THE ROLE OF JUDGES IN A DEMOCRATIC SOCIETY

> *I have been in a minority of one as to the proper administration of the*
> *Sherman Act. I hope and believe that I am not influenced by my opinion*
> *that it is a foolish law. I have little doubt that the country likes it and I*
> *always say, as you know, that if my fellow citizens want to go to Hell I will*
> *help them. It's my job.*

> — Oliver Wendell Holmes, Jr.[1]

Any judicial decision implicitly raises questions about the role of judges in a democracy. How much freedom does a judge have, or can a judge take? Is a judge's function only to help us on our way to Hell? If it is not, then must we fear being led there nonetheless by a well-meaning but misguided judiciary?

Through their decisions, judges are always answering these questions implicitly. Sometimes they answer them explicitly, usually with well-worn platitudes about deference to the other branches of government. Rarely, though, does the outcome of a case actually turn on a determination of the governmental role of the judiciary. In this chapter, we will examine two of these rarities — statutory cases in which the Supreme Court was directly confronted with the question, "What is a judge?"

The first of these is *Gregory v. Ashcroft*, which presented the question of whether judges are "on the policymaking level" and therefore excluded from the coverage of the Age Discrimination in Employment Act. You read portions of this case in Chapters 10 and 12, which you should review at this point.

GREGORY v. ASHCROFT
501 U.S. 452 (1991)

Justice O'Connor delivered the opinion of the Court. * * *

Governor Ashcroft relies on the plain language of the statute: it exempts persons appointed "at the policymaking level." The Governor argues that state judges, in fashioning and applying the common law, make policy. Missouri is a common law state. The common law, unlike a constitution or statute, provides no

---

[1] Letter from Oliver Wendell Holmes, Jr. to Harold Laski (Mar. 4, 1920), *in* 1 Holmes-Laski Letters, 1916-1925, at 248–249 (Mark DeWolfe Howe ed., 1953).

definitive text; it is to be derived from the interstices of prior opinions and a well-considered judgment of what is best for the community. As Justice Holmes put it:

> "The very considerations which judges most rarely mention, and always with an apology, are the secret root from which the law draws all the juices of life. I mean, of course, considerations of what is expedient for the community concerned. Every important principle which is developed by litigation is in fact and at bottom the result of more or less definitely understood views of public policy; most generally, to be sure, under our practice and traditions, the unconscious result of instinctive preferences and inarticulate convictions, but nonetheless traceable to views of public policy in the last analysis." O. Holmes, The Common Law 35–36 (1881). * * *

The Governor stresses judges' policymaking responsibilities, but it is far from plain that the statutory exception requires that judges actually make policy. The statute refers to appointees "on the policymaking level," not to appointees "who make policy." It may be sufficient that the appointee is in a position requiring the exercise of discretion concerning issues of public importance. This certainly describes the bench, regardless of whether judges might be considered policymakers in the same sense as the executive or legislature. * * *

[Given the need for a clear statement of congressional intent to apply the statute to these employees, the Court resolved the ambiguity against statutory coverage.]

Justice WHITE, with whom Justice STEVENS joins, concurring in part, dissenting in part, and concurring in the judgment. * * *

"Policy" is defined as "a definite course or method of action selected (as by a government, institution, group, or individual) from among alternatives and in the light of given conditions to guide and usu[ally] determine present and future decisions." Webster's Third New International Dictionary 1754 (1976). Applying that definition, it is clear that the decisionmaking engaged in by common-law judges, such as petitioners, places them "on the policymaking level." In resolving disputes, although judges do not operate with unconstrained discretion, they do choose "from among alternatives" and elaborate their choices in order "to guide and . . . determine present and future decisions." The quotation from Justice Holmes in the majority's opinion is an eloquent description of the policymaking nature of the judicial function. Justice Cardozo also stated it well:

> "Each [common-law judge] indeed is legislating within the limits of his competence. No doubt the limits for the judge are narrower. He legislates only between gaps. He fills the open spaces in the law. . . . [W]ithin the confines of these open spaces and those of precedent and tradition, choice moves with a freedom which stamps its action as creative. The law which is the resulting product is not found, but made." B. Cardozo, The Nature of the Judicial Process 113–115 (1921).

Moreover, it should be remembered that the statutory exception refers to appointees "on the policymaking level," not "policymaking employees." Thus, whether or not judges actually *make* policy, they certainly are on the same *level* as

policymaking officials in other branches of government and therefore are covered by the exception. * * *

Justice BLACKMUN, with whom Justice MARSHALL joins, dissenting. * * *

Although it may be possible to define an appointed judge as a "policymaker" with only a dictionary as a guide,[2] we have an obligation to construe the exclusion of an "appointee on the policymaking level" with a sensitivity to the context in which Congress placed it. * * *

The policymaker exclusion is placed between the exclusion of "any person chosen by such [elected] officer to be on such officer's personal staff" and the exclusion of "an immediate advisor with respect to the exercise of the constitutional or legal powers of the office." See 29 U.S.C. § 630(f). Reading the policymaker exclusion in light of the other categories of employees listed with it, I conclude that the class of "appointee[s] on the policymaking level" should be limited to those officials who share the characteristics of personal staff members and immediate advisers, *i.e.*, those who work closely with the appointing official and are directly accountable to that official. * * * Because appointed judges are not accountable to the official who appoints them and are precluded from working closely with that official once they have been appointed, they are not "appointee[s] on the policymaking level" for purposes of 29 U.S.C. § 630(f).

NOTES AND QUESTIONS

(1) *Judges as policymakers.* The Justices are highly reluctant to describe judges as "policymakers." Only Justices White and Stevens actually state that judges make policy, and even they soft-pedal by (1) noting that the statute required only that judges be "on the policymaking level," not that they actually be policymakers, (2) focusing solely on judges' common-law functions, and (3) using a dictionary definition of "policy" that was quite broad and might include a good many other state employees as well. The five Justices in the majority skirt the issue, and Justices Blackmun and Marshall deny that policy is an important factor in judicial decisionmaking. Why this reluctance? Is it accurate? Does it reflect humility? Public relations?

(2) *Liberal vs. conservative.* The Court's two most liberal members argued for a broader application of this anti-discrimination statute. Perhaps that is not surprising. Yet is the outcome in this case "liberal" or "conservative"? The former legal director of the ACLU has written:

---

[2] Justice WHITE finds the dictionary definition of "policymaker" broad enough to include the Missouri judges involved in this case, because judges resolve disputes by choosing " 'from among alternatives' and elaborate their choices in order 'to guide and . . . determine present and future decisions.' " I hesitate to classify judges as policymakers, even at this level of abstraction. Although some part of a judge's task may be to fill in the interstices of legislative enactments, the primary task of a judicial officer is to apply rules reflecting the policy choices made by, or on behalf of, those elected to legislative and executive positions. A judge is first and foremost one who resolves disputes, and not one charged with the duty to fashion broad policies establishing the rights and duties of citizens. That task is reserved primarily for legislators. * * *

Gregory at first glance appears to be a defeat for civil rights. * * * Viewed from the pragmatic perspective of enhancing opportunities for minorities and women to become judges, however, the case is no worse than a tie and may well be a win. The overwhelmingly white, male composition of our current state and federal courts reflects an historically inadequate minority participation in the selection process. If the court had adopted the EEOC's reading [in] *Gregory*, the ordinary processes of judicial renewal in appointive states, this time with minority input, would have been delayed for a decade.[3]

Is it a "win" to trade the rights of the elderly for those of women and minorities? If so, is it a lasting victory?

Note also that the judicial portrait painted by Justices Blackmun and Marshall — that of a deferential dispute-resolver, humbly applying rules laid down by others to the minor and limited disputes that happen to come before them — is generally seen as the "conservative" view of judging. Think about the dispute over the legitimacy of *Roe v. Wade*. Ironically, Justice Blackmun wrote the majority opinion in *Roe*, over a dissent by Justice White objecting that the decision was "an improvident and extravagant exercise" of "raw judicial power" with "scarcely any reason or authority." Here Justice White asserts that judges are policymakers whereas Justice Blackmun diffidently shies away from any such claim. What happened?

(3)   At the time this case was decided it did not escape notice that the two dissenters were the Court's two oldest members. Is this coincidence?

(4)   Counterfactually, suppose that *federal* judges were subject to mandatory retirement and that the statute covered federal employees. What outcome? (Note that the clear statement approach taken by the majority, see Chapter 10, drops out, since there are no federalism concerns when Congress regulates to protect federal employees as opposed to state.) With rare exceptions, federal judges do not decide common-law cases; their docket is almost exclusively statutory and constitutional. Does this mean that federal judges (including those on the Supreme Court) are not "on the policymaking level," even though state judges are or might be? Does the interpretation of statutes involve policymaking? Is *Gregory* itself an example of judicial policymaking?

(5)   In *Bob Jones* the Court observed that "it cannot be said that educational institutions that * * * practice racial discrimination * * * should be encouraged by having all taxpayers share in their support by way of special tax status." In making that statement, is it acting as a court or a legislature? Consider the following criticism of the opinion:

In its analysis of congressional inaction in the face of the 1971 revenue ruling, the Court takes Congress's failure to act as a decision to acquiesce in — that is, to permit — the IRS's denial of tax exemptions to racially discriminatory schools. Yet in concluding that federal public policy is

[3] Burt Neuborne, *Of Sausage Factories and Syllogism Machines: Formalism, Realism, and Exclusionary Selection Techniques*, 67 NYU L. Rev. 419, 431 (1992).

offended by the practices of such schools — and that therefore governmental support (in the form of tax-exempt status) should be denied to them — the Court ignores much similar governmental inaction [namely, Congress's failure to outlaw such discrimination]. Why should congressional silence toward the IRS imply acquiescence in its behavior, while congressional silence toward the practices of discriminatory private schools imply precisely the opposite attitude toward their behavior? By the logic of the *Bob Jones* approach to legislative inaction, this tissue of prohibitions and the silences that surround it could just as easily be construed, not as declarations of a public policy against discrimination in private education, but as decisions to tolerate such discrimination. * * *

"Public policy" that is not law is completely ambivalent; it suggests equally and simultaneously that certain conduct should and should not be allowed. "Public policy" in this context is an empty idea. A rule that forbids the granting of tax exemptions to organizations that violate public policy is not a rule at all.[4]

Accepting the foregoing criticism, does it show that *Bob Jones* was wrongly decided but *Gregory* rightly decided?

(6)   To put it most bluntly, are judges simply legislators in robes? Consider the following cynical assessment, offered by a state Supreme Court Justice: "The major difference between courts and other political institutions * * * is that it is not usually smart to try to bribe appointed judges."[5]

CHISOM v. ROEMER
501 U.S. 380 (1991)

JUSTICE STEVENS delivered the opinion of the Court.

[The Louisiana Supreme Court consists of seven elected judges. Two are elected at-large from one multi-member district; that is, voters in this district vote for two Justices. The other five are elected from smaller single-member districts; that is, voters in each of these districts vote for a single Justice. (By way of illustration: U.S. Senators are elected from multi-member "districts"; Representatives come from single-member districts.) Petitioners are black registered voters in Orleans Parish. Orleans Parish is the largest of the four parishes that comprise the multimember district and contains about half of that district's registered voters. Although more than one-half of Orleans Parish's registered voters are black, over three-fourths of the voters in the other three parishes are white, so that a majority of the voters in the district as a whole are white.

Petitioners filed an action in Federal District Court against the Governor and state officials alleging that the use of the multi-member district impermissibly

---

[4]   Mayer G. Freed & Daniel D. Polsby, *Race, Religion, and Public Policy: Bob Jones University v. United States*, 1983 SUP. CT. REV. 1, 10–12.

[5]   RICHARD NEELY, THE PRODUCT LIABILITY MESS: HOW BUSINESS CAN BE RESCUED FROM THE POLITICS OF STATE COURTS 14 (1988).

diluted minority voting strength in violation of § 2 of the Voting Rights Act of 1965. As amended in 1982, § 2 reads:

(a) No voting qualification or prerequisite to voting or standard, practice, or procedure shall be imposed or applied by any State or political subdivision in a manner which results in a denial or abridgement of the right of any citizen of the United States to vote on account of race or color, or in contravention of the guarantees set forth in section 4(f)(2), as provided in subsection (b).

(b) A violation of subsection (a) is established if, based on the totality of circumstances, it is shown that the political processes leading to nomination or election in the State or political subdivision are not equally open to participation by members of a class of citizens protected by subsection (a) in that its members have less opportunity than other members of the electorate to participate in the political process and to elect representatives of their choice. The extent to which members of a protected class have been elected to office in the State or political subdivision is one circumstance which may be considered: Provided, That nothing in this section establishes a right to have members of a protected class elected in numbers equal to their proportion in the population.

Plaintiffs' argument was that combining Orleans Parish with the other, predominantly white, parishes for purposes of selecting two Justices meant that black votes were always swamped by white votes. Only if Orleans Parish were a single district and the other three parishes a separate single district would black voters be able, in the words of § 2(b), to "participate in the political process and elect representatives of their choice."

The Court of Appeals, relying on its earlier decision in *League of United Latin American Citizens Council v. Clements*, 914 F.2d 620 (5th Cir. 1990) (*LULAC*), held that § 2(b) does not apply to judicial elections.]

The text of § 2 of the Voting Rights Act as originally enacted read as follows:

"SEC. 2. No voting qualification or prerequisite to voting, or standard, practice, or procedure shall be imposed or applied by any State or political subdivision to deny or abridge the right of any citizen of the United States to vote on account of race or color."

The terms "vote" and "voting" were defined elsewhere in the Act to include "all action necessary to make a vote effective *in any primary, special, or general election.*" The statute further defined vote and voting as "votes cast with respect to candidates for public or party office and propositions for which votes are received in an election."

At the time of the passage of the Voting Rights Act of 1965, § 2, unlike other provisions of the Act, did not provoke significant debate in Congress because it was viewed largely as a restatement of the Fifteenth Amendment. * * * Section 2 protected the right to vote, and it did so without making any distinctions or imposing any limitations as to which elections would fall within its purview. As Attorney General Katzenbach made clear during his testimony before the House,

"[e]very election in which registered electors are permitted to vote would be covered" under § 2.

Justice Stewart's opinion for the plurality in *Mobile v. Bolden*, 446 U.S. 55 (1980), which held that there was no violation of either the Fifteenth Amendment or § 2 of the Voting Rights Act absent proof of intentional discrimination, served as the impetus for the 1982 amendment. One year after the decision in *Mobile*, [Congress passed the present version of the statute.] * * *

Under the amended statute, proof of intent is no longer required to prove a § 2 violation. Now plaintiffs can prevail under § 2 by demonstrating that a challenged election practice has resulted in the denial or abridgement of the right to vote based on color or race. Congress not only incorporated the results test in the paragraph that formerly constituted the entire § 2, but also designated that paragraph as subsection (a) and added a new subsection (b) to make clear that an application of the results test requires an inquiry into "the totality of the circumstances."

The two purposes of the amendment are apparent from its text. Section 2(a) adopts a results test, thus providing that proof of discriminatory intent is no longer necessary to establish *any* violation of the section. Section 2(b) provides guidance about how the results test is to be applied.

Respondents contend * * * that Congress' choice of the word "representatives" in the phrase "have less opportunity than other members of the electorate to participate in the political process and to elect representatives of their choice" in section 2(b) is evidence of congressional intent to exclude vote dilution claims involving judicial elections from the coverage of § 2. We reject that construction because we are convinced that if Congress had such an intent, Congress would have made it explicit in the statute, or at least some of the Members would have identified or mentioned it at some point in the unusually extensive legislative history of the 1982 amendment.[6] * * *

Both respondents and the *LULAC* majority place their principal reliance on Congress' use of the word "representatives" instead of "legislators" in the phrase "to participate in the political process and to elect representatives of their choice." When Congress borrowed the phrase from [an earlier Supreme Court case], it replaced "legislators" with "representatives."[7] This substitution indicates, at the

---

[6] Congress' silence in this regard can be likened to the dog that did not bark. See *A. Doyle, Silver Blaze*, in *The Complete Sherlock Holmes* 335 (1927). Cf. Harrison v. PPG Industries, Inc., 446 U.S. 578, 602 (1980) (REHNQUIST, J., dissenting) ("In a case where the construction of legislative language such as this makes so sweeping and so relatively unorthodox a change as that made here, I think judges as well as detectives may take into consideration the fact that a watchdog did not bark in the night").

[7] The word "representatives" rather than "legislators" was included in Senator Robert Dole's compromise, which was designed to assuage the fears of those Senators who viewed the House's version, H. R. 3112, as an invitation for proportional representation and electoral quotas. Senator Dole explained that the compromise was intended both to embody the belief "that a voting practice or procedure which is discriminatory in result should not be allowed to stand, regardless of whether there exists a discriminatory purpose or intent" and to "delineate what legal standard should apply under the results test and clarify that it is not a mandate for proportional representation." Hearings on S. 53 et al. before the Subcommittee on the Constitution of the Senate Committee on the Judiciary, 97th Cong., 2d Sess., 60 (1982). Thus, the compromise was not intended to exclude any elections from the coverage of

very least, that Congress intended the amendment to cover more than legislative elections. Respondents argue, and the [*LULAC*] majority agreed, that the term "representatives" was used to extend § 2 coverage to executive officials, but not to judges. We think, however, that the better reading of the word "representatives" describes the winners of representative, popular elections. If executive officers, such as prosecutors, sheriffs, state attorneys general, and state treasurers, can be considered "representatives" simply because they are chosen by popular election, then the same reasoning should apply to elected judges.[8] * * *

The *LULAC* majority was, of course, entirely correct in observing that "judges need not be elected at all," and that ideally public opinion should be irrelevant to the judge's role because the judge is often called upon to disregard, or even to defy, popular sentiment. The Framers of the Constitution had a similar understanding of the judicial role, and as a consequence, they established that Article III judges would be appointed, rather than elected, and would be sheltered from public opinion by receiving life tenure and salary protection.[9] Indeed, these views were generally shared by the States during the early years of the Republic. Louisiana, however, has chosen a different course. It has decided to elect its judges and to compel judicial candidates to vie for popular support just as other political candidates do.

The fundamental tension between the ideal character of the judicial office and the real world of electoral politics cannot be resolved by crediting judges with total indifference to the popular will while simultaneously requiring them to run for elected office. When each of several members of a court must be a resident of a separate district, and must be elected by the voters of that district, it seems both reasonable and realistic to characterize the winners as representatives of that district. Indeed, at one time the Louisiana Bar Association characterized the members of the Louisiana Supreme Court as representatives for that reason: "Each justice and judge now in office shall be considered as a representative of the judicial district within which is situated the parish of his residence at the time of his election." Louisiana could, of course, exclude its judiciary from the coverage of the Voting Rights Act by changing to a system in which judges are appointed, and in that way, it could enable its judges to be indifferent to popular opinion. The reasons why Louisiana has chosen otherwise are precisely the reasons why it is appropriate for * * * the Voting Rights Act to continue to apply to its judicial elections. * * *

Congress enacted the Voting Rights Act of 1965 for the broad remedial purpose of "ridding the country of racial discrimination in voting." [W]e [have] said that the

---

subsection (a), but simply to make clear that the results test does not require the proportional election of minority candidates in any election.

[8] Moreover, this Court has recently recognized that judges do engage in policymaking at some level. See *Gregory v. Ashcroft* ("It may be sufficient that the appointee is in a position requiring the exercise of discretion concerning issues of public importance. This certainly describes the bench, regardless of whether judges might be considered policymakers in the same sense as the executive or legislature"). A judge brings to his or her job of interpreting texts "a well-considered judgment of what is best for the community." As the concurrence notes, Justice Holmes and Justice Cardozo each wrote eloquently about the "policymaking nature of the judicial function."

[9] [Ed. Fn.] The Constitution provides that federal judges "shall hold their Offices during good Behaviour, and shall, at stated Times, receive for their Services, a Compensation, which shall not be diminished during their Continuance in Office." U.S. CONST., art. III, § 1.

Act should be interpreted in a manner that provides "the broadest possible scope" in combating racial discrimination. Congress amended the Act in 1982 in order to relieve plaintiffs of the burden of proving discriminatory intent, after a plurality of this Court had concluded that the original Act, like the Fifteenth Amendment, contained such a requirement. Thus, Congress made clear that a violation of § 2 could be established by proof of discriminatory results alone. It is difficult to believe that Congress, in an express effort to broaden the protection afforded by the Voting Rights Act, withdrew, without comment, an important category of elections from that protection. Today we reject such an anomalous view and hold that state judicial elections are included within the ambit of § 2 as amended.

The judgment of the Court of Appeals is reversed and the case is remanded for further proceedings consistent with this opinion.

It is so ordered.

JUSTICE SCALIA, with whom The CHIEF JUSTICE AND JUSTICE KENNEDY join, dissenting.

Section 2 of the Voting Rights Act is not some all-purpose weapon for well-intentioned judges to wield as they please in the battle against discrimination. It is a statute. I thought we had adopted a regular method for interpreting the meaning of language in a statute: first, find the ordinary meaning of the language in its textual context; and second, using established canons of construction, ask whether there is any clear indication that some permissible meaning other than the ordinary one applies. If not — and especially if a good reason for the ordinary meaning appears plain — we apply that ordinary meaning.

Today, however, the Court adopts a method quite out of accord with that usual practice. It begins not with what the statute says, but with an expectation about what the statute must mean absent particular phenomena ("we are *convinced* that if Congress had . . . an intent [to exclude judges] Congress would have made it explicit in the statute, or at least some of the Members would have identified or mentioned it at some point in the unusually extensive legislative history,") and the Court then interprets the words of the statute to fulfill its expectation. Finding nothing in the legislative history affirming that judges were excluded from the coverage of § 2, the Court gives the phrase "to elect representatives" the quite extraordinary meaning that covers the election of judges.

As method, this is just backwards, and however much we may be attracted by the result it produces in a particular case, we should in every case resist it. Our job begins with a text that Congress has passed and the President has signed. We are to read the words of that text as any ordinary Member of Congress would have read them, see Holmes, The Theory of Legal Interpretation, 12 Harv. L. Rev. 417 (1899), and apply the meaning so determined. In my view, that reading reveals that § 2 extends to vote dilution claims for the elections of representatives only, and judges are not representatives.

* * * The foundation of the Court's analysis, the itinerary for its journey in the wrong direction, is the following statement: "It is difficult to believe that Congress, in an express effort to broaden the protection afforded by the Voting Rights Act, withdrew, without comment, an important category of elections from that protec

tion." There are two things wrong with this. First is the notion that Congress cannot be credited with having achieved anything of major importance by simply saying it, in ordinary language, in the text of a statute, "without comment" in the legislative history. As the Court colorfully puts it, if the dog of legislative history has not barked nothing of great significance can have transpired. Apart from the questionable wisdom of assuming that dogs will bark when something important is happening, see 1 T. Livius, The History of Rome 411–413 (1892) (D. Spillan translation), we have forcefully and explicitly rejected the Conan Doyle approach to statutory construction in the past. See *Harrison v. PPG Industries, Inc.*, 446 U.S. 578, 592 (1980) ("In ascertaining the meaning of a statute, a court cannot, in the manner of Sherlock Holmes, pursue the theory of the dog that did not bark"). We are here to apply the statute, not legislative history, and certainly not the absence of legislative history. Statutes are the law though sleeping dogs lie.

The more important error in the Court's starting-point, however, is the assumption that the effect of excluding judges from the revised § 2 would be to "withdr[aw] . . . an important category of elections from [the] protection [of the Voting Rights Act]." There is absolutely no question here of *withdrawing* protection. Since the pre-1982 content of § 2 was coextensive with the Fifteenth Amendment, the entirety of that protection subsisted in the Constitution, and could be enforced through the other provisions of the Voting Rights Act. Nothing was lost from the prior coverage; *all* of the new "results" protection was an add-on. The issue is not, therefore, as the Court would have it, whether Congress has cut back on the coverage of the Voting Rights Act; the issue is how far it has extended it. Thus, even if a court's expectations were a proper basis for interpreting the text of a statute, while there would be reason to expect that Congress was not "withdrawing" protection, there is no particular reason to expect that the supplemental protection it provided was any more extensive than the text of the statute said. * * *

The Court, petitioners, and petitioners' *amici* have labored mightily to establish that there is a meaning of "representatives" that would include judges, and no doubt there is. But our job is not to scavenge the world of English usage to discover whether there is any possible meaning of "representatives" which suits our preconception that the statute includes judges; our job is to determine whether the *ordinary* meaning includes them, and if it does not, to ask whether there is any solid indication in the text or structure of the statute that something other than ordinary meaning was intended.

There is little doubt that the ordinary meaning of "representatives" does not include judges, see Webster's Second New International Dictionary 2114 (1950). The Court's feeble argument to the contrary is that "representatives" means those who "are chosen by popular election." On that hypothesis, the fan-elected members of the baseball All-Star teams are "representatives" — hardly a common, if even a permissible, usage. Surely the word "representative" connotes one who is not only *elected by* the people, but who also, at a minimum, *acts on behalf of* the people. Judges do that in a sense — but not in the ordinary sense. As the captions of the pleadings in some States still display, it is the prosecutor who represents "the People"; the judge represents the Law — which often requires him to rule against the People. * * * The point is not that a State could not make judges in some senses

representative, or that all judges must be conceived of in the Article III mold, but rather, that giving "representatives" its ordinary meaning, the ordinary speaker in 1982 would not have applied the word to judges, see Holmes, The Theory of Legal Interpretation, 12 Harv. L. Rev. 417 (1899). It remains only to ask whether there is good indication that ordinary meaning does not apply. * * *

As I said at the outset, this case is about method. The Court transforms the meaning of § 2, not because the ordinary meaning is irrational, or inconsistent with other parts of the statute, but because it does not fit the Court's conception of what Congress must have had in mind. When we adopt a method that psychoanalyzes Congress rather than reads its laws, when we employ a tinkerer's toolbox, we do great harm. Not only do we reach the wrong result with respect to the statute at hand, but we poison the well of future legislation, depriving legislators of the assurance that ordinary terms, used in an ordinary context, will be given a predictable meaning. Our highest responsibility in the field of statutory construction is to read the laws in a consistent way, giving Congress a sure means by which it may work the people's will. We have ignored that responsibility today. I respectfully dissent.

NOTES AND QUESTIONS

(1) *Subsequent developments.* Following this decision, the parties settled the lawsuit, with the state agreeing to create seven single-member districts for Supreme Court justices, which it did, effective in 2000. (The transition to the new regime proved complex and litigation-producing, but need not be gone into here.) Most of Orleans Parish is now in the new District 7; some is in District 1. The Justice from District 7 is Bernette Johnson, the first African-American ever to sit on the Louisiana Supreme Court.

(2) *The meaning of "representatives."* Chisom turns on the definition of "representative" and whether it applies to judges. Justice Stevens reads "representatives" to refer to "the winners of representative, popular elections." Is this circular? Is the winner of an election by definition a representative? Are all representatives necessarily elected?

Justice Scalia insists that the ordinary meaning of "representatives" cannot extend to judges. How would you argue against him?

(3) *The role and obligations of a "representative".* The nature of representation is a matter of longstanding dispute in political theory. Under one model, a representative should be an "agent," directly implementing the will of her constituents (the "principal"). On another, a representative should be a "trustee," acting for the benefit of the public but exercising independent judgment as to how those interests are best furthered. Under either model, there is a further question as to whether the representative should take instructions from, or seek to further the interests of, her own constituency in particular or the citizenry in general. This discussion dates back to the debates on ratification of the Constitution in this country, and much further back than that elsewhere. If judges *are* representatives, are they agents or trustees? Of whom?

(4) *Should judges be representatives?* If judges are policymakers, basic democratic principles would seem to require that they be representatives, implementing the public will. Justice Holmes seemed to endorse this sort of judicial responsiveness when he wrote that "[t]he first requirement of a sound body of law is, that it should correspond with the actual feelings and demands of the community, whether right or wrong."[10] Yet the other branches are better suited to that task, and tracking popular opinion seems inconsistent with a commitment to the rule of law and an independent judiciary.

How would the *Chisom* Justices respond to these concerns? Does Justice Stevens believe that judges *should* respond to public opinion, or only that they *do*? Does Justice Scalia believe that they *do not*, or only that they *should not*? Would the answers differ for elected and appointed judges? A former California Supreme Court Justice once said that for an elected judge to ignore the political consequences of a visible decision is "like ignoring a crocodile in your bathtub."[11] Is that good or bad?

(6) *Representativeness.* At its most basic, the fight in *Chisom* was about the fact that the Louisiana Supreme Court was, had always been, and, given the electoral structure, was likely to remain, all white. Is that a problem? Is it as much a problem as an all-white Louisiana legislature would be?

For much of the 20th century, there was understood to be a "Jewish seat" on the U.S. Supreme Court. In the 21st, it is generally perceived that there are de facto African-American and female seats. What is the value, if any, of such diversity quotas?

If representativeness in judges is important, is that because judges *are* representatives or because they are not? It has been argued that representativeness is especially important if judges are *not* representatives in the sense of being accountable to the public; precisely because they are unconstrained, the legitimacy and acceptability of their decisions will hinge at least in part on their representativeness:

> [A] distinction should be drawn between "accountability" and "representativeness." Some people have assumed that because judges make policy decisions in deciding cases — e.g., the abortion and reapportionment decisions of the Supreme Court — judges should be accountable, in apparently the same way that legislators are thought to be accountable. The legislative analogy should be rejected, however, because it assumes that the task of the judge is no different from that of the legislator. [In fact,] the jury analogy, suggesting that the second major goal of judicial selection, [the first being quality,] is representativeness and not accountability, is more appropriate than the legislative analogy.[12]

---

[10] Oliver Wendell Holmes, Jr., The Common Law 41 (1881).

[11] Julian N. Eule, *Crocodiles in the Bathtub: State Courts, Voter Initiatives and the Threat of Electoral Reprisal*, 65 U. Colo. L. Rev. 733, 739 (1994), quoted in *Republican Party v. White*, 536 U.S. 765, 789 (2002) (O'Connor, J., concurring).

[12] Robert P. Davidow, *Judicial Selection: The Search for Quality and Representativeness*, 31 Case W. Res. L. Rev. 409, 419–420 (1981).

Consider John McGinnis's objection to arguments for *jurisprudential* diversity on the Supreme Court:

> It would certainly be controversial to claim that, whatever the advantages of jurisprudential diversity, they outweigh the advantages of correct Supreme Court decisions. It may be the highest commendation for a legislature that it represents the diverse views of the citizenry and thereby serves as a vehicle for democratic compromise. Under the traditional view that the law is distinct from politics, it is hardly the highest commendation, however, that a court is representative. Indeed, in a structure with constitutional judicial review [i.e., in which courts can set aside legislative acts as unconstitutional], one of the essential tasks of the Court is to enforce constitutional provisions against the will of a representative legislature.[13]

How would Professor McGinnis view the claim that *racial* diversity is important to the Court?

When Richard Nixon nominated G. Harold Carswell for the Supreme Court, a chorus of objections arose in light of Carswell's wholly undistinguished credentials. Senator Roman Hruska leapt to Carswell's defense:

> Even if he is mediocre there are a lot of mediocre judges and people and lawyers. They are entitled to a little representation, aren't they, and a little chance. We can't have all Brandeises, Cardozos, and Frankfurters, and stuff like that there.

Hruska's argument assured the good Senator a certain immortality but failed to persuade his colleagues, who refused to confirm Carswell's nomination. What exactly is its flaw? Why not a mediocre seat on the Supreme Court?

(7) *The ideal versus the real.* One of us has written that all the Justices in *Gregory* and *Chisom* agree both that judges should be apolitical, neutral dispute-resolvers and that in practice they fall short of that ideal. Their disagreement in the cases results from some looking to the normative (ideal) and others to the descriptive (real) version of the judicial role.

> [In *Gregory*, the Court's reluctance to label judges "policymakers"] stems from the fact that the view of judges as policymakers conflicts with the present Court's highly majoritarian and deferential description of its own role. Unelected judges are not accountable to the public and policy choices may legitimately be made only by the people's representatives. Against the background of its statement that what distinguishes courts is that they lack an electoral constituency and, therefore, do not make political decisions, it would have been quite awkward for the Court to suddenly announce that judges *do* make policy. * * * The Court hewed closely to the image of judges as expositors rather than creators of the law, or at least as closely as it could without actually affirming it. * * *

---

[13] John O. McGinnis, *The President, the Senate, the Constitution, and the Confirmation Process: A Reply to Professors Strauss and Sunstein,* 71 TEX. L. REV. 633, 651 (1993).

[L]ike the majority in *Gregory*, *Chisom* ultimately looked not to a theoretical model, but to a perceived practical reality. The extent to which elected judges do in fact respond to popular pressure is unclear. * * * Nonetheless, there is some support, both intuitive and empirical, for Justice Stevens's view of the world. * * *

While Justice Stevens focuses on the link between elections and accountability, Justice Scalia latches on to * * * the idea of an apolitical judiciary. For Justice Scalia, neither an elected judge nor an appointed one is a popular representative * * *. But his argument is not that elections do not actually have an effect on judicial independence. He seems uninterested in whether they do; it is enough that they are not supposed to. * * *

The difference between the majority and the dissent at the abstract level is minute. They share a theoretical commitment to an independent judiciary. Despite its holding, the majority stresses that "ideally public opinion should be irrelevant to the judge's role," and it plainly disapproves of electing judges. The majority is unable to rely on "the ideal character of the judicial office," however, given "the real world of electoral politics." In contrast, the dissent looks to the ideal.[14]

Do you agree that the justices in these two cases share a single normative vision of the judicial role? In both *Gregory* and *Chisom* the Court was interpreting a statute; in deciding whether judges fit within a statutory term or phrase, which should count, the "ideal character of the judicial office" or the practical reality?

(8) Chisom *redux.* The themes in play in *Chisom* resurfaced in *Republican Party v. White*, 536 U.S. 765 (2002). In that case, a badly divided Court struck down Minnesota's "announce rule" under the First Amendment. The rule prohibited any candidate for judicial office to "announce his or her views on disputed legal or political issues." The state defended the rules as a measure to protect the reality and appearance of judicial impartiality and open-mindedness.

Anyone would agree that a restriction such as this would be a flagrant First Amendment violation were it applied to speech by candidates for political office, such as governor or member of the legislature. The question for the Court was whether judicial elections are sufficiently different to allow greater restriction of candidates' speech. In an opinion by Justice Scalia, the majority observed that in shaping the common law and interpreting state constitutions judges are significant governmental actors, and judicial elections are not so fundamentally different than elections for other officials. Minnesota might have doubts about the propriety of judicial elections, but "the First Amendment does not permit it to achieve its goal by leaving the principle of elections in place while preventing candidates from discussing what the elections are about." Justice O'Connor concurred, writing separately to express her dislike of judicial elections, stressing the risk of making judges too susceptible to popular pressure in their decisionmaking or beholden to campaign contributors. Justice Stevens and Justice Ginsburg each wrote a dissent, joined by each other and Justices Souter and Breyer, in which they stressed the

---

[14] Michael Herz, *Choosing Between Normative and Descriptive Versions of the Judicial Role*, 75 MARQ. L. REV. 725, 726–729, 736–737, 742–743 (1992).

differences between judicial and political officials. As Justice Stevens wrote, "[i]n a democracy, issues of policy are properly decided by majority vote; it is the business of legislators and executives to be popular. But in litigation, issues of law or fact should not be determined by popular vote; it is the business of judges to be indifferent to unpopularity." Both dissents argued that because judges are not political actors serving a constituency, the state must be left free to regulate elections to ensure as much as possible that judges are, and will be perceived to be, neutral servants of the law.

White was a constitutional rather than a statutory case, and the specific legal issue lies outside the scope of these materials. However, consider whether the positions of individual justices in *White* were consistent with their positions in *Chisom*.

Assignment

Judicial selection in the states varies significantly, but there are three basic methods: (1) appointment by the governor, sometimes with some sort of legislative confirmation, or by the legislature — this is the least common method; (2) appointment by the governor from a short list submitted by a nonpartisan nominating commission (this is generally known as "merit selection" or "the Missouri Plan"); or (3) popular election, with the states split between partisan and non-partisan elections. State judges generally serve for specified terms of years, at the end of which they must be reappointed; frequently that occurs through a retention election, even for judges who were initially appointed. Almost every state holds initial and/or retention elections for at least some of its judges.[15]

Under the U.S. Constitution, *federal* judges are appointed by the President with the advice and consent of the Senate. The opinions in *White* indicate that Supreme Court Justices like the system. (Since it is the system through which they were selected, that is perhaps not surprising.) Each displays a deep antipathy to judicial elections.

Our methods for picking judges should reflect our conception of what judges do. The standard justification for electing judges is that judges make policy and, in a democracy, should be accountable to the public like any other powerful government official. The standard justifications for appointing judges are that (a) judges ought to be independent from politics and popular pressure, (b) the public is not well-equipped to evaluate judicial qualifications, and, increasingly, (c) that soliciting and receiving campaign contributions can cast doubt on a judge's impartiality.[16]

---

[15] A summary and state-by-state survey of the methods of judicial selection has been prepared by the American Judicature Society and is available on its website; as of this writing it can be found at http://www.ajs.org/selection/docs/Judicial%20Selection%20Charts.pdf.

[16] In *Caperton v. A.T. Massey Coal Co.*, 129 S. Ct. 2252 (2009), a badly divided Supreme Court ruled that in some circumstances due process requires a judge to recuse herself in a case in which a campaign contributor is a party. *Caperton* involved a $50 million jury verdict in a fraud case. By a vote of 3-2, the West Virginia Supreme Court set aside the verdict. One of the three justices in the majority, Brent Benjamin, had been elected to the court after the trial but before the appeal. Candidate Benjamin had received $3 million in campaign contributions (more than 60% of the total amount he spent on the campaign) from the CEO of the defendant. The plaintiffs requested that Justice Benjamin recuse

During debate over the ratification of the U.S. Constitution James Madison wrote that, while in general high-ranking governmental officers ought to be selected by the people,

> [s]ome deviations * * * from the principle must be admitted. In the constitution of the judiciary department in particular, it might be inexpedient to insist rigorously on the principle: first, because peculiar qualifications being essential in the members, the primary consideration ought to be to select that mode of choice which best secures these qualifications; second, because the permanent tenure by which the appointments are held in that department must soon destroy all sense of dependence on the authority conferring them.[17]

Should judges be elected? Explain.[18]

---

himself; he refused. In an opinion by Justice Kennedy, a 5-Justice majority ruled that on the "extreme" facts of this case, the Due Process Clause required Justice Benjamin to recuse himself because there was "a serious risk of actual bias — based on objective and reasonable perceptions."

[17] THE FEDERALIST No. 51, at 321 (James Madison) (Clinton Rossiter ed., 1961); *see also id.*, No. 78, at 466, 471 (Alexander Hamilton) (describing judges as "the citadel of the public justice and the public security" and asserting that anything other than life tenure would be "fatal to their necessary independence").

[18] A useful overview of arguments pro and con, along with an assessment of modern judicial elections, is David E. Pozen, *The Irony of Judicial Elections*, 108 COLUM. L. REV. 265 (2008).

EPILOGUE

On April 10, 1959, Judge Learned Hand of the United States Court of Appeals for the Second Circuit was honored for his 50 years of judicial service. After lengthy and effusive encomiums from the judicial luminaries of the day, Hand spoke:

> I confess when I look at my service it seems to have been for the most part trivial. It amounted to a good deal to the people at the moment, but when one takes it in bulk, it does not seem to have been much. That gives me a little sense of fatuity. And then I reflect that though this may be true, having judges is absolutely essential. We all agree to that. Without them we should be even more of a cut-throat community than we are. That is our excuse; and it is an adequate defense.
>
> What do we judges do? There are two kinds — I do not mean two kinds of judges; there are more than two kinds of judges; but there are two kinds of work, it seems to me. There are some laws that I like to think of as open ended: statutes or rules that merely say: "Do what you think is right." We cover this up decently by saying that one should be "reasonable," which really does not mean anything, except that you should take the conflicting values and probabilities, and make the best guess you can. I do not know why that is any different from legislation.
>
> But there is the other kind of law: far the greatest part. This consists of the interpretation of words. Of course, as you know, there have been many sages who have spoken on this, and I do not know that it has got us very much further. Aristotle said it pretty well, but not quite in these words. However, the substance was that when you are interpreting words, you must remember that they cover many diverse instances, which cannot be foreseen. Interpretation is necessarily an act of creative imagination; you must try to put yourself in the place of the author of those words and fabricate how he would have dealt with the instance that has arisen. Is the occasion before you within what you impute to him? That is what most of our work is; and to me it remains, old man as I am, an undertaking of delightful uncertainty.
>
> I do not know what are the qualities which one should bring to it; but I know some. The first one, I suggest, is complete personal detachment. You must keep, as far as it is possible — it is never quite possible — but as far as it is possible, you must keep your personal choice out of the frame you select to impose upon the written words. You must be detached almost to the point of being aloof. I know, this is often deemed very heretical; I am only telling you the way it seems to me. Then you must have as much imagination as is possible. You must try to fix before your mind the

455

different possible patterns that will fit on to those words, and among those patterns in the end you must choose.

And that, as I say, is to me and has been a delightful — that is a little strong — a most engaging and pleasant occupation. After all, why isn't it in the nature of an art? It is a bit of craftsmanship, isn't it? It is what a poet does, it is what a sculptor does. He has some vague purposes and he has an indefinite number of what you might call frames of preference among which he must choose; for choose he has to, and he does.

So I like to think that the work of a judge is an art[.]*

---

* Proceedings of a Special Session of the United States Court of Appeals for the Second Circuit, April 10, 1959, at 27–29, *reprinted in* 264 F.2d.

Appendix A

THE FEDERAL COURTS

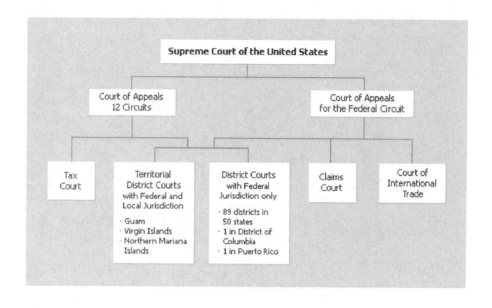

NEW YORK STATE COURTS

CIVIL COURTS

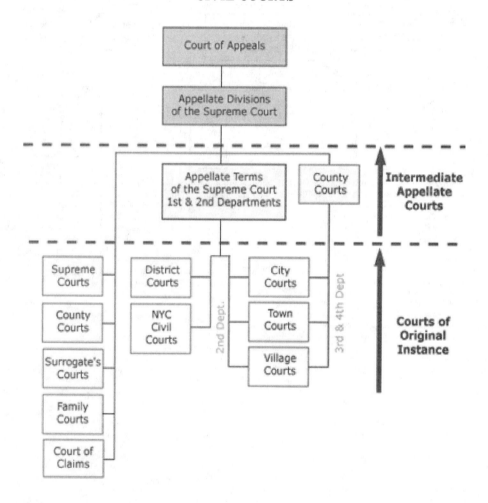

CRIMINAL COURTS

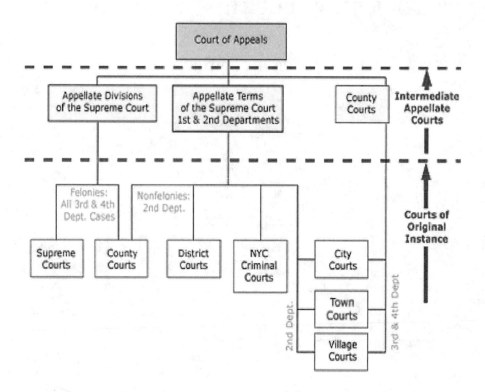

Appendix C

CALIFORNIA STATE COURTS

CALIFORNIA COURT STRUCTURE

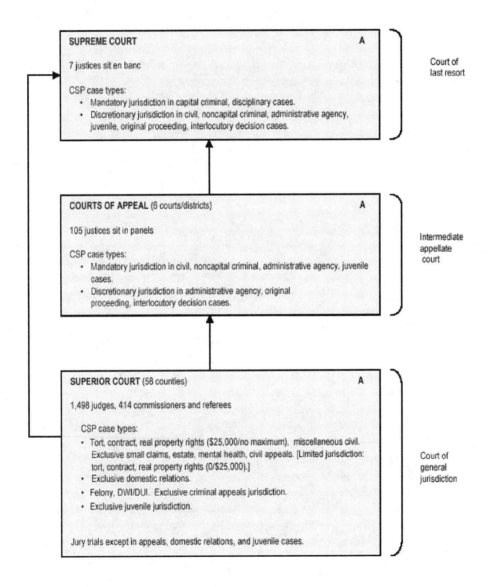

SUPREME COURT   A

7 justices sit en banc

CSP case types:
- Mandatory jurisdiction in capital criminal, disciplinary cases.
- Discretionary jurisdiction in civil, noncapital criminal, administrative agency, juvenile, original proceeding, interlocutory decision cases.

Court of last resort

COURTS OF APPEAL (6 courts/districts)   A

105 justices sit in panels

CSP case types:
- Mandatory jurisdiction in civil, noncapital criminal, administrative agency, juvenile cases.
- Discretionary jurisdiction in administrative agency, original proceeding, interlocutory decision cases.

Intermediate appellate court

SUPERIOR COURT (58 counties)   A

1,498 judges, 414 commissioners and referees

CSP case types:
- Tort, contract, real property rights ($25,000/no maximum), miscellaneous civil. Exclusive small claims, estate, mental health, civil appeals. [Limited jurisdiction: tort, contract, real property rights (0/$25,000).]
- Exclusive domestic relations.
- Felony, DWI/DUI. Exclusive criminal appeals jurisdiction.
- Exclusive juvenile jurisdiction.

Jury trials except in appeals, domestic relations, and juvenile cases.

Court of general jurisdiction

Appendix D

GEOGRAPHIC BOUNDARIES OF THE FEDERAL COURTS

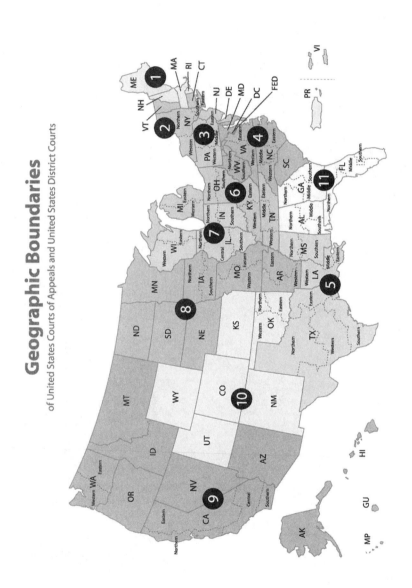

Geographic Boundaries
of United States Courts of Appeals and United States District Courts

Appendix E

THE LEGISLATIVE PROCESS

This Appendix reviews the legislative process at the federal level. Most states have a comparable set of procedures, although the details can vary meaningfully.

Proposed Legislation

When a piece of legislation is formally proposed in the United States House of Representatives or the Senate it is known as a "bill." (Some items are designated "resolutions"; these primarily concern internal matters, but for present purposes the distinction is not important.) Here is an annotated copy of a bill as it appears after having been introduced, while pending in the United States House of Representatives; notes corresponding to the numbers added to the bill follow the bill itself.

103D CONGRESS[1]
1ST SESSION[2]

H. R. 2880 [3]

To permit the prevailing party in a civil action in Federal court to recover attorneys' fees from the losing party.

IN THE HOUSE OF REPRESENTATIVES

AUGUST 5, 1993

Mr. Cox[4] introduced[5] the following bill; which was referred to the Committee on the Judiciary.[6]

A BILL

To permit the prevailing party in a civil action in Federal
court to recover attorneys' fees from the losing party.[7]

1[8]   *Be it enacted by the Senate and House of Representa-*
2   *tives of the United States of America in Congress assembled,*[9]
3   **SECTION 1.**[10] **SHORT TITLE.**
4   This Act may be cited as the "Loser Pays Act".[11]
5   **SEC. 2. FINDINGS**[12]
6   The Congress makes the following findings:
7   (1) Reforming the civil justice system in the
8   United States is imperative if that system is to re-
9   main truly open and accessible to all Americans. De-
10   spite the fact that the United States is home to 70

2

1   percent of the world's lawyers, Americans do not

2   have access to simple justice as do citizens of other

3   countries.   Delays,   over-crowded   court   dockets,

4   harassing   suits   designed   to   extort   "settlements",

5   and   increasingly   costly   proceedings   have   made   it

6   nearly impossible for honest litigants to survive until

7   trial.

8   (2) Despite this enormous expenditure of time

9   and money, almost none of these cases will come to

10   trial. In over 96 percent of the cases that came to

11   an end in Federal court during 1992, the parties did

12   not get a single day of trial before a judge or jury.

13   The image of an honest judge or jury applying the

14   law to particular facts in order to determine who is

15   right is only that—imaginary.

16   (3) Cutting the costs and the length of civil

17   lawsuits is vitally necessary for consumers and busi-

18   nesses alike. They cannot afford the years of ex-

19   pense now necessary to maintain an honest case in

20   the current system. Until this problem is addressed,

21   America's free enterprise system will continue to be

22   at risk.

23   (4) Awarding the prevailing party his or her at-

24   torneys' fees in civil lawsuits will do much to end the

25   improper incentives for lawsuits that are inflating

3

1   litigation costs dramatically. It will give meritorious

2   plaintiffs the full measure of the damages they de-

3   serve, without deduction for the lawyers' costs of

4   suit. And it will give defendants whose rights are

5   vindicated, often after years of wasted time and

6   money, a chance to be made whole.

7   **SEC. 3. PAYMENT OF ATTORNEYS' FEES.**[13]

8   (a) AWARD OF FEES.—The prevailing party in any

9   civil action brought in or removed to a court of the United

10   States shall be entitled to attorneys' fees to the extent that

11   such party prevails on any position or claim advanced dur-

12   ing the action. Attorneys' fees under this subsection shall

13   be paid by the nonprevailing party.

14   (b) RECORDS.—Attorneys' fees may not be awarded

15   under subsection (a) unless counsel of record in the action

16   involved maintained accurate, complete records of hours

17   worked on the matters involved in the action, regardless

18   of the fee arrangement with his or her client.

19   (c) LIMITATION ON FEES.—The fee award under this

20   section shall not exceed the attorneys' fees of the

21   nonprevailing party with respect to the particular position

22   or claim. If the nonprevailing party received services under

23   a contingent fee agreement, then the fee award to the pre-

24   vailing party shall not exceed the reasonable value of those

25   services, as determined by the court at the time the final

4

1 judgment is entered. In addition, the court may, in its dis-

2 cretion, limit the fees awarded under subsection (a) to the

3 extent that the court finds exceptional, unusual, and spe-

4 cial circumstances that make payment of such fees unjust.

5 (d) DEFINITION.—As used in this section, the term

6 "prevailing party" means a party to an action who obtains

7 a favorable final judgment (other than by settlement), ex-

8 clusive of interest, on all or a portion of the claims as-

9 serted in the action.

10 **SEC. 4. EFFECTIVE DATE**[14]

11 This Act and the amendments made by this Act shall

12 take effect 90 days after the date of the enactment of this

13 Act, and shall not apply to any action or proceeding com-

14 menced before such effective date.

---

1. A "Congress" lasts two years, i.e. from the January after one election until the January after the next. The first Congress assembled in 1789, the second in 1791, and so on. Thus, the 111th Congress began its work in January 2009.

2. Each Congress is in turn divided into two sessions, corresponding to the calendar year. The Twentieth Amendment to the U.S. Constitution specifies that "Congress shall assemble at least once in every year, and such meeting shall begin at noon on the 3rd day of January, unless they shall by law appoint a different day." Since Congress has not "by law appoint[ed] a different day, each new Congress commences at noon on January 3 of odd years, and the second session of each Congress commences at noon on January 3 of even years.

3. Bills are numbered sequentially as they are introduced, with a prefix indicating whether it has been introduced in the House or the Senate; the numbering begins all over again with each Congress. Thus, this was the 2,880th bill introduced in the House of Representatives during the 103d Congress. A bill keeps the same number through the entire legislative process until either it is enacted or the Congress in which it was introduced concludes.

Note if this was the 2,880th House bill, legislation was being introduced at the rate of roughly 700 bills a month, or more than 30 every business day. The flow of bills is greatest at the beginning of a Congress, and trickles down to almost nothing by the end. This is because a bill that has not been acted on by the end of a Congress simply disappears; it is no longer pending. To be considered by the next Congress, it must be introduced again. Thus, at the beginning of a Congress, many members will have bills ready to go that they had introduced without success in the previous Congress and now are introducing again. Furthermore, precisely because proposals do not survive the end of a Congress, bills introduced late in the game have no chance of even being considered except in the most extraordinary circumstances. A member who introduces a bill toward the end of a Congress is doing so for some purpose other than getting it enacted.

4. Mr. Cox (R–Cal.), who introduced (see note 5) the bill, is referred to as its "sponsor." A bill's fate will depend in part on who its sponsor is. For the bill to have the best chance of success, the ideal sponsor would be a well-respected, well-liked Member from the majority party who chairs the relevant committee and is actually committed to getting the bill passed rather than just providing the symbolic value of introducing legislation. In most instances, of course, the sponsor lacks at least some of those attributes.

Bills very often have multiple sponsors; there is no cap on the permissible number of co-sponsors. Multiple sponsorship may be good for the bill; bi-partisan sponsorship in particular gives an important endorsement and signal to the house as a whole. Multiple sponsorship can also be good for the sponsors. Members of Congress like to associate themselves with popular causes and are pleased to jump on the bandwagon. Furthermore, individual members may want to associate themselves with nationally *un*popular causes that play well at home. Sponsoring a bill that has no chance of passage is an effective and cheap way of appeasing local interests.

The sponsor is often referred to as the "author" of a bill, although almost never does a legislator actually sit down and compose legislative language. That is the work of staffmembers. Moreover, the exact language of a bill is often suggested by the executive branch or lobbyists. The final wording of most bills tends to be drawn from numerous sources.

5. The actual process of introducing a bill is straightforward. In the House, the sponsor (or an aide, or a page) drops the bill into a "hopper," a special wooden box located beside the rostrum. In the Senate, the bill is placed into a tray beside the bill clerk, who sits at the foot of the rostrum in the front of the chamber. The bill is then assigned a number and printed. This is the printed version of H.R. 2880, not the original version as introduced.

H.R. 2880 was introduced, i.e., placed in the hopper, on August 5, 1993. In legislative strategy, timing is critical. This is not the place to go into the strategic considerations, but the timing was probably not an accident.

6. After introduction, almost all bills are referred to a committee for initial consideration. Usually, the committee then refers the bill to a subcommittee.

In the House, referral to committee is mandatory; in the Senate it is occasionally, but rarely, forgone. As of the 111th Congress, the Senate has seventeen Standing (i.e. permanent) and three Special or Select Committees (i.e. ad hoc committees charges with grappling with specific complex issues), the House has twenty Standing Committees and two Select Committees, and there are four Joint Committees (i.e. committees with members from both the House and the Senate). Most of these committees are further subdivided into subcommittees, of which there are 74 in the Senate and 102 in the House. Many have lamented the proliferation of subcommittees, and their number has decreased somewhat in recent years.

Committee jurisdiction is according to subject matter; that is, legislation about the courts goes to the Judiciary Committee, legislation about air pollution goes to the Committee on Environment and Public Works, etc. Although the assignment of H.R. 2880 to the Judiciary Committee was straightforward, it is not always clear where the bill should be routed. (It is possible to send a bill to more than one committee, but that is very much the exception.) Formally, it is the Speaker of the House or the presiding officer in the Senate who determines to which committee a bill should be sent; in practice it is generally the parliamentarian that makes the decision. The choice of committee can have very real consequences for a bill's chances of passage. Because the committee chair controls the agenda and the discussions of the committee, a friendly chair is essential to getting a bill through committee. A hostile chair can easily bottle up pending bills. While there are methods by which the committee or the house as a whole can force the bill out of committee for a floor debate even without committee consideration, these are rarely attempted and even more rarely successful.

If a bill is actually considered and ultimately approved by the committee (again, usually after it has been approved by the subcommittee to which it was referred), it is "reported" to the full House or Senate. If voted on favorably by *both* the House and Senate *and* signed by the President (or passed by two-thirds of the House and two-thirds of the Senate over the President's veto, or neither signed nor vetoed by the President within ten days (assuming that Congress is in session)) it is then said to be "enacted," transformed from a "bill" to an "Act." This process is described more fully in the following section, *Enacting Legislation*.

The huge majority of bills go no further than referral to committee. For example, in the 110th Congress, which was in session in 2007 and 2008, 7335 bills and resolutions were introduced in the House, of which 308 ultimately became law. In the Senate the corresponding figures were 3724 and 134. Thus, out of 11,059 introduced bills, a grand total of 442, or under 5%, were enacted. These figures are a bit misleading; many bills overlap or virtually duplicate one another (almost always, related or identical bills are introduced in both the House and the Senate, for example), and enacted legislation often contains ideas or provisions borrowed from unenacted bills. Nonetheless, the overwhelming majority of legislative proposals go nowhere — more precisely, they go to a committee, where they die.

7. This is the official title of the bill; if the legislation is enacted into law, and assuming there is no change to this language, this will be the official title of the Act.

8. Each line is numbered to facilitate discussions over changes in wording. If the Loser Pays Act does survive the committee consideration, it is unlikely to do so without amendment.

9. This "enacting clause" is standard and automatic. In fact, Congress itself has passed legislation requiring this particular formulation. *See* 1 U.S.C. § 101.

10. All bills, and thus all Acts, are divided into sections; longer ones are divided into titles, and the titles are divided into sections. At least in theory, each section contains only a single "proposition of enactment." The titles are like floors in a building (1, 2, 3, etc.) and the sections like rooms on each floor (101, 102, 103, 201, 202, 203, etc.). For example, you may have heard of "Title VII." That is the basic federal law against employment discrimination. It consists of a series of sections, each beginning with the number 7, that are found within Title VII of a particular piece of legislation, namely the Civil Rights Act of 1964. There are actually many "Title VII's"; the others are just not as famous at Title VII of the Civil Rights Act.

11. Many bills specify a short title. Enacted legislation is generally known by this title rather than the official title. Since the mid-1990s, short titles have increasingly read as if they had been penned by advertising or PR firms rather than legislators. One turning point was the 1994 "Contract with America," which led to, among others, the "American Dream Restoration Act" (which was mainly about the income tax rates for married couples) and the "Personal Responsibility and Work Opportunity Act" (which limited the amount of time a person could receive welfare benefits). A more recent example was the controversial USA PATRIOT Act, passed in the wake of the September 11 attacks to give federal authorities more powerful investigatory and enforcement tools for the so-called War on Terror. That Act's familiar name is an acronym from its "short title": the "Uniting and Strengthening America by Providing Appropriate Tools Required to Intercept and Obstruct Terrorism Act of 2001." Similarly, in the spring of 2009 bills were introduced in both the House and Senate designed to prevent use of the internet to find and exploit children. Both had the same short title: "Internet Stopping Adults Facilitating the Exploitation of Today's Youth Act of 2009" — that is, "Internet SAFETY." *See* H.R. 1076, S. 436, 111th Cong. 1st Sess. (2009).

Some pieces of legislation are better known by some other, wholly unofficial title (for example, everyone refers to the Federal Water Pollution Control Act as the Clean Water Act), and some come to be known by the name of their sponsors (the Sherman Act, or the McCain-Feingold campaign finance legislation), by a hyphenation of the Senate and House sponsors of corresponding bills (the McCarren-Ferguson Act, the Gramm-Rudman-Hollings Act), or by the name of a private individual with whom the legislation is particularly associated (the Comstock Act, the Lindbergh Act, the Brady Bill).

12. Bills often include a statement of findings and/or a statement of purposes, but there is no requirement that they do so and many do not. Like, for example, the Preamble to the U.S. Constitution, such findings have no direct or formal legal effect. But they can be influential or provide a peg for an interpreter (judicial or otherwise) aiming for a particular outcome. Statements of Findings or Purpose are aimed primarily at three audiences: (1) legislators, with regard to whether to vote for the bill; (2) interest groups, which may be somewhat mollified by the symbolic

victory of ringing, though not substantive, legislative language; and (3) courts, with regard to how to interpret it if enacted. Occasionally, a court will rely heavily on findings. For one example of a court placing extraordinary weight on congressional findings, see *Sierra Club v. Ruckelshaus*, 344 F.Supp. 253 (D.D.C. 1972), *aff'd*, 4 Env't Rep. Cases 1815 (D.C. Cir. 1972) (per curiam), *aff'd by an equally divided court*, 412 U.S. 541 (1973).

13. This is the heart of the Loser Pays Act; indeed, it is the only section that actually does something. It would eliminate the "American Rule" for litigation in the federal courts, requiring that, subject to certain limitations and judicial oversight, the loser in any civil lawsuit that is litigated to judgment pay the winner's attorneys' fees.

14. This provision does two things. First, it establishes a specific date as of which its provisions take effect. Such a provision is not required; if an Act is silent as to its effective date, it is deemed to take effect immediately upon enactment.

Second, this provision makes clear that the new rules are prospective only, not retroactive. They apply only to lawsuits filed (not decided) after 90 days after the law is passed and thereafter. This too is not a required provision, and is not found in every piece of legislation. The general presumption is that statutes are prospective only. But Congress can, within certain vague constitutional limits, legislate retroactively. The general rule is that a statute will be read to be retroactive only if Congress expressly so provides.

Enacting Legislation

The Constitution lays out the basic procedures for enacting legislation in article I, section 7:

> Section 7. [1] All Bills for raising Revenue shall originate in the House of Representatives; but the Senate may propose or concur with Amendments as on other Bills.

> [2] Every Bill which shall have passed the House of Representatives and the Senate, shall, before it become a Law, be presented to the President of the United States; If he approve he shall sign it, but if not he shall return it, with his Objections to that House in which it shall have originated, who shall enter the Objections at large on their Journal, and proceed to reconsider it. If after such Reconsideration two thirds of that House shall agree to pass the Bill, it shall be sent, together with the Objections, to the other House, by which it shall likewise be reconsidered, and if approved by two thirds of that House, it shall become a Law. But in all such Cases the Votes of both Houses shall be determined by Yeas and Nays, and the Names of the Persons voting for and against the Bill shall be entered on the Journal of each House respectively. If any Bill shall not be returned by the President within ten Days (Sundays excepted) after it shall have been presented to him, the Same shall be a Law, in like Manner as if he had signed it, unless the Congress by their Adjournment prevent its Return, in which Case it shall not be a Law.

Beyond these bare bones, the details of the legislative process are determined by each chamber's own rules. *See* U.S. Const. art. I, sec. 5 ("Each House may determine the Rules of its Proceedings"). These rules are quite detailed and complex; indeed, each chamber has a full-time employee, the parliamentarian, who in turn has a group of assistants, whose task it is to know the rules backwards and forwards, understand them, and explain them to the Members. The rules also vary in significant respects between the House and the Senate.

Now that the Loser Pays Act has been referred to the Judiciary Committee, what happens next? The most likely action is no action. A small fraction of introduced legislation stirs the interest of the Committee (or, more precisely, the chair). If it does choose to proceed, the Committee or, more likely, the relevant subcommittee will hold a hearing or hearings on the proposal. These are usually but not always held in Washington. The Committee chair determines the agenda and selects the witnesses (although members of the minority party are allowed to invite some witnesses). The witnesses submit prepared written testimony, make brief oral statements, and answer questions from the committee members. A transcript is made.

The next step is a committee "markup," a meeting at which the committee debates, considers amendments, and makes revisions to the bill. The committee or subcommittee that is considering the bill sits down with a draft (which draft to work from is often itself an important and controversial decision) and goes through it, often line by line. In some cases, markups are closed to the public. More often, they take place in the presence of not only the legislators and their aides, but interested lobbyists and observers as well. While only the legislators speak and participate, there is constant discussion, signaling, and handing of notes and suggested language between the legislator, staffmembers, and lobbyists. Depending on the complexity of and controversy surrounding a bill, a markup can last a few hours, a few days, or many months. No transcript is kept of the markups, and traditionally they have been the least visible "official" part of the legislative process. Increasingly, however, subcommittees take place with the cameras rolling and are streamed over committee websites. Of course, the more that markups take place in public, the more the actual discussion and hammering out of compromises takes place outside the markup.

At the conclusion of deliberation, a vote of committee or subcommittee Members is taken to determine what action to take on the measure. It can be reported, with or without amendment, or tabled, which means no further action on it will occur. If the committee has approved extensive amendments, it may decide to report a new bill incorporating all the amendments. This is known as a "clean bill," which will have a new number. If the Committee votes to send the bill to the full house — to "report it out of committee" — it will prepare a written report to accompany the bill. The report, which is written by full-time staffmembers employed by the Committee, is supposed to describe and explain the bill's provisions to those who will be voting on it. Though the nominal audience is the Senate or the House, as the case may be, the report's authors well know that if the bill is enacted the report will be read by lawyers and judges and write it accordingly.

Should a bill escape from committee, it is very likely that it will pass the full house. This is not automatic, and the proposal remains subject to debate and amendment, but most favorably reported bills are then passed. Bills that are reported out go to the full house for debate, possible further amendment, and a vote. House and Senate procedures, though both arcane, differ in their specifics. The essential difference is that there is more opportunity for debate and amendment on the Senate side. In the House, debate is strictly limited. In addition, the powerful House Rules Committee establishes the rules for debate and amendment for each bill individually.

Floor debate is transcribed in the *Congressional Record*. In theory, the *Record* is "substantially a verbatim report of proceedings," 44 U.S.C. § 901, but in reality the gap between what was said and what gets printed can still be meaningful. First, Members can "revise and extend" their remarks, though such additional material appears in a separate section from the transcript of floor proceedings. In 1978 both houses began to indicate subsequently added statements with a bullet; in the House such additions also appear in a slightly different typeface. This eliminated the most fictionalized versions of congressional proceedings. However, it remains the practice to give members a transcript of their remarks, prior to publication in the *Record*, so that any "transcription errors" can be corrected. As long as they are editing a statement actually made, as opposed to adding a whole new statement, significant alterations can be made, and it is impossible to tell whether or how the words in the publication differ from the words actually spoken on the floor.

At the conclusion of debate, which can include votes on individual amendments, there is an up or down vote on the bill. A bare majority suffices for passage, although in the Senate the filibuster rule (which does not exist in the House), means that as a practical matter 60 affirmative votes are often necessary for passage, otherwise the bill will never come to a vote.

The House and the Senate go through this process in parallel. In general, identical or very similar legislation is introduced more or less simultaneously in both houses. Although what goes in is similar, what comes out may be quite different. For a bill to be enacted and presented to the President for his signature or a veto, however, the Senate and House must have passed precisely identical versions. If this has not happened, representatives of the relevant House and Senate committees meet together as a "conference committee." The conference hammers out a mutually acceptable compromise, if it can, produces another report, and then the new version of the bill returns for a vote to both the House and Senate. Only if both houses approve identical bills does the legislation go to the President. Most important legislation (but a minority of all legislation) requires a conference committee to resolve differences in the versions approved by each chamber.

Once Congress presents a bill to the President, three things can happen, as per Article I, Section 7 of the Constitution. First, the President can sign the bill, in which case it becomes law. Second, he can veto it. If he does so, he returns the bill, with an explanation for the veto, to the house in which it originated. Only if the House and the Senate each vote by a 2/3 majority to override the veto does the bill become law. Third, he can do nothing. In that case, the bill becomes law, just as if the President had signed it, after ten days of inaction, *provided* that the Congress

has not adjourned. If Congress has adjourned, and thus is deemed not available to receive a vetoed bill from the President, the bill does not become law through the President's inaction. Instead, it quietly dies; this is the "pocket veto." Because Congress is especially active in the waning days, if not the waning hours, of a session, the pocket veto is more important than one might think. There has been significant disagreement between the legislative and executive branches over what constitutes an "adjournment" for these purposes.

This process produces a good deal of paper that can be reviewed after the fact. The statements of witnesses at hearings will give a sense of the problems to which Congress sought to respond; the statements of legislators at hearings may give a sense of what concerned them and what they were trying to do; different drafts of bills will show what ideas were specifically rejected; discussion on the floor of the Senate or the House may reveal the understanding of Congress (or at least of particular members) of the meaning of the bill; there will often be three separate reports (House, Senate, and Conference) discussing the bill's meaning and purpose and summarizing its provisions; and the President is likely to set out his own understanding of the legislation when signing it. All of this material constitutes "legislative history," which may be consulted by later interpreters trying to understand what the enacted statute means.

Enacted Legislation

Assume that a bill has been enacted. It is now law and is identified by a Public Law Number rather than a bill number. Public Laws are numbered sequentially within a Congress in order of passage; the Public Law Number has a prefix indicating the number of the enacting Congress.

Public Laws are published by the Government Printing Office (GPO) in three forms. First, the GPO publishes a "slip law"; an unbound pamphlet (like a court's "slip opinion") containing nothing other than the Act itself. A slip law looks very much like a printed bill, such as the Lower Pays Act set out above, though with a few obvious differences ("An Act" in place of "A Bill," for example). Second, all the laws from each session of Congress are then published, in chronological order, in *Statutes at Large*. Finally, the Office of the Law Revision Counsel of the House of Representatives (http://uscode.house.gov) publishes the *United States Code*. The U.S. Code is where the bulk of federal legislation is "codified," that is, set out in a current, organized, and comprehensive fashion. The U.S. Code thus gathers together all laws on a particular topic, eliminates repealed or expired statutes, and incorporates amendments into the original statute. It contains only the "general and permanent" laws enacted by Congress — not private laws, appropriations legislation, resolutions declaring national home-baked bread day, and the like. And not every provision within a Public Law makes it into the U.S. Code. For example, were the Loser Pays Act to be enacted Section 3 would definitely be codified; section 2 would probably be codified; and sections 1 and 4, which do not actually impose legal requirements, would be left out.

A new edition of the Code appears every six years, with cumulative supplements issued annually. (One measure of the growth of statutory law is the increase in the sheer length of the U.S. Code. The 1964 compilation consisted of 9797 pages. The 2006 edition, the most recent as of this writing, is over 41,000 pages long.)

Unlike *Statutes at Large*, the U.S. Code is not organized Act by Act. The Code is divided into 50 Titles, arranged alphabetically by subject matter. Thus, Title 15 covers "commerce," title 16 "copyright," title 17 "conservation," title 18 "crimes," and so on. Title 28 is devoted to the judiciary; title 42, entitled "public health and welfare," contains a diverse range of provisions falling roughly within that general heading: laws concerning pollution, social security, and civil rights. As a result, the provisions of a single Act may be scattered through different sections, and even different titles, of the U.S. Code.

Acts are divided into titles and sections; so is the U.S. Code. Unfortunately, the title and section numbers of the one have little to do with the title and section numbers of the other. For example, consider Title VII of the Civil Rights Act of 1964. The provisions of Title VII (which, as noted, are all sections of the 1964 Act itself — what you would find in the slip law or Statutes at Large — beginning with the number "7") are *not* found in title 7 of the U.S. Code. They are in Title 42, along with the rest of the civil rights laws. And within title 42, they are assigned new section numbers. So, to pick a particular provision at random, Section 702 of the Civil Rights Act of 1964 is not found in title 7 of the U.S. Code, or even at § 702 of 42 U.S.C.; as it happens, it is 42 U.S.C. § 2000e-1. It is the same provision; but it has one section number in the Act and another in the U.S. Code. Courts tend to cite the U.S. Code; lawyers who work primarily with a particular statute tend to refer to the sections in the Act itself.

So assume the Loser Pays Act was enacted. It would be issued as a slip law, which would look very much like the bill reproduced above, and published in *Statutes at Large* sequentially with the other laws from that session of Congress. Only sections 2 (probably) and 3 (definitely) would then be inserted into the U.S. Code. These provisions would presumably be placed in Title 28 of the Code, which covers judicial matters, and assigned new, unrelated section numbers.

Strictly speaking, the U.S. Code contains authoritative versions (or "legal evidence") of federal statutory law only if and to the extent it has been enacted into positive law — that is, it has gone through the legislative process, with Congress passing, and the President sign into law, parts of the Code. As of mid-2009, this had occurred for 24 of the 50 titles. The remaining 26 titles are only "prima facie evidence" of what the law actually is. 1 U.S.C. § 204.

Appendix F

TWO STATUTORY PROBLEMS

Problem 1

The first, and often hardest, task in the real world is to locate all relevant provisions. That much we have already done for you. Section 83 applies to this transaction, which involves the transfer (from Super to Smith's son) of property (the Super stock — note § 83 does not say "real property") "in connection with the performance of services" (the employment contract itself provided for the transfer). While the property did not go to Smith, the person who actually performed the services, that is irrelevant; § 83 applies whenever property is transferred "to any person other than the person for whom such services are performed."

What, then, does § 83 provide? First, we know that Smith herself will be taxed; § 83 income "shall be included in the gross income of the person who performed such services," i.e., Smith. The fact that she did not receive the stock herself does not matter. The income attributed to her is the excess of the property's fair market value over the amount paid for it. Neither Smith nor her son paid anything for the property (the initial *value* of the stock is thus irrelevant to the problem, since no one *paid* that amount). Because the amount paid is zero, Smith's income is the full fair market value of the stock.

As of the initial transfer to her son, however, Smith does not yet have income from this transaction. She only has income when there is no longer a "substantial risk of forfeiture." Under the statute's express terms, such a risk exists as long as "rights to full enjoyment of such property are conditioned upon the future performance of substantial services by any individual." Here, the risk continues for the first three years of Smith's employment; were she not to stay on the job (which clearly requires "substantial services" from her), her son would lose the stock. After three years (i.e., in 2004), however, the substantial risk of forfeiture disappears, and the full market value of the property is included in Smith's gross income. Smith therefore has no income from this transaction until 2004, and $50,000 ($500/share times 100 shares) of income in that year.

In 2007, the son sells the stock for $70,000 ($700/share times 100 shares). Is this income attributable to Smith? No. Section 83 essentially drops out of the picture; it has nothing to say about what happens after the value of the property has been included in the income of the person performing the services. The gain from the sale would therefore be included in the income of Smith's son. Does he have $70,000 in income? That is, after all, how much he has gained from this whole deal. No. Under § 1001(a), his gain (i.e. his income) from the sale is the difference between the "amount realized" ($70,000) and his "basis." "Basis" is a term of art in tax law. The concept is easiest to explain by an example, but its essential function is to avoid taxing the same income. Its application is clear enough here. Under the regulations, in a "subsequent sale" of § 83 property, which is what we have here,

the property's basis is the amount paid plus the amount included in gross income under § 83. Here, nothing was paid for the property, and $50,000 was "included in [Smith's] gross income under § 83." The stock therefore has a basis of $50,000. The son's gain (the excess of the amount realized ($70,000) over the basis) is $20,000. In this way taxes on the $70,000 of income that flowed from this stock are divided between Smith and her son, and the government does not collect taxes twice on the same income.

In short, the answer to the question is that Smith has $50,000 of income in 2004 and her son has $20,000 of income in 2007.

Problem 2

This is a real-world sort of problem, but this exact scenario would not arise. There are few if any incinerators this small, and the emissions numbers are invented. Also, in the real world there are a bunch of EPA regulations that also apply, and the state might impose additional limitations of its own under its State Implementation Plan. Finally, in the real world we would never still be asking about the design of the facility after construction has already begun. Financial and engineering realities would preclude it, not to mention the fact that the § 165 permit is a pre-construction permit.

The heart of the problem is whether either of two separate provisions of the Act that might regulate an incinerator just beginning construction applies here. Under § 111(b)(1)(B) of the Act, the EPA Administrator is supposed to issue New Source Performance Standards — regulations imposing emission limits for pollutants of concern from new stationary (as opposed to mobile) sources. The Act itself imposes no obligations on private parties; it tells the EPA to write regulations, and it is the regulations that actually operate on private parties. The regulations must, of course, be consistent with the Act. The regulations apply to categories of facilities; that is, there is an incinerator NSPS, a coal-fired power plant NSPS, a paper mill NSPS, and so on. § 111(b)(1)(A). So one part of the question is whether there is an applicable incinerator NSPS.

A completely separate part of the Act requires new stationary sources over a certain size to obtain a permit and meet certain emissions control requirements. The Act has two parallel sets of provisions; one for clean air areas and one for dirty air areas. The provisions in the problem are from the former, the so-called Prevention of Significant Deterioration (PSD) provisions. The basic requirements for new sources in clean air areas are evident from the excerpted provisions: they must obtain a "PSD permit" and they must hold emissions to a level that reflects use of the Best Available Control Technology (BACT).

So the questions here are: (1) Do either of the NSPSs (one old, one only proposed) apply to this new incinerator? (2) Does the facility have to use BACT (and if so, what would that require)?

A would be right if the new incinerator were wholly unregulated. However, at a bare minimum, it must comply with the NSPS that EPA issued in 1975. There's no indication from the facts or hint in the statute that the NSPS applies only to certain incinerators, say those above a certain size. The only limitation that the

statute or the facts reveal is that the NSPS applies only to new sources (i.e. post-1975), which this facility clearly is.

B would be right if the 1975 NSPS applies but nothing else does. As noted, at a bare minimum the 1975 NSPS does apply. Other requirements do as well, however, as we shall see.

C is the right answer, though it is not initially apparent what it is doing here. The incinerator will have to get a permit and use BACT if it is a "major emitting facility." § 165(a). Major emitting facility is defined in § 169(1). There are two categories: a facility that is on the list of 28 types and at full capacity would 100 TPY of a regulated pollutant (1st sentence), and any facility which at full capacity would emit 250 TPY of a pollutant (2nd sentence).* The proposed new incinerator does not fall within the first category, which includes only incinerators that will handle 50 or more tons of garbage per day. This facility will handle 40 TPD. Thus, it is a major emitting facility only if it will emit 250 TPY of any pollutant. If designed to emit only 249, then it is not in the second category either. Therefore it is not a major emitting facility, and therefore it does not have to use BACT (which would bring emissions down below 249 TPY).

D is wrong for the same reason that C is right. D would be right if the facility were a little larger (i.e. charging more than 50 TPD of waste or emitting over 250 or more TPY of a regulated pollutant). Then it would be a major emitting facility and have to use BACT. BACT is defined in § 169(3); it clearly includes the "now quite common devices" that would limit emissions to 100 TPY. The question is whether it requires going all the way down to 75 TPY. If the new NSPS is valid and applicable, then it does, since an NSPS sets a minimum of stringency for BACT. See last sentence of § 169(3). As discussed below, however, the NSPS does not apply.

E would be right if the new NSPS applied. (Note it could apply directly, and/or indirectly via BACT. So if there is an NSPS that would translate to 75 TPY of particulates for this facility, and it was a major emitting facility, then § 165 and § 111 would *both* require that limitation). But the NSPS does not apply. An NSPS applies to new sources. This is not a new source. This is *not* because the NSPS has only been proposed, not issued in final form. The triggering date is the date the regulation is proposed, not the date it is finally promulgated. § 111(a)(2). But construction began 6 months ago; the proposal came out 2 months ago. Because construction predated the proposal, the NSPS doesn't apply. (Assuming, of course, that the final version of the NSPS is consistent with the proposal. If the final

---

* In fact, we have taken a small liberty with the actual statutory language here. The Act in fact does not use the phrase "at full capacity would emit"; rather, it refers to facilities with "the potential to emit" more than 100 or 250 TPY. "Potential to emit" is an ambiguous term. A major emitting facility is one with the "potential to emit" 250 tons per year; the proposed facility might be said to have the potential to emit 1000, because that's what it would emit if without controls, or if the controls were broken for a year. The meaning of "potential to emit" was litigated in the D.C. Circuit, which held that it refers to emissions at full capacity *with the pollution control equipment in place and functioning.* "Potential" (as opposed, implicitly, to "actual" or "anticipated") thus refers to operation at full capacity, not to operation while malfunctioning. In the problem, we wrote that definition into the statute.

version is different, then sources that began construction prior to final promulgation are not "new.")

If groundbreaking was tomorrow, then the proposed NSPS would apply, and E would be the correct answer, except for a pretty strong argument that the new NSPS is invalid. The question doesn't really give enough information, but there's a decent argument that up-to-the-minute technology requirement reflected in the new NSPS goes beyond the "best system of emissions reduction . . . adequately demonstrated" standard of § 111(a)(1). The usual understanding, reflected in the language of the statute and in the fact that the NSPS is a floor for BACT and not vice versa, is that the § 111 Best Demonstrated Technology standard is laxer than BACT. Note that if indeed BACT is 100 TPY, then the NSPS has to be invalid. (Alternatively, if the NSPS is valid, then BACT must be at most 75, and so D is incorrect even if the incinerator were a major emitting facility.)

TABLE OF CASES

[References are to pages]

A

Aldridge v. Williams 287; 381
Alyeska Pipeline Service Co. v. Wilderness Society. 350
American Trucking Ass'ns; United States v.. . . .285; 330
Anastasoff v. United States 196
Anderson v. Reith-Riley Const. Co.. . . . . .134; 137
Angle v. Chicago, St. Paul, Minneapolis & Omaha Ry. Co.. 176
Anslinger v. Martinsville Inn, Inc. 36
Apfelbaum; United States v.. 330
Arizona v. Roberson 202

B

Bailey v. State Workmen's Compensation Commissioner. 419
Barnhart v. Sigmon Coal Co. 326
Baron Bramwell in Andrews v. Stytrap. 139
Barrett v. Southern Pacific Co.. . 106; 109; 113; 135
Barrett v. United States. 329, 330
Beeson v. City of Los Angeles 125
Behrens v. Pelletier. 350
Bellew v. Dedeaux. 283
Blanchard v. Bergeron 382
Bloch v. Hirsh .232
Block v. Community Nutrition Institute. 336
Bob Jones University v. United States. . . .415; 428
Boutilier v. INS 437
Bowen v. Georgetown Univ. Hosp.. 400
Bramblett; United States v. 330
Brockamp; United States v.. 333
Brooklyn Nat'l Corp. v. Commissioner. 264
Brown v. Board of Education of Topeka. 7; 415; 430
Brown; United States v.. 330
Bryant; United States v.. 330
Burnet v. Colorado Oil and Gas Co. 184
Butler v. Acme Mkts., Inc. 33
Butler v. Aiken .204
Butler v. McKellar. 202
Butler v. South Carolina. 203
Butler v. South Carolina. 203
Butler v. State .203
Butler; State v.. 203

C

Caminetti v. United States. 369
Caperton v. A.T. Massey Coal Co. 453
Cheatle v. Cheatle 245
Chevron U.S.A. Inc. v. NRDC 397
Chicago, B. & J.R. v. Chicago 210
Chicago, B. & Q. R. Co. v. Krayenbuhl 135
Chisom v. Roemer 387; 443
Christiansburg Garment Co. v. EEOC. 351
Church of The Holy Trinity v. United States. . . 275
Circuit City Stores, Inc. v. Adams. 268; 288
City and County of (see name of city and county)
City of (see name of city)
Clearview Coal Co.; Commonwealth v.. 209
Collopy v. Newark Eye & Ear Infirmary. 40
Commonwealth v. (see name of defendant)
Congini v. Portersville Valve Co.. . . . . . . .36; 43
Congress. Train v. Colorado Public Interest Research Group, Inc. 330
Conroy v. Aniskoff 381; 384; 386
Cook; United States v.. 330
Copfer v. Golden 121; 124; 149
Corbett; United States v.. 330
Cotton, In re Estate of. 251
Courtell v. McEachen. 153–155; 157
Craig v. Finch 330
Craig; United States v.. 277
Crane v. Smith 122
Culbert; United States v.. 330
Cullings v. Goetz. 152

D

Dalton v. St. Luke's Catholic Church. 40
Darrow v. Hanover Twp. 38
Deem v. Millikin 241, 242
Dudley; United States v.. 329
Dunn v. United States 329

E

Edwards v. Arizona 204
EEOC v. Massachusetts 377
EEOC v. Wyoming. 339
Egger, Tax Court in Estate of v. Commissioner. .346
Environmental Defense Fund v. City of Chicago.371
Estate of (see name of party)
Ettin v. Ava Truck Leasing Inc.. 33
Ex rel. (see name of relator)

[References are to pages]

Exxon Mobil Corp. v. Allapattah Servs., Inc.. . .369

F

Fay v. Noia. 205
Faylor v. Great Eastern Quicksilver Mining Co..118; 138
FDA v. Brown & Williamson Tobacco Corp.. . .410
Figuly v. Knoll 33; 36
Filmore v. Metropolitan Life Ins. Co.. 239
Flint v. Robins Dry Dock & Repair Co. 175
Flora v. United States 330
Fogerty v. Fantasy Inc.. 353
France v. A.P.A. Transport Corp.. . . . . . . .40, 41
Franklin v. Hill. 434
Friedrich v. Chicago 354; 357
Fyfe, People ex rel. v. Barnett. 427

G

Garcia v. Soogian. 152; 157
Garcia v. United States. 370
Geiger v. President of Perkiomen & R. Turnpike Road. 314
Georgia Ass'n of Retarded Citizens v. McDaniel.308
German Alliance Insurance Co. v. Home Water Supply Co.. 176
Gillespie v. McGowan. 114
Goldberg v. Housing Auth. of Newark. 34
Gonzales v. Carhart 206
Grant v. Hipsher. 236
Green, Moore & Co. v. United States. 331
Gregory v. Ashcroft. 337; 376; 439
Guste, State of Louisiana ex rel. v. M/V TESTBANK. 177
Gwartz v. Superior Court. 29

H

Hargreaves v. Deacon 114
Harrison v. PPG Industries, Inc.. . . . . . .445; 448
Hart v. Massanari. 181; 199
Hattaway v. United States. 330
Hattie v. Shaheen. 314
Hill v. INS 438
Huddleston v. United States. 329
Hutchinson v. Chase & Gilbert, Inc. 156
Hynes v. New York C. R. Co.. . . . . . . .91; 108

I

Immer v. Risko 40, 41

In re Estate of (see name of party)
In re (see name of party)

J

Jaskolski v. Daniels 361
Jermane v. Forfar. 314
Johnson v. Railway Express Agency 314
Johnson v. Southern Pacific Co.. 330
Jones v. Alfred H. Mayer Co.. 418
Justifying the Judge's Hunch: An Essay on Discretion. 88

K

Kahn v. James Burton Co.. 138
Kallen, In re. 43
Kelly v. Gwinnell. 32; 33; 50; 68
Keystone Bituminous Coal Ass'n v. DeBenedictis 229
King v. Lennen. 156
Kirby; United States v.. 276
Klein v. Raysinger. 33; 43
Klix v. Nieman. 114
Knight v. Kaiser Co.. . 132; 145–148; 154, 155; 164
Koons Buick Pontiac GMC, Inc. v. Nigh. 369

L

Lake v. Ferrer. 125; 138
Lamie v. United States Trustee 344
League of United Latin American Citizens Council v. Clements 444
Levy; United States v.. 330
Li v. Yellow Cab Co.. 422
Linn v. Rand. 35; 43
Lochner v. New York 207
Locke; United States v.. 340
Long v. Standard Oil Co. 137
Long v. State of New York 255
Longstaff, In re. 438

M

Malone v. Jersey Central Power & Light Co.. . . 42
Marbury v. Madison 196; 237
Massachusetts v. EPA 402
Matthews v. Delaware, L. & W. R.R. 42
Maxwell; Commonwealth v.. 427
McBoyle v. United States 315; 319
McKelvey v. United States 331

[References are to pages]

Mead Corp.; United States v. 400
Melendez v. City of Los Angeles.125; 136; 147, 148
Merenoff v. Merenoff 38
Metro. Stevedore Co. v. Rambo 400
Meyer v. General Electric Company 126
Miller v. Allstate Insurance Co. 313
Miller v. Moran 44
Mississippi Valley Co.; United States v.. 330
Missouri v. Jenkins. 354
Mobile v. Bolden. 445
Montana v. Stanko. 80
Morse v. Douglas. 138
Mugler v. Kansas. 211
Mut. Life Ins. Co. v. Armstrong. 240

N

New York v. Shore Realty Corp. 373
Nix v. Hedden 317

O

Ould v. Washington Hospital for Foundlings . . .429
Overholt v. Vieths 114

P

Palsgraf v. Long Island R.R. Co.. . . . . .34; 93
Patterson v. McLean Credit Union 413
Pekin, City of v. McMahon 116
Penn Central Transportation Co. v. New York
    City 232
Pennsylvania v. Union Gas Co. 266
Pennsylvania Coal Co. v. Mahon 208; 218
Pennsylvania Dep't of Corrections v. Yeskey. . .339
Penry v. Lynaugh. 204
People ex rel. (see name of relator)
The People v. Ruggles. 279
Perin v. Carey 429
Perrin v. United States. 330
Peters v. Bowman 116; 124; 125; 133; 136
Petition of (see name of party)
Philbrook v. Glodgett 330
Planned Parenthood v. Casey 189; 206
Plessy v. Ferguson 430
Plymouth Coal Co. v. Pennsylvania. 209
Polk v. Laurel Hill Cemetery Ass'n. 124
Powell v. Pennsylvania. 211
Public Citizen v. United States Dep't of Justice. 286;
    292; 343; 363; 387; 389

Q

Quindlen v. Prudential Insurance Co. of
    America .330

R

Rainwater v. United States. 330
Rappaport v. Nichols 33; 35; 43
Reardon v. Spring Valley Water Co.. 125
Rector of the Church of the Holy Trinity; United
    States v. .284
Reid; United States v. 315
Reiter v. Sonotone Corp.. 331
Republican Party v. White 450; 452
Ressam; United States v.. 323
Reynolds v. Willson 142; 149; 153–155
Richards v. Connell 114
Richardson v. Town of Danvers. 314
Richmond Medical Center for Women v.
    Gilmore .192
Rideout v. Knox 208
Riggs v. Palmer 242
Ristan v. Frantzen 42
Robins Dry Dock & Repair Co. v. Flint 175
Rodriguez v. United States. 360
Roe v. Wade 188
Ruckelshaus v. Sierra Club 360
Runyon v. McCrary 414, 415; 418; 426

S

San Diego Gas & Electric Co. v. San Diego . . .207
Sanchez v. East Contra Costa Irrigation Co.. . . .118;
    125; 137; 145
Savings Bank v. Ward 176
Scharton; United States v. 331
Schooner Paulina's Cargo v. United States 255
Schreiner v. High Court of Illinois Catholic Order of
    Foresters. 240
Schwegmann Bros. v. Calvert Distillers Corp. . .370
Scrimgeour; United States v.. 329
SEC v. Collier 383
Second National Bank of North Miami; United States
    v.. 330
Shaare Tefila Congregation v. Cobb 427
Shrader v. Equitable Life Assurance Soc.. 250
Sinclair, In re. 382
Sioux City & Pacific Railroad Company v.
    Stout. 135

[References are to pages]

Skidmore v. Swift & Co. 395
Smith, Petition of. 322
Soronen v. Olde Milford Inn, Inc. 35, 36; 39
Southern Pac. Co. v. Jensen. 87
Spicer v. Spicer. 163
St. Francis College v. Al-Khazraji. 426
Standard Oil Co.; United States v.. 330
Stark v. Advanced Magnetics, Inc. 322
Stasio; State v.. 44
State v. (see name of defendant). . . . .
State Farm v. Butler 313
State of (see name of state)
Sturges v. Crowninshield. 343

T

Taylor; United States v. 387
Town of (see name of town)
Towne v. Eisner 305
Turley; United States v. 330
TVA v. Hill. 399

U

United Savings Ass'n v. Timbers of Inwood Forest
    Assocs. 323
United States v. (see name of defendant)
University of Utah Hosp. & Medical Ctr. v.
    Bethke. 320
Unzueta v. Ocean View School Dist. 303

Updegraph v. The Commonwealth 279

V

Van Horn v. Blanchard Co. 40

W

Wadsworth v. Siek. 246
Weems v. United States 360
Wells Fargo Bank; United States v.. 346
Welsh v. United States. 295
Wesson v. Washburn Iron Co. 209
West Virginia Univ. Hosps. v. Casey 356; 420
Wiener v. Gamma Phi Chapter of Alpha Tau Omega
    Fraternity. 33
Wilford v. Little 124; 138
Willis v. Department of Conservation & Economic
    Dev.. . . . . .38; 40
Woods v. San Francisco 138

Y

Young v. Community Nutrition Institute 321

Z

Zuber v. Allen 370
Zuni Public School District No. 89 v. Department of
    Education 283; 385; 364

INDEX

[References are to chapters and sections.]

A

ADMINISTRATIVE AGENCIES
Generally . . . 13: A
Deference to agency interpretations by courts
    . . . 13: C
Inaction by agencies . . . 13: D
Interpretation of laws
    Generally . . . 13: B
    Deference to agency interpretations . . . 13: C
    Inaction by agencies . . . 13: D

B

BRIEFING CASES
Generally . . . 2: B
Additional information . . . 2: B–9
Dissents . . . 2: B–8
Facts of case . . . 2: B–3
Heading . . . 2: B–1
Holding . . . 2: B–5; 2: B–6
Issues . . . 2: B–5; 2: B–6
Procedural history . . . 2: B–4
Reasoning . . . 2: B–7
Sample brief . . . 2: C
Separate opinions . . . 2: B–8
Statement of case . . . 2: B–2

BURKE, EDMUND
Precedent and Burkean conservatism . . . 5: D–3

C

CANONS OF CONSTRUCTION
Generally . . . 10: B–6
Expressio unius, use of . . . 10: B–6(c)
Invoking canons . . . 10: B–6(a)
Linguistic canon . . . 10: B–6(c)
Presumption against interference with governmental
    operations . . . 10: B–6(d)
Substantive canons . . . 10: B–6(d)
Types of canons . . . 10: B–6(b)

CASES
Generally . . . 1: B
Briefing cases (See BRIEFING CASES)
Disputes distinguished . . . 1: E
Eminent domain and police power case; illustrative
    example . . . 6: B
Gregory v. Ashcroft (See *GREGORY V. ASHCROFT*)
Sequence of . . . 2: A; 4

COMMON LAW
Generally . . . 1: A
Statutes and (See STATUTES AND THE COM-
    MON LAW)

CONTEXT AS CAUSE 10: B–5

COURTS
Generally . . . 1: C
California state courts . . . App C
Decisions by (See JUDICIAL DECISIONS)
Federal Courts
    Generally . . . App A
    Geographic boundaries of . . . App D
Geographic boundaries of federal courts . . . App
    D
New York state courts . . . App B
State courts
    California . . . App C
    New York . . . App B

D

DISPUTES
Cases distinguished . . . 1: E

E

EMINENT DOMAIN
Jurisprudence of takings . . . 6: C
Precedent in eminent domain case; illustrative ex-
    ample . . . 6: B

F

FEDERAL COURTS
Generally . . . App A
Geographic boundaries of . . . App D

G

GRAMMAR, FAULTY USE OF 10: B–4

GREGORY V. ASHCROFT
Legislative history as factor in . . . 12: B–3(c)
Presumption against interference with state opera-
    tions as factor in . . . 10: B–6(d)
Role of judges in democratic society as factor in
    . . . 15: A

I

IGNORING UNAMBIGUOUS MEANING 10: C

J

JUDGES
Generally . . . 1: D
Decisions by (See JUDICIAL DECISIONS)
Role in democratic society . . . 15: A

JUDGMENTS (See JUDICIAL DECISIONS)

JUDICIAL DECISIONS
Generally . . . 1: F; 3: C; 6: A; 6: I
Administrative agencies, deference to interpretations
   by . . . 13: C
Bases of . . . 3: A
Briefing cases, in . . . 2: B–5; 2: B–6
Democracy as factor in . . . 6: H
Economics as factor in . . . 6: D
Empathy as factor in . . . 3: B
"Law of rules" as factor in . . . 6: G
Overruling of . . . 1: F–1
Passion as factor in . . . 3: B
Politics as factor in . . . 6: E
Precedent as factor in (See PRECEDENT)
Property rights as factor in . . . 6: F
Reason as factor in . . . 3: B
Res judicata . . . 1: F–2
Reversals of . . . 1: F–1
Stare decisis . . . 1: F–2

L

LACK OF CLARITY, REASONS FOR 10: B–1

LEGISLATIVE HISTORY
Generally . . . 9: A–6; 12: A
Age Discrimination in Employment Act, applicabil-
   ity to . . . 12: B–3(c)
Air quality standards, as factor in . . . 12: B–3(a)
CERCLA, as factor in . . . 12: B–3(b)
Clean Air Act, applicability to . . . 12: B–3(a)
Cost of researching . . . 12: C–4
"Democratic exegesis" . . . 12: C–4
Hazardous waste cleanup laws, as factor in . . . 12:
   B–3(b)
Hierarchy of legislative sources . . . 12: B–2
Inaccurate evidence of actual views, effect of
   . . . 12: C–2
Indeterminacy in . . . 12: C–3
Intent of legislators as irrelevant . . . 12: C–1
Judicial reliance on, attack against
   Cost of research . . . 12: C–4
   "Democratic exegesis" . . . 12: C–4
   Inaccurate evidence of actual views . . . 12:
     C–2
   Indeterminacy . . . 12: C–3
   Intent of legislators as irrelevant . . . 12: C–1
   Unavailability of history . . . 12: C–4
Plain meaning rule . . . 12: B–1
Practical use of . . . 12: B–3(a)
Unavailability of history . . . 12: C–4

LEGISLATURES
Common Law, response to . . . 7: C
Legislative history (See LEGISLATIVE HISTORY)
Legislative process . . . App E
Statutory interpretation and (See STATUTORY IN-
   TERPRETATION)

LITIGATION
Generally . . . 1: E

O

OVERRULING OF JUDGMENTS
Generally . . . 1: F–1

P

PRECEDENT
Generally . . . 1: F–2; 5: A
Adherence as constitutional requirement . . . 5:
   D–4
Advantages and disadvantages compared . . . 5: E
Appeals cases . . . 6: A
Assimilation, categories of . . . 5: C–4
Binding nature of . . . 5: B–2
Burkean conservatism and . . . 5: D–3
Categories of constraints imposed by . . . 5: C–2
Characterizations constraints imposed by . . . 5:
   C–2
Constitutional requirements as constraints . . . 5:
   D–4
Constraints imposed by
   Generally . . . 5: C–1
   Assimilation, categories of . . . 5: C–4
   Categories . . . 5: C–2
   Characterizations . . . 5: C–2
   Constitutional requirements . . . 5: D–4
   Decisions without characterizations . . . 5:
     C–3
   Degrees of constraint . . . 5: C–5
Criticisms of use of . . . 5: D–1
Defenses of use of
   Efficiency . . . 5: D–2(c)
   Fairness . . . 5: D–2(a)
   Legitimacy . . . 5: D–2(d)
   Predictability . . . 5: D–2(b)
Definition of precedent . . . 5: B–1; 5: B–2
Degrees of constraint . . . 5: C–5
Efficiency of . . . 5: D–2(c)
Eminent domain and police power case; illustrative
   example . . . 6: B
Fairness of . . . 5: D–2(a)
Legitimacy of . . . 5: D–2(d)
Predictability of . . . 5: D–2(b)
Rule, as . . . 5: B–1
Stare decisis
   Generally . . . 1: F–2
   Statutory cases, in . . . 14: A
Statutes and precedents . . . 7: C

PUNCTUATION AS CAUSE 10: B–4

R

READING STATUTES
Generally . . . 10: A
Armed Career Criminal Act . . . 10: A–3
Arson statutes . . . 10: A–6
Clean Air Act . . . 10: A–2
House, law as to use of . . . 10: A–6
Incinerator construction, regulations as to . . . 10:
   A–2
Internal Revenue Code . . . 10: A–1

[References are to chapters and sections.]

READING STATUTES—Cont.

Primacy of text . . . 10: A

Suspension of teacher for drug use, law as to . . . 10: A–4

Use of weapons during commission of crime, law as to . . . 10: A–5

Violent felony statute . . . 10: A–3

Weapons, laws as to use of
    Use of weapons during commission of crime . . . 10: A–5
    Violent felony statute . . . 10: A–3

RES JUDICATA

Generally . . . 1: F–2

REVERSALS

Generally . . . 1: F–1

RULINGS (See JUDICIAL DECISIONS)

S

SOURCES OF STATUTORY INTERPRETA-TION

Generally . . . 9: A–9

Administrative agencies (See ADMINISTRATIVE AGENCIES)

Canons of construction (See CANONS OF CON-STRUCTION)

Historical context . . . 9: A–5

Later amendments . . . 9: A–7

Legislative context . . . 9: A–5

Legislative history (See LEGISLATIVE HISTORY)

Public policy . . . 9: A–8

Purpose of statute . . . 9: A–4

Reading texts (See READING STATUTES)

Societal values . . . 9: A–8

Text of statute
    Generally . . . 9: A–1
    Beyond . . . 9: A–2
    External sources . . . 9: A–2
    Reading texts (See READING STATUTES)

Title of statute . . . 9: A–3

STARE DECISIS

Generally . . . 1: F–2

Statutory cases, in . . . 14: A

Theory of precedent (See PRECEDENT)

STATE COURTS

California . . . App C

New York . . . App B

STATUTES

Administrative agencies and (See ADMINISTRA-TIVE AGENCIES)

Canons of construction (See CANONS OF CON-STRUCTION)

Changing statutory meaning . . . 14: B

Common Law and (See STATUTES AND THE COMMON LAW)

Illustrative examples of statutory problems . . . App F

Legislative history (See LEGISLATIVE HISTORY)

Legislative process . . . App E

STATUTES—Cont.

Obsolete statutes . . . 14: C

Precedent and . . . 7: C

Purpose of . . . 11: A

Reading statutes (See READING STATUTES)

Sources of statutory interpretation (See SOURCES OF STATUTORY INTERPRETATION)

Stare decisis . . . 14: A

Statutory uncertainty
    Generally . . . 10: B
    Ambiguity . . . 10: B–3
    Canons of construction (See CANONS OF CONSTRUCTION)

Theories of statutory interpretation (See STATU-TORY INTERPRETATION)

Uncertainty as to (See STATUTORY UNCER-TAINTY)

STATUTES AND THE COMMON LAW

Generally . . . 7: A

Complications caused by statutes . . . 7: B

Legislative response . . . 7: C

STATUTORY INTERPRETATION

Generally . . . 8: A

Administrative agencies, by (See ADMINISTRA-TIVE AGENCIES)

Broadening intentionalism . . . 8: A–3(a)

Courts and legislatures as lawmaking partners
    Generally . . . 8: B
    Dynamic statutory interpretation . . . 8: B–2
    Independent judicial judgment . . . 8: B–1
    Legislative supremacy . . . 8: B–3

Dynamic statutory interpretation . . . 8: B–2

Imaginative reconstruction . . . 8: A–3(a)(i)

Independent judicial judgment . . . 8: B–1

Intentionalism
    Narrowing intentionalism . . . 8: A–3(b)
    Traditional intentionalism . . . 8: A–1

Legislative history (See LEGISLATIVE HISTORY)

Legislative intent, use of
    Doubts as to . . . 8: A–2
    Fictional intent . . . 8: A–2(a)
    Public choice . . . 8: A–2(b)

Legislative supremacy . . . 8: B–3

Narrowing intentionalism . . . 8: A–3(b)

New textualism . . . 8: A–3(b)

Principals without intent, application of
    Generally . . . 8: A–3
    Broadening intentionalism . . . 8: A–3(a)
    Imaginative reconstruction . . . 8: A–3(a)(i)
    Narrowing intentionalism . . . 8: A–3(b)
    New textualism . . . 8: A–3(b)
    Purposivism . . . 8: A–3(a)(ii)

Purposivism . . . 8: A–3(a)(ii)

Reading statutes (See READING STATUTES)

Sources of (See SOURCES OF STATUTORY IN-TERPRETATION)

Traditional intentionalism . . . 8: A–1

STATUTORY UNCERTAINTY

Generally . . . 10: B

Ambiguity . . . 10: B–3

[References are to chapters and sections.]

STATUTORY UNCERTAINTY—Cont.
Canons of construction (See CANONS OF CON-
   STRUCTION)

T

TAKINGS
Illustrative case . . . 6: B

TAKINGS—Cont.
Jurisprudence of . . . 6: C

V

VAGUENESS 10: B–2